Refurbishment Manual

MAINTENANCE
CONVERSIONS
EXTENSIONS

GIEBELER   MUSSO

FISCH   PETZINKA

KRAUSE   RUDOLPHI

Birkhäuser
Basel · Boston · Berlin

Edition Detail
Munich

Authors

Georg Giebeler
Prof. Dipl.-Ing. Architect
Department of Building Construction, Wismar University of
Technology, Business & Design

Rainer Fisch
Dr.-Ing. Architect
Federal Office for Building & Regional Planning, Berlin

Harald Krause
Prof. Dr. rer. nat. Dipl.-Phys.
Department of Building Physics & Building Services,
Rosenheim University of Applied Sciences

Florian Musso
Prof. Dipl.-Ing. Architect
Department for Building Construction & Science of Materials, Munich TU

Karl-Heinz Petzinka
Prof. Dipl.-Ing. Architect
Department of Design & Building Technology, Darmstadt TU

Alexander Rudolphi
Prof. Dipl.-Ing.
Gesellschaft für Ökologische Bautechnik mbH, Berlin

Editorial services

Project Manager:
Steffi Lenzen, Dipl.-Ing. Architect

Editor:
Julia Liese, Dipl.-Ing.

Editorial assistants:
Claudia Fuchs, Dipl.-Ing. Architect; Carola Jacob-Ritz, M.A.;
Eva Schönbrunner, Dipl.-Ing.; Nicole Tietze, M.A.

Editorial assistant English edition:
Daniel Morgenthaler, lic. phil.

Drawings:
Marion Griese, Dipl.-Ing; Martin Hämmel, Dipl.-Ing.;
Daniel Hajduk, Dipl.-Ing.; Caroline Hörger, Dipl.-Ing.;
Claudia Hupfloher, Dipl.-Ing.; Nicola Kollmann, Dipl.-Ing.;
Simon Kramer, Dipl.-Ing.; Elisabeth Krammer, Dipl.-Ing.;
Dejanira Ornelas, Dipl.-Ing.

Translation into English:
Gerd H. Söffker, Philip Thrift, Hannover

Proofreading:
Raymond D. Peat, Alford, UK

Production & layout:
Roswitha Siegler

Reproduction:
Martin Härtl OHG, Martinsried

Printing & binding:
Kösel GmbH & Co. KG, Altusried-Krugzell

Co-authors:

Petra Kahlfeldt, Dipl.-Ing. Architect
Kahlfeldt Architekten, Berlin
Florian Lang, Dipl.-Ing. Architect
Lang+Volkwein Architekten & Ingenieure, Darmstadt

Bernhard Lenz, M.Eng. Dipl.-Ing. Dipl.-Ing. Architect
Department of Design & Building Technology, Darmstadt TU

Jochen Pfau, Prof. Dr.-Ing.
Department of Interior Design, Rosenheim University of
Applied Sciences

Ulrich Schanda, Prof. Dr. rer. nat. Dipl.-Phys.
Department of Building Physics & Building Services, Rosenheim
University of Applied Sciences

Elmar Schröder, Dipl.-Phys.
Müller-BBM, Planegg

Jürgen Volkwein, Dipl.-Ing. Architect
Lang+Volkwein Architekten & Ingenieure, Darmstadt

Johann Weber, Dipl.-Ing.
Department for Building Construction & Science of Materials,
Munich TU

Library of Congress Control Number:
2009927456 (hardcover)
2009927457 (softcover)

Bibliographic information published by the German National
Library.
The German National Library lists this publication in the Deutsche
Nationalbibliografie; detailed bibliographic data are available
on the Internet at http://dnb.d-nb.de.

This book is also available in a German language edition
(ISBN 978-3-7643-8874-4)

Editor:
Institut für internationale Architektur-Dokumentation GmbH &
Co. KG, Munich
www.detail.de

© 2009 English translation of the 1st German edition
Birkhäuser Verlag AG
Basel · Boston · Berlin
PO Box 133, 4010 Basel, Switzerland
Part of Springer Science+Business Media

Printed on acid-free paper produced from chlorine-free pulp.
TCF∞

ISBN: 978-3-7643-9946-7 (hardcover)
ISBN: 978-3-7643-9947-4 (softcover)

9 8 7 6 5 4 3 2 1   www.birkhauser.ch

Contents

Preface

"A change that is not an improvement is a degradation."   Adolf Loos

Many books have already appeared in the Construction Manual series and all deal in detail with one area of construction: concrete, timber, facades, etc. The *Refurbishment Manual*, on the other hand, covers all areas of construction: from the foundations to the final coat of paint inside, from preliminary planning to site supervision. Bringing all this together on just 280 pages would seem to be a daring exercise because there are extensive writings available on each one of these themes. And indeed, this book is based on the knowledge every architect should have at his or her fingertips. It is not intended to replace any of the standard works on building or building materials that have already been published; but it adds something: forms of construction and building materials that we – the planners, the design team – have to deal with during conversion and refurbishment projects.

The reason for this is that the essential difference between conversion work and new work is that in the former case the building is already standing. Even if it is not immediately evident, this facile-sounding statement contains questions such as: Is it necessary to distinguish between the architectural planning for conversion work and new work? If the answer to that is yes, then do the differences pervade all phases of the design and construction work? Do we need additional knowledge in order to master conversions?

The answer is: yes, there are fundamental differences in the planning methods, evaluation models and specialist knowledge that we as planners and designers must acquire in order to realise a conversion, successful in itself and for the client.

The following chapters are therefore mainly dedicated to the differences between the methods used for new building work and conversion work. This presumes that we already have experience in the design of new structures, which we can normally expect to be the case because the planning of new works is part of every architect's training. However, the courses of study generally on offer these days seldom include information on the planning of conversion and refurbishment projects, which is all the more surprising because working with the building stock dating from all previous ages used to be customary and, in addition, was handled very pragmatically: what could be used was used; what could be converted was adapted to suit our own tastes, our own uses; what was "left over" was demolished. It was the Modern Movement that forced us to divorce ourselves from the building stock: the new town, the new house, the new society. Sometime later, after the devastation of World War 2 had made these "new" towns feasible, we noticed that by taking this path we were in danger of losing something. The tide turned. In the early 1960s there was a remarkable alliance between reformers like Alexander Mitscherlich and conservationists like Hans Sedlmayr, who both demanded the conservation of the old towns. The conservation order is a child of that age; its idea of protection and retention resulted in the publication of specialist literature and also corresponding, new courses of study. But economically feasible only in the case of special inheritances from bygone architectural ages, the refurbishment and conversion of seemingly trivial structures was not regarded as a worthwhile pastime for ambitious architects. This attitude did not change until quite recently – certainly partly attributable to the fact that the volume of new build orders has declined significantly. Today it is just such building projects that find their way into trade journals and architectural presentations.

Closing the gap between books dealing with the conservation of historic buildings and monuments and those dealing with the construction of new buildings is the aim of this Construction Manual. Many of the statements found here are based on personal experience. Quite obviously, there will be many other alternative solutions to those suggested here.

A manual that is arranged according to periods and contains historical drawings
Part C of this book is divided into four time periods: founding years, inter-war and post-war years, and prosperous years. A different breakdown, e.g. according to the components of the building such as walls and floors, would have been truer to the standard layout in the other Construction Manuals. However, in order to

understand the building to be refurbished in its entirety, the respective components of one particular age are addressed in a direct relationship. The division into components serves as a subdivision within the four time periods; so there are four chapters for each component, e.g. the suspended floors of the founding years, the suspended floors of the inter-war years, etc. Forms of construction for suspended floors specific to a certain period are therefore presented directly alongside the associated forms of wall construction typical of that age. Besides the descriptions, all components are illustrated by way of historic drawings, most of which have been taken from the works on design and construction that were standard at that time. We are less interested in the – admittedly wonderful – illustrations themselves and more in the information they convey. The reader is recommended to study the drawings very carefully because they often contain much more than the associated caption might suggest, and thus represent a valuable planning and design aid. The reason behind the description of long outdated methods of construction is simple: these techniques belong to, are part of, the building to be refurbished. They therefore form the starting point for our planning assignment: historic details, specific material properties and the materials used at the time of the original construction are key parameters on which to base our design work. Only knowledge of old forms of construction enable us to make sensible decisions regarding their upkeep, replacement or refurbishment.

A manual that dispenses with standard details
No two conversions are alike. Even the attempt at a holistic study of the structure within its time period of course represents a considerable simplification. On the one hand, the time periods are not clearly defined, but instead form a continuum, a fact that also applies to the forms of construction used; on the other hand, there are – especially in periods with deficiencies in the transport infrastructure – regional differences in the styles of building, a fact that is attributable to the materials available locally. So if there is no standard historic detail, e.g. for a timber joist floor, then there can be no standard detail

for the refurbishment of such a component – quite apart from the fact that today's demands themselves are not uniform, but instead are responses to different uses and legislation. Instead of making specific and hence preclusive suggestions, this book highlights the common technical flaws in historic forms of construction. Most of these were certainly known to the architects of the time, but owing to the respective state of the art or monetary pressures they were tolerated. Despite the aforementioned problem, this book contains suggestions for improving such "historical" weaknesses – again in the field of conflict between modern legislation, innovations and costs.

A manual that contains much more than just "old" forms of construction
Despite all these limitations, we do meet with very similar and recurring tasks and framework conditions in refurbishment projects. These are mainly collated in Part B. And although the attempt to find definitions, provide advice for the planning of conversions, energy-efficiency upgrades, changes to the technical infrastructure, conservation of historic structures, materials and decontamination are also dependent on the existing building make-up, they are placed in separate chapters to improve overall clarity. This is supplemented by overriding, recurring refurbishment themes such as damp-proofing or thermal insulation measures. The historic forms of construction in Part C only achieve their full potential as a planning aid when considered in conjunction with the information contained in Parts A and B.

In addition to the countless institutions and individuals who provided vital information for this book, I would like to thank the authors of standard works on construction. I recommend that every planner, every designer read those books – in addition to this manual! – because they are not only informative, but in most cases also highly enjoyable.

Georg Giebeler
Cologne, August 2008

Part A   Introduction

Fig. A   Palais Langhans, Prague (CZ), Ladislav Lábus

Definitions

Georg Giebeler

A 1.1

There is no universally applicable term that covers all building measures on existing buildings and is also understood as such. Instead, we have a number of terms that exist alongside the word refurbishment and mean something similar, indeed, even the same thing: conversion, maintenance, modernisation, total refurbishment, deconstruction, works in the building stock, restoration, renovation. There are several reasons for this vagueness. On the one hand, the degree of change, compared to the extent of the building fabric to be retained, varies greatly – from minor repairs to total refurbishment of the entire building. On the other hand, the intervention in the existing building fabric is carried out for totally different reasons – aesthetic, technical or functional. In addition, a "traditionally" imprecise choice of words makes it impossible to assign the words exactly to the measures involved.

Nevertheless, this chapter will attempt to define the various terms and distinguish them from each other. The purpose of this is not to achieve irrevocable definitions, but rather a classification that will provide architects with a planning aid.

Different types of intervention in the building stock call for both different planning methods and different building measures. If the architect is in the position to be able to assign a certain term to his task, this can help to clarify the planning and construction processes. The terms will therefore be explained and defined below. In addition, practical advice for the realisation of the planning assignment will be given.

The classification will be carried out according to two aspects: firstly, the extent of the intervention in the existing building fabric; secondly, the scale of the building work. The planning methods and the building measures can be derived from this combination. The degree of intervention begins with the rebuilding of a structure that no longer exists, or at best only as a ruin, includes complete demolition and subsequent rebuilding, plus different levels of conservation (from renovation to gutting):

- Reconstruction
- Restoration
- Deconstruction
- Demolition
- Renovation/maintenance
- Repairs/maintenance
- Partial refurbishment
- Refurbishment
- Total refurbishment
- Conversion
- Gutting/rebuilding with partial retention

We can add further terms to this list for works that occur in conjunction with refurbishment but do not fit into this classification:

- Modernisation
- Decontamination
- Extension/additions
- Fitting-out
- Change of use

In many cases more than one term applies to a building project because either the terms overlap to a certain extent or several measures are carried out simultaneously. By contrast, the classification of the project size is relatively conclusive. It can be subdivided into five categories:

- XXL: town/district
- XL: block/complex
- M: building
- S: part of building/storey
- XS: dwelling/room

The expressions "further building work" or "works in the building stock" could be used for the classification. Neither expression describes measures in the technical sense, but rather indicates an approach. The former reflects the continuous process of building: after the conversion is also before the conversion. It also makes it clear that every measure has to react to the existing structures. So strictly speaking "works in the building stock" should really be called "works *with* the building stock".

A 1.1   "Kolumba", art museum of the archbishopric of
        Cologne, Cologne (D), 2007, Peter Zumthor
A 1.2   Frauenkirche, Dresden (D), 1743/2005,
        George Bähr
A 1.3   The planning work required for various types of
        refurbishment work

A 1.2

Reconstruction

Reconstruction is the rebuilding of a structure that no longer exists, i.e. strictly speaking it is new building work. In the case of a serious reconstruction, however, use is made of old forms of construction, too. Reconstructions always invite controversial discussions, with the criticism becoming fiercer as the degree of actual reconstruction decreases, i.e. as faithfulness to the original diminishes. For example, whereas the planning of the Stadtschloss in Berlin is being followed extremely critically, the reconstruction of Dresden's Frauenkirche met with much approval (Fig. A 1.2).

Although reconstructions are based on old designs, they are always new works without original parts. The acknowledged regulations for new building works therefore generally apply. Standards, statutory instruments, manufacturers' recommendations, sequence of building operations, time on site, form of tender and site management mostly correspond to those of new construction projects. The methods used during the planning phase are also similar because only rarely are historic structures documented in such detail that the architect does not need to plan or design anything new. Besides, many European, especially German, archives of drawings and documents concerning the building stock were destroyed in World War 2, meaning that illustrations and/or photographs have to be used for reconstruction projects instead of engineers' and architects' scale drawings. During planning work, reconstruction means not only working through the available sources for the original structure but also that today's architects have to mimic the building style of a certain period, i.e. it is not an exclusively scientific assignment. Contemporary specialist literature is an important aid throughout the planning when the goal is to reproduce historic constructions as accurately as possible using the means at our disposal today.

Restoration

Restoration means finishing an incomplete structure. The term first appeared during the romantic period as people became aware of the cultural monuments of the past. It was essentially coined by the French architect and art historian Eugène Viollet-le-Duc, who in the early 19th century arranged for the restoration of palaces dating from the Middle Ages. Cologne Cathedral is another example of a structure being completed after almost 300 years of inactivity (Fig. A 1.4). Restoration is very similar to reconstruction except that in the former original building elements are still available, which are then supplemented by appropriate additions. Its close relationship with reconstruction means it is similarly disputed: "The process of restoration is a highly specialized operation. Its aim is to preserve and reveal the aesthetic and historic value of the monument and is based on respect for original material and authentic doc-

	Planning work required for building (M) compared to new build[1]					Planning work required in comparison to M (building)[2]			
	Prelim. design, design	Approval	Detailed drawings	Tenders	Award, site management, cost accounts	XL: Block/complex	S: Part of building/storey	XS: Dwelling/room	
Reconstruction/restoration	++	○	+	+	+	/	/	/	Costly, time-consuming planning because research is necessary
Demolition/deconstruction	n/a	n/a	n/a	-	-	-	+	n/a	Often carried out by specialised contractors
Renovation/maintenance	n/a	n/a	n/a	-	+	○	○	○	Costly, time-consuming organisation (When can work be carried out?) and accounting (many management services)
Repairs/maintenance	n/a	n/a	--	-	+	○	○	○	Costly, time-consuming organisation/accounts, often no planning services
Partial refurbishment	--	n/a	+	++	++	n/a	n/a	n/a	Costly, time-consuming organisation and accounting, frequently disputes with neighbours
Refurbishment	--	n/a	○	+	++	○	+	+	Great demands placed on site management because of many uncertainties
Total refurbishment	--	n/a	+	+	+	○	+	n/a	In total slightly higher costs/more works reqd. at new/existing interface
Conversion	+	○	++	++	++	○	++	++	High design costs due to adaptation to suit the existing; high construction costs
Gutting/rebuild with part retention	○	+	○	+	+	/	/	/	Extra costs for safety measures only
Extension	+	○	+	○	○	/	/	/	Measures in the existing account for only a small part of the total budget
Fitting-out	+	+	++	++	++	n/a	n/a	n/a	Many parts of existing bldg. continue to be used; partial fit-out; costly, costly, time-consuming organisation/accounts, often disputes w. neighbours
Change of use	n/a	+	n/a	n/a	n/a	○	○	○	Only an approval required, but can be very extensive

++ much more	-- much less	/ no comparison, cannot be evaluated (e.g. owing to major fluctuations)	[1] Provides a guide as to how much higher the conversion surcharge must be or where it can be ignored.
+ more	n/a hardly or never required		[2] Necessary increase in the conversion surcharge depending on the size of the project.
○ about the same			
- less			

A 1.3

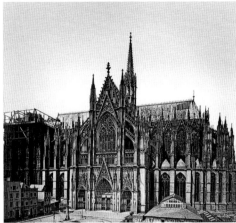

A 1.4

uments. It must stop at the point where conjecture begins…" [1]

However, this well-intentioned piece of advice is often disregarded, also because original documents are frequently unavailable. Moreover, it is not always possible to deduce what should be classed as original: the first building, the first extension, the first refurbishment, or the first conversion? This conflict has pervaded the discussions surrounding this subject in recent decades and the answers tend to reflect the respective *zeitgeist* instead of being generally acknowledged approaches. The reason for this may also be that the term "original" has been transferred – wrongly – from the visual arts to the discussions concerning architecture, where this term was unknown.

Deconstruction

It was around the year 2000 when urban planners rediscovered the theme of demolition as "negative building" and repackaged this in the term "conceptual deconstruction". What triggered this was the huge scale of the vacant housing in the towns and cities of former East Germany following unification. But similar problems occur in other regions as well; they are mostly the result of radical, structural processes that give rise to an economic decline and hence the sudden departure of the local inhabitants, e.g. in Detroit following the collapse of car production there. Deconstruction is intended to cure the urban problems of vacant properties through the targeted demolition of individual buildings, blocks or districts, i.e. control the process of negative growth. However, these concepts often fail because of a lack of funding – demolition without subsequent replacement with a new building can never show a profit.

Demolition

Besides deconstruction on a large scale, individual buildings are often demolished in order to erect a new structure on the same site. This is not an original architectural service because it is frequently carried out by specialist contractors before the project development even gets fully underway. Demolition contractors are the only ones with the appropriate specialist knowledge. Factors that need to be considered in addition to the building regulations (demolition permit) are structural aspects (special demolition engineering), safety regulations for the site operatives and the public (local residents and passers-by) and environmental protection measures if any pollutants or hazardous substances are involved. In Germany demolition work has been covered by DIN 18007 since 2000.

Renovation/maintenance

Renovation does not add anything new to the building stock nor does it replace old with new. Instead it maintains the value and the function of the existing building through competent "upkeep". Rented premises are typically renovated. Germany's 2nd Calculation Act (*Berechnungsverordnung*) specifies the following for this situation: "Cosmetic repairs include only wallpapering, painting or whitewashing the walls and ceilings, the painting of floors, radiators and heating pipes plus internal doors and the inner surfaces of windows and external doors." [2] In

Trade	Component	Inspection	Interval
Earthworks	Drainage	Check for sanding up and flush out, root damage	5 years
	Buried pipes and cables	Breakage due to settlement and roots, sludge build-up	5 years
Loadbearing structure	All components	Settlement cracks	First inspection 5 years after completion
Carpentry items	Truss joints	Check bolts for tightness	5 years
	All components	Check for rot (swimming pools etc.) and water damage	5 years
Roof covering	Flat roof	Gullies, flues, penetrations, remove growths, embrittlement cracking	Annually, at start of winter
	Pitched roof	Gutters, downpipes, visual inspection of roof covering	Annually, at start of winter
Heating	Boiler	Measure emissions	Annually, at start of winter
	Pipes	Sludge build-up, seals – especially with automatic top-up	5 years
	Radiators and valves	Valves for operation and seals	5 years
Plumbing	Hot-water provision	Calcification	5 years
Electrics	Circuit-breakers	Function	Annually
Fire protection	Smoke detectors	Function	Annually
	Fire extinguishers	Check, refill	2 years
	Escape routes	Stored objects, wedged doors	Continually
Windows	Wooden windows	External protective finishes	2 years
	All windows	Seals for brittleness and cracks	2 years
Insulation	Constructions with vapour barrier	Moisture	Once only 5 years after completion
Wood-block flooring	Oiled surfaces	Care instructions: clean and oil	Annually
Renovation intervals for rented apartments[1]		Kitchens, bathrooms, showers	3 years
		Living rooms, bedrooms, halls, toilets	5 years
		Other ancillary rooms	7 years

[1] According to the model rental contract of the German Federal Ministry of Justice dating from 1976, but these are not rigid intervals.

A 1.5

A 1.4   Cathedral, Cologne (D), 1248/1880, Gerhard von
        Rile/Ernst Friedrich Zwirner, Karl Eduard Voigtel
A 1.5   Maintenance intervals (proposal)
A 1.6   Panel construction building after deconstruction,
        Leinefelde (D), 1961/2004,
        Stefan Forster Architekten
A 1.7   Conversion of a department store, Eschweiler (D),
        2006, BeL Architekten

the same publication, maintenance is defined as follows: "Maintenance costs are the costs that must be expended during the period of use in order to maintain the intended use and eradicate properly the constructional or other defects caused by wear and tear, ageing and the effects of the weather." This includes work that actually already falls under the heading of maintenance: "The minor maintenance measures cover only the rectification of small defects in the electricity, water and gas installations, the heating and cooking facilities plus window, window shutter and door hardware."

Neglecting maintenance can lead to major damage, especially for those areas that are not generally visible, e.g. flat roofs. The design team should therefore provide the building owner with a list of suitable maintenance measures together with a schedule of maintenance intervals and maintenance instructions – a service that should be remunerated separately according to the German HOAI scale of fees for architect/engineers. The construction materials used should also be listed because, for example, mineral paints for interior use are then only advisable when mineral paints are used again in all subsequent renovation work. Fig. A 1.5 shows a typical checklist with the intervals at which the inspections or maintenance work should be carried out.

Repairs/maintenance

Maintenance in this case is limited to the replacement or repair of defective building components. Maintenance work is necessary at regular intervals between the total refurbishment intervals and is usually the responsibility of the building manager, not requiring any assistance from the design team. Whether the maintenance work for identical building components coincides should be investigated for economic reasons. A leak from a water pipe, for instance, may occur from time to time, certainly not simply once a year. But in the case of regular leaks, it may be advisable to replace all the water pipes above basement level. The leak may indeed have been caused by earlier maintenance work, e.g. a system of iron pipework being partly replaced by copper.

Maintenance measures inevitably lead to follow-up costs that may far exceed the actual cost of

the repairs, e.g. if intact ceramic tiles have to be chiselled off when searching for the source of a leak. In this case we must ask ourselves the question of whether we take the step to complete refurbishment, e.g. renewing all the bathrooms. In rented accommodation, the costs can then be passed on to the tenants, at least partly.

Refurbishment

In contrast to maintenance, refurbishment measures also include intact but, for example, outdated components or surfaces. The difference between refurbishment and conversion, however, is that refurbishment does not involve any major changes to the loadbearing structure or interior layout. It therefore lies exactly between maintenance and conversion, but the extent of refurbishment works can vary enormously.

Partial refurbishment

Partial refurbishment involves only one component or one part of the building, e.g. the facade, the ground floor or the east wing. Such projects are among the most difficult to organise because they are carried out while the rest of the building is still in use. Conflicts with users are inevitable because partial refurbishment measures cannot be carried out in isolation; the technical infrastructure, for example, extends throughout the building. One effective strategy is to provide detailed information about the intended measures at an early stage. For example, cutting and chasing work in occupied buildings is very annoying, especially when it starts at seven o'clock in the morning! A little consideration in the form of specifying working hours in the contract plus communications regarding the duration of the building work offer some relief here: the work remains annoying but limiting the duration increases the acceptance. The same is true for setting up a scaffold, cutting off services (especially the television!), work in internal and external access zones and all measures where excessive dust, noise or vibration is to be expected.

More generous time and cost buffers should be allowed for when planning partial refurbishment in particular, also a budget to cover collateral damage to areas and components that were not included in the refurbishment plans. Such

damage is unavoidable and its rectification should be carried out quickly and without bureaucratic fuss. In addition, the owners of rented premises should certainly be warned about the possible risk of lost revenue from rents. For when the "suitability of the rented premises for the use as stated in the contract" is revoked or reduced, German legislation permits rent reductions of 20% on average. This clause comes into play as soon as an apartment cannot be ventilated because there is too much dust, or when the telephone in an office cannot be used because of excessive noise.

"Normal" refurbishment

Normal refurbishment measures encompass an entire building or least a part of the building that already exists as a clearly separate, autonomous element. Any demolition work necessary is mostly limited to surfaces or preparatory work for upgrading fire protection, noise control or thermal performance. Additions and changes to the existing infrastructure are typical, but

A 1.8

their complete replacement less common. Refurbishment cycles for individual components have been relatively well determined empirically (see "Planning refurbishment works", p. 23, Fig. B 1.2). True refurbishment without a change of use does not require building authority approval and is safeguarded by the notion of toleration of the building stock, but this concept is usually no longer valid for total refurbishment or conversion works.

Total refurbishment

Demolition measures during total refurbishment projects are very extensive. The demolition returns the building more or less to its loadbearing carcass. The primary structure remains essentially unaltered. Typical measures include the complete replacement of the infrastructure and the upgrading of all building components to meet the requirements of the latest legislation and standards. Owing to the extent of the work, total refurbishment is an expensive undertaking, especially when decontamination is involved as well. But in the end the refurbished building comes very close to a new one in terms of its facilities and safety. This is also expressed by the fact that upon completion all the components are covered by the warranty, also with respect to current standards and legislation. Such an all-embracing warranty is often missing from simple refurbishment projects because many components are left untouched, still in their original condition. In terms of planning, a total refurbishment is not so very different to a new construction, partly because many uncertainties are eliminated, so to speak. It may be that certain weaknesses in the carcass, e.g. the lack of a damp-proof course, excessive deflections of the suspended floors, or acoustic weaknesses due to a low weight per unit area, remain because their rectification is uneconomic. During the planning, the flatness tolerances should be considered. These usually lie well outside those of current standards, which have been covered by DIN 18202 supplement 1 only since 1969.

Conversion

Conversions always affect the structure of a building. They extend the concept of refurbishment to interventions in the loadbearing mem-

bers and/or the interior layout. In conversion projects it is therefore always essential to appraise the existing loadbearing structure. Total refurbishment measures almost always involve conversion work, meaning that many construction projects are best described by using more than one term, e.g. "total refurbishment plus conversion". Changes to the structure always require structural calculations, which must also take into account the existing building fabric. This makes early, often destructive, investigations of the materials and methods used unavoidable, e.g. cutting open a concrete slab to establish the position and nature of the reinforcement. Furthermore, true design services are necessary for conversion projects because they involve changes to the interior layout or the access/circulation concepts. Such additional planning input is covered in the German HOAI scale of fees for architects/engineers in the form of a surcharge for conversion work. Partial conversion should be treated similarly to partial refurbishment.

Gutting/rebuilding with partial retention
Gutting comes close to providing a new building. Quite frequently the project involves retaining the facades of an existing building – resulting from a disputed understanding of the conservation of historic buildings – but demolishing and rebuilding the interior completely.

Modernisation
The term modernisation is in the first place relevant in landlord and tenant legislation. According to the German Civil Code, the annual rent may be increased by 11% of the costs incurred for modernisation if the measures are carried out according to the statutory stipulations (including advance warning, detailed description of intended measures). Modernisation can add up to partial refurbishment, e.g. upgrading the thermal insulation or replacing windows, but also conversion work, e.g. the subsequent addition of balconies. In any case, modernisation serves to improve the lettable floor space by increasing the level of comfort or decreasing the running costs. The following measures are

A 1.9

A 1.10

regarded as modernisations in the meaning of German landlord and tenant legislation:

- Upgrading thermal/sound insulation, also internally (e.g. between stairs and apartments)
- New sanitary facilities
- Installation of central heating (to replace individual appliances) or central hot-water supply (instead of separate water heaters)
- Additions to electrical installations, also the provision of cable television or the installation of a door intercom
- The erection of balconies or conservatories
- Installing a lift

Decontamination

This is the proper elimination of pollutants and hazardous substances from buildings and their correct disposal. The contamination of the interior air by hazardous substances has been a constant topic in refurbishment since the late 1970s due to the presence of PCP-based wood preservatives and asbestos fibres. In the meantime, the risks of many other substances have become known; the options for dealing with these are discussed in the chapter on hazardous substances (see pp. 102–115). Various statutory instruments and different limit values exist depending on the use of the building: the maximum workplace concentration, for instance, is applied to commercial uses, recommended values I and II of the Environmental Issues Committee, on the other hand, are relevant for housing and public buildings. If the values established in measurements of the interior air exceed the prescribed limit values, decontamination must be carried out, which can take place before or during the building works. For the building owner, such decontamination measures often result in higher costs and a substantial increase in the time needed for the work. Carrying out measurements well ahead of any proposed building works is therefore imperative where hazardous substances are suspected. In buildings built or refurbished between 1960 and 1990, the chance of finding contamination is relatively high.

Extensions/additions

An extension is a new structure that is directly connected with the use of the existing building. The planning work should consider the fact that conversion work at the junction with the existing building is usually unavoidable and therefore structural issues are involved. A frequent cause of problems is the differential settlement that can occur between the old and new parts of the building, especially in the following cases:

- Different foundation levels
- Building the foundations for the new works in the region of the previous excavation
- Building the foundations in different soils
- Adding extra storeys to only part of the existing building (subsequent settlement)
- Dewatering measures for the new works, e.g. lowering the water table

Fitting-out

Fitting-out is all the works carried out after erecting the structural carcass plus roof structure and roof covering. One typical measure is converting the roof space into one or more habitable rooms, i.e. fitting-out an attic storey not originally in use. The constructional problems that can occur are described in the chapters "General refurbishment tasks" and "Buildings of the founding years" (see pp. 127–129 and p. 153). Added to these are the loss of protection afforded by the notion of toleration of the building stock, which complicates the building authority approval process, especially with respect to fire protection, means of escape, distance to neighbouring buildings and car parking requirements. Further problems result from the fact that the work has to be carried out while the rest of the building is occupied (see "Partial refurbishment", p. 13). Such fitting-out projects are therefore very demanding from the planning point of view and should be remunerated accordingly.

Change of use

A change of use is subject to construction legislation stipulations. In the first instance this concerns obvious changes like converting an apartment block into offices, even if only part of the building is involved. However, also minor changes of use within the same usage group, e.g. from baker to hairdresser, require approval by the authorities in certain cases, and especially when there are differences with respect to occupational safety and health issues, emissions, car parking, etc. For this reason, more intensive uses represent changes of use that require approval, e.g. if an existing office floor used as a company headquarters is let to a call centre operator. One problem here is the associated loss of protection afforded by the notion of toleration of the building stock. This means that a change of use can have far-reaching consequences because the current building regulations may need to be complied with, and the existing building may not be adequate. This legal situation has been criticised many times because it hinders the long-term use of buildings and is hence questionable in terms of both economics and ecology.

Notes:

[1] The Venice Charter, 1964
[2] Zweite Berechnungsverordnung, cl. 28

A 1.11

Further building work – thoughts on works *with* the building stock

Georg Giebeler, Petra Kahlfeldt

A 2.1

The refurbishment of a building always means adapting it to meet current standards, too, whether because of changes in users' demands or new technical regulations. The building measures required here call for knowledge of both current and historical building methods. Based on an understanding and appraisal of historic structures, this task is solvable in the technical sense. It would appear to be that the focal point in the first place is the technical and not the architectural side, from which we could conclude that refurbishment and conversion projects are purely engineering services. This widely held opinion is probably due to the fact that a major part of the architecture has ostensibly already been completed: the volume essentially set, the structure of the building fixed by the loadbearing members, and even the appearance seemingly predetermined, especially in the case of concrete and masonry structures. The planner's task therefore appears to be reduced to solving the purely technical problems of the existing building, e.g. thermal performance, noise control, with the architecture playing no role at all. This point of view is reinforced by the way that the conservation of historic buildings and monuments has been carried out for many years: the details to be constructed, the techniques to be used and the surface finishes chosen were very often specified by art historians. Such persons are undoubtedly scientifically trained for such tasks, but their very conception of the job means they avoid integrating any of their own design ideas.

But even the simplest of refurbishment tasks calls for an equal amount of architectural input. Very small measures and changes can result in a substantial change to the existing building – mostly spoiling the appearance as well – as the following examples will show.

Adding extra thermal insulation to the outside of a building is a very common upgrading measure these days and in most cases results in much deeper window reveals on the outside and the unsatisfactory effect of "holes for windows". This adulteration of the architecture is even more noticeable when the windows were originally flush with the outside face of the original facade. Furthermore, the new insulation to the reveals themselves reduces the size of the window openings, i.e. the ratio of window area to wall surface changes. The roof overhang at the eaves also decreases – even disappears altogether in some cases – due to the additional thermal insulation on the external wall. Another effect is that any relief or details on the facade – small but perhaps significant, e.g. stone door jambs or moulded window surrounds – are also levelled off. For reasons of cost, labour-intensive methods such as stone plinths worked with masonry tools disappear behind new render and the narrow window surrounds common on the rendered facades of the post-war years are simply forgotten. Even the surfaces of existing rendered facades disappear with the refurbishment work because instead of older sprayed and scratched render finishes, the lack of skilled, experienced workers means that now only trowelled finishes are on offer.

Likewise, the replacement of windows – necessary for technical reasons – almost inevitably by new products with wider frames is accepted virtually without any comment; and the greenish, reflective float glass as a substitute for the thinner, wavy cast glass is then particularly alarming when you compare the old and new elevations. Re-covering a steep pitched roof with wide concrete roof tiles can disfigure a gable because a delicate verge detail is replaced by crude verge tiles bedded in mortar.

Another example is the way facing masonry is treated in northern Europe; inexpensive external thermal insulation composite systems are causing more and more characteristic clay brick facades to disappear from the urban landscape. But even if an expensive double-leaf solution with new facing brickwork is chosen instead, the colouring, the imperfections and hence the character of the old facade can never be regained.

Inside the building, new ceilings needed for sound insulation or fire resistance purposes alter not only the proportions of rooms but also cover old plaster coves between wall and ceiling, even ornamental mouldings on the ceiling itself – quite apart from the fact that the difference between the hand-crafted old plaster on the walls and the perfectly flat plasterboard ceiling is unpleasantly conspicuous even to the uninitiated. Simply improving the impact sound

A 2.2

insulation calls for changes such as covering up nailed floorboards and removing the high, painted and profiled skirting boards, which for reasons of cost are replaced by simple timber battens. Following refurbishment, old panelled doors frequently look out of proportion because they have been shortened to accommodate the new floor construction. Even purely technical adjustments often leave behind a peculiar, alienated overall feeling in an old building. For example, in old surroundings simple sheet steel radiators appear mundane in contrast to the massive original radiators, and on staircases skirtings of ceramic tiles or other special finishes are irreparably damaged when cutting chases for new electrical or fire safety installations. There are many more, similar examples, and the refurbishment measures always appear unavoidable. To be sure, many of the building measures described here are inescapable where noise control, thermal performance or fire protection have to be upgraded to meet statutory requirements. But the result is a different one

when the planning work is carried out according to architectural principles, i.e. with a conceptual, formal, technically holistic approach, instead of planning exclusively in accordance with the technical and economic feasibility. The aforementioned measures are among the typical tasks of refurbishment and that means what has been said applies even more so to more extensive interventions in the building stock such as total refurbishments, conversions and extensions, in other words complex architectural assignments that demand a synthesis between architecture and technology. The design approach with respect to such planning tasks seems to be changing, maybe has even changed already. Reconstructive adaptation or contrasting new elements – until recently these two approaches were irreconcilable opponents. In the meantime, the experience gained on a multitude of planning tasks involving the building stock – particularly for buildings not protected by conservation orders, but not only these – has seen the development of a new approach

that gives priority to the unity of the building – no longer old and new as opposites, but instead old and new as a harmonic whole (Fig. A 2.1). This notion of "works within the building stock" will be enlarged upon in the following two sections.

Further building work? Further building work!

Building, whether new works or conversions, always means further building work – continuing to build at a certain site, building, street, district, town, landscape.

It always involves tackling the existing situation. No site is unoccupied or undescribed. Our living spaces are cultural spaces full of visible and invisible, but in every case detectable, references, i.e. historical, spiritual/cultural, spatial, social/emotional, functional and physical traces. These are either visible on the surface or can be made legible.

To build is to live. This is why architecture is founded on permanence and continuity. Getting to grips with our own social and architectural history is therefore an essential prerequisite for everything new. Every architectural project is based on what the architect finds and its complex past – spiritually and materially (Figs. A 2.2 and 2.3). Consequently, every change is assigned an importance and a responsibility that goes way beyond the individual design of the architect.

The architectural theme of further building work is as old as architecture itself. At the start we ask the existential question: "Building?" – a simple hut with a roof of leaves, a house between trees or a bird's nest? Sometime after we get the answer: "Further building?" What do we do when our hut, house or nest has to be altered to suit different functional demands, totally different requirements?

Further building always calls for a sensitive weighing-up between preserving and renewing. We expect architects to show interest, knowledge, empathy and self-imposed constraints. For in the end what this entails is – initially – becoming involved with the constructional language and the three-dimensional text of the building stock. Moreover, the design approach called for is one that solves the dilemma of conservation or renewal appropriately.

But what is appropriate? It is not simply provid-

A 2.3

a

b   A 2.4

ing an answer to the functional, technical question regarding the connection between old and new in the design. The architectural and spatial task demands a change to the existing building, i.e. a composed, designed treatment. The Italian architect Francesco Collotti sees this as understanding an assignment as being provided "with internal living forms in order to achieve an interpretation, a subtle but at the same time technical and literary act of creative composition". This field of conflict into which the architect is drawn is quickly defined: on the one side the existing building with its idea of space created by constructions and materials, and on the other side the ingredient seen as necessary, which results from a change in demands or a change of use.

In a consequential further development of the catchphrase that appeared during the debate about fundamentals around 1900, "conservation instead of restoration", the approach that has become established in contemporary conservation work, i.e. that the different periods of building work must be clearly evident on a building and readily discernible, means that new and old must be rigorously separated. This notion of a "dual" system – there the old, here the new – has become a general guideline for works in the building stock, irrespective of whether the building is covered by a conservation order. Propagated by architects and the curators of monuments, this categorical separation between old and new has remained the guiding principle right up to the present day– albeit with totally different intentions. For the conservation of historic buildings and monuments based on scientific findings, the integrity, authenticity and legibility of the construction must be preserved; for many architects this is a criterion – thankfully accepted – that enables them freedom to express their own artistic, individual preferences, which at all costs must be distinguished from those of their anonymous architecture colleagues of history. This separation, fragmentation, breakdown into layers – adding new to old in a clearly identifiable way – is widespread. A conversion based on this principle understandably calls for major changes to the existing works in order to be able to establish the figuratively, materially and also constructionally contrasting ingredient.

The result is, however, inhomogeneous and discordant.

The basis for the debates about the success or otherwise of further building work, which are heard not only in architecture circles, can only be architectural criteria themselves. The image of a recognisable town, street or district, one with which people can identify as a cultural community of buildings and spaces, forms as a holistic thought that includes and accepts the existing objects as a matter of fact.

Meanwhile, despite all the efforts at separation, an understanding and a practice of further building has emerged that does not place the celebration of time periods in the foreground but rather emphasizes the architectural unity of the building. Is the connection – transcending time – that brings together our modern constructions and those surviving from the past not a good way of illustrating tradition? In the awareness of an ongoing cultural inheritance and taking into account architectural traditions, the design task "works in the building stock" is an explicit invitation to instigate coexistence and cooperation, an aesthetic and figuratively sensitive correspondence, the search for a coherent, cohesive design language. Miroslav Sik, a prize-winning Swiss architect known for his high-quality further development of historically mature European towns and cities, regards the search for a coherent design language as "the middle way between flagrantly trite statements and over-ambitious design antics. Plan the necessary, leave the unnecessary and address the needs of buildings and their occupants as an architect." [1]

This is the only way to create the pictorial metaphor of unification as a transformation consisting of preserved and renewed without changing the origins or losing them altogether. In a design concept of the "new whole", the old is not used as a setting for the new. It is the search for architectural coherency that enables the existing and the new intervention to be equal partners in an overall architectural form, to go beyond the sheer insurmountable categories of new and old without the complexity and diversity needed to master the building task being lost at the same time. The new seen as a transformed whole has a little of both in it with-

out it being seen as a separate layer: a continuous, homogeneous whole. [2]

Works in the building stock? Works *with* the building stock!

But we could understand further building work as the uncritical continuation of a long since outdated era, as a retro wave, engulfing the construction industry in the same way as it has done the design departments of car and furniture manufacturers. Copies of the past – apparently legitimate since the reconstruction of Dresden's Frauenkirche (an understandable act of reconstruction) – are unfortunately also the starting point for architectural monstrosities such as the "Palace Arcade" shopping centre in Braunschweig and all the many small, apparently trivial examples in the tradition of the Bauhaus or other marketable eras.

For "historic architecture" is, as it says, "historic" and cannot be "present-day". Reproducing a building from Germany's *Gründerzeit* "true to the original" is destined to fail to the same extent as its conversion into a palace of glass. Several insurmountable obstacles stand in the way of such projects:

- Different political and social conditions
- A different environment – in terms of both architecture and urban planning
- Different legislation and regulations
- Different manual skills
- A different state of the art
- Planners are not "historic" – consequently, they cannot build in a historic way

For these reasons, the dogmatic copying of history must fail. But where is the aforementioned middle way, the "reconciliatory coexistence and cooperation"? It begins where further building work is no longer regarded as works "in" the building stock, i.e. as something new "within" the existing, but rather as works "with" the building stock, i.e. fusing the existing with the new to form a holistic new object, like, for example, the Feyferlik/Fritzer architectural practice has succeeded in achieving with the new building and conversion works for the Mariazell pilgrimage site (Figs. A 2.4 and 2.5). However, the use of the existing presupposes

A 2.5

A 2.4   Archive rooms in the roof space, ecclesiastical
        building, Mariazell (A), 2001, Feyferlik/Fritzer
A 2.5   Refurbishment of liturgy area and organ installation,
        basilica, Mariazell (A), 2000, Feyferlik/Fritzer

an understanding of the existing in its entirety. Only in this way is it possible to understand the entire structure instead of individual pros and cons. Further building work is not limited here to understanding the technical features, but rather to discovering the original conception and liberating this from factual and taste-related constraints, i.e. separating the historical concepts from the necessary, the prescribed, the technically restricted aspects, or the typical fashions of the time. This is different to the case of a new building, which can be adjusted to a position (also known as "style"), something an existing building cannot do. The building stock cannot be subsequently squeezed into a position. Conversions cannot be forced. If the planner sees only the disadvantages of the existing building, satisfactory results will hardly be possible. Further building means using the best ingredients you have at your disposal, discovering the positive sides of the existing structure and shutting out the negative ones, loving the existing structure.

Understanding the existing, learning to love and using the new to form a whole could be likened to a team: the partnership between the architects responsible for the existing building – possibly all totally different – and those of the new works. However, this partnership in actual fact consists of only one – sort of schizophrenic – person, i.e. the architect appointed to carry out the latest work. In order that the partnership can succeed despite different initial conditions, the current planner can refer to a common experience, which was valid for the architects of the past just as much as it is for the architects of the present: costs have to be kept to a minimum and everything must be constructed on time and without defects. Historic constructions and the resulting architecture are usually a demonstration of this set of problems and not the manifestation of independent artistic expressions as often claimed by the curators of historic monuments (a claim thankfully accepted by the retro designers). The delicacy of a window with glazing bars lies not in its design, but rather in its well-functioning, inexpensive construction which, however, no longer meets today's demands. If further building means finding a contemporary solution that fits into the overall concept, neither

the fixed glazing without glazing bars in an aluminium frame nor a "looks-from-a-distance-almost-like design" will be adequate. It is the window that the architect of the existing building would have designed if he had had today's technical options at his disposal and could have stood back and viewed the whole from the same distance as today's architect. Empathy with the creator of the existing is not possible outside our own experience, which rules out an uncritical acceptance of every historical concept right from the very start. Empathy in further building means: How would the architect of history have solved this detail? Which constructions would he have used to implement the Energy Conservation Act, comply with or circumvent the Rosenheimer window-building guidelines? The planning of further building with the new works and conversions necessary for this presupposes modern constructions and modern manual skills, which themselves imply totally different architecture. The texture and waviness of a rendered facade dating from the 19th century – as an inexpensive, good-quality construction – can no longer be imitated because today's bricks are far too accurate, today's workers have little or no experience of lime renders and – made careful through constant complaints – no longer perform manual work.

Further building or works with the building stock means acknowledging the building stock and trying to understand it, identifying and assessing its structure and its position. Only after that is it possible for the architect to develop his own position, as a response to the existing. And a personal position is always related to the present day: current political and social circumstances, current costs, current constructions. So designing according to modern standards – not being forced to create a contrast, not being forced to make the new legible, as is often and wrongly requested – is not objectionable but instead convincing. Why should something be separated when it forms a whole? In other words wishes to be "one" building and not a didactic 1:1 exhibition of various architectures. All we demand, quite rightly, is good architecture, i.e. a conceptually coherent, functioning whole. So in further building the exclusivity of contrast

or adaptation is not suitable as a design approach. Both merge into the "team of understanding equals"; that means today's planners exercising respect towards the work of the architects of the past, but also the posthumous consent of those architects for further building according to modern principles.

Notes:

[1]   Speech held on the occasion of awarding the
      Heinrich Tessenow Medal in 2005.
[2]   This section is the work of Petra Kahlfeldt,
      an architect in Berlin.

Part B   Principles

Fig. B   SUVA Building, refurbished building envelope,
Basel (CH), 1993, Herzog & de Meuron

Planning refurbishment works

Georg Giebeler

B 1.1

The planning of conversions is fundamentally different from the planning of new works. For example, the entire planning process for a new structure is abstract until work commences on site: discussions with clients and other members of the design team can be structured by employing interim targets, external obligations exist only as a result of statutory provisions. The client can prescribe unambiguous objectives with respect to costs, completion date and his functional requirements, sometimes even his aesthetic preferences.

But the starting point for a conversion is an existing building, which alters the situation completely. Planning work departs from the abstract level right at the start and delves into the problems of the existing construction. The client's demands remain the same, however: reliable costs and deadlines, functional requirements and architectural requests. The procedure when planning a conversion must take this conflict into account if a satisfactory result is to be achieved.

Analysis

The planning process begins with an analysis of the existing construction – an ongoing task that is repeated many times as design and construction proceeds. The more comprehensive the investigations, the greater is the reliability of the planning and hence also the costs and deadlines. However, for reasons of his fee alone, the architect would never carry out a complete analysis. So it is important to select the critical points. For example, to check the serviceability of a timber joist floor, it is always the supports that are investigated; it is not necessary to remove the ceiling completely. Besides knowledge of the defects typical at the time the building was constructed and our own experience, a decent portion of commonsense is helpful: a major cause of damage is water in all its forms, so the components that deserve attention are those that could have been damaged in some way by rainfall, splashing water, groundwater, water vapour (organic infestation, rot) or leaking water pipes.

Archives

The first step should always be to study old documents. Drawings and calculations provide an overview of the design and construction process at that time and serve as the foundation for further investigations or inspections. Possible sources are the client himself, previous owners, the architect and structural engineer originally responsible, and the archives of the local building authority.

Research

Researching the building means carrying out a detailed historical analysis of the existing construction with the aim of being able to trace the history and the planning of the building when it was first designed and built. Archive material collected from various sources plus random examinations of components provide the starting point for this. This approach allows different phases of the construction, later extensions and conversions, older and newer refurbishment work or superficial maintenance to be identified and recorded. Knowledge of the building methods used is helpful when trying to assess their typical strengths and weaknesses, but also evidence of constructional deficiencies, e.g. concealed joints between the original structure and an extension.

The cost and work involved in such research is, however, only realistic for buildings with a historic value. But the approach as such can be transferred to simple planning tasks as well.

On-site measurements and as-built drawings

The measurement of structures or components accompanies the conversion measures during all phases of the work. Here, too, the difference between this and a new-build project must be considered. Again and again, the inaccuracies of the existing structure lead to conflicts with the new planning work. So the trick is to interpret the on-site measurements, i.e. deliberately draw other dimensions to those measured in order to achieve a consistent overall picture. For example, deviations from right-angles amounting to only a few degrees are seldom important when planning a conversion and should be ignored. It is also necessary to interpolate the differences in length amounting to several centimetres measured in a room. The aim of on-site measurement is not to create an exact likeness, but rather to achieve a consistent basis for planning.

B 1.1   Conversion of an industrial building into an office building, Cologne (D), 2001, 4000architekten
B 1.2   Lifetime expectancies of various building components
B 1.3   The make-up of the building stock in Germany (residential buildings only)

Component	Lifetime [years]	
	min.	max.
Render, facades	30	60
Pitched roofs	40	60
Flat roofs	20	40
Windows	25	40
Insulating glass units	20	35
Building envelope as a whole	20	60
Heating	12	35

B 1.2

Period	Detached houses [m²]	Apartment blocks [m²]	Total floor area [m²]	Proportion of total floor area
before 1918	305 000	227 000	532 000	18 %
1919–1948	244 000	145 000	389 000	13 %
1949–1957	209 000	185 000	394 000	13 %
1958–1968	252 000	223 000	475 000	16 %
1969–1978	303 000	258 000	561 000	19 %
1979–1983	383 000	246 000	629 000	21 %
total	1 696 000	1 248 000	2 980 000	100 %

B 1.3

For this reason, automated systems that can generate CAD data from 3-D measurements are only recommended for very special applications, e.g. the conservation of important historic buildings.

Notwithstanding, to achieve proper, interpretable documents, inaccurate measurements should be avoided. A laser measuring instrument is indispensable for this because it supplies exact dimensional data and in contrast to a tape measure can be used by one person alone (Fig. B 1.6). Additional tools are a folding one-metre rule, a plumb line and a compass. The following recommendations are helpful when carrying out on-site measurements:

• If possible, use chain dimensions instead of starting from zero again each time.
• Measure through open doors etc. in order to obtain the total internal dimensions of the building.
• Measure heights in the staircase and record storey heights.
• Measure the total external dimensions.
• Door openings etc. need be measured on one side only.
• In rooms with walls at odd angles, measure the diagonals; the minimum or maximum dimensions obtained with laser instruments are helpful here because the target can be "run along" an edge.
• Look at the underside of the floor above: heights, downstand beams, etc. are often forgotten when measuring.
• Measure all wall thicknesses.
• Window openings usually include a masonry stop, so two clear opening dimensions are required.
• Take horizontal dimensions at the same height wherever possible because no wall is perfectly vertical.
• If possible, remove wall and soffit linings in order to obtain the dimensions of the structural carcass.

Begin drawing the as-built drawings with the most dependable dimensions, i.e. the overall sizes, and then try to fit the interior layout into this as logically as possible (Fig. B 1.4). Interpreting the information means drawing what should be repetitive dimensions identically, e.g. window openings, and possibly also checking whether the wall sections between windows should not also be identical, even though you may have noted different dimensions. The idea behind this is to reveal the thinking of the building's original architect and not the vagaries in the skills of the construction workers involved. At the start of the planning phase, drawings to a scale of 1:50 are adequate. During the later stages, especially when fitting new into old, further measurements will be necessary. As a rule, accurate on-site measurements should not be carried out until after any demolition work has been completed – in order to prevent duplicating the work (see "Clearance" p. 29).

Dimensional coordination
The attempt to standardise the dimensions of components has been a feature of all periods in the history of building. But just like with many other products, different standards have existed in different regions. Harmonisation on a national level took place similarly to the current introduction of Euronorms, i.e. rather sluggishly. Knowledge of the dimensional coordination customary at the time the building was erected can assist in the interpretation of the existing structure, i.e. in order to estimate the dimensions of the underlying structure, e.g. masonry wall thicknesses and their linings, without having to open up the construction (Fig. B 1.5).

Visual inspections
Many patterns of damage and forms of construction can be determined purely by visual inspections and feeling, touching the surfaces. As this is an inexpensive approach, a thorough inspection and full documentation is advisable. As part of this, it is helpful to note the positions at which photographs were taken on the as-built drawings because this is the only way to assign the photographs unequivocally at a later date. The partial opening-up of components is also highly recommended. For example, when assessing a timber joist floor, the nature and construction of the ceiling and infill materials are important, especially when considering load-bearing capacity, sound insulation and fire resistance. In this situation it is usually sufficient to open up the floor beneath one joist support. The position of the joists is easy to determine from above via the positions of the nails securing the floorboards.

Measurements and laboratory tests
The measurement of component properties and laboratory tests can supply further information regarding suspected problems, but because this is costly a full investigation is not feasible. Generally, individual examinations are used to draw conclusions about the entire construction, which does leave some room for errors.
Simple instruments for measuring the moisture content of components measure the electrical resistance in the material by means of two electrodes (Fig. B 1.7). If the material is known, tables can be used to reach conclusions regarding the degree of saturation in terms of percentage by volume. As this method is relatively imprecise and prone to errors, a series of measurements should be carried out. The measurements are carried out on the surface of the component, which means that no statements can be made regarding the moisture in the middle of the component, e.g. a masonry wall. The same applies to dielectric measurements, i.e. those based on measuring electromagnetic waves. Nevertheless, in practice both types of measurement are adequate because normally the intention is only to estimate whether a component is wet or dry.
If accurate values or measurements in the centre of a component are required, taking a sample is the only option. In this case the water content can be established exactly with the help of the Darr method, which uses three weight measurements: first of all, the sample as taken on site is weighed, then the completely dried sample, and finally the saturated sample. This method allows the moisture content to be determined in terms of percentage by volume. In order to classify the causes of surface moisture, e.g. damp, warm summer air on cool surfaces (basement masonry), measurements of the moisture content in the component should be supplemented by interior humidity, interior temperature and surface temperature values. Determining the dead loads of components and constructions can be useful when planning

conversions. For example, if we replace the loam filling to a timber joist floor by sound-insulating batts, the weight saved can be offset against floor constructions using floating screeds or suspended ceilings. This is useful for the structural analysis.

Many component analyses cannot be cleared up by way of simple in situ inspections. In such cases samples must be taken and tested in suitable laboratories. This is necessary not only in cases of damage, but also when the material properties are required for new calculations, e.g. grade of concrete and yield stress of steel in a reinforced concrete floor slab. And for decontamination assignments measurements of the interior air to check for parameters such as VOC, PCB, asbestos, formaldehyde and mould are standard (see also "Dangerous substances in the building stock", pp. 102–115).

Evaluation

The evaluation of the existing construction is an intrinsic part of the architect's services. Very early on, a decision must be made as to whether the objectives of the client can be achieved with a reasonable budget. Using the analysis of the existing construction as our starting point, a study is carried out to establish to what extent existing components can be used in the refurbished building and the cost of refurbishing such parts. Only afterwards is it possible to conclude whether or not the property is suitable for conversion.

In order to be able to reach a reasonably reliable decision at an early stage, the architect should concentrate on the following three issues.

Usage – new usage
Not every representative of the building stock is suitable for every new type of use. This will always be a problem where very specific, unalterable user interests are involved. For example, the circular saw in a carpentry shop needs a certain amount of space, and no alternative concept will suffice. If essential, i.e. generally loadbearing, components, are in the way, the cost of the conversion will rise substantially. Partial conversions, e.g. a single storey, can lead to further problems. For example, any supports required in the floor below – if occupied – may be just as impossible as the repositioning of a waste-water discharge stack.

The discrepancies between users' wishes and the survey of the existing construction therefore result in constraints. Identifying and reconciling these is part of the evaluation process.

Conversion potential
The architect should estimate the inherent conversion potential of the structure taking into account the constraints. In other words, to what extent it is possible to intervene in the existing fabric so that it can be adapted to the new user requirements? The conversion potential depends on the type of construction and therefore also on the period in which the building was erected.

"Forcing" a conversion on a building will always lead to an unsatisfactory result – both financially and architecturally.

Patterns of damage, principal problems
The analysis usually results in a number of patterns of damage that cannot be fully appraised at this early stage of the planning. The aim must be to establish the principal problems and estimate their costs and completion dates. Fig. B 1.8 shows the economic appraisals of a number of typical refurbishment and conversion measures.

Planning process

Conversions exhibit a number of idiosyncrasies, both in terms of the sequence of operations and the boundary conditions. If the architect has been mainly concerned with new structures up until now, he must learn to rethink the planning process. One thing that is very clear is that the planning and site supervision of conversion projects is more involved than that of new-build projects, which is allowed for in the German scale of fees for architects/engineers (HOAI) by way of the conversion surcharge.

Phase 1: clarification of design brief
Clarification of the design brief covers the initial preliminary work and discussions between the client and the architect in which the nature of the future cooperation, the costs of the building work, the completion date and general user require-

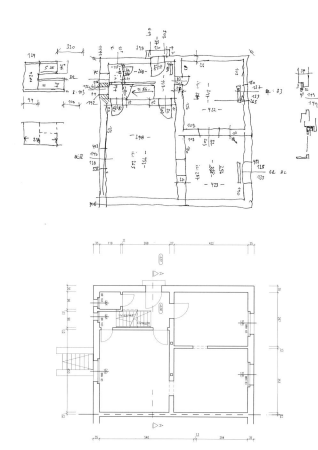

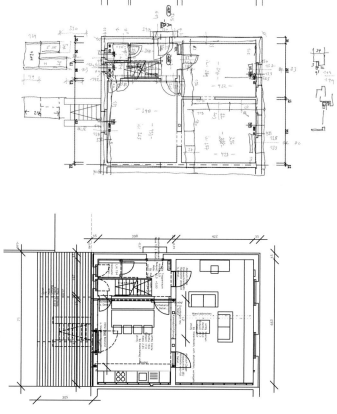

B 1.4

ments are discussed. This phase is considerably different to the equivalent phase for a new-build project. Right from the start, the client expects a report on the quality and conversion potential of the building; so the client's questions are much more specific. On the other hand, requirements concerning usage and targets regarding costs and deadlines are attached the same importance as for a new building.

It is imperative to explain to the client that with a conversion the latter two issues cannot be answered at this early stage. Which measures may need to be taken in the future in order to achieve even only a vague target cannot be clarified until after a detailed analysis of the existing structure has been carried out – and in the worst case not until after the structure has been purchased. The client is taking a considerable risk in this latter case because he is buying a property without knowing exactly how much a refurbishment will cost and when it will be completed. And he also has to accept that he may possibly have to modify his usage concept.

It is therefore vital to answer the following questions unambiguously and confidently: Is it worth refurbishing this building? What difficulties are we likely to face?

The initial discussions very often take place as part of a site visit, the purpose of which is to view, not to appraise. Not until the project has been reduced to an abstract level – and subsequent partial analyses have possibly been carried out – is it possible to make a relatively reliable statement as to whether or not conversion is worthwhile. The architect should never forget that answering this question in the affirmative is at that moment a decision regarding a large portion of the total cost of the project. The architect is therefore recommended to include services from the preliminary planning and possibly also the final design phases in this phase of the work. Such consultancy services should also be reflected in the level of the fee. A survey of the existing structure, for example, can be invoiced as a "special service" according to the German scale of fees for architects/ engineers.

Phase 2: preliminary planning

Besides further work originating from phase 1, the main new areas of work in this phase are developing the planning concept, conducting the first meetings with the other specialists in the design team and the authorities, plus estimating the costs.

The loadbearing capacity is an important point in the appraisal of the existing building because upgrading the loadbearing structure can be a very expensive undertaking. And it would be foolhardy to appraise the existing structure without the help of a structural engineer. Estimates of possible spans based on experience of new-build work are not reliable in conversions because the serviceability of historical constructions often has to be investigated according to the latest standards.

Cost estimates according to building volume are also destined to fail in the case of conversion projects because there are insufficient statistics available to use as a basis. The reason for this is that owing to the fact that all conversion projects are different, they are harder to categorise. It is therefore advisable to bring forward the cost estimate from phase 3 or at least carry out a detailed examination of individual components.

Phase 3: final design

If some of the costing has already been carried out in phase 2, the primary task of the final design phase is working through the planning concept, including the provision of drawings. One obvious approach is to use the as-built drawings as a basis for the final design. However, those drawings contain too much information, which could result in apparent constraints. Such drawings also have "graphical" limits, which are then regarded as part of the existing structure and thus generate further constraints. The outcome is consequently often closer to a refurbishment than a new start.

So like with urban planning studies, an attempt should be made to remove small details from the drawings. The most radical method in the planning of conversions is to gut the entire building theoretically: What is left when we demolish all components that are not loadbearing? Left with this drawing of the "structural carcass", it is easier to plan and think without constraints. After this concept phase, the second step is to investigate which non-loadbearing components can be integrated into the concept. One advantage of this method is that it is possible to avoid interventions in the fabric of the building.

Starting with the basic fabric of the building also means delving into the original design and eliminating possibly disruptive interventions at a later date.

Phase 4: building permission application

This phase of the project involves all the work that leads to gaining approval to go ahead with the project from the relevant authorities. But contrasting with a new-build project, the aim of negotiations with the building authorities is to achieve a number of exemptions. These concern both urban planning regulations, e.g. clearance to neighbouring buildings, and building technology regulations, e.g. fire resistance, thermal performance, sound insulation. Possible exemptions required should be specially investigated from the very start in order to avoid problems at this stage.

Phase 5: working drawings

This phase includes all the fabrication and detailed planning work prior to issuing tenders. The basic differences between new-build and conversion projects disappear at this stage, apart from a few significant exceptions: accuracy, presentation and technical fundamentals. Taking inaccuracies into account represents

Clay brick format	Length [cm]	Width [cm]	Height [cm]
Oldenburg format	22	10.5	5.5
North German thin format	22	10.5	5.2
Hamburg format	22	10.5	6.5
Flensburg format	22	10.5	4.8
Kiel format	23	11	5.5
Hamburg format	23	11	5.6
Holstein format	23	11	5
Imperial format	25	12	6.5
"Ilse" format	25	12	4.6
Old Bavarian format	29	14	6.5
Old Württemberg format	29	14	6.5
Viennese format	29	14	6.5
Baden format	27	13	6
Monastery format	28.5	13.5	8.5
Monastery format II	29	14	9
Württemberg format	29.8	14.3	7.2
Bavarian format	30	14	7

B 1.5

B 1.4   Preparing an as-built drawing: from the in situ freehand sketch to the finished CAD drawing
B 1.5   Common clay brick formats prior to 1940
B 1.6   Laser measuring instrument
B 1.7   Moisture measuring instrument
B 1.8   Economic effectiveness of typical refurbishment and conversion measures

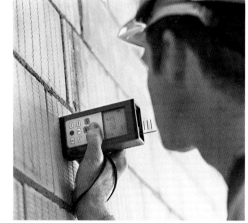

B 1.6

B 1.7

one great difference in the planning process. Planners with no experience of conversion work often try to implement the fabrication and detailed planning techniques they have applied in new-build projects. The sometimes glaring inaccuracies in the existing structure, e.g. lack of right-angles, lack of verticality, walls not in line vertically, excessive plaster/render thicknesses, sagging floors, bowing walls, etc., all have to be taken into account in the fabrication and detail drawings. Joints between components – especially those between existing and new components – are sometimes totally different to corresponding details for new projects.

Two methods have proved to be very helpful: bringing forward the demolition work and visiting the site together with specialist companies and specialist consultants from industry, whose experience in conversion measures is very useful for the planning and tendering. Quite naturally, working together with long established, local companies whose employees are familiar with the old methods of building, even partly from their own experience, is worthwhile.

On the drawings for conversion projects the use of the colours grey (for existing), red (for new) and yellow (for demolition) is widespread. Black is sometimes used for denoting existing elements, but solid shading can mask annotation etc. The shading conventions for the materials of existing components drawn in section should only be used when the material is known for certain. In all other cases, the components should be shaded without signifying the material so that the design team and site workers are not led astray.

The subject of dimensioning is not without its problems either. As already mentioned, the dimensions measured in situ often do not match those on the as-built drawings. If we project complete chains of dimensions through a whole building, these – man-made – differences become apparent and lead to confusion among the contractor's personnel. One remedy is to distinguish between "binding" and "uncertain" dimensions; the latter serve only for approximate orientation, determining quantities, etc., "binding" dimensions, on the other hand, specify dimensions of new components or details regarding interventions in the existing fabric (Fig. B 1.4).

Phases 6 and 7: tender, award of contract
Compiling specifications and awarding contracts are other areas where aspects peculiar to conversion projects must be considered. The greatest difficulty is to be found in the uncertainties that characterise the planning process. Not all the components to be retained can be recorded and appraised in full. This calls for a certain flexibility in terms of itemising and also calculating the quantities, a situation that should be avoided at all costs in tenders for new-build projects. In order to avoid unpleasant additional negotiations, optional items should be included for works that are perhaps only suspected. Inaccuracies in the specification cannot be totally avoided because it is not possible to "x-ray" every component. It is therefore necessary to establish whether the problems associated with conversions are adequately covered in the contract documents. Standards and building regulations have been developed with new buildings in mind and may well need to be restricted or even suspended by way of special contractual clauses. Classic examples of this are warranty issues when including parts of the existing building, or adaptive measures in the case of inaccuracies exceeding the standard tolerances. More reliable costs can be achieved by including ancillary works typical of new-build projects, i.e. works to be remunerated separately, among the standard items. One widespread but risky approach is to base many items on daywork rates. In conversion work this is harder to avoid than in new projects, but is just as difficult to keep under control. On conversion projects it is normal to have to invest much more time in site supervision in order to achieve acceptable quality standards and dependable costs and timetables. Nevertheless, predicting all these aspects is still less precise than is the case with new structures.

Component	Pattern of damage/refurbishment measure	Economic appraisal	Appraisal required in individual case[1]	Non-destructive analysis by...
General	House fungus or extensive infestation of timber components		--	Odour, mould pores (laboratory test if suspected)
General	Removal of hazardous substances		--	Not possible (laboratory test required)
General	Reconditioning of worn but intact surface finishes (e.g. floor coverings)	+		Visual inspection
General	Additions to or replacement of water and electric installations	o		Visual inspection of heating and electric installations, visual inspection of valves below wash-basins/sinks (lead pipes)
General	Replacement of waste-water pipes and drains	-		Video camera
Foundations	Underpinning because of settlement	-		Not possible
Foundations	Underpinning for deeper extensions	--		Not applicable
Basement floor	Subsequent waterproofing, no hydrostatic pressure	o		Moisture measurement of ground slab (24-hour measurement with device below plastic sheet)
Basement floor	Subsequent waterproofing, hydrostatic pressure	--		Visual inspection or moisture measurement of ground slab (24-hour measurement with device below plastic sheet)
Basement floor	Subsequent deepening below formation level	--		Not applicable
Basement ext. wall	Subsequent damp-proof course	-		Moisture measurements as series of vertical measurements
Basement ext. wall	Subsequent vertical waterproofing, drainage	o		Moisture measurements as series of vertical measurements
Basement ext. wall	Sealing joints in existing waterproof basement		+	Visual inspection
Flr. over basement	Corroded steel beams to jack arch floor		+	Visual inspection
Flr. over basement	Severe settlement of vaulting	--		Visual inspection
Flr. over basement	Exposed reinforcement	o		Visual inspection, check for hairline cracks and voids
Grd. floor ext. wall	Subsequent damp-proof course	-		Moisture measurements as series of vertical measurements
Grd. floor ext. wall	Efflorescence, salt deposits	+		Visual inspection (possible additional laboratory test in order to rule out house fungus)
Grd. floor ext. wall	Subsequent thermal insulation	+		Visual inspection
Grd. floor ext. wall	Settlement cracks (legacy)	+		Visual inspection (legacy settlement cracks recognisable by way of dirt deposits)
Grd. floor ext. wall	Refurbishment of render, conservation order		o	Not possible (research required)
Grd. floor ext. wall	Exposed reinforcement in fair-face conc. elements, balconies	o		Visual inspection, check for hairline cracks and voids

[1] Normal works for refurbishment measures which, however, are subject to severe fluctuations and therefore require an appraisal in every individual case.

a

B 1.8

Phase 8: construction management
The planning phase accompanying the construction on site is often referred to as site management. However, it also includes supervising the budget and timetable right up to the time of defects-free handover.
The main difference between the planning of new structures and conversions lies in the quantity of existing building fabric that must be retained and refurbished. As long as existing components are being used in some form, the cost of supervision must multiply if "surprises" – which arise from the less precise planning that is inevitable – are to be minimised. This means that working hours are shifted from the planning to the building phase, meaning that a larger buffer is required when planning the time on site. The fact that the loadbearing structure – at least – is already in place might lead us to suspect that conversions can be realised quicker, but this is not true. Trades with many interfaces with the existing fabric require generous time reserves; a typical example of this is plastering/rendering. Decisions recorded in detail and without delay reduce the risk of later disputes when the work has to be paid for! But it is a well-known fact that you should not make any hasty decisions on the building site. Complex relationships are often not identified until planning work is adjusted to suit on site. As the work on site progresses, so the site supervision for a conversion becomes more and more similar to that of a new-build project because the problems typical to conversion work decrease. One activity often neglected is joint measurement work, which should always be carried out promptly. The additional claims typical of conversion work, e.g. adjusting for inaccuracies or increased quantities for demolition work, cannot be checked unless the measurements have been taken beforehand.

Costs
Longer construction times always mean higher costs. Allowances should certainly be built into the trades at risk so that the total budget is not exceeded in the end. Besides extra costs typical to certain trades, additional costs specific to conversion work can also occur, e.g. rectifying collateral damage as a result of demolition or cutting/chasing work. The uncertainties encountered with, for example, structural requirements or damp-proofing are almost impossible to calculate (Fig. B 1.8).
The accuracy of cost estimates and calculations typical in Germany and required by legislation cannot be upheld in conversion projects. The only solution is to add a generous allowance to the total cost, which can only be reduced during the course of the work on site.

Strategies for increasing flexibility
Less dependable planning can be offset by greater flexibility. Manoeuvrability with respect to costs and time on site can compensate for the inevitable problems that will be encountered. Such strategies can take on the following forms:

- Work based on direct labour or daywork rates: This method frequently leads to disputes, also between client and design team. Such work can never be ruled out completely, but it should not exceed 10 % of the value of the contract.
- The inclusion of allowances, as mentioned above: The difficulty here lies in convincing the client on the one hand and the contractor on the other. "Visible" allowances are happily accepted by workers as "already included", which means they lose their effectiveness. The time and money buffers should disappear during the course of on-site work to give the client more planning and financial security.

The work of some trades is very similar to that in new-build projects, in particular those involved in the later stages of fitting-out, e.g. floor and wall finishes, painting and joinery work, because by this stage there is hardly any need to adjust to the existing fabric of the structure. Such work requires only a very small allowance. The time and money reserves here can be minimised and based on the experience gained with new-build projects.

Component	Pattern of damage/refurbishment measure	Economic appraisal	Appraisal required in individual case	Non-destructive analysis by...
Window	Replacement of windows in fenestrated facade	+		Visual inspection of bottom part of window frame and seals, also year of manufacture in the case of insulating glass units
Window	Replacement/refurbishment, conservation order	-		Visual inspection of bottom part of window frame and seals, also year of manufacture in the case of insulating glass units
Window	Replacement of curtain wall		o	Not applicable
Window	Partial upgrading of existing curtain wall, thermal and sound insulation, fire resistance		-	Visual inspection, establish year of manufacture, study archive documents
Internal wall	Refurbishment of plaster, repairing cracks	+		Visual inspection, tap to discover voids, especially at base of wall
Internal wall	Chimney refurbishment, sooting up	+		Visual inspection, especially attic floor and cleaning openings in basement
Structural frame	Exposed reinforcement	o		Visual inspection, check for hairline cracks and voids
Structural frame	Upgrading fire resistance		-	Establish year of manufacture, study archive documents (concrete cover)
Structural frame	Corroded rolled steel sections		o	Visual inspection
Structural frame	Corroded cast stanchions	+		Visual inspection
Suspended floor	Upgrading load-carrying capacity/deflection		--	Measure at edge and mid-span in the case of long spans
Suspended floor	Upgrading fire resistance	o		Establish year of manufacture, study archive documents (concrete cover)
Suspended floor	Upgrading sound insulation	o		Not possible, maybe ask users
Suspended floor	Thermal bridges due to cantilevering balconies		--	Visual inspection
Suspended floor	Timber joist floor rotten at supports (no fungus)	o		Not possible (supports must be opened up)
Suspended floor	Exposed reinforcement	+		Visual inspection, check for hairline cracks and voids
Roof/roof space	Some rot at the eaves	+		Visual inspection
Roof/roof space	Upgrading load-carrying capacity/deflection of roof structure	o		Visual inspection and measure deflection
Roof	Replacement of roof covering	+		Visual inspection, especially nibs on underside
Roof/roof space	Fitting-out of previously unused roof space		-	Not applicable

+ non-critical   - critical
o less critical   -- very critical
b

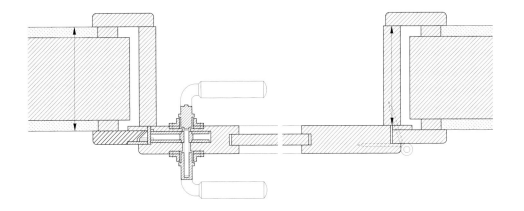

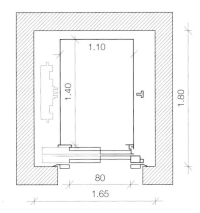

B 1.9

B 1.10

*Standards and statutory instruments, toleration
of the building stock*
In principle, the newest standards, directives
and statutory instruments apply to a change of
use or a conversion. Quite obviously, however,
trying to comply with such a requirement will
lead to problems in many areas.
Whether the notion of toleration of the building
stock applies can only be decided on a case-
by-case basis. In Germany a distinction is made
between "active" and "passive" toleration of the
building stock. Whereas the passive form protects an originally legally compliant structure
against changes due to later legislation, the
active form secures the approval of measures
designed to retain passive toleration. For the
notion of toleration of the building stock to
apply, the following conditions must be met:

• A usable existing structure suitable for its
  function
• Compliance with previous legislation
• Continuation of the usage

Preserving the toleration of the building stock is
linked with very strict stipulations; it is intended
to safeguard conservatory measures and expires...

• upon a change of use if other building regulations apply to the new use (i.e. possibly
  even only a minor change of use),
• if there are major qualitative and quantitative
  changes, e.g. changes to the loadbearing
  structure,
• the building has not been used for more than
  12 months or is structurally "worn out", e.g.
  structures at risk of collapse.

Private-law requirements or personal criteria do
not affect toleration of the building stock. For
instance, a small workshop in the middle of
town cannot invoke the notion of toleration of
the building stock when an extension to the
premises is required. But for the very same reason, i.e. toleration of the building stock, the
workshop's neighbours might have to endure
any emissions even if they do not comply with
current legislation.

The following legislation especially often conflicts
with planned conversion measures, meaning
that special exemptions must be obtained:
• Clearance to adjacent structures, plot ratio:
  Many existing structures, primarily in densely
  built-up areas, do not comply with the current
  legal or statutory requirements regarding plot
  ratios or minimum distances to site boundaries. In most of these cases toleration of the
  building stock is interpreted very generously.
  Often problematic, however, are extensions,
  e.g. the addition of balconies or converting a
  roof space into habitable rooms, with the
  associated change in the enclosed volume.
  Clearances to neighbouring structures will
  then have to be verified, at least for the new
  works. In such a case either the infringement
  of the clearance will be entered in the register
  of public obligations – with the consent of the
  neighbours affected – or the absorption of
  the clearance must be entered into the land
  registry entry for that building.
• Thermal performance: Measures to improve
  thermal performance, e.g. attaching external
  insulation, fall under the heading of passive
  toleration of the building stock. And in the
  light of the need to achieve reductions in
  carbon dioxide emissions, there may exist
  exemption clauses regarding the infringement of the clearance to adjacent buildings
  (which have already been incorporated into
  building legislation in some instances).
• Noise control: The forms of construction used
  in the past very often do not come even close
  to meeting today's requirements regarding
  insulation against airborne and structure-
  borne sound. A good example of this is the
  timber joist floor common in 19th century
  buildings. Improvement measures are possible
  in principle, but the low loadbearing capacity
  of the existing construction means that the
  options are limited. If a change of use is also
  planned (e.g. from residential to office
  space), the inadequacy of the sound insulation values will have to be negotiated with the
  authorities and the client and exempted because in this case the change of use means
  that the notion of toleration of the building
  stock no longer applies.

• Fire protection: Taking the example of the
  timber joist floor again, such a floor need not
  be checked for its fire resistance according
  to current legislation because the frequent
  demand for a floor construction consisting of
  incombustible materials is impossible to comply with. As replacing the floor would be uneconomic, an exemption must be negotiated,
  in this case with the local fire brigade, which
  can ask for a report from a fire safety expert
  and/or compensatory measures. Such measures can be expensive and so this issue must
  be clarified as soon as possible.
• Stability, serviceability: The loadbearing
  structure will have to comply with the latest
  standards and codes of practice as well if the
  notion of toleration of the building stock no
  longer applies. The standards applied to the
  materials used, however, are exempted from
  this. Instead, the standards valid at the time
  of erecting the building and the permissible
  material properties of that period can generally be used. The loading assumptions for
  any new calculations necessary are, however,
  taken from the latest regulations. A building
  component can very quickly lose the protection afforded by the notion of toleration of the
  building stock if the loads increase due to
  changes to the construction or changes of use,
  e.g. adding new floor screeds or suspended
  ceilings to upgrade the sound insulation.

When considering old buildings in the light of
new legislation and standards, it is important to
establish whether public or private law is involved. Regulations and statutory instruments
are certainly public law and must be complied
with once the protection afforded by toleration
of the building stock no longer applies. Private-
law standards, on the other hand, may not
apply in certain conditions, provided they are
not included by law in the approval procedure.
However, deviations of any kind must be approved by the client in writing so that any
claims for damages at a later date, e.g. due to
loss of rental income, can be dismissed.

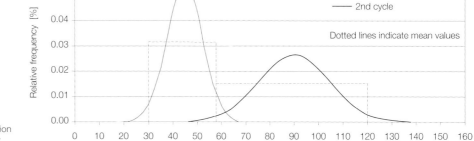

B 1.11

B 1.9 Historic door frame: the width of the lining is equal to the thickness of the wall plus plaster
B 1.10 Minimum dimensions for a lift suitable for disabled persons
B 1.11 Frequency distribution for two normal-distribution renovation cycles using the example of render (see Fig. B 1.2)

Retrofitting of technical infrastructure
The usually unavoidable improvements to or replacement of the technical infrastructure is more a question of standards than one of legal rights. This primarily concerns flues and ventilation ducts, heating pipes, sanitary installations and waste-water pipes, but also low-voltage systems in offices. The retrofitting of such technical infrastructure items in existing buildings is often difficult because the buildings were often not designed accordingly. The horizontal distribution – generally unproblematic in new buildings – frequently causes problems which lead to architectural and constructional difficulties. Early conception with the help of specialists is therefore strongly advised.

Building physics
The refurbishment of existing structures is always associated with a change to their building physics characteristics. It is almost always necessary to upgrade the thermal and sound insulation. But even the apparently harmless installation of legally compliant, tightly sealing new windows can lead to subsequent damage to building components that had never experienced any problems over the past 100 years or more. Building physics considerations – preferably with the help of a specialist – must be included in the planning work at an early stage, even when apparently standard measures are involved. Components recommended as non-critical by their manufacturers should be investigated because although such components may well be non-critical for new buildings, they may not be suitable for every application when converting an existing building.
Primarily critical are any measures that alter the vapour pressure equalisation between inside and outside, i.e. any form of insulation (also sound insulation), cladding, lining and surface finish.

Barrier-free design
Some European countries have strict rules regarding the accessibility of and within buildings, especially those used by the public. Even though in Germany there is no general obligation to carry out barrier-free upgrades, it remains disputed as to whether there should be a mandatory obligation to create a barrier-free building once the protection afforded by the notion of toleration of the building stock has been lost. It is advisable to examine all design elements to see whether an alternative barrier-free design is possible because this not only ensures legal compliance, but also offers additional convenience for all users. The usual problems are:

• No lift: The installation of a lift suitable for disabled persons presents major constructional and architectural problems, e.g. contrast between technical structure and historic building fabric, accommodating the volume (also above and below lift shaft) within the building, floor penetrations, insulating against propagation of structure-borne sound to adjoining rooms (Fig. B 1.10).
• Minor level differences with steps: Ramps suitable for wheelchair users require a gradient of no more than 6 %, which means they are about 3 m long per step and apart from the change to the layout and the architecture, become unfeasible even if only a few steps are involved. If a lift cannot be positioned so that it can serve several stops per storey (doors both sides), stair lifts are the only answer.
• Door thresholds: A barrier-free design for wheelchair users means that thresholds may be no higher than 20 mm; the wooden door thresholds in old buildings are often higher. Deciding between the historic effect of the door and barrier-free requirements should always be decided in favour of the latter.
• Inadequate clear widths: Widening a door opening always involves replacing the lintel as well, i.e. interfering with the stability of the structure. But as a clear structural opening of approx. 1 m is usually adequate, the cost of such a measure is not unreasonable.

Demolition
The fabric of the building to be retained – which should not be confused with the building as it exists as such – forms the basis for the conversion. How much of the existing building should be demolished must be established during the planning process. The basis for this decision rests on three questions:

• How valuable is the existing structure?
This question should not be answered only with respect to objective, conservationist aspects, but also as part of the design concept. Existing components may be worthless in terms of the history of building, but nevertheless critical for the building's "image". In particular, if the building's origins or past uses are to remain evident, components that may otherwise have been demolished or removed may need to be retained.
• Is it worth retaining the existing structure? Sometimes it can be cheaper to demolish a wall and build a new one in the same position, e.g. if the wall would otherwise have to be repaired, or many layers of unserviceable surface finishes and/or plaster/render would have to be removed.
• Does the existing structure conflict with the new use?
This concerns all measures designed to upgrade the stability, building physics and building services. For example, the intact timber joist floors in a multi-tenant residential building when the conversion to a low-energy building can only be achieved by installing underfloor heating and the sound insulation must be upgraded to comply with current standards. The cost of upgrading the existing floors structurally and acoustically may be only a little less than that of providing new reinforced concrete floors, and the new floors would offer greater safeguards against possible defects.

These questions should be asked for every component in the existing structure so that a sensible demolition plan can be drawn up. Purely pragmatic considerations show that, when in doubt, demolition should be preferred. Retaining the existing always involves uncertainties for planners and clients – both during the construction phase and throughout the period covered by the warranty. By contrast, new components are controllable in terms of costs, technology and warranty. But these aspects should always be checked against the first question regarding the value of the existing. Every demolition process represents an intervention in the loadbearing structure of the

B 1.12

B 1.12 Demolition of an office building
B 1.13 Electric wall saw
B 1.14 Core drill
B 1.15 Demolition methods

building – in the form of changing loads, the temporary storage of debris in the building and vibrations during the work. All this can lead to damage, especially cracks, in existing components even if only non-loadbearing components are directly affected by the demolition measures.

"Clearance"

The first phase of demolition concerns all works on non-loadbearing components. All surface finishes and materials that are definitely unserviceable are removed. In the case of a total refurbishment this could mean, for example, partitions, floor coverings, wall finishes, ceilings, insulation (if no longer adequate), sanitary appliances, electrical installations and water pipes. Once "clearance" of the existing structure has been carried out, it is much easier to appraise and measure; we are not far away from the aforementioned structural carcass drawing. As these measures have to be carried out anyway and do not require any building authority approval, they should be carried out as soon as possible, best of all right at the start of the final design stage.

During these demolition works it is vital to protect any surfaces that are to be retained because the work is mostly carried out by unskilled labour and the demolition contractor is usually no longer on site during the actual conversion work itself.

Gutting

B 1.13

B 1.14

Gutting means demolishing the entire insides of a building, leaving only the external walls standing; even loadbearing and bracing components in the building are removed completely. The new insides are usually in the form of a separate, loadbearing structure which, once complete, also carries the loads of the retained external walls even if those walls were originally loadbearing themselves. Gutting calls for extensive, expensive safety measures, and apart from that, building fabric already paid for and actually usable is removed, which increases the overall costs considerably. This is also the main problem of gutting, which is only worthwhile for private-sector clients when the usage can be substantially intensified. That could be the case, for example, when the original building has low storey heights or several buildings are to be combined into one. The resulting discrepancy between facade and internal structure is almost impossible to conceal and is again and again the subject of strong criticism in the construction industry. This approach is therefore used only occasionally, when no other method is possible, e.g. when a facade is protected by a conservation order.

Complete demolition

In the event of the complete demolition of a structure, it is necessary to observe not only DIN 18007 but also building regulations (demolition permit), structural aspects (special demolition engineering), safety regulations for the site operatives and the public (local residents and passers-by) and environmental protection measures if any pollutants or hazardous substances are involved. Many different methods are used in complete demolition, and which is used in any particular case essentially depends on two circumstances: the construction of the vertical loadbearing elements (masonry, reinforced concrete, steel) and the location of the structure (open or confined development). The construction of the suspended floors plays only a subsidiary role. In most cases hydraulic excavators with attachments such as demolition shears, pulverisers and steel shears are used. Such plant can be employed on building heights of up to 40 m. The considerably more spectacular demolition by explosives only ccounts for some 4 % of all demolition projects and is an option primarily reserved for large masonry industrial buildings or special structures such as bridges, cooling towers or football stadiums. The demolition of the many panel construction buildings in the east of Germany is also carried out primarily with hydraulic plant. Fig. B 1.15 lists the various techniques and their applications.

Economy

The question of whether a conversion is worthwhile can be calculated approximately as an overall measure. To do this, a number of individual costs must be determined:

- The purchased price of the existing structure or its potential selling price (excluding the land)
- The cost of demolition back to the loadbearing structure
- The cost of special refurbishment measures, e.g. damp-proofing, installation of damp-proof courses, upgrading the stability
- The cost of a comparable structural carcass based on the volume approach for a new building

If the calculated cost of a new structure is well below the sum of the first three items, a conversion is not favourable from the economic viewpoint, and complete demolition may be worth considering. This can happen when the fabric of the building is in a very poor condition or the planned new usage is incompatible with the existing structure.

But if many fitting-out components can be used again without being refurbished, we can assume that a conversion is worthwhile. Surfaces and components to be refurbished should not be listed on the credit side because the cost of refurbishment is often close to that of procuring new materials.

Ecology

The debris from demolition work plus excavated material (160M t/year) represents the largest item (245M t/year) in the total waste flow in Germany. Some 76 % of building debris (53.4M t in total) is recycled, only 8 % (4.2M t) ends up in landfill sites. The relatively high proportion of recycling is due to the large amount of mineral debris that occurs during demolition. Some 98 % by weight of a completely demolished apartment block can be classed under this heading. Recycling of metals has reached 100 %, but large quantities occur only in industrial buildings. Materials such as timber or glass, which can only be recycled at great expense, are disposed of in landfill sites. However, this quantity is destined to rise in the future because many of the building materials used over the past 40 years are harder to recycle than those used prior to 1965. This concerns, for example, thermal insulating materials, aerated concrete blocks, plastic coverings, plasterboard, gypsum and synthetic plasters/renders. It is frequently the "indivisible" connection between the materials – like with external thermal insulation composite systems – that complicates the recycling. Building materials and components that cannot be recycled or are difficult to recycle increase the cost of demolition, either because of the fees incurred for disposal in landfill sites (e.g. PVC coverings) or the need to sort components into their constituent materials (e.g. plasterboard walls) on the building site, which is labour-intensive. However, sorting on the building site is worthwhile, even for small demolition projects, when this means that the mineral debris can be taken away separately. It should be remembered, though, that although ceramic tiles and plaster can remain on a wall that is to be demolished, several layers of wallpaper, or wooden or PVC linings, cannot.

The group of hazardous building materials is small in terms of quantities, but can cause enormous costs. It should not be forgotten that the demolition personnel are in close contact with such materials, the hazards of which – because they are often untrained workers with temporary contracts – are unknown to them. From the ecological viewpoint it is important to investigate whether certain components could perhaps remain in the structure instead of being disposed of, and back this up with the economic argument. Also worth considering is the direct recycling of components, i.e. the reuse of whole building components. For instance, reusing intact roof tiles on a new roof structure is no more expensive than re-covering with new concrete tiles, but is more sensible from the ecological viewpoint. Good experience has been gained in the reuse of elements from panel construction, apparently achieving a savings potential of up to 20 % of the cost of a new structural carcass.

After the conversion is also before the conversion
Sustainability is one of the buzzwords of recent years, and it is heard again and again in conjunction with conversion measures. The continued usage of existing buildings and structures is advisable for ecological and economic reasons, for social and cultural motives, too. We should not forget that even the best conversion can be used only for a limited time. Technical progress, changing legislation and standards, new demands regarding comfort and convenience and obsolete functions are not only the reasons behind today's conversions, but those of the future as well. This situation can be taken into account in the planning by way of a number of principles:

• Avoid major interventions in the original, especially the structural, building fabric. Interventions that go beyond the design concept of the original architect are irreversible and should be well-founded.
• New components can be planned so that they are easy to remove later (e.g. steel-concrete composite floors instead of reinforced concrete floors). This applies even more so when such components are only useful for specific purposes.
• Surfaces that would disturb present functions but are perhaps valuable or typical of the period can be covered up instead of being removed.
• New buildings and conversions should be comprehensively documented – both electronically and on paper – so that they can form the basis for the work of later design teams.
• New materials should be chosen so that they do not harm the existing structure and can be disposed of or recycled without problems at a later date

Renovation cycles also mean that some components may well have been replaced already, others not yet. Buildings dating from the 19th century – even those that did not suffer in the intervening wars – will certainly have been refurbished several times and can therefore be a mixture of the building techniques of different periods.

Type of structure	Case	Manual demolition	Wire rope	High-pressure water jet etc.	Demolition hammer	Demolition and sorting grab	Explosives	Dismantling/ lifting equipment	Long-reach excavator	Demolition shears	Demolition-class hydraulic excavator
High-rise buildings Frame structure	1	–	–	o	–	–	+	o	+	+	–
	2	–	–	–	o	–	+	o	+	+	–
	3	–	o	o	–	–	o	+	+	+	–
	4	o	–	o	–	–	–	+	–	–	–
High-rise buildings Wall structure	1	–	o	o	–	–	+	o	+	+	+
	2	–	o	o	–	–	+	o	+	+	+
	3	–	+	o	–	–	o	o	+	+	+
	4	o	–	o	–	–	–	+	o	o	o
High-rise buildings Hybrid structure	1	–	o	o	–	–	+	o	+	+	+
	2	–	o	o	–	–	+	o	+	+	+
	3	–	o	–	–	–	+	o	+	+	o
	4	o	–	–	–	–	–	+	+	+	o
Low-rise buildings	1	–	o	o	–	+	+	o	o	+	+
	2	–	o	o	–	+	+	o	o	+	+
	3	–	o	o	–	+	+	o	o	+	+
	4	o	+	–	–	–	o	–	o	+	+
Tower-type structures	1	–	–	–	–	–	+	–	+	–	–
	2	–	–	–	–	–	+	o	o	–	–
	3	–	–	o	–	–	o	+	+	–	–
	4	–	–	o	–	–	–	+	–	–	–

Case 1: Open demolition site, structure for demolition free-standing   + = preferred
Case 2: Open demolition site, structure for demolition confined   o = justifiable
Case 3: Confined demolition site, structure for demolition free-standing   – = not justifiable / not practicable
Case 4: Confined demolition site, structure for demolition confined

Note: Dismantling, steel shears or wire ropes are the methods preferred for demolishing steel structures.

B 1.15

Building physics

Harald Krause, Jochen Pfau,
Ulrich Schanda, Elmar Schröder

B 2.1

Refurbishing a building always has an influence on its thermal and moisture balance, and hence the interior climate as well. The aim of an energy-efficiency upgrade is to reduce the heat flows from inside to outside in winter and vice versa in summer. Besides installing thermal insulation, improving the airtightness of the building is another very important aspect. Both measures plus the appropriate heating and ventilation systems should be coordinated with each other in order to achieve an agreeable interior climate, save energy and avoid damage to the fabric of the building. Only then can refurbishment work be successful over the long-term.

Besides investigating the energy-efficiency aspects, a refurbishment project should also involve upgrading the sound insulation and fire protection, so that they comply with current standards where necessary. Improving the sound insulation concerns primarily the impact sound insulation, but also the airborne sound insulation and preventing noise from building services. Fire protection involves drawing up a complete concept, which includes escape routes, properties of building components and fire-fighting.

It should be remembered with all measures that the refurbishment should satisfy the requirements of the next 30 years. Shorter refurbishment intervals are certainly uneconomic. Whether complying with the minimum standards is the right objective must be checked before starting any planning work.

Energy efficiency, thermal performance, moisture control

Energy efficiency has in the meantime become a focal point in the planning work for refurbishment projects as well as for new structures. In Germany approx. 30 % of the primary energy consumption is used for heating purposes in buildings (Fig. B 2.3). Improving the energy efficiency in this area would make a noticeable contribution to sparing resources and protecting the climate.

Most of the energy is consumed in the building stock, especially those buildings built before the 1st Thermal Insulation Act (WSVO) came

into force in 1977. Owing to their age, refurbishment measures can be expected for those buildings in the coming years; and that is the chance to upgrade the fabric of those buildings so that they can meet the challenges we can expect over the next 30 years with regard to the careful husbandry of our planet's resources. Fig. B 2.2 shows the different energy standards in Germany, in this case for the final energy consumption for hot-water provision and space heating plus domestic electricity consumption. A factor of 10 separates the heating consumption of an old building and the passive house standard already in widespread use. Although it is not always possible to achieve the passive house standard – an annual floor space-related heating requirement of 15 kWh/m²a – in a refurbishment project, there are many examples of projects that prove that reducing energy consumption by 75–80 % is also economically viable [1]. Owing to the sharp increase in energy costs over recent years, the statutory stipulations regarding thermal insulation measures according to the current edition of the Energy Conservation Act (EnEV) are no longer up to date from the economic viewpoint. The insulation thicknesses required and the component parameters are based on the energy costs of 10 years ago. The next edition of the EnEV, planned for 2009, will apparently call for a further approx. 30 % reduction in energy, plus another 30 % later on. Improving the energy efficiency of the building stock by up to 80 % presumes a total refurbishment, which – like for new building work – requires an integrated planning approach. But such a refurbishment results in several advantages for owners and users in the long-term:

- Realisation of a holistic concept for thermal performance and building services
- Minimisation of thermal bridges at all building details
- Claiming subsidies
- Maintaining and increasing the value of the property

In economic terms the right time for an energy-efficiency upgrade is when the modernisation of important components, e.g. roof or render, is due. Current studies show that it is worth insu-

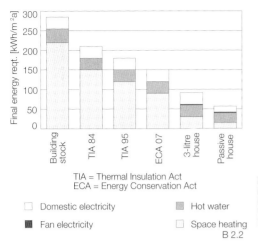

TIA = Thermal Insulation Act
ECA = Energy Conservation Act

☐ Domestic electricity
■ Fan electricity

■ Hot water
☐ Space heating

B 2.2

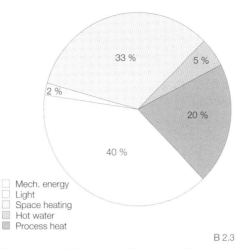

☐ Mech. energy
☐ Light
☐ Space heating
☐ Hot water
☐ Process heat

B 2.3

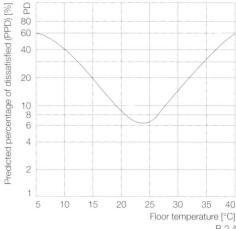

B 2.4

lating an external wall even in conjunction with a new coat of paint [2].

Which refurbishment measures represent the optimum solution for any particular building can only be decided following a detailed analysis of the energy balance of the building and the costs of potential upgrading measures. In the meantime, well-documented reference projects can be referred to and corresponding design software can be employed [3].

Thermal performance and comfort

Too little importance is attached to the aspect of better comfort when considering the advantages of a well-insulated building. The studies carried out by Ole Fanger, professor at the Technical University of Denmark, proved that the well-being of people depends on the conditions of their surroundings and the influencing factors can be derived from quantifiable variables [4]. The findings were brought together in DIN EN ISO 7730 [5]. The German Energy Agency (dena) has published current studies for the low-energy house standard in a planning directive [6].

The perceived room temperature plays a major role in thermal comfort. This can be approximated as the mean value of the interior air and the surface temperatures of the enclosing surfaces. Low surface temperatures can therefore be compensated for by higher air temperatures, although the maximum difference between the mean surface and air temperatures should not exceed 1.5–3.0 °C (Fig. B 2.5).

Another factor influencing comfort is the radiant temperature asymmetry. This is caused by different surface temperatures within a room, e.g. a cold window on one side and an internal wall at the interior air temperature on the other. Owing to the radiation exchange with the surroundings, parts of the body facing the cold surface cool more noticeably.

The velocity of the air, which is perceived as a draught, also influences our comfort. Air movements near the floor are particularly critical, which is why these should not exceed 0.15 m/s. Draughts can be caused by ventilation systems, leaking seals around doors and windows and air descending on cold surfaces. The temperature stratification in a room can also contribute

to a feeling of discomfort. The vertical temperature gradient in a room should not exceed 2 °C per metre; with such a gradient, a seated person will usually notice the difference between the temperature at his ankles and the temperature on the back of his neck. The surface temperatures of floors should lie between 19 and 29 °C. These values are used as fixed factors when planning insulation measures and designing underfloor heating systems.

In addition to these purely thermal influencing variables, the humidity of the interior air is also critical. For sedentary activities and an interior air temperature of 20 °C, a relative humidity of 35–65 % is regarded as comfortable.

DIN EN ISO 7730 expresses the global comfort in terms of the PMV and PPD values. The PMV (Predicted Mean Vote) value designates the predictable average assessment of the interior climate. The PPD (Predicted Percentage of Dissatisfied) value is derived from this and specifies the number of persons who can be expected to be unhappy with the prevailing interior climate. For the local comfort (draughts, temperature asymmetry, surface temperatures, temperature gradient), this number can be read off diagrams, as shown in Fig. B 2.4 for the example of floor temperature.

Thermal comfort categories are defined in ISO 7730 for specific requirements. It is necessary to comply with the global and the local comfort criteria in each case.

The energy-efficiency upgrading of a building can contribute to optimising the thermal comfort in a number of ways. Better insulation values result directly in higher internal surface temperatures and hence reduce the risk of radiant temperature asymmetry and blocks of cold air descending the walls; the heating system's influence on the comfort is thus reduced. Better seals around doors and windows reduce the risk of draughts. In a passive house, the layout and nature of the heating surfaces has become almost irrelevant. Consequently, a holistic planning approach results in lower costs for the heating systems and greater freedom for the interior design because even with large windows there is no need to include a radiator below the window to compensate for the lower surface temperature at the window.

In summer better thermal insulation prevents overheating, especially in the rooms directly below the roof. The guideline here is the frequency of excessive temperatures, which specifies how often a specified interior temperature is exceeded with respect to the length of time the room is occupied. According to DIN 4108-2 in housing the temperature should exceed 25 °C for no more than 10 % of the year. [7].

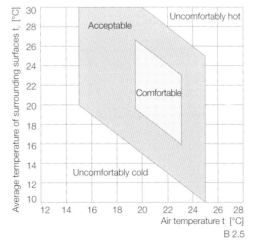

B 2.5

B 2.6

Survey of existing structure

The aim of the survey is to determine the relevant thermal and moisture data, including details of the respective forms of construction, materials and layer thicknesses. Particular care must be taken when analysing thermal bridges with respect to energy losses, but also to avoid damage caused by moisture after the refurbishment.

U-values for external components

The U-value describes the thermal quality of a component. It specifies how much heat energy passes through 1 m^2 of the component for a temperature difference of 1 K. DIN EN 6946 [8] specifies the method for calculating the U-values of external components, excluding doors and windows.

Accurate thermal performance data for existing buildings is not usually available. If the materials are not immediately identifiable, the first step is to find out which materials were used in the region at the time the structure was originally built so that the correct thermal conductivity values can be applied. The thermal conductivity of a material is a measure of its ability to transport heat energy and so this serves as the input variable for calculating U-values. Only the thermal conductivity design values, which have replaced the thermal conductivity groups (WLG) used in the past, may be used for establishing U-values [9].

When carrying out an energy-efficiency upgrade designed to achieve a higher standard than that required by legislation, the existing U-values can usually be neglected because the thermal resistances of the layers of thermal insulation are generally much greater than those of the fabric of the building. The U-values after refurbishment are primarily determined by the layers of insulation. Determining a U-value by direct measurement is generally very involved and, moreover, imprecise, so such an approach is generally inadvisable; a corresponding standard was withdrawn.

In practice, building physics experts, architects and planners base their U-values on typical forms of construction, which are also specified in a publication [10] (Figs. B 2.9, 2.15 and 2.17). In the meantime, databases are also available in the Internet [11].

U- and g-values for doors and windows

The U-values for doors and windows are calculated according to DIN EN 10077 [12]. To do this it is necessary to know the U-values of the glass to DIN EN 673 and the frame, plus the properties of the spacer between the panes of insulating glass and the dimensions of the window [13]. All these values can be supplied by the respective manufacturer. The DIN 4108 method results in simplifications [14]. Glazing bars dividing up the area of glass must be included in the U-value calculations.

The total energy transmittance g specifies that proportion of the solar energy incident on the glazing that passes through into the interior and hence is available as an energy gain during the cold months of the year. It is calculated according to DIN EN 410 [15].

On the whole, windows in the building stock can be reduced to a few types. The calculation of the energy balance requires the g-values as well, which depend on the make-up of the glazing. The U-values of solid wooden doors can be approximated from the thickness, and for metal doors with glass panels the values given in figure Fig. B 2.8a can be used.

Moisture parameters

In the well-established Glaser method to DIN 4108-6, the occurrence of interstitial condensation for steady-state interior and exterior climate conditions is investigated and assessed with respect to damage to the component. In this method it is only the vapour permeability that is considered as a transport mechanism. But surface diffusion and capillary transport play a critical role with higher levels of moisture. And in a dynamic analysis the moisture storage, i.e. the sorption capacity of building materials, is also taken into account. Serious damage is often caused by the transport of moisture by convection via joints or faulty seals. The main moisture parameters of a material are:

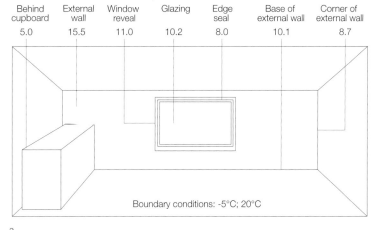

Behind cupboard	External wall	Window reveal	Glazing	Edge seal	Base of external wall	Corner of external wall
5.0	15.5	11.0	10.2	8.0	10.1	8.7

Boundary conditions: -5°C; 20°C

a

Behind cupboard	External wall	Window reveal	Glazing	Edge seal	Base of external wall	Corner of external wall
16.5	19.5	16.0	17.7	13.0	16.7	17.8

Boundary conditions: -5°C; 20°C

b   B 2.7

Window type	Year of manufacture	Window U_w [W/m^{2}K]	Glass U_g [W/m^{2}K]	Frame U_f [W/m^{2}K]	Total energy transmittance, g-value [–]
Wood frame with single glazing	bis 1960	5.0	5.8	1.6–2.2	0.9–0.85
Coupled window with 2 No. single glazing	1870–1945	2.6–2.8	2.8	1.6–2.3	0.8–0.76
Single-glazed window with secondary single glazing	1950–1965	2.5–2.7	2.8	1.6–2.2	0.8–0.76
Wood frame with double glazing	1960–1985	2.6–2.7	3.0–2.8	1.6–2.0	0.8–0.76
Plastic frame with double glazing	1965–1985	2.6–3.0	3.0–2.8	1.6–2.5	0.8–0.76
Aluminium frame with double glazing	1965–1985	3.2–4.3	3.0–2.8	3.5–7.0	0.8–0.76

a

Window type	Glazing [mm]	Gas filling	Window U_w [W/m^{2}K]	Glass U_g [W/m^{2}K]	Frame U_f [W/m^{2}K]	Total energy transmittance, g-value [–]
Wood, IV 68	4-16-4	argon	1.4–1.5	1.2	1.5	0.60–0.64
Plastic, 3-chamber	4-16-4	argon	1.5–1.6	1.2	1.7–1.8	0.60–0.64
Plastic, 5-chamber	4-16-4	argon	1.4	1.2	1.2	0.60–0.64
Wood, IV 68	4-16-4-16-4	argon	1.1–1.2	0.6	1.5	0.45–0.55
Plastic, 5-chamber	4-16-4-16-4	argon	1.1	0.6	1.2	0.45–0.55
Passive house frame	4-16-4-16-4	argon	0.8	0.6	0.8	0.45–0.55
Passive house frame	4-12-4-12-4	krypton	0.75	0.5	0.8	0.45–0.55

b   B 2.8

Ground floor slab/floor over basement	Typical construction	Period	U-value before refurbishment [W/m²K]	Construction after refurbishment	U-value after refurbishment			
					Insulation thicknesses with $\lambda_B = 0.040$ W/mK			
					12 cm	16 cm	20 cm	25 cm
					[W/m²K]			
Ground floor slab	Floor covering 40–50 mm screed Reinforced concrete	Prior to 1870	1.6	Floor covering 40 mm screed Insulation/waterproofing 180 mm concrete slab Insulation	0.30	0.23	0.19	–
Steel beams with infill	Floor covering Support. construct. Loose fill Steel beams and hollow bricks	1920–45	0.80	Floor covering Screed Insulation Vap. barrier/airtight mem. Steel beams & hollow bricks Insulation	–	0.21	0.18	0.16
Reinforced concrete slab	Floor covering Screed 20 mm insulation 180 mm reinforced concrete	1960–72	1.15	Floor covering Screed 20 mm insulation 180 mm reinforced conc. Insulation	0.26	0.21	0.17	–
Reinforced concrete slab	Floor covering Screed 50 mm insulation 180 mm reinforced concrete	1972–85	0.76	Floor covering Screed 50 mm insulation 180 mm reinforced conc. Insulation	0.23	0.19	0.16	–

B 2.9

- Vapour permeability resistance index (μ-value); the equivalent air layer thickness (s_d-value) is used for the moisture control calculations for building components according to the Glaser method.
- Moisture storage function, moisture-related thermal conductivity and transport coefficients for the transport of fluids for dynamic calculations.

The DIN 4108 series of standards contains fundamental building material parameters. More detailed data for dynamic calculations can be obtained from, for example, a database (materials database for energy-efficiency upgrade projects) or is included in software used for energy calculations [16].

Thermal bridges
Generally, thermal bridges occur at adjoining components with one-dimensional, calculable U-values. The influence of such a junction between components on the heat losses and the surface temperatures can be determined only with programs employing a two-dimensional approach such as the finite element method (FEM) or the finite difference method (FDM) (Fig. B 2.6). If the junctions are linear, the influence is characterised by the thermal transmittance per unit length (Ψ-value). Point thermal bridges usually influence the energy requirements to only a small extent, but can lead to moisture problems. The majority of thermal bridges in older buildings are obvious or can be derived from the building practices of the time. The thermal bridges catalogue for existing buildings is a useful aid [17]. Infrared thermography can be useful when trying to identify and assess the significance of thermal bridges (Fig. B 2.1); it can also be used as a quality control method during or after refurbishment. When adding

external insulation to an existing facade, the thermal bridges are mostly automatically eliminated. A more accurate analysis therefore seems sensible only in the case of partial refurbishment, cantilevering elements or when internal insulation has been installed. Critical thermal bridges can be expected at the following details:

- Junctions between suspended floors and external walls
- Continuous cantilevering balcony slabs
- Roller shutter housings and window lintels
- Window sills and window reveals
- Junctions between interior walls and ground floor slabs or interior walls and floor slabs over basements

In a partial refurbishment the low surface temperatures at thermal bridges should be given special attention because moisture damage can occur unless there is an overall concept for thermal performance, sealing and ventilation. The appearance of mould on component surfaces essentially depends on the inner surface temperature and the humidity of the interior air. The former can be increased by improving the thermal insulation (Fig. B 2.11). The humidity of the interior air is influenced by the in situ moisture loads and the air change rate (Fig. B 2.12). Replacing the windows often improves the airtightness of a building and therefore reduces the basic air change rate, which inevitably leads to higher interior humidity levels and hence to mould problems around thermal bridges. In order to be able to assess the risk of mould growth on internal surfaces around thermal bridges, DIN 4108-2 defines the temperature factor f_{Rsi}, which is calculated from the internal surface temperatures plus the interior and exterior air temperatures (Fig. B 2.10). The temper-

B 2.7 a Typical internal surface temperatures in an old building
b Internal surface temperatures after refurbishment (passive house standard)
B 2.8 a Parameters of old window constructions
b U-values of current window constructions for the standard size 1.23 x 1.48 m
Glazing: glass thickness - cavity - glass thickness
Passive house frame: window frame with U_f-value < 0.8 W/m²K, available in timber and plastic with special insulating measures
B 2.9 Typical U-values of old ground floor slabs and floors over basements plus improvement options by using thermal insulation
B 2.10 Determining the temperature factor f_{Rsi} to DIN 4108-2
B 2.11 Inner surface temperatures at an external wall corner depending on the thickness of the thermal insulation for a clay brick wall, $\lambda = 0.8$ W/mK, with external insulation
B 2.12 The internal humidity depends on the amount of moisture and the inflow of external air

$$f_{Rsi} = \frac{\Theta_{Si} - \Theta_e}{\Theta_i - \Theta_e}$$

f_{Rsi}: Temperature factor
Θ_{Si}: Inner surface temperature
Θ_i: Room temperature
Θ_e: External temperature

B 2.10

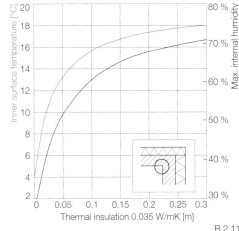

B 2.11

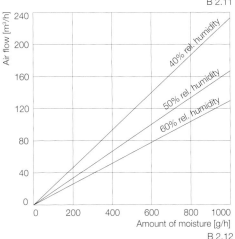

B 2.12

B 2.13 Schematic construction of an external thermal insulation composite system (ETICS)
B 2.14 Example of insulation in the form of an external thermal insulation composite system (ETICS)
B 2.15 Typical U-values of old wall constructions plus improvement options by using thermal insulation
B 2.16 Temperature progression: junction between internal and external walls (clay bricks)
    a   without insulation
    b   with internal insulation
    c   with internal insulation and insulation wedges
B 2.17 Insulating materials and their parameters (selection):
The three columns on the right show the insulation thicknesses needed to achieve the respective U-value for a 300 mm thick solid clay brick wall, $\lambda = 0.8$ W/mK (insulation over whole area).

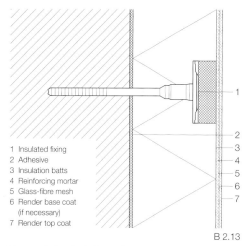

1 Insulated fixing
2 Adhesive
3 Insulation batts
4 Reinforcing mortar
5 Glass-fibre mesh
6 Render base coat (if necessary)
7 Render top coat

B 2.13

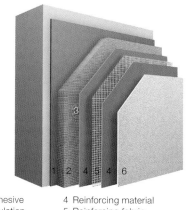

1 Adhesive   4 Reinforcing material
2 Insulation   5 Reinforcing fabric
3 Fixing   6 Render finish

B 2.14

ature factor should be ≥ 0.7. Such a figure ensures that the internal surface temperature does not drop below 12.6 °C during normal internal and external climate conditions. With an interior air humidity of 50 % and a room temperature of 20 °C, temperatures below 12.6 °C lead to a relative humidity greater than 80 %, which encourages the growth of mould.
In older buildings the temperature often drops below 12.6 °C at many points, which contributes to an increased occurrence of mould growth (Fig. B 2.7a). Fig. B 2.11 shows the internal surface temperature as a function of the thickness of thermal insulation for the example of an external wall corner. Better thermal insulation always raises the internal surface temperatures and hence reduces the risk of condensation or mould. Surface temperatures > 12.6 °C at critical points as well can only be achieved by using the forms of construction and insulation thicknesses required for passive house standards (Fig. B 2.7b).

Refurbishment measures
A holistic refurbishment must satisfy the following standards from the building physics viewpoint:

• Continuous thermally insulated envelope
• Continuous airtight membrane
• Adapted ventilation concept

If one of these three points is not given adequate consideration, problems can occur, above all with moisture control. Ventilation represents the interface with the building services and the ventilation requirements are derived from the building physics. The new standard for the ventilation of dwellings therefore calls for ventilation not reliant on the user intervention in order to control moisture [18], which means that a flow of external air, calculated according to standard of thermal insulation and size of dwelling, must be guaranteed without any action being taken by the occupants, i.e. with the windows closed. This air change rate is generally achieved not via infiltration, i.e. through the joints, but rather by way of ventilation measures, e.g. a natural ventilation concept or a fan-assisted solution.

Most existing buildings do not have a continuous envelope of thermal insulation. This must be established prior to an energy-efficiency upgrade. Staircases, access to basements and partly heated areas represent particular challenges in this respect. Penetrations through the thermally insulating envelope cannot always be completely avoided in the floor slab over a basement or around the basement perimeter and in most cases it is only possible to reduce the negative effects.

Airtightness
The airtightness concept is just as important as the thermal insulation. Consideration has to be given to matching up the thermal insulating envelope with the airtight envelope as far as possible. An airtight form of construction represents the prerequisite for proper functioning of the ventilation system and results in numerous advantages for users:

• Reduced heating energy consumption due to a lower air change rate through the joints
• No unpleasant draughts
• No moisture damage due to condensation caused by warmer interior air flowing through components
• Better sound insulation

External wall	Typical wall construction	Year of construction	U-value before refurb.	U-value after refurbishment [W/m²K] with ETICS, $\lambda_B = 0.035$ W/mK, $\lambda_B = 0.040$ W/mK			
				Minimal 12 cm	Average 14–16 cm	Geared to future needs 20 cm	Internal insulation 8 cm
Timber-frame wall, rendered and plastered	20 mm plaster 140 mm masonry 20 mm render	Prior to 1870	1.6	0.25	0.19–0.21	0.16	0.38
Facade dating from the founding years	15 mm plaster 250 mm masonry 150 mm sandstone	1870–1920	1.5	0.24	0.19–0.21	0.16	0.38
Solid clay brick masonry, imperial format bricks	15 mm plaster 375 mm masonry 20 mm render	1920–1945	1.5	0.24	0.19–0.21	0.16	–
Vertically perf. clay brick masonry (1400 kg/m³)	15 mm plaster 300 mm masonry 20 mm render	1952–1977	1.4	0.24	0.19–0.21	0.16	–
Hollow blocks (lightweight conc. 1400 kg/m³)	15 mm plaster 300 mm masonry 20 mm render	approx. 1946–1970	1.8	0.25	0.20–0.22	0.16	–
Aerated concrete masonry	15 mm plaster 300 mm aerated concrete masonry, 20 mm render	1946–1972	1.3	0.24	0.19–0.21	0.15	–
Concrete sandwich	15 mm plaster 150–200 mm concrete 40–60 mm insulation 60 mm concrete facing leaf	1960–1985	0.7	0.21	0.17–0.18	0.14	–
Masonry with ETICS	15 mm plaster 240 mm cs masonry 50 mm insulation 20 mm render	1972–1985	0.7	0.21	0.17 0.18	0.14	–

B 2.15

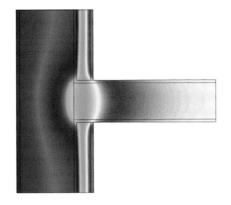

a

Achieving airtightness subsequently calls for various measures, which are explained below.

Masonry

In principle, the plaster provides an airtight layer. However, this is often interrupted, especially in the vicinity of timber joist floors. Leaks around power sockets or other building services components represent further problems. External insulation, if bonded over its entire area, can be used to create a further airtight layer when this is not possible on the inside. Concrete walls can be regarded as airtight.

b

Timber constructions and roofs

The airtight membrane can be formed by plastic sheeting, building paper, wood-based board products, plasterboard or gypsum fibreboard. Care must be taken to ensure that all joints and junctions are sealed appropriately; mechanical fasteners and adhesives are among the methods recommended.

Masonry–timber junctions

This interface must also be able to accommodate possible movements of the components with respect to each other. Airtight seals with mechanical fasteners and adhesives have proved to be good solutions.

c   B 2.16

Window and door frames

As windows and doors are non-loadbearing components and therefore rigid connections between these and the surrounding structure are not permitted, movement at this interface cannot be ruled out. Bonding plastic sheeting to the inside is a popular solution. Where internal doors form part of the airtight layer, an airtight installation and airtight seals around the door itself are essential.

Building services

Pipes, cables and ducts penetrating the airtight layer should be avoided right from the start of the planning. In masonry it is primarily power sockets in the external walls or unplastered external walls behind linings concealing pipework to sanitary appliances that constitute the weaknesses in the airtightness. Distribution networks for a building should therefore always lie within the airtight envelope in order to minimise troublesome penetrations.

Thermal insulation

The aim of thermal insulation is to reduce heat losses and raise the surface temperatures on the inside and hence improve the thermal comfort.

Insulating materials

Many different insulating materials are available today (Fig. B 2.17). Besides their thermal and moisture-related properties, the choice of material is also dictated by fire resistance, sound insulation and compressive strength considerations. Every approved insulating material carries a DIN 4108 marking which is based on its suitability for certain applications. The processing, installation and ecological aspects can also affect the choice.

External insulation to walls

Several systems are used for applying external insulation to walls (Fig. B 2.15), but the most common method is to use an external thermal insulation composite system (ETICS). In this system the insulation is attached to the existing facade directly using mechanical fasteners or adhesive, or is attached to a metal or timber framework fixed to the facade (Figs. B 2.13 and

Insulating material	Density	Thermal conductivity	Water vapour diffusion resistance index	Forms available	Insulation thickness [cm] for U-value [W/m²K] of		
					0.3	0.2	0.15
	ρ [kg/m³]	λ [W/mK]	μ [–]				
Flax	20–50	0.040–0.050	1–2	Batts, blown material, loose fill	11–14	18–22	24–31
Hemp	20–150	0.040–0.080	1–2	Batts, blown material, loose fill	11–22	18–36	24–49
Wood fibres	30–250	0.040–0.080	5–10	Batts, blown material	11–22	18–36	24–49
Wood-wool boards	60–600	0.090–0.100	2–5	Boards	25–28	40–45	55–61
Calcium silicate foam	200–290	0.040–0.070	2–6	Boards, loose fill	11–20	18–31	24–43
Cork	65–160	0.040–0.055	2–8	Granulate, boards	11–15	18–25	24–34
Mineral wool	20–220	0.035–0.050	1–2	Batts, blown and caulking material	10–14	16–22	21–31
Mineral foam	20–130	0.035–0.045	3–6	Boards	10–13	16–20	21–28
Perlite	60–160	0.045–0.080	2–5	Loose fill, boards	13–22	20–36	28–49
Expanded polystyrene (EPS)	15–30	0.035–0.040	20–100	Boards	10–11	16–18	21–24
Extruded polystyrene (XPS)	20–50	0.030–0.040	80–250	Boards	8–11	13–18	18–24
Polyurethane	30–80	0.025–0.040	30–100	Boards, in situ foam	7–11	11–18	15–24
Cellular glass	105–165	0.040–0.055	∞	Boards, loose fill	11–15	18–25	24–34
Reeds	190–220	0.045–0.065	2	Batts	13–18	20–29	28–40
Vacuum insulation panels	150–180	0.006–0.010	∞	Boards, no approval yet	2–3	3–4	4–6
Cellulose	25–65	0.040–0.045	1–2	Loose fill, batts, blown material	11–13	18–20	24–28

B 2.17

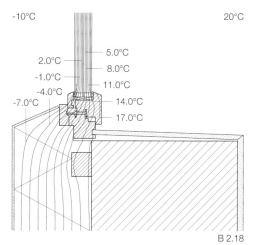

-10°C   20°C

5.0°C
2.0°C   8.0°C
-1.0°C   11.0°C
-4.0°C   14.0°C
-7.0°C   17.0°C

B 2.18

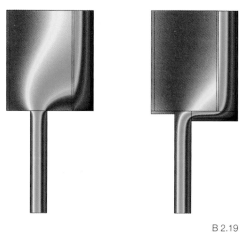

B 2.19

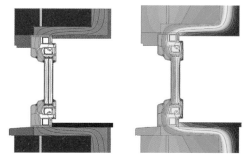

B 2.20

B 2.18   Window installation optimised for thermal per-
         formance with the help of an insulating frame
B 2.19   Examples of the isotherms at a window–wall
         junction with and without insulation to the reveal
         (schematic)
B 2.20   Window–wall junction with uninterrupted internal
         insulating layer
B 2.21   Typical U-values for old roof and attic floor con-
         structions plus improvement options by using
         thermal insulation

2.14). The approved ETICS differ in terms of
their layers, thermal conductivity, fire resistance
characteristics and the building heights for
which they are approved; foamed and fibrous
insulating materials are used. A flat, stable
substrate is important for refurbishment work.
A layer of render may be necessary to compensate for larger discrepancies in the quality
of the existing surface.
Systems with building authority approval have
also been tested with respect to moisture control. Requirements regarding the exterior paint
finish must nevertheless be taken into account.
External insulation increases the temperature
within the existing wall considerably, which
generally provides better protection against
moisture damage because the temperature
only falls below the dew point within the thermal
insulation. Thermal insulation in front of a cavity
open to the external air, which cools the masonry
as well, must be avoided at all costs.
Retrofitted curtain wall facade systems made
from timber, ceramics or stone protect the insulating material against the direct effects of the
weather so a whole range of fibrous insulating
materials can be employed. The ventilation
cavity prevents any moisture diffusion problems.
Systems for refurbishing timber structures are
also the subject of ongoing development. Prefabricated wall elements with integral windows
are designed to be affixed to or suspended
from the existing facade. I-beams as the loadbearing framework for different types of insulating materials can be used here as well.

Internal insulation to walls
Adding internal insulation to walls places high
demands on the designer and the contractor. If
an existing facade and hence the character of
a building is to remain intact, internal insulation
is the only option for an energy-efficiency upgrade.
The following problems must be considered at
the planning stage:

- Attaching insulation to the inside leads to
  lower temperatures within the existing wall
  and hence the risk of interstitial condensation.
- Warm interior air flowing behind the internal
  insulation due to leaking joints and junctions
  in the lining or the vapour barrier leads to
  substantial condensation between insulation
  and wall.
- Moisture due to driving rain or rising damp
  (capillary action) cannot dry out as easily
  because of the lower wall temperature.
- Internal insulation entails a loss of floor
  space, although the area with an acceptable
  thermal comfort level is enlarged.

The repercussions for moisture control should
be checked in every case, and the Glaser
method is the first port of call. When insulating
materials exhibit a high sorption capacity and a
high liquid water diffusivity, e.g. cellulose or
calcium silicate foam boards, only dynamic
methods of calculation can supply reliable values.

Such methods are advantageous because they
include the following:

- Several transport mechanisms (diffusion,
  surface diffusion, capillary action)
- Sorption properties of the materials
- Moisture-related material data
- Initial moisture contents
- True weather situations, including rain
- True moisture loads in the interior
- Coupling between heat and moisture transport
- Phase transitions within the construction

The results can be presented as a chronologi-
cal progression, and validated programs from
various manufacturers are available in 1-D and
2-D versions [19].
A vapour barrier must be used with insulating
materials that do not exhibit any capillary action.
The new vapour barriers with adaptive moisture
properties, which permit easier drying-out in
summer towards the inside as well, have proved
to be worthwhile.

Overcoming thermal bridges
Most thermal bridges, e.g. continuous concrete
balcony slabs, are eliminated by adding external insulation. Critical points here, though, are
primarily the junctions between the floor over a
basement or a ground floor slab and the external and internal walls. This problem can be
considerably diminished, however, by affixing
insulation below the floor over the basement
and around the outside of the basement walls.
An isotherm calculation is certainly advisable in
order to reveal the internal surface temperatures (Fig. B 2.6). Alternatively, the forms of
construction shown in DIN 4108 supplement 2
or a thermal bridges catalogue can be used to
provide ideas for building without thermal
bridges [20].
Generally speaking, all joints and junctions that
penetrate the layer of insulation are critical in
the case of internal insulation. Wedges of insulating material can be used to raise the surface
temperatures at junctions between internal and
external walls or floor slabs and external walls
(Fig. B 2.16). With concrete floor slabs, eliminating the penetration of the insulation should
begin with the floor finishes and screed, i.e. the
internal insulation should not simply begin
above the floor covering. This problem is usually
solved only by removing the floor finishes and
the screed and installing a layer of insulation
beneath the screed, which, however, is advisable for improving the impact sound insulation
anyway.
Party walls often continue right up to the underside of the roof covering. Decreasing the thermal bridge effect can be achieved by removing

the masonry and insulating this area, or by adding some insulation in the ventilation cavity between the two leaves of the party wall.

Thermal insulation to the roof
The following options are possible for (close) couple roofs:

- Insulation between the rafters
- Insulation between and below the rafters
- Insulation above the rafters
- Combinations of insulation between, below and above the rafters

Insulation between the rafters usually requires the depth of the existing rafters to be doubled because the common rafter depths of 140–150 mm are usually inadequate for the insulation thicknesses required these days (Fig. B 2.21). Achieving a decent summertime thermal performance also requires insulation at least 200 mm thick. Moisture control analyses plus a carefully designed, airtight layer are essential.
A vapour barrier with adaptive moisture properties is suitable in conjunction with bitumen roof sheeting or sheet metal roof coverings so that the condensation that builds up in the winter can dry out more easily towards the inside. Fibrous and blown insulating materials are the most popular forms for insulation between the rafters.
When adding insulation on top of the rafters, which always involves re-covering the roof and increasing the height of the building, one alternative to fibrous insulating materials is to use PU-based insulation boards; these boards exhibit thermal conductivities of up to 0.025 W/m²K, which means the thickness of the insulation can be reduced substantially (Fig. B 2.21). However, the junction between the roof and the external walls must be carefully detailed to avoid thermal bridges.
For the topmost floor beneath an unheated roof space the simplest solution for the insulation is to use flooring-grade insulating boards. An airtight installation is very important so that no cold air can flow between the boards. As the insulation is laid on the cold side, moisture problems are unlikely, provided the airtightness is guaranteed.
On a flat roof it is normally possible to add additional insulation on top of the existing waterproofing. If no further waterproofing is added on top of the insulation we speak of an upside-down or inverted roof. In this case a surcharge should be added to the thermal conductivity of the insulating material according to DIN 6946 [21]. Any thermal bridges at parapets can be eliminated by insulating the entire construction.

Thermal insulation to ground floors
Ground floor slabs laid directly on the ground cannot normally be insulated on the underside once they have been constructed, which means that insulation on top of the slab is the only option (Fig. B 2.9). The internal walls inevitably penetrate the layer of insulation and hence cre-

ate thermal bridges. It is therefore important to ensure that the internal walls are fully insulated as well. In addition, an isotherm calculation is recommended. Owing to the fact that the temperature of the soil is higher than that of the outside air, surface temperatures are not usually in the critical range, i.e. they lie above 12.6 °C. Around the perimeter of the slab, the external insulation to the wall must extend down at least to the soil zone unaffected by frost.
If there is no ground floor slab, a complete new construction is required anyway. The inevitable excavation can be enlarged to allow for a layer of insulation below the new floor slab.
Adding insulation to the underside of a ground floor slab over a basement is recommended, provided there is enough height in the basement. If height is a problem, vacuum insulation panels can be used which are much thinner than conventional insulating materials. Otherwise, it will be necessary to add insulation on top of the ground floor, although here again, the clear ceiling height, especially in buildings

built from the 1950s onwards, could place a limit on the maximum thickness of insulation feasible.

Window constructions and their integration
Windows, as sources of daylight, provide passive solar energy gains and can also be used as ventilation elements, making them the most complex components in the building envelope. But in terms of thermal performance, they represent weaknesses at first glance because the U-values possible are considerably poorer than those of the wall or roof constructions. Choosing a suitable window construction is therefore a very important exercise. Standard windows these days comprise two panes of glass with a low-E coating and argon-filled cavity. The U_W-value for the window as a whole is approx. 1.4 W/m²K. With current designs and triple glazing, U_W-values as low as 0.8 W/m²K can be achieved. Using such windows in frames with an improved thermal performance, the window becomes an energy supplier over the heating period owing to the solar gains. Fig. B 2.8b lists the para-

Roof/attic floor	Typical construction	Year of construct	U-value before refurb. [W/m²K]	Construction after refurbishment	U-value after refurbishment [W/m²K] $\lambda = 0.040$ W/mK			
					15 cm	20 cm	30 cm	40 cm
(Close) couple roof	Lining 140 mm rafters Sheeting Counter battens, battens Roof covering	Prior to 1870	1.4	Lining 140 mm rafters Extra rafter depth/insulation Sheeting Counter battens, battens Roof covering	–	0.24	0.17	0.12
Mansard roof	Plaster Wood-wool lightweight boards 140 mm rafters Sheeting Counter battens, battens Roof covering	1870–1920	1.1	Plaster Wood-wool l/w boards 140 mm rafters Extra rafter depth/insulation Sheeting Counter battens, battens Roof covering	–	0.20	0.13	0.10
Timber joist attic floor	Plaster Plaster background Joists/soundboarding Floorboards	1920–1945	0.75	Plaster Plaster background Joists/soundboarding Floorboards V. barrier/airtight membrane Insulation Screed/boards	–	0.16	0.13	0.11
Converted (close) couple roof	Plaster 40 mm wood-wool lightweight boards 150 mm rafters Sheeting Counter battens, battens Roof covering	1945–1960	0.9	Plaster 40 mm wood-wool l/w boards 150 mm rafters Extra rafter depth/insulation Sheeting Counter battens, battens Roof covering	–	0.20	0.13	0.10
Reinforced concrete attic floor	Plaster 160 mm reinforced concrete slab 20 mm existing insulation 40 mm screed	1960–1972	1.3	Plaster 160 mm RC slab 20 mm existing insulation 40 mm screed Insulation Screed/boards	0.22	0.17	0.12	–
Flat roof (warm deck)	Plaster 180 mm reinforced concrete slab Levelling layer 60 mm existing insulation Bitumen waterproofing Gravel	1972–1985	0.5	Plaster 180 mm RC. slab Levelling layer 60 mm existing insulation Bitumen waterproofing Insulation Optional waterproofing Gravel	0.17	0.14	0.11	–

B 2.21

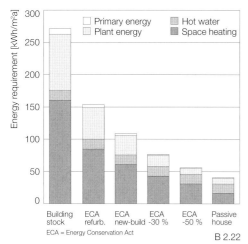

B 2.22

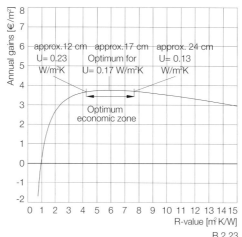

B 2.23

Additional insulation to an old component up to the optimum U-value: 0.17 W/m²K

B 2.24

meters of typical window constructions. Besides the construction of the window itself, its integration into the wall is also critical. In principle, the junction between the window and the wall should not interrupt the insulating layer, and in the case of external insulation the outer part of the frame must be covered with insulation, too. An uninsulated window reveal inevitably leads to very low surface temperatures and mould problems (Fig. B 2.19). An ideal installation leads to Ψ-values approaching zero and hence to a detail that avoids any thermal bridges (Fig. B 2.18).

A continuous layer of insulation is also necessary for internal insulation (Fig. B 2.20). An airtight junction between the window frame and the wall is essential so that the warm interior air cannot flow behind the insulation.

EnEV 2007 requirements – EPCs

The level of requirements in the 2007 edition of the Energy Conservation Act (EnEV) was not changed from the 2004 edition [22]; the component values valid in the past continued to apply. However, a primary energy analysis according to the method given in the Act is possible as an alternative, and the limit values to be complied with in an existing building are approx. 40 % higher than those for a new building. What is new is the obligation to record the energy-efficiency quality of a building by way of an energy performance certificate (EPC). This also applies to the building stock. The intention is to provide buyers and tenants with an easily understood way of assessing the quality of a property. A scale is used to classify the building according to its energy consump-

tion, and to make this even easier to follow, the scale is provided with typical consumption figures for various buildings, right up to passive house standard (Fig. B 2.28).

A certificate can be issued on the basis of the measured energy consumption or the calculated energy requirement. Up until 1 October 2008 either type of certificate was possible for residential buildings with less than five dwellings. But since then such buildings require a certificate based on the energy requirement.

When a building is to be given an energy-efficiency upgrade, the possible measures should always be evaluated with the help of an energy requirement calculation. Basically, for mapping the building and determining the energy-efficiency quality of the components, it is possible to use the method given in the EnEV, which initially takes into account the thermal bridges by means of a global surcharge of 0.1 W/m²K added to the U-values of the total thermally relevant enclosing surface. In the case of extensive energy-efficiency upgrading measures involving passive house components, the use of

Component	Measure	Current economic solution		Forward-looking solution	
		U-value [W/m²K]	Equivalent price of energy-saving [cent/kWh]	U-value [W/m²K]	Equivalent price of energy-saving [cent/kWh]
Pitched roof	Insulation below and between rafters	0.16[1]	2.0	0.16[1]	2.0
	Insulation above rafters	0.16	1.7	0.11	2.0
	Insulation above and between rafters	0.15	1.9	0.10	2.1
Flat roof	Extra insulation in warm deck construction	0.18	3.2	0.12	3.5
	Inverted roof on waterproofing	0.22	2.9	0.16	3.3
Attic floor	Thermal insulation (not trafficable)	0.14	0.7	0.12	0.9
	Thermal insulation (trafficable)	0.14	1.6	0.12	1.7
External wall	ETICS when renewing render	0.17	1.3	0.13	1.6
	ETICS when repainting	0.17	2.3	0.13	2.5
	Curtain wall facade with extra insulation when renewing facade	0.18	2.0	0.13	2.3
	Internal insulation with airtight membrane when renewing wallpaper	0.28[1]	1.0	0.28[1]	2.0
	Internal insulation with airtight membrane when renewing plaster	0.28[1]	1.0	0.28[1]	1.0
Basement wall	Internal insulation with airtight membrane when renewing plaster	0.27[1]	2.5	0.27[1]	2.5
Floor over basement	Insulation below floor	0.27[1]	2.5	0.27[1]	2.5
Space-heating and hot-water pipes	Subsequent lagging[2]	1× DN	0.9	2× DN	1.5

[1] Insulation thicknesses limited because otherwise excessive loss of floor space
[2] Lagging thickness is related to nominal diameter DN

B 2.25

B 2.22 Comparison of the energy requirements of various building standards
B 2.23 Annual gains due to energy-savings plotted against thermal resistance R
B 2.24 Comparison of costs for energy saved after adding insulation to an external wall expressed as a function of the U-value of the existing component
B 2.25 Economics of insulating measures: comparison of energy-saving (equivalent prices of energy-saving based on price of energy in 2007)
B 2.26 Apartment block dating from 1930, Nuremberg (D), 2002, Burkhard Schulze Darup
 a before refurbishment
 b after refurbishment
 c calculated and measured energy consumption figures
B 2.27 Comparison of the energy balance of an apartment block dating from 1930
 a before refurbishment
 b after refurbishment with passive house components
B 2.28 Sample energy performance certificate for a residential building in Germany

a

b

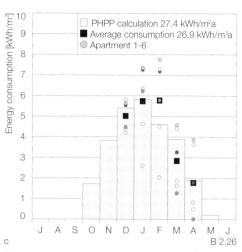

c

B 2.26

the Passive House Planning Package (PHPP) is recommended [23]. The PHPP is an MS Excel application that has proved worthwhile for planning energy-efficiency projects. Software based on DIN EN 832 is also available, which enables a detailed analysis without the global surcharge of the EnEV.

Desirable level of energy efficiency
When carrying out a total refurbishment, the first question to ask is: What level of insulation is desirable from the economic viewpoint? Currently, the following designations have established themselves:

• EnEV new-build level
• EnEV minus 30 %
• EnEV minus 50 %
• Refurbishment with passive house components

The EnEV minus 30 % and EnEV minus 50 % levels result from the current upgrade incentives available from the Kreditanstalt für Wiederauf-

bau (KfW) and describe the primary energy-savings related to the EnEV new-build level. If these standards are achieved, subsidies are guaranteed in addition to a low-interest loan. Savings in primary energy in this order of magnitude call for improvements to the building services, the use of renewable energy sources and a ventilation system with heat recovery in addition to an energy-efficiency upgrade for the building envelope itself.
Fig. B 2.22 shows the energy requirements associated with the various levels of efficiency. EnEV minus 50 % comes close to what can be achieved with passive house components. If internal insulation is the only option, it is possible to reach almost new-build level. Efficient building services result in a reduction in the running costs of those services, as Fig. B 2.22 illustrates. Irrespective of the requirements of the Energy Conservation Act, it is worthwhile investigating which insulation thicknesses are economic at current prices. The Passive House Institute in Darmstadt has investigated several insulation measures on the basis of an economic feasib-

ility study using the discounted cash flow method [24]. The study identified the economically viable insulation thicknesses and those U-values of external components in the building stock where insulation measures would be helpful (Figs. B 2.23 and 2.24).
Fig. B 2.25 lists possible insulation measures in terms of their economic effectiveness. All the measures listed are economic in the medium-term because current energy prices make the energy-savings worthwhile. It should be remembered that from the economic viewpoint, additional insulation should always be combined with other measures which are probably necessary anyway, e.g. a new coat of exterior paint.

Energy-efficiency upgrades – What is feasible?
The energy-efficiency upgrade possibilities will be illustrated using the example of a multi-occupancy building in Nuremberg dating from 1930 [25]. The building with a total floor area of 895 m² was completely refurbished in 2002 (Fig. B 2.26). Using the energy balance soft-

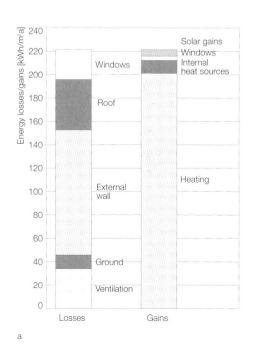

a

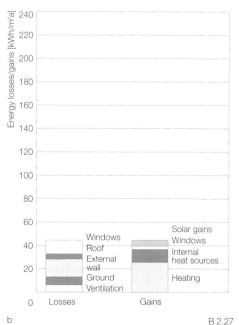

b

B 2.27

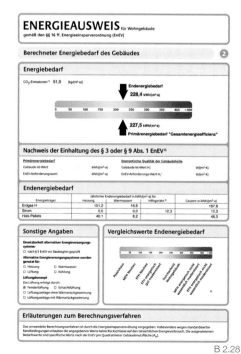

B 2.28

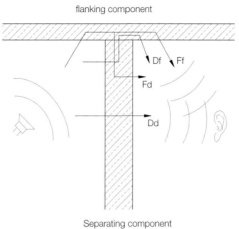

flanking component

Separating component

B 2.29

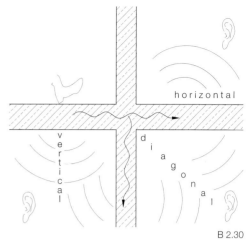

horizontal

vertical

diagonal

B 2.30

ware of the Passive House Planning Package (PHPP) [26], the energy consumption before and after refurbishment was calculated, which resulted in an enormous savings potential (Fig. B 2.27). The following energy-efficiency upgrade measures were implemented:

- A thermal upgrade of the external wall by means of a 200 mm ETICS having a U-value of 0.15 W/m²K; floor over basement: 0.19 W/m²K; roof: 0.12 W/m²K
- Installation of passive house-grade windows (U-value 0.85 W/m²K) avoiding all thermal bridges
- Installation of a ventilation system with heat recovery
- Installation of gas-fired condensing boilers and a solar thermal energy system

Quite decisive here is the fact that the calculated values have been confirmed in practice. The results of the measurements are shown in Fig. B 2.26c, which reveals that the refurbished building performs exactly as predicted. Deviations due to the influences of the users are in the same order of magnitude as for normal apartment blocks.

The lessons learned from numerous buildings refurbished with passive house components is clear: the measures carried out offer better safeguards against moisture-related damage, improve the thermal comfort thanks to higher surface temperatures and double the energy-savings possible compared with a refurbishment according to the EnEV standard.

The Passive House Institute in Darmstadt, the scientific partner, sums up the situation as follows: "The appeal of a high-value modernisation increases when we use highly efficient components because the quality of life for the occupants rises noticeably. Furthermore, modernisation measures in the building stock are a decisive driving force in the economy. The measures shown enable considerable CO_2 reductions to be achieved – more than 75 % in the pilot refurbishment projects. The improvement in efficiency is such that the reduced consumption at the same time enables the more sensible use of renewable energy sources."

Sound insulation

According to DIN 4109 "Sound insulation in buildings", a standard that is also incorporated into building legislation, sound insulation means insulating against airborne and impact sound from areas occupied by other users, insulating against noises from building services (e.g. water pipes) and commercial operations, and protecting against noise from outside. The principal part of this standard lists the parameters necessary for assessing sound insulation. Supplement 2 of the standard contains suggestions for enhanced sound insulation between the living and working areas of different units plus recommendations for normal or enhanced sound insulation within the same unit. Another set of regulations for stipulating contractual requirements is VDI 4100 "Technical rule – Noise control in dwellings – Criteria for planning and assessment".

Whereas in new buildings the sound insulation aims are mostly specified according to the aforementioned standards, conversion or refurbishment projects often require a differentiated approach. Where a change of use is not planned and the parts of the construction relevant to acoustics will not be altered, toleration of the building stock applies initially. So the requirements currently valid may not have to be complied with. But as soon as a change of use is involved or parts of the construction relevant

to acoustics are to be renewed, the requirements of the latest edition of DIN 4109 must usually be applied.

Irrespective of the legal situation, where apartments are involved the occupants often expect an appropriate level of sound insulation following conversion or refurbishment measures – even if this has not been explicitly expressed – because they will have paid large sums of money for the apartments or the rents will have been increased. The willingness to except poor sound insulation is markedly lower with higher rents or purchase prices. According to DIN 4109, the task of sound insulation is "to protect people in habitable rooms against unreasonable annoyance caused by sound propagation". The sound insulation requirements formulated in this standard are often no longer adequate for many of the occupants of apartments. The statement "it cannot be expected that noises from outside or neighbouring rooms can no longer be heard" is not identical with the expectation of complete silence and confidentiality, which is often not feasible from a constructional viewpoint anyway. For all those involved in the building process it is therefore important to quantify sound insulation by means of parameters. Otherwise, in the case of a dispute a court will apply its own interpretation of "appropriate sound insulation" based on the specification – and court verdicts in such instances tend to favour the occupants.

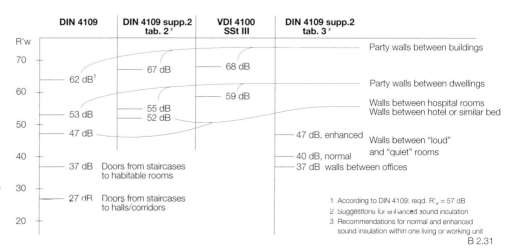

	DIN 4109	DIN 4109 supp.2 tab. 2 [2]	VDI 4100 SSt III	DIN 4109 supp.2 tab. 3 [3]	
R'w					
70		67 dB	68 dB		Party walls between buildings
	62 dB[1]				
60			59 dB		Party walls between dwellings
	53 dB	55 dB 52 dB			Walls between hospital rooms Walls between hotel or similar bed
50	47 dB			47 dB, enhanced	Walls between "loud" and "quiet" rooms
40				40 dB, normal	
	37 dB	Doors from staircases to habitable rooms		37 dB walls between offices	
30					
	27 dB	Doors from staircases to halls/corridors			
20					

1 According to DIN 4109: reqd. R'w = 57 dB
2 Suggestions for enhanced sound insulation
3 Recommendations for normal and enhanced sound insulation within one living or working unit

B 2.31

Source of noise	Sound pressure level of source [dB(A)][1]	Background noise level in room [dB]	
		20	30
Oil-fired heating	25	hardly disturbing	not disturbing
Flushing WC	28	disturbing	hardly disturbing
Running a bath	32	very disturbing	hardly disturbing
Closing a garage door	35	very disturbing	hardly disturbing
Using a bath	35	very disturbing	hardly disturbing

[1] Guidance values

B 2.32

Main parameters for sound insulation and values required

The parameter for the airborne sound insulation requirements between rooms is the weighted sound reduction index R'_w. The weighting (index "w") means that the frequency of the sound reduction index R is weighted by a frequency-related function designed to take account of human hearing characteristics, which is based on a noise spectrum typical of housing situations (see "Glossary", p. 266). For instance, a small amount of sound insulation for low frequencies is not attached great significance in the assessment because the human ear is less sensitive to low frequencies. The advantage of this variable is that it represents a numerical reference point that is easy to use in planning sound insulation and does not depend on frequency. Sound reduction indexes should always be as large as possible.

The sound insulation between two rooms actually achieved in practice depends not only on the constructional properties of the separating component, but also on the constructional situation (Fig. B 2.29). Airborne and impact sound propagation to adjacent rooms takes place not exclusively via the component separating the two rooms. The soundwaves propagate in the form of structure-borne sound in flanking components as well and are radiated from these in the form of airborne sound. The dash (') in the weighted sound reduction index R'_w denotes that the sound insulation also takes into account sound propagation via flanking components. A difference of 3 dB between the weighted sound reduction index of the component R_w and the weighted sound reduction index of the component R'_w in the as-built condition means that 50 % of the sound energy propagates via flanking paths (Fig. B 2.29). The requirements always apply to the as-built situation, i.e. R'_w, and $R'_w < R_w$, a fact that must be considered during the planning.

The weighted airborne sound improvement index $\triangle R_w$ is the parameter used to measure the improvement (= enhancement) to the sound reduction index of a separating component by the inclusion of a wall lining, suspended ceiling or hollow floor.

In the case of external components, the sound reduction index achievable is made up of a weighting of the energy transmission through the individual components, e.g. external wall, windows and roof, adjusted to take account of the different areas of these components. The resultant weighted sound reduction index $R'_{w,res}$ is the acoustic parameter used for this situation. The requirement placed on this variable depends on the external noise load to which the building is subjected. The latter can be specified by means of the so-called critical external noise level. The noise level must be known before designing the building envelope and can be obtained from the local building authority or determined by an acoustics consultant based on calculations or measurements.

The parameter used for the impact sound insulation requirements of components (suspended floors, stairs) is the weighted normalised impact sound (pressure) level $L'_{n,w}$; in this expression the term "weighted" has the same significance as with the weighted (airborne) sound insulation index (see above). The dash (') again stands for the propagation of impact sound via the suspended floor itself plus the flanking components, e.g. walls. It should be remembered that impact sound can propagate not only vertically, but also horizontally and diagonally into other rooms (Fig. B 2.30). In contrast to the sound insulation index, however, the normalised impact sound level should be as small as possible, and here $L'_{n,w} > L_{n,w}$ always applies.

The weighted impact sound reduction index $\triangle L_w$ is used for assessing to what extent an impact sound reduction measure, e.g. a floating screed or other floor finish, helps to optimise (= reduce) the normalised impact sound level of the structural floor construction.

The R'_w and $L'_{n,w}$ values required are generally designated by the abbreviation "reqd.", which stands for "required". Figs. B 2.31 and 2.33 enable a comparison of a number of values for certain sound insulation requirements and recommendations.

To gain an overall picture of the actual sound insulation that exists in buildings built in recent decades, a few comparative figures, derived from measurements, will be given here [27]. For party walls in 1950 the maximum of the frequency distribution for the measured sound reduction index R'_w was 48 dB, and by the mid-1960s this figure had already risen to 54 dB. For the airborne sound insulation of party floors in 1950 the maximum of the frequency distribution for R'_w was 46 dB, by 1966 it had risen to 55 dB and in 1987 had reached 58 dB. For the impact sound insulation of party floors a value of $L'_{n,w}$ = 73 dB was given in the literature in the 1950s, but this had come down to 49 dB by the mid-1960s, a figure that was still valid in 1987 (all figures refer to former West Germany) [28]. When assessing noises from building services, we use the maximum, A-weighted sound pressure level (see "Glossary", p. 266).

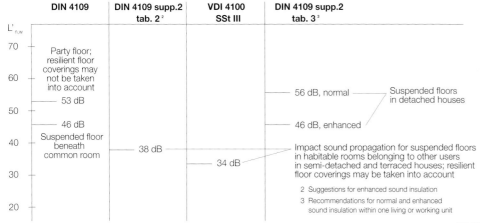

B 2.33

2 Suggestions for enhanced sound insulation
3 Recommendations for normal and enhanced sound insulation within one living or working unit

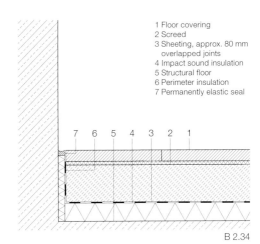

1 Floor covering
2 Screed
3 Sheeting, approx. 80 mm
   overlapped joints
4 Impact sound insulation
5 Structural floor
6 Perimeter insulation
7 Permanently elastic seal

B 2.34

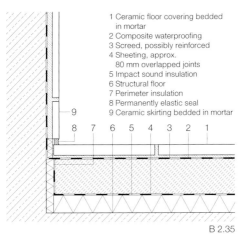

1 Ceramic floor covering bedded
   in mortar
2 Composite waterproofing
3 Screed, possibly reinforced
4 Sheeting, approx.
   80 mm overlapped joints
5 Impact sound insulation
6 Structural floor
7 Perimeter insulation
8 Permanently elastic seal
9 Ceramic skirting bedded in mortar

B 2.35

The A-weighting here means that the sensitivity of the human ear with respect to frequencies is taken into account, i.e. the physical sound pressure level is "adjusted" to a value relevant to the physiology of the human ear. This adjustment is designated by the dB(A) unit of measurement. A sound level of 20 dB(A) is suitable for bedrooms, 55 dB(A) is necessary for concentrated working (and should never be exceeded) and 70 dB(A) is the level of excited, loud conversation. The perceived disturbance always depends on the background noise level (Fig. B 2.32). The maximum permissible sound pressure level for flushing a toilet – according to legislation – is 30 dB(A) and can certainly be annoying in a quiet location, but against a background noise level of 40 dB(A) will be inaudible. Sound pressure levels due to water systems that lie well below 25 dB(A) are not always feasible in apartment blocks using standard systems. Finally, it should be mentioned that the planned standard DIN 4109-1, which has already been published in draft form, intends to change the parameters used hitherto for describing sound insulation. The requirements would then no longer be determined depending on the parameters R'_w and $L'_{n,w}$, which designate the sound insulation of components independently of their surface area, but rather depending on the weighted standardised sound level difference $D_{nT,w}$ for the airborne sound insulation and the weighted standardised impact sound level $L'_{nT,w}$ for the impact sound insulation. Obviously, a large component surface area can transmit more sound than a small area. In order to take this into account, the new DIN 4109-1 would describe sound insulation in terms of the parameters $D_{nT,w}$ and $L'_{nT,w}$. The advantage of these new parameters is that the sound insulation that could be actually expected between two adjacent rooms can be defined. The disadvantage is that a differentiated planning approach becomes necessary because the actual surface areas of the separating components have to be taken into account. If and when DIN 4109-1 is introduced, it will become necessary to assess the different uses (specifying which of the rooms is loud and which is quiet) and sensitivities (disturbing effect of transmitted sound and confidentiality) and include the

actual size of the separating component plus the volumes of the rooms.

Procedure in the case of refurbishment
The first step when planning sound insulation measures is to assess the acoustics of the parts of the existing structure affected by the conversion or refurbishment measures. Only after that can a sound insulation concept be drawn up.

Survey of existing structure
If detailed information on the existing constructions is available, the acoustic parameters R'_w and $L'_{n,w}$ can be calculated. The acoustic behaviour of forms of construction for which detailed information is unavailable, e.g. specific hollow-core slabs, and acoustic deficiencies (dry linings or floating screed with acoustic bridges), however, can usually be ascertained only through in situ measurements. Questioning users about conspicuous acoustic aspects can be very helpful, too.

Sound insulation concept
The second step consists of listing the acoustic requirements according to DIN 4109 and, if applicable, client and user requirements that exceed those of the standard. The constructional feasibility must always be checked, especially in the case of conversion or refurbishment projects. Sometimes the cost of achieving a high standard of sound insulation exceeding the minimum requirements of DIN 4109 is disproportionately high. Frequent problems that occur are:

· The introduction of the additional loads of floating screeds
· The associated increase in the depth of the floor construction
· The rigid connection between stairs and stair shaft walls which is difficult to eliminate subsequently
· Restrictions due to the stipulations of conservation orders

Promising the client that enhanced sound insulation requirements will be achieved may be very foolhardy without carrying out a survey of the existing structure first because such sound

insulation may be impossible to achieve, at least with a reasonable budget.
But in every case the acoustic requirements should be recorded in writing. For example, if after refurbishment only the minimum sound insulation to DIN 4109 can be complied with, but the specification promises especially high-value housing (e.g. luxury apartments), the owner is very likely to be successful if he sues the builder or developer at a later date for better sound insulation. Such a situation can only be prevented by including information in the specification regarding the actual acoustic standard of the building.
Where conversion or refurbishment measures include changes to the interior layout, an acoustically more favourable layout of the individual rooms should be considered. What this means is avoiding placing rooms that need to be protected from loud noise adjacent to those where loud noises can be expected, e.g. bathroom, WC, plant room, staircase. Planning the interior so that rooms such as halls, corridors and kitchens act as "acoustic buffers" is to be recommended.
The exposure to external noise must also be taken into account. If the prevailing external noise level at the building has changed, this fact must be taken into account when planning the sound insulation of the external components, also considering any potential external noise developments in the coming years. In particular, rooms that need to be protected from noise, e.g. bedrooms, should preferably be situated on the side of the building facing away from the main noise sources.
Finally, the desired level of sound insulation must be implemented by specifying the forms of construction. In the case of any ambiguity, which mainly results from the fact that it was not possible to carry out a proper survey of the existing structure, especially with older buildings (lack of documents describing design and construction), specialists should be appointed to specify the refurbishment measures and/or the recommendations of materials or system suppliers (e.g. dry construction) or trade associations should be sought [29].

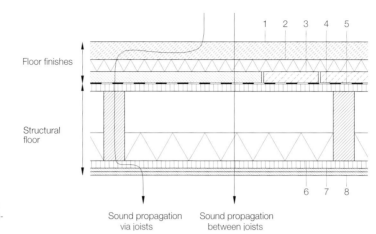

1 Screed
2 Impact sound insulation
3 Ballast to structural floor in the form of small-format concrete flags or bonded loose fill
4 Sheeting to prevent loss of loose fill
5 Flooring grade particleboard
6 Attenuation to void
7 Battens or resilient bars
8 Boards forming ceiling

Floor finishes

Structural floor

Sound propagation via joists

Sound propagation between joists

B 2.36

B 2.34 Detail of floating screed–wall junction
B 2.35 Detail of floating screed–wall junction in wet rooms
B 2.36 Construction of a timber joist floor showing sound propagation paths
B 2.37 Screed and subfloor thicknesses and compressibility of insulation layer for floating screed without heating pipes (selection) to DIN 18560-2

Acoustic weaknesses in existing buildings and their rectification

Some of the more common acoustic problems encountered will be discussed below. The problems are usually connected with the building methods customary at the time the original building was erected (which may show regional variations), the construction options and materials available at that time and any differences between the noise control requirements valid then and now. Specific, detailed forms of construction are shown in Part C (see pp. 116–205).

Suspended floors
Timber joist floors, lightweight reinforced concrete slabs and hollow-core slabs represent the main sources of acoustic problems in old buildings. In most cases adding a floating screed to all these three types of suspended floor in order to improve the impact sound insulation is the only practical solution in housing. Although floating screeds have been standard practice in housing for many decades, structure-borne sound bridges often ensue due to poor workmanship.
The most frequent cause of acoustic bridges around the perimeter of suspended floors is the lack of or poorly installed strips of insulation – needed to isolate the screed from other parts of the construction. Floor tile adhesive and levelling courses that infiltrate into the gap between screed and wall represent other, typical causes (Figs. B 2.34 and 2.35). A single acoustic bridge between screed and structural floor can increase the weighted normalised impact sound level by several decibels and hence determine whether the construction complies or fails to comply with the requirements (Fig. B 2.39). So even today, laying a screed without any acoustic bridges is still a challenge for any contractor.

Timber joist floors
A few figures are necessary in order to understand the problem. In existing buildings timber joist floors without a ceiling exhibit a weighted normalised impact sound level of $L'_{n,w} = 65$ dB and higher, depending on the floor finishes and the presence of any ballast, e.g. pugging. Adding a floating dry subfloor can improve the situation by approx. 10 dB, and a mineral screed

will be even better. So in order to reach the minimum requirement in housing of reqd. $L'_{n,w} \leq 53$ dB, further measures are generally necessary. A reasonable prognosis of the impact sound insulation to be achieved is only possible with relevant planning aids or through a comparison with measured forms of construction [30]. A research project of the German Society for Wood Research (DGfH) included an investigation of many different types of old suspended floor constructions with proposals for their refurbishment [31]. When using planning values it is essential to check whether the $L_{n,w}$ or the $L'_{n,w}$ value is specified for tested forms of construction.
Fig. B 2.36 shows a popular, inexpensive and up-to-date form of construction for a timber joist floor. Which of the components can be implemented during refurbishment depends on the particular situation, especially the deconstruction usually necessary, the loadbearing capacity of the joists and, in the end, the depth available for the upgraded floor construction.
A floating screed is indispensable here. Mineral screeds improve the impact sound insulation but are much heavier and must dry out before further work can continue, thus prolonging the construction process. Manufacturers' special system components can be used to reduce the depth of a floating subfloor.
Adding ballast to a structural floor is always worth considering. Pugging can be introduced

to reduce the depth of the additional floor finishes, although the acoustic effectiveness is much lower because the structure-borne sound transmitted by the joists is not reduced at all (Fig. B 2.36). However, the timber joists are often of such a size that adding ballast without increasing the loadbearing capacity of the floor by some means is out of the question.
A suspended ceiling will be required in addition to a screed if good sound insulation is to be achieved. It is important here to mount the ceiling on resilient hangers, and the ceiling material itself should be as heavy as possible. The type of hanger must be chosen very carefully because the desired improvement to the sound insulation is only achieved when the load on the hanger due to the suspended ceiling approaches the hanger's maximum permissible load. Alternatively, in smaller rooms it is possible to build a completely separate ceiling spanning between the walls. Improvements in the weighted normalised impact sound level $L_{n,w}$ of up to 15 dB are possible when using a ceiling decoupled from the timber joist floor instead of a ceiling attached directly to the underside via battens, or the layer of plaster on a backing of reed batts so often found in older buildings.
In order to optimise a timber joist floor for the low frequencies of impact sound as well, there should be a generous clearance, normally at least 100 mm, between the suspended ceiling and the underside of the floor.

Vertical imposed loads	Point loads	≤ 2 kPa	≤ 2 kPa	≤ 3 kPa	≤ 4 kPa
	Distributed loads	–	≤ 3 kPa	≤ 4 kPa	≤ 5 kPa
Compressibility		≤ 5 mm	≤ 5 mm	≤ 3 mm	≤ 3 mm
Min. thickness	Self-levelling calcium sulphate screed (CAF)	30 mm[2]	40 mm	45 mm	50 mm
	Calcium sulphate screed (CA)	35 mm[1,2]	50 mm[1]	55 mm[1]	60 mm[1]
	Cement screed (CT)	40 mm[1,2]	55 mm[1]	60 mm[1]	65 mm[1]
Compressibility		≤ 3 mm	≤ 3 mm	≤ 3 mm	≤ 3 mm
Min. thickness	Asphalt (AS)	25 mm[2]	30 mm	30 mm	35 mm

[1] With an insulation thickness ≤ 40 mm, the thickness may be reduced by 5 mm in the case of calcium sulphate and cement screeds.
[2] The screed thickness must be increased by 5 mm in the case of a higher compressibility (≤ 10 mm).

B 2.37

Lightweight reinforced concrete slabs
In housing a floating screed is indispensable for improving the impact sound insulation of reinforced concrete floor slabs where these are used in conjunction with masonry flanking walls. With lightweight reinforced concrete floor slabs having a mass per unit area < 300 kg/m² (slab depth < 140 mm), it is often not possible to achieve the airborne sound and impact sound insulation values required by legislation just by adding a floating screed. Whether and which additional measures are necessary depends on the flanking walls. Lightweight flanking walls with a mass per unit area < 250 kg/m² are unhelpful in such situations. Suspended, non-rigid ceilings (which can achieve an improvement of max. 3 dB), independent wall linings or replacing masonry walls with plasterboard-clad stud walls represent possible supplementary measures.

The dynamic stiffness of the insulating material plays a key role when selecting impact sound insulation, the actual material itself is less important. Impact sound insulating materials with a low dynamic stiffness result in a greater reduction in the impact sound level. However, a higher compressibility of the insulation must be accepted, which generally means that a lower permissible imposed load and/or a slightly greater nominal screed thickness must also be accepted (Fig. B 2.37).

Lightweight wood-wool boards plus a layer of plaster on the underside of the suspended floor can have a negative effect on the sound insulation because these form a resonant system together with the reinforced concrete slab. Possible remedies are to remove the plaster and wood-wool boards completely or to remove just the plaster and add a suspended, non-rigid ceiling. Like with timber joist floors, minimising the connection between the ceiling and the structural floor results in the best sound insulation.

Hollow-core slabs
Hollow-core slabs (waffle slabs, ribbed slabs, etc.) normally have a much lower mass per unit area than homogeneous solid slabs. In addition, the voids within the floor slabs result in thin shells

that have a negative effect on the acoustics, making such slabs even worse than solid floor slabs with the same mass per unit area, especially for the impact sound insulation. Like with all heavyweight floor slabs, adequate impact sound insulation requires the addition of a floating screed, which, planned and laid carefully, can compensate for the deficiencies of the hollow-core slabs in the medium- and high-frequency ranges. The main problem with hollow-core slabs, however, is the airborne sound insulation. Owing to their (usually) low mass per unit area, there is a strong connection between the floor and the flanking masonry walls. The architect is therefore recommended to remove masonry walls wherever possible and replace them with stud walls clad with wood-based board products or plasterboard. Alternatively, independent wall linings can be built in front of the masonry walls.

In any case measurements will be necessary because there are many different types of hollow-core slabs in the building stock, and their acoustic behaviour can vary quite significantly.

Floor coverings
Carpets are frequently replaced by laminate or wood-block floor coverings these days. Where impact sound insulation is guaranteed by a functioning floating screed, this change of floor covering does not usually present any problems, although the impact sound level will rise. If, however, the carpeting was part of the original acoustic concept, as was permitted in the past, replacing the carpet with a different type of floor covering can lead to an inadmissible impact sound level. According to civil law, laying a new floor covering may not worsen the impact sound insulation. That is not feasible with a laminate or wood-block floor covering simply laid in adhesive, and where a laminate floor covering is laid loose on impact sound insulation this results in a smaller reduction in the impact sound level than would be the case with carpet (Fig. B 2.40).

Staircases
When considering stairs we must distinguish between the stair flights and the landings. The

minimum requirements for the impact sound insulation of the stair flights in multi-storey housing according to DIN 4109 only apply when there is no lift and there are more than two dwellings in the building. The subsequent addition of a lift therefore exonerates the developer from upgrading the acoustics of the stair flights. Improving the impact sound insulation of reinforced concrete stair flights that are rigidly connected to the walls is usually extremely problematic. If no change of use is involved, the notion of toleration of the building stock can be exploited. Adding carpet can achieve a worthwhile improvement. Alternatively, ceramic tiles or similar floor finishes can be glued to a resilient underlay laid on the stair treads. Like with a floating screed, complete separation between the tiles and the walls, treads and risers is essential if structure-borne sound transmissions are to be suppressed.

The landings in multi-storey housing must comply with minimum sound insulation requirements according to DIN 4109 – unless the notion of toleration of the building stock applies. The impact sound insulation to landings can be improved sufficiently with a floating screed, like with suspended floors, or with carpet.

Lightweight masonry walls
Existing lightweight masonry walls can lead to two types of problem:
Firstly, the sound insulation at junctions between suspended floors and party walls where the mass of the masonry wall is < 200 kg/m². The masonry wall flanking component in this case leads to an undesirable reduction in the sound insulation (see p. 46).
Secondly, the improvement in the airborne sound insulation of a single-leaf solid wall with a mass per unit area < 450 kg/m² as a party wall (Fig. B 2.41). Adding a second solid wall is not a solution, even when a cavity is created between the new and existing walls. To improve the sound insulation, the new solid masonry wall must be built off a resilient bearing pad on the suspended floor and completely decoupled from the surrounding walls and floor above by means of joints. This form of construction is common in, for example, music studios, but not

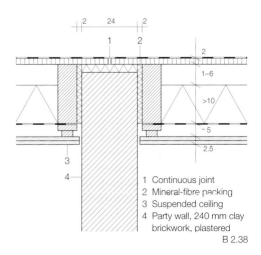

1 Continuous joint
2 Mineral-fibre packing
3 Suspended ceiling
4 Party wall, 240 mm clay brickwork, plastered

B 2.38

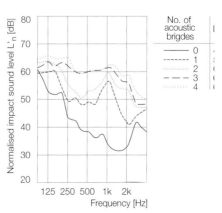

No. of acoustic bridges
— 0
--- 1
···· 2
–·– 3
–– 4

B 2.39

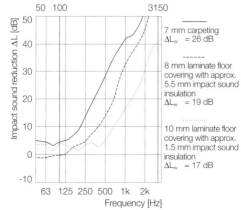

7 mm carpeting
ΔL$_w$ = 26 dB

8 mm laminate floor covering with approx. 5.5 mm impact sound insulation
ΔL$_w$ = 19 dB

10 mm laminate floor covering with approx. 1.5 mm impact sound insulation
ΔL$_w$ = 17 dB

B 2.40

B 2.38 Sketch showing the principle behind the minimisation of flanking transmissions when building a party wall up to the underside of the roof covering and to interrupt continuous components

B 2.39 Normalised impact sound level of a floating calcium sulphate screed on polystyrene impact sound insulation boards with different numbers of discrete acoustic bridges

B 2.40 Impact sound reduction of carpet and laminate floor coverings on solid floors

B 2.41 Weighted airborne sound improvement index ΔR_w as a parameter for improving the impact sound insulation of a solid wall by using a wall lining on separate studs and attenuation in the void

B 2.42 Construction of a coupled window after refurbishment; inner glazing replaced by double-glazed window

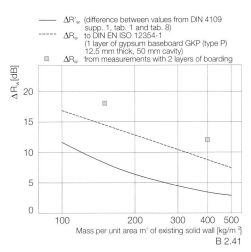

—— $\Delta R'_w$ (difference between values from DIN 4109 supp. 1, tab. 1 and tab. 8)
----- ΔR_w to DIN EN ISO 12354-1 (1 layer of gypsum baseboard GKP (type P) 12.5 mm thick, 50 mm cavity)
▢ ΔR_w from measurements with 2 layers of boarding

B 2.41

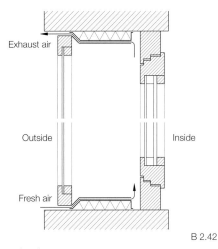

B 2.42

in housing. In the latter case it is possible to build an independent wall lining comprising non-rigid boards (e.g. plasterboard or gypsum fibreboard), which will improve the airborne sound insulation. The optimisation achievable with an independent wall lining depends on the sound insulation quality of the existing wall (Fig. B 2.41). Independent wall linings achieve the best sound insulating effect when the distance between the non-rigid boards and the existing wall is as large as possible (min. 50 mm), the boarding is as heavy as possible (at least two layers of boards), the stud construction is free-standing in front of the wall (fixed at floor and ceiling only – hence the use of the term "independent") and the cavity is attenuated with an insulating material (e.g. mineral fibres). A second independent wall lining on the other side of the wall achieves a further improvement of max. 3 dB where there are flanking masonry walls attached to the party wall itself.

Party walls in roof space conversions
The subsequent conversion of roof spaces into habitable rooms with party walls between the dwellings must be considered very carefully with respect to flanking transmissions (Fig. B 2.29). In order to upgrade a wall so that it acts as a party wall, it is necessary to extend the wall up to the underside of the roof covering and interrupt any lining on the underside of the roof at the wall (Fig. B 2.38). This is also necessary for fire protection. The lining to the underside of the roof covering should also be interrupted at the walls within a dwelling and the space filled with a fibrous insulating material (absorbent bulkhead). And in cases where additional rigid, non-porous insulating material has been subsequently laid over the rafters this should be replaced by, for example, porous insulating materials to minimise the flanking transmissions. Such measures must be checked by a specialist.

Water pipework
Direct-flush and wall-mounted WCs often lead to complaints regarding the noise of flushing transmitted through the water pipework. A direct-flush WC should be replaced by a cistern. In the case of a floor-mounted WC, fixing it to a floating screed is the only answer. A wall-mounted

WC, a form that is becoming more and more popular, requires a suitable wall lining to conceal cistern and pipework.
The manufacturer must supply details of which product and system satisfies which sound insulation requirements. It should not be forgotten here that the manufacturer's tests will have been carried out in a standardised setup, and the figures may need to be converted to take account of the actual situation on site; some manufacturers provide information for standard cases. The installation instructions should be followed exactly because such systems usually represent well-conceived assemblies in which the effects of changes are unpredictable. Furthermore, the manufacturer's warranty will otherwise be invalid.
The use of tested systems is also recommended for all other components of water pipework systems, e.g. drinking-water, heating, waste-water and internal rainwater pipes, baths and shower trays, vanity units, bidets, fittings, etc. Fittings that do not comply with the requirements of fittings group I (noise level ≤ 20dB(A)) should be replaced.

External noise
When determining the sound insulation necessary for the external components, is also necessary to take into account the fact that not only the windows, but also the external wall and possibly even the roof contribute to sound propagation. With high external noise levels (road, rail, water and air traffic), calculations will be necessary and the resulting sound insulation requirements must be adhered to.

Windows
Secondary glazing, and coupled windows in particular, with tightly sealing joints achieve good sound insulation values compared with insulating glass units with two or more panes. When the former are replaced by modern insulating glass units, a noticeable drop in the sound insulation quality is often the result. This is especially noticeable in the case of low-frequency sound sources such as slow HGVs. With a coupled window it is best to replace either the inner or outer window with the insulating glass necessary for achieving the thermal performance required by the latest legislation. Make sure, however, that the cavity within the coupled window is adequately ventilated because otherwise moisture problems can occur. And the ventilation openings required should be designed so that they do not impair the sound insulating effect of the second window unit too severely (Fig. B 2.42).

External thermal insulation composite systems
The subsequent addition of an external thermal insulation composite system (ETICS) can either improve or worsen the insulation against external noise, depending on the system used. The reason for this is the formation of a resonant system. When the product used has a resonant frequency below that relevant for building acoustics, the result is an improvement; otherwise, the result will be worse (up to 6 dB at the resonant frequency) or at least no better than before the ETICS was added (admittedly for other reasons). The sound insulating effects of each system in conjunction with a solid external wall are described in the national technical approvals of the system manufacturers. ETICS do not have any negative impact on the flanking transmissions of an external wall.

Roofs

Where a roof space is to be converted into habitable rooms, it should be remembered that roof structures with exposed rafters (insulation above the rafters) exhibit a low airborne sound insulation figure owing to the low mass of the roof structure. Roof structures with insulation between the rafters plus one or more layers of boarding forming a lining beneath the rafters result in much better sound insulation figures. The manufacturers of rigid foam boards have started to add an additional layer of fibrous insulating material to their products in order to provide an acoustically non-rigid (elastic) layer between the roof covering and the lining, which improves the sound reduction index by a few decibels. The forms of construction used for roofs in refurbishment projects are mostly only slightly different to those used for new-build projects. The relevant planning information and publications of the materials suppliers can therefore be referred to [32]. Windows in the roof can impair the sound insulation, and as yet there is no answer to reducing the noise of rain on Velux-type windows.

Fire protection

Many existing buildings exhibit deficits in terms of protection against fire. These are usually the result of a combination of insufficiently protected escape and rescue routes in conjunction with combustible materials in the building and subsequent changes to the building. Typical fire protection deficiencies are:

- Escape and rescue routes not in accordance with the requirements (e.g. timber staircases)
- Fire compartments not sufficiently subdivided according to current usage (no or excessively large fire compartments)
- Combustible materials in loadbearing construction and surface finishes
- Components and separating components with inadequate fire resistance
- Proper fire-fighting techniques (accessibility, systems) impossible

In particular, there is the risk that subsequent changes will infringe the fire protection requirements. This is especially the case with the following:
- The construction of new openings
- The removal of walls to create larger rooms
- The provision of additional windows, glazing, doors, etc.
- Changing the uses of rooms

Fire protection concept and measures

Improvements to the fire protection often have to be carried out in the course of refurbishment and conversion work. The constructional, conceptual or installation-related steps required can only be established by considering the existing building as a whole, and depend on the level of risk, the stipulations of conservation orders and economics.

Solutions should be worked out within the scope of a fire protection concept during the planning phase and should specify any existing risks and the measures required to reduce those risks (Fig. B 2.43). As the fire protection concept is drawn up, it becomes clear as to whether the level of fire protection required can be achieved through additional measures (e.g. upgrading the fire resistance of loadbearing components or lining escape/rescue routes with incombustible materials), or whether any deficiencies must be compensated for in some other way. The addition or improvement of escape/rescue routes should represent a primary aim in the fire protection measures. It should also be ensured that the boundaries to the fire compartments fulfil their function in terms of preventing the spread of smoke and fire. The intended measures must always be submitted to and approved by the building authorities, possibly also the local fire brigade and a specialist fire safety consultant. Fig. B 2.44 shows the approach in principle, together with the main factors, measures required and parties involved. The structural fire protection requirements placed on new buildings and existing buildings are essentially identical – it is their realisation that can be very different. Whereas for a new structure the building itself, its components, junctions and penetrations are planned right from the start with fire protection in mind, in an existing structure it is frequently necessary to upgrade the existing components or implement other, equivalent measures. It is often impossible to transfer the fire protection details of verification documentation (primarily national technical approvals or national test certificates) to every part of an existing building or form of construction.

A reduction in the level of safety required can be applied for in individual cases, but this must be approved by the building authority responsible. In certain situations – not usually the case for a change of use – the notion of toleration of the building stock applies to refurbishment measures. Forms of construction and materials that would not be approved for a new building are accepted in an existing building, but mostly only in combination with other fire protection measures. For example, when refurbishing an apartment block with no change of use, no change in the density of occupancy, a timber staircase can remain in place provided additional measures such as a fire extinguishers and/or smoke vents are provided.

Component/ actual condition	Requirements			Deviation	Risks	Measures	
	Fire compartment	LBO[1]	Conservation order			Installations	Construction
Timber-frame wall F30-B	Vertical separation	F90-AB	Retention of timber-frame wall	yes	Spread of fire Spread of smoke Stability	None	Fire-resistant cladding both sides → F90-BA
Timber joist floor < F30-B	Horizontal separation	F90-AB	Retention of historic wood-block floor finish	yes	Stability	Sprinklers	Self-supporting ceiling → F60-B
Mild steel columns < F30-A	No separation	F90-AB	None	yes	Stability	None	Fire-resistant casing → F90-A

[1] Federal State Building Regulations

B 2.43

Model Building Regulations/Federal State Building Regulations
Aims of protection and requirements of structural fire protection

Catalogue of criteria	**Risk analysis** Usage Fire loads Form of construction	Prerequisites for cladding/fire-resistant casing Definition of risks Upgrading requirements	Specialist planner Architect Developer Building authority Fire brigade
Catalogue of measures	**Fire protection planning** Fire compartments Escape/rescue routes F class Building materials class	Fire detectors/alarms Fire-extinguishing installations Smoke and heat vents Urban configuration	Specialist planner Architect Building conservationist Developer Building authority Fire brigade Insurers
Specifications	**Fire protection implementation** Specialist contractors	Quality assurance	Specialist planner Architect Building conservationist Developer

B 2.44

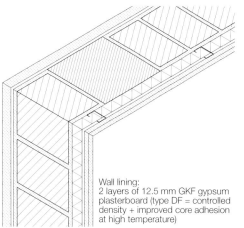

Wall lining:
2 layers of 12.5 mm GKF gypsum plasterboard (type DF = controlled density + improved core adhesion at high temperature)

B 2.45

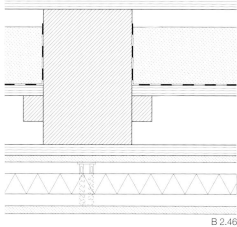

B 2.46

Upgrading existing walls to achieve better fire protection

We must distinguish here between non-loadbearing enclosing walls, loadbearing enclosing walls and loadbearing non-enclosing walls.

Solid walls

The fire resistance of the existing wall construction can be estimated by comparing it with the constructions given in DIN 4102-4. The following tables contain details of solid walls:

· Tab. 35: walls of plain and reinforced concrete
· Tab. 38: walls of masonry and wall panels (non-loadbearing)
· Tab. 39: walls of masonry (loadbearing)

In the case of intact masonry walls, the fire resistance of the existing wall is generally sufficient. Gaps should be filled or plastered over on at least one side. In the case of reinforced concrete walls, it is the concrete cover to the steel reinforcement and the overall thickness that are critical.

If the fire resistance of the existing wall does not meet the building legislation requirements, an "additive improvement", e.g. a suitable independent wall lining that is not reliant on the fire resistance of the existing wall, is one possible solution. The principle of "existing fire resistance (wall) + fire resistance (lining) = total fire resistance" is used here, although the approval of the building authority must be obtained. Other undefined or unclassified wall types must be treated like components with zero fire resistance (F = 0). Such situations will require the construction of independent wall linings with fire resistances of F 30 to F 90 which fulfil the fire safety requirements independently, regardless of the existing wall.

Another way of achieving better performance in fire is to apply a coat of a suitable plaster to one or both sides of a concrete or masonry wall.

Timber-frame walls

The construction of timber-frame walls with in-filled panels is covered in DIN 4102-4, section 4.11, up to fire resistance class F 30-B. According to the standard, the members of the timber frame must measure at least 100 x 100 mm for exposure to fire on one side only, 120 x 120 mm for exposure to fire on two sides. The panels between the frame members must be filled completely with wattle and daub, wood-wool lightweight building boards to DIN 1101 or masonry to DIN 1053-1, and at least one side of the wall must be clad. The materials used for the planning include the following:

· Gypsum fire-resistant board (GKF) to DIN 18180, d ≥ 12.5 mm
· Gypsum plasterboard (GKB) to DIN 18180, d ≥ 18 mm
· Gypsum fibreboard, d ≥ 10 mm, based on tests
· Plaster to DIN 18550-2, d ≥ 15 mm

In addition, there are many special, approved, fire-resistant boards available which generally enable the construction of particularly slender or highly fire-resistant walls.

The classification F 90-B (F 90-BA) always presumes additive cladding and independent wall linings (Fig. B 2.45). Verification is by way of test certificates or a specialist report. A fire-resistant lining can generally be mounted on timber or metal framing that is attached directly to the timber-frame wall or erected as a free-standing element in front of the wall. It is important to realise that the cavity between a fire-resistant lining and the existing wall should not be ventilated because this would lead to a stack effect. Additional sheeting, e.g. vapour barrier material, does not have any negative effect on the fire resistance. If the wall also has to satisfy thermal and sound insulation requirements, the addition of insulating materials must be checked, also which insulating materials may be used (building materials class, melting point). A fibrous insulating material, e.g. mineral wool, is advisable as cavity attenuation when sound insulation is important.

Upgrading existing suspended floors to achieve better fire protection

The fire resistance of suspended floors is described in DIN 4102-4 in terms of type of floor and features of the construction. We distinguish between solid structural floor types I to III

(described in DIN 4102-4, section 6.5) and timber floors (timber joist or timber panel floors). Where a roof construction is identical to that of a suspended floor, its fire protection properties are regarded as identical (Fig. B 2.49). Solid structural floors are dealt with in DIN 4102-4 sections 3.4 – 3.11, timber joist floors in sections 5.2 and 5.3.

If the fire performance of the existing suspended floor is inadequate, it must be upgraded to a higher fire resistance class (Figs. B 2.47 and 2.50). In certain circumstances a reinforced concrete slab can be improved by adding coats of plaster to the soffit. But in most cases the fire resistance class of a suspended floor is improved by adding ceilings and soffit linings, and – where the fire comes from above – by changing the floor finishes (e.g. screed).

DIN 4102-4 requires a suspended floor construction to be assessed as a whole in order to allocate it to a fire resistance class. This applies to structural floors with a soffit lining or a suspended ceiling. Sometimes it is sufficient when a ceiling alone satisfies the fire resistance requirements for a fire from below and/or above. Test certificates must prove the adequacy of such an independent ceiling system.

When used as fire protection, ceilings and soffit linings have to satisfy different requirements depending on the protection required and the risks expected:

· As a lining required for fire protection in conjunction with the structural floor: improvement in the reaction to fire of a complete floor construction
· As an independent component or element required for fire protection: protecting the ceiling void, possibly containing important services items, and the structural floor above that against fire from the room below
· As an independent element required for fire protection: protecting the room below from a fire in the ceiling void (e.g. fire load due to cable insulation)
· Isolation of fire loads (e.g. in escape routes)

According to DIN 4102-4 solid floor slabs type I and II in conjunction with ceilings can achieve a maximum fire resistance class of F 30. Rein-

B 2.47

B 2.48

B 2.47 Change of use: conversion of army barracks protected by conservation order into offices, Düsseldorf (D), 2008, Petzinka Pink Architekten; upgrading the fire resistance of existing suspended floors by means of self-supporting F 90 ceilings

B 2.48 St. Elisabeth Hospital, Stuttgart (D), 1985; conversion of the kitchen into a bistro, fire-resistant casings to steel beams and columns

B 2.49 Conversion of roof space showing fire-resistant lining to underside of rafters

B 2.50 Conversion of an old warehouse into a music college, Volkach (D), 2001, Reinhold Jäcklein; system ceiling below suspended floor, acoustic ceiling with random perforations below fire-resistant ceiling, separation of room acoustics and aesthetics functions (lower ceiling) from building acoustics and fire protection functions (upper ceiling)

forced concrete floor slabs type III can achieve fire resistance classes up to F 90, although insulating materials in the ceiling void are not permitted.

The restrictions of DIN 4102-4 can be overcome by providing test certificates and special reports verifying the improved fire protection given by ceilings and soffit linings. The advantage of the systems described in the test certificates and expert reports over those described in the standard is that they are economic and also satisfy building acoustics requirements. Generally, all solid suspended floors types I to III satisfy the F 30, F 60 and F 90 requirements when we employ the equation "solid floor + ceiling = classified floor construction". Here, the thickness of the material used for the ceiling depends on the fire resistance of the existing structural floor.

Fire and timber joist floors
The various types of timber floors found in existing buildings can be divided into three forms from the fire protection viewpoint:

· Suspended floors with concealed timber joists
· Suspended floors with semi-exposed timber joists
· Suspended floors with fully exposed timber joists

If the timber joists are to remain fully or partly exposed even after refurbishment, the fire resistance classification achievable depends on the cross-section of the joists and the load on the floor. Assessment guidelines for floor joists can be found in DIN 4102-4, section 5.5; complete floor constructions up to class F 60-B are given in section 5.4 of the same standard. Intact old timber joist floors with a false ceiling (e.g. sand fill on pugging boards in the ceiling void) and timber joists at least 100 mm wide with a corresponding boarded ceiling can achieve a fire resistance exceeding 30 minutes, which means they can be classified as F 30-B without the need for any upgrading measures. On the other hand, very lightweight timber joist floors without a false ceiling are poorer from the fire viewpoint. Such a form of construction can

lose its integrity after 15 or 20 minutes and therefore has no classifiable fire resistance. When planning the refurbishment, consideration should be given as to whether the fire resistance of an existing timber joist floor can be optimised "additively" or whether a more drastic intervention is necessary. Removing a false ceiling can be considered in individual cases.

An additive upgrade can make use of the fire resistance – if any – of the existing suspended floor (Fig. B 2.46). The additional measures necessary are therefore less costly and it is not necessary to intervene in the existing floor. This generally leads to economic solutions (no deconstruction, no debris, lighter ceiling and flooring systems).

When considering the fire resistance of an old timber joist floor, the following aspects must be taken into account within the scope of the refurbishment in order to reach the F 90 classification:

· The floorboards on the timber joists should be tongue and groove boards at least 21 mm thick or wood-based board products at least 19 mm thick.
· Timber joist floors must be checked structurally for the additional loading due to the fire upgrading measures; an analysis of the existing structure should always form the starting point for a refurbishment.
· Any damage to any plaster beneath a timber joist floor must be made good; if a suspended ceiling is more than 250 mm below the soffit, wire mesh must be fitted below the old plaster and fixed to the loadbearing timber joists.
· Generally, ceilings must be fixed to the loadbearing timber joists with approved wood screws; the screws should be designed for a tensile load such that the embedment depth in the timber is at least 50 mm.
· All joints between ceilings and peripheral components should be sealed.

Ceilings may need to be modified or, in extreme cases, removed completely, back to the joists. Besides the reduction in weight, the assessment of the suspended floor based on the "new" timber joist floor (see DIN 4102 for fire protection and DIN 4109 for sound insulation) is advantageous. The costs for the manual work and the disposal of the debris are, however, higher, and the sound insulation may be worse and

susceptibility to vibration may be greater due to the removal of the false ceiling, and measures will have to be taken to compensate for this. The fire resistance for exposure to fire from above depends mainly on the type, thickness and construction of the subfloor and insulation. According to DIN 4102-4 gypsum screeds and gypsum boards can be used up to fire resistance class F 60. Where suspended floors have to comply with the requirements of class F 90, the suitability of dry subfloors must be ensured by way of test certificates or specialist reports.

Upgrading columns and beams to achieve better fire protection
It is normally necessary to clad or encase columns and beams of steel and timber in order to achieve a certain fire resistance classification (Fig. B 2.48). The following requirements profile must be assessed in order to design the fire protection required:

· Type of member to be protected (column, beam)
· Fire resistance required
· Nature of exposure to fire (on one, two, three or four sides)
· Steel sections: determining the relationship between perimeter and cross-sectional area (so-called section factor U/A)
· Timber: species, cross-section, width-to-depth ratio
· Type of cladding, thickness
· Fire protection verification (DIN 4102-4 or test certificate)

DIN 4102-4 includes information on columns and beams clad with gypsum fire-resistant board (GKF). In addition, there are many tested fire-resistant cladding systems that are more economic or offer better fire protection than the DIN solutions. The following board types can be used as fire-resistant casings to beams or columns:
· Special gypsum boards
· Cement-bonded fire-resistant boards
· Calcium silicate foam boards
· Mineral-fibre boards

B 2.49

B 2.50

The structure and strength of some of these boards is such that mechanical fasteners (screws or clips) can be driven into their edges and so no separate framing is required.

Besides the aforementioned upgrading measures for walls, floors, columns and beams by means of "two-dimensional" cladding forms, fire protection measures in existing structures must also take account of the building services (penetrations, encapsulation, shafts).

Notes:

[1]   German Energy Agency (ed.): Besser als ein Neubau: EnEV minus 30 %. Planning aid. Berlin, 2007
[2]   Kah, Oliver; Feist, Wolfgang: Wirtschaftlichkeit von Wärmedämmmaßnahmen im Gebäudebestand. Darmstadt, 2005
[3]   ibid. [1]
[4]   Fanger, Ole: Thermal Comfort – Analysis and Applications in Environmental Engineering. Copenhagen, 1970
[5]   DIN EN ISO 7730: Ergonomics of the thermal environment – Analytical determination and interpretation of thermal comfort using calculation of the PMV and PPD indices and local thermal comfort criteria. Jun 2007
[6]   German Energy Agency (ed.): Thermische Behaglichkeit im Niedrigenergiehaus – Teil 1: Winterliche Verhältnisse. Berlin, 2007
[7]   DIN 4108-2: Thermal protection and energy economy in buildings – Part 2: Minimum requirements to thermal insulation. Jul 2007
[8]   DIN EN ISO 6946: Building components and building elements – Thermal resistance and thermal transmittance – Calculation method. 2007
[9]   ibid. [1]; DIN V 4108-4: Thermal insulation and energy economy in buildings – Part 4: Hygrothermal design values. Jun 2007 (pre-standard)
[10] Institut für Bauforschung e.V. (ed.): U-Werte alter Bauteile. Hannover, 2005
[11] Internet database: www.masea-ensan.de
[12] DIN EN 10077: Thermal performance of windows, doors and shutters – Calculation of thermal transmittance. Dec 2006
[13] DIN EN 673: Glass in building – Determination of thermal transmittance (U-value) – Calculation method. Jun 2003
[14] ibid. [9]
[15] DIN EN 410: Glass in building – Determination of luminous and solar characteristics of glazing. Dec 1998
[16] ibid. [11]
[17] Stiegel, Horst; Hauser, Gerd: Wärmebrückenkatalog für Modernisierungs- und Sanierungsmaßnahmen zur Vermeidung von Schimmelpilzen. Stuttgart, 2006

[18] DIN 1946-6: Ventilation and air conditioning – Part 6: Ventilation for residential buildings; General requirements, requirements for measuring, performance and labelling, delivery/acceptance (certification) and maintenance. Dec 2006 (draft standard)
[19] Fraunhofer Institute for Building Physics (ed.): WUFI und WUFI 2D. Holzkirchen, 2007; Institute for Building Climatology, Dresden TU (ed.): Delphin
[20] ibid. [14]; DIN 4108 supp. 2: Thermal insulation and energy economy in buildings – Thermal bridges – Examples for planning and performance. Mar 2006
[21] ibid. [8]
[22] Energy Conservation Act 2007
[23] Feist, Wolfgang et al.: PHPP 2007 – Passivhaus-Projektierungspaket. Passive House Institute (ed.). Darmstadt, 2007
[24] ibid. [2]
[25] Passive House Institute (ed.):24th proceedings of the inexpensive passive house study group. Einsatz von Passivhaustechnologien bei der Altbau-Modernisierung. Darmstadt 2003; Passive House Institute (ed.): 32nd proceedings of the inexpensive passive house study group. Faktor 4 auch bei sensiblen Altbauten – Passivhauskomponenten + Innendämmung. Darmstadt, 2005
[26] ebd. [23]
[27] Veres, Eva et al.: Bauphysik 11. Berlin, 1989, pp. 37–43; Gösele, Karl: Schallschutz-Entwicklungen in den letzten 30 Jahren. In: Deutsche Bauzeitung 122 (1988). No. 1, pp. 75–82
[28] ibid. [24]; Scholze, Jürgen: Bauphysik 17. Berlin, 1995, pp. 138–143; Kötz, W.-D.: Erhebung zum Stand der Technik beim baulichen Schallschutz. Fortschritte der Akustik. DAGA 1988, pp. 75–82
[29] Informationsdienst Holz (ed.): Holzbau Handbuch. Reihe 1, Teil 14, Folge 1 – Modernisierung von Altbauten. Munich, 2001; Informationsdienst Holz (ed.): Holzbau Handbuch. Reihe 7, Teil 3, Folge 1 – Erneuerung von Fachwerkbauten. Munich, 2004; Informationsdienst Holz (ed.): Holzbau Handbuch. Reihe 3, Teil 3, Folge 3 – Schalldämmende Holzbalken- und Brettstapeldecken. Munich, 1999
[30] ibid. [29]; Informationsdienst Holz (ed.): Holzbau Handbuch. Reihe 3. Teil 3. Folge 4 – Schallschutz Wände und Dächer. Munich, 2004
[31] Rabold Andreas et al.: Forschungsvorhaben – Holzbalkendecken in der Altbausanierung. Final report, available from the German Society for Wood Research
[32] DIN 4109: Sound insulation in buildings; requirements and testing. Nov 1989

Building services

Karl-Heinz Petzinka, Bernhard Lenz,
Jürgen Volkwein, Florian Lang

B 3.1

As the development of new technologies and combinations thereof are progressing rapidly, building services become out of date more quickly than the building itself these days. The importance of the building services is therefore growing. Maintenance of building services has a substantial impact on the economics and value of a building because defective building services lead to a loss in efficiency and also a risk of damage to the building fabric. The objectives of refurbishing the building services are therefore as follows:

- Maintaining functionality and reliability
- Prolonging the remaining lifetime of existing installations
- Increasing the efficiency
- Improving the ease of use (adapting to current needs)

Achieving these objectives within a reasonable economic framework requires a systematic approach when building services are due for refurbishment. Only in this way is it possible to devise a checklist as a decision-making aid and distinguish between the need for repairs, additions or replacement. An accurate survey of the existing plant and installations is essential and should include all the main items in the building services inventory (Fig. B 3.2). In this chapter the investigation of the building services is limited to the main, or rather the more usual, elements and does not consider any special technical installations.

Ages of individual components in existing systems
Often the only way of gauging the age of the building services is via the year of construction of the building itself; this represents a starting point for estimating the remaining lifetime of the existing installations. In doing so it must be remembered that the oldest components in a subsystem (e.g. incoming water pipes) probably represent the weakest links in the installation and are therefore the critical elements when estimating the remaining lifetime, unless a subsystem (e.g. water supply) and all its components has already been replaced completely at sometime in the past (Fig. B 3.3).

Survey of existing structure
During the survey of the existing structure, all the forms of construction, materials, joints, connections and junctions are recorded. The quality of the building services can be derived from this and hence the standards that applied when the systems were installed. Additions or modernisation work should also be taken into account. Furthermore, the distribution networks for the individual subsystems must be ascertained: horizontal, vertical, surface-mounted, concealed, central distribution lines, shafts, space utilisation, retrofitting options, etc. (Fig. B 3.6). This information must be supplemented by a differentiated assessment of the degree of wear and/or damage to the components (e.g. incrustation, obvious leaks, mechanical stresses, etc.).

Efficiency of the existing installations
It may be advisable to renew installation components because they cannot handle changing needs or their technology is outdated. The properties of components and systems are noted in order to enable an assessment. The first priority here is the direct energy consumption (e.g. lighting or heating) and the consumption of auxiliary energy (e.g. ventilation system). The efficiency of the system components such as waste-water drainage (backflow) or the air change rate of a mechanical ventilation system should also be checked.

Controllability of systems
Besides the simple functionality of technical installations, the controllability of the systems has a considerable influence on their acceptance by users. Taps, temperature controls and air outlets all fall under this heading.

Evaluation catalogue
The refurbishment needs as a whole and for individual components are decided on the basis of the survey of the existing structure and installations according to the following evaluation catalogue. The criteria should be regarded as a prioritised list to be worked through in this order. If the outcome of the evaluation is positive for all the points for the respective components, subsystems or installations, then the

B 3.1   Corroded pipes and fittings
B 3.2   Overview of the main elements of building services
B 3.3   Service lives of various building services components

52

```
                    ┌─────────────────────────────────────┐
                    │    Main elements of building services│
                    └─────────────────────────────────────┘
```

Water supplies	Water drainage	Space heating	Building cooling	Ventilation	Electricity supply	Special building services
• Connection to public main • Water treatment • Distribution pipework, routing of pipework • Materials, lagging • Using rainwater • Using grey water	• Waste-water sources • Drainage pipework, routing of pipework • Materials, lagging • Inspection options • Connection to public sewer network • Rainwater drainage • Waste-water treatment	• Fuels, storage • Heating plant • Exhaust-gas flues • Hot-water provision, storage • Distribution of heat and hot water • Pumps, special elements • Heat output • Regulation and control	• Thermal mass • Room cooling • Decentralised/central plants • Solar cooling	• Natural ventilation • Mechanical ventilation • Air handling • Ventilation systems with heat recovery	• Connection to public grid • Distribution, fusing • Installation zones • Materials, installations • Earthing, equipotential bonding • Lightning protection	• Fire protection systems • Travel and transport systems • Media supplies • Waste disposal systems

B 3.2

components are in a good condition and do not need to be refurbished. The respective severity and the weighting of any deficiencies or damage established form the basis for deciding on the nature and scope of refurbishment measures.

1. Legal stipulations
Generally, like the building itself, the existing building services enjoy the protection offered by the notion of toleration of the building stock, provided the building services complied with the technical codes of practice valid at the time of their installation. In other words, the building services may continue to be used without having to adapt them to the requirements of more recent legislation and/or standards.
However, in the event of changes or additions to the existing installations, the parts of the systems affected must then comply with the current codes of practice. And depending on the particular situation, other existing components not directly affected by the changes may also need to be upgraded to satisfy the latest requirements. This can happen, for example, with the electrical distribution network.
Moreover, there are some legal stipulations that override the toleration of the building stock concept and make it necessary to upgrade existing installations even outside of planned refurbishment measures. The owner or operator, or a person appointed by the owner/operator, is responsible for ensuring compliance with the technical regulations. In Germany the legal requirements include, for example, the Drinking Water Act (TrinkwV) and the Energy Conservation Act (EnEV).

2. Lifetime
The anticipated remaining lifetimes of the individual components are determined from the information regarding their age and condition based on a comparison with the average lifetimes. It is worth pointing out here that the service lives represent a rough guide only, which depends very much on year of manufacture, material properties, design, utilisation, joints and connections, intensity of use, maintenance and care, and not least of all, the products themselves (Fig. B 3.3). Deviations from the norm are certainly encountered in practice.

As soon as several individual components in a subsystem have reached the end of their anticipated useful lives, complete replacement of the subsystem must be considered as an alternative. But how many individual components can be sensibly replaced can only be assessed on a case-by-case basis.

3. Options for increasing the efficiency of the building services
A comparison of the existing performance features of components and/or subsystems with the current demands and technical possibilities reveals differences that may make refurbishment appear advisable.
On the one hand, the reason for refurbishment may be the specific desire to improve the performance of a subsystem, but on the other, a profitability calculation may be sufficient incentive to compare future savings in the running costs and the cost of a new investment.

4. User acceptance: controllability and ease of use
The decision in favour of refurbishment can also be triggered by user acceptance – or the lack thereof. In most cases it is possible to retrofit control and regulatory devices, ranging from simple, additional light switches right up to electronic indoor climate controls.
Besides the essential measures, other constraints and factors must be considered in order

to devise a final refurbishment concept. For instance, all interventions must be agreed with users and occupants because the building services have a considerable influence on usability; an unoccupied building requires a totally different refurbishment concept to an occupied one. The work is further complicated by the fact that many building services installations are concealed behind finished surfaces, which means that renewing or upgrading the systems usually involves damaging those surfaces. The costs of making good any damage must be taken into account in the planning.
The scope of the building measures is decisive in this context. If numerous surfaces in different rooms and storeys have to be renewed as part of a larger refurbishment project, it is advisable to use the opportunity to upgrade the building services as well. And vice versa: intelligent, minimally invasive modernisation concepts must be devised in order to avoid damaging valuable surfaces where this is possible and worthwhile, which may mean preparing different refurbishment strategies for a building.
Where central, readily accessible shafts or distribution lines (e.g. in corridors) are available, these can be used for replacement or retrofitting measures, which minimises the damage to existing surfaces and simplifies the refurbishment work. Unused chimneys, shafts and voids are ideal for installing pipes and cables, provided the rules for installing the pipe/cable

Heating plant	Service life[1]	Mechanical ventilation, cooling and air-conditioning systems	Service life[1]
Low-temperature boiler[2]	20–25 years	Pipework[2]	30–40 years
Condensing boiler[2, 3]	10–15 years	Air outlets[2]	20–30 years
Burner[2]	10–15 years	Fans[2, 6]	5–15 years
Pumps	10–15 years	Heat exchanger (air/air)[6]	15–25 years
Pipes (heating)[4, 5]	20–40 years	Electrical installations	30–40 years
Radiators[6]	25–35 years	**Water supply and drainage**	
Underfloor heating[3, 4]	25–35 years	Water supply[5]	30–40 years
Solar collectors[3]	20–25 years	Water drainage	30–40 years

[1] Average values based on information supplied by trade associations, craft guilds and manufacturers.
[2] Assuming regular inspection/servicing/cleaning.
[3] Longer experience with such systems is not yet available.
[4] Service life according to approval tests for pipes = 50 years.
[5] Heavily dependent on temperature, water quality and materials (see also Fig. B 3.5).
[6] Depends on model.

B 3.3

Metal	Voltage with reference to hydrogen [V]
Aluminium	- 1.67
Zinc	- 0.76
Iron	- 0.44
Tin	- 0.14
Lead	- 0.13
Hydrogen	± 0.00
Copper	+ 0.34

B 3.4

Type of pipe	Service life, copper	Service life, galvanised steel
Hot water	40 years	20 years
Cold water	80 years	40 years

B 3.5

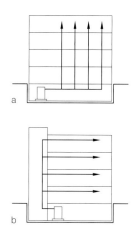

B 3.6

materials and the fire regulations regarding fire stops between storeys and different occupancies are complied with. Intervening in the construction of a building itself in the form of wall chases, floor penetrations or holes through downstand beams must be properly planned and checked by the appropriate specialists within the refurbishment concept.

In order to minimise the intervention in surfaces and structural components, the refurbishment should make use of independent installation zones wherever possible.

Building services and conservation

When refurbishing buildings subject to conservation orders, it should not be forgotten that the building services might also belong to the cultural treasures of the building that are to be preserved. This applies not only to obvious items such as stoves or bathroom fittings, but to concealed items as well.

In addition, renewing or adding building services components entails a considerable intervention in the surface finishes and interior architecture, e.g. through the laying of pipes and cables. The aim is to develop specific concepts for the installations and their locations. The following options can be considered:

- Concealing behind surface finishes
- Integration into the architecture of the building, e.g. through the use of matching fascia panels
- Intentional architectural featuring in order to define a new element clearly different from the existing

In the case of a building protected by a conservation order, these points must also be agreed with the authorities responsible.

Water supplies

In principle, drinking-water systems in existing buildings are protected by the notion of toleration of the building stock, provided health and hygiene aspects are not at risk. As drinking water is a foodstuff, the Drinking Water Act must be complied with in all respects. If the prescribed limit values for the contents of the water are exceeded at the draw-off points in the building (e.g. due to contamination caused by old lead pipes), the causes must be found and eliminated.

Modern drinking-water systems must generally be designed and installed in accordance with the stipulations of DIN 1988, DIN EN 1717, DIN EN 806 and DIN 50930. The data sheets of the DVGW (German Technical & Scientific

Association for Gas & Water) and the VDI directives, all acknowledged codes of practice, must also be adhered to. Depending on the materials used, a drinking-water system will certainly need to be totally refurbished after 0–50 years, and a partial refurbishment may be necessary for systems 30–40 years old (Fig. B 3.5). The condition of the system is checked by cutting pieces out of the distribution pipework at random and inspecting them for incrustation and corrosion. When refurbishing occupied apartment blocks, an overall concept must be drawn up first before commencing with individual measures so that apartments can be vacated successively to enable the work to be carried out.

Connection to public main

If there is not one already, residential and commercial properties should be provided with a room for incoming services according to DIN 18012 within the course of any refurbishment work to house all the services on the road side of the building. However, residential buildings with up to four dwellings do not normally require a separate room. The size of the room depends on the number of consumers to be supplied. When carrying out a total refurbishment, individual service connections can be replaced by one multi-service connection (Fig. B 3.11). The service pipe in an existing building should be checked to establish whether the water meter is fixed to a meter board and includes two shut-off valves correctly installed in the direction of flow that enable the meter to be replaced easily. The pipe must also be fitted with a back-siphonage preventer (backflow valve) and a drain valve. If there is no means of preventing backflow, DIN 1988 states that a suitable valve must be retrofitted. If the other fittings mentioned here are also lacking, these should also be installed.

Installation situation of cold-water pipe	Lagging thickness [1] [mm]
exposed, in unheated room in duct, without hot pipes in chase, rising main; on concrete slab	4
exposed, in heated room	9
in duct or masonry chase, adjacent to hot pipes	13

[1] based on λ = 0.040 W/mK

Internal diameter (DN) of hot-water pipe [mm]	Lagging thickness [1] [mm]
≤ 22	20
> 22 and ≤ 35	30
> 35 and ≤ 100	DN
> 100	100
Pipes and fittings • in wall and floor penetrations • at crossings and junctions • at central pipe manifolds	50 % of requirement listed above

[1] based on λ = 0.035 W/mK

B 3.7

Water treatment
Filters protect the installation in the building against contamination. If installed subsequently, the pipes must always be flushed out first. The installation of a water-softening unit is recommended for water hardness values of 16 °dH and higher, and for values ≥ 20 °dH such a system is vital if detrimental incrustation (furring) is to be avoided in refurbished pipes (Fig. B 3.8).
Dosing units can be installed to protect against corrosion, furring or excessive liberation of heavy metals. But as such devices release chemicals into the system, they should only be retrofitted when the drinking water is already contaminated.

Distribution pipework
Existing pipework should be checked for leaks, materials, dimensions and compliance with the valid regulations and standards. Excessively large pipe diameters mean that the water remains in the pipes for longer, which leads to higher metal concentrations in drinking water. As water must flow through all parts of the system, any pipes still connected to the system but no longer in use are not permitted and must be removed. Excessively small pipe diameters can suffer erosion of their inner surfaces due to excessive flow velocities.
Specialist contractors can check for leaks by using pressure tests. DVGW data sheets W 551 and W 553 should be consulted for information on preventing a possible build-up of legionella bacteria, especially in large systems. A large drinking-water system is one with a hot-water tank with a capacity > 400 l or a pipework volume containing > 3 l of water between the outlet of the water heater and the draw-off point (see also pp. 59–65). According to this definition, even a detached house could have a large system.

Routing of pipework
A backflow of fluids into the drinking-water system should not be possible under any circumstances. A direct connection between drinking water and other types of water is not permitted and must be separated immediately.
On upper floors, the bottom edge of a draw-off point must be at least two times the pipe's nominal diameter (DN) or ≥ 20 mm above the edge of the sink or basin and in a basement at least 300 mm above the basement floor slab. There should be no connections between hot and cold drinking water at any point in the systems. Existing installations must be checked to ensure that these requirements are complied with.
The retrofitting of installations in unused rubbish chutes, sewers, seepage trenches, etc. is not permitted. However, unused chimneys may be used for new installations.
The drinking-water supply pipe (DWC) must be laid at a sufficient distance from hot-water pipes (DWH) or hot-water secondary circuits (DWS), heating systems and chimneys in order to prevent heating the drinking water (risk of

legionella bacteria). The drinking-water supply pipe should always be positioned below all other pipes in order to prevent corrosion of the other pipes in the case of condensation. Freezing and condensation are possible risks for pipes mounted in or on external walls. As condensation can damage timber, metal and other building materials, all accessible water pipes should be lagged subsequently (Fig. B 3.7). The fire protection requirements must be maintained wherever pipes penetrate components required for fire protection. Pipe ducts and shafts may include room ventilation elements and electrical cables provided the provisions of Germany's Model Pipe & Cable Routing Directive (MLAR) are adhered to. Pipes may not be cast into concrete or gypsum filler materials. Pipes should be lagged to guarantee thermal expansion and minimise structure-borne sound transmissions.

Materials
In older buildings water pipes are mainly made of galvanised steel, copper and, occasionally, lead. The electrochemical potential series should be taken into account at a change of material (Fig. B 3.4). A "nobler" material may only be installed in the direction of flow because otherwise galvanic corrosion may occur. The choice of material must be based on the properties of the local water supply and the desired operating temperature. When changing the use of an existing water system, care should be taken to ensure that the future flow velocity, water temperature and stagnation time are compatible with the previous use.
Galvanised steel pipes that are bent must be replaced because the zinc coating on the inside can flake off and leave the pipe unprotected against corrosion. Contamination in the zinc coatings of older galvanised steel pipes can lead to harmful amounts of lead and cadmium in the drinking water. If this is suspected, the water should be tested for these substances and the pipes replaced if necessary.
If water from galvanised pipes is cloudy or exhibits a rusty colouring after several days of stagnation, this indicates damage to the internal galvanising and corrosion of the steel pipe. In this case the pipework affected should be replaced without delay. If the existing building contains hot-water pipes (> 60 °C) made from galvanised steel, these, too, must be replaced because the high temperature can lead to increased pitting (Fig. B 3.10).
Where the drinking water has a relatively low pH value, galvanised steel pipes should also be replaced by other, more suitable materials because excessive internal corrosion is likely. Direct connections between stainless and galvanised steel must be replaced by connections with suitable fittings in order to prevent galvanic corrosion (Fig. B 3.13).
In the past hemp or flax was wound around the external threads of screwed joints and a sealing paste (mostly based on talcum or oils) was also applied. In some cases the hemp was also

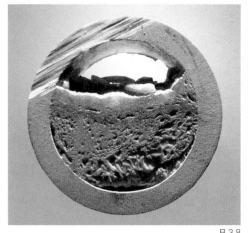
B 3.8

B 3.9

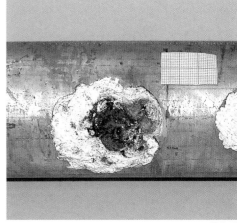
B 3.10

B 3.11

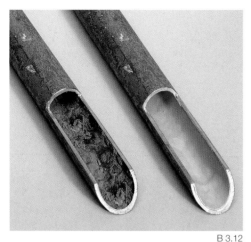

B 3.12

B 3.13

B 3.14

prepared with red lead before it was wound around the thread. Which sealing material was actually used can only be determined by un-screwing the joints. If there is any trace of red lead, the sections affected must be replaced because otherwise lead is absorbed into the drinking water.

Copper pipes are characterised by their easy bendability and are therefore ideal for refurbish-ment tasks. Their smooth surfaces mean they are suitable for hot-water pipes. But where the pH value of the drinking water lies below 7.4, copper pipes should be avoided because other-wise excessive surface corrosion can be ex-pected. Alternative copper pipes with a tinned internal surface are available and these can be used anywhere. The local water supply company can provide information on the pH value.

Lead pipes were still being used in some regions up until the mid-1970s, in isolated instances even as late as 1990 (Fig. B 3.14)! Generally, however, lead pipes are found in buildings erected before 1935. All lead pipes must be replaced because otherwise it is impossible to comply with the maximum lead concentration values specified in the Drinking Water Act. Lead pipes are easy to identify because they are relatively soft, non-magnetic and emit a dull sound when tapped; and scratching the surface reveals their unmistakable matt silver-grey colouring.

Plastic pipes were not used in former West Germany before the 1980s, but in former East Germany PVC pipes were first introduced in the early 1960s. Such pipes usually consist of un-plasticised PVC-U, PE-HD or PE-LD and are suitable for cold-water applications only. Glued, welded or clamped (compression joint) connections are usual. Materials such as PE-X may be used for new hot-water pipes. Owing to the thermal expansion of plastic pipes, special expansion arrangements must be included for hot-water pipes.

Stainless steel pipes have only been in use for about 15 years and therefore are found only in newer buildings. They are characterised by their minimal corrosion plus the extremely low release of chromium and nickel into the drink-ing water. Stainless steel pipes should not be used where the drinking water exhibits a high

chlorine content because this increases the risk of crevice corrosion and pitting. In an installation containing galvanised and stainless steel pipes, direct contact between the two materials can lead to galvanic corrosion. The direction of flow of the water is irrelevant and so even parts of the system can be replaced by stainless steel.

Lagging

Lagging around drinking-water pipes is a rarity, but where pipes were laid outside, lagging made from felt, hemp, peat, asbestos or diatomite can be found. Asbestos lagging should be removed by a specialist contractor (see "Dangerous sub-stances in the building stock", p. 112). Accord-ing to the Energy Conservation Act, in unheated rooms all accessible hot-water and heating pipes plus their fittings must be lagged (Fig. B 3.7).

Maintenance

Special precautions must be taken when con-version and refurbishment work leads to longer stagnation times in the drinking-water pipes. DIN 1988 calls for the pipework to be flushed out if the stagnation time exceeds four weeks. And according to VDI Directive 6023, a micro-biological examination is recommended when the stagnation time reaches six months. If the stagnation time will exceed 12 months, the drinking-water system must be isolated from the water supply and drained. The installation may only be reconnected and put into service again by the local water supply company or a specialist contractor. Where minor damage to the inside of the pipes has occurred, the refur-bishment measures can include providing an internal coating to VDI Directive 6001 (Fig. B 3.12), a method that can be used on pipes of 5–150 mm diameter. But before an internal coating can be applied, all fittings must be re-moved and the pipes cleaned of all deposits by forcing a granulate through the pipes under pressure. Afterwards, an epoxy resin mixture is applied under pressure to seal the internal sur-face. This method is worth considering because it overcomes the need to remove and dispose of old pipes.

Using rainwater

Rainwater harvesting systems are rare in the building stock, but adding such a system can be investigated as part of a larger refurbish-ment project. Rainwater can be used as a sub-stitute for drinking water for flushing toilets, watering gardens and – with restrictions – for washing machines as well. A rainwater system does not require any approvals, but the Drink-ing Water Act specifies that the authorities be notified. A system according to DIN 1989 con-sists of collecting areas, filters, storage tank with overflow, pump and pipework with draw-off points. If the water is to be used in the washing machine as well, bitumen roof sheet-ing and untreated copper roofs cannot be used for collecting the rainwater. And owing to the risk of oil and fuel residues, car parking areas and similar hardstandings should never be used as collecting areas. Roofs covered with asbestos-cement tiles are a major health risk and green roofs are also unsuitable because of the particles that are washed out.

Adding a rainwater system in the course of re-furbishment work should not present any prob-lems. However, additional pipework must be allowed for because connections between drinking-water and rainwater systems are not permitted. Existing systems should be checked to establish whether all pipes and draw-off points are provided with clear "not drinking water" signs. It is also necessary to check that the drinking-water top-up arrangement for the rainwater cistern has sufficient clearance to the maximum filling level of the tank so that it is impossible for rainwater to enter the drinking-water system. The quantities of waste water may be calculated and paid for differently depending on the local authority.

Type of pipe	Min. fall	Standard
Unvented discharge pipe from single appliance	1.0 %	DIN EN 12056-2, DIN 1986-100,
Vented discharge pipe from single appliance	0.5 %	DIN EN 12056-2, DIN 1986-100
Unvented discharge pipe from multiple appliances	1.0 %	DIN 1986-100
Buried pipes for waste water and waste water + rainwater		
• within the building	0.5 %	DIN 1986-100
• outside the building	1 : DN	DIN 1986-100
Buried and discharge pipes for rainwater in the building	0.5 %	DIN 1986-100

B 3.15

B 3.16

B 3.12 Pipe with deposits before refurbishment (left) and with new internal lining after refurbishment (right)
B 3.13 Galvanic corrosion due to contact between different pipe materials
B 3.14 Leak in old lead pipe repaired with sleeve
B 3.15 Minimum falls for waste-water pipes
B 3.16 Compact grey-water system for installing in an existing building

Using grey water

So-called grey water contains no faecal material or excessively dirty kitchen waste water. Once treated, like rainwater it can be used for flushing toilets instead of drinking water. Grey-water systems are similar to rainwater systems but includes additional, elaborate cleansing components (Fig. B 3.16). And whereas a rainwater system requires separate supply pipes, a grey-water system requires separate drain pipes as well. Such systems have only been around for about 10 years and there are not very many in use. Retrofitting such a system is very complex and costly owing to the need for the separate waste-water pipework.

Water drainage

We can divide waste water into black water (foul water) containing faecal material, and the non-faecal grey water and rainwater (surface water). Changes or additions to existing waste-water systems and new systems all generally have to be approved by the authorities. New systems within a building must be designed to DIN EN 12056, outside the building to DIN EN 752. The provisions of DIN 1986 also apply, and DIN 1986-3 contains recommendations regarding maintenance and inspections. Furthermore, there may also be local byelaws that must be complied with and these may also call for inspections or upgrading of the existing systems.

The system of public sewers is designed as a combined or separate system, and where a separate system is used, waste water and rainwater must be drained separately from a building plot. If a waste-water system is to be completely renewed, it is important to establish whether a separate system on the public side has been installed in the meantime, making it necessary to drain the waste water and rainwater via separate systems.

Connection to public sewer network

In buildings erected prior to 1940 it can be assumed that the connecting drains are too small for today's requirements and over the years will have become at least partly blocked and will have developed some leaks. In accordance with the provisions of the applicable Federal State Building Regulations (LBO), the local authority can demand that drains be checked for leaks at regular intervals. There may also be local byelaws that prescribe inspections and tests at certain intervals. It is therefore possible, especially in the case of old installations, that a drains test – as required by the LBO – is long since overdue. Vacuum or pressure tests can be used to check for leaks.

Drainage pipework

The sanitary appliances drain via branch discharge pipes into vertical discharge stacks, which are normally ventilated via a vent pipe above roof level. The discharge stacks drain into drains that are usually below the foundation and no longer accessible once installed. The owner of the building plot is responsible for the drainage pipework within the plot. Connection to the system of public sewers is via a drain from the boundary of the building plot or an inspection chamber.

Routing of pipework

The drains are laid below the basement floor slab of the building or in the ground. Horizontal pipes must be laid with a minimum, constant fall, which depends on their diameter, such that they are self-cleansing (Fig. B 3.15).

The recommended minimum nominal internal diameter for a buried drain is 125 mm. The cross-sectional area of the pipe may not decrease in the direction of flow. Inappropriate cross-sections and incorrect falls are the causes of many blockages in existing systems. Changes of direction in drains and discharge pipes may not exceed 45°. More severe changes of direction represent another cause of blockages and should be replaced by more gradual bends and junctions during refurbishment. If drains below the ground slab are the source of permanent problems, it may be easier and cheaper to lay new discharge pipes throughout the

building and connect these to a buried drain outside the building instead of refurbishing the existing system.

When connecting additional toilets to a horizontal discharge pipe it is important to make sure that the vertical distance between the invert of the discharge pipe and the water level in the trap to each toilet is at least equal to the nominal size of the discharge pipe (normally 100 mm). Where pipes penetrate components required for fire protection, the penetrations must comply with the fire protection requirements. Drainage pipes may be routed together with room ventilation elements and electrical cables provided the provisions of Germany's Model Pipe & Cable Routing Directive (MLAR) are adhered to. Condensation is a possible risk for pipes mounted in or on external walls. And where pipes pass through timber joist floors or timber stud walls, any condensation that occurs can lead to saturation and damage to the building fabric, which is why drainage pipes should be subsequently lagged. Even if no condensation has been observed in the past, a change to the construction (e.g. cladding a pipe) leads to a new situation and hence to the possibility of condensation in the future. Lagging the pipes also improves the sound insulation. Adequate lagging to discharge stacks is also important where these are to be clad.

If a waste-water pipe is to be accommodated in a historic suspended floor construction within the course of the refurbishment, the planning should take account of the fact that, for example, there may be a false floor in the construction that considerably reduces the depth available for the pipework. Where pipes are concealed within timber joist floors, it is usually necessary to remove the floorboards and replace any loose fill locally in order to guarantee the sound insulation.

In existing installations that lie below the backflow level, it is necessary to establish whether a back-siphonage preventer (backflow valve) is fitted. If such a valve is missing, a blockage in the sewer or an excessive load in a public combined sewer due to heavy rain can lead to a backflow that can in turn lead to flooding in the building itself. A back-siphonage preventer should therefore be inspected at regular intervals.

B 3.17

B 3.18

If condensate is to be drained from a condensing boiler, it is important to ensure that the drain pipes are made from a suitable material; otherwise, a neutralisation unit must be retrofitted (see pp. 59–62).

Materials
Existing drainage systems must be checked to ensure that their materials, dimensions and design comply with current standards and regulations. Diverse materials based on stoneware, concrete, fibre-cement, plastics and metal can be used for waste-water pipes, although not all pipe materials are approved for all parts of the drainage system (Fig. B 3.19). Unsuitable pipes must be replaced.

Most of pipes in the building stock are made of cast iron or stoneware. Undamaged stoneware pipes may continue to be used in most cases. Cast iron pipes have been used since the middle of the 19th century. These, too, may continue to be used for all parts of waste-water systems, provided no condensate from condensing boilers is to be drained. The "lightweight German waste pipe" has been used in Germany since the 1930s. Although these pipes (to DIN 19500 – DIN 19513) are no longer available, it is possible to connect new pipes to them.

Well into the 1960s, connections between pipes were often sealed with hemp soaked in bitumen, which was forced into the spigot and socket joints. This was then covered with cement mortar. Where old pipes are to be replaced, the materials specified in DIN 1986-4 may be used (Fig. B 3.19). Stainless steel pipes and hot-dip galvanised steel pipes with an internal coating of synthetic resin are approved for all parts of waste-water systems, but additional corrosion protection is required where these pipes are to be buried in the ground. Fibre-cement pipes are suitable for all parts of waste-water systems apart from those sections buried in the ground. Plastic pipes can also be used for waste water because they are characterised by high discharge coefficients and low susceptibility to incrustation. Their thin walls make them particularly suitable for subsequent installations. Although plastic pipes are regarded as non-flammable, fire protection precautions according to the MLAR may need to be taken.

Maintenance
When refurbishing occupied apartment blocks, an overall concept must be drawn up first before commencing with individual measures so that apartments can be vacated successively to enable the work to be carried out. The positions of the spigot and socket joints and the branches must be carefully considered during the planning so that subsequent connections are still possible. If only parts of an existing pipework system are to be removed or replaced, any incrustation in the pipes could become detached and block bends, elbows or inlets. Deposits and incrustation are to be expected in systems that have been used for 30 years or more, meaning that an inspection of the entire drainage system is to be recommended as part of the refurbishment work. A mirror test is the simplest inspection method: a lamp at one position in the system and a mirror at another. An endoscope can be used to achieve much more precise results: a small hole approx. 2 mm in diameter is drilled in a pipe through which a mini borescope is inserted. Alternatively, a remote controlled trolley fitted with a camera can

be sent through the pipes (Fig. B 3.18), a method that is generally possible for pipes with a nominal diameter of DN 100 or more; there are, however, special systems that can be used in pipes as small as DN 50. The results of the inspection can be categorised according to a scale of urgency ranging from 0 (= immediate action required) to 4 (= no action required). Immediate action is necessary when, for example, the function of a buried pipe is no longer guaranteed or the groundwater could be contaminated by leaking waste water.

But before a drainage system can be refurbished, the waste water must be diverted for the duration of the work.

Incrustation or root penetration can be rectified with the help of a grinding robot (Fig. B 3.17). Such devices can be used in pipes with a nominal diameter of DN 80 or more and can perform other tasks in addition to grinding, e.g. drilling, grouting and repairing damage. Leaks from the drainage system can be repaired using injection or lining techniques, both of which can be used in pipes with a nominal diameter of DN 100 or more. Attaching sealing sleeves externally is

Pipe material	Permissible applications							
	DPS	DS	DPM	BPI	BPS	RWiB	RWoB	CP
Stoneware (STZ)	+	+	+	+	+	+	–	+
Concrete (BT)	–	–	+	+	+	–	–	–
Fibre-cement (FZ)	+	+	+	–	–	+	+	–
Metal (zinc, copper, aluminium, galvanised steel)	–	–	–	–	–	–	+	–
Cast iron without socket (SML)	+	+	+	+	+	+	+	–
Steel (ST)	+	+	+	+	+	+	+	–
Stainless steel (CrNi)	+	+	+	+	+	+	+	+
PVC-U (KG)	–	–	–	+	+	+	–	+
PVC-C (HT)	+	+	+	+	–	+	+	+
PE (PE-HD)[1]	+	+	+	+	–	+	+	+
PE (PE-HD)[2]	–	–	–	+	+	–	–	+
PP (PP-HT)	+	+	+	+	–	+	+	+
ABS (HT)	+	+	+	+	–	+	–	+

DPS Discharge pipe from single appliance
DS Discharge stack
DPM Discharge pipe from multiple appliances
BPI Buried pipe, inaccessible below ground floor slab
BPS Buried pipe in soil

RWiB Rainwater pipe in building
RWoB Rainwater pipe outside building
CP Pipe for condensate from firing appliances
[1] DIN 19535-10, DIN EN 1519-1
[2] DIN 19537-1, DIN 19537-2, DIN EN 12666-1

B 3.19

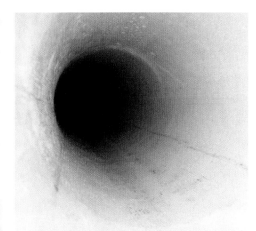

B 3.20

B 3.21

another way of repairing leaks, at least temporarily.

In the injection method a so-called packer is inserted into the pipe, positioned at the location of the damage and inflated pneumatically. The damaged area is thus temporarily sealed off from the inside of the pipe and the damage can be repaired by injecting synthetic resin. Once the resin has cured, the packer is deflated and withdrawn from the pipe.

In the lining method a hose-like partial lining made from laminated glass fibre is positioned at the location of the damage with the aid of a packer (Fig. B 3.20). The packer is then inflated pneumatically, which presses the lining onto the damaged inside wall of the pipe. Once the resin has cured, the packer is deflated and withdrawn from the pipe. This produces a stable, durable partial lining to the inside of the pipe at the location of the leak.

Stainless steel sleeves with a compression seal are also transported to the location of the damage by means of a packer and permanently anchored in position by inflating the packer. Such internal sleeves can be used in pipes with a nominal diameter of DN 150 or more.

Repairs to particularly small pipes or longer sections of pipe can be carried out using various techniques based on the inversion method. In this method a hose-type pipe liner is impregnated with a synthetic resin, placed inside-out in a special cylinder and then connected to the pipe to be refurbished. Pressure is then applied to roll over the laminated liner onto the inside of the pipe (Fig. B 3.21). Steam or UV light is used to cure the liner, which produces a permanent, homogeneous pipe lining. The system can be used for pipe diameters of DN 50 and greater. Leaking pipe inlets can be repaired by inserting an inflatable lining with the help of a packer which is then subsequently bonded in place with an epoxy resin.

If a drain can no longer be refurbished, one replacement option is the burst lining method, which permits trenchless renewal of a pipe while retaining the same route. In this method a bursting tool is pulled through the old pipe, which breaks open the pipe and forces the fragments into the surrounding soil. This is immediately followed by a new pipe with the

same or a larger diameter to replace the old one. This method is suitable for drains with a diameter of DN 100 or more, but a minimum clearance to adjacent pipes must be maintained. DIN 1986-30 prescribes verifiable leakage tests for buried pipes that require major alterations or refurbishment, unless such tests have already been carried out. A CCTV inspection is useful for when minor alterations or refurbishment work is planned.

Rainwater drainage
During a refurbishment project, consideration should certainly be given to whether in future rainwater falling on the building and the building plot should be used as a substitute for drinking water or simply allowed to seep into the ground. If the rainwater is to be used, it must be collected in a cistern and distributed as required throughout the building by means of a pump (see "Water supplies", pp. 54–57). Seepage can take place above ground, e.g. via trenches. Such systems do not require approval. Underground seepage systems, however, require approval.

Waste-water treatment
In situ waste-water treatment can only be regarded as an emergency or temporary solution unless there is no system of public sewers or connection to the nearest one would be unreasonably expensive. Waste-water treatment plants must be approved according to the Water Management Act (WHG) and installed according to DIN 4261 and DIN EN 12566. The operation of such plants is also subject to building and water management regulations. Any existing small waste-water treatment plants should always include a biological treatment stage or should have one retrofitted. Cesspits should be partially drained at regular intervals depending on the sludge accumulation, the percolating filter of the biological treatment stage flushed out depending on the degree of sludge accumulation and seepage trenches checked for proper operation at regular intervals according to DIN 1986. The provisions of DIN EN 752-5 must be taken into account during refurbishment work.

Hot-water heating systems
Reducing energy consumption and running costs are the reasons for renewing or upgrading hot-water heating systems. The individual components of the heating system must be coordinated with each other as well as with the building envelope in order to achieve the best-possible efficiency.

In all the member states of the European Union, the legal requirements for building heating are based on EU Directive 2002/91/EG, and in

Germany that takes the form of the Energy Conservation Act.

Where a boiler is more than 15 years old, regular inspections by a specialist company and measurement of the exhaust gases are specified in the EU Directive, which also prescribes an improvement to the overall energy efficiency of a building in the case of major refurbishment measures, i.e. those in which the cost of the work to be carried out on the building services and the building exceed one-quarter of the value of the building (excluding the value of the building plot itself) or in which more than one-quarter of the building envelope is to be refurbished.

Various measures can be employed to improve the efficiency of a heating installation. For example, individual components, e.g. solar collectors, can be retrofitted, or outdated parts replaced before the end of their useful service lives. The remaining lifetime of individual installation components can be determined from their service lives (Fig. B 3.3). An estimate of the degree of wear can be made on the basis of a visual inspection of the main components.

If several installation components have to be renewed and the estimated remaining lifetime of the boiler is less than five years, serious consideration should be given to replacing the entire system.

The total efficiency of a heating system always depends on its design and the coordination of the technical components with each other. It is generally true to say that the lower the operating temperature of a system, the more efficiently it can be operated and the more effective will be the integration of renewable energy sources. The choice of the right heating system essentially depends on the heating requirements of the whole building, which is why insulating measures for the building envelope should be investigated – and instigated where applicable

– within the scope of refurbishment before replacing the heating. The following factors are critical when redesigning the heating installation:

- The choice of new heating plants for space heating and hot water
- The choice of central or decentralised heating plants
- The selection of a type of energy based on these choices

The new heating systems that can be considered are those based on combustion or heat pumps for exploiting environmental energy. These can be supplemented by solar technologies. The design of a ventilation system with heat recovery and reheating is another possibility, either as a supplementary or even as a replacement system.

The decision whether to opt for central or decentralised heating plants as part of the refurbishment essentially depends on the existing system components and the extent of the intervention in the existing building fabric. Central heating systems are very efficient for heating purposes, but require extensive distribution networks. Whether central or decentralised hot-water provision is the better choice depends on requirements and the distances to the draw-off points. In office buildings with very low hot-water requirements, decentralised appliances are certainly more economic than hot-water tanks and distribution pipework. But in a detached house the length of pipework is comparatively short, when planned properly, and the hot-water requirement comparatively high. The same can apply to an apartment block if the system is designed properly (lagging to pipes and components) and so here, too, central hot-water provision may prove to be the more economic system in terms of total energy

consumption. Central hot-water provision also lends itself better to the integration of a solar thermal system.

Both fossil fuels and renewable energy media are available for operating the heating system. Priority should always be given to using renewable energy sources. Where heating systems for fossil fuels with all the necessary supply or storage facilities are available and can continue to be used, the consumption should be reduced as far as possible (insulating the building envelope, optimising the ventilation) and the technology be made as efficient as possible. Whether a new connection for a fossil fuel supply should be considered or an existing oil-fired system converted to gas-firing are questions that must be considered very carefully taking into account the above criteria and those given in Fig. B 3.23.

When using renewable energy media, smaller amounts of harmful exhaust gases or residues are released than is the case with fossil fuels. The ensuing carbon dioxide emissions result in a zero-carbon overall balance. Various raw materials can be considered as renewable fuels (Fig. B 3.23). When choosing a system, however, the primary energy consumption of the production should be taken into account.

Provision of fuel

If the building already has a gas connection or a tank for heating oil, these should be checked for proper operation and safety. The service pipe to the gas main can be checked for leaks and any non-standard connections by a qualified technician. Exposed gas pipes in the building must be firmly fixed to the wall and painted yellow (RAL 1012) in order to rule out mistakes. The outside of an LPG tank should be inspected every two years by a qualified person according to the Operational Safety Act, and the inside every five years (commercial systems) or every

B 3.22

Properties	Natural gas	Liquid gas	Heating oil (extra light)	Wood pellets	Wood chippings	Electricity mix	District heat	Solar radiation	Environmental energy[2]
Renewable				•	•		o	•	•
Connection to public network required	•					•	•		
No connection to public netw. required		•	•	•	•			•	•
Depends on supplier	o	o				o	•		
Storage room necessary		•	•	•	•				
Suitable for condensing technology	•	•	•	o	o				
Simple metering of consumption	•					•	•	o	o
Cumulative energy cost[1] [kWh$_{prim}$/kWh$_{fin}$]	1.14	1.11	1.11	1.16	1.07	2.99	0.77–1.85		
Greenhouse gas CDE[1] [g/kWh$_{fin}$]	249	263	303	42	35	647	217–408		
Primary energy factor to DIN V 4701-10:2006-12	1.1	1.1	1.1	0.2	0.2	2.7	0.0–1.3		

[1] Carbon dioxide equivalent according to data from GEMIS computer program.
[2] Energy from ground, groundwater or outside air that can be exploited with the help of a heat pump.

B 3.23

B 3.24

B 3.25

10 years (private systems), including the pipe connections, by technicians from the German technical inspections body TÜV. Other aspects to be checked are the stability of the installation plus compliance with the clearances to adjoining buildings (see TRF 1996, TRB 610 and TRB 801, annex 25).

Heating oil tanks must be built with double walls when they are to be buried in the ground or set up in buildings, and fitted with a leak indicator. Single-wall tanks require a sealed bund wall on all sides. With regular maintenance, a service life of approx. 40–45 years can be assumed. Pipes buried in the ground should be laid as suction lines or in a protective duct. Heating oil tanks with a volume < 10 m³ must be inspected by TÜV technicians every 10 years, all larger tanks every five years. Before being used for the first time, every above-ground installation with a volume > 1 m³, every underground heating oil tank and all underground pipes must be checked by an approved person according to the Water Management Act (WHG). Every above-ground installation with a volume ≥ 10 m³, every underground heating oil tank and all underground pipes must be serviced every five years. If the tank is installed in a building, the tank room must also be inspected. Stricter regulations apply in regions where the groundwater has to be protected against contamination. Every decommissioned above-ground installation with a volume ≥ 10 m³ (in groundwater protection regions ≥ 1 m³) and every underground installation must be appraised by an approved person according to the WHG. Rooms for storing wood pellets should be inspected to ensure that they remain permanently dry and dust-tight. In the case of a conversion from oil- to wood pellet-firing, the former tank room can usually be used for storing the pellets. flexible fabric silos, buried tanks or converted steel tanks can be used as alternatives.

Boiler room

The Heating Plant Act (HeizanlV) specifies the requirements placed on boiler rooms. For this reason, the existing boiler and the room itself must be checked to ensure that they comply with the Act. In doing so, the following points must be clarified in particular:

- Nature of heating (e.g. space heating only, heating with hot-water provision, heating/ventilation)
- Boiler output
- Location and size of central heating plant
- Choice of fuel
- Location and size of fuel store
- Accessibility of boiler room
- Enclosing walls, floors above and below, doors
- Size of fresh-air inlets
- Exhaust-gas flues
- Fire detector/alarm system
- Emergency-stop switch for heating
- Safety of installation (including electric cables)
- Noise emissions

VDI Directive 2050, sheet 1, contains reference values for the minimum sizes of boiler rooms which can be used as a starting point for the planning, although a separate boiler room is only specified for boiler outputs of 300 kW and more. If a boiler is replaced in the course of an energy-efficiency upgrade, the boiler output can frequently be reduced, and this may well mean that the new boiler does not need a separate room.

Heating plant

The heart of any heating system is the heating plant, which provides the thermal energy that is distributed throughout the building. It is the heating plant that is mainly responsible for the energy requirements, efficiency and environmental impact of the heating system.

Individual stoves

Individual stoves, fired by oil, gas or wood and designed for heating just one room, can still occasionally be found in old buildings. Such stoves may still be used provided the chimney sweep certifies that the exhaust-gas limits are not exceeded. Replacing such stoves is, however, advisable for reasons of energy efficiency.

Night storage heaters

From the 1950s to the 1970s one widespread form of heating individual rooms was the night storage heater, which was operated with cheap off-peak electricity. This form of heating is extremely inefficient from the primary energy viewpoint. In the light of the rising price of electricity and the successive abolition of the special off-peak electricity tariffs, the operation of such heaters is no longer economic over the long-term. Many local authorities and electricity providers therefore pay subsidies for the decommissioning of night storage heaters. In addition, heaters fabricated prior to 1980, in a few cases even newer units, may contain asbestos (Figs. B 3.24 and 3.25), meaning that the release of asbestos particles into the air in the room cannot be ruled out. Information as to whether a heater constitutes a hazard can be obtained from the manufacturer by stating the type number. Contaminated heaters must be disposed of without delay by certified contractors.

Standard boilers

Boilers with flow and return temperatures of 90/70 °C or 70/55 °C are designated standard or constant-temperature boilers. They exhibit considerable energy losses in standby operation especially and should therefore be replaced. The Energy Conservation Act (EnEV) prescribes that boilers installed before 1978 and not fitted with a new burner must be replaced by 31 December 2008 (Fig. B 3.22). The repair of such boilers is not recommended because they are uneconomic according to today's standards.

Low-temperature boilers

Low-temperature boilers operate with lower flow and return temperatures of 55/45 °C and are therefore considerably more efficient. Every standard boiler in a central or decentralised heating system can be replaced by a low-temperature boiler. Degrees of efficiency up to 97 % are normal. The heating system as a hot-water system with distribution and heat output components (e.g. radiators) can generally con-

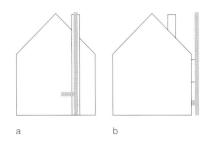

a   b

B 3.26

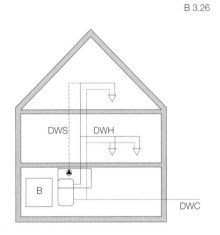

a

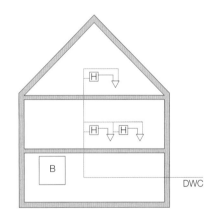

b

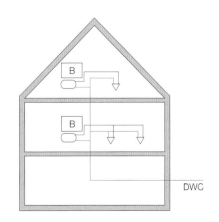

c

B 3.27

tinue to be used. Low-temperature boilers can be fired by fossil fuels or renewable energy media, but the chimney may need to be refurbished in conjunction with the boiler replacement because the temperature of the exhaust gases is lower than that of standard boilers and a build-up of condensate in the chimney must be prevented in order to preclude damage. A chimney sweep can advise on the need for this.

Condensing boilers
A condensing boiler is a highly efficient heating system with a degree of efficiency exceeding 100 % because it uses the latent heat contained in the steam of the exhaust gases. Such a boiler can be fired by fossil fuels or renewable energy media and, like with the low-temperature boiler, it can be used to replace any old boiler (central or decentralised systems). The existing heating circuits can continue to be used in most cases. The distribution losses in the system are reduced by the lower flow and return temperatures of 35/28 °C. The heating output surfaces in the rooms must be larger – the ideal solution is to combine a condensing boiler with underfloor heating. The condensate produced by the combustion must be drained into the wastewater system. A chimney refurbishment or a new flue will be necessary unless there is a moisture-resistant, pressure-tight chimney available for the fan-assisted exhaust-gas discharge. Very small exhaust-gas flues (≤ 100 mm O.D., plastic) can be used, depending on the boiler output, which can be advantageous in refurbishment projects.

Heat pumps
Heat pump systems powered by gas or electricity draw their energy from the air, the soil or water and raise this to a higher temperature level. Heat pumps with ground couplings are not usually suitable for refurbishment projects because a correspondingly large open area is required. Boreholes are, however, possible. Air/water heat pumps can be set up outside the building if space is at a premium. Cheaper electricity tariffs are available for operating heat pumps. No chimney is required. When operated in reverse, a heat pump system can be used for cooling (see pp. 65–67). The operation of a heat pump presumes a very good standard of insulation (EnEV standard at least). Coil heating systems (floor, wall, ceiling) are ideal for use with heat pumps.

Co-generation plants, combined heat and power (CHP)
Compact co-generation plants based on internal combustion engines can produce heat and generate electricity. The waste heat is used for heating purposes and the electricity is fed into the public grid, which is remunerated at an agreed rate. Co-generation plants can be operated with fossil fuels or renewable energy media and are suitable for including in refurbishment projects provided there is a long-term, high heating requirement.

These plants are inefficient if the operating time is less than 4000 h/year. Where long operating times can be guaranteed, e.g. by interconnecting several housing units, such plants represent a good alternative to conventional systems. The high exhaust-gas temperatures mean that the existing chimney can usually continue to be used without any problems, but the location of the plant must be chosen carefully to limit the noise emissions.

Exhaust-gas flues
Replacing an old boiler by a new one results in a higher efficiency primarily because the operating temperature is lowered. This leads to lower exhaust-gas temperatures which in some circumstances may mean that the existing chimney has to be refurbished. If the existing chimney is not adapted to handle the lower exhaust-gas temperatures, it will not be possible to prevent the ensuing condensation causing the formation of shiny soot and an accumulation of soot (saturation from the inside) in the existing chimney. The chimney sweep can specify the refurbishment needs depending on the particular system.
Two solutions can be considered for refurbishing the chimney (Fig. B 3.26). In both cases the inside of the chimney must be absolutely moisture- and corrosion-resistant (possible materials include stainless steel, aluminium, glass, plastics or vitrified clayware). The condensation that collects must be drained away from the base of the chimney.
A chimney refurbishment is always necessary when a condensing boiler is installed because condensate occurs at the boiler and in the chimney. The condensate must be drained into the waste-water system, and any pipes that carry condensate must be suitable for a pH value < 6. Condensate neutralisation is always required with oil- and wood-fired boilers, but with gas-fired boilers only for an output ≥ 200 kW. As the buoyancy of the cooled exhaust gas is lacking here, a fan (integrated into the boiler) is needed to drive the gases out of the chimney. Such fan-assisted exhaust-gas discharge requires a pressure-tight chimney design with a corresponding test for leaks.

Hot-water provision
The drinking water is heated centrally in conjunction with the main heating plant or locally at the draw-off points. In the latter case, with a gas-fired or electric instantaneous water heater or a storage water heater, an extensive system of hot-water pipes is unnecessary (Fig. B 3.27b). That means there are no losses in the pipework and no energy is required for distribution (pumps). However, such heating appliances should be used only at places remote from the main heating plant where only small amounts of hot water are required. Existing storage water heaters should be lagged or replaced by a self-regulating electronic instantaneous water heater. Central hot-water systems can be operated in

B 3.26 Chimney refurbishment options
  a Internal lining (flue) inserted into existing
    chimney
  b New, external flue
B 3.27 Various systems for providing hot water
  a Central heating with central hot-water heating
    and secondary circuit
  b Central heating with decentralised hot-water
    heating (e.g. instantaneous water heater)
  c Decentralised space heating for each dwelling
    with integral central hot-water heating (combi-
    nation boiler)
B 3.28 Integration of a hot-water tank – as hot-water,
    space heating and solar storage tank – into a
    heating system with solar collectors
B 3.29 Schematic illustration of a one-pipe system
  a with bypass pipes
  b with forced circulation
B 3.30 Schematic illustration of a two-pipe system

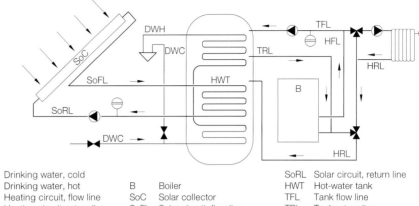

DWC	Drinking water, cold			SoRL	Solar circuit, return line
DWH	Drinking water, hot	B	Boiler	HWT	Hot-water tank
HFL	Heating circuit, flow line	SoC	Solar collector	TFL	Tank flow line
HRL	Heating circuit, return line	SoFL	Solar circuit, flow line	TRL	Tank return line

B 3.28

conjunction with the space heating for one or more dwellings and represent particularly energy-efficient solutions. Furthermore, a solar-powered hot-water system can be integrated.
Existing systems should be optimised by regulating any secondary circuits and by adding a hot-water tank (Fig. B 3.27a). The greatest energy losses occur at the tank and in the distribution. Maximum insulation and the best appliance efficiency classes are essential here.

Hot-water tanks
Hot-water tanks are used for both the space heating and the hot-water requirements. Many existing buildings have a hot-water tank that – depending on the level of convenience required – provides between 25 and 40 l of hot water per person (at 50–60 °C) and is heated directly by the boiler (Fig. B 3.27c). Systems that produce heat and have to store this until it is needed or other systems that are difficult to regulate, e.g. wood-fired stoves, heat pumps or solar systems, should be operated with a means of buffering the thermal energy (Fig. B 3.28). Incrustation (furring) can build up on the heat exchanger in the middle of a hot-water tank due to the heating of the water, and such deposits can lead to a drop in performance. In a tank fitted with an cleaning eye, deposits can be detected and removed. The internal coating of the tank should also be inspected for corrosion, which is often caused by oxygen infiltrating the heating water. The oxygen finds its way into the water either via an open expansion tank or pipes that are oxygen-permeable (e.g. old plastic pipes, especially in underfloor heating systems). Whereas an open expansion tank can be replaced by a sealed expansion vessel, if the old pipes are inaccessible and therefore cannot be replaced, a rustproof stainless steel tank (including all pipes and fittings) must be installed.
Both hot-water tank types are often characterised by high energy losses due to inadequate insulation. It is possible to insulate tanks subsequently, although prefabricated insulating jackets are available only rarely. If the tank is located outside the heated part of the building, the location of the tank can be insulated instead. Reducing the temperature of the stored water

is another way of minimising losses. Where drinking water is involved, the provisions of DVGW Data Sheet W 551 must be complied with because it is imperative to avoid encouraging the growth of legionella bacteria. Appropriate insulation, pipe sizes to suit demands and heating plant designed to suit the operating times and the flow/return temperatures are all essential points to be considered when planning a new installation. If a new hot-water tank is to be installed, heating the water by solar energy should always be considered, at least the integration of such a system at a later date.

Distribution of heat from hot-water heating systems
The heat produced by the heating plant has to be distributed throughout the building by a system of pipes. The pipes must be properly dimensioned, lagged and hydraulically balanced in order to guarantee efficient distribution.

Heating circuit
The circuit can be provided with an open or sealed expansion tank to equalise the pressure. Open systems can still be found in some buildings; these allow oxygen to infiltrate the system which can cause internal corrosion in some circumstances. As the pipes of sealed systems usually last longer, an open system should be converted into a sealed one. Corrosion generally occurs at joints between pipes or between pipes and radiators in the region of the maximum system pressure, i.e. in the lower storeys. If damage is discovered in an older heating circuit, all the factors should be weighed up in order to decide whether repairs should be carried out or the whole system completely replaced because isolated damage often indicates a generally worn system.
In the case of a one-pipe system, new pipework for flow and return lines should be installed in order to balance the system hydraulically and enable the radiators to be controlled individually. Control valves and bypass pipes can be installed in particularly large systems in order to achieve some improvement (Figs. B 3.29 and 3.30).

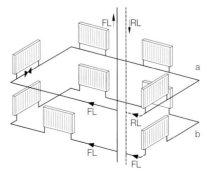

FL Flow line
RL Return line

B 3.29

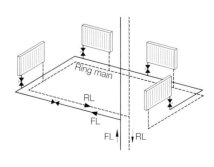

B 3.30

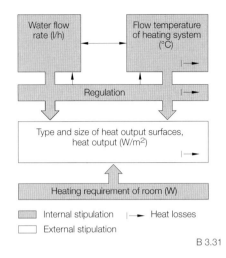

Internal stipulation |→ Heat losses
External stipulation

B 3.31

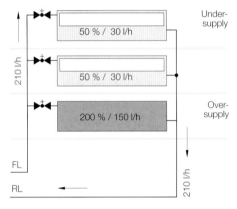

a

b

c

B 3.32

The efficiency of the distribution and the fittings and radiators installed can be severely impaired by the "silting-up" due to corrosion processes. This problem can be rectified by flushing out the system.

Hot-water circuit
Hot-water pipes are subject to the same requirements as cold-water pipes. In the building stock, hot water heated centrally is provided at the draw-off points usually by way of secondary circuits driven by a circulation pump. There may be considerable energy losses in the pipes due to the high water temperature, but this can be reduced with appropriate lagging (Fig. B 3.7). Alternatively, or in addition, the circulation pump can be fitted with a timer so that the circulation takes place only at the times when hot water is mainly required. This reduces the line losses and also cuts the amount of electricity required for the pump.
Annex 5 of the Energy Conservation Act requires that heating pipes and fittings that are located in unheated areas – but are still accessible (in economic terms) – must be insulated. Bends, branches and penetrations are also affected by this regulation. From the heating viewpoint, lagging the pipes – especially long ones – in heated areas is also to be recommended.
The lagging to the pipes depends on the ambient conditions (moisture, mechanical stresses) and the fire protection requirements (building materials class according to the Federal State Building Regulations).

Pumps in the heat distribution system
The pumps required for distributing the hot water for space heating and other purposes are generally only replaced upon failure. The current edition of the Energy Conservation Act, however, calls for the retrofitting of self-regulating pumps. Many of the pumps in the building stock are oversized in terms of their electrical power; their replacement would achieve energy-savings. When installing new pumps, it is important to make sure that low-energy, electronically controlled pumps with an EC drive are installed which can be controlled depending on the flow and return temperatures.

Solar thermal systems
If the existing building has a solar thermal system, the first task should be to inspect the collectors for damage and leaks. The recommendations for heating pipes also apply to the pipes of solar thermal systems. All air must be bled out of the system, pipes must be lagged and the pumps checked. A solar thermal system can be used for providing hot water or to assist the space heating. Such a system can provide up to 60 % of the annual hot-water requirements and up to 30 % of the space heating requirements, depending on the energy consumption of the building.

Heat output in hot-water heating systems
The output of heat to rooms that require heating can be achieved with a hot-water heating system via radiators, coil heating or activation of the building components.
Most existing buildings requiring refurbishment are heated by way of convectors or radiators, occasionally coil heating systems. Leaks in radiators are easily detected by way of a visual inspection, but leaks in coil heating systems can lead to considerable damage if the leak remains undetected for a long time. Thermographic imaging can be used to detect the source of a leak.
According to the Energy Conservation Act, new heating systems must be fitted with "automatic devices for the individual control of the temperature in each room" [1]. This means that, for example, thermostat valves must be installed if not already fitted, preferably with an optimised actuation. Another way of saving energy is to reduce the flow temperature of the heating system, but the size of the heat output surfaces must be coordinated with this reduction (Fig. B 3.33). Most existing buildings are fitted with large radiators that actually turn out to be oversized following an energy-efficiency upgrade, but that allows a lower flow temperature to be set (Fig. B 3.31).

Regulating and controlling heating systems
Heating systems can be fitted with numerous control devices. The Energy Conservation Act stipulates that new systems should be fitted with "central, automatic devices for reducing and shutting off the flow of heat and starting and stopping electrical drives depending on the external temperature, or another suitable command variable, and the time" [2].
New control systems can be added to old boilers depending on the their type and age. Modulation, or rather the timer-controlled shutdown of the system (e.g. reducing the output during the night or during periods of absence), results in considerable energy-savings.

For efficient, energy-saving operation, the following basic settings for regulating the heating system must be carried out by a qualified person and checked at regular intervals:

· Target temperatures for all operating conditions
· Heating curve (matched to the system)
· Threshold temperature levels for regulating the system
· Time periods for operating conditions
· Recording of command of variables via sensors (actual values)

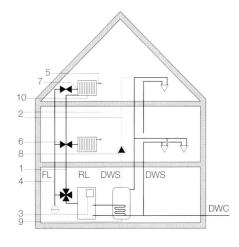

1 Lagging the heating pipes in unheated areas
2 Lagging the DWH and DWS pipes
3 Improving the heating controls
4 Adjusting the pump output
5 Bleeding the air out of the system
6 Fitting thermostat valves (with low regulating characteristic)
7 Hydraulic balancing (valve presets)
8 Adding a timer for the circulation pump
9 Insulating the water tank
10 Cleaning the components to improve flow

B 3.33

B 3.31 Variables influencing the type and size of heat output surfaces
B 3.32 Heat distribution in comparison
    a Heating system without hydraulic balancing = uneven heat distribution
    b Heating system incorrectly regulated by increasing the pump output
    c Heating system with proper hydraulic balancing = even heat distribution
B 3.33 Central heating with central hot-water heating and secondary circuit; highlighting the components in the existing system that can be optimised

Hydraulic balancing of heating systems

The constant and correct heat distribution throughout the entire system is regulated by the hydraulic balancing of the heating system. Limiting the flow rate of the hot water to the value of the heating requirement of the individual heat output components rules out the problem of the under- or over-supply to individual heat output components. In a poorly balanced system, rooms near the heating plant are overheated, those further away inadequately heated (Fig. B 3.32). Hydraulic balancing is the only way of avoiding this problem, and in existing buildings controllable heating circuits are required in order to achieve hydraulic balancing, which requires the installation of new valves.

Cooling the building

The internal temperature of a building can be reduced by way of ventilation, cooling or airconditioning. The situation normally encountered in existing buildings is a central plant with a network of ducts. Decentralised units are rare and then are mostly used for individual rooms or premises.

The service lives and maintenance intervals of central plants depend on the type of plant, the operating times and the location. Maintenance must be carried out according to DIN EN 378 and the recommendations of the German Engineering Federation (VDMA Data Sheet 24186); filters must be renewed regularly, ventilation ducts and outlets cleaned as required. Only a specialist can decide whether individual defects should be rectified or the complete system replaced, and then only on a case-by-case basis.

Cold-air system, night-time cooling

On hot summer days additional ventilation (natural or mechanical) does not usually help to lower the temperature. However, increasing the air velocity does lead to a decrease in the perceived room temperature. Night-time cooling, on the other hand, is an effective way of lowering the interior temperature, but does require an adequate amount of thermal mass in the interior of the building. With an optimum amount of thermal mass and a high air change rate, cooling to about 3 K above the minimum nighttime temperature is possible.

Thermal mass

Where an existing building has only little thermal mass available, the installation of phase change materials (PCM) can be considered. Paraffins, for example, undergo a change of state at 25–28 °C, absorbing considerable energy as they do so without experiencing an increase in their temperature; this curtails the temperature peaks. The latent energy stored in a PCM must be released later, e.g. during night-time ventilation with cool outside air. PCMs can be filled into sealed plastic bags and laid on suspended ceilings, included as an additive in gypsum-based boards, or mixed into plaster in microencapsulated form.

Room cooling

Various systems are available for cooling without mechanical ventilation in combination with a central chiller plant, should such a system be required as part of a refurbishment project. Those systems that feed cold water through cooling elements, capillaries or pipes are particularly suitable for installing in an existing building. Besides the use of standard components, capillary tube mats can be fixed to the underside of a structural floor or a suspended plasterboard ceiling and then plastered over. Fixing such mats directly to a solid floor slab enables the slab to be used as thermal mass as well (cooling through activation of the building component). The mats are thin and so can even be retrofitted in rooms with a low ceiling height. Where the mats are to be fitted in office buildings, it is advisable to attach them to match the spacing of the windows so that partitions can still be installed at a later date. Capillary tube mats must be connected to the coldwater system of the chiller plant. A cooling output of about 80 W/m² is feasible; there are no fire protection problems. Capillary tube mats can also be fitted to an existing suspended metal ceiling by fixing them above the panels. The cooling output fluctuates in this situation depending on the presence of any attenuating acoustic fleece.

It is also possible to erect a metal cooling ceiling in an existing building, but this changes the interior architecture completely because the cooling panels remain visible below the soffit.

A metal cooling ceiling can also be installed between a soffit and a suspended ceiling with at least 35 % air permeability. A cooling output of up to 200 W/m² is possible with such an arrangement.

Owing to their high degree of prefabrication, cooling panels are especially suitable for the refurbishment of occupied office buildings. These panels, too, are connected to the central cold-water supply and change the interior architecture completely. Cooling outputs of up to 250 W/m² are possible.

Convector fans can be retrofitted locally; again, these require a connection to the cold-water system. They operate with recirculated air and do not need a fresh-air duct. The cooling output depends on the size of the unit and generally lies between 0.75 and 9 kW.

All the aforementioned systems can be integrated into the hot-water heating system of a building and therefore can be used for heating as well.

If a higher cold-water requirement is expected after refurbishment, e.g. due to different plant or a change of use, the use of groundwater for cooling the building should be considered, depending on the size of the building. Cooling the building by means of groundwater must be approved by the authorities. It is also possible to operate a heat pump in reverse.

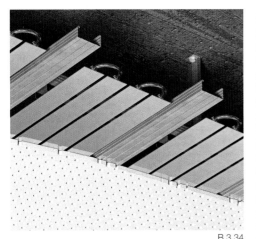

B 3.34

B 3.35

B 3.36

B 3.34 Heating/cooling ceiling
B 3.35 Facade appearance spoiled by decentralised split air-conditioning units
B 3.36 Example of a decentralised facade-mounted ventilation system, usually fitted into the spandrel panel or below a raised access floor
B 3.37 Aluminium honeycomb structure for open evaporative cooling in a wet cooling tower
B 3.38 Recommended ventilation times for natural ventilation via the windows depending on the time of year in order to guarantee a hygienic air change rate, taking into account a reduction in the ventilation heat losses (within the heating period)
B 3.39 Diagram showing the principle of "Cologne ventilation" via separate fresh-air and exhaust-air shafts for the rooms to be ventilated
B 3.40 Compact design for an adsorption-type refrigeration unit with low output

Split air-conditioning units
Split air-conditioning units do not require a central chiller plant. Generally, these permanent wall-mounted units used in residential and commercial premises consist of a convector fan installed on the inside and a cold-water element on the outside (Fig. B 3.35). This type of unit can usually be used for heating and cooling. The distance between the two parts of the unit should be as short as possible. Cooling outputs lie in the range approx. 1.5–5.5 kW. Split air-conditioning units are relatively small and are ideal for retrofitting to the individual parts of a building. However, their high energy consumption makes them inefficient and the external components substantially impair the appearance of the facade. Prior to installing such units, it is important to check whether more energy-efficient air-conditioning measures can be realised.

Decentralised ventilation and air-conditioning
Decentralised ventilation units are fitted directly into the facade and operate with a direct intake of external air at the unit itself (Fig. B 3.36). Heating and cooling functions can be added to such units, which means they have to be connected to a two- or four-line system; the latter consists of flow and return lines for both heating and cooling.
Such units can be added to an existing building by integrating them into a spandrel panel, raised access floor or suspended ceiling. They do not need any large air ducts and so are suitable for refurbishment projects. One particular advantage is that they can be controlled individually by users. Although these systems are fitted with filters, they are not suitable for use in highly polluted inner-city areas. Generally, the cooling output achievable is not sufficient to cover the entire cooling needs of a building. It is usually advisable to combine such units with a system of cooling surfaces.
An alternative to decentralised air-conditioning with a central cold-water supply is a system based on adiabatic cooling, which operates much more efficiently than decentralised air-conditioning units. However, such a system requires a cold-water supply (not a cold-water supply with a defined flow temperature) plus expelled-air outlet and fresh-air inlet, factors that must be considered during refurbishment. These systems are good for refurbishment projects from the energy viewpoint; their water consumption is low. They can be installed as roof-mounted units or in the void between suspended ceiling and underside of structural floor.

Central air-conditioning
In principle, air-conditioning systems need large duct cross-sections for conveying the amounts of air required, which means it often appears impossible or inadvisable to fit such systems into existing buildings. Twin-duct air-conditioning systems generate different air temperatures which – routed parallel – are first mixed at the outlet. Where an existing building contains such a system, a check should be carried out to establish whether this can be replaced by a single-duct system because this is better from the energy viewpoint.
If the clear ceiling height in a building is to be increased during the refurbishment work, an existing low-pressure system can be replaced by a high-pressure system, which allows the duct cross-sections to be reduced by up to 75 %. Existing systems with indirect humidity control (dew point control) should be replaced by systems with direct humidity control because these are much more efficient. Conventional control systems for complex installations should be replaced by DDC (direct digital control). When servicing or repairing central compression-type refrigeration units, it is vital to ensure that refrigerants containing CFCs, e.g. R12 or R22, which are often found in older systems, are replaced by zero-CFC products. The refrigerants R12 and R22 have been banned in new systems since the year 2000, but may still be used in existing systems up until 2014.
According to EU Regulation 2037/2000, stationery chiller and air-conditioning plants with > 3 kg of refrigerant must be checked for leaks every year, systems with ≥ 30 kg of refrigerant every six months. Moreover, the Energy Conservation Act stipulates that air-conditioning systems must be serviced and their energy-efficiency checked at regular intervals.
The recooling unit needed to remove the heat from refrigeration plant is often provided in the form of a wet cooling tower (Fig. B 3.37). Recooling within a wet cooling tower takes place through the evaporation of water to the open air, which provides an optimum habitat for legionella bacteria. For reasons of hygiene, it is advisable to check that there is sufficient clearance between any existing wet cooling towers and any air intakes.
In the ideal case a refurbishment project should include the integration of geothermal recooling into the system. However, geothermal recooling requires corresponding external areas that can be subsequently activated – an expensive, involved undertaking. The possible use of groundwater and boreholes for recooling should always be investigated, however; VDI Directive 4640 provides planning advice. If there is the chance of accommodating a ground coupling on the site for preconditioning the incoming fresh air, this option should be explored in detail.

Solar cooling

There are more sustainable alternatives to compression-type refrigeration units. For example, absorption-type and adsorption-type refrigeration units can be used that are powered by district heat, solar energy or a co-generation plant (Fig. B 3.40). Systems of this kind are available with cooling outputs starting at approx. 5.5 kW. Owing to the correspondence between cooling output and external cooling load, solar-powered systems are ideal for air-conditioning. A solar cooling system requires a sufficient area of suitably oriented surfaces for the collectors, or waste heat.

Another alternative is to use sorption-assisted conditioning – a desiccant cooling system (DCS). In contrast to the absorption-type and adsorption-type refrigeration units, this produces cold air instead of cold water. The water consumption of such a system is low and the use of solar energy means that there is a high correspondence between external heat loads and cooling requirements and the performance influenced by the incident solar radiation. In solar systems without storage options it must be remembered that there are a few hours during which the comfort criteria cannot be met with such a system. An alternative is to use central plants with permanent supplies of waste heat. Only substances with zero ozone depletion potential (ODP) are used in a DCS. Water is used as the refrigerant; only the ventilators and pumps require electrical energy and therefore contribute only minimally to anthropogenic CO_2 production, with the amount depending on how the electricity is generated. With appropriate provision of electrical energy, we can assume a relatively low global warming potential (GWP).

Ventilation

Ventilation of the interior must be guaranteed for hygiene reasons. Ventilation is essential for dissipating odours, emissions of harmful substances and moisture, reducing the concentration of carbon dioxide in the room, and avoiding damage to the building fabric (e.g. saturation of components or mould growth with the associated health risks).

The hygienic air requirement of a person depends on the ambient conditions and their activities, and for housing is approx. 20–40 m^3/h, which can be achieved with an air change rate of 0.4–0.6 h^{-1}.

Natural ventilation

Natural ventilation is the designation given to the non-mechanically assisted exchange of air in buildings. Older buildings frequently exhibit considerable air leaks in the building envelope. The causes of the leaks are doors and windows plus poor workmanship where voids are concerned (e.g. converted roof spaces, roller shutter housings, etc.). The leaks lead to a permanent exchange of air between inside and outside (ventilation via the joints), and although this guarantees a high interior air quality in terms of hygiene, it also leads to cold interior surfaces and draughts plus huge uncontrolled ventilation heat losses and, furthermore, damage to the fabric of the building due to convective water transport. When carrying out refurbishment work it is vital to ensure that the enclosing thermal envelope is airtight in order to avoid damage to building components and to minimise ventilation heat losses.

In residential refurbishment projects (e.g. new windows) it is frequently the case that problems with mould occur that are mostly attributable to a high interior humidity and an inadequate air change rate. In "airtight" buildings users are obliged to guarantee a hygienic air change rate in order to prevent unhygienic conditions and the risk of damage to the building components as a result of inadequate ventilation.

Natural ventilation via the windows is readily accepted by users, but it is difficult to achieve controlled ventilation in this way. Users must therefore devote considerable attention to the matter in order to avoid serious heat losses and cooling of the components due to excessive ventilation (Fig. B 3.38).

Rooms without opening lights must be ventilated in some other way. In old buildings, especially apartments, there may be shaft systems for rooms located away from the facade which enable ventilation via the thermal currents generated by warm waste air. The replacement fresh air for these rooms is guaranteed either via a separate shaft ("Cologne ventilation") or via neighbouring rooms that adjoin the facade ("Berlin ventilation") (Fig. B 3.39).

The systems encountered in the building stock often do not function properly without the assistance of a fan and should be improved during refurbishment. Hygiene, fire protection and sound insulation aspects should be checked where there are shafts, which should be either cleaned or lined with a new ventilation pipe so that they can continue to be used. Noises or odours from other dwellings can be overcome by installing baffles and flap valves. In addition, fire stops for the individual storeys may need to be integrated depending on the fire protection requirements.

Besides these ventilation techniques there are also diverse, functioning solar ventilation systems (e.g. solar chimney), some with preheating of the air by solar energy. Most are assisted by specific mechanical air handling. Such systems can be integrated into existing buildings but must be designed to suit the individual situation.

B 3.37

Month	Surge ventilation[1] [min]
December to February	4–6
March and November	8–10
April and October	12–15
May and September	16–20
June to August	25–30

[1] Frequency: at least 3–4 times daily

B 3.38

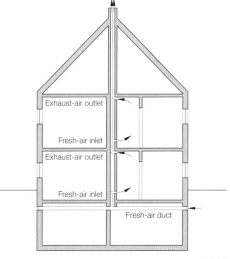

Exhaust-air outlet

Fresh-air inlet

Exhaust-air outlet

Fresh-air inlet

Fresh-air duct

B 3.39

SorTech AG

B 3.40

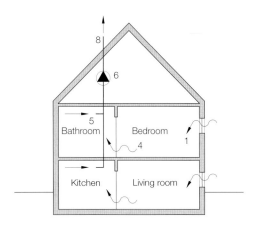

B 3.41

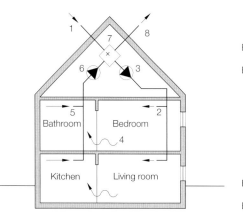

B 3.42

B 3.41 Schematic illustration of an extract system for
        housing
B 3.42 Schematic illustration of a controlled ventilation
        system with heat recovery for housing
        1 Fresh air
        2 Fresh-air ducts
        3 Fresh-air fan
        4 Ventilation between rooms
        5 Exhaust air
        6 Exhaust-air fan
        7 Heat exchanger
        8 Expelled air
B 3.43 Heat recovery system with two heat exchangers
        and a fluid medium in a so-called run-around coil
B 3.44 Colour coding for electrical installations

Mechanical ventilation systems
If the transmission heat losses of the building envelope are substantially reduced as a result of refurbishment measures, it is then the ventilation heat losses in particular that make up a large part of the total energy consumption of the building. A controlled ventilation system can help to overcome this problem. An existing ventilation system must be inspected to establish the condition of the plant, the ventilation ducts and the air outlets, and checked to establish whether the system is designed to meet requirements.

Dirty ducts provide habitats for microbes, dusty deposits can become detached and contaminate the interior air, greasy deposits can ignite in the event of a fire. Existing cleaning eyes offer one method of assessing the condition. Cleaning (e.g. dry steam, low-pressure equipment or rotary brushes) is usually carried out by a specialist contractor.

Ventilation ducts that can be inspected visually from the outside should be checked for leaks by means of a smoke test. All leaks must be sealed and components or routing that lead to unfavourable air flows should be replaced or modified.

Besides duct cross-sections and duct routing that favour good air flows, it is the fans that are mainly responsible for the energy consumption of a ventilation system. The fans must be designed for the volume of air required – ideally, flow-controlled fans should be retrofitted. In the system control the settings and all the command variables should correspond to the performance profile and every sensor should operate properly; additional command variables or adjustments to the system settings may be possible in order to improve the efficiency.

One primary requirement for the successful operation of controlled ventilation systems is the construction of an airtight building envelope. The Energy Conservation Act demands that this be verified by means of an airtightness test (blower door test). Where ventilation systems are to be installed in existing buildings it is important to ensure that the plan layout of the building enables efficient routing of the ducts on all floors. Unused chimneys can be exploited here for vertical ducts. Adequate ceiling heights must

be available to accommodate horizontal ducting. In a detached house it is reasonable to assume circular ducts approx. 8–15 cm in diameter.

Extract system
Extract systems are not usually encountered in the building stock. If a central extract system is to be installed, the extraction must take place in kitchens and bathrooms (Fig. B 3.41). The fresh-air inlets can be integrated into the external walls of living rooms etc. Leakage-air openings (grilles in the internal doors) guarantee a flow of air through the dwelling to the extract rooms. The system should be fitted with flow-reducing valves in the extract rooms and flow-controlled fans at the rooftop exhausts. Extract systems guarantee optimum interior air quality permanently without any user intervention. They constitute an alternative to natural ventilation via the windows and can achieve notable energy-savings.

Ventilation systems with and without heat recovery
Ventilation systems are only found in more recent buildings. If a controlled ventilation system is to be added to a building, systems of supply and extract ducts must be incorporated. Such a system allows the fresh-air and exhaust-air flows to be precisely controlled for individual rooms as well as the entire building. In addition, such systems offer the chance of preheating the incoming fresh air via a heat recovery installation that uses the waste heat of the expelled air (Fig. B 3.42).

To do this, it is not essential for the fresh-air and exhaust-air ducts to cross, which can result in considerable expense. There are also systems available that – in the form of recuperative heat exchangers – used fluid media to transfer the waste heat over long distances from the exhaust-air duct (e.g. on the roof) to the fresh-air duct (e.g. in the basement) (Fig. B 3.43). Furthermore, the integration of a heat pump enables further energy to be recovered.

Decentralised ventilation units with heat recovery, which are ideally installed in pairs, are also available for retrofitting. They are built into the external wall of a room and are therefore directly

connected to the outside air. At regular intervals, the unit switches on for a brief period (15–45 seconds) in order to blow outside air into the room and subsequently extract the same amount of waste interior air. The second unit operates at staggered intervals. The air flows through a regenerative heat exchanger in the unit which absorbs the heat of the expelled air and transfers it to the incoming fresh air so that no system of ducts is necessary.

The use of a ventilation unit guarantees a permanently regulated air change rate controlled by the quality of the interior air and suited to the requirements of the individual rooms. With heat recovery, more than 90 % of the waste heat can be transferred to the incoming fresh air.

Electrical installations
Existing electrical installations that do not present any immediate danger are protected by the toleration of the building stock concept and may continue to be used provided they comply with the regulations that were current at the time of their installation. Consequently, they may also be serviced and repaired according to the outdated standards. However, if parts of a system are replaced or supplemented, the entire section of the system involved must be updated to comply with the latest codes of practice.

It is generally true to say that an electrical installation should be renewed after 30–40 years. The wire cross-sections used in electrical installations built prior to 1950 are mostly too small for modern electrical power requirements. Installations dating from before 1940 often include distribution and safety elements that should be renewed without delay, and pre-1930 installations can include unusable distribution and safety elements. An adequately sized electrical connection to the building can only be assumed for buildings built after 1950. If the connection is older, it is worthwhile checking whether a new connection is necessary. Fig. B 3.45 (overleaf) lists typical electrical component standards depending on the period of construction.

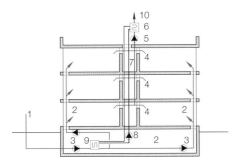

1 Fresh air
2 Fresh-air ducts
3 Fresh-air fan
4 Exhaust air
5 Exhaust-air fan
6 Heat exchanger, exhaust air/fluid medium
7 Heat exchanger circuit (run-around coil)
8 Heat exchanger pump
9 Heat exchanger, fluid medium/fresh air
10 Expelled air

B 3.43

Colour coding for three-core electric cables

	current	pre-1967
phase L1	brown (black[1])	black
neutral	light blue	grey
earth (PE or PEN)	green-yellow	red

Colour coding for five-core electric cables

	current	pre-2003
phase L1	brown	black
phase L2	black	brown
phase L3	grey	black
neutral	blue	blue
earth	green-yellow	green-yellow

[1] up to 2003

B 3.44

Connection to public grid

The electrical connection to a building is generally in the form of an incoming cable that is connected to the intake unit housing the main fuses. This unit represents the transition from the public side of the system to the private side. There should be no gas and water pipes within 1 m of the incoming electricity supply. If the distance is less, the positions of the pipes/cables should be adjusted or appropriate protective measures must be integrated. Where the incoming electricity supply is realised by way of an overhead line, it is recommended to lay a conduit with a minimum internal diameter of 36 mm between the roof space and the basement in order to prepare for an underground connection to the public grid in the future. The main cable from the intake unit to the electricity meter(s), which normally contains all five conductors (three phases, one neutral, one earth) of the three-phase system, should include the appropriate protective fuses and be laid in accessible rooms, preferably adjacent to the staircase. During refurbishment work it is advisable to incorporate an additional conduit to accommodate any further cables that may be necessary in the future. The consumer unit in a dwelling should ideally be located in the entrance hall, but in the pre-1990 building stock of former East Germany it is often found in the bathroom, kitchen or an installation shaft. A consumer unit in a bathroom must be relocated.

Distribution, fusing

A minimum number of circuits – depending on the type of dwelling – is a requirement of DIN 18015 for new electrical installations. The distribution board in houses and apartments takes the form of a so-called consumer unit. A separate circuit is prescribed for communal areas and basements and also appliances with a consumption exceeding 2 kW (e.g. cooker). Automatic fuses and cables with adequate cross-sections are essential requirements for all circuits. The minimum cross-section for permanent copper cables is 1.5 mm², permanent aluminium cables 2.5 mm² (former East Germany). DIN VDE 0100 provides an overview of the load ratings and fusing for the multi-core cables used in buildings. Protection against

direct and indirect contact is usually required. Effective protection against direct contact is provided by installing circuit-breakers in the form of residual current devices (RCD) with a $\triangle I$ of 30 mA. Electrical circuits in bathrooms and outdoors must always be fitted with an RCD (see "Equipotential bonding", p. 70). When installing a new electrical system according to DIN 18015, a minimum number of power sockets and connections for individual consumers up to 2 kW must be provided. RAL-RG 678 can also be used to define the number of electrical fittings (Fig. B 3.46). When routing cables through existing timber-frame buildings, the members of the timber frame may not be chased to accommodate the cables. The cables can be laid in the plaster if it is sufficiently thick. Otherwise, it is possible to drill holes through the timber members, but their size should not exceed about one-sixth of the cross-sectional area of the timber. Conduits should be used where cables pass through the infill panels.

Installation zones

Cables that are to be concealed in the walls may only be laid in the installation zones defined in DIN 18015. In floors and ceilings, however, the principle of the "shortest route" applies. In buildings in which the electrical installation was supplemented during the war and post-war years, diagonal cables can also be found in the walls. These cables should be located with the help of a cable detector and then permanently disconnected from the electricity supply. Special protective zones apply in bathrooms: electrical installations in these areas are either prohibited or subject to strict safety regulations.

Cables

Besides cables containing the copper wires customary these days it is possible to find cables with aluminium wires in the building stock. The risk with the latter is that they may have built up high contact resistances over time. Here and there in former East Germany aluminium wires with a copper casing have been encountered. Galvanic corrosion is possible with this mixture of aluminium and copper. Aluminium cables should therefore be replaced for reasons of safety during any refurbishment work. The colour coding of the wires found in the building stock can differ from the colour coding used these days depending on the year of installation (Fig. B 3.44).
DIN VDE 0100-520 provides advice on assessing whether cables in the building stock are suitable for modern requirements; DIN VDE 0100-737 provides similar advice for wet rooms. Where existing installations include cables with textile sheathing or brittle plastic insulation, all such cables should be replaced by modern cables without delay for reasons of safety. Connections between cables in the form of screw terminals covered by adhesive tape should also be replaced by approved terminals.
Flat cables of type NYIF/NYIFY, or NYM cables buried in the plaster, or a conduit installation can be found in dry rooms (including bathrooms) in housing. Individual PVC single-core non-sheathed cable of type H07 V-U (formerly NYA) may be laid loose in conduits or trunking. Flat cables must be laid completely within the plaster, but may not be cast into concrete. Plastic-sheathed cables of type NYM must be used for components consisting primarily of combustible materials; flat cables are not permitted (Fig. B 3.47). According to VDI Directive 3817, flat cables of type NYIF and NYIFY may not be used in buildings protected by conservation orders. Damp-proof cables, sockets, junction boxes and switches must be used in wet rooms, although bathrooms and kitchens in residential buildings are not classed as wet rooms.

Building services in housing	1890–1920	1920–1930	1930–1940	1950–1960	1960–1970	1970–1980
Gas-fired instantaneous water heater				o	•	•
Electric instantaneous water heater					o	•
Electrical installation						
Small cable across-sections	•	•	•	•		
Surface-mounted cables	•	•				
Concealed cables		o	•	•	•	•
Surface-mounted junction boxes/switches	•	•				
Concealed junction boxes/switches			•	•	•	•
Central screw-in fuses	•	•	•	•	o	
Circuit-breakers					•	•
Consumer units					o	•

• = mainly encountered
o = also encountered

B 3.45

Room		1	2
Bedroom, living room	≤ 12 m²	6	2
	12–20 m²	8	2
	> 20 m²	11	3
Kitchen		10	3
Kitchenette		7	2
Bathroom		4	3
WC		2	1
Utility room		8	2
Corridor/hall	length ≤ 3 m	2	2
	> 3 m	3	2
Patio/terrace	length ≤ 3 m	1	1
	> 3 m	2	2
Storage room		2	1
Workshop		6	2
Basement/attic belonging to dwelling		2	1

1 Earthed power socket
2 Lighting outlet

B 3.46

Method of laying	Cable type			
	NYA¹	NYIF	NYM	NYY
behind plaster	–	•	•	•
in plaster	–	•	•	•
on plaster	–	•	•	•
in combustible voids	–	•	•	•
in concrete	–	–	–²	•
in conduits behind plaster	•	–	•	•
in conduits in plaster	•	–	•	•
in conduits on plaster	•	–	•	•
in conduits in concrete	•	–	•	•
in trunking on plaster	•³	–	•	•
in trunking below floor	–	–	•	•

– = no   • = yes
1 New designation H07V-U or H07V-K
2 When concrete is vibrated or tamped; permitted in chases or below plaster
3 Only trunking that requires tools for access

B 3.47

Installations

Connections between cables should be placed in junction boxes, and switches, power sockets and permanent connections should be housed in appropriate boxes. Existing switches can generally continue to be used.
Where two-core cables are replaced by three-core cables, power sockets without an earthing contact must be replaced by earthed power sockets. All existing earthed power sockets must be wired correctly. Installations in a room that has lost its insulating property, e.g. through the subsequent installation of central heating (earthing), must be carried out according to the current edition of DIN VDE 0100 and a suitable earthing contact must be provided if this does not exist already.

Earthing

TN-C-S earthing (protective multiple earthing, PME) was not prescribed for kitchens and bathrooms in the pre-1990 building stock of former East Germany. Proper protective earthing in kitchens and bathrooms was common practice in former West Germany from about 1960 onwards and prescribed for cables after 1973. Prior to that, TN-C earthing was used, i.e. the directly earthed conductor was connected via the earthing contact to the neutral conductor and thus took on the functions of the earthing and neutral conductors. This meant that all cables required only two cores, which is extremely dangerous if the directly earthed conductor fails. Installations in other areas could still be laid as two-core cables with TN-C earthing even after 1984. Installations employing this earthing principle in kitchen and bathroom floors in the building stock must be permanently disconnected from the electricity supply for safety reasons and replaced by three-core cables with TN-C-S earthing laid in, for example, conduits at the base of the walls.

Equipotential bonding

To protect against different potentials, which can build up between different conductive systems, an equipotential bonding installation is required near the intake unit. The protective earth conductor of the electrical installation, the earthing wires from antennas and telephone systems plus all metallic systems (e.g. gas and water pipes) must be connected via an equipotential bonding conductor to an appropriately earthed equipotential bonding rail according to DIN EN 62305 (see below). During refurbishment work a check should be carried out to ensure that all equipotential bonding connections are in place and functioning properly. If there are any signs of corrosion, the contact resistances of the screw terminals should be checked. Since 2002 local equipotential bonding for a bath has no longer been necessary (see DIN VDE 0100), but this is nevertheless still recommended. It should be implemented only when an RCD is installed at the same time because in the event of an electrical fault in conjunction with functioning equipotential bonding, higher shock currents can flow than is the case without an earthing connection.

Lightning protection

A functioning lightning protection installation is protected by the toleration of the building stock notion. Where the authorities make no stipulations, the installation of a lightning protection system is left to the discretion of the building owner. However, lightning protection installations may be required by the Federal State Building Regulations or the building's insurers. Such systems should certainly be installed – and checked for completeness and proper functioning – in tall buildings and those with a high fire risk, also buildings with soft roof coverings. In the case of a change of use or a conversion, a lightning protection installation may become necessary and a decision has to be made as to which protection class applies.
We generally make a distinction between internal and external lightning protection. The latter essentially consists of an air termination network, down conductors and an earth electrode. Depending on the risks involved, the lightning protection can be categorised into protection classes which prescribe different sizes for lightning protection zones.

Lightning protection zones

Different methods can be used to determine the protection zones. The most common method is the grid method to EN V 61024 in which the air terminations are arranged like a grid on the roof of the building. The grid size depends on the lightning protection class (Fig. B 3.48). Components that project more than 300 mm beyond the grid, e.g. chimneys, must be provided with their own air termination(s). Air terminations should be routed as close to the perimeter of the building as possible and their ends should be bent vertically upwards at least 300 mm. There should be a clearance of at least 500 mm between down conductors and openings in the building.

Down conductors

Galvanised steel wire, copper or aluminium may be used as conductors (Fig. B 3.49). The maximum distance between conductors depends on the lightning protection class and ranges from 10 to 25 m. Constructions such as steel stanchions or escape ladders can be used as conductors in the course of refurbishment measures, provided they are continuous and will remain electrically conductive permanently. Metallic installations such as water pipes less than 500 mm from the lightning protection system should be avoided, or removed, above the equipotential bonding installation. If this is not possible, the installation must be connected to the lightning conductor.

Earth electrode
New structures are generally provided with an earthing connection in the foundations. Where an existing building has such an earthing connection, the rest of the earthing system may be connected to this provided it exhibits the appropriate maximum resistance and has not become corroded.
In refurbishment projects it is mostly necessary to install a ring or individual earth electrode. A ring earth electrode in the form of a steel cable in lead sheathing can be used around a freestanding building; it should be laid at a distance of 1 m from the outside edge of the foundation. If the subsequent installation of a ring earth electrode is not feasible, individual earth electrodes in the form of rods or strips may be employed.

Internal lightning protection
The internal lightning protection consists of the equipotential bonding and the overvoltage protection installations. Equipotential bonding is provided in the form of a combined equipotential bonding rail that serves the electrical low-voltage system and the lightning protection. If there are any signs of corrosion, resistance measurements should be carried out. The equipotential bonding must be in the form of a connection between all the earthing terminals, the main protective conductor of the electrical installation, the earthing to antennas and telephone systems and all metallic installations (e.g. gas and water pipes, baths, steel staircases) and the equipotential bonding rail. In existing buildings a check should be carried out to establish whether there is a continuous bond between all installations. In order to achieve this subsequently, it is possible to use continuous electrically conductive pipes (but not gas pipes!) as connecting elements. The equipotential bonding installation should not be positioned above the level of the surrounding ground and is generally installed alongside the other incoming services.
Additional overvoltage protection safeguards sensitive electronic equipment against direct or indirect lightning strikes. Such additional protection can be installed subsequently, either centrally in the building installation or decentralised to protect individual appliances.

Prefabricated supply and disposal systems
Standardised, prefabricated installation components, manifolds and elements are characterised by quicker on-site installation times, which is especially advantageous when refurbishing occupied buildings. Customised prefabricated complete systems are generally only economically viable when a large number of identical systems is required.

False wall installations
Systems with frames to which all the installation elements can be fixed are ideal for refurbishment purposes. Once installed and all pipes, cables, etc. have been fitted, the frames are clad with gypsum-based boards or infilled with masonry. A false wall requires a depth of about 150 mm.

Installation manifolds
Installation manifolds consist of pipework designed to be self-supporting and stable in itself. Depending on requirements, a manifold can comprise water and waste-water pipes, heating pipes, ventilation ducts and possibly also electrical installations. The manifold is installed in the building as a complete prefabricated unit and the other elements are then connected to it. Lugs and brackets enable the installation manifold to be clad with suitable materials in situ.

Plumbing units
If the entire sanitary installation is to be replaced in the course of refurbishment, room-high plumbing units can be employed. These consist of self-supporting framed constructions that include the entire supply and disposal installations and fixings for attaching sanitary fittings. They are erected in front of an existing wall, or actually form a dividing wall themselves, and are subsequently clad in situ.

Prefabricated bathrooms
The individual components of a prefabricated bathroom consist mainly of lightweight concrete, glass fibre-reinforced plastics or sandwich panels. As the components are assembled on site, the maximum transport dimensions within the building must be considered in the case of a refurbishment project (Fig. B 3.50).

Sanitary units
Where complete bathrooms are to be prefabricated, compact and extension systems are worth considering. Compact bathrooms are factory-prefabricated bathroom units that are subsequently built into the building on site; however, this type is rarely used in refurbishment work (Fig. B 3.51). Factory-prefabricated extension or tower systems that are built onto the outside of the building facade are suitable for refurbishment projects but do constitute a considerable change to the appearance of the facade.

Notes:

[1] Energy Conservation Act 2007, cl. 14
[2] ibid.

Lightning protection class	Effectiveness of lightning protection	Grid size	Radius of rolling sphere
SK I	98%	5 × 5 m	20 m
SK II	95%	10 × 10 m	30 m
SK III	90%	15 × 15 m	45 m
SK IV	80%	20 × 20 m	60 m

B 3.48

	Galvanised steel	Aluminium	Copper
round	Ø 8 mm	Ø 10 mm	Ø 8 mm
flat	20 × 2.5 mm	20 × 4 mm	20 × 2.5 mm

B 3.49

B 3.45 Building services depending on year of construction (housing)
B 3.46 Number of power sockets and lighting outlets, electrical fittings level 2 to RAL-RG 678 (levels 1–3; DIN 18015 corresponds to level 1)
B 3.47 Different methods of laying cables (selection)
B 3.48 Lightning protection classes to EN V 61024-1
B 3.49 Materials for air terminations and down conductors
B 3.50 The parts of a prefabricated bathroom
B 3.51 Sanitary unit in composite construction

B 3.50

B 3.51

Conservation

Rainer Fisch

We understand conservation to be all those measures required for the investigation, protection and upkeep of natural landmarks, archaeological sites, art treasures, historic buildings and even movable items (e.g. paintings, books, vehicles, trains). This chapter, however, deals exclusively with historic buildings and conservation areas. In order to be able to understand better the current definition of the heritage concept and the principles and working methods of conservation, it is necessary to trace the historical evolution of this subject. Conservation is principally the task of demonstrating and preserving cultural identities. The interpretation of that has kindled a discussion that has been ongoing for centuries and shows no sign of abating.

Historical development since the dawn of the modern age
The roots of today's European notion of conservation stretch back to the Renaissance. This does not mean that prior to that time no consideration at all was given to the building cultures of earlier periods. However, prior to that time the motivation to preserve the buildings of the past did not stem from an awareness of history: the continuity of a place or the reverence shown to a benefactor, e.g. in the case of religious buildings, led to a respect that prevented certain structures from being demolished. Pragmatic considerations such as the good quality of the building fabric or the valuable artistic design also played a decisive role. This also explains the thoughtless remodelling and adaptation of old structures to suit new circumstances, the demands of new users. It was not the preservation of a contemporary document that was the principal goal at that time, but rather the retention of the memory or the reuse of structures that had been erected using enormous material and human resources. In Trier, for example, after the victory over the Romans at the end of the 5th century, many buildings were converted: from the 11th century until 1795, the Porta Nigra served as a collegiate church, a monastery was established in the Roman grain stores, and the Aula Palatina, today called the Constantine Basilica, was reused as a place of refuge for the local inhabitants and later converted into an electoral residence for the archbishops of Trier (Fig. B 4.2).

It was not until the Renaissance that ancient buildings and their parts were first regarded as the cultural heritage of past, worthy epochs. But there was a lack of general interest and it was mainly the popes and a small group of intellectuals who carried out archaeological investigations. These were limited exclusively to ancient times but were devoted to maintaining the ancient heritage permanently.

First decrees for the protection of historic buildings (17th to 18th C.)
Wide public interest in the productive efforts of bygone ages first emerged during the Enlightenment. Crucial for this was certainly a growing interest in history and the simultaneous recognition that not only writings but also coins, tombstones, monuments and buildings could serve as historical sources. It was in 1796 that Gottfried Herder (1744–1803) suggested no longer considering only political events and wars as the focus of historical research. He pleaded for a holistic assessment with the aim of understanding the thoughts and actions of the people of earlier times.
The first legislation for the protection of heritage – "Act Concerning the Monuments and Antiquities of our Nation" of Friedrich II, Landgrave of Hesse-Kassel (1779) and the "Sovereign Announcement" of Margrave Alexander von Bayreuth (1780) – appeared roughly at the same time as Herder's *Letters for the Advancement of Humanity*. But in both texts the goal is not the preservation of buildings as such, but merely the safeguarding of inscriptions, coats of arms and boundary stones.
It is none other than Johann Wolfgang von Goethe (1749–1832) who can be regarded as the pioneer of the modern heritage concept. His euphoric essay "German Architecture" appeared in 1773. In that he heaps praise on Erwin von Steinbach and admires his work, Strasbourg Cathedral, as the most glorious historic monument. Goethe describes the building as the witness to a spirit and an authentic act and not, as hitherto, merely as the source of history for en epoch. He therefore places the individual work of an artist at the centre of attention. But Goethe's essay initially had no significance for the treatment of historical struc-

B 4.1 Roman Room, New Museum, Berlin (D), 2009,
David Chipperfield Architects
B 4.2 Constantine Basilica, Trier, after a drawing by
Alexander Wiltheim, c. 1616
B 4.3 West facade of the Marienburg, drawing by
Friedrich Frick after Friedrich Gilly, 1799
B 4.4 Festivities surrounding the laying of the foundation
stone for the extension to Cologne Cathedral,
4 September 1842, lithograph after Georg Rudolf
Daniel Osterwald

tures. Rather, it was an early, small step that pointed the way towards our current understanding of heritage.

The national heritage (late 18th to mid-19th C.)
In the Romantic period, following the turmoil of the French Revolution and the associated decline in values, the spirit of the Middle Ages came to the fore as an expression of a natural unity between art and piety. The general opinion was that virtue, morals and faith could be regained by emulating the examples of the Middle Ages and its Gothic architecture. As the works of the Middle Ages were also seen as reproducible, the completion of famous structures of the Middle Ages was regarded as consequent. The goal became the continuation of unfinished places of worship such as the cathedrals at Cologne and Ulm, the restoration of the partially destroyed Speyer Cathedral and the extension of well-known fortifications such as Wartburg Castle at Eisenach.

These hectic building activities involving historic buildings can also be explained by the growing national awareness. The buildings of the past, particularly those from the Gothic period, were seen as typically German and served to distinguish Germany from its European neighbours. The national heritage was born: a document and expressive witness to a distinct national identity and, as such, worthy of preservation. Gothic became the German national style. Paradoxically, the French regarded Gothic as most definitely French, the English as particularly English!

In 1794 Chief Building Surveyor David Gilly (1748–1808) surveyed the Marienburg Castle in West Prussia (now Malbork, Poland), formerly the seat of the Teutonic Order. His son Friedrich (1772–1800), who was accompanying him, took the opportunity to provide idealised drawings, which he exhibited at the Berlin Academy of Arts in 1795 (Fig. B 4.3). The people of Berlin were enthralled and perceived the forgotten fortress as a genuine German construction. In 1804 Friedrich Wilhelm III, King of Prussia, bowed to public pressure and prohibited the planned demolition. After the Napoleonic Wars, the systematic reconstruction of the first German national monument began, supported by a large proportion of the population.

However, the half-finished, great Gothic cathedral alongside the "German Rhine" was soon to become the most important national monument. Its completion would be an expression of the newly found unity and freedom following Napoleon's capitulation. After the Rhineland was succeeded to Prussia in 1815, the Protestant Prussian royal family realised that completion of the cathedral represented an opportunity to win popularity in the Catholic Rhineland. Cologne Cathedral became the German national monument per se. In his speech on the occasion of the laying of the foundation stone in 1842, King Friedrich Wilhelm IV of Prussia declared: "Germany has built her, and so with God's mercy let her be the gateway to a new, great and good age!" [1] (Fig. B 4.4).

The establishment of conservation (19th C.)
Karl Friedrich Schinkel (1781–1841), a student of Friedrich Gilly, studied the architecture of the Middle Ages in depth and supplied designs for the restoration of the Marienburg. In 1810 he became a civil servant in the "Higher Building Deputation", which had been founded in 1770 as the "Higher Building Department" and in 1804 had been changed into an authority with an advisory remit only. Being responsible for the aesthetic aspects of public buildings, he was able to travel throughout Prussia. Countless churches had been blown up, demolished or ravaged during the Napoleonic Wars. The consequences of the "Final Report of the Imperial Deputation" of 1803 were, however, more serious. The abolition of almost all ecclesiastical princedoms, abbeys and monasteries and the confiscation of church property led to an unprecedented wave of destruction. Schinkel was appalled at the condition of historical buildings, and in 1815 presented a memorandum on conservation to King Friedrich Wilhelm III in which he complained about the disorderly assignment of responsibilities and called for separate authorities that would be "entrusted with the welfare of these objects" [2]. According to Schinkel the staff of these protective authorities would be drawn from local communities, from various social classes. Their primary duty would be "to compile lists of everything they find in their districts and to provide reports on the conditions of those objects and the ways in which they could be preserved" [3]. Schinkel also proposed that, wherever possible, the heritage assets should be left where they are found, and not preserved in museums in the capital because changing their location would cause them to lose a great part of their significance.

Although Schinkel's proposals were not implemented during his lifetime, they did not remain completely ineffective. In that same year, King Friedrich Wilhelm III decreed that the Higher Building Deputation be consulted in the case of changes to public or historic buildings. What this meant in practice that was that Schinkel was informed about all building measures. He dedicated himself intensely to the retention and upkeep of historic buildings in Prussia's territories and also became a proponent of the buildings of the Baroque and Renaissance periods, even though he did not feel they were particularly worthy of merit.

Two years after Schinkel's death, his student Ferdinand von Quast (1807–1877) was appointed the first "Conservator of Cultural Heritage in Prussia" in 1843 by "supreme order of the Cabinet". In the Kingdom of Bavaria there had already been an "Inspector General for the Cultural Heritage of the Middle Ages" since 1835; King Ludwig I of Bavaria had been following the example of France in this matter, where an "Inspection Générale des Monuments historique" had been set up as early as 1830. However, the first Inspector General in Bavaria, Sulpiz Boisserée (1782–1854), had to resign from his office for health reasons after only a year and his successor, Friedrich von Gärtner (1792–1847), understood his role as that of a design architect rather than a conservator. After 1847 the post remained vacant.

Ferdinand von Quast can therefore quite rightly claim to be the first professional conservator in Germany who really practised his profession (Fig. B 4.5). His title was "Building Surveyor" and he was directly responsible to the Minister of Cultural Affairs. His tasks were the compiling of an inventory, the preparation of reports on the restoration of historic buildings and maintaining contact with societies concerned with

B 4.2

B 4.3

B 4.4

73

B 4.5   The Ferdinand von Quast Medal has been awarded
in Berlin every year since 1987 in remembrance of
the first Prussian building conservator.
B 4.6   Current edition of the "Manual of German Cultural
Heritage"
B 4.7   Heidelberg Palace, Ottheinrich Building, destroyed
in 1689
B 4.8   Carl Schäfer's proposal for the reconstruction of
the Ottheinrich Building, 1900
B 4.9   Protective structure for the "Golden Portal" of the
cathedral in the style of the art nouveau movement,
Freiberg (Saxony) (D), 1903, Schilling & Graebner,
drawing by Bruno Schmitz, competition entry for
the extension to the cathedral in Freiberg (Saxony)

B 4.5

history and antiquities. Building measures on
cultural heritage assets had to be approved by
the Ministry of Cultural Affairs before work
could commence – unless they were inviolable
private property. Where heritage was threatened
by building measures, the "Conservator of Cultural Heritage" had the right to halt the building
works. Following the example of Prussia, although
not with the same power of authority and personnel resources, the Grand Duchy of Baden
and the Kingdom of Württemberg set up similar
departments in 1853 and 1858 respectively.
The registration of all historic buildings and
cultural heritage had already begun during
Schinkel's time, although the lists were not systematic and not uniform. Ferdinand von Quast,
too, neglected to compile a proper list even
though an inventory is indispensable for the
retention and upkeep of cultural heritage. It
was for this reason that Ferdinand von Quast
was again appointed to carry out a survey; the
project failed in the end, however, because of
a lack of responses.
Nevertheless, the first volume of a heritage
assets inventory was published in 1870; shortly
before this, in 1867, a directory of heritage
assets in the district of Kassel had been submitted in Berlin. Thereupon, the Ministry of
Cultural Affairs appointed the "Society for the
History and Regional Studies of Hesse" to draw
up an inventory for the region.
But the first – and to this day only – directory of
heritage assets for the whole of Germany did
not appear until 1905–1912, under the title of
Handbuch der deutschen Kunstdenkmäler
(Manual of German Cultural Heritage). Affec-
tionately known as "the Dehio" after its first
compiler, the art historian Georg Dehio (1850–
1932), it has been updated continuously since
then (Fig. B 4.6). It contains not only lists of all
heritage assets, but also an critical selection. In
the preface to the first volume, Dehio describes
his objectives as the consistent treatment of the
entire range of German art and a brief, specific
description of the heritage assets. In addition,
he states that this compilation should serve as
a reference work for deskbound studies and as
a guide book, and should be available at a

price anyone can afford.
And indeed, it found favour with a wide public.
Since the start of the 19th century, groups
devoted to the study and upkeep of local history
and cultural assets had been forming in the
German-speaking countries. It was the activities
of these mainly voluntary groups, financed by
more prosperous citizens, that were responsible
for ensuring that public appreciation of heritage
grew over the following years. Societies dedicated to history and antiquities were founded,
which in 1852 merged with the "Historic Com-
missions" and the regional history institutes and
study groups to form the "Umbrella Organisation
for the German History and Antiquities Societies"
in order to emphasize the unity of German history in its diversity and stimulate research into
regional and local history.

*Changes to the interpretation of heritage (late
19th to early 20th C.)*
People gradually learned to appreciate the
architecture styles that had emerged after the
Middle Ages, too. But, as in the past, purity of
style was still the goal of restoration. Later additions were replaced by styles that matched the
original, unfinished structures were completed.
Conservators – and it was mostly architects
that were at work here – understood restoration
to mean supplementing the building first and
foremost in the style of the respective period.
The French architect and art theorist Eugéne
Emmanuel Viollet-le-Duc (1814–1879) took on
the function of a role model in this field. He
undertook detailed investigations and also
made use of historical sources and literature in
order to comprehend the constructions, techniques and ornamental forms of the Middle
Ages. The results of his research were published in his 10-volume work *Dictionnaire raisonné
de l'architecture française du XIe au XVIe siècle*.
He and many contemporary architects thus
achieved a perfection in their designs and constructions that made it difficult to distinguish
between historic and new components at first
glance. At the close of the 19th century this led
to fierce disputes about the right way to handle
historic buildings – a debate that had raged in
England 50 years previously. The dispute had
been triggered by the Ottheinrich Building at

Heidelberg Palace: destroyed by soldiers in
1689 and again in 1693 and, following make-
shift repairs, ravaged by fire in 1764, Heidelberg Palace was regarded as a symbol for the
ignominious defeat by France (Figs. B 4.7 and
4.8). Soon after the triumphal war of 1870/71,
plans were drawn up for the reconstruction of
the palace. The architect Carl Schäfer (1844–
1908) initially devoted his time to the Friedrich
Building and finished restoring this in 1903,
which meant that he replaced about one-third
of all the facade components and rebuilt the
missing top storeys according to his own interpretation.
In 1901 Georg Dehio, a professor at the University of Strasbourg, protested against this approach with his essay "What shall become of
Heidelberg Palace?". He demanded rigorous
retention of the existing ruins and rejected
Schäfer's reconstruction plans, using the French
expression "vandalisme restaurateur" to describe
them. "We would lose the genuine and gain the
imitation; lose what has become historical and
gain the timeless arbitrariness" [4]. In his opinion conservation had overtaken the reconstructions of the 19th century and "had now reached
the principle that it could never depart from
again: preserve and only preserve! And only
supplement when preservation has become
materially impossible; re-creating the lost only
under very specific, limited circumstances" [5].
The fact that the art historian Dehio finally triumphed
as an advocate for protecting the building fabric and using methods committed to authenticity can certainly be attributed to the circum-
stance that the acceptance of historicism was
steadily declining. An intense exchange regarding the tasks and aims of conservation
began. The first issue of the journal *Die Denkmalpflege*, which is still the mouthpiece of the
German Association of Conservators, was published in 1899. And just one year later, the first
"Conference on Conservation" took place.
Another protagonist of the new definition of the
conservation task, besides Dehio, was the
Austrian Alois Riegl (1858–1905), from 1897
onwards professor of art history at the University
of Vienna. Although Dehio and Riegl had different ideas about what constituted the historical
value of a building, their constructional and

B 4.6

practical rigorousness led to a new way of handling the historic building stock. No longer in the sense of an imitative epoch, but rather consciously detached from the original substance, which resulted in, for example, the protective structure to the "Golden Portal" of the cathedral in Freiberg in Saxony in the art nouveau style (Fig. B 4.9).

At the same time, the realisation that structure and surroundings form a coherent whole led to a broadening of the conservation concept. It was in 1889 that Camillo Sitte (1843–1903), a colleague of Riegl in Vienna, published a book with the title *City Planning According to Artistic Principles*, which turned out to be a ground-breaking publication both for 20th century urban planning and for conservation. Henceforth, it was no longer simply individual heritage assets that were considered worthy of preservation, but also urban locations. It was realised that the standard practice up until that time, i.e. robbing the cathedral of the Middle Ages of its surrounding built environment to liberate the preserved structure, no longer conformed to the original concept.

Movements to protect the local environment, which had emerged as a consequence of industrialisation and its sweeping social changes towards the end of the 19th century, expanded the conservation concept even further. The highly popular trend was based on traditional values, opposed urbanisation and technification, and favoured nature and folk art. Handed-down customs and traditions, landscapes, flora and fauna, geological features, simple monuments to local history, farmhouses and urban houses all seemed worthy of preservation.

Conservation as a state responsibility (20th C.)
The growing importance of conservation was reflected in the constitution of the Weimar Republic of 1919. Conservation is stipulated as an objective of the state in article 150. The separation between state and church, however, led to an ambiguous situation with respect to religious heritage assets.

The seizure of power by the National Socialists initially had little effect on the treatment of heritage, apart from isolated cases like the conversion of Braunschweig Cathedral and the collegiate church in Quedlinburg into "shrines" to National Socialism. In the opinion of Adolf Hitler, only the cathedrals, palaces and town halls of the Middle Ages were worthy of preservation. Without hesitation, entire city districts in Berlin dating from the founding years were demolished to make way for "Germania". The clearances of timber-framed houses that had started in the 1920s proceeded apace. Apart from that, the 19th-century additions to historic buildings, described as "disfigurements", were also removed wholesale.

The devastation of World War 2 annihilated not only countless individual heritage assets, but also entire historic districts, e.g. in Cologne, Lübeck, Dresden and Trier, which were lost forever. After the abuses of the National Socialists, it was no longer opportune to return to Germany's own history; people wanted to look to the future. So the years of reconstruction were used to modernise the towns and cities ready for the future. Many damaged historic buildings were demolished, especially if they were not seen as especially valuable. The growing desire for a higher standard of living led to a migration from the historic centres to the suburbs. Whole streets were sacrificed in the attempt to satisfy demands for "car-friendly towns and cities". At the same time, conservation did not distance itself from its attitude and accepted its share of responsibility for the measures in the Third Reich. Historicism remained a hated concept. These days we therefore speak of a second wave of destruction in which allegedly more historical building fabric was lost than was destroyed by the bombs and shells of World War 2 (Figs. B 4.10a and 4.10b).

In 1964 international specialists adopted a set of theses known as the "Venice Charter", which had a decisive influence on the definition of conservation and its practical realisation. This pioneering guideline was, however, not embraced by the public at first. It was not until 1970 that the general criticism of the negative effects of modern urban planning, its consequences for nature and the built environment led to a protest movement from which conservation and other factors would draw sustenance. Starting with bodies of students, public cam-

B 4.7

B 4.8

B 4.9

B 4.10   City centre, Dresden
             a Photograph taken after the air raid of
                13/14 February 1945, view from tower of city hall
             b Photograph taken today from the same position
B 4.11   A volume from the "Heritage Topography" series
B 4.12   Conservation area: Hufeisen Estate, Berlin (D),
             1933, Bruno Taut and Martin Wagner
B 4.13   Völklingen Ironworks, Saarland, an example of a
             complex protected by a conservation order but
             difficult to preserve and use

a

b   B 4.10

paigns emerged to oppose the demolition of historic buildings. The long since overdue recognition of historicism and urban conservation gradually became established. Between 1971 and 1980, all the federal states of former West Germany passed heritage protection legislation. The demolition of the fully intact late-Gothic university church in Leipzig in 1968 led to criticism in the former GDR. In the end, the importance of the historical built environment for the population was acknowledged even here. The "Act for the Preservation of Heritage in the GDR" came into force in 1975.

The year 1975 was also declared the "European Architectural Heritage Year" by the Council of Europe. Thereupon, the German Association of Conservators decided to compile a uniform inventory of all heritage assets within 10 years. This appeared in the form of the so-called Heritage Topographies. However, the original objective of a complete list has still not been accomplished. And the volumes published so far also differ in terms of layout and content; all they have in common is the generous use of

photographs. Even the uniform black cover originally adopted has not been used by all federal states (Fig. B 4.11).

The unification of former East and West Germany has presented conservation in Germany with major challenges. Although, on the one hand, the lack of building maintenance in the former East Germany over many decades has protected historic buildings against detrimental modernisation, on the other hand, many buildings are in acute danger. Rural and religious buildings are especially at risk. The federal states of the former East Germany adopted heritage protection legislation between 1991 and 1995. An attempt was made to save the historical heritage with immediate measures and a great injection of funds. The Deutsche Stiftung Denkmalschutz (German Foundation for Monument Protection), founded in 1985, became especially active in the former East Germany. Besides the conservation of heritage assets at risk, the task of this privately funded organisation is to make people aware of the objectives of conservation. For example, based on a Council of Europe initiative, every year on the second Sunday in September the foundation organises "Heritage Open Day" in Germany, on which approx. 4.5 million visitors reflect the population's wide acceptance and interest [6].

The denationalisation of conservation (21st C.)
Despite the widespread public awareness of the need for conservation, the trend among the politicians is to curtail state involvement in conservation or to abandon it completely. Once again, it is the old question: How do we decide whether a building is worthy of preservation? An interim climax in the discussion surrounding the denationalisation of conservation can be found in a polemic pamphlet by the publicist Dieter Hoffmann-Axthelm, published in 2000 on behalf of Antje Vollmer, a member of Bündnis 90/Die Grünen (the German Green Party). In his remarks he comes to the following conclusion: "If no one is bothered, why should we save it?" [7] Quite obviously, heritage is no longer seen as a representative of its time. According to Ms. Vollmer, "by their very nature, historic and cultural identities [must be] changeable and rectifiable" [8]. This is a completely new definition of the conservation concept which admittedly no longer needs a state-run institution but in the final consequence also no further scientific research either. Industrial facilities, the structures of National Socialism, the ex-GDR and the Modern Movement are trenchantly considered by Mr. Hoffmann-Axthelm to be unworthy of preservation because they are not beautiful. He calls for the abolition of conservation by the state and local authorities in favour of private initiatives. His remarks sparked off a broad debate about conservation which filled the arts pages of German newspapers for many weeks. The Bündnis 90/Die Grünen parliamentary faction arranged for a consultation in the Bundestag in March 2000. However, through the political influence of lobby groups and persons in the public limelight it was possible to avert the idea of the denationalisation of conservation. Nevertheless, like in all public institutions, the number of personnel and the funds available to conservation bodies and authorities has been and is still being successively reduced. At the same time, the conservation concept is expanding on the international stage. In the opinion of international lobbies it is no longer solely the historical fabric that is worth saving, but also intangible cultural assets. When we hear that we undoubtedly initially think of oral traditions such as myths and tales, the perform-

B 4.11

B 4.12

ing arts such as theatre and dance, and social practices such as customs and festivals. But interpreting the definition of heritage in this way in the end leads to consequences for the conservation of buildings. Specifically, it results in other factors that have to be considered in addition to the historic building stock, e.g. the memories of the people. This development is also interesting in the light of the current debate surrounding reconstruction.

The prerequisite for such a chain of reasoning, however, is that there must be such a genuine memory. This is certainly always the case immediately after the destruction of a popular historic building as a result of a natural disaster or an armed conflict. But the fact that a building can continue to exist intangibly, merely in people's imaginations, over a long time was proved by, for example, the vigorous – and finally successful – public demand for the rebuilding of the Frauenkirche in Dresden. And even though such public demand is alleged again and again by those in favour of the rebuilding of the Berlin Stadtschloss, the public is not moved in the same way.

The modern understanding of conservation

The conservation concept is not static. It is changing and will always be re-appraised. Different nations have different views as to what constitutes heritage. On the one hand, this is due to different historical and cultural developments, on the other, certainly also the different political systems. For instance, in Japan besides buildings that embody a high historic or artistic value for the country, intangible cultural assets, e.g. handicrafts, are also protected by the state. This also means that persons with those particular skills can receive financial support from the state [9]. All too often our European understanding of the conservation concept is regarded as internationally applicable. In October 2003 the UNESCO General Conference adopted the "Convention for the Safeguarding of the Intangible Cultural Heritage". In the Federal Republic of Germany the definition of a building of historic interest is laid down in the heritage protection legislation of the individual federal states.

The features of a heritage asset
"A building of historic importance is a constructed facility or part thereof whose preservation because of historical, artistic, scientific or urban significance is in the public interest. A building of historic importance includes its fittings and furnishings in so far as they contribute to the historic value of the structure." [10]
Even though the individual heritage protection acts of the German federal states are formulated differently, the assessment criteria for a building of historic importance are basically identical throughout the legislation. Besides the four reasons mentioned in the "Act for the Protection of Heritage in Berlin" – historical, artistic, scientific, urban –, some heritage protection legislation also includes technical or folkloric reasons. The protection of historic structures must be decided upon exclusively according to these criteria. According to the definition, buildings are worthy of preservation when they bear witness to the past and are of interest to the general public. Our current aesthetic sense is just as irrelevant as the question regarding the retention and usage options. Conservation has to deal with those problems; heritage protection only assesses whether or not a building satisfies the aforementioned criteria (Fig. B 4.13).

Conservation areas
A conservation area is, for example, a group of buildings, a city district, a street, the overall appearance of a place, farms, but also industrial production plants that seen as a complete built facility (frequently in conjunction with their natural surroundings) attest to certain historical, urban or technical developments. The area could be one that has grown over time or one entity that was planned and built in one process. The criterion is not that every building within the conservation area must possess heritage features (Fig. B 4.12).

B 4.13

B 4.14

B 4.15

Heritage protection

In the specialist literature the two terms conservation and protection are frequently treated as synonyms. Protection, however, is only one aspect of conservation. It ensures the correct compliance of the sovereign measures of the state for preserving the historico-cultural inheritance, which is guaranteed by laws, procedures and administrative structures.

Statutory provisions and procedures
The Federal Building Code (BauGB) regulates building planning law in Germany. In paragraph 1 "Task, concept and principles of physical planning" it states that the objective of "sustainable urban development ... and socially fair use of the land serving the welfare of the general public" is to be fostered. In order "to secure a humane environment and to safeguard and cultivate the natural resources essential to life ... the issues of building culture, heritage protection and the conservation of exemplary districts, streets and open areas of historical, artistic or urban importance and the constitution of the urban and rural landscape" are to be especially considered [11]. When drawing up land-use and development plans, the specialist heritage authorities must therefore be consulted. They can place restrictions on approvals. Owing to the cultural sovereignty of the federal states in Germany, every state has its own heritage protection legislation. But unlike the Federal State Building Codes, for example, which are based on a Model Building Code, there has never been a "model heritage protection code", and so not only the overriding legislation, but also the associated regulations concerning the procedures for granting conservation orders and the powers of the authorities and organisations involved differ considerably. In principle, we distinguish between the so-called constitutive and informative systems when it comes to granting conservation orders.

In the constitutive system a structure that fulfils the heritage criteria according to the legal definition must be recorded in the list of heritage assets by way of an administrative act. Only after this is legally binding and has been announced does the structure enjoy the protection offered by the respective heritage protection legislation. Prior to that, the owner must be consulted. Conservation areas are excluded from this regulation. The heritage protection legislation of North Rhine-Westphalia, Rhineland Palatinate, Schleswig-Holstein, Bremen and Hamburg employ this procedure. But as it is very time-consuming and costly and every formal error nullifies the validity of the conservation order, there is a risk that the owner will try to circumvent the aims of protection. Therefore, apart from Hamburg, all the above federal states include the possibility of granting a provisional conservation order.

The principle of the informative heritage directory assumes that a building with the corresponding features is per se covered by the provisions of heritage protection legislation without any further sovereign act. The owner's rights and obligations have to be complied with even if he is not informed about the heritage aspects of his building. In this system letters of notification are not regarded as administrative acts. Brandenburg, Berlin, Baden-Württemberg, Bavaria, Hesse, Mecklenburg-Western Pomerania, Lower Saxony, Saarland, Saxony, Saxony-Anhalt and Thuringia make use of this system.

Authorities in Germany
In accordance with the general internal governance of the German federal states, the structure of the heritage protection authorities is built on three levels in most instances. The tasks of the lower heritage protection authorities are carried out by local government. The higher heritage protection authorities are the regional or district chief executives, in Rhineland Palatinate the supervisory and services departments, in Saxony-Anhalt and Thuringia the state administration offices. The supreme heritage protection authority in each case is the ministry responsible. Schleswig-Holstein, however, employs a different system, with the district chief executives and the mayors of the boroughs as the lower heritage protection authorities and the State Conservation Agency as the higher heritage protection authority. Berlin, Brandenburg, Hesse, Mecklenburg-Western Pomerania and Lower Saxony forego the intermediate level of administration. Owing to their size, Saarland, Bremen and Hamburg employ a different administrative structure. In Hamburg it is the Heritage Protection Department of the Cultural Affairs Authority that is responsible for heritage protection matters, in Saarland the State Heritage Department in the Environment Ministry. The "Act for the Upkeep and Protection of Cultural Monuments" of the Free Hanseatic City of Bremen is administered by the State Conservation Agency in Bremen itself and by the municipal authorities in Bremerhaven. The Senator for Cultural Affairs represents the higher heritage protection authority.

The supreme heritage protection authorities are responsible for executing the heritage protection legislation through their subordinate authorities. They provide the functional supervision for the lower level(s) of administration. They draft bills and regulations and are responsible for enacting executive provisions. The higher heritage protection authorities provide the functional supervision for the lower authorities and are therefore responsible for dealing with objections to decisions made by the latter. Where the federal heritage protection legislation does not provide otherwise, the lower heritage protection authorities initially carry out all sovereign measures. They are the local contacts and the approval bodies for changes to historic buildings. In addition to the heritage protection authorities, there are also the State Conservation Agencies, which act as the specialist state authorities for all matters of heritage protection and conservation [12]. The tasks of the specialist heritage authorities are generally specified in the herit-

B 4.14 The designation plaque for a historic monument according to the Hague Convention
B 4.15 The logo of the German Foundation for Monument Protection
B 4.16 Machu Picchu (PE), the Inca city discovered in 1911, today a World Heritage Site

age protection legislation of each individual federal state. The "Act for the Protection of Heritage in Berlin" contains the most comprehensive list of all [13], specifying that the specialist heritage authority – in addition to assisting with the execution and realisation of regulatory duties – is responsible for the following according to the heritage protection legislation:

• The systematic registration of heritage assets and the production of a Heritage Topography and its publication.
• The recording of heritage assets in a directory for information, and the regular updating of the directory.
• The scientific examination of heritage assets and the maintenance of collections relevant to heritage as a contribution to regional history.
• Advising and assisting the owners and proprietors of heritage assets with respect to their care, maintenance and restoration.
• Working towards the consideration of heritage assets in urban developments.
• The publication of newsletters on the upkeep of heritage assets.
• Providing specialist advice and reports on all conservation issues.
• Awarding subsidies for conservation.
• The publication and dissemination of findings relevant to heritage assets.
• Representing the public in matters concerning the protection and conservation of heritage assets.

B 4.16

Some German federal states also include advising the heritage protection authorities, carrying out restoration work (possibly in workshops set up for this purpose) and issuing certificates for tax purposes according to heritage protection legislation among the obligations of the specialist heritage authorities. The State Conservation Agencies frequently divide up their jurisdictions into areas (matching the rural districts and boroughs), each of which is the responsibility of a local conservator. The most senior civil servant in such an authority is the State Conservator.

Voluntary conservators
The participation of voluntary conservators is provided for in the heritage protection legislation of the 16 federal states in order to help and advise the aforementioned authorities. With the exception of Mecklenburg-Western Pomerania and Lower Saxony, the heritage protection legislation allows for the establishment of an Antiquities & Monuments Board, the members of which are officially appointed for a certain period. Furthermore, the legislation usually provides for the participation of voluntary building and artistic heritage conservation officers. Some heritage protection legislation embodies the notion that organisations and persons with legal status that are involved with heritage protection and conservation tasks, e.g. societies concerned with local history, culture, etc., should become involved. Voluntary conservators are always independent and not bound by directives.

Organisations and associations
The sovereignty of the German federal states in cultural matters and, as a result, the 16 different heritage protection acts do not automatically mean that there are 16 different ideas about the right way to handle heritage and 16 different administrative procedures! Like with education policies, it is the task of the "Standing Conference of the Ministers of Education and Cultural Affairs of the Federal States in the Federal Republic of Germany" to formulate a common approach to heritage protection. Moreover, numerous national and international organisations and associations are active in this field and contribute to standardisation through the exchange of information and views.

Vereinigung der Landesdenkmalpfleger in der Bundesrepublik Deutschland (VLD)
The German Association of Conservators, an alliance of the state heritage departments, was formed in 1951 under the umbrella of the aforementioned Standing Conference. The association uses its annual meetings to carry on the "Conference on Conservation" tradition and publishes the journal *Die Denkmalpflege* twice a year. In addition, it is the co-publisher of the *Handbuch der deutschen Kunstdenkmäler*. The VLD advises the Standing Committee at the aforementioned Standing Conference, produces statements on fundamental issues of conservation and ensures functional coordination

on a national level. Since 1990 all the conservators in the federal states of the former East Germany also belong officially to the VLD.

International Council on Monuments and Sites (ICOMOS)
This organisation, responsible to UNESCO, was founded in Warsaw in 1965. It is an international, non-governmental lobby group that campaigns worldwide for the study and preservation of historical cultural assets and advises the World Heritage Committee. ICOMOS promotes an international exchange through colloquia and conferences. National committees exist in more than 120 countries. The "German ICOMOS National Committee" has been constituted as an unincorporated body since 1965. Its tasks include the determination, monitoring and notification of World Heritage Sites in Germany.

Deutsches Nationalkomitee für Denkmalschutz (DNK)
Founded in 1973 as an interdisciplinary forum, it is the objective of the German National Committee for Heritage Protection to promote the protection of heritage assets in all areas of life by way of information policies, influencing legislation, strengthening the commitment of citizens and public dialogue. National and state governments, the German parliament, local umbrella organisations, the Church, trade unions, the media and various cultural organisations are represented on this national committee. The DNK normally awards the "German Prize for Heritage Protection", donated in 1977, annually: the "Karl Friedrich Schinkel Ring" and the "Silver Hemisphere" are bestowed on persons who have contributed in some special way to the preservation of historic buildings. A prize for journalists is also awarded.

Deutsche Stiftung Denkmalschutz (DSD)
Originally intended as an industry-funded foundation, the German Foundation for Monument Protection gradually developed into a privately funded body and now has more than 170 000 private supporters. Founded in 1985, it is now the best-known and most influential private conservation organisation in Germany (Fig. B 4.15). Besides producing numerous specialist publications, it publishes the journal *Monumente* bimonthly. Since 2001 the Dehio office has been incorporated into the DSD, supervising the continued publication of the *Handbuch der deutschen Kunstdenkmäler* [14].

The "Kommunale Denkmalpflege" working group of the Deutscher Städtetag

The German Association of Cities is a municipal umbrella organisation that represents the common interests of the bodies involved in dealings with the German government, the German parliament (Bundestag and Bundesrat) and the European Union. Its primary tasks are participating in the drafting of important bills and providing a forum where its members can exchange their ideas and experiences. The "Municipal Conservation" working group was set up in 1982 under the umbrella of the German Association of Cities. It informs and takes up a position regarding current problems in urban conservation. For example, the "Göttingen Appeal" is the result of a conference on the theme of the "conservation of large-scale retailing" organised jointly with the VLD (see above) in November 2007.

International treaties

Throughout the history of the world, the destructiveness of armed conflicts has always led to a great loss of valuable historic fabric. The devastation of World War 2, which led to the loss of entire historic city centres such as those of Frankfurt and Dresden in Germany, Coventry in England, Rotterdam in the Netherlands and Warsaw in Poland, to name but a few, made this very clear. But even now, cultural heritage is threatened by the effects of war, like the old part of Dubrovnik (UNESCO World Heritage Site) which suffered terribly in the Serbo-Croatian war of 1991/92, or the historic stone bridge over the Neretva in Mostar, which collapsed in 1993 after being badly damaged in the Bosnian Civil War. International treaties are intended to highlight the national responsibility for and importance of cultural assets and prevent their obliteration.

Hague Convention for the Protection of Cultural Property in the Event of Armed Conflict

The second section of the Hague Convention, Laws and Customs of War on Land, adopted in 1899 and amended in 1907, contains a passage requiring that historical monuments should be spared wherever possible during armed conflicts. The effects of the two World Wars led to an international conference in 1954 during which 56 states drew up the "Hague Convention for the Protection of Cultural Property in the Event of Armed Conflict". The treaty came into force on 7 August 1956. It is an internationally valid contract to which more than 100 states have added their signatures to date. Switzerland ratified the convention in 1962, Austria in 1964, and the Federal Republic of Germany in 1967. The ex-GDR signed the convention in 1974.

Worthy of protection in the meaning of the convention is "movable or immovable property of great importance to the cultural heritage of every people, such as monuments of architecture, art or history, whether religious or secular; archaeological sites; groups of buildings which, as a whole, are of historical or artistic interest;

works of art; manuscripts, books and other objects of artistic, historical or archaeological interest; as well as scientific collections and important collections of books or archives or reproductions of the property defined above" [15]. The same applies to "buildings whose main and effective purpose is to preserve or exhibit the movable cultural property defined [above] such as museums, large libraries and depositories of archives, and refuges intended to shelter, in the event of armed conflict, the movable cultural property defined [above, which are] to be known as 'centres containing monuments'". The parties to the contract are obliged to safeguard cultural assets during peacetime as well. Plaques fixed to the protected buildings serve to identify them (Fig. B 4.14). The USA and the UK both signed the treaty in 1945 but have not yet signed the conventions. In the past the USA gave as its reason the impossibility of complying with the conventions in the event of nuclear weapons being used. However, in 1999 the then President, Bill Clinton, recommended that the US Senate ratify the treaty because in his opinion the American military forces would act in accordance with the principles of the Hague Conventions anyway. The British government was of the opinion that the original text of the 1954 convention contained serious weaknesses and ambiguities. These were, however, rectified in the second protocol of 1999, and in 2004 the UK announced that it would sign the treaty and the second protocol. But to date neither the USA nor the UK have ratified the convention.

In addition to the Hague Convention there is the so-called Roerich Pact, an agreement that came into force in 1935. Although it pursues the same objectives, the obligations of the signatory states are considerably more modest. The pact remains valid to this day, but its significance is limited to the Americas.

European Cultural Convention

This treaty, which was signed in Paris by the member states of the Council of Europe on 19 December 1954 and came into force on 5 May 1955, calls in article 1 for each contracting party to "take appropriate measures to safeguard and to encourage the development of its national contribution to the common cultural heritage of Europe". The wording is not very specific and therefore has little practical significance. More than 40 European states have ratified the convention to date.

UNESCO Convention Concerning the Protection of World Cultural and Natural Heritage

At the 1972 General Conference of the United Nations Educational, Scientific and Cultural Organisation, the recognition that parts of our cultural and natural heritage are of international significance and hence must be preserved as part of a world inheritance for the whole of humankind led to the "UNESCO Convention Concerning the Protection of World Cultural and Natural Heritage". Monuments, groups of

buildings and sites of outstanding universal value are regarded as our cultural heritage. These can be included in the "World Heritage List". The 21 members of the World Heritage Committee decide on the applications of the individual signatory states based on their own set of standards.

The World Heritage Committee also decides on how to apply the World Heritage Fund. More than 750 cultural sites have been entered in the World Heritage List so far. Those include, for example, the old city of Sana'a, Canterbury Cathedral, the Convent of St. Gall, the Grand Canyon National Park and the Inca city of Machu Picchu (Fig. B 4.16). Heritage assets on the World Heritage List that require extensive measures for their maintenance and need financial assistance can be added to the "List of World Heritage in Danger" ("red list"). The Dresden Elbe Valley has been on the red list since July 2006 because of the plans to build the so-called Waldschlösschen Bridge.

Convention for the Protection of the Architectural Heritage of Europe

According to this agreement signed in Granada on 3 October 1985 by the member states of the Council of Europe, architectural heritage is defined as monuments, groups of buildings and sites. The latter are "the combined works of man and nature, being areas which are partially built upon". The parties to the contract are obliged to draft legislation to protect the architectural heritage, "to prevent disfigurement, dilapidation or demolition" and wherever possible "to provide financial support ... for maintaining and restoring the architectural heritage on its territory". In addition, they undertake to prepare inventories and documentation, to allow

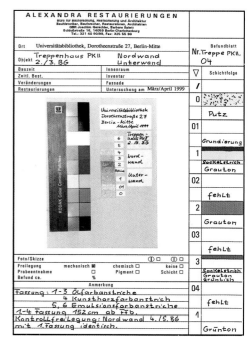

B 4.17

the removal of a protected property only under very strict conditions, "to promote measures for the general enhancement of the environment" in the vicinity of monuments, and to promote and support scientific research and private initiatives. To guarantee these and other requirements, legislation plus supervisory and approval procedures are obligatory. More than 30 European states have signed the convention so far.

Practical building conservation

Where do the works on a historic building differ from other building measures? Considering the definition of the heritage concept, the differences very quickly become obvious. The objective of conservation is to preserve a building as a witness to a past age. Conservation is not about rectifying an aesthetically dissatisfying situation or improving a building's energy balance. An investor, for example, considers a property from the economic viewpoint; he wishes to create as much lettable or saleable space as possible. By contrast, the conservator behaves like a lawyer representing the interests of the public at large, which wishes to retain a remembrance of a bygone age with as little change as possible. Inevitably, a conflict of aims is the result, the solution to which frequently requires compromises on both sides.

Research

Intensive research supplies important findings for the maintenance and hence makes an important contribution to the success of the intervention. Incorrect assumptions can therefore be avoided and costs reduced as a result. Supposed constructional mistakes, damage or illogical constructions often turn out to be delib-

erate decisions taken during planning for some reason that is not immediately obvious. Therefore, research marks the start of any building measures involving a historic structure. The first question is whether or not this really is a heritage asset! The first clues can be found in the heritage topographies and the *Handbuch der deutschen Kunstdenkmäler* (Dehio) mentioned above. It is also possible to consult the lower heritage protection authority (local government). But caution is necessary here: if a building is not declared as a heritage asset, in some federal states it may be the case that it is nevertheless declared to be one (see p. 78).

The building records, which are normally archived by the building authorities, or in the case of older buildings in the town or city archives, provide information about the original plans and later changes to the construction. Further sources of information can often be found in local libraries and archives. Not only drawings, but also old invoices for building work or fire insurance policies shed further light on the building. In the land surveyor's offices, in some regions called land registry offices, it is possible to study the original land register. It is important to collate all information in one document. The finishes schedule is an ideal way of handling the information. Such schedules are being increasingly kept in digital form. Crucial for success is the use of a systematic, consistent standard. The surface finishes in all rooms plus the windows, doors, fixtures and fittings, construction details and building services must be described exactly, recorded by means of photographs or drawings and supplemented by the results of previous researches. A finishes schedule is not static; it is added to in the course of the ongoing

investigations and planning and therefore at the end of the building measures provides a record of all changes and an up-to-date picture of the structure.

A comprehensive photographic record, which should form part of every finishes schedule, specifies the in situ situation. The photographs must be designated according to a standard system and the camera positions marked on the general arrangement drawings. Special details are recorded on a findings and colour chart (Fig. B 4.17).

A detailed survey of the existing structure in the form of on-site measurements is still indispensable even when as-built drawings are available. This is because, firstly, it is often the case that the drawings do not match the in situ situation, and, secondly, there are frequently dimensional differences and deformations, due to building physics problems or structural damage. The individual levels of accuracy and various methods that can be used in the survey will not be explored any further here.

The acquisition of all data relating to the structure in the form of researches, photographs and surveys is only the first step. The architect has to evaluate all this information and initiate appropriate further investigations. These could take the form of, for example, archaeological, dendrochronological [16] or restorative analyses. An assessment of the loadbearing system and any possible deformations is also essential. Concealed components can be revealed these days with the help of active thermography, ultrasound or radar. It may be necessary to carry out additional investigations such as the removal of cores of material for analysis, but such destructive procedures may be carried out only

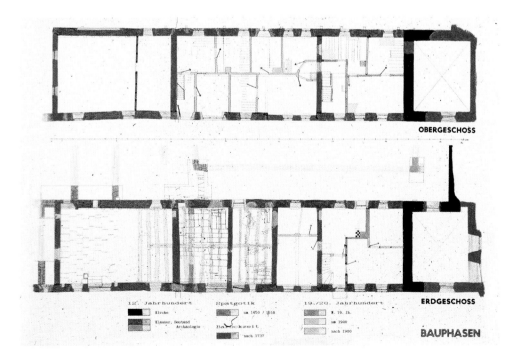

B 4.18

B 4.17 Example of a findings and colour chart showing different wall finishes to the State Library in Berlin
B 4.18 Example of a building phases drawing (bottom: ground floor; top: upper floor) with different colours indicating the differen phases of construction

B 4.19 Glass corridor in the Marienkirche, Berlin (D), 1992, Klaus Block; as the tower room could not function as an entrance lobby owing to the historic painting, a glass corridor was built to protect against temperature and moisture fluctuations.
B 4.20 The former abbey of St. Mary's, Lobbach-Lobenfeld (D), 1997, Hans Stadtler; the new elements stand out clearly from the historic fabric.
B 4.21 New Museum, Berlin (D), 2009, David Chipperfield Architects; the repairs are visible but still match the colouring of the historic structure.
B 4.22 Liebermann House, Pariser Platz, Berlin, 1901
B 4.23 Vacant site at Pariser Platz, Berlin, 1959
B 4.24 Sensitive reconstruction of Liebermann House, Berlin (D), 1997, Josef Paul Kleihues

B 4.19

B 4.20

B 4.21

after consulting the heritage protection authority responsible. Which survey specialists are appointed depends on the particular building and situation. The architect enters all the information into the finishes schedule.

Basis for planning
The first goal of the research should be to prepare building phases drawings, which shows the individual periods of construction plus any conversions in the form of plans, sections and elevations so that they are easy to follow. On coloured drawings older parts are coloured darker, newer parts lighter (Fig. B 4.18).
The mapping of the damage includes the constructional and building physics examinations and describes the materials used, their condition and their properties. Deformations such as deflections of suspended floors, bulges in facades, cracks in masonry, efflorescence or rotten timber beams are only the results of constructional or building physics problems. Patterns of damage frequently have their own history, which is often recorded in old tradesmen's invoices and other written documents. Such documents can help when searching for the causes of damage. The mapping of the damage includes checking the foundations and the structural system and also provides information about the thermal and acoustic performance of the construction.
The surfaces worthy of preservation are marked on the so-called fitting-out drawing. Coloured boundaries to wall surfaces, historic floors, plaster ceilings or fixtures and fittings permanently attached to the structure represent especially sensitive areas that must be protected during the building work and taken into account in the future planning work.
Another step on the way to planning and design is the conservation drawing. This document provides an overview of where interventions need to be made in the historic building fabric for constructional reasons and which areas should not be altered if at all possible. The conservation drawing reveals the architectural consequences of all the knowledge obtained. It therefore corresponds directly with the preceding stages in the work and rates or weights their results.

Approval for conservation
When a planning application is submitted to the appropriate building authority, the lower heritage protection authority responsible automatically becomes involved in the case of a historic building. The architect or developer is, however, advised to contact the authority beforehand and inform them about the intended building measures. Once the planning application is ready, the plans will already be far advanced and changes to reflect any stipulations imposed by the heritage protection authority will be expensive. If the architect has based his design on the aforementioned researches and planning basis, it will be easy for him to explain and provide reasons for his approach. The

principle to follow should be therefore: the better the research and the clarification of the design brief, the more rewarding will be the discussions with the representatives of the heritage protection authority. The knowledge gained about the building in no way stifles the creativity of the architect. Quite the contrary: this building task cries out for creative solutions! There are different opinions – in architectural circles but also among conservators – as to which architectural stance should be taken in this case. For instance, new components may represent a stark contrast to existing ones or may not even be detectable at first glance. Without doubt, these different design strategies depend on the building, but also on the individuals involved (Figs. B 4.20 and 21).
A good design is characterised by the fact that it respects the existing and engages in a dialogue with it. To do this it is necessary to adhere to certain principles that have become established in conservation:
Irrespective of whether the work involves extending or simply maintaining an existing historic structure, all unavoidable additions should express a current architectural style. If we consider the fact that historic buildings are witnesses to bygone ages, then every pseudo historical fashioning is certainly out of the question because it adulterates or blurs the character of the evidence. It is therefore important that modern additions are authentic for our times and can be clearly recognised as such. It should be possible to separate them from the historic components without damaging the latter. Components that do not meet modern requirements because of their dimensions or properties should not be replaced by new ones, but rather supplemented in such a way that the original components are upgraded; for example, delicate trussing can be relieved by a beam, further rafters added to strengthen a roof structure. This "additive principle" means that all building measures automatically comply with the reversibility requirement (Fig. B 4.19).
Article 11 of the Venice Charter states: "The valid contributions of all periods to the building of a monument must be respected, since unity of style is not the aim of a restoration" [17]. But in situ, on the building site itself, this unambiguous appeal is frequently much more difficult to handle. Superimposed, different historical, scientific and aesthetic values are not unusual. The additions of later times, to reveal an earlier phase, may only be sacrificed under very strict conditions.
Unlike in France, for example, historic buildings are not categorised in Germany. Nevertheless, not all owners of historic buildings have to satisfy the same stipulations laid down by the approving heritage protection authorities. This disparate treatment, which is frequently misunderstood by the public and condemned as arbitrariness, is drawn from the characteristics of a building that enable it to be classed as a historic monument. Decisive for the practical building operations is whether a building should be pro-

tected for historical, artistic, scientific or technical reasons, or owing to its urban or folkloric
significance. The actual approval process is
generally a compromise between the different
demands of the parties involved and frequently
ensues from a joint dialogue. For instance, if
the long-term retention of a historic building
can only be guaranteed through a new usage,
but this calls for interventions in the building
fabric, this leads to a trade-off process even
among state conservators themselves. How
much historical building fabric must be sacrificed in order to realise the new usage? Is the
usage concept unsuitable for the building or is
it only the architectural realisation that is lacking? Are there other usage options or must the
shortcomings be accepted in order to retain
the historic building? What constitutes the heritage value of the building and what priorities
arise out of this? Where the decisions are especially difficult, the lower heritage protection
authorities can contact the specialist heritage
authorities for help and advice. An optimum
decision is a rarity in conservation. The very
nature of historic buildings means that decisions
can only be made on a case-by-case basis.

Realisation of the building works
Building measures in or on a historic structure
call for special precautions to be taken. The
workers must be made aware of the special
needs of this type of building task. Choosing
specialist contractors with experience of conservation work can be a great advantage here.
On larger projects complete encapsulation
creates a workshop-like situation in which the
workers can achieve more precise results
thanks to the better working conditions. In addition, such a situation automatically fosters a
different attitude to that normally encountered
on an open building site. Nevertheless, components and finds must be protected against further damage and labelled. It is often forgotten
that vibrations can also represent a danger for
historic buildings.
Even if the detailed drawings are especially
precise and the detailed planning matches
each specific situation, unforeseen situations
always occur in historic buildings which call for
corrections to the plans. It is important that the
state conservator responsible is involved in
such adjustments; firstly, to find an acceptable
solution to new issues, and, secondly, to check
the implementation of the original plans. So on-
site meetings with the representative of the heritage protection authority will always take place
during the building work. Moreover, many decisions cannot be taken until in situ samples are
available. During such sampling work carried
out by the specialist contractors and restorers
on the building site, the conservator should of
course be present. The specialist heritage
authorities can consult other specialists, e.g.
stone or glass restorers, in addition to their
local conservators, all of whom can be involved
in the on-site meetings when specific problems
occur. Through their scientific backgrounds

and practical building experience, these specialists can frequently help to find mutually
acceptable solutions (Fig. B 4.28).
A historic building with many historic features,
e.g. an elaborately sculpted facade or walls
decorated with coloured figures, consequently
calls for a greater site presence by both the
architect and the conservator responsible.
Special details demand increased coordination
not only between the planning team and the
specialist contractors – the presence of the
conservator is also necessary at the regular
site meetings. However, as the personnel available to the specialist heritage authorities can
these days no longer guarantee such a level of
supervision, private consultants are being used

for these tasks, especially on large public
projects, but of course only in agreement with
the authorities, which in such situations retain a
primarily regulatory function. This function must
be carried out in close consultation with the
freelance conservator appointed by the developer.
One important aspect often neglected is the
documentation of all constructional interventions in the historic fabric. This requirement is
vital for conservation work. Many developers
nevertheless try to evade this requirement because it results in costs but no apparent direct
return for their money. For the upkeep of the
construction and later repairs, however, owners
come to appreciate such records.

B 4.22

B 4.23

B 4.24

B 4.25   The Emperor Hall of the "Esplanade" Hotel at
         Potsdamer Platz, Berlin, was raised by 2.5 m and
         then transported 75 m in 1996.
B 4.26   The Emperor Hall of the "Esplanade" Hotel in the
         new Sony Center, Berlin
B 4.27   Conversion of the former Catholic parish church
         "The Three Wise Men" into premises for an
         architectural practice, Cologne (D), 1990,
         Link Architekten
B 4.28   Colour-matching trials in the Nubian Room of the
         New Museum, Berlin
B 4.29   Conversion of a crane structure built in 1950 with
         a steel crane dating from 1966, Berlin (D), 2002,
         Sven Thomsen

B 4.25

B 4.26

Reconstruction and relocation

In the conservation of historic monuments, reconstruction is the rebuilding of a structure or part thereof that no longer exists. The work is carried out on the basis of old drawings, photographs, engravings and written documentation. The outcome is a reproduction that attempts to emulate a certain condition, frequently by including original parts, but just as often by using other materials and techniques.

Reconstructions are very controversial because they undermine the true sense and purpose of conservation. Because they deny facts like war and devastation, they are the exact opposite of historical documents. Furthermore, buildings are generally not so well documented that an identical copy of the original is feasible. However, this is sometimes not the aim of a reconstruction, as the rebuilding of the marketplace in Münster or the new market in Dresden illustrate. Modern usage requirements result in different interior layouts behind reproductions of historic facades.

So-called sensitive reconstruction does not even try to create an image of a historic building already lost. The overall architectural form, the volume and the segmentation of the facade of a certain preceding construction or style constitute the guidelines. In its constructional and architectural details, this building expresses a current, modern architectural language (Figs. B 4.22–4.24).

One special form of reconstruction is the anastylosis. This Greek term borrowed from archaeology designates the reconstruction of a building from the remains of the original ruins at its original location. The addition of missing pieces and the use of auxiliary structures are generally indispensable. The anastylosis, however, does not strive to re-create an intact structure, but simply present the remaining original fragments in their original context.

Transporting a historic building to a different place should represent the absolute exception in conservation. Such relocation causes the building to lose part of its substance and its link with its historic surroundings. In addition, the local topographical context is lost. Relocating a historic building is an option when there is no alternative to demolition. Such relocated build-ings often find a permanent new home in open-air museums (e.g. in Detmold, Hessenpark near Frankfurt or Vogtsbauernhof in the Black Forest). The best-known example of relocation is the temples of Abu Simbel, the relocation of which was initiated by UNESCO and took place between 1964 and 1968. They were originally located in what is now Lake Nasser.

Instead of documenting the dismantling of a structure so that it can be rebuilt faithfully, it is also possible to relocate a complete structure as a whole, as was done in 1996 in the case of the Emperor Hall of the former "Esplanade" Hotel in Berlin (Figs. B 4.25 and 4.26). The most recent example of such a relocation project is the Romanesque Emmaus Church, which dates from the 13th century and is thus probably one of the oldest churches in Saxony. It originally stood in Heuersdorf but in 2007 the planned open-cast mining of lignite made it necessary to move it from its original location to Borna some 12 km away. By using a special vehicle it was possible to relocate the 665 tonne, 14.5 m long, 8.9 m wide and 19.6 m high hall church with its little chancel in one complete piece!

Use, change of use

In the past changes of use have protected historic monuments from certain demolition. The Porta Nigra in Trier was converted into a two-storey church in the Middle Ages. In Rottenburg the Carmelite church, after the profanation in the course of secularisation, was first used as stables and since 1817, after building intermediate floors, as a residence for the cathedral's canons. So changes of use are not a new topic in conservation. But every adaptation to a usage different from the original one takes its toll on the historical fabric and therefore the sustainability of usage concepts must be questioned.

One current problem is the conversion of churches and industrial buildings that are no longer required for their original purposes [18]. From the viewpoint of conservation, it is important to find new uses for these structures that handle the existing elements carefully and preserve the original concept plus the architectural and artistic statements. Churches are characterised, for instance, by their spacious interiors. Reusing them for housing means erecting intermediate floors and hence losing the impression of the spaciousness of the original interior. For conservators, such usage is generally unacceptable. But again here, the crucial aspect is to determine what constitutes the actual historic value of the building (Fig. B 4.27).

Article 5 of the Venice Charter outlines the problem of the usage of historic buildings thus: "The conservation of monuments is always facilitated by making use of them for some socially useful purpose. Such use is therefore desirable but it must not change the layout or decoration of the building." [19]

On the one hand, usage guarantees the ongoing upkeep and therefore the long-term retention of the structure; on the other, usage places specific demands and requirements on the structure. So when drawing up a usage concept, it is important to apply a few principles: the inherited historic fabric results in constraints for the usage, not vice versa. Normally, the retention of the original purpose is the most protective approach in the meaning of conservation. One exception to this rule is, at best, the use as a museum. This does not mean using the historic building in the usual sense of a

B 4.27

B 4.28

museum, i.e. to display interesting, historic artefacts, but rather to present the building itself together with its fixtures and fittings as an exhibit. However, the necessary infrastructure calls for a not inconsiderable need for adaptation. In order that the statement of the historic building is not minimised and its fabric is not threatened, the scale of the usage is very important. Over-usage damages any building. In the case of a historic building, the constraints due to over-usage of a building increase exponentially (Fig. B 4.29).

Historic buildings must be constantly maintained and cared for. Maintenance schedules with checklists for the regular inspection of certain components have proved worthwhile in the past, also service contracts with specialist companies. In the Netherlands and Belgium, "Monumentenwacht" (monument watch) is an established organisation. It inspects nearly 20 000 monuments in the Netherlands, including almost all the churches. The staff inspect the heritage assets and produce records of any damage. They carry out small repairs themselves, clean out the gutters and refix loose roof tiles, and they advise the owners when larger maintenance measures are necessary. There are such organisations in Germany, too, e.g. "DenkmalWacht Brandenburg und Berlin", or "Monumentendienst", organised by the non-profit-making Kulturschatz Bauernhof Foundation (partly funded by an EU programme), the Federal State of Lower Saxony, the Foundation of Lower Saxony and various local authorities.

Notes:

[1] Friedrich Wilhelm IV of Prussia: speech during the laying of the foundation stone for the completion of Cologne Cathedral, 1842. In: Huse, Norbert (ed.): Denkmalpflege, Deutsche Texte aus drei Jahrhunderten. Munich, 1996, pp. 56–57

[2] Schinkel, Karl Friedrich: Memorandum zur Denkmalpflege, 1815. In: ibid. [1], p. 70

[3] ibid. [2], p. 71

[4] Dehio, Georg: Was wird aus dem Heidelberger Schloß werden?, 1901. In: ibid. [1], p. 115

[5] ibid. [4], p. 110

[6] Visitor figures from 2006

[7] Hoffmann-Axthelm, Dieter: Kann die Denkmalpflege entstaatlicht werden? Report for Bündnis 90/Die Grünen (the Green party) parliamentary faction. In: Vereinigung der Landesdenkmalpfleger in der Bundesrepublik Deutschland (ed.): Entstaatlichung der Denkmalpflege? Von der Provokation zur Diskussion. Berlin, 2000, p. 31

[8] Vollmer, Antje: Zwölf Thesen zum Thema Denkmalschutz, Reformbedarf, Veränderungsmöglichkeiten. In: ibid. [7], p. 34

[9] For an understanding of the concept of conservation in Japan see: Enders, Siegfried; Gutschow, Niels (ed.): Hozon – Architectural and Urban Conservation in Japan. Stuttgart/London, 1998

[10] Act for the Protection of Heritage in Berlin (Denkmalschutzgesetz Berlin – DSchG Bln) of 24 April 1995, cl. 2, para. 2

[11] Federal Building Code (BauGB) in the edition notified on 23 September 2004, cl. 1, para. 5 & 6

[12] see: Act for the Protection and Upkeep of Historic Monuments (Denkmalschutzgesetz – DSchG) – last amended by the Act of 24 July 2003, Bavaria, Art. 12, para. 1

[13] ibid. [10], cl. 5, para. 2

[14] The Handbuch der deutschen Kunstdenkmäler is today published jointly by three institutions: the "Dehio-Vereinigung. Wissenschaftliche Vereinigung zur Fortführung des kunsttopographischen Werkes von Georg Dehio e.V.", the "Vereinigung der Landesdenkmalpfleger in der Bundesrepublik Deutschland", and the "Deutsche Stiftung Denkmalschutz".

[15] Hague Convention for the Protection of Cultural Property in the Event of Armed Conflict, edition of 11 April 1967, Art. 1, Definition of cultural assets

[16] Dendrochronology is a method for dating timber by comparing the growth rings.

[17] The Venice Charter for the Conservation and Restoration of Monuments and Sites. Venice, 25–31 May 1964, 1989 edition, Art. 11

[18] see: Fisch, Rainer: Umnutzung von Kirchengebäuden in Deutschland. Bonn, 2008

[19] ibid. [17], Art. 5

B 4.29

Building materials in refurbishment projects

Florian Musso, Johann Weber

Refurbishment and new construction are building assignments with different emphases. Ageing processes will have become visible on buildings needing refurbishment, and some of those processes may well lead to an attractive patina. In a special form of recycling, the refurbishment should enable as many parts of the existing building to be incorporated in the new plans – an economically and culturally viable approach. Like with new construction, there is a direct relationship between material and construction, and the two can only be treated separately to a certain extent.

Consequently, questions of building materials for refurbishment projects must be considered in conjunction with the building components. A rough breakdown into loadbearing structure, envelope and fitting-out results in groups of building materials to match these profiles. This chapter is intended to give the reader the chance to find solutions – starting with the specific building component and its specific problems. Existing and new materials are considered in a constructional context for refurbishment, i.e. elimination of the underlying problems and transformation into a state that will remain free of problems for as long as possible.

Loadbearing structure

Stability is crucial for every construction and must be assured during and after refurbishment as well. Damage and changes of use must be harmonised with the applicable standards within the scope of the refurbishment.

Timber

Timber is a building material with a long service life provided it remains dry and air can circulate around all sides. Norwegian stave churches dating from the 13th century are impressive proof of this. Only a few species of timber are strong, economic and durable enough to be considered for loadbearing and bracing components. In Central Europe, softwoods such as spruce, fir, Scots pine, larch and Douglas fir are the softwoods that have been regularly used, and oak the only hardwood, owing to its high loadbearing capacity and natural resist-

ance to fungi and insects. Timber exhibits a high strength for a low self-weight, has a high elasticity and insulates relatively well (but about four times worse than genuine insulating materials). The various species of timber are distinguished by way of their durability to fungi and insects.

Timber is a hygroscopic building material, i.e. it absorbs moisture and then releases it again. A changing moisture content also means a changing volume: timber swells as it absorbs moisture and shrinks as it dries out. However, this phenomenon applies only to the range between oven-dry (moisture content $u = 0\%$) and fibre saturation ($u \sim 30\%$). Above the fibre saturation point, practically no further deformation occurs. The dimensional changes for indigenous species are largest in the tangential direction, about half that radially, and negligible longitudinally. The swelling and shrinkage of timber can be reduced by applying a coating that limits the absorption of moisture.

Timber should always be installed with the moisture content expected during its service life, otherwise cracks and/or deformation can be expected:

- Fully enclosed,
  structures heated: approx. 9 % (± 3 %)
- Fully enclosed
  structures unheated: approx. 12 % (± 3 %)
- Roofed-over
  open-sided structures: approx. 15 % (± 3 %)
- Structures fully-
  exposed to the
  weather: approx. 18 % (± 6 %)

Damage

Timber is mainly damaged by excessive absorption of moisture due to constructional and building physics shortcomings, but also poor maintenance (Figs. B 5.2 and 5.4). Inadequate sizing, whether due to the wrong choice of timber or a change of use, leads to deflections and deformations. Undersized members are particularly common in buildings built in the 1930s and the years immediately following World War 2 – times in which there were shortages of suitable building materials. The durability of wood and wood-based products can be

B 5.1 Refurbishment, conversion and extension of a timber-framed house and barn in Urbach (D), 2005, Heydorn Eaton Architekten
B 5.2 Rust marks due to iron nails, wattle-and-daub infill gradually decaying, moss growing on the wood due to permanent moisture
B 5.3 Solid timber's natural resistance to fungi according to DIN EN 350-2
B 5.4 Softwood cladding that has rotted due to splashing water

B 5.2

Resistance class	Species of wood
Resistance class 1	teak, afzelia, greenheart, mansonia, jarrah, makoré
Resistance class 1–2	robinie, merbau, iroko, afrormosia
Resistance class 2	oak, western red cedar, basralocus, azobé, bubinga, wenge
Resistance class 3	walnut, keruing
Resistance class 3–4	Douglas fir, Scots pine, larch, elm
Resistance class 4	spruce, fir, hemlock, southern pine
Resistance class 5	beech, maple, alder, birch, ash, lime

The durabilities given in the table relate only to the heartwood; the sapwood of all species corresponds to resistance class 5. The durability decreases from 1 to 5.

B 5.3

endangered by harmful plants (fungi) and animal pests (insects). Infestation can change the appearance, performance and loadbearing capacity of timber structures, even lead to their complete destruction.

Without using chemical preservatives, fungal infestation is likely if the moisture content remains permanently above 20 % and the temperature fluctuates between +3 and +40 °C. Wood-destroying fungi consume the organic material in the wood as they grow. They thrive especially well in areas cut off from the air. Dry rot is the fungal species most feared. It extracts the cellulose from the wood and leaves behind the lignin as a brown substance. Masonry can also be infested as well as softwood. Fungal species such as wet rot, oak mazegill, conifer mazegill, etc. break down the substance of the wood. Wood-discolouring fungi such as blue stain or mould spoil the appearance but do not damage the timber itself. They can, however, destroy coatings and hence initiate other damage due to the subsequent infiltration of moisture. Insects – mainly beetles, e.g. house longhorn beetle (authorities must be notified), death-watch beetle, common furniture beetle – use timber (primarily the sapwood of softwoods) as a source of nutrients and as nests for their larvae. The boring and burrowing can destroy the timber completely. The mature beetles leave the wood via characteristic exit holes. Both living trees and dry wood already installed in a building can be infested. A moisture content exceeding just 10 % provides optimum conditions for infestation.

Refurbishment

Undersized timber members can be upgraded or reinforced by attaching components made from wood, wood-based products (e.g. parallel strand lumber, laminated veneer lumber, glued laminated timber) or steel. Polymer concretes based on epoxy and polyester resins can also be used for the upgrading and reinforcing of existing timber members. To do this, holes are drilled in sound timber into which glass-fibre rods are inserted for stability. The missing timber and the holes are then filled with polymer concrete (with quartz sand as aggregate). Timber joist floors can be reinforced by adding

a concrete topping that is anchored to the existing timber construction (timber-concrete composite floor). The damaged ends of timber beams and joists can also be repaired. Splicing new timber sections into the existing timber cross-section comes closest to retaining the original appearance (heritage protection). The damaged joints and small members of timber frames can be upgraded by splicing, or replaced by infill members or posts and rails provided with special spigots.

Timber components infested by the house longhorn beetle must be refurbished by removing the infested parts right back to sound timber, provided the remaining cross-section has the necessary loadbearing capacity. If that is not the case, the hot-air method can be used to combat the infestation. This method involves blowing heated air at a temperature of > 55 °C into an enclosed space (e.g. roof structure) for one hour in order to eradicate all the eggs and larvae. The surface temperature of the timber should not exceed 120 °C, however (fire protection). Afterwards, a chemical wood preservative should be applied to prevent further infestation. In the case of a wood-destroying fungal infestation, the only refurbishment option is to replace the components affected. Besides employing constructional protective measures, a chemical wood preservative must be used to prevent further infestation. Where dry rot is encountered, it is not only necessary to remove all the timber components affected, but also the

adjacent masonry as well. In some federal states, e.g. Hamburg, Hesse, Saxony, Thuringia, the authorities must be notified when this dangerous fungus is found.

Timber can be protected by active measures (for existing infestation) and preventive measures (to prevent infestation). Prevention is achieved by choosing the right timber (well-dried, properly stored timber members made from a durable species), passive constructional measures and chemical wood preservatives. According to DIN 1052 the heartwood of spruce and fir is less durable (class 4), Scots pine and larch moderately durable (class 3 – 4) and oak durable (class 2) (Fig. B 5.3). The sapwood of all species of wood is unsuitable for long-term applications.

Passive constructional measures to protect timber should be preferred when carrying out refurbishment work. Contact with the soil, the accumulation of condensation and permanent saturation should all be avoided; damp timber members should be ventilated so that they can dry out. According to DIN 68800-3 timber components can be assigned to risk classes from GK 0 (no chemical wood preservative required) to GK 4 (extreme risk). Chemical wood preservative is not essential for classes GK 1 – 4 provided "naturally durable" species are used. Wood with a moisture content < 20 % is a prerequisite if fungal infestation is to be avoided, and insect infestation can only be ruled out when the moisture content drops below 10 %.

B 5.4

B 5.5

B 5.6

B 5.7

B 5.8

Where the timber is exposed and can be inspected for infestation (e.g. in open roof spaces), chemical wood preservatives are unnecessary. With careful planning, all loadbearing components apart from sole plates (GK 2) can be assigned to risk class GK 0. Chemical wood preservatives are also unnecessary when using Scots pine, larch or Douglas fir that is free from sapwood.

Chemical wood preservatives are designed to prevent infestation by fungi and insects. Preventive protection is a prerequisite for loadbearing components, but chemicals are only necessary for certain risk classes. Preventive chemical wood preservatives inhibit insect and fungal infestation either by way of water-soluble toxic salts applied by steeping or pressure-impregnation, or organic solutions with oils or solvents applied to the outer surfaces. Active chemical wood preservatives are used after infestation. In this situation applied coatings and steeping (possibly under pressure) are both possible options. Chemical treatment is undesirable for non-loadbearing, dimensionally accurate components. In this case a written agreement between architect and building owner is recommended. In the interior fitting-out, the widespread use of wood preservatives should never be permitted. Provided durable heartwood is used for windows and external doors, preservatives are unnecessary.

Iron and steel

Steels are alloys of iron and carbon with a carbon content < 2.1%. Unavoidable accompanying elements are phosphorus, sulphur and nitrogen. Other additives such as manganese, silicon, chromium, nickel and molybdenum are sometimes used. Mild steel (known as wrought iron up to about 1900) is a non-hardenable steel with a carbon content < 0.5 %; it cannot be cast and has only moderate elasticity. Hardenable steels (alloyed with, for example, manganese, chromium, silicon, tungsten) have a carbon content of 0.5–1.5 % and can be forged or cast; they exhibits good elasticity, ductility and tensile strength. Cast iron has a carbon content of 2.3–5.0 %; it can only be worked cold, is brittle, and weldable to a limited extent only. The type of metal can be determined by inspecting the sparks during gentle grinding of the surface:

• Red rays with stars = cast iron
• Yellow lines with drops = mild steel
• Bright yellow sparks with stars = tool steel

Depending on the quantities of the alloying elements (L) and the carbon (C), steel is classed as carbon steel (C < 0.2 %), low-alloy steel (C > 0.2 %, L < 5 %) or high-alloy steel (L > 5 %). Non-rusting steel is a high-alloy variety and is known as stainless steel (chromium content > 12 %). Higher chromium contents and other alloying metals such as nickel, molybdenum, titanium or niobium improve the corrosion resistance.

Damage
Owing to the great affinity between steel and oxygen, corrosion takes place in the presence of oxygen and moisture (air humidity > 70 %) (Figs. B 5.5, 5.6 and 5.11). This so-called rusting is associated with a loss of steel, which means that steel must be well protected, especially outdoors. Corrosion classes C 1 – 5 specify the corrosion rates of unprotected steel components (e.g. C 5: industrial atmosphere with sulphur dioxide, chloride, fumes, fly ash, or marine climate, 650 – 1500 g/m²a). In reinforced concrete the steel reinforcement is protected against corrosion by the alkaline environment of the surrounding concrete until the concrete is damaged by carbonation.

Refurbishment
Rusting can be prevented by applying diverse protective coatings (e.g. by brush, roller, immersion, spraying) and by galvanising processes. The surfaces must first be cleaned of all rust, oil, grease and old paint by way of grinding, blasting or acid treatments. Immersion and galvanising cannot be carried out in situ. The combination of galvanising and painting (duplex method) offers better protection. Joints and small cracks can be made good with putty (formerly containing red lead) and boiled linseed oil, for example (Figs. B 5.32 and 5.34). Paints consist of a thinner undercoat and a thicker final or finish coat. Natural pigments, graphite or silicate paints are mixed with water glass, tar and asphalt and bonded with linseed oil and varnish.

Reinforced concrete
Concrete consists of cement, coarse and fine aggregates, water and possibly additives or admixtures depending on its function. The cement paste sets to give concrete it is well-known properties. Reinforced concrete is a composite building material in which the concrete resists the compression forces and the steel the tension forces. It was first used at the start of the 20th century.

Damage
Carbonation is a chemical reaction that causes the $Ca(OH)_2$ (calcium hydroxide) in the cement paste of the concrete to be converted into $CaCO_3$ (limestone) (Fig. B 5.8). This causes the pH value in the pore water to drop from more than 13 to less than 9. At pH values > 10, a protective passivation layer forms on the steel reinforcement. But if the pH drops below 9, the reinforcement can corrode. The carbonation process slows as the concrete ages and depends on the weather exposure and the surface structure of the concrete. It can be made visible by spraying fresh damage with a phenolphthalein solution containing ethanol. The appearance changes suddenly from colourless (neutral) to violet (alkaline) at pH values between 8.2 and 9.8 respectively. Chlorides (de-icing salts) in the pore water can cause rusting of the reinforcement, too. White patches due to

B 5.5 Bitumen waterproofing turned up a reinforced concrete plinth to protect against splashing water; steel stanchion painted with red lead
B 5.6 Inadequately coated steel handrail with excessive corrosion due to water draining down the facade
B 5.7 Hollow clay block floor supported by steel beams divided into segments for easier erection
B 5.8 Spalling of concrete due to carbonation; inadequate cover to reinforcement
B 5.9 Repaired clay brickwork damaged by rising salt water, paint on window shutter flaking off near window sill
B 5.10 Loosening of finishes due to vegetation
B 5.11 Corrosion due to permanent moisture in the open joint of a steel plate laid in the formwork to a concrete column

B 5.9

B 5.10

washed-out calcium hydroxide can build up on adjacent components.

Refurbishment
The cause of the damage must be known and the right repair technique chosen if concrete is to be refurbished successfully. Various methods can be used to analyse the damage: from a visual inspection to destructive and non-destructive evaluations and examinations of samples in the laboratory.
DIN 1504 describes 11 strategies for repairing damaged concrete:

- IP: Protection against ingress
- MC: Moisture control
- CR: Concrete restoration
- SS: Structural strengthening
- PR: Physical resistance
- RC: Resistance to chemicals
- RP: Preserving or restoring the passivity
- IR: Increasing resistivity
- CC: Cathodic control
- CP: Cathodic protection
- CA: Control of anodic areas

Concrete is generally repaired by applying substitute or protective layers. The substrate is prepared by methods such as chiselling away loose concrete, cleaning with wire brushes or needle guns, grinding, sand-blasting, shot-peening, high-pressure water jets or flame-cleaning treatments. Cracks up to a width of 0.3 mm are regarded as unproblematic and are repaired by filling and sealing, ensuring that the materials used create an elastic, stress-transferring connection between the flanks of the crack. Impregnation or injection with epoxy resin, polyurethane resin, cement paste or cement emulsion can be considered as repair methods depending on the size, location and nature of the crack and any movement to be expected and the state of the concrete.
With adequate concrete cover to the reinforcement, surface damage is made good by applying a polymer-modified, cement-bonded grout by hand or a pure cement-bonded sprayed grout. Existing reinforced concrete structures can be supported by steel beams, for example (Fig. B 5.7). Components with inadequate load-

bearing capacity can also be upgraded by attaching additional reinforcement in the form of space-saving steel- or carbon-fibre plates. Surfaces can be protected by sprayed grout, hydrophobic agents, impregnation treatments and coatings. If the steel reinforcement is still exposed to corrosive conditions despite a protective surface finish, the reinforcement itself can be coated or protected electrochemically. The ambient conditions are defined by exposure classes.

Masonry
Masonry can consist of natural or man-made units. We distinguish natural stone according to its origins as sedimentary (e.g. limestone, shelly limestone, sandstone), igneous (e.g. granite) and metamorphic (e.g. marble) rocks. The man-made masonry units include fired (clay bricks) and unfired units such as granulated slag aggregate, concrete, calcium silicate and aerated concrete bricks (from 1929 onwards). Clay bricks are formed (hand-moulding, extrusion) from clay, loam or clay-like substances, possibly with additives (e.g. fragments), then dried and finally fired at about 900–1200 °C. Solid and vertically perforated clay bricks are used for loadbearing and non-loadbearing masonry. They can also be used as a backing wall to rendered or faced masonry. Lightweight clay bricks are produced with the addition of aerating substances (sawdust, polystyrene foam); their thermal conductivity and compres-

sive strength are lower than those of standard clay bricks. Facing and so-called engineering (= high-strength) bricks – fired above the sintering point (1150–1300 °C, depending on the raw materials) – are suitable for frost-resistant facing brickwork. In order to comply with stricter insulation standards, facing brick walls with cavity insulation are becoming common these days in addition to lightweight clay brickwork. Following the use of many local brick formats and the imperial format (RF, 250 x 120 x 65 mm) introduced in 1871, the "octametre" module (normal format: 240 x 110, 50 x 70, 10 mm, 10 mm joint vertical, 12 mm horizontal) based on a modular grid of 125 mm (= 1/8 metre) became established for masonry construction after World War 2.
Similar to concretes, screeds or renders, mortars consist of fine aggregate, a binder and water. Mortar groups are used to distinguish the different types of binder used: MG 1 lime mortar (sand + quicklime), MG 2 lime-cement mortar, MG 3 cement mortar (sand + cement) and MG 4 gypsum mortar (sand + gypsum). As cement products were developed in the 19th century, lime mortar became less popular because of its lower compressive strength compared to cement mortar. However, lime mortar has disinfectant and moisture-regulating properties because it releases moisture about 10 times faster than cement mortar and is therefore suitable for repairs and internal use. Hybrid products combine the benefits of both

B 5.11

B 5.12 Partially refurbished copper flashings on an accessible flat roof

B 5.13 Sheet copper capping to patched synthetic rubber parapet waterproofing suffering from embrittlement and slippage

B 5.14 Laying bitumen roof sheeting on a flat roof with the help of a propane gas torch

B 5.15 Interlocking clay tiles damaged by sliding snow at the eaves, with moss beginning to grow

B 5.16 Distorted profiled sheet aluminium roofing

B 5.17 Old clay roof tiles after several years of exposure to the weather (left) and a new clay tile roof covering (right)

B 5.12

B 5.13

B 5.14

products, overcoming the disadvantages. For example, MG 2 lime mortar combines two parts quicklime with one part cement and six parts sand. Lightweight and thin-bed mortars are used for lightweight vertically perforated clay brickwork.

Damage

Moisture is the main cause of damage to masonry. It washes out deposits such as endogenous efflorescence (wall/lime saltpetre, lime bloom/weeping), serves as a means of transport for exogenous soiling and incrustation, and accelerates the weathering of the surface (discoloration, fading, blemishes, patination). Salt crystallisation and frost can also lead to the disintegration of the masonry units through lamination, loss of cohesion with formation of blisters, crumbling and voids due to the dissolving of binder in the joints (Fig. B 5.9). Biological growths due to plants, mosses, lichens, algae and mould are encouraged by a high moisture content in the masonry (Fig. B 5.10). In basements and at the bases of walls, water can rise through the masonry by way of capillary action (rising damp). Cracks, on the other hand, are mainly caused by shrinkage, temperature fluctuations and structural movements. Facing leaves are exposed to high temperature fluctuations, are therefore at risk of cracking and must be able to expand and contract without restraint. Inadequate bonding dimensions in the masonry bond (min. 4 mm high, 45 mm wide) can lead to cracking which in some circumstances can lead to collapse.

Refurbishment

After first cleaning the masonry dry, wet-cleaning (high-pressure) is employed. Lime bloom/ weeping is removed by brushing and, if necessary, acid treatments. Defective joints and units are removed, voids and cracks filled by injecting grout, units replaced and joints pointed (min. 15 mm deep). Prior to pointing, the surface must be cleaned and wetted with high-pressure equipment, afterwards given a water-repellent (not sealing) treatment if required. Movement joints (planned cracking points) prevent problematic cracking of the masonry but are difficult to install subsequently. The moisture load can be reduced by constructional measures such as increasing the eaves overhang. Rising damp can be checked by the subsequent installation of injected and other types of damp-proof course.

Building envelope

The loadbearing structure and the enclosing envelope can be fully separated from each other only rarely. The primary function of the envelope is to control the passage of water from outside and inside (in the form of vapour). Rising energy costs have led to forms of construction that are mainly determined by the parameters insulation and airtightness. The adaptation of existing structures to conform to current boundary conditions represents an immense energy-savings potential.

Flat roofs

Primarily for economic reasons, the warm deck with polystyrene foam (from about 1960 onwards) or mineral wool insulation covered by a waterproofing material represents the most common type of flat roof. On an inverted roof with the waterproofing below the water-resistant insulation made from extruded polystyrene foam (from about 1970 onwards), the roof covering is better protected. Insulation laid to falls is not possible here, however, because the insulation is very expensive and the contact with the cold rainwater makes it less efficient. On a "compact roof" cellular glass boards are laid in hot bitumen on all sides and also covered with waterproof sheeting. The "Duo-roof" combines the advantages of warm deck and inverted roof and is a good choice when refurbishing flat roofs. Since the beginning of the 20th century, bitumen, a byproduct of crude oil distillation, has replaced the hazardous tar products used hitherto for roof waterproofing. Flexible bitumen sheeting consists of a backing material soaked in bitumen that is coated both sides with an additional layer of bitumen (mostly polymer-bonded bitumen) and given a mineral finish (e.g. talcum, sand, slate granules). The backing is made from polyester fleece, jute cloth, glass cloth or glass fleece (from about 1950 onwards), and determines the mechanical properties such as strength, flexibility and tear resistance. A durable, sealed roof covering using flexible bitumen sheeting can only be achieved by bonding the sheeting together. It is therefore laid in two or three parallel layers with the seams offset and min. 80 mm overlaps between adjacent rolls of material, and bonded together over the entire surface. Various methods are used:

- Pouring and rolling: the material is rolled out into hot bitumen.
- Felt-torching: the underside of the material is melted with a propane gas torch (Fig. B 5.14).
- Mopping: hot bitumen compound is spread over the surface before unrolling the sheeting.
- Cold application: the rolls of material are coated on the underside with adhesives made from bitumen or polyurethane.

Asphalt roof coverings can be used only on stable surfaces, but can accept foot and vehicular traffic immediately.

B 5.15

B 5.16

B 5.17

Flexible synthetic sheeting, e.g. made from plasticised polyvinyl chloride (PVC-P) or elastomers, are available with or without a backing material (glass fleece). After early problems with such sheeting in the 1970s, they were modified in various ways and since then have been used mainly for industrial and commercial buildings. They are bonded with hot adhesive and held in place with mechanical fasteners or a ballast material. Their compatibility with bitumen must be checked where applicable.

Damage
Compared with pitched roofs, flat roofs experience fewer, but more expensive, cases of damage. Inadequate falls lead to ponding, which stresses the waterproofing and sealing of the roof covering unnecessarily. A lack of protection to the surface of the waterproofing material can lead to damage caused by UV radiation or mechanical damage. Depending on the waterproofing system and materials, fatigue, embrittlement, the formation of blisters and corrugations, growths or cracks due to high movement stresses are all possible problems.

Refurbishment
Adding further insulating and waterproofing layers improves the thermal performance. Falls can also be integrated in this upgrading work. In the case of more severe saturation, the complete roof system (above the loadbearing structure) should be replaced. If the damage is limited to certain areas, bonding or felt-torching an additional layer of waterproofing, either over the whole area or just locally, is mostly sufficient. Flashings, gullies and the sealing at joints and junctions should be inspected and maintained (Figs. B 5.12 and 5.13).

Clay and concrete roof tiles
Pitched roofs are primarily covered with overlapping materials such as clay or concrete roof tiles, slate and fibre-cement sheets, or organic materials such as thatch, wood shakes/shingles and bitumen strip slates. Clay roof tiles are made from a mixture of loam, aluminium oxide and sand. They are extruded (bullnose tiles) or moulded, with various forms, colours and surface textures, and then subsequently dried and

fired. Concrete roof tiles made from Portland cement, water and quartz sand are available in similar forms and colours. Slate is a sedimentary rock that can be split into thin sheets. Fibre-cement (corrugated) sheets these days consists of a cement mixture reinforced with polyvinyl alcohol fibres, the surface of which can be finished with a water-repellent colour coating. Older sheets may well contain asbestos-fibre reinforcement, which can cause lung cancer and must be dealt with appropriately.

Damage
All roofing materials should be checked to ensure proper laying with the recommended roof pitches. Nevertheless, problems in the form of, for example, mechanical damage caused by falling branches, careless access or wind can occur (Figs. B 5.18 and 5.19). Efflorescence (salts) is often a sign of permanently saturated roof tiles. Lime inclusions cause spalling due to their increase in volume. Sulphur gases in the air can cause efflorescence and large-pore clay mixtures can encourage vegetation. Fibre-cement sheets can suffer colour changes, efflorescence and leaching of caustic substances (which damages glass). Vegetation often causes embrittlement of uncoated sheets.

Refurbishment
Repairs to damaged roofs can take the form of the replacement of damaged or missing small-format clay or concrete roof tiles, slates, shakes/shingles or sheets (Fig. B 5.17). Brittle and incorrectly fixed bitumen strip slate roofs often have to be re-covered completely because the overlapping makes it impossible to achieve adequate sealing and fixing subsequently.

Metal roof coverings
Metals (from the Greek *Metallon* = mine) are divided into ferrous and non-ferrous types. The former are metal alloys in which the iron content is higher than that of any of the other alloying elements. The best-known metal alloys include brass (alloy of copper and zinc) and bronze (alloy of copper and tin). Non-ferrous metals are divided into heavy metals (density > 4.5 g/cm^2, e.g. lead, copper, zinc, tin, chromium, nickel) and light metals (density < 4.5 g/

cm^2, e.g. aluminium, magnesium, titanium). Aluminium is one of the light metals but is comparatively strong. Owing to its potential of - 1.67 V it is regarded as a base metal. It owes its corrosion resistance to the hard, transparent layer of oxide that forms on the surface. Aluminium can be worked hot and cold (Fig. B 5.16), welded (depending on the content of alloying metals), soldered, bonded with adhesive and forged. In addition, it is a good conductor of heat and electricity.
Copper, like aluminium, is a very important non-ferrous metal. It is relatively soft and malleable and can be rolled, drawn, forged, soldered and welded, but is difficult to cast. Exposure to the weather changes the colour suddenly from reddish to brownish red and then to black (Fig. B 5.12). Furthermore, copper is corrosion-resistant and not sensitive to cement, lime and gypsum. The oxygen in the atmosphere causes brown copper oxide to form on the surface and over time the effects of carbon dioxide and moisture cause the formation of a green patina on the surface. This consists of alkaline copper carbonate which protects the copper against further oxidation and should not be confused with the toxic verdigris, which only forms in contact with acetic acid.
Zinc is alloyed with small amounts (< 0.5 %) of titanium, copper and aluminium to create a roof covering material. It is a soft, silvery white material. Exposed to the atmosphere, the reaction between carbon dioxide and the primary corrosion product zinc hydroxide produces alkaline zinc carbonate, which is highly resistant and forms a protective layer. This changes the colour of the zinc from silvery white to a matt greyish blue.
Sheet lead consists of commercial-grade lead (99.94 %), a small amount of copper (0.04 – 0.05 %) and additives. It has little tensile strength, undergoes significant changes in length as the temperature rises and falls, but is highly resistant to almost all acids. This soft, matt grey metal can be formed while cold (drawing, rolling, casting, soldering), leaves marks on other materials and is corrosion-resistant in the air: a coating of oxide first forms on the surface which later becomes a light grey patina of lead carbonate ($PbCO_4$) due to the reaction with the

B 5.18 Shallow-pitched dormer window, with standing seam galvanised steel sheet roof covering and inadequate verge detail
B 5.19 Subsequent damage (detail from Fig. B 5.18) at the saturated verge
B 5.20 Window with defective edge seals (condensation in cavity), chalking paint finish and lichens growing on aluminium glazing bars, failing jointing
B 5.21 Moisture damage to bottom rail and window frame, render damaged by expansion of window sill
B 5.22 Refurbished wooden window with bottom rail made from oak and louvre sunshade in cavity between panes
B 5.23 Flaking and fading of the paint to a wooden door caused by UV radiation

B 5.18

B 5.19

carbon dioxide in the atmosphere. After the quick formation of the carbonate in the early years, a linear corrosion rate can be expected after five years exposure.

Damage
Galvanic corrosion can occur with copper in conjunction with aluminium, titanium-zinc or galvanised steel. These latter metals should therefore not be used downstream of copper products in the flow direction of rainwater. The erosion products caused by wind, weather and rain are seldom pure metals, but rather metal compounds because of the environmental influences. The erosion reduces the thickness of the metal, which may require some form of protection. The rate of corrosion category (C1 = insignificant to C5 = severe) depends on the local atmospheric conditions (to DIN EN ISO 12944-2). Rates of corrosion that can be expected:

- Aluminium: up to 10 g/m²a
- Copper: up to 50 g/m²a
- Zinc: up to 60 g/m²a
- Lead: up to 7.4 g/m²a

The erosion allows compounds to reach the soil and the waste water, and so the compounds must be carefully checked for their environmental compatibility. At the same time, oxidation in the atmosphere leads to the formation of a protective layer (patina), which reduces the rate of loss of the material.
Aluminium can, on the one hand, be attacked by more noble metals like copper, but on the other hand, also be attacked by alkaline masonry lime (mortar) due to the formation of calcium aluminate. Once the layer of oxide on the surface has been broken down, the metal decomposes. In the electrochemical potential series, copper is among the noble metals below silver and gold. It is, however, resistant to non-oxidising acids such as hydrochloric acid. Sulphuric and nitric acid cause copper to oxidise due to the formation of corresponding copper salts. Zinc can be attacked by acids and alkalis and then gives off hydrogen gas and oxidises (e.g. due to tannic acid, formerly also tar). It is resistant to neither hydrochloric nor sulphuric acid, nor

sodium hydroxide solution, and dissolves. With so-called white rust, the lack of carbon dioxide and the effect of moisture prevents the formation of a protective layer of zinc carbonate, and instead creates corrosion products, which in the worst case can lead to the sheet metal rusting through at isolated places. The corrosion of exposed galvanised surfaces has declined over the last 20 years as a direct result of the decrease in the acid content of the air (primarily sulphur dioxide). Lead is attacked by organic acids (including those ensuing from hardwoods), condensation and the alkaline constituents of wet mortar and concrete, but can be protected by non-porous protective coatings or appropriate intermediate layers. Some 10–20 % of old water pipes are still made of lead. Soft water with a degree of hardness of 8 °dH can dissolve hazardous $Pb(OH)_2$ out of lead. With hard water, however, a protective layer of alkaline lead-calcium carbonate forms which prevents lead compounds entering the water supply. Using lead solder on copper pipes may also be the cause of lead in drinking water.

Refurbishment
Following thorough mechanical cleaning of the sheet metal, some form of surface protection can be applied to prevent contact with water and oxygen. Isolated flaws can be repaired by soldering or soldering in new materials. Patination oils compensate for variations in colour.

Wood and wood-based products
The indigenous species spruce, fir, Scots pine, larch and Douglas fir plus cedar species and tropical species, e.g. afzelia, are used in the facade. Wood-based products are boards and linear elements that are produced by joining together smaller pieces of wood (e.g. boards, veneers, battens, chippings, fibres, wool) with the help of binders or adhesives and additives such as hardeners, wood preservatives, flame retardants, water repellents, etc. Reducing the size of the wood by sawing, rotary cutting, splitting, chipping, chopping or defibration and the subsequent bonding process results in consistent characteristics instead of the anisotropic properties of timber, meaning that wood-based products, in contrast to solid timber, exhibit less scatter in their properties and to a large extent isotropy in the plane of the product. Solid timber, plywood and cement-bonded fibreboards are suitable for facades.
Plywood consists of at least three layers (plies) of veneer bonded together cross-wise with adhesive. This cross-wise bonding compensates for the different shrinkage behaviour in the longitudinal and transverse directions. The nature of the central ply enables us to distinguish between veneer plywood with veneers exclusively parallel to the plane of the board, laminboard with a central core of strips of solid wood glued together on edge and blockboard with a central core of sawn, glued solid timber battens. Laminated veneer lumber (LVL) consists of veneer plies glued together with waterproof adhesive parallel to the fibres. To improve stability, transverse veneers are included on large widths. Parallel strand lumber (PSL) consists of thin strips of veneer bonded together with waterproof adhesive to form T-beams and cut to form beams with standard dimensions. Compound sections consist of individual, narrow laminations, finger-jointed to create longer lengths, that are glued together to produce sections with various dimensions. Glued laminated timber (glulam) is a softwood product consisting of at least three laminations whose planed sides are placed one above the other and glued together to form a complete timber section.

Fibreboards are classed according to their density as porous (with/without bitumen impregnation), medium hard (also known as medium density fibreboard, MDF) and hard or extra hard. Mainly used for interior work, they are produced by two methods: the wet method, in which the bond between the fibres and bundles of fibres is essentially based on the wood's own binder, lignin, and the natural bond between the fibres due to felting (interlocking); or the dry method, which employs synthetic resins. Depending on the type of binder, we distinguish between organic boards (synthetic resin) and mineral boards (Portland or magnesia cement, gypsum). Coarse particleboards consist of larger, layered chips, one particular type being known as oriented strand board (OSB). Wood-wool lightweight building boards are produced using low pressure from long-fibre mineralised wood wool from spruce trees and a mineral binder (Portland cement, magnesite). On facades they are used primarily as a substrate for render.

Damage
Only the surface of the wood is affected by the weather. The depth of this effect can be up to 4 mm, depending on the species and the length and type of exposure. The causes of this weathering are photochemical, biological and physical processes that are superimposed and interdependent. The biological processes also include infestation by plant and animal pests. The development of a grey colouring on the outside of the wood is evidence of the weathering process. Depending on the orientation, a slow degradation of the wood fibres can take place, and the wood itself near the surface can be degraded by UV radiation. Brownish, water-soluble and/or leachable decomposition products are formed (from lignin). If these are removed by the effects of wind and rain, whitish cellulose remains, which is less sensitive to radiation (bleaching effect).
Down to a depth of 0.5 mm, timber surfaces wetted by rain or dew can be colonised by dark-coloured moulds which feed off photochemical decomposition products. These dark fungi are another cause of the grey colouring of the wood. Colonisation by mould represents a "natural pigmentation" of the timber surface which slows down the further degradation of the timber by light. The different densities of the xylem lead to the growth rings becoming highlighted as erosion continues. When directly exposed to the weather, the reduction in cross-section can be up to 0.1 mm per year.
Wood-based board products can bulge, crack, become saturated and decay, starting at the edges, due to incorrect adhesive bonding and the effects of swelling and shrinkage (Fig. B 5.4). Corrosion of mechanical fasteners frequently causes unsightly blemishes (Fig. B 5.2). Plant and animal pests have already been discussed in the section on timber under "Loadbearing structure" (see pp. 86–88).

Refurbishment
Timber components can be protected against direct exposure to the weather by appropriate coating systems, but these must also be maintained. In the case of advanced weathering of the surface, the surfaces can be repaired by sanding. If this is no longer possible, replacement is the only option, while improving the passive protection to the timber at the same time. If certain colouring effects are to be achieved and the wood is to be protected against UV radiation, a coating with a varnish or glaze is necessary, which must be renewed at regular intervals.

Doors and windows
In Germany spruce, fir, Scots pine, larch and oak are used for wooden doors and window frames, but also tropical woods such as the reddish meranti (resistant and free from knots). The quality of the wood used is critical for the durability and performance of doors and windows.

Damage
The bottom rail and the lower parts of wooden window frames are particularly affected by moisture (Figs. B 5.21 and 5.22). Serious damage – right up to irreparable damage to the wood itself – can even take place with a vapour-tight external coating. The appearance of gaps at corners due to shrinkage and swelling leads to moisture infiltration and fungal growth.
The edge seals of insulating glass units these days last about 25–30 years. Damage appears in the form of improper functioning and condensation in the cavity between the panes (Fig. B 5.20). Deposits from other building materials, e.g. rust, hydrofluoric acid from wood preservatives or silicate from cement-bonded facade materials containing lime (e.g. fibre-cement), can etch and stain the surface of the glass. With older, putty-fixed glazing the linseed oil putty is often hard and cracked. Newer joint sealing compounds based on silicone (service life 10–20 years) or acrylic (suitable for painting) can be used to replace polysulphide synthetic resins such as "Thiokol" containing PCP (used approx. 1955–1975). Cracking, embrittlement and loss of adhesion or cohesion in the joints make refurbishment unavoidable. With patent glazing systems and gaskets made from synthetic rubber (from 1930 onwards), embrittlement and damaged corner joints can be encountered.

Refurbishment
The exposed bottom rail of a wooden window can be made from oak in order to prolong the service life of this component. Regular inspections (every 3–5 years) – in order to detect and rectify premature coating and moisture damage – are essential if the full service life is to be realised. Besides polishing the glass surfaces, breakages or edge seal failures can only be dealt with by replacing the complete glass unit or window. But the much better U-values of the

B 5.20

B 5.21

B 5.22

B 5.23

B 5.24

B 5.25

B 5.24 Salt damage in the splashing water zone of a plinth made from Brannenburger nagelfluh (sedimentary rock), repaired by replacing the side cladding
B 5.25 Travertine facade panels (no ventilation cavity) becoming detached due to frost action at the plinth
B 5.26 Render damaged between plinth made from Untersberger limestone and the rendered clay brick wall protected against rising damp by a bitumen damp-proof course, Glyptothek Museum, Munich (D), 1815, Leo von Klenze
B 5.27 Reconstruction of a sandstone/clay brick facade in simplified form using reclaimed bricks, Alte Pinakothek Art Museum, Munich (D), 1957, Hans Döllgast

B 5.26

windows available these days (e.g. customary insulating unit in 1975: U = 2.8 W/m²K, today U-values as low as 0.5 W/m²K) may make replacement desirable from the thermal viewpoint anyway. The thermal performance of windows can be upgraded by adding additional panes. Infestation by insects or fungi can be solved by constructional protection measures or wood preservatives (see pp. 86–88).

Stone

The huge variety of natural rock types found throughout the world is divided into three large rock divisions according to their origins:
Igneous rocks are formed from cooled and crystallised magma from deep within the earth (e.g. granite, diorite, syenite, gabbro, trachyte, rhyolite and basalt).
Sedimentary rocks are formed from the erosion products of older rocks through cementation and diagenesis (e.g. conglomerate, sandstone, mudstone, limestone, dolomite, travertine, tuffaceous limestone).
Metamorphic rocks are formed when submerged sedimentary rocks or transformed and molten igneous rocks are subjected to high pressures and temperatures (e.g. gneiss, quartzite, slate, serpentinite, marble).
Choosing the wrong rock and surface treatment is the reason behind many damage scenarios. The minerals contained in each particular type of rock are critical here. For example, unstable iron compounds can lead to discoloration in the form of brown streaks (rust). Minerals and elements can discolour and stain other constituents or components, also decompose, decay completely, form holes, increase soiling and encourage the growth of undesirable flora. The frost resistance of the rock is another critical factor in Central European latitudes. Many stone quarries contain a mix of rock types, with both weathering-resistant and more vulnerable varieties. A blanket decision based on a few samples is often insufficient owing to the scatter in the values. And whereas it is possible to draw on a great wealth of experience in the use of indigenous rocks, for the many types available these days from elsewhere in the world there is often no appropriate experience concerning their long-term behaviour.

Damage

Water in its vapour, liquid and frozen states is the cause of most of the damage found in natural stone. Water fills voids such as cracks, capillaries and pores, and can cause spalling when it freezes. This is because water expands as it turns into ice, the volume increasing by about 9 %. Especially damaging are frequent freeze-thaw cycles. The problem with facade panels becoming detached because of the freezing of the mortar bed in which they were laid (mainly during the 1970s) is encountered much less these days thanks to the use of ventilation cavities and mechanical fasteners (Fig. B 5.25).

Some rock types also lose much of their strength when saturated with water (sandstone about 70 %). In addition, water can dissolve the binder out of the rock. The leaching material forms a compact sinter crust that damages the microstructure of the natural stone. Efflorescence occurs whenever the substances dissolved in water, mostly salts, are transported to the surface by capillary action and then crystallise as the water evaporates. Where the salts form a crust on the surface, there are also salt deposits below these. This salt concentration leads to spalling due to the pressure of crystallisation similar to that of freezing water (Fig. B 5.24). Water also transports damaging salts, contamination and gases into the rock, where they cause chemical changes. In contrast to efflorescence, the accumulation of washed-out cement particles creates so-called cement laitance. The unsightly grey layer left after the evaporation of the water can be removed with cement laitance remover without causing any damage.
Accumulations of dirt consist of particles of quartz, calcareous spar/calcite, gypsum, clays and rust that are blown by the wind. This soiling is worse on soft rocks such as limestone and sandstone. What is at first only a problem for the appearance, can lead – through the effects of moisture and a chemical reaction – to the particles becoming firmly attached and a change in the surface. If the surface remains moist, layers can spall off. Well known is the damage caused by accumulations of bird droppings and also that caused by urine, e.g. on plinths (dogs) or in sanitary facilities with urinals.
Plants can etch the structure of the stone and crack it as their roots grow. Bacteria, algae and lichens cause chemical transformation processes through their metabolic products and acids. The effects of sunshine, rain and wind can lead to colour changes in the surface. It is this patination that gives the stone its character and relief.
Weathering causes some constituents of the stone to be washed out depending on climate, orientation, height of building, rock type, temperature, radiation, air, moisture and the constituents and organisms in air and water. This can result in different weathering patterns even within one facade. Weathering and the formation of a gypseous crust on the surface of carbonatic rock types leads to progressive roughening of ground or polished surfaces, which then appear to have faded due to the diffuse reflections. Hard rocks like granite are resistant to weathering and decay. Dense materials weather on the surface and lose some of their substance. The typical representatives of this group are marble and dense limestones, whose surfaces become powdery or covered in a covering of gypsum (which gradually disintegrates). Where absorbent materials are involved (e.g. sandstones), contamination can infiltrate deeper into the microstructure. Crusts and zones of differing strengths are produced,

characterised by the conversion and loss of binder.

Rocks with porous microstructures and binders containing lime or dolomite are endangered by air pollution. Sulphur dioxide (SO_2) reacts with moisture on the surface of the stone, or in the stone itself, to form sulphurous acid, which dissolves the stone. The calcium sulphate solution evaporates from the surface of the stone and efflorescence is the result. If the calcium sulphate crystallises in the stone, gypsum is formed, but the increase in volume leads to spalling. Air pollution in the form of carbon dioxide causes less damage, dissolving the lime in porous limestones and sandstones. Where different stone types are combined or stone has been used with other materials, their compatibility with each other must be checked. Rusting steel components can lead to discoloration and spalling due to the increase in volume. Mechanical fasteners must therefore be made from stainless steel. Outdoors, the natural substances in wood species such as oak can cause discoloration of natural stone which is difficult to remove.

Refurbishment

Facades facing the prevailing weather direction are generally cleaned sufficiently by natural processes, whereas on other sides there is often a serious accumulation of dirt. The aim of cleaning is to remove the damaging and unsightly deposits as carefully as possible using water (with or without additives), pressurised water jets, steam, etc. The means and methods must take into account the long-term protection of the original building fabric.

Constructional measures such as the formation of projections and mouldings plus careful drainage of rainwater minimise the damage caused by water and the weather; coarsely worked surfaces are more vulnerable here than polished ones. Dirty gypseous crusts and other worn areas can be removed by sand-blasting or bush-hammering the surfaces. Acids or chemical cleaning agents are dangerous and should be used only by specialist contractors following preliminary tests. When replacing stones and slabs, the colours and textures must be matched.

Treatment with substances that reduce the water absorption through the surface (pores, capillaries) also reduce wetting and soiling and accelerate the water run-off. The prerequisite is an absorbent stone type and a vapour-permeable impregnation treatment that alters neither the surface nor the colour. The chemicals industry can supply products that strengthen, protect and preserve the natural stone. The action of UV radiation means, however, that most impregnation treatments have only a limited lifetime.

Render

Renders are finishes applied to walls in one or more coats of a certain thickness. They are made from render mixes or other materials that gain their final properties after hardening in situ. Render mixes are made from binders, aggregates (sand) and water, possibly special additives as well. In the case of calcined gypsums and anhydrite binders for interior use only, additives are unnecessary. We generally distinguish between renders with mineral and organic binders (synthetic resin products/dispersions). Like mortars for masonry, mineral renders are divided into groups according to their binders. The non-hydraulic and hydraulic lime types of group I have little compressive strength but can absorb and release considerable amounts of water. Products made from masonry lime and cement belong to group II and are the standard materials used for facades these days. Group III materials (cement/lime hydrate and pure cement) are very strong, absorb little moisture and are therefore suitable for use as water-repellent layers and in areas likely to suffer mechanical damage (e.g. plinths, stairs). The gypsum and anhydrite materials of groups IV/V may be mixed with lime and are for internal applications. Organic materials are divided into group POrg 1 (outside and inside) and POrg 2 (inside only).

We distinguish between site-mixed and ready-mixed materials depending on where the mixing takes place, and between ready-mixed and premixed dry materials depending on whether the water (for mixing the raw materials together) is added at the works or on the building site. The latter has been produced since the late 19th century, and its advantages are the accurate mixing of the different materials and the supervision during production. Ready-mixed

materials were used for finish coats until the 1960s. Later, machine-applied materials became more popular for undercoats. It was primarily the development of lighter, highly insulating wall materials that led to the development of lighter and softer renders. Lightweight, or insulating, renders are applied to lightweight masonry and reduce the risk of cracks.

Besides contributing to the styling of a facade, renders also protect the underlying wall against water. This property is guaranteed through a combination of strength, water-repellent properties and thickness. The durability of a render depends on various factors, e.g. composition, strength, water absorption capacity, deformation modulus, substrate and preparation, application, edge details, surface treatment, coating, maintenance and care. Depending on the render system, spatterdash, undercoat and finish coat (possibly pigmented) will be necessary. Smooth surfaces such as concrete need a coat of bond enhancer first. Curing should take place at temperatures between 0 and 30 °C in order to prevent rapid drying-out and frost problems.

Insulating renders are those with a thermal conductivity < 0.2 W/mK. This is the case where the oven-dry density of the hardened mortar is < 0.6 kg/dm³ (aggregates: expanded polystyrene or mineral lightweight materials such as expanded perlite/mica/clay, foamed glass, exfoliated vermiculite and pumice). Organic and mineral aggregates may be combined. Insulating renders are not suitable for the bases of walls where mechanical damage is likely. Renovation renders should not seal the surface, but rather exhibit high porosity and vapour permeability while reducing the water absorption through capillarity. As such renders contain considerable amounts of cement, an air en-

B 5.27

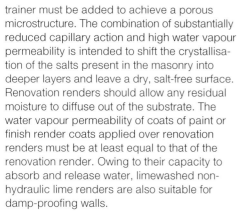

B 5.28

B 5.29

B 5.30

trainer must be added to achieve a porous microstructure. The combination of substantially reduced capillary action and high water vapour permeability is intended to shift the crystallisation of the salts present in the masonry into deeper layers and leave a dry, salt-free surface. Renovation renders should allow any residual moisture to diffuse out of the substrate. The water vapour permeability of coats of paint or finish render coats applied over renovation renders must be at least equal to that of the renovation render. Owing to their capacity to absorb and release water, limewashed non-hydraulic lime renders are also suitable for damp-proofing walls.

Coating materials made from organic binders, generally in the form of aqueous dispersions, plus aggregates or fillers with the majority of particles > 0.25 mm are used for producing resin renders. However, such products require a coat of primer and are also applied to mineral renders as a finish coat. They are easy to mix and apply and are mostly applied by machine (coat thickness: 2–3 mm). Resin renders based on aqueous dispersions cure through the evaporation of the water in the material, which causes the distances between the dispersed polymers to vanish, giving rise to cross-linking. The resulting film is then no longer water-soluble. Organic products are used for the renders in external thermal insulation composite systems (ETICS), sometimes as textured finishes or for finish coatings.

In an ETICS the thermal insulation (boards or lamella products) is attached to the existing substrate (e.g. clay bricks, calcium silicate bricks, concrete) by means of adhesive and/or mechanical fasteners, and covered by a layer of tough render (Fig. B 5.28). The render consists of an undercoat with a reinforcing mesh embedded in the upper third of its thickness. The ETICS is completed with a finish coat of render, which may be painted, but it is important that all components are fully compatible. An ETICS was first used in Berlin in 1957. At that time rigid polystyrene foam boards were used for the thermal insulation, and that is still the case for nearly 90 % of the systems used today. ETICS have been widely used throughout Germany since 1965, and since the late

1970s with mineral-fibre insulating boards as well. Polyurethane foam (PUR), cork, wood fibres, hemp and reeds are possible alternative insulating materials these days. For reasons of cost, mineral renders are preferred to the resin products with their better thermal characteristics.

Damage

The causes of damage and cracking in render can be found in the render itself or in the substrate, or may be due to structural movements. Blemishes and discoloration are often attributable to constructional weaknesses such as thermal bridges and splashing water. Permanent moisture in areas that cannot dry out properly encourage the growth of algae and fungi and can cause chalking, dusting, erosion and spalling (Figs. B 5.26 and 5.29).

Where render becomes detached from the substrate, this is due to permanent wetting/drying, heating/cooling and poor adhesion due to an absorptive substrate or the lack of a primer. Varying, unsound substrates and those subjected to creep or shrinkage can lead to coats becoming detached and cracked. Mineral products are more brittle than organic ones and so may crumble and crack. But the disadvantage with organic materials is that blisters can form and whole coats can become detached. ETICS can suffer from cracking (poor workmanship), damage due to impacts, failure of the adhesive, discoloration and algal/fungal growth. In the complete systems offered these days it is soiling of the surface and algae that are the main problems. On older buildings with an unsuitable substrate, insulating materials not attached with mechanical fasteners can become detached, together with the render. The insulating materials must be tightly butted together or any gaps filled with in situ foam in order to avoid temperature differences in the render. Uneven insulation can lead to cracks; any difference in levels must be made good.

Refurbishment

If damp render is to be repaired permanently, the moisture infiltration into the wall must be prevented by horizontal damp-proof courses or other appropriate waterproofing measures. As damp walls dry out, damaging salts are carried

to the surface. The water evaporates, leaving behind the salts as crystals on the surface. Compressive stresses of 50–200 N/mm^2 ensue during this crystallisation process. An open-pore render system is therefore essential with damp walls. Loose coats of render must be removed back to sound material and repaired or completely replaced as necessary; the render should not have a higher strength than the substrate.

At cracks where no further movement is expected, the crack should first be widened, coated with bond enhancer or provided with reinforcement and then filled with grout. Detached coats and larger cracks can be repaired by applying insulating or lightweight render materials (check low-temperature elasticity) to the existing materials, consolidated and treated with a water-repellent agent (Fig. B 5.30).

Smaller cracks can be bridged over and filled with a coating system or suitable filler plus finish coat. Where further movement at cracks is to be expected, an expansion joint should be incorporated and covered by a suitable profile. ETICS with algal infestation can be treated with fungicidal or biocidal coatings and cleaned. For older systems with problems in the insulation, mechanical fasteners, render, etc., often the only solution is complete replacement.

Paints and coatings

Coatings consist of binders, fillers, pigments, solvent or thinners and other additives. Depending on the degree of coverage, we distinguish between impregnation, sealing, glazes and opaque paints. According to DIN 18363 the substrate can be made ready for coating by using preparatory materials (sealants, strippers, cleaning agents, impregnation treatments, wood preservatives, water repellents, biocides), primers and fillers. The coating systems are divided into those that contain solvents and those that can be thinned with water (colourless varnishes, lacquers, glazes with oil-based and lacquer binders).

Priming coats, varnishes and glazes must be compatible with the respective substrate (mineral, timber, metal). In the water-thinnable systems (binder, lime, sizes, emulsions and dispersions), those suitable for mineral substrates are lime, lime-cement, silicate, dispersion silicate, synthetic dispersion, distemper, silicon resin emulsion and dispersion lacquers. Water-thinnable synthetic dispersions, dispersion varnishes, synthetic dispersion and acrylic glaze paints are available for timber, and synthetic dispersion paints for metals. Coatings for mineral and wooden substrates may include fungicides or biocides. Intumescent paints applied to metal expand to form an insulating foam in the event of a fire.

Lime paints use calcium hydrate (quicklime slaked with water as binder and pigment) as a binder; they can be used internally and also in protected external areas. Other binders such as casein or synthetic resin dispersions can be added to improve durability. Carbonation (absorption of CO_2 from the air) causes the formation of a hard white layer of lime. Only pastel shades are possible because lime can bind only a few pigments. Lime paints can be applied to plaster/render that has not fully cured (al fresco). Owing to their alkaline properties, they act as a disinfectant and kill fungi, do not form a film and can only be applied to mineral substrates and those containing lime (but not gypsum plasters).

Silicate paints consist of potassium water glass as a binder, water and a dye powder made from water glass-resistant pigments and fillers. Water glass is a glass-like compound made from silicon and oxygen which, dissolved in water as a salt with sodium or potassium, forms a colourless, gelatinous mass. Two-part silicate paints contain neither organic solvents nor synthetic dispersions to improve their workability. They do not form a film and are applied only to mineral, silicating substrates as an exterior finish when restoring buildings protected by conservation orders because their use calls for good workmanship and is therefore costly. One-part silicate paints represent a further development of the two-part products; they use synthetic dispersions (acrylate, styrene/acrylate) and organic solvents to improve their workability and properties. They are used mainly on mineral substrates externally, provided sufficient protection from the weather can be guaranteed, and internally. When using lime and silicate paints, glass, stone, facing bricks, aluminium

components, etc. must be covered and any splashes washed off immediately. Any porous lime layers (sinter crust) must be removed with chemicals and the stone subsequently rinsed with water.

In dispersion paints the binder is finely dispersed in water. The evaporation of the water causes the dispersed synthetic particles to combine and form the film of binder. In normal dispersion paints this film is less tough but more impact-resistant than with dispersion lacquers. The properties can be controlled through the choice of binder (synthetic resins). Dispersion paints are used on exposed walls and facades. The less vapour-permeable dispersions should not be applied to lime plaster/renders. Solvent-free dispersion paints for interiors are the most widely used product group of the paints and varnishes. Synthetic resin plasters/renders are bonded with synthetic dispersions.

In natural resin paints (e.g. for plaster) the binder is finely dispersed in water. These products contain small amounts of solvent for forming a film. Animal and vegetable oils, resins and waxes in various combinations are used as binders. Natural resin paints are used on less exposed mineral walls and ceilings. Gypsum-based boards and highly absorbent or sandy substrates must be primed with a paint thinned with water (max. 1:1) or a natural resin primer (possibly mixed with 10–20 % paint).

Size, the binder in distempers (e.g. for plasterboard), does not lose its water-solubility even after drying out. Distempers therefore remain sensitive to moisture. Sizes are based on animal (mostly lactic acid/casein) or vegetable (mostly cellulose) products. Casein paints are more water-resistant than cellulose paints (mixed with whitewash they are no longer water-soluble). Cellulose paints represent one of the most inexpensive paint systems. Distempers can be used internally on less exposed mineral substrates (ceilings, some walls). They are also suitable for wallpaper and plasterboard. Casein-tempera paints can also be used for less exposed timber components.

Silicon resin paints (e.g. for render) combine the advantages of silicate binders (quartz, chemical silication with the mineral substrate) and synthetic resins. Pure silicon resin paints

are water-repellent and vapour-permeable, but do not form a film. As the proportion of synthetic dispersion increases, so the film formation and strength increase, too, but water absorption and vapour permeability decrease. Silicon resin paints can be applied to almost all mineral substrates internally and externally, but owing to their CO_2 permeability are not suitable for reinforced concrete. The main applications are severely exposed mineral facades.

Polymer resin paints are products in which the binder (combinations of synthetic resins such as acrylate, styrene, vinyl toluene, polyvinyl chloride) is dissolved in organic solvents (not water). Owing to the particle size and the solvent, they form more compact films than dispersion paints, although they contain binders that are chemically related. Polymer resin paints penetrate deep into the substrate with small synthetic resin particles, which substantially improves the adhesion and cleanability of the paint film. They are used for coating mineral facades, but can also be applied to hot-dip galvanised or primed steel surfaces externally and exposed mineral substrates internally.

Until the development of synthetic resins in the middle of the 20th century, oil-based paints were the only paint systems that provided substrates with an impact-resistant, tough film coating. To this day, boiled linseed oil obtained from flax is used as the binder. Oil-based paints and natural resin varnishes are regarded as environment friendly, even though the majority of systems contain solvents. They are mostly used on exposed internal and external wood and wood-based products. Oil-based paints are also suitable as a primer to protect against rust because they enclose any residual rust on rusty metal surfaces.

Alkyd resin lacquers were developed from oil-based paints through chemical modification. Alkyd resins with an oil content > 60 % are regarded as high-quality decorators' products, whereas alkyd resins with a lower oil content tend to be used for industrial purposes (e.g. stove enamels). Alkyd resin lacquers are mainly used for exposed timber and metal components internally and externally, e.g. windows, doors, shutters, cladding (Figs. B 5.32 and 5.33).

In dispersion lacquers the binder is finely dis-

B 5.28   Structure of an external thermal insulation composite system (ETICS)
B 5.29   Serious spalling of render undercoat and finish coat due to the crystallisation pressure of salts dissolved in rising damp, example from Venice
B 5.30   Grooved render finish to art nouveau facade made good with repair mortar
B 5.31   Flaking of paint and damage to timber substrate caused by moisture and UV radiation plus inadequate maintenance

B 5.31

B 5.32

B 5.32   Renewing the coating to sheet metal cable trunking using alkyd resin paint
B 5.33   Steel door frame repaired with filling material prior to final painting with alkyd resin paint
B 5.34   Rusting below the paint finish to a steel component
B 5.35   Thermal conductivity of various insulating materials
B 5.36   Acoustic ceiling made from plasterboard
B 5.37   Acoustic insulation in the form of laminated mineral-fibre batts

B 5.33

B 5.34

persed in water and ensures an impact-resistant film after drying. Considering the need for hygienic air and hygienic working conditions, dispersion lacquers represent an alternative to synthetic resin varnishes, and contain both solvents and water. They are used on exposed mineral substrates (walls) internally, also wood or wood-based products internally and externally. Dispersion lacquers for metal generally contain anti-corrosion pigments, whereas wood primers for exterior use are mixed with biological substances. Water-thinnable polyurethane resins are suitable where high demands are placed on mechanical and chemical resistance. In buildings they are primarily used together with water-thinnable one-part systems, also two-part systems containing solvents. Polyurethane resins are used on exposed timber, metal or concrete interior components (furniture, industrial and sports floors, wood-block flooring), also metals indoors and outdoors. Owing to their low water vapour permeability, their suitability for mineral substrates is limited.

In water-thinnable clear varnishes the binder is dispersed in water. In contrast to normal dispersion paints the binder is modified in such a way that it forms an impact-resistant film after curing. Clear varnishes have a high binder content and contain no pigments or fillers. Water-thinnable clear varnishes are used in buildings primarily for furniture and other exposed wooden components (e.g. door frames, windows), for coating industrial and sports floors and for sealing wood-block floors. Applications outdoors are possible with specially modified polyurethane resins. Without special additives, however, clear varnishes are permeable to UV light, which means that the lignin in the wood – and hence the substrate for the varnish – is destroyed.

In glazes, also thinned with water, the binder (acrylate and alkyd resin/acrylate combinations) is dispersed in water. Wood glazes are runny, porous and penetrate into the substrate. The structure on the surface of the wood remains intact. To improve their properties, water-repellent and pest-resistant additives can be included. Besides thin-film glazes with their easy workability and consistent weathering properties, high-build glazes are also available which form a thicker film and provide good protection against moisture. Wood glazes are similar to clear varnishes, but protect against UV light as well (pigmentation). They last longer than synthetic and natural resin glazes, but still not as long as other products. They are used to protect wood indoors and outdoors (moisture content < 18 %, windows < 12 %).

Nitrocellulose varnishes first gained significance on an industrial scale in the early 20th century. As environmental protection became a more important topic, they were used less and less because they contain plasticisers and up to 80 % solvents. Synthetic resin varnishes containing solvents are used mainly internally to protect timber and metal surfaces (after priming) against mechanical impacts.

Although natural resin varnishes contain less oil than oil-based paints, they still dry like the latter, i.e. chemically-oxidatively. Combinations of vegetable oils with tree resins or shellac are common. They dry quickly, but must be applied carefully. Owing to their alcohol content they are known as spirit varnishes and are used for protecting wood internally (moisture content <14 –15 %), but they do not protect the wood against UV light.

Damage

Most problems with paints on facades can be attributed to moisture, poor substrates and too rapid drying of the coating. The paint should prevent moisture infiltrating from the outside, but should also allow moisture to escape from the wall or the interior. Condensation can cause mould growth in interiors. Saturation of the masonry causes paint to flake off and the crystallisation of salts. Water-soluble paints can be degraded over the long-term. Moisture that has infiltrated the wall may be responsible for discoloration, efflorescence, flaking, blisters (especially resin plasters and dispersion paints) and the transportation of salts that crystallise on the surface. Likewise, growths of mould or algae at permanently damp places. Incompatibility between undercoats and top coats result in incomplete drying, creasing and cracks. Loss of shine and chalking due to exposure to the weather are problems that occur mainly with lacquers. The repainting intervals of five to eight years specified for the majority of paint systems are, however, often far exceeded in practice (Figs. B 5.31 and 5.34).

Refurbishment

Old coats of paint can usually be removed by grinding or sanding and the surfaces then repainted, chalky linseed oil paints can be refreshed by re-oiling (Fig. B 5.32). If a coat of paint is completely degraded or a mineral paint is to be used on organic layers, an analysis (flame test, solvent test, etc.) should be carried out and the old coats then removed as follows:

• mechanically (scraping, brushing, grinding, sanding))
• thermally (hot air)
• chemically (strippers or caustic solutions, biologically degradable whenever possible, for polymers and coatings containing solvents)

Pure acrylates from dispersion paints are thermoplastic and therefore very difficult to remove. The uppermost layer of an oil-based paint can be removed with ammonia through a saponification reaction. Distemper and lime paint can be washed off. Where coats of paint on metal are badly degraded, strippers are often the only solution. After allowing the components to dry out (moisture below equilibrium moisture content, plaster/render requires 28 days) and preparing the substrate (sound, bond enhancer on absorbent substrates), new coats of paint can be applied. Where mould or algae infestation is anticipated, most paints can be mixed with biocides.

Insulating materials

Insulating materials are those building materials that owing to the presence of countless voids exhibit a large volume for a low weight. Stationary air is a poor conductor of heat. Thermal insulation materials have a thermal conductivity < 0.1 W/mK (Fig. B 5.35). Specific insulating materials are a development of the 20th century. Cork boards were first produced in 1896. The Dyckerhoff company started its production of "Torfoleum" insulation boards made from pressed and impregnated peat in 1912, which were superseded in 1958 by rigid polystyrene foam boards. Nowadays, insulating materials are made from organic and mineral materials in many forms (felt, batts, boards, loose fill). The common products are coordinated with respect to moisture behaviour, fire protection, elasticity and heat storage for internal, external, impact sound, basement and roof insulation applications. Diagonal cuts and tongue and groove joints ease installation. Besides mineral wool and rigid foam materials, natural insulating materials (e.g. flax, cotton, sheep's wool) are becoming ever more significant.

Owing to its low price, the most popular synthetic insulating material is expanded polystyrene (EPS). Extruded polystyrene (XPS) has a closed-pore structure and is therefore suitable for applications in damp environments such as an inverted roof and in the ground. Rigid polyurethane foam (PUR) has good insulating values but also a high primary energy content. Mineral wool (glass wool, rock wool) is suitable for almost all everyday applications (but not when moisture is involved) and owing to its compressibility is popular as an insulating material between timber studs and timber rafters. Cellular glass consists of foamed silicates. It is vapour-tight, waterproof and heat-resistant, and can be used in applications where moisture is present, e.g. terraces, flat roofs, in the ground (also with hot bitumen). Vacuum insulation panels (VIP) are excellent insulators. They consist of several layers of foil-covered pyrogenic silicic acid from which the air has been evacuated. VIPs are expensive and vulnerable to mechanical damage, and can therefore be used only in conjunction with conventional insulating materials and for special applications (e.g. insulation for a level terrace access). Among the natural insulating materials, cellulose products in the form of boards, pellets and flakes (for blowing into voids) made from scrap paper have proved worthwhile in timber construction. Cotton, sheep's wool, flax and hemp are currently still expensive and also vulnerable to infestation; they are used in a similar way to mineral wool. Wood fibres and cork are among the oldest insulating materials. Wood-fibre insulating boards are ideal for combined protection against heat and cold. Cork is obtained from the bark of the cork oak and is used in the form of insulation cork board (ICB), natural cork and cork granulate. Perlite is an insulating material obtained from volcanic rock (loose fill). Calcium silicate internal insulating boards are made from calcium, quartz sand, cellulose fibres and water glass. They are used as thermal insulation on the inside of an external wall and are therefore ideal for subsequent internal insulation where the appearance of the original facade must be retained (Fig. B 5.38). Their porous structure allows them to absorb condensation, which can then evaporate. If applying a coating, care must be taken to ensure that the porous structure remains intact.

Damage

Many insulating materials lose some of their insulating effect because water infiltrates from outside or condensation from inside. Pigments in the materials can lead to discoloration of adjoining components. Above all, "natural insulating materials" can be infested by animal pests and possibly degraded completely. Settlement of loose fill or other soft insulating materials can lead to voids, defective fixings can cause insulating material to become detached. Old materials are often not thick enough to comply with current standards.

Refurbishment

Damaged insulating materials must be replaced, smaller voids can be filled with in situ foam. Upgrading the thermal performance usually involves installing additional layers of insulating material at suitable places (outside, inside, in the plane of the loadbearing members). On very intricate facades, internal insulation is preferred to external insulation (mostly ETICS these days), even though the latter is much more sensible from the building physics viewpoint.

Insulating material	Thermal conductivity [W/mK]
Expanded polystyrene (EPS)	0.025–0.045
Extruded polystyrene (XPS)	0.032–0.041
Polyurethane foam (PUR)	0.025–0.040
Mineral wool	0.033–0.045
Cellular glass	0.040–0.050
Vacuum insulation panel (VIP)	0.0042
Cellulose products	0.037–0.070
Cotton	0.040–0.045
Sheep's wool	0.039–0.046
Flax	0.037–0.040
Hemp	0.042–0.046
Wood-fibre insulating boards	0.036–0.051
Cork	0.036–0.055
Perlite	0.044–0.070
Calcium silicate insulating boards	0.050–0.070

B 5.35

B 5.36

B 5.37

B 5.38

B 5.39

B 5.40

Fitting-out

Fitting-out components sometimes show signs of damage such as cracks and saturation, which are attributable to loadbearing structure and envelope problems. This is exacerbated by the fact that many of the building materials used in fitting-out are less resistant to moisture and loads. Coatings, casings and linings are often replaced and therefore not dealt with in detail here.

Plaster and gypsum materials
Plaster should adhere well to the substrate so that it provides a sound, flat surface for finishes such as wallpaper, paint, etc.; it should also be able to absorb water and allow the passage of water vapour. Plaster can also help to improve the sound insulation and fire protection properties. Lime, gypsum or lime-gypsum plasters (group P I or P IV) are mainly used. Cement plasters can be used where mechanical impacts are expected. Gypsum plasters of group P IV (gypsum, gypsum sand, gypsum lime and lime gypsum mortars) employ calcined gypsum as a binder (also in combination with lime); they can be used for internal walls and ceilings in rooms where the humidity is not excessive, which includes domestic kitchens and bathrooms (Fig. B 5.39). Plasters of group P I (non-hydraulic and hydraulic lime mortars) contain lime as the binder and they are used both indoors and outdoors. The use of pure lime mortar declined between the 1950s and the 1970s, but it is becoming more popular again because of its ecological benefits and the damage reported with building chemicals products. Owing to its very long setting time, pure non-hydraulic lime mortar is seldom used. Plasters with non-hydraulic or hydraulic lime as the binder are often modified with small amounts of cement and synthetic resin additives nowadays so that they set quickly and are water-repellent. Cement and lime-cement plasters are suitable for interior work to only a limited extent. They are perceived as cold and hard, have limited sorption capacity and hardly help to regulate the interior humidity. Acoustic plasters exhibit an open-pore structure to improve the sound insulation. Loam plasters are generally used to replace similar plasters on timber-framed walls. Plasterboard consists of a gypsum core with a covering of paper both sides. Gypsum fibre-board contains cellulose fibres as well as gypsum and can be used for the same applications as plasterboard. Plasterboard is divided into various groups (Fig. B 5.41):

- Plasterboard B for general applications
- Plasterboard F with improved fire resistance
- Plasterboard I with improved moisture resistance

All boards can be affixed to existing walls with dabs of mortar or screwed to timber or metal stud constructions to form an inner lining or casing which is subsequently given a skim coat of plaster (Figs. B 5.36 and 5.40). : Solid gypsum-based boards are suitable as non-loadbearing internal walls and linings but they are not widely used in Germany. Finishes can be applied directly.

Damage
Damage to plaster is caused by structural movements, inconsistently and poorly repaired substrates, mechanical impacts and moisture. Prior to refurbishment, the cause of the damage should be established and rectified. Shortcomings in workmanship such as missing or inadequate movement joints, lack of consideration for the movements of the structure, e.g. deflections of suspended floors, lead to cracks in plasterboard walls and linings. As gypsum components do not have a high impact resistance, they should not be used in areas where mechanical damage is likely, e.g. staircases. Persistently high moisture levels can lead to mould growth, efflorescence and degradation of the material.

Refurbishment
When moisture and movements are the cause of the damage, these must be rectified during the refurbishment work. Cracks and spalling can often be attributed to too rapid drying. Small cracks and damage can be repaired by cutting back to sound material and filling with a suitable material, if necessary providing reinforcement in the form of cloth or tear-resistant wallpaper. Plasterboard can be painted with highly elastic dispersion paints after the cracks have been repaired in order to suppress the formation of new cracks. But expansion joints can be retrofitted if required. Mould can be dealt with by installing insulation, reducing the moisture loads and applying disinfectant plasters and paints (lime).

Wooden floors
Floorboards are made from softwoods such as spruce, fir, Scots pine and larch. Wood-block flooring employs many different indigenous hardwoods (oak, maple, ash, beech, cherry, walnut) and tropical species (owing to their hardness and abrasion resistance).

Damage
Besides mechanical damage and wear, changes of colour, discoloration and burn marks are common. Bulges, depressions and shrinkage caused by drying out become noticeable by way of loose pieces and widened joints.

Refurbishment
Wood-block flooring and floorboards can be sanded and re-sealed more often than parquet laminate flooring. Badly damaged or worn pieces can be replaced individually. In contrast to oiled and/or waxed floors, sealed wooden floors cannot be partially repaired; instead, the whole area must be sanded and the system of finishes renewed.

Subfloors and terrazzo
Subfloors are laid directly on a loadbearing substrate or a separating or insulating layer. They can be in the form of in situ materials (screeds, asphalt) or dry materials (plasterboard, flooring-grade particleboard). A bonded screed is laid directly on the loadbearing substrate. An unbonded screed is laid on a separating material for constructional or building physics reasons (e.g. waterproofing). A floating screed is laid as a load-distributing, rigid layer on various resilient thermal or sound insulating materials and must be able to move independently ("float"). Separating layers between insulation and subfloor are necessary, and peri-

B 5.38 Calcium silicate boards as internal insulation,
with double layer of plasterboard as inner lining
B 5.39 Gypsum plaster internal wall finish
B 5.40 Metal stud wall with mineral fibre insulation and
plasterboard cladding
B 5.41 Colour-coded plasterboard
B 5.42 Cracked terrazzo floor after repair

B 5.41

B 5.42

meter components must be separated from the subfloor by strips of insulating material.

The thickness of a screed depends on the materials used and should increase as the thickness of the insulation increases. Self-levelling screeds are very runny and can therefore be pumped. Rapid-hardening screeds are improved cement screeds with particularly short curing times. Heated screeds contain heating coils (hot water or electricity) and are generally laid on a layer of insulation and can only be completed after a controlled heating and cooling process. Granolithic screeds are cement screeds with a hard aggregate and a finished surface.

Cement and calcium sulphate screeds dominate the market. In the form of a floating screed, the following thicknesses are necessary (plus heating coil): calcium sulphate ≥ 30 mm, cement ≥ 40 mm; heating coil cover ≥ 30 mm. Cracking is a problem with cement screeds (joint spacing 4–7 m for a bay size of max. 40 m²). Under normal conditions a cement screed is ready for use after 28 days (residual moisture). Calcium sulphate screeds are usually laid in the form of self-levelling screeds. They also require approx. 28 days, although a rate of about 10 mm per week can be used as a guide to the drying time. As calcium sulphate screeds are sensitive to moisture, the surface of the screeds must be waterproofed and proof of only minimal residual moisture is necessary.

Asphalt consists of bitumen, sand/chippings and stone dust and is laid "dry" at a temperature of approx. 200–250 °C. Once it has cooled it can accept traffic immediately and is therefore first choice in refurbishment projects where time is short. Flooring cement was widely used for reconstruction work in the post-war years. It is made from caustic magnesium, an aqueous solution (generally magnesium chloride), additives (pigments) and aggregates such as soft wood chippings and wood flour, but also cork granulate, paper powder, quartz dust and fibres. Synthetic resin screeds can be very thin when laid as bonded screeds and are highly resistant to mechanical impacts and chemicals. Terrazzo floors are in situ, seamless floor finishes, mostly in the form of two layers. The upper layer is known as the topping, the lower the

setting bed. Together the two layers form a hardwearing floor finish. Coloured stone aggregates, pigments and white or grey Portland cement can be used to colour the topping. Once hard, the compacted topping is ground with different grits until the largest particle size is visible, then subsequently waxed or oiled.

Damage
In addition to shrinkage cracks due to the drying process, cranks, bulges, unevenness, damage caused by loads and dusting (up to total disintegration) are possible problems. Terrazzo floors may suffer from loss of individual pieces, cracks and discoloration.

Refurbishment
Adhesive residue and unevenness can be eliminated by grinding. Minor damage can be repaired by cutting back to sound material and filling with appropriate material, small cracks or voids by injection or coating with a synthetic resin solution. To join the flanks of very small cracks such that stresses can be transferred across them, they are cut back to sound material, cleaned out and then filled with a synthetic resin or synthetic resin mortar. When anchoring wider cracks, it is necessary to drill through the crack into the screed every 200 mm (down to the separating layer in the case of a floating screed, into the loadbearing floor for a bonded screed). The drilled holes are then cleaned out and filled with a synthetic resin mortar. "Riveting" is similar: the holes drilled in the vicinity of the crack are filled with synthetic resin until a "rivet head" forms. In the case of "wiring", the screed is cut back every 200 mm at 90° to the crack; after cleaning out, a wire is laid in this cut-out which is then filled with synthetic resin mortar and struck off flush. Pressure-grouting of bonded screeds involves closing off cracks by injecting synthetic resin using packers. Terrazzo floors can be made good or renewed. Cracks are chiselled out, widened and then filled with terrazzo material. After grinding the whole floor, it is re-impregnated with waxes and oils (Fig. B 5.42).

Dangerous substances in the building stock

Alexander Rudolphi

Up until the end of the 19th century the use of chemical products in the building industry was essentially limited to wood preservatives, corrosion protection products, seals and paints. However, it is wrong to believe that none of the buildings built more than 150 years ago are contaminated by substances harmful to humans. For instance, there is a long tradition of using arsenic and mercury compounds in wood preservatives. Even now arsenic is used in pressure impregnation methods in the form of chromium-copper-arsenic (CCA) wood preservative salts and has not yet been completely banned for certain applications. In 1988 Germany produced 380 t of arsenic oxide and imported approx. 100–200 t [1].

Wood and coal tar oils (low-viscosity tar oil derivatives) have been used since very early times. The production of paints from lead and copper oxide, also mercury sulphide, is even described in the books on architecture by the Roman master-builder Vitruvius [2]. From the Middle Ages to the 19th century there were numerous toxic compounds involving arsenic (orpiment – yellow) or lead (red lead – orange, white lead). Toxic paints, e.g. lead chromate and chromium oxide (yellow and green respectively) or copper arsenite (green – the most toxic paint ever produced!) were primarily used in art and only occasionally in the building industry. In the 20th century the highly toxic cadmium was added to the repertoire (for neon yellow and red pigments), and was used up until the 1980s.

Since the advent of the chemicals industry, numerous synthetic substances and concoctions in various combinations have been developed and used in the building industry over the last 150 years. The product diversity for the construction sector first reached a peak in the 1960s and 1970s – and today modern synthetic products and resins are ubiquitous on building sites. Up until the 1980s new products suitable for the construction industry were in most cases not investigated any further with respect to their potential danger for persons or the environment; instead, they appeared on the market without delay, heralded as innovative achievements. In some instances the use of substances such as coal tar oils, which are now acknowledged as

dangerous and banned, were included in technical codes of practice as representing the state of the art (e.g. DIN DVM 2122 "Coal tar in roofing felts", DIN 281 – until 1973 – "Cold-applied wood-block flooring compounds"). Pesticides like DDT were used for eradicating lice in open powder sprays in the home.

Only gradually did the hazards of individual substances come to light – mostly through the occurrence of job-related diseases or industrial accidents, which resulted in the first prohibitory legislation.

During the 1950s and 1960s hundreds of people in Japan suffered from the so-called itai-itai disease, a form of cadmium poisoning caused by pumping industrial, contaminated waste water into coastal waters. In December 1984 some 27 t of methyl isocyanate, used in the production of pesticides, leaked into the environment from the Union Carbide chemicals factory in the Indian city of Bhopal. The accident caused the deaths of approx. 20 000 people and is responsible for the disorders of a further 120 000. In July 1976 in northern Italy near the small town of Seveso large quantities of the dioxin TCDD were released in an industrial accident in connection with the production of trichlorophenol at a plant belonging to the Icmesa company (a subsidiary of Roche). More than 200 people were taken severely ill with chloracne.

Thereafter, compounds including cadmium, lead, mercury or arsenic were gradually restricted or banned. The same had happened to pesticides such as DDT and PCP (pentachlorophenol) in Western European and Scandinavian countries during the 1960s, although they remained in widespread use in the Comecon (Council for Mutual Economic Assistance) countries until the 1980s and 1990s. Polycyclic aromatic hydrocarbons (PAH) including the carcinogen benzo[a]pyrene (BaP) as an indicator substance, which were used in floor adhesives, wood preservatives and asphalt products up until the 1960s, were also banned. These substances were first recognised to be problems in the 1980s and disappeared from most building products during the 1990s – once again, only in the countries of the western industrialised world.

B 6.1   Refurbishment work in the presence of contamination by wood preservatives
B 6.2   Categories of danger (selection) and their symbols

Explosive E

 Dangerous for the environment N

 Toxic/very toxic T/T+

 Flammable F

 Irritant Xi

 Harmful Xn

B 6.2

The timespan between the detection of health problems and the adoption of corresponding legislation was, however, very long in some cases. For example, the asbestos fibres known to the ancient Greeks reappeared in numerous industrially manufactured products from the mid-19th century onwards. It was primarily the enormous tensile strength of the fibres and their fire resistance that was exploited. Asbestosis, a disease caused directly by asbestos fibres, was described as early as 1900. As advances in medicine were made, so the connection between lung cancer and asbestos fibres was recognised in the 1940s. Further restrictions did follow, but was not until 1993 that the use of asbestos was banned completely in Germany, and the ban in all other EU member states did not come into effect until 2005. The consequence of this historical development is that almost all existing buildings built prior to 1995 are contaminated with at least one dangerous substance – usually more. And the corresponding products are not always directly visible, but instead often concealed in the layers of building components or combinations of materials in such a way that without specific preliminary investigations they are not detected until the refurbishment or conversion works are in progress.

Definition, declaration and handling of dangerous substances

In everyday speech we generally make no distinction between dangerous substances and harmful substances.
Generally, we distinguish between biogenic (natural) and anthropogenic (man-made) harmful substances. They are defined as "substances that are released into the environment through the actions of people and damage ecosystems or parts thereof" [3]. The term "harmful substances" therefore tends to have a general significance and is used in various federal state directives and occupational safety publications. The legal definition in the German Criminal Code is: "Harmful substances ... are substances which are capable of harming the health of another, animals, plants or other property of significant value; or polluting or otherwise negatively and permanently altering a body of water, the air or the soil." [4]

The legislation surrounding chemicals and dangerous substances uses the term "dangerous substances" exclusively. The term is defined in cl. 1 and 3 of the Chemicals Act (ChemG), which describes them as substances with the following properties:

- flammable, highly flammable, combustible, explosive
- harmful, toxic, very toxic
- corrosive, irritant, sensitising
- carcinogenic
- reprotoxic, mutagenic
- dangerous for the environment

Biocides are subject to a special regulation with respect to classification and usage. In the European directive covering biocidal products they are defined as "active substances and preparations [that are] intended to destroy, deter, render harmless, prevent the action of, or otherwise exert a controlling effect on any harmful organism by chemical or biological means" [5]. Based on this definition we can generally assume that such a substance is dangerous.
Generally, the use of chemicals in Europe and Germany is regulated by the Chemicals Act (ChemG) [6]. The use of substances that have one or more of the aforementioned harmful characteristics is specified in the Dangerous Substances Act (GefStoffV) [7]. The purpose of these two acts is "to protect people and the environment against the harmful effects of dangerous substances and preparations, make them identifiable, avoid their use and prevent their occurrence" [8]. The new edition of the Dangerous Substances Act (2005) also incorporates the European dangerous substances directive in German law [9]. Restrictions and bans concerning substances considered to be especially dangerous are specified in the Chemicals Prohibition Act (ChemVerbotsV) [10].
An important requirement alongside the detection and description of the properties of materials is the obligation to declare dangerous substances (regulations covering information, labelling and packaging). Every dangerous property is assigned so-called risk phrases (R)

and safety precautions (S) described in the Dangerous Substances Act. The designations and definitions have been standardised in all the European languages and are binding. The great number of risk phrases and combinations thereof is not reproduced here, but is readily available in the Internet. Risk phrases can be combined as required and can be roughly divided into the following risk categories:

- R 01 – R 19: various degrees of fire and explosion risk
- R 20 – R 28: various degrees of toxicity
- R 29 – R 33: risk of chemical reactions with dangerous consequences
- R 34 – R 39: various irritant and corrosive effects
- R 45: may cause cancer
- R 50 – R 59: various environmental risks
- R 60 – R 64: mutagenic damage

In addition, substances whose properties can cause particularly acute health risks must be labelled with the appropriate danger symbols, which are generally known because of the binding regulations (Fig. B 6.2).
There is no labelling obligation for sensitising properties or those dangerous for the environment, only risk phrases. An additional regulation applies to substances classified as carcinogenic, mutagenic and/or reprotoxic (so-called CMR substances) in category 1 or 2 (properties proven in humans or animals). If products already declared as toxic and very toxic (categories of danger T, T+, Xn) contain these substances, they must be labelled with an "E" as well.
The Dangerous Substances Act allocates safety precautions to every risk, which must be clearly identifiable together with the material properties. Here are some examples:

- R 7 (may cause fire)
  → S 7 (keep container tightly closed)
- R 17 (spontaneously flammable in air)
  → S 17 (keep away from combustible material)
- R 23 (toxic by inhalation)
  → S 23 (do not breathe gas/fumes/vapour/ spray)

Like the risk phrases, the safety precautions can also be combined as required.
Substances and preparations that owing to their danger for people or the environment may not be marketed or used, or at best only with considerable restrictions, are listed in detail in both the Chemicals Prohibition Act (cl. 1 with regulations for individual substances in the appendix) and the Dangerous Substances Act (cl. 18 with a list in appendix IV).
Bans or significant restrictions exist for numerous substances and preparations that were – and in some cases even today still are – used in the building industry. Those include, in particular, arsenic, asbestos, PCP, PCB, DDT, tar oils, biopersistent fibres, formaldehyde, diverse heavy metal compounds, organotin compounds, etc. (see pp. 110–115).
The so-called Material Safety Data Sheets (MSDS) have been introduced in Europe to enable full declarations of the categories of danger of new products containing dangerous or harmful substances [11]. In Germany this safety information is covered by the "Technical Rules for Dangerous Substances" (TRGS), an annex to the Dangerous Substances Act. The TRGS describes all the constituents and properties that must be declared, together with handling and safety advice for all application, transport, storage and accident situations.
Apart from that, the TRGS represents an important basis for working with and source of information for dangerous substances in existing buildings. The precise implementation requirements for specific dangerous substances, rules for risk assessment, safety requirements, training and certification requirements for the persons involved in practice, etc. are described here in detail. Some of the most important TRGS documents for refurbishment and conversion work in existing buildings are:

- TRGS 201 – Classification and labelling of wastes during handling
- TRGS 400 – Determination and assessment of risks caused by dangerous substances at places of work
- TRGS 519 – Asbestos: demolition, refurbishment or maintenance measures
- TRGS 520 – Establishment and operation of collecting depots and interim storage for small quantities of dangerous wastes
- TRGS 521 – Fibre dust
- TRGS 524 – Refurbishment and working in contaminated areas
- TRGS 551 – Tar and other pyrolysis products originating from organic material
- TRGS 555 – Operating instructions and guidance according to cl. 20 of the Dangerous Substances Act
- TRGS 560 – Air recirculation during handling of carcinogenic dangerous substances

Based on the statutory instruments covering the handling of dangerous substances on building sites, the requirements in Germany, anchored centrally in German law, are implemented by the BG Central Office for Health and Safety at Work (BGZ), the "prevention arm" of the German Federation of Institutions for Statutory Accident Insurance and Prevention (HVBG), through the BG Regulations (BGV) and BG Rules (BGR). (BG stands for the "institutions responsible for statutory accident insurance and prevention".)
Besides the specific health and safety tasks on construction sites, e.g. buildings, civil engineering works, cranes, machines, BGR 128 is the most important binding document when carrying out building work in areas contaminated by dangerous substances. It contains exact requirements regarding the persons, organisation and procedures necessary for all demolition and conversion works in contaminated existing buildings, e.g. the provision of airlocks for contaminated areas (Fig. B 6.3). One key requirement of BGR 128 is the compulsory appointment of a coordinator, whose competence is demonstrated by appropriate qualifications, when the work exceeds a certain volume. This requirement applies to building and demolition work in areas in which "an as yet unknown level of dangerous substances is to be expected", i.e. in most existing buildings [12]. The only exceptions are the handling of asbestos, for which special certification according to TRGS 519 is necessary, and man-made vitreous fibres (MMVF), which are covered by TRGS 521.
All these regulations for the handling of dangerous substances of course presume that testing, evaluation and classification of substances, chemical products, preparations, etc. have been carried out first. In the past this was essentially a task for the state or state institutions, e.g. in Germany Division II – Environmental Health and Protection of Ecosystems – at the Federal Environment Agency (UBA) or the German Institute for Building Technology (DIBt), whose primary task, similar to German building law, is to protect the public against risks. In this setup, however, the institutions can only respond to instances of damage and risks that are already known. The number of (as yet) inconspicuous products not examined for potential risks was unknown until the introduction and gradual implementation of the REACH regulation (Registration, Evaluation, Authorisation and Restriction of Chemicals). For example, European law made a distinction between existing substances (up until September 1981) and new substances in industrial chemicals. Only the latter had to be tested and assessed for possible risks to human health and the environment by manufacturers or distributors. The number of existing substances, on the other hand, was estimated to be at least 100 000! According to information supplied by the Federal Environment Agency, further estimates reveal that of the approx. 30 000 industrial chemicals currently in use, up until 2006 only 140 substances had been adequately tested for their effects.
It was for this reason that the European union introduced the so-called REACH regulation in January 2007, a compulsory reform of European chemicals legislation. The main innovation is that the burden of proof is now on the manufacturer. Also new is the requirement that all applications across the entire supply and fabrication chain must be checked, and not just the raw materials themselves. All chemicals produced in a quantity exceeding 1 t/year must be registered. And a Chemical Safety Report (CSR) must be produced by the manufacturer when the quantity exceeds 10 t/year.
Approvals are mandatory for all substances for which a particularly high risk potential has been acknowledged, and the European Commission reserves the right to invoke a ban or restrict usage. In Germany registration is managed by the Federal Institute for Occupational Safety & Health. The first lists with substances requiring approval were planned for 2008; following an appropriate assessment, those substances will be banned or their use restricted.
A similar intention was behind the publication of the EU's Biocide Directive in May 1998, which was adopted in Germany in June 2002 [13]. In contrast to "normal" industrial chemicals, biocides are always considered to present a risk, meaning that the substances generally require approval without the need for a classification phase. But even in the case of biocides we still have to assume a large number of unknown, as yet inadequately tested substances. Here again, the testing obligation has been transferred to the manufacturer or distributor.
According to the Biocide Directive all substances functioning as biocides must be registered, identified, tested and evaluated by 2009. The intention is to review and evaluate the substance portfolio submitted, starting in 2009. In Germany this will be carried out by the Federal Institute for Risk Assessment (BfR), work which includes the recording and evaluating of "old biocide active substances" used up until the year 2000.
The substances used as preservatives in the building industry fall into Main Group 2, which lists the most important types of product, e.g. wood, film and masonry preservatives, separately. In the course of reviews planned for the future, wood preservative substances frequently used in the past and now present in the building stock e.g. pyrethroid (active toxic ingredient:

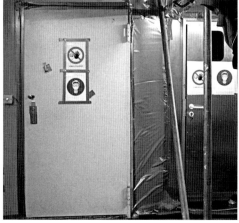

B 6.3

permethrin, a contact and stomach poison), may be reappraised.

The significance of dangerous substance contamination in the building stock

The risks that result for the building owner or the architect and planning team due to combinations of dangerous substances when working in the building stock have grown constantly over recent years. There are several reasons for this:

- Stricter evaluation standards for risk assessment
- New appraisals of existing substances by public bodies, in the future by REACH and the Biocide Directive
- The growing health and safety demands of users
- Major cost increases for occupational safety and organisation when working in contaminated areas
- Major cost increases for the disposal of contaminated building wastes

In each one of these points, important progress has been achieved in recent years with respect to better protection for human health and the environment, better occupational safety and transferring the costs according to the "polluter pays principle".

One example with considerable consequences for the cost of refurbishment in the building stock is the pan-European classification of man-made vitreous fibres (MMVF) – used primarily in insulating materials – as potentially carcinogenic (Fig. B 6.4). In Germany this classification led to the amendment of the list of so-called biopersistent fibres in the list of dangerous substances in the Dangerous Substances Act in the early 1990s and to the formulation of TRGS 905 with rules for allocating MMVF to carcinogenicity categories [14], and TRGS 521 was published to cover the everyday handling of MMVF.

From 1994 onwards, the manufacturers gradually adjusted the formulations of the glass and rock melts in order to improve the biosolubility of the fibres to a maximum half-life of 40 days

in the lungs. As the verification methods are very involved and cannot be easily followed by consumers (or even specialists), a certification method for insulating products made from mineral fibres was introduced, indicated by RAL quality mark GZ 388. This is intended to guarantee the improved properties (Fig. B 6.5) [15]. Today there are practically no non-certified European insulating products available on the market. Difficulties are experienced with construction projects outside Europe and the imported products because these are not subjected to any restrictions.

As the gradual changeover and certification of the insulating products could not be completed until 2000, the old product types may well be encountered in older buildings even today – with consequences for occupational safety on the building site.

A direct consequence of classifying categories of danger is the increased planning, time and costs for occupational safety when carrying out refurbishment work in buildings. If significant dangerous substances are first detected after refurbishment work has commenced, considerable cost increases and time delays can be expected.

The sensitivity of residents, office workers and other building users has steadily risen over recent decades. This can be seen in, for example, the increase in allergy-related disorders, respiratory diseases and unspecified symptoms. More and more, refurbishment work in rooms or buildings is necessary when high concentrations of dangerous substances are established through measurements following an accumulation of complaints from users, or other conspicuous aspects. Whereas a refurbishment obligation is anchored in law for a number of known dangerous substances, e.g. weakly bonded asbestos or PCB (polychlorinated biphenyls), for the majority of dangerous substances encountered, e.g. formaldehyde, numerous biocides, PAH (polycyclic aromatic hydrocarbons), phenols and many others, there is no corresponding legislation; the risk assessments can only be carried out on the basis of recommendations (see pp. 110–115). A number of German courts have confirmed rent reductions

when formaldehyde contamination has been discovered in rented accommodation.

Over the past 10 years there has also been a noticeable change in the way building wastes are handled – primarily determined by the Cradle-to-Grave Economy & Waste Act (KrW/AbfG) of 1996. This has led to considerable increases in the cost of utilising and disposing of contaminated building wastes and calls for great care to be taken when selecting refurbishment methods, sorting the waste streams, intermediate storage and transport. Since 2000 untreated residual wastes may no longer be disposed of in landfill sites, and since May 2005 the landfill options have been further restricted, even discontinued completely in some regions. In the light of ever scarcer resources, the utilisation precept of the above act is sensible. The proportion of unusable wastes has dropped drastically since then. It is also logical that owing to the considerable cost to the public of dealing with legacy pollution from landfill sites and other uncontrolled waste disposal the costs for organised waste management should be borne by the producers of that waste. This therefore calls for a rethink on the part of building owners when planning and executing refurbishment and conversion work.

B 6.4

B 6.5

B 6.3   Airlocks as a protective measure in a contaminated building
B 6.4   Man-made vitreous fibres (MMVF) – classed as carcinogenic – revealed during demolition work
B 6.5   Mineral wool certification symbols on the packaging

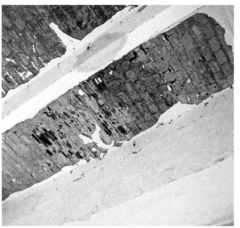

B 6.6

B 6.7

The aims of assessing dangerous substances contamination in the building stock

The chance of encountering contamination by dangerous substances in existing buildings is important in various phases and for various reasons. Therefore, diverse situations and perspectives will be explored below.

Risks to users and curtailment of usage
Curtailment of usage manifests itself in various ways, e.g. noticeable annoying odours, an accumulation of "unspecific" illness symptoms, reports of allergic reactions. This usually begins with complaints to public or private building owners, housing cooperatives, employers, etc., which turns into a protracted dispute about the assessment and the causes. Those affected are first accused of being hysterical, or of having caused the problem themselves, or of trying to seek some advantage. Aggravating this matter is the fact that most doctors cannot provide satisfactory answers regarding causes when confronted with unspecific symptoms. More and more, those affected make use of the better options now available and themselves appoint an environmental specialist to carry out measurements. The ensuing legal disputes generally lead to tedious, costly expert witness proceedings.

With the exception of asbestos, PCP (pentachlorophenols) and PCB (polychlorinated biphenyls), recommended target and intervention values (concentrations at which immediate action to eliminate the causes is imperative) are the only ways of assessing dangerous substances concentrations in rooms:

- PCP Directive with an intervention value ≥ 1 mg/kg new dust or 5 mg/kg old dust
- PCB Directive with an intervention value ≥ 3000 ng/m³ room air
- Asbestos Directive with a refurbishment requirement when weakly bonded asbestos is present
- Formaldehyde Directive (recommendation of the Federal Environment Agency) with an intervention value of 0.12 mg/m³ room air
- PAH with the indicator substance benzo[a]pyrene (BaP), intervention value 10 mg/kg new dust

The Federal Environment Agency is successively publishing so-called recommended interior air values for individual substances [16]. They are divided into recommended value RW I = target value (i.e. no health problems expected), and RW II = intervention value (i.e. health problems can be expected). A value higher than RW II means action must be taken. These recommended values are, however, just that, but have already been used by the courts as a basis for assessment. Interesting for existing buildings, however, is the RW II value of 1 µg/m³ room air for PCP; other recommended values for toluene, styrene, naphthalene and terpenes occur in this order of magnitude only in the first one to two years in new buildings.

In principle, if a risk to usage is suspected, the situation should be investigated without delay by a specialist in order to prevent speculation, fears and costly disputes. If corresponding concentrations are established, the causes must be clarified and the necessary refurbishment and replacement works initiated.

Valuation and value depreciation of a building
When financing or selling properties, ascertaining capital assets, etc., it is generally necessary to carry out a valuation of the property. As described by the Valuation Directive (WertR) such a valuation has up until now included the basic data of a property, an appraisal of the location, a description of the existing construction and an assessment of the condition provided by a specialist [17]. In recent years an energy-efficiency appraisal has been added to this. Whereas contamination of the soil is already included in the Valuation Directive (annex 1), dangerous substances contamination caused by building materials has not been listed as a criterion affecting value.

Rising costs in conjunction with the conversion and refurbishment of contaminated buildings has meant that banks and buyers are increasingly asking for a preliminary appraisal of the most significant types of contamination. The reaction to this in recent years has been the inclusion of quick appraisals and the listing of a few dangerous substances in building portfolios. The information, however, is limited to contamination by asbestos and – mostly properties in

former East Germany – wood preservatives and PCB.

As financial risks rise, clients are asking for detailed surveys depending on region and type and size of building. In addition to the building data, we are seeing more and more offers with "package solutions" prepared by experts:

- Energy-efficiency report, energy performance certificate
- Building and timber damage reports
- Dangerous substances and contamination reports

The main problem here lies in not recognising types of concealed contamination that occur frequently. Such a preliminary appraisal demands very experienced personnel.

In practice, however, the sale and auction offers usually include a clause stating that the property has not been surveyed and may contain dangerous substances. An incalculable risk therefore remains. In the worst case it can happen that the planned change of use for an otherwise intact building may have to be reconsidered. One example is the roof space conversions in timber roof structures planned in former East Germany and Berlin after 1989. For a long time the degree of contamination caused by wood preservatives was vastly underestimated. In those schemes where it was intended to retain the basic roof structure, the plans had to be completely rethought after work on site commenced, and in some cases abandoned completely after contamination by wood preservatives was discovered subsequently (Fig. B 6.9). The appraisal of existing wood preservative contamination can be carried out according to the so-called Bremen List for timbers where direct, constant contact is normal (e.g. housing, offices) [18] (see pp. 110–115).

B 6.6   Damage caused to a historic hollow clay block floor due to the wrong choice of refurbishment method
B 6.7   Floor screed stripped correctly
B 6.8   Lightweight screeds containing phenol removed as a complete layer from the floor construction
B 6.9   Wood preservatives containing DDT and lindane from the ex-GDR

B 6.8

B 6.9

Cost controls for refurbishment projects

A client has a duty to ensure that those in his employ work in safe conditions. The prerequisite for this is the obligation to ascertain and notify. In the case of dangerous substances first detected during the building work, there is a risk of delaying the on-site operations. If additional refurbishment work is necessary, this is handled via supplements to the contract without comparing market prices. In the worst case the client has no influence on the method of refurbishment selected, waste separation and disposal. Optimisation of the costs, e.g. with respect to the wastes caused by each refurbishment method, is then no longer possible.

In normal cases for buildings built before 1995 a dangerous substances expert is generally appointed. This results in direct costs during the planning for investigating the dangerous substances and, if applicable, providing a complete catalogue of dangerous substances. The estimate for the cost of the building work also increases depending on the findings. However, through errors of judgement, but mainly through ignorance or poor advice, these costs are often shunned. Where the investigations are carried out, the risks for the cost estimates are considerably reduced. Harmful substances detected can be rated in terms of concentration, quantity and separation methods, and tendered for, including the necessary safety measures and disposal of the building debris. Where a dangerous substances expert is not appointed, the building is not examined for potential dangerous substances, probably because there was "no cause for suspicion". This means there are also no direct extra costs during the planning phase and the estimate of the cost of the building work remains unaffected. Depending on the type of building, however, a risk remains regarding incalculable supplements to the contract and time delays, with the corresponding rise in the cost of the building work. In some circumstances the methods of separating the materials on site and means of disposal can no longer be optimised, no new tenders can be invited and hence the costs and methods are no longer under control. In the worst case the contractor appointed with the refurbishment work will be unfamiliar with this

type of work and considerable damage to the building can result. There are plenty of examples where this has happened, especially with undiscovered asbestos contamination in steel and reinforced concrete buildings. PAH contamination (adhesives and waterproofing) or phenol contamination (binders in lightweight screeds or secondary loads due to cleaning agents, Fig. B 6.8) of (mostly) solid suspended floor slabs can sometimes be just as involved and costly. The problems are usually on the top of the floor and require removal of finishes and screed. Without an exact investigation of the floor type, the wrong choice of refurbishment method can result in considerable damage to the building (Figs. B 6.6 and 6.7).

In order to guarantee optimum planning of the refurbishment with respect to the cost of the work and the disposal when dealing with contaminated floor constructions, accurate information about the components must be acquired when preparing the catalogue of dangerous substances:

- Determining and presenting the floor construction types in a building (e.g. according to periods and layers).
- Taking random samples from the individual areas without distinguishing between depths in the first stage of the dangerous substances catalogue.
- In the case of negative findings, preparing a room catalogue with checking of the depths or the layers affected.
- Checking the detachability of layers and the load-carrying capacity of the floor structure.
- Opting for refurbishment or encapsulation.
- Specifying the refurbishment method.

Safety during building measures

When carrying out refurbishment and other work in contaminated areas, safe handling of dangerous substances can only be guaranteed when all the factors that could lead to a risk for personnel are determined and evaluated, and appropriate protective measures are specified and adhered to.

The employer has overall responsibility for determining and assessing the risks due to dangerous substances at a place of work. The duty of the employer, or his client, to ascertain

and notify where risks are suspected stems from cl. 16 of the Dangerous Substances Act. When carrying out work in areas with known contamination, the client is obliged to carry out or arrange for the determination of the types, quantities and states of the anticipated dangerous substances, plus the potential risks of the contamination to be encountered in the meaning of health and safety at work. In doing so, he must record the results of investigations and make these available to all those in his employ. Before work can commence in potentially contaminated areas, the client must also investigate the suspected dangerous substances and estimate and classify the ensuing risks in the meaning of health and safety at work. Here again, the results must be recorded and made available to all those in his employed.

According to cl. 37 of the Dangerous Substances Act, the handling of carcinogenic substances must be submitted to the authority responsible at the latest 14 days before beginning any work. In addition, the employee (i.e. the contractor) must notify the employers' liability insurance association of the work according to BGR 128 four weeks in advance.

Furthermore, special duties/regulations apply to demolition and refurbishment work:

- BGR 128 (rules for contaminated areas)
- Building Sites Act
- Safety at work regulations to be specified in each case
- Establishment of black/white areas (airlocks) depending on degree and nature of contamination
- Obligation to notify the employers' liability insurance association of the work
- Ensuring the technical competence of the contractors appointed through certification to BGR 128 and/or TRGS 524 (Technical Rules for Dangerous Substances – Refurbishment and Works in Contaminated Areas)
- In the case of more than one contractor: obligation to appoint a health and safety officer and the preparation of a health and safety concept

Safeguarding usage and value in the case of renewing the construction

Once decontamination and demolition work in a building has been completed, conversion and renewal work can begin. In doing so it should be remembered that the classification and appraisal of dangerous substances is an ongoing process depending on the respective level of knowledge. For example, in many cases these days it is no longer possible – technically or economically – to refurbish houses dating from the 1960s and 1970s that are contaminated with formaldehyde, older mineral-fibre insulation and asbestos fire protection. Although the buildings are only 30 or 40 years old, they have no value, indeed even lower the value of the plot. On buildings just 10 years old, the contamination by old mineral-fibre insulation has to be taken into account in the form of more work and higher costs. The implications of REACH and the Biocide Directive mean that many substances used in the building industry will be subjected to a reappraisal with respect to their risk potential following their registration in the next 5 – 10 years. This fact must be taken into account during design and construction. The modern catchphrase "sustainable building" embraces ecological, economic and social protection aims, which also include sustainable utilisation and the long-term retention of a building's value. It is principally the health- and environment-related properties of buildings that

must be considered in this context. The use of potentially risky substances should be avoided whenever possible.

That also applies to the use of biocides in wood preservatives, and jointing compounds and paints containing fungicides. Constructional protective measures in the form of sound building physics solutions or permanent protection against moisture have proved to be fundamentally more suitable, more long-lasting. The Interiors of buildings should be kept as free as possible from organic halogen compounds, e.g. in the form of flame-retardant additives, in order to rule out secondary risks in fires due to corrosive fumes or dioxin in fire soot. Growing demands on the hygiene and health characteristics of building interiors can be taken into account at an early stage by selecting zero-emissions materials and designing to avoid emissions of fibres in interiors. And for external areas, too, the Federal Environment Agency recommends refraining from using heavy metals such as zinc and copper sheet over large exposed areas because of the risk of compounds of those metals entering the soil or waste water [19]. The topicality and growing demand for buildings that retain their value and the use of nonhazardous, environmentally friendly materials have led to corresponding aids, certificates, advice and directives becoming available and being deployed.

The Federal Ministry of Transport, Building & Urban Affairs (BMVBS) intends to publish guidelines for sustainable building within the building stock in which corresponding recommendations will be summarised [20]. The "Blue Angel" quality mark (RAL environment symbol) initiated by the Federal Environment Agency is awarded to products (e.g. paints and varnishes, woodbased products, wallpaper, etc.) that avoid or comply with limits for risky substances. Environment labels have also been introduced for building materials in which precautionary requirements have been taken into account. The building industry carries out its own certification for important product groups (Fig. B 6.11).

Necessary works and the refurbishment planning sequence

The first steps in a provisional appraisal of an existing building are to carry out a visual inspection and make a rough assessment of whether any dangerous substances could be present. Moreover, when planning conversion and refurbishment work a competent assessment of the boundary conditions (type and age of building, location, history of usage, building measures carried out in the past) is necessary as well as a survey, and where there are suspicions also sampling – at least in the form of mixed samples from several locations.

The age of the building alone and the original building fabric does not permit an assessment of whether contamination by dangerous substances is or is not likely because practically all buildings undergo conversions, repairs or other constructional changes at different points in their history. It is frequently the case that when renewing roof waterproofing, floor finishes or building services, the old materials and components are simply covered over and so left in the structure. Fig. B 6.10 shows the complete refurbishment sequence for a contaminated area in the form of a flow chart.

Where surveys or dangerous substances catalogues are to be provided for a building, the quotations should be compared. The services of such specialists are not generally defined with respect to scope and completeness or the consideration of analysis costs as is the case, for example, for reports on timber damage to quality mark RAL GZ 832. As far as possible, tenders should therefore include unambiguous information regarding the services required and the structure of the quotation. The exact number of samples and analyses required can only be determined during the preparation of the report itself and so such services should be quoted separately as unit prices.

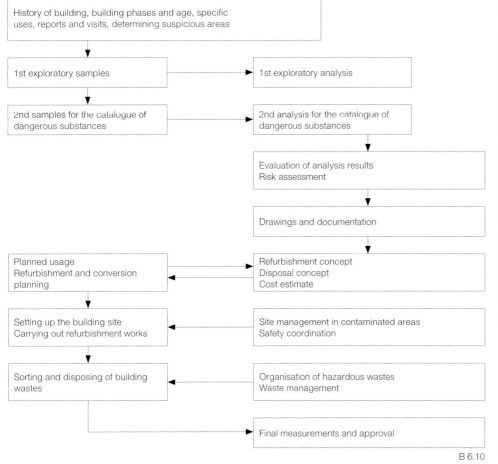

B 6.10

B 6.10   Flow chart showing the refurbishment sequence

The detection of contamination in an existing building and the integration into the planning and tendering can be carried out in three stages depending on situation and complexity:

In the first step a specialist carries out a preliminary inspection of the building. To do this, a compilation of the most important building data with details of age, former uses and known conversions or repairs is essential. The result of such an inspection is the specification of suspicions in the meaning of the Dangerous Substances Act. Owing to the fact that dangerous substances are often concealed within the construction, the appraisal of each situation demands considerable experience and special knowledge of historic building materials. The appraisal should in no way be included in the architect's standard services.

Once there is a suspicion or contamination has been actually observed, further, more far-reaching investigations are vital.

Depending on the purpose of the investigation (planning a conversion, building valuation, checking alternatives, etc.), it may be advisable to carry out a dangerous substances survey as a second step in order to draw up a complete list of the dangerous substances encountered in the building. This initially involves only establishing their presence, not exact quantities, risk assessments, refurbishment concepts, etc. This second step can save money, especially with large projects. In practice an initial survey is frequently carried out. If during this survey there is no evidence of, for example, wood preservatives in the roof, a mixed sample (made up of several individual samples from timber components) is examined for determining the presence of any wood preservatives (with the aim of making a yes/no statement) (Fig. B 6.13). If the result is negative (no contamination detectable), the high cost of differentiated sampling and individual analyses can be saved. If the result is positive (contamination detected), this already indicates the first safety requirements to the specialist and the planning team. In addition, the detailed investigations can be carried out more efficiently and hence also more cost-effectively.

A complete dangerous substances catalogue is necessary in the case of specific planning work for an existing building. Where possible the catalogue should include the following aspects depending on scope and situation:

- It is advisable to establish and describe all the products or building component layers affected as comprehensively as possible by carrying out a dangerous substances survey of the building (unless this has been carried out already).
- Where sampling is necessary, the sampling positions should be based on experience and distributed over the surfaces concerned.

The sampling and analysis work must be carried out competently.

- The individual degrees of contamination established are to be evaluated afterwards with respect to potential risks and refurbishment needs. An exact description of the building component at the place of discovery forms one part of the appraisal. Additional examinations and statements regarding the detachability of the building component layers (e.g. suspended floors, roofs, fire-resistant coatings, etc.) are advisable.
- A dangerous substances report should be supplemented by refurbishment recommendations, including the choice of optimum separation and removal methods for contaminated products, components or component layers, and a risk assessment for the work connected with those refurbishment measures.
- The risk assessment is used to determine the occupational safety requirements necessary for the work according to the stipulations of the relevant TRGS or BGR.
- Only after these investigations and appraisals are available is it possible to provide an estimate of the cost of refurbishment and the quantities of waste, including the cost of removal/disposal, within the scope of the report.

The individual services that contribute to preparing a dangerous substances report are closely linked and should not be awarded or carried out separately. Only exact knowledge of the building components allows a suitable refurbishment method to be selected. At the same time, the method has a direct impact on the occupational safety requirements and the composition, distribution and quantities of wastes generated. Consequently, the dangerous substances appraisal and the chosen refurbishment method have a considerable influence on the cost of occupational safety and waste disposal (Fig. B 6.10).

RAL Deutsches Institut für Gütesicherung und Kennzeichnung e. V.

RAL UZ 12 a:	Low-pollution paints
RAL UZ 38:	Low-emissions elements made from wood and wood-based products
RAL UZ 76:	Low-emissions wood-based board products
RAL UZ 102:	Low-emissions wall paints

DIBU Deutsches Institut Bauen und Umwelt e.V.

The DIBU is an association of manufacturers who provide their products with environmental product declarations (EPD) according to the European guidelines for declaring building products.

GUT Gemeinschaft umweltfreundlicher Teppichboden e. V.

The GUT certificate means that the carpeting product satisfies a series of requirements, e.g. low emissions, no harmful dyes, no heavy metals, etc.

natureplus Internationaler Verein für zukunftsfähiges Bauen und Wohnen e. V.

The natureplus® quality mark stands for products without health hazards, environmentally compatible production, the careful use of finite resources and serviceability.

B 6.11   Certification of important product groups (selection)

B 6.11

B 6.12

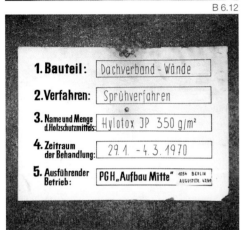

B 6.13

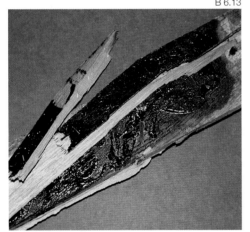

B 6.14

B 6.15

The most common dangerous substances in the building stock

DDT

Dichloro-diphenyl-trichloroethane (DDT), a blend of various isomers plus the by-products DDD and DDE, is a synthetic insecticide which is still used today in many countries (Fig. B 6.12). It was banned in former West Germany in 1972. DDT is essentially ecotoxic, damaging living organisms that live in the soil, air and water. Chronic toxicity has been observed in humans, but not evaluated conclusively. The substances can lead to pulmonary oedemas and damage liver, kidneys, heart and bone marrow. It is also a neurotoxin. In the building industry DDT was mainly used as an active substance in wood preservatives. DDT came to the attention of the public again after 1989 because up until then it had still been used in former East Germany and therefore can be encountered in correspondingly high concentrations in timber structures.

Lindane

Gamma-hexachlorocyclohexane (lindane) is produced synthetically through an additive chlorination of benzene (Fig. B 6.9). This was first achieved in 1825 but its insecticide effect was not recognised until 1935. Industrial production began in 1942 and rose continually until the late 1960s, the product being used mainly as an insecticide in agriculture and forestry. Since then production and usage have been declining steadily.

Lindane is suspected of being carcinogenic and harmful to the nervous system when normal values are exceeded, and being responsible for a number of serious diseases of the internal organs. Building usage can also be affected because lindane is released into the air from wood preservatives.

From 1980 onwards its use in former West Germany was restricted to the contact and stomach poison used in wood preservatives; it has not been produced or used at all since 1984. According to EU Regulation 850/2004, lindane may not be used in Europe since 1997; however, it is still used in medical applications. In former East Germany, lindane was used as a wood preservative mainly in combination with DDT and PCP up until 1989 and can still be frequently encountered in timber structures.

PCP

Pentachlorophenol, one of the compounds in the chlorophenols group, is a colourless solid in its normal state and functions as a disinfectant and fungicide. It was banned from use in interiors as early as 1978 by the German Institute for Building Technology (DIBt) and this ban was incorporated in the Dangerous Substances Act in 1986. Until its production, import and use in Germany was banned in 1989 by the Pentachlorophenol Prohibition Act, it was used in disinfectants and wood preservatives. In other countries it continues to be used in the textiles and cosmetics industries.

PCP is ecotoxic. Toxicity in humans has been observed, but not evaluated conclusively. The substances can lead to pulmonary oedemas and damage liver, kidneys, heart and bone marrow. It is also a neurotoxin. The problems are aggravated by the fact that technical PCP products can contain up to 0.1 ppm dioxin impurities (TCDD – tetrachlorodibenzodioxin). It is classed as a category 2 carcinogen according to TRGS 905 and has mutagenic and reprotoxic effects. PCP must be labelled with the categories of danger N (dangerous for the environment) and T+ (very toxic).

The DIBt produced the "Guidelines for assessing and refurbishing PCP-contaminated building materials and components in buildings" (PCP Guidelines) in 1996, which proposed evaluating any contamination found on the basis of measurements (dust and interior air) and biomonitoring. Fig. B 6.16 shows the appraisal sequence in the form of a flow chart. As an assessment basis for measured contamination due to wood preservatives (mostly in combined formulations), TRGS 900 is hardly practicable and the PCP Guidelines very involved when trying to describe the refurbishment requirements. In order to be able to carry out a consistent appraisal and classify the extent of necessary measures, the risk assessment of the Bremen Environment Institute can be used as an alternative [21] (Fig. B 6.17).

PAH

The polycyclic aromatic hydrocarbons (PAH) make up a group of more than 100 individual compounds which are produced upon heating or incinerating organic materials in an atmosphere lacking in oxygen, e.g. car exhaust fumes, industrial processes. They never occur as individual substances, but instead always in the form of complex mixtures. Measurements in solids generally take into account 16 individual PAH which have been specified by the American Environmental Protection Agency (EPA). Benzo-[a]pyrene (BaP) is the indicator substance.

In high concentrations PAH are mainly found in products that are produced using coal tars, coal tar oils and coal pitches. Those include coal tar oils, asphalt floor tiles and tar adhesive. Bitumen, too, which is produced from crude oil, contains PAH, albeit only traces, provided it is not mixed with tar. The following products are regarded as especially critical: paints based on tar oil (for waterproofing to wet rooms and roofs), building papers soaked in tar oil (roofing felts, fish paper for HV cables and heating pipes), adhesives for wood-block flooring, mastic asphalt and wood preservatives (Fig. B 6.14). Numerous representatives of the PAH group have been proved to be carcinogenic and mutagenic, toxic for the immune system and the liver, and to cause irritation of mucous membranes. Apart from the carcinogenic effect of certain PAH, it cannot be ruled out that in rooms containing coal tar products (floor tiles, adhesives, impregnation treatments) certain sensitive persons may suffer from unspecific symptoms such as headaches, discomfort, etc.

Waterproofing products containing PAH are mainly concealed below screeds, in masonry or below external roof finishes (Fig. B 6.15). In these cases the question concerning removal options is usually limited to demolition (observing the necessary safety precautions) and proper disposal (waste codes EWC 17 04 10, EWC 17 03 03). When using floor and wood-block flooring adhesives in interiors, it is also necessary to decide whether the whole floor must be removed as a result of the PAH contamination. To help here, a study group at the Federal Environment Agency has drawn up the following recommendations:

• If the wood-block flooring adhesive has a BaP content < 10 mg/kg, no further measures are necessary.
• With a BaP content of 10–3000 mg/kg in the wood-block flooring adhesive, the house dust should be tested. If the house dust exhibits > 10 mg/kg BaP, measures to minimise the concentration should be taken quickly.
• With a BaP content > 3000 BaP in the wood-block flooring adhesive and a BaP content > 10 mg/kg in the house dust, measures to minimise the concentration should be taken quickly.
• With a BaP content > 3000 mg/kg in the wood-block flooring adhesive and a BaP content < 10 mg/kg in the house dust, the BaP concentrations in the interior and exterior air should be measured. If the BaP concentration in the interior air is more than twice as high as the exterior concentration but at least 3 mg/m^3 higher, measures to minimise the concentration should be taken quickly.

Naphthalene
This substance is generally assigned to the PAH group, which is not correct chemically, however. It is indeed also a constituent of coal tar oil, but occurs naturally in only a few crude oils and in certain essential oils. Naphthalene is produced primarily through incomplete combustion (e.g. car exhaust fumes, cigarette smoke) and during the dry distillation of coal. Although in the past it was used completely openly, e.g. in mothballs, the Dangerous Substances Act now classes it as harmful to the environment and human health. Naphthalene can be ingested or inhaled and in TRGS 905 is therefore classed as a category K 3 substance (suspected of causing cancer). In addition, naphthalene vapours irritate the eyes and respiratory tract.
Naphthalene is mainly perceived as an unpleasant odour when it occurs as an impurity in building products or when products containing tar are covered to a large extent by other building components such as screeds, PE sheeting, ceramic tiles, thermal insulation (roof). Where it is not covered, the odour is superimposed on other higher-valency PAH, producing the typical tar smell.
Other sources, specifically for (poly)chlorinated naphthalenes (PCN), are wood preservatives

and the typical applications of polychlorinated biphenyls (PCB). PCN exhibit similar properties to PCB and, in addition, were previously used as wood preservatives. However, later they were essentially replaced by PCB and other types of wood preservative. Yet further sources are naphthalene impurities in recycled waste rubber products (e.g. impact sound insulation). Where naphthalene concentration occurs in buildings, measurements of the interior air are always necessary because with a concentration ≥ 0.02 mg/m^3 in the interior air the Interior Air Hygiene Commission of the Federal Environment Agency recommends carrying out refurbishment measures.
As little research has been carried out into this problem, no encapsulation methods for naphthalene have yet been properly tested, apart from aluminium foil, meaning that demolition is the only safe refurbishment strategy. Both the source of the contamination, the layer containing tar and possibly also any components such as screeds, insulation or separating materials that have been contaminated should all be removed. A classification as hazardous waste purely because of naphthalene is unknown.

Arsenic
In chemical terms, arsenic belongs to the metalloids, which depending on the bond exhibit either metallic or non-metallic properties. It occurs mainly as a by-product during the production of copper, lead or gold. The arsenic sulphide compounds orpiment and realgar were already known in ancient times. Arsenic is added to copper alloys to improve their workability. Its pesticide effect was already known in the Middle Ages, and arsenic preparations were used for protecting plants in the 18th century, but were banned in 1808 because of their high toxicity. Around the same time, arsenic was being used as a dye in the form of copper arsenates – and here again poisoning was common. At the start of the 20th century arsenic was used as a chemical weapon known as "Blue Cross". Even today, arsenic is used in various countries for pest control or as a wood preservative. And it is still used in medical applications. Since 2003 the commercial processing of preparations containing more than 0.3 % by wt. arsenic has been banned in Europe. The WHO has specified limit values for its use in electroplating (e.g. galvanising) – a common use worldwide.
In the building industry arsenic occurs most frequently in wood preservatives, mostly in copper-chromium-arsenic compounds (CCA salts). The use of these compounds for timbers in habitable rooms and in contact with foodstuffs or natural waters (e.g. as anti-fouling paints) has been banned since 2003. Arsenic contamination is relevant for the classification of scrap wood waste because to qualify for reuse, suitable waste wood may not have an arsenic content exceeding 2 mg/kg dry substance. If scrap wood with a protective treatment containing arsenic is incinerated without waste-

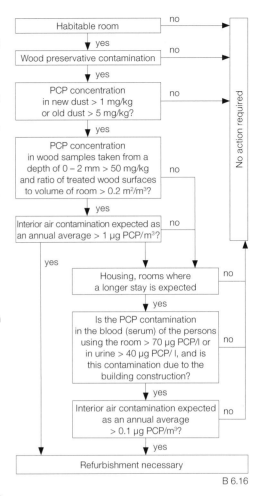

B 6.16

PCP and DDT [mg/kg]	Lindane [mg/kg]	Assessment
< 30	< 5	low contamination
30–200	5–30	moderate contamination
200–1000	30–100	high contamination
> 1000	> 100	very high contamination

B 6.17

B 6.12   DDT crystals on the surface of wood
B 6.13   Example of a declaration of wood preservative measures on a roof structure (mandatory throughout Germany)
B 6.14   Old adhesive containing PAH adhering to a piece of wood-block flooring
B 6.15   Waterproofing material containing PAH in a jack arch floor with screed topping
B 6.16   Classification of PCP contamination for estimating the refurbishment requirements
B 6.17   Assessment of wood preservative concentrations in wood

B 6.18

B 6.19

Phenol index [mg/kg]	Assessment
< 0.01–1	no contamination
1–5	low contamination
5–10	moderate contamination
> 10	high contamination

B 6.20

B 6.18 Scanning electron microscope image of an asbestos fibre
B 6.19 Jointing compound containing PCB
B 6.20 Assessment of phenol contamination
B 6.21 PCB capacitor as a closed system
B 6.22 Formaldehyde in building materials: adhesive and synthetic foam
B 6.23 Establishing the refurbishment urgency in the case of contamination by weakly bonded asbestos

gas scrubbing, some 20–80 % of the arsenic (a proven carcinogen) escapes into the air, which is why arsenic contamination is frequently found in the soil near former impregnation plants. The waste code for arsenic is EWC 17 02 04.

Asbestos
Asbestos is the collective name for fibrous minerals of magnesium silicate and the dioxides of iron, calcium, aluminium and silicon (Fig. B 6.18). We distinguish between two main forms depending on the chemical composition: chrysotile and amphibole (actinolite, amosite, anthophyllite, tremolite). Asbestos initially proved to be an outstanding material for the building industry, with important technical properties (incombustible, resistant to chemicals, electrical and thermal insulation properties, elastic, good tensile strength). But the use of asbestos fibres was banned owing to the health risks, which were realised quite soon; building products with asbestos fibres are, however, common in old buildings and can be encountered in many functions. Special care should always be taken when a building component forms part of the fire protection concept (fire-resistant hatches and doors, coatings on steel, etc.).
Chrysotile has the greatest practical significance for building products. The toxic effect is due to the geometry of the mineral fibres, so-called respirable fibres measuring 5–500 µm long and 1–3 µm thick (WHO definition). The fibres are not biosoluble and cause asbestosis and lung cancer. In Europe asbestos is classed as a category 1 carcinogen according to annex 1 of directive 67/548/EEC (substances known to cause cancer in humans; 15th amendment of directive 67/548/EEC, 28 Oct 1991). According to the 1991 Asbestos Act, import, use and production in Germany has been essentially banned since 1993.
Where demolition, refurbishment or repair work is to be carried out in buildings with asbestos contamination, statutory instruments must be observed in order to protect the workers, the population and the environment. We distinguish between weakly bonded applications, e.g. pipe lagging, gaskets, fire-resistant coatings (sprayed asbestos), fire protection blankets, and strongly bonded applications, e.g. plaster, fibre-reinforced cement products such as roof and wall sheeting, pipes, floor panels. The release of fibres into the environment is to be expected with weakly bonded products. In order to protect users, the Asbestos Act (directive for the appraisal and refurbishment of weakly bonded asbestos products) contains a refurbishment obligation for corresponding applications and products which is divided into three urgency categories; Fig. B 6.23 illustrates the urgency assessment process in the form of a flow chart.
Strongly bonded asbestos products can initially remain in place provided no maintenance or repair work is to be carried out and depending

on the risk assessment for the particular technical function.
TRGS 519 (Technical Rules for Dangerous Substances – Asbestos) forms the legal basis for asbestos refurbishment. Demolition and refurbishment work may only be carried out by appropriately certified contractors. The aim of protective measures during the work is to use screens, airlocks and negative pressure working conditions to prevent any fibres escaping into the environment. The authorities must be notified of the work. The waste is classed as hazardous: waste codes EWC 16 02 12, EWC 17 06 01 and EWC 17 06 05.

Formaldehyde
This colourless gas also known as methanal is a simple carbon-oxygen-hydrogen compound and belongs to the group of volatile organic compounds (VOC). It has a pungent smell, is highly reactive and readily soluble in water. Contact with formaldehyde causes symptoms such as irritation of the eyes, bronchial problems and headaches. In the building industry formaldehyde is best known as a binder in wood-based board products – which can still emit the gas even after 20 years (Fig. B 6.22). Owing to the serious and frequent illness symptoms, the formaldehyde content in new wood-based board products is limited by the 1996/1998 Chemicals Prohibition Act and the Formaldehyde Directive (DIBt Directive 100). The following values for the interior air of habitable areas may not be exceeded:

• Federal Health Agency/Federal Environment Agency recommended value 1977/1990: 0.1 ppm (corresponds to 120 µg/m³)
• Refurbishment target value: 0.05 ppm (corresponds to 60 µg/m³)

PCB

Polychlorinated biphenyls form a group totalling 209 chemical compounds (so-called PCB congeners) composed of biphenyl and chlorine. These compounds have been produced artificially since 1929/30 and are very widely used owing to their interesting technical properties. They are non-flammable, durable and resistant to acids and alkalis. This is why they have been used extensively, e.g. as electrical insulators in transformers and capacitors, as plasticisers in synthetic materials, in sealants for building expansion joints, and in hydraulic systems.

PCB is a category 3 carcinogen according to TRGS 905 (substances that owing to their possible carcinogenic effect in humans give cause for concern). PCB also has a reprotoxic effect. Health risks are mainly due to a chronic toxicity caused by an accumulation in the body. We distinguish between open (sealing compounds, coatings) and closed (capacitors, transformers) applications.

Following severe massive poisonings (Japan in 1968, Taiwan in 1969), the use of PCB in open applications was banned in Germany in 1978. In 1989 the use of the substance was further restricted by the PCB Prohibition Act, which was superseded in 1993 by the Chemicals Prohibition Act. Capacitors containing PCB have been completely banned since 2000. Devices made from or containing PCB must be disposed of by 31 December 2010 at the latest (Figs. B 6.19 and 6.21).

In 1996 the federal state of North Rhine-Westphalia brought into force a "Directive for the assessment and refurbishment of PCB-contaminated building materials and components in buildings" (PCB Directive NRW), which was aimed at protecting users. Like in the Asbestos Act, the refurbishment requirement is divided into three urgency categories based on an assessment of the interior air measurements to discover the effect of open applications. An interior air contamination value of 0.3 µg/m³ is defined as the precautionary value that should not be exceeded. When the concentration in the interior air lies between 0.3 and 3.0 µg/m³, the source must be investigated and regular ventilation, cleaning and dusting are prescribed in order to reduce the contamination. A higher concentration is regarded as an intervention value and signals immediate refurbishment. The waste code for PCB is EWC 17 09 02.

Phenols

A pungent lignite smell was noticed in many buildings in former East Germany that were refurbished after 1991, a smell that led to frequent complaints. The main source of the contamination was quite clearly the floors. Initial examinations of material samples taken from the floors indicated a comparatively high phenol content. The group of phenolic substances (phenols and alkyl phenols), which cause such unpleasant odours, comprise a mixture of substances that can be isolated from coal or lignite or produced synthetically on an industrial scale. Owing to the excellent bactericidal effects, the mixture and its aqueous soap solution was for a long time used as an antiseptic or disinfectant. In the GDR this group of substances was widely used in the chemicals industry as a phenol-based group of chemicals owing to its strong lignite fixation and could be found in diverse applications in daily life. According to western standards, on the other hand, phenols had been disappearing from everyday life since the 1960s.

From the toxicological viewpoint phenols should certainly be classed as critical. Although they are quickly excreted from the body in the urine, studies have revealed their acute toxicity in various ways. Tests on animals showed that phenols can damage the central nervous system, kidneys and liver, weaken the immune system and cause changes to haematological parameters [22]. Phenols are classed as category 3 carcinogens [23].

Phenols can also be absorbed directly through the skin, which can lead to very gradual, unspecific poisoning phenomena because the poisoning-pain-warning effect fails to materialise due to an anaesthetising effect. Longer exposure often results in an increased sensitisation to chemical substances (allergy-like reactions).

Uniform test methods or acknowledged criteria with respect to the appraisal of phenol-contaminated building materials or interior air are not yet available. The phenol contaminations established in buildings manifest themselves mainly in the form of slight to intense unpleasant odours preventing long-term use of the rooms. To enable an assessment of the physical contamination and hence a decision regarding refurbishment, a recommendation with guidance values – the phenol index in contaminated material – was formulated in 2004 on the basis of odour threshold values. According to this recommendation, when a noticeable contamination exceeds a certain level, the layer of material containing phenols should be removed (Fig. B 6.20).

B 6.21

B 6.22

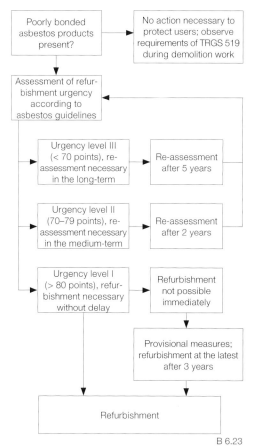

B 6.23

B 6.24

B 6.25

B 6.26

Mineral oils

Mineral oils are liquid distillation products obtained from crude oil or coal. Contamination caused by diesel, heating or lubricating oils is undesirable in residential buildings for hygiene reasons. If the contamination is more recent, intense odours are usual. In addition, mineral building materials contaminated with oil result in enormous constructional difficulties because oil separates materials and hence destroys the adhesion. A mineral hydrocarbon (MHC) content < 100 mg/kg in a building material is regarded as harmless, but with ≥ 1000 mg/kg oil the building waste is classed as hazardous (waste code EWC 17 04 10). Building components contaminated with oil should always be cleared from interiors. To do this, it is normally necessary to remove/demolish the elements concerned.

MMVF

Man-made vitreous fibres (MMVF) are manufactured from rock or glass melts (Fig. B 6.25). In larger quantities they are suitable for thermal/sound insulation and fire protection applications in buildings (Fig. B 6.26). Like asbestos, up until about 1995 MMVF products contained split fibres with critical dimensions (diameter < 3 µm, length > 5 µm, L/D ratio > 3), which are respirable and can therefore cause lung diseases and cancer. This risk is worsened by fibres with a high biopersistence which do not dissolve in the pulmonary fluid and can accumulate over time. MMVF fibres with these properties have been classed as carcinogens since 1995 and corresponding provisions can be found in TRGS 905. Classification and assessment is carried out by means of the biopersistence, which is influenced by the formulation of the melt and other factors (Fig. B 6.24).

The overriding applicable EU Directive 67/548/EEC was amended to take account of the current state of knowledge in October 1997. It differs from the TRGS 905 valid in Germany in a number of points. The fibre property KI > 40, as a criterion for the carcinogenicity index (KI) of a product, is not included in the EU directive. Instead, the directive describes the test method for biosolubility of the fibres with respect to the fibre geometry used (fibre length/thickness in test).

When using insulating materials made from MMVF, the manufacturer must submit a declaration of the carcinogenic potential according to cl. 4a and 5 of the Dangerous Substances Act. It is only permitted to use those products from which fibre dusts cannot be emitted during handling or use. According to cl. 4a of the Dangerous Substances Act and the criteria specified in TRGS 905, such dusts are regarded as carcinogenic or possibly carcinogenic. The declaration must include a corresponding certification of the product, e.g. "mineral wool quality mark" (RAL GZ 388).

Insulating materials made from mineral fibres that were installed prior to 1996 must always be classified as carcinogenic or possibly carcinogenic and therefore require appropriate refurbishment and treatment. The fibres of insulating materials from the period between 1996 and 2000 must be investigated and classified in every individual case because this was a transitional period and various conventional fibres were installed, even in the year 2000. Since then it is almost certainly the case that the fibre products installed already complied with the current requirements.

The main problem with MMVF products is that with the decreased bioresistance only one of numerous health hazard properties was reduced. The irritation of the respiratory tract, especially in persons who have suffered in the past, remains unchanged, just like the irritation of mucous membranes and the skin. For this reason, MMVF products should generally be encapsulated in such a way that no fibres can escape into the interior air.

TRGS 521 (Technical Rules for Dangerous Substances – Fibre Dusts) specifies the handling of old MMVF products during refurbishment and processing. Three protection levels (S 1 – S 3) are specified, each with different occupational safety and environmental protection criteria. Classification depends on the quantity found in situ, the type of use and the method of dismantling required. Protection levels S 2 and S 3 require extensive protective measures and screens around the working area. The old material must be transported in dust-tight containers and is classed as hazardous waste (waste code EWC 17 06 03).

Heavy metals

The term heavy metal as a collective name has no standard definition. The group comprises metals from the fourth period of the periodic table onwards and having a density exceeding 5 g/cm3. Contrary to general beliefs, not all heavy metals are toxic (e.g. gold). In small amounts, "trace elements", various heavy metals such as copper, chromium, iron, zinc, etc. are vital for the human organism.

Lead, cadmium, chromium, copper, zinc and mercury are the heavy metals encountered most frequently in building products. They occur mostly in the form of formulation or alloying constituents and in this form do not represent a direct threat to the environment. Only copper, zinc and lead are used in their pure form as sheets, pipes, etc. Here again, it is not the metal itself that constitutes a risk for humans or the environment, but rather the dissolution of the metal and the removal of metal ions or the subsequent formation of metal salts. Well known are the health problems caused by copper (from copper pipes) dissolved in drinking water and soil contamination due to the long-term dissolution of copper and zinc (sheet metal on roofs/facades) by rain.

Lead is used as a stabiliser and biocide in polymer plastics, as a pigment or desiccant in paints and anti-corrosive treatments, and in older buildings as drinking-water pipes, roof coverings and cable sheathing. Lead is absorbed into the human body through the food chain or in the form of dust; it accumulates and is very difficult for the body to break down (half-life in the body > 20 years). The toxic effect causes problems for the kidneys, testicles, central nervous system and the biosynthesis of haemoglobins. During refurbishment measures in particular, the release of lead in the form of dust or vapour should be taken into account, e.g. when using hot-air or grinding machines to remove old coats of paint. When classifying excavated material (soil contamination) and scrap wood in waste, the lead content is limited. Sheet lead and lead pipes are removed in their entirety and represent a valuable raw material. To avoid future contamination of the environment, the use of products containing lead should be reduced in building works.

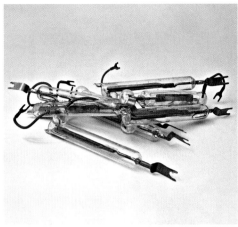

B 6.27

B 6.28

B 6.24   scanning electron microscope image of mineral
          fibres
B 6.25   MMVF insulating materials: soft blanket (back),
          laminated acoustic insulating material (front)
B 6.26   Insulating material above a suspended ceiling
B 6.27   Mercury in technical switching elements
B 6.28   CFC in situ foam

Cadmium is used in various compounds, as a pigment in paints, as a plasticiser and stabiliser (PVC) in plastics and in rustproofing treatments. Cadmium and its compounds are toxic (even in small concentrations), carcinogenic, mutagenic and reprotoxic. It accumulates easily because the biological half-life in humans is 10–30 years. Cadmium occurs exclusively as a formulation or alloying constituent and the risk potential only develops through processing or combustion. For cadmium, too, there is also a limit for excavated material (soil contamination) and for scrap wood. Apart from that, it does not occur as a dangerous substance in existing buildings. To avoid future contamination of the environment, the use of products containing cadmium should be reduced in building works. In the building industry, mercury is found in older building services systems, in switching elements, in mercury vapour lamps and occasionally as a pigment and biocide in lacquers, paints and plastics (Fig. B 6.27). It is mainly absorbed into the human body in the form of mercury vapour via the lungs. Mercury causes damage to the kidneys and the central nervous system. If technical appliances containing mercury are discovered when preparing the dangerous substances catalogue, they must be removed very carefully (waste codes EWC 17 09 01, EWC 20 01 21). Apart from that no special action is normally required.

CFC

Chlorofluorocarbons (CFC) cause massive damage to the ozone layer. The CFC-Halon Prohibition Act has banned the production, marketing and in certain cases the use of some CFC in Germany since 1991. This was superseded by the Chemicals-Ozone Layer Act (law concerning substances that damage the ozone layer) in 2006. CFC are used as propellants in insulating foams and as refrigerants (Fig. B 6.28). The Prohibition Act covers only 17 substances, e.g. trichlorofluoromethane (R 11), dichlorodifluoromethane (R 12), chlorotrifluoromethane (R 13), tetrachlorodifluoroethane (R 112), trichlorotrifluoroethane (R 113), dichlorotetrafluoroethane (R 114) and chloropentafluoroethane (R 115). Substances used for technical applications such as H 1201 halon or R 134a

CFC are not included but likewise have a global warming potential that is, respectively, 6300 or 3300 times that of CO_2 and should therefore be avoided.
Only certified contractors may remove and dispose of cooling systems containing CFC. Refrigerants containing more than 1 % by wt. CFC may no longer be used, but insulating materials containing CFC do not have to be removed. In some regions (e.g. Berlin) such insulation is regarded as hazardous waste and must be disposed of in a special way.

Notes:

[1]   World mineral statistics, 1988
[2]   Wissenschaftliche Buchgesellschaft Darmstadt (ed.): Vitruvius – The Ten Books on Architecture – 7th book. Darmstadt, 1991
[3]   Streit, Bruno: Lexikon Ökotoxikologie. Weinheim, 1994
[4]   German Criminal Code cl. 325
[5]   Directive 98/8/EC of the European Parliament and of the Council of 16 February 1998 concerning the placing of biocidal products on the market, last amended on 29 Nov 2007
[6]   ChemG: Gesetz zum Schutz vor gefährlichen Stoffen of 20 Jun 2002, last amended on 31 Oct 2006
[7]   GefStoffV: Verordnung zum Schutz vor Gefahrstoffen; federal law decree within enabling scope of ChemG of 23 Dec 2004, last amended on 26 Oct 2007
[8]   ChemG cl. 1
[9]   Council Directive 98/24/EC of 7 April 1998 on the protection of the health and safety of workers from the risks related to chemical agents at work
[10]   ChemVerbotsV: Verordnung über Verbote und Beschränkungen des Inverkehrbringens gefährlicher Stoffe, Zubereitungen und Erzeugnisse nach dem ChemG of 16 Mar 2003, last amended on 12 Oct 2007
[11]   Previous regulation: EU Safety Data Sheets Directive 91/155/EEC, superseded by EC REACH Regulation No. 1907/2006 since 1 Jun 2007
[12]   BGR 128 cl. 1 "Scope"
[13]   Biocides are "active substances and preparations containing one or more active substances, put up in the form in which they are supplied to the user, intended to destroy, deter, render harmless, prevent the action of, or otherwise exert a controlling effect on any harmful organism by chemical or biological means." The principal subgroups are fungicides and pesticides. Directive 98/8/EC of the European Parliament and of the Council of 16 February 1998 concerning the placing of biocidal products on the market
[14]   Biopersistence is the solubility of inhaled fibres in pulmonary fluid.

[15]   RAL: Deutsches Institut für Gütesicherung und Kennzeichnung e.V.
[16]   Ad hoc working group "Interior Air Hygiene Commission" (IRK) of the Federal Environment Agency and AOLG
[17]   Directive for determining the market values of building plots (WertR) in the March 2006 edition
[18]   Ed. Bremen Environmental Institute
[19]   Federal Environment Agency (ed.): Leitfaden für das Bauwesen – Reduktion von Schwermetalleinträgen aus dem Bauwesen in die Umwelt, Berlin, 2005
[20]   The free guidelines entitled "Nachhaltiges Bauen im Bestand" are expected to be published in 2008 by the Federal Ministry of Transport, Building & Urban Affairs. The objectives and advice for new construction, some of which are identical, have been available from the ministry since 2002.
[21]   Bremer Umweltinstitut e.V.: Gift im Holz. Bremen, 1994
[22]   BUA: Phenol – BUA Material Report 209 of the advisory council for environmentally relevant legacy materials, German Chemical Society (GDCh), 1998
[23]   Deutsche Forschungsgemeinsaft: MAK- und BAT-Werte-Liste 2000. Senate Commission for investigating materials hazardous to health, Memorandum 36. Weinheim, 2000

Classification of building tasks

Georg Giebeler

This part of the book is divided into chapters that correspond with four periods in the history of Germany since about 1870:

- Buildings of the founding years 1870–1920
- Buildings of the inter-war years 1920–1940
- Buildings of the post-war years 1950–1965
- Buildings of the prosperous years 1965–1980

Most of the standards and regulations referred to in the text are also of German origin. Crucial to the choice of this method of classification – instead of a breakdown according to components or materials – is the attempt to see the building requiring refurbishment as a whole. Depending on the period in which it was built, every building exhibits typical shortcomings – due to new requirements regarding usage, design, construction or serviceability – that must be rectified or minimised during the refurbishment. It is therefore necessary to be familiar with or at least be able to understand the typical forms of construction of past times in order to be able to respond appropriately in the case of conversion or refurbishment.

The reader is therefore recommended to read the corresponding chapter completely instead of only the sections that may be immediately relevant. Such an approach can direct the attention to potential weaknesses in the construction that are not obvious at first glance, and hence avoid problems during the planning work. Firstly, the periods are not nearly so distinct as the classification might lead us to believe because forms of construction develop continuously, i.e. they do not suddenly appear on the market and then just as suddenly disappear. Secondly, the building regulations and standards and forms of construction applicable in Germany do not necessarily apply throughout Europe, not to mention the rest of the world. One example of this is the timber joist floor, which was not completely superseded by the reinforced concrete slab until the post-war years and so crops up in several time periods; in developing countries, however, similar floors are still built today. It is a similar story with concrete containing clay brick aggregate, which is a peculiarity of the German post-war years that owes its brief boom to the enormous amounts of clay brick rubble available at that time. The tables on the next three pages are intended to compensate for the structural disadvantages of the classification to some extent.

Fig. C 0.1 attempts to assign the building task to a certain chapter by means of the evolution of building methods – even if the developments did not actually take place in Germany. The idea behind this is the assumption that every building is erected as inexpensively as possible taking into account technical possibilities and user demands. The critical parameter here is the ratio of the cost of labour to the cost of materials. If labour is comparatively cheap, there is little incentive to employ time-saving methods of construction, and ways of saving materials are favoured. On the other hand, rising wages encourage time-saving forms of construction and hence technological developments as well. This applied to Germany in the post-war years just as much as it applies to Mexico today. The expression "post-war years" therefore describes both a German time period and a lean economic period applicable on a wider scale.

Fig. C 0.3 lists typical methods of building that can be assigned to the various time periods. The table shows which methods were used in which periods, when those methods were most prevalent and where more detailed information can be found. Here again, a classification of non-German structures is also possible, provided the methods of building used are known. To do this, compare the agreement between the individual columns.

Fig. C 0.2 has a similar structure to Fig. C 0.3, but instead of being based on the customary forms of construction used in the past, it lists the typical refurbishment tasks of the present, e.g. thermal insulation to an external wall. This allows the reader to see how often the particular refurbishment measure is necessary for buildings of a particular period; the page numbers for further information are also given.

C 0.1   Matrix for the development of building methods
C 0.2   Matrix for components/refurbishment measures today
C 0.3   Matrix for former methods of building

Criteria	Comparative standards	prior to 1870	Founding years 1870–1920	Inter-war years 1920–1940	Post-war years 1950–1965	Prosperous years 1965–1980	later than 1980
Customary suspended floor methods	Prefabricated elements, use of cranes, composite building methods						•
	In situ concrete floor slabs, precast concrete					•	
	In situ concrete floor slabs, in situ concrete			•	•		
	Timber joist floors	•	•	•			
Customary loadbearing external wall methods	Reinforced concrete walls, formwork systems						•
	Large-format masonry units					•	•
	Normal-format masonry units	•	•	•	•		
Excavation methods	Multi-level, also dewatering					•	•
	Single-level, excavators, trucks				•	•	
	Also manual work			•	•		
	Manual work	•	•				
Customary concrete formwork methods	Formwork systems, use of cranes						•
	Solid timber formwork sheeting, manual transport					•	
	Plank formwork				•		
	Hardly any concrete construction	•	•	•			
Bulk transport, use of machinery	Complete logistics chains, large plant						•
	Trucks, large plant (cranes, excavators)					•	
	Trucks, also manual transport			•	•		
	Mainly manual transport	•	•				

C 0.1

Component	Refurbishment measure	prior to 1870	Founding years 1870–1920	Inter-war years 1920–1940	Post-war years 1950–1965	Prosperous years 1965–1980	later than 1980	General refurbishment tasks
Ground floor slabs	Replace water-permeable (tamped loam, clay brick pavings)	•	p. 134	o				
	Replace partly watertight (concrete screed)			o	•	o		
	Waterproof partly watertight (concrete slab)				o	•	o	
Waterproofing in the ground	Masonry, install horizontal and vertical waterproofing for first time	•	•	•	o			p. 125
	Masonry, renew horizontal and/or vertical waterproofing			o	•	•		
	Concrete wall, install vertical waterproofing for first time			o	•	o		
	Concrete wall, renew vertical waterproofing					•	o	
Loadbearing walls	Masonry, upgrade resistance to driving rain	o	o	o				
	Masonry, upgrade thermal performance	•	•	•	•	•	o	p. 122
	Concrete wall, upgrade thermal performance				o	•	o	p. 122
	Timber wall, upgrade thermal performance and waterproofing	•				o	o	
Frame, vertical	Cast iron or steel frame, upgrade fire protection	•	•	p. 167	o			
	Reinforced concrete frame, exposed reinforcement			•	o	p. 195		
	Reinforced concrete frame, upgrade fire protection			p. 167	•	o		
	Reinforced concrete frame, upgrade thermal performance					p. 195	o	
Suspended floors, solid	Concrete floor slab, upgrade loadbearing capacity			p. 167	o			
	Concrete floor slab, upgrade acoustic performance			p. 168	p. 185	o		
	Concrete floor slab, exposed reinforcement			•	o	p. 195		
	Timber joist floor (solid floor), refurbish supports	•	o					
Suspended floors, frame-type	Timber floor, upgrade loadbearing capacity	•	p. 147	•	o			
	Timber floor, upgrade acoustic performance	•	p. 148	•	o			
	Timber floor, upgrade fire protection	•	p. 149	•	o			
	Timber floor, refurbish supports	•	•	•	o			p. 129
Roof	Pitched roof, install secondary waterproofing layer for first time	•	•	•	•	o		p. 128
	Pitched roof, upgrade loadbearing capacity	o	o	o	•			
	Flat roof, replace all layers			•	•	o		
	Flat roof, upgrade thermal performance					•	•	
Windows	Single-glazed windows, replace completely	o	p. 141	•	•	o		
	Single- and double-glazed windows, replace glass	o	o			o	o	
Curtain walls, cladding	Replace completely				p. 180	p. 198	o	
	Upgrade thermal performance by replacing glass					o	o	
Non-loadbearing walls	Masonry, refurbish plaster	o	o	o	o			
	Lightweight construction, upgrade acoustic performance	o	o	o	•			
Floor finishes	Install impact sound insulation for first time	•	•	•	o			

C 0.2

Component	Typical form of construction	prior to 1870	Founding years 1870–1920	Inter-war years 1920–1940	Post-war years 1950–1965	Prosperous years 1965–1980	later than 1980
Foundations			p. 133	p. 156	p. 174	p. 192	
	Rubble stone	•	•	o			
	Masonry, stepped footing	•	•	•	o		
	Tamped concrete		o	•	o		
	Plain concrete			o	•		
	Reinforced concrete				o	•	
	Raft foundations					o	•
	Deep foundations		o	o	o	•	•
Basement, ground floor slab			p. 134	p. 156	p. 175	p. 192	
	Compacted soil	•	o				
	Clay brick pavings	o	•				
	Plain concrete up to 100 mm thick			•	o		
	Plain concrete				•	•	
	Reinforced concrete					o	•
Floor slab over basement			p. 135	p. 157			
	Masonry vaulting	•	•	o			
	Jack arch floor		•	•			
	In situ concrete slab			o	•	•	•
External walls in contact with the ground			p. 134	p. 157	p. 175	p. 193	
	Heavyweight masonry	•	•	•			
	Tamped concrete			•	o		
	Reinforced masonry, concrete-filled blocks				•	o	
	Plain concrete, formwork to one side			•	•		
	Reinforced concrete					•	•
Waterproofing in the ground			p. 134	p. 157	p. 175	p. 193	
	Simple vertical waterproofing			o	•		
	Secure vertical waterproofing				o	•	
	Secure horizontal waterproofing				o	•	
	Secure tanking in ground water					o	•
Loadbearing walls			p. 138	p. 157	p. 176	p. 193	
	Masonry, solid masonry units	•	•	•		o	
	Masonry, hollow and lightweight masonry units			o	•	•	
	Concrete-filled blocks				•	o	
	No-fines plain conc., conc. with clay brick agg.				•		
	Reinforced concrete					•	•
	Timber construction, system houses					•	•
Frame, vertical			p. 142	p. 161	p. 179	p. 197	
	Cast iron	•	•	o			
	Steel, riveted			•	o		
	Steel, welded and bolted				•	•	o
	Reinforced concrete with haunches			•	•		
	Reinforced concrete				o	•	•
	Precast concrete elements					•	•
Suspended floors			p. 144	p. 165	p. 182	p. 199	
	Timber joist floor	•	•	•	o		
	Steel beams with infill elements, jack arch floors			o	•		
	Precast concrete elements with infill elements				•	•	
	Reinforced concrete					•	•

a

C 0.3

Component	Typical form of construction	prior to 1870	Founding years 1870–1920	Inter-war years 1920–1940	Post-war years 1950–1965	Prosperous years 1965–1980	later than 1980
External walls			p. 138	p. 157	p. 176	p. 193	
	Single-leaf		•	•	•	•	o
	Cavity wall (unventilated cavity)		o	•	o		
	Double-leaf with cavity insulation					o	•
	Full thermal insulation					o	•
Roof covering			p. 151	p. 170	p. 187	p. 201	
	Pitched roof, bullnose tiles	•	•	o			
	Pitched roof, interlocking clay tiles			o	•	•	•
	Flat roof without insulation		o	•	•	o	
	Flat roof with insulation					•	•
Windows, facade			p. 140	p. 160	p. 179	p. 197	
	Coupled windows	o	•	o			
	Secondary glazing			•	o	o	
	Single windows	•		o	•	o	
	Single windows, double glazed					o	•
	Curtain wall facades				o	•	•
Non-loadbearing walls			p. 142	p. 160	p. 180	p. 199	
	Masonry, solid masonry units		•	•	o	•	o
	Masonry, hollow and lightweight masonry units				•	•	•
	Lightweight partitions, fabricated in situ		•	•	o		
	Lightweight partitions, partly prefabricated				o	•	•
Floor finishes to suspended floors			p. 150	p. 168	p. 185	p. 200	
	Floorboards, nailed	•	•	•	o		
	Subfloors with finished wearing surface (terrazzo)	o	•	•	•		
	Unbonded subfloors		o	o	•	o	
	Floating subfloors				o	•	•
Ceilings			p. 146		p. 177		
	Plaster on background ("Rabitz" type)	•	•	•			
	Plaster on wood-wool lightweight boards				•		
	Plaster on solid suspended floor			o	•	•	•
	Suspended ceiling, partly prefabricated					o	•
Insulation				p. 159	p. 177	p. 194	
	Natural materials (peat, cork)	o	•	•	•	o	
	Wood-wool lightweight boards			o	•	•	
	Man-made vitreous fibres				o	•	•
	Foamed plastics					o	•
Chimneys, heating			p. 143	p. 163	p. 181	p. 200	
	Masonry chimneys	•	•	•	o		
	Masonry chimneys with flue pipes			o	•		
	Special flue bricks				•	•	
	Individual stoves		•	•	•		
	Central heating			o	o	•	•

• common, standard   o may be encountered

General refurbishment tasks

Georg Giebeler

C 1.1

Not all refurbishment tasks can be unequivocally assigned to a certain time period. Many apply to more than one of the time periods in the following chapters and are therefore treated separately on the next few pages.

Energy-efficiency upgrades
One of the most common refurbishment tasks at the moment is improving the energy efficiency of the building stock, and a number of problems occur again and again when adding thermal insulation to external components.
On a new-build project, the decision to install the insulation internally or externally is in the first place based on economics, technical and use-related conditions. But this applies to refurbishment projects to a limited extent only. For example, an ornamented facade dating from the founding years rules out external insulation even though that is best for a residential building and external insulation is the only way of avoiding thermal bridges at junctions with internal walls. Despite the technical problems and the lower standard of interior comfort, internal insulation is the only solution in such a case. If the facade is protected by a conservation order, additional insulation may not be necessary at all. However, from the point of view of the successful long-term marketing of the property, quite apart from our responsibility towards the environment, this is not to be recommended. Nevertheless, it is possible – in consultation with the building owner – for the heritage protection authority responsible to have the building exempted from the requirements of the Energy Conservation Act (Fig. C 1.2). However, conformity with the minimum thermal performance specified in DIN 4108 is obligatory because this standard is included in building legislation. The subsequent installation of thermal insulation may also be taken as a chance to give everyday buildings a contemporary character. However, the risk here is that features typical of certain periods may be lost. Such features include, for example, the window surrounds of many post-war buildings, where the render is usually trowelled smooth to contrast with the rougher render finish of the rest of the facade. The reason for this feature was a purely practical one: the surrounds could be repainted readily

from inside without having to renovate the entire facade – necessary in those days because of the soot deposits caused by coal-fired stoves and boilers. However, as these surrounds also form part of the architectural style of the period, refurbishing without reproducing or restoring these surrounds – a frequent occurrence – represents an insensitive intervention in the facade design. This together with the deep reveals resulting from the subsequent addition of external insulation ruins the typical character of the facades of that period.
A new layer of thermal insulation alters more than just the appearance – the moisture balance of the building changes, too. In buildings with timber joist floors in particular, a system with a very low resistance to vapour diffusion should be chosen so that any construction moisture present can continue to dissipate to the outside. This is especially important at the bases of walls, where the moisture rising from the ground is released into the outside air. A barrier to this moisture transport, e.g. in the form of an unsuitable render or perhaps even a bituminous waterproofing material, can lead to damage such as rotten timber floors or effluorescence and mould growth in a previously dry ground floor.

External insulation
So-called external thermal insulation composite systems (ETICS), i.e. a rendered insulating material, represent especially cost-effective external insulation solutions. Thanks to the many years of experience with such external insulation, there are now reliable, tried-and-tested systems available that can also be applied to difficult substrates. Nevertheless, large areas of loose old render should always be removed first because these can form downright "piles of debris" behind the new layer of insulation, which then manifest themselves on the outside. Any impermeable barriers such as ceramic tiles, resin plasters or synthetic coatings applied during previous refurbishment work should also be removed. In the case of such barriers, partial removal by scouring the surface is usually sufficient.
The reaction to fire of the expanded foamed insulating materials normally used should also be considered. If the respective federal state

C 1.1 Conversion of a stable block into two homes, Bergün (CH), 1997,
Daniele Marques and Bruno Zurkirchen
C 1.2 Minimum U-values for customary refurbishment measures according to the Energy Conservation Act

building regulations call for the use of not readily flammable building materials (class B1) for external wall cladding applications (usually building category 4 and higher), the use of such insulating materials alone is not permitted. There are two possible solutions in such a situation: either the use of rock wool around windows and doors, or the inclusion of a fire stop at every second floor, i.e. an approx. 200 mm high, horizontal, continuous strip of fire-resistant material at the level of the intermediate floor, for instance. The base of the wall needs special attention, as already mentioned. The customary standard insulating systems are designed for new buildings and their suitability for old buildings – i.e. very low vapour diffusion resistance – must be checked. Another detail that must be examined in every individual case is the junction with the window. Until well into the post-war years, most window openings were built such that the outer frame is partially covered by a masonry nib (see Fig. C 1.3 overleaf); only 20–30 mm of the frame is visible externally, meaning that it is impossible to insulate the reveals. Two solutions are possible here:

The first option is to cut off the masonry nib, usually approx. 60 mm thick, and replace this with insulation of the same thickness. This must be carried out on all sides, however, i.e. beneath the window sill and under the lintel as well. And the detail at the lintel almost always leads to structural problems because the nib here is often loadbearing. This is frequently the case with the concrete lintels of the post-war years, which were cast together with the suspended floor above, also the arches of the founding and inter-war years. It is worthwhile checking the window details at an early stage because if this solution is not possible, the costs will rise considerably.

The second option is to simply replace the windows by new ones with a wider outer frame. The disadvantages of this solution are the higher costs – collateral damage to window board and plaster internally is virtually inevitable – and the decrease in the size of the glass area. In conjunction with deeper reveals and coated glass, this leads to a noticeable reduction in the amount of incoming daylight. Alternatively, the new windows can be fitted further forward within the new wall thickness, which overcomes the lighting problem but may prevent the installation of roller or other shutters. Depending on the thickness of the insulation and the details, this solution can either retain the old facade appearance by setting the windows back by half a brick and then accepting the lower level of daylight, or change the appearance of the facade completely by fitting the windows on the outside (Figs. C 1.3a–c).

It is not advisable to omit the insulation to the window reveals or to reduce it to just a few centimetres because with the insulation thicknesses necessary these days for external walls the result will almost certainly be mould growth on the inside around the bathroom and kitchen windows. Some manufacturers of insulating

materials permit the window reveals to be left uninsulated, contending that a temperature exceeding 12.6 °C has been measured on the internal surfaces around the windows. However, this dew point calculation is based on a relative air humidity of 50 % at 20 °C air temperature – a value that is regularly exceeded in practice given the ventilation and heating behaviour usual these days, especially in kitchens and bathrooms.

Similar problems concerning the windows occur when adding insulation to single-leaf clay brick or facing masonry that is to be given a second leaf made from the same material: if the windows are left in their old positions, they must be replaced and even if the existing masonry nibs are cut off, the size of the window is reduced considerably. This has an effect on both the daylight entering the room and the proportions of the facade.

The aforementioned problems can be diminished by placing the windows in the plane of the new thermal insulation. However, the architectural and technical problems of the detail at the eaves and junctions with other components, e.g. stone cladding, canopies, that result from the single-leaf masonry plus the thermal insulation (min. 200 mm) still have to be solved. Cladding made from fibre-cement sheets, wooden boards, etc. can represent a thinner and less expensive alternative when a conscious decision is taken to refrain from reproducing the current facade design. The ventilated cavity that is then possible – sometimes essential – ensures a vapour-permeable construction that is safe for the existing building (Fig. C 1.3d).

Internal insulation
Buildings with external facades worthy of preservation can only be insulated on the inside. Not unreasonably the Energy Conservation Act specifies lower requirements for the U-value (0.45 instead of 0.35 W/m²K) in this case because the thermal bridges at junctions with internal walls and floor slabs cannot be completely eliminated.

The new internal insulation reduces the surface temperature of the original inside face of the external wall, which results in additional cooling of the internal wall and floor surfaces at the junctions and thus the risk of condensation forming. Thin layers of insulation – approx. 80 mm should be regarded as a maximum – reduce the problem so that in rooms with normal uses the dew point limit of 12.6 °C can generally be verified by calculation and further measures are unnecessary. Care is required, however, with wet rooms and walls where the air circulation is poor, e.g. behind built-in cupboards. As an alternative to accepting the thermal bridges, a 1 m width of insulation – also available in wedge form – can be affixed to both sides of each internal wall. This option is, however, rather theoretical because there is no satisfactorily aesthetic or functional solution for dealing with the ensuing step in the wall surface. By contrast, cutting a continuous slit in the internal wall (provided it is non-loadbearing and is not required for the stability of the building) to create a thermal break represents a genuine alternative. However, even non-loadbearing internal walls must be secured against horizontal loads, e.g. by fixing them with indi-

Component	Planned refurbishment measure	Min. U-value [W/m²K] for heated rooms (> 19 °C)
External walls	Provision of new external cladding, attaching external thermal insulation or renewing render when U-value of existing wall > 0,9 W/m²K	0.35
	Where the above does not apply	0.45
External walls in the ground	Installation of waterproofing or drainage Installation of new inner lining	0.40 0.50
Windows	Replacement of windows or addition of further glazing	1.70
	Replacement of glazing	1.50
Windows with special glazing (sound insulation > 40 dB, bulletproof, fire-resistant)	Replacement of windows or addition of further glazing	2.00
	Replacement of glazing	1.60
Curtain walls, cladding	Replacement of glass, panels, or complete replacement with special glazing (see above)	1.90 2.30
External doors	Replacement of external doors	2.90
Roofs and suspended floors (outside air above or below)	Replacement of roof covering to pitched roofs above or floors below habitable rooms	0.30
Suspended floor over (unheated) basement	Installation of thermal insulation on underside	0.40
Flat roofs	Renewal	0.25
Ground floor slabs (in contact with soil)	Renewal of floor finishes	0.50

C 1.2

C 1.3 Adding new thermal insulation to an existing
external wall: details at window reveals
a External thermal insulation composite system,
masonry nib cut off (left: original detail), but
window left in original position
b As for a, but without removing masonry nib,
new window with wider outer frame
c As for a, but position of window altered to
maintain existing external appearance
d Facade panels with ventilated cavity, masonry
nib removed, window repositioned
e Internal insulation, masonry nib retained, new
window with wider outer frame

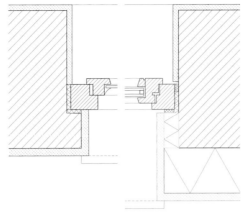
a

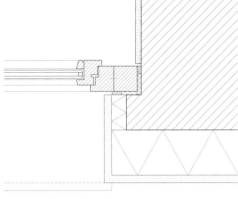
b

vidual steel anchors. In addition to damage
caused by condensation, excessive thicknesses
of internal insulation can also lead to tension
cracks. Such cracks are caused by the disparate expansion of the warmer internal wall and
the now (because of the refurbishment) much
colder external wall.
Another problem is the displacement of the
dew point into the internal insulation. Depending on the insulating material used, irreversible
saturation of the insulation can be caused if
there is no vapour barrier or it has been poorly
installed. Saturated insulation is no longer effective as insulation and will lead to mould growth
within the construction. As, however, vapour
barriers cannot be fully inspected during construction, poor workmanship is the rule rather
than the exception; junctions with floors and
soffits, pipe and cable penetrations etc. are
especially critical. It is therefore advisable to
install internal insulation either without any vapour
barrier at all or with a "smart" vapour barrier
whose membrane function prevents a build-up
in the moisture level so that the insulation can
dry out towards the inside again and again
over the course of the year (Fig. C 1.3e).

Thermal bridges
Irrespective of whether internal or external insulation is planned, as the complexity of the building geometry grows, so do the problems of installing subsequent thermal insulation. Balcony
slabs cannot usually be reliably insulated on all
sides without impairing both the aesthetics
(chunky appearance on elevation) or the functions (inadequate clearance and step at balcony
door). The same is true for loggias. Passages
through the building cannot be adequately insulated on the inside (removal and replacement
of floor finishes, step inside building) and are
therefore insulated on the underside. Swapping
from internal to external insulation also occurs
at party walls between buildings of different
sizes; the result is potentially damaging thermal
bridges and therefore such details are always
problematic.
In principle, potential damage can be avoided
– assuming toleration of the building stock applies – by not providing any additional thermal
insulation in heated buildings that show no signs

of mould growth. If we adhere to this principle,
the answer would seem to be to provide nothing
more than the statutory minimum – undoubtedly
a piece of advice that is open to criticism. Only
rarely can thermal bridges be completely avoided
when adding thermal insulation at a later date,
and the greater the difference between the insulated and the uninsulated component, the
more likely it is that such thermal bridges will
give rise to problems such as tension cracks,
moisture in the components and mould.

Windows
Besides problems confined to specific periods,
there are also general aspects concerning
types of glass and sealing that must be considered when refurbishing windows.
Since the 1970s more types of float glass have
been processed, and since 1995 insulating
glasses have been coated with metal oxides as
well, which enabled the U-value to be reduced
from 3.0 to 1.3 W/m²K virtually overnight. The
different effect of the glass plays a major role in
conversion work: uncoated rolled glass appears
white and reflections are always "wavy" – a
total contrast to coated float glass. Replacing
the glass or the windows changes the look of
the building. This presents a problem for facades
protected by conservation orders in particular,
but also when adding additional storeys or carrying out a partial refurbishment, i.e. when perhaps only one storey is involved.
In terms of the sealing of windows, it is true to
say that the windows installed these days are
much more airtight than those of the past. The
Energy Conservation Act prescribes class 3
joint permeability, or class 2 for buildings with
no more than two storeys; standard windows
frequently achieve even class 4. This means
that the exchange of air normal in the past –
essentially a form of forced ventilation through
the gaps between the separate parts of the
window – can no longer take place, which can
lead to increased air humidity and higher moisture contents in components and hence to
mould problems.

Render and plaster
Voids behind old plaster are common. Theoretically, this does not represent a problem because

if the plaster has not yet become completely
detached, it will probably continue to stay in
place. In practice, however, cutting and chasing for pipes and cables, even just repairing
the walls, leads to large areas of plaster coming away from the substrate. If the voids are
only local, they can be made good at reasonable cost. But the situation is different if the
flaws account for more than one-third of the
area. The huge coat thicknesses regularly
encountered and the matching-up and ancillary
works required make reliable costing almost
hopeless. In addition, tension cracks between
old and new plaster are virtually inevitable,
especially when – out of ignorance – new gypsum
plaster is placed alongside existing lime plaster.
And whether all voids have really been found or
whether users will find them when they hammer
a nail into the wall will always remain an uncertainty. The complete removal of old plaster
(even where it is still firmly attached) therefore
represents a sensible alternative, especially
when new internal finishes (internal insulation to
external walls, linings to improve the sound insulation of party walls, new partitions) mean
that only a few areas of old plaster would remain.
In contrast to this, where there are voids behind
old render, it should certainly be removed back
to the substrate because damage to the building fabric is almost certainly the cause. The
problems at the interfaces between new and
old render are similar to those between new
and old plaster. Exacerbating this problem,
however, is the fact that old decorative render
finishes can no longer be reproduced these
days. Even if the rendering methods are the
same, a consistent appearance following partial repair is often impossible to achieve. The
reason for this is the many coats of paint that
have changed the original structure over the
years. Where damage extends over a large
area, a complete covering with a new finish
render coat is the only remedy.
Besides removing all loose render, all surfaces
that reduce adhesion, e.g. loose coats of paint,
must also be removed. Render that shows signs
of dusting but is still adhering can in some circumstances be repaired by applying a coat of
penetrating primer. Afterwards, the areas to be
repaired are rendered coarsely and a mesh is

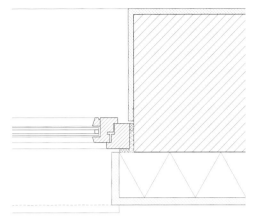

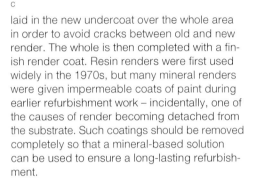

c

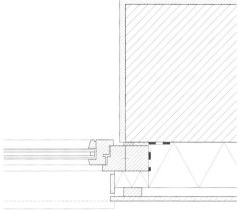

d

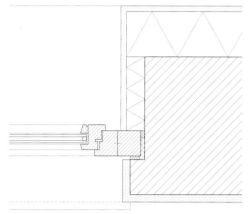

e   C 1.3

laid in the new undercoat over the whole area
in order to avoid cracks between old and new
render. The whole is then completed with a finish render coat. Resin renders were first used
widely in the 1970s, but many mineral renders
were given impermeable coats of paint during
earlier refurbishment work – incidentally, one of
the causes of render becoming detached from
the substrate. Such coatings should be removed
completely so that a mineral-based solution
can be used to ensure a long-lasting refurbishment.

Moisture from the ground
Almost all buildings built before the war show
signs of saturation of the components in contact with the ground. The cause is nearly always
the lack of waterproofing to the external walls
and floor of the basement, and the missing
damp-proof course in the masonry walls as
they emerge from the ground. Such waterproofing was not usual in those days because the
basement served only as a storage place for
coal and potatoes, and as such also functioned
satisfactorily when it was damp. The architects
of the time responded to this in constructional
terms by specifying heavyweight floor slabs at
ground floor level, i.e. forms of construction that
were not adversely affected by dampness, and
also by raising the ground floor clear of the
splashing water zone. The inclusion of unglazed
openings in this plinth allowed basement walls
and basement air to dry out. Damp-proofing is
therefore unnecessary; indeed, it can even
cause damage in the form of settlement as
masonry joints dry out subsequently. However,
if the ground floor is suffering or the basement
rooms are to be used for other purposes, which
should be avoided if at all possible, damp-
proofing is the only – usually expensive – solution.
Basement floor slabs are usually not very thick,
which means they are easy to remove. Excavat-
ing deeper – but certainly no lower than the underside of the foundations – allows a new basement floor slab to be cast in impermeable concrete, which should be at least 250 mm thick.
Manual work (removing the excavated material)
and other ancillary costs (concrete pump hire)
make such work expensive. The joint between
the masonry and the new floor slab remains an

uncertainty. It can be pressure-grouted but the
unevenness of the rising wall means that a
watertight seal cannot be guaranteed.
Where the external walls to a basement are
damp, an investigation should be carried out
first to establish whether this is just local wetting
or the moisture is evenly distributed over the
inner surfaces. Only in the latter case can we
assume that the moisture is infiltrating from the
surrounding soil. If the level of moisture is higher
at ground level, this indicates the presence of
rising damp, and local damp patches point to
defective buried water pipes or rainwater down-
pipes.
The installation of vertical waterproofing around
an existing basement is carried out in a similar
way to a new building: after cleaning the surfaces a bituminous waterproofing compound is
applied, mostly in the form of a thick coat, which
is then covered by permeable insulation. Additional drainage is advisable on sloping sites.
Vertical waterproofing is often less expensive
than might be first assumed, provided machines
can be used for the excavation. What increases
the cost over comparable measures for a new
basement is the presence of a very uneven wall
surface, which leads to a high consumption of
waterproofing compound or the need for a coat
of render to level the surface.
The most common and at the same time most
expensive damp-proofing measure is the subsequent installation of a damp-proof course
(dpc) in the masonry. There are three methods
in common use: mechanical, injection and
electro-osmosis.
Mechanical methods can be regarded as the
most reliable in many instances – not because
they are carried out flawlessly every time, but
because workers and building owners can see
exactly what is being done. Different methods
are used for installing the damp-proof course,
but common to all methods is that the work is
carried out in sections, and the quality of the
system depends primarily on the quality of the
overlaps between these sections. The waterproofing materials used certainly conform to
new-build standards. The problem with all
mechanical methods is the intervention in the
loadbearing structure. The chasing, cutting,
drilling or pressure-injecting and the poor work-

manship (excessively large sections, filling
material with inadequate structural strength)
can lead to settlement and cracking. The most
significant methods are described below.
The masonry replacement method is the oldest
method and at the same time the most reliable,
but also the most time-consuming and expensive. The first step is to cut slots in the masonry
(max. 500 mm long, but this depends on the
vertical loads), leaving sections of intact masonry in between. Flexible bitumen sheeting is
inserted into the slots, which are then bricked
up (non-shrink grout) such that the structural
properties of the wall are retained. Slots are
now cut in the remaining intact masonry, the
flexible bitumen sheeting inserted, overlapped
with and bonded to the adjacent pieces and
the slots bricked up. A structural engineer should
determine the positioning and size of the slots.
The height of the slots depends on the thickness of the masonry because there must be
sufficient room to bond together the bitumen
sheeting and lay the bricks. This method can
therefore only be considered for masonry up to
approx. 500 mm thick (Fig. C 1.4 overleaf).
A special masonry saw can be used to cut a
slit approx. 10 mm high and approx. 800 mm
long through the masonry. The damp-proof
course is created either by forcing wedges of
synthetic damp-proofing material into the slot
or by inserting flexible bitumen sheeting similarly to the masonry replacement method. The
advantage of the synthetic wedges is that they
also carry the vertical loads. The wedges overlap by 50 % to create quasi a seamless damp-
proof course. Again, this method is really only
suitable for masonry up to approx. 500 mm
thick (Fig. C 1.5).
In the sheet steel method, corrugated stainless
steel sheets 300 – 400 mm wide are vibrated
into a bed joint by means of a pneumatic hammer. The sheets overlap approx. 50 mm in
order to create a watertight barrier, but this is
especially difficult at corners (Fig. C 1.6). The
connection to bituminous vertical waterproofing
is also difficult. Both these disadvantages also
apply to the synthetic wedges.
The contiguous boring method is also regarded
as very reliable and can be used in masonry up
to about 4 m thick! Holes approx. 120 mm in

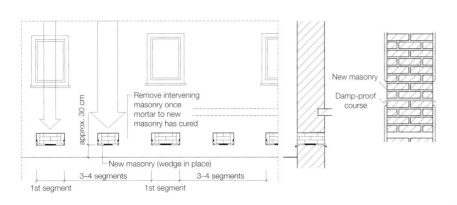

C 1.4

Remove intervening masonry once mortar to new masonry has cured

New masonry

Damp-proof course

New masonry (wedge in place)

approx. 30 cm

3–4 segments   3–4 segments

1st segment   1st segment

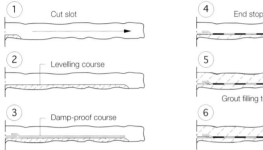

1 Cut slot

2 Levelling course

3 Damp-proof course

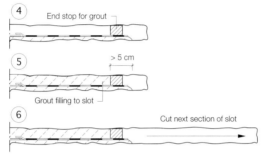

4 End stop for grout

5 > 5 cm

Grout filling to slot

6 Cut next section of slot

C 1.5

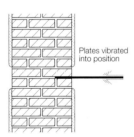

Plates vibrated into position

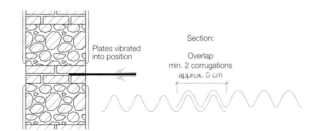

Plates vibrated into position

Section:

Overlap min. 2 corrugations approx. 5 cm

C 1.6

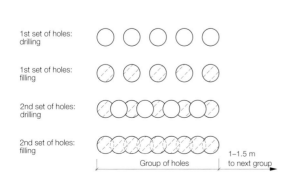

1st set of holes: drilling

1st set of holes: filling

2nd set of holes: drilling

2nd set of holes: filling

Group of holes

1–1.5 m to next group

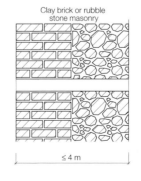

Clay brick or rubble stone masonry

≤ 4 m

C 1.7

C 1.4   Masonry replacement method after completing the first stage of the work
C 1.5   Sawing method carried out six steps
C 1.6   Corrugated steel plate inserted into a masonry bed joint
C 1.7   Contiguous boring method carried out in four steps

diameter are drilled through the wall every approx. 100 mm. These are then filled with a non-shrink grout (based on cement or epoxy resin, with additives). After the grout has cured, holes are drilled through the intervening intact masonry, overlapping with the first set of (filled) holes. The advantages of this method are that it is hardly susceptible to settlement, does not cause any vibration and can be used in composite masonry walls (Fig. C 1.7).

Injection methods differ in terms of their technology – non-pressurised infiltration or pressure-injection – and also their materials (Figs. C 1.9 and 1.10). All the materials are in fluid form when they are injected and cure within the masonry. They spread through the capillaries horizontally and vertically, i.e. form a "cloud" around the point of injection, which is supposed to overlap with the other "clouds". And this is precisely where the two most frequent shortcomings are to be found: if the masonry is more than 50 % saturated, the capillaries are already full of water and cannot accommodate any more waterproofing fluid; and as the true spread of the fluid cannot be checked, overlapping is not guaranteed. Another common problem is that the masonry is not properly investigated prior to injection. In composite masonry, for example, i.e. clay brick leaves plus a cavity filled with rubble stone and mortar, the waterproofing fluid seeps away uncontrolled into joints and voids instead of spreading out. Owing to these uncertainties, injection methods should therefore be referred to as horizontal moisture checks, not moisture barriers. One advantage of these methods over the majority of mechanical methods is, however, that the work involves no vibrations, a criterion that is sometimes very important with buildings protected by conservation orders. Another area where injection methods are helpful is with masonry thicknesses exceeding 500 mm because this is where many mechanical methods reach their limits. Injection methods can also be used while buildings remain in use because the horizontal barrier in the external walls can usually be installed from just one side, i.e. outside (Fig. C 1.10).

Electro-osmosis is based on the physical law that fluids in capillaries can be moved by applying an electric field (nanopump). Its effectiveness in damp masonry has not been proved, however, and so this method can be disregarded, an approach that also applies to some of the "miracle cures" available on the market.

Efflorescence

Saturated masonry often leads to the formation of damaging salts (Fig. C 1.8). In areas that have dried out, woolly, usually white, gossamer-

C 1.8 Salts that can damage building materials and
lead to efflorescence on masonry
C 1.9 Effects and injection methods of various injection
fluids
C 1.10 Injection methods
a Holes for non-pressurised injection
b Holes for pressure-injection

like formations build up – the efflorescence of
the salts that were previously dissolved in water.
These can enter the masonry in various ways:
through their natural occurrence in the subsoil,
their presence in the groundwater (e.g. excessive fertilisation), defective sewers, de-icing
salts or urine. Such efflorescence is not only
unsightly; it can also damage clay brickwork or
mortar in certain circumstances. Following
damp-proofing, the quantity of damaging salts
should therefore be reduced. It is usually sufficient to remove the render or plaster completely
once the masonry is dry, brush the surface of
the masonry thoroughly and rake out the joints.
It may be necessary to replace the masonry
locally where the problem is severe. If that is
not adequate, electrical or vacuum methods
can be used to remove the salts from the masonry. Contrasting with this is the dry method of
applying so-called sacrificial plaster or render:
a coat of absorbent lime or desalination mortar
is applied and then removed again after a few
months after it has soaked up the salts.

Roof space conversions

Critical when selecting the type of roof insulation to be installed are the planned use of the
roof space, the other associated conversion
measures and architectural issues. Irrespective
of these criteria, these days the installation of a
secondary layer below the roof covering –
missing in most roofs – is obligatory. Removing
and re-laying the roof covering is therefore unavoidable, even if for aesthetic and ecological
reasons reusing the existing roof tiles is a possibility.
Starting with this premise, various methods of
insulating the roof space can be considered.
What all methods have in common is the need
to compensate for the unevenness of the roof
structure, which can sometimes be considerable because as the roof space was not intended
to be a habitable room, there were no stipulations
regarding the dimensions of the roof members.
Furthermore, the structural members would
often not pass a deflection analysis to a modern
code of practice.
Where there is no lining to the rafters or the lining is not worth keeping, the simplest solution
is to attach timber sections to the sides of the
rafters to deepen them. This creates enough
depth for insulation between the rafters, provides the framing for a level lining and solves
the structural problems. In addition, the outer
edge of the roof structure is not changed so all
eaves and verge details remain unaltered, thus
avoiding both technical and architectural problems. The only disadvantage is the loss of space
in the roof space, which the designer should
assume to be 100 mm on average. This shift in

Salts that can damage building materials

Chlorides	Calcium chloride	$CaCl_2 \cdot 6\ H_2O$
	Common salt (sodium chloride)	$NaCl$
Sulphates	Epsom salt (magnesium sulphate)	$MgSO \cdot 7H_2O$
	Gypsum (calcium sulphate)	$CaSO_4 \cdot 2\ H_2O$
	Glauber salt (sodium sulphate)	$Na_2SO_4 \cdot 10\ H_2O$
	Ettringite	$3\ CaO \cdot Al_2O_3 \cdot 3\ CaSO_4 \cdot 32\ H_2O$
Nitrates	Magnesium nitrate	$Mg(NO_3)_2 \cdot 6\ H_2O$
	Calcium nitrate	$Ca(NO_3)_2 \cdot 4\ H_2O$
	Lime saltpetre	$5\ Ca(NO_3)_2 \cdot 4\ NH_4NO_3 \cdot 10\ H_2O$
Carbonates	Soda (sodium carbonate)	$Na_2CO_3 \cdot 10\ H_2O$
	Potash (potassium carbonate)	K_2CO_3
	Lime (calcium carbonate)	$CaCO_3$

C 1.8

Injection compound	Principle behind method		Injection method	
	sealing	hydrophobic	with pressure	without pressure
Cement suspension	•		•	
Fines suspension	•		•	
Bitumen solution	•		•	
Synthetic resin solution	•		•	•
Siloxane solution		•	•	•
Silicone resin solution		•	•	•
Silicic acid ethyl ester hydrophobe		•	•	•
Molten bitumen	•		•	
Molten paraffin	•			•
Bitumen emulsion	•		•	
Silicone micro-emulsion		•	•	•
Alkali silicate	•		•	•
Methyl siliconate		•	•	•
Higher alkylated siliconate		•	•	•
Akali siliconate/alkali silicate	•	•	•	•

C 1.9

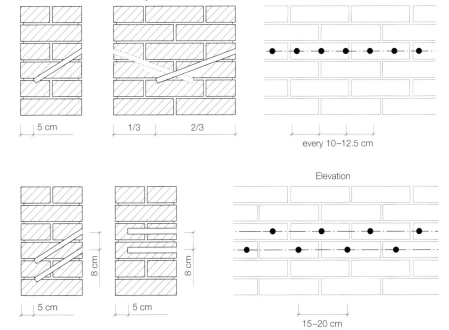

a

Masonry thickness d > 60 cm   Elevation

5 cm   1/3   2/3   every 10–12.5 cm

b

8 cm   8 cm
5 cm   5 cm

Elevation

15–20 cm

C 1.10

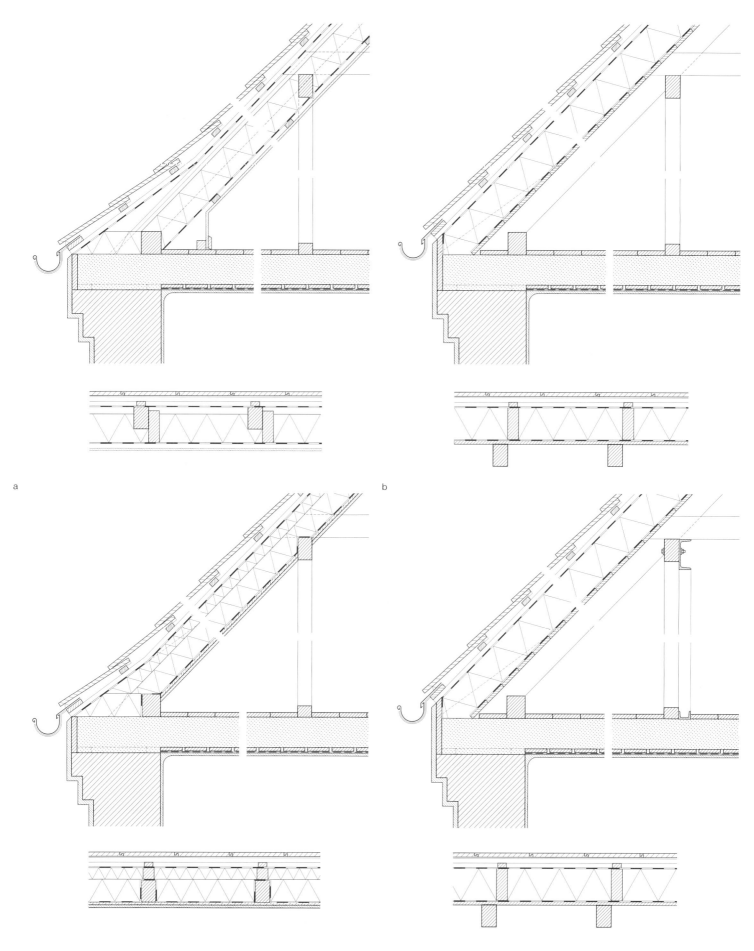

a

b

c

d

C 1.11

the position of the inner surface also frequently leads to an unsatisfactory interior architecture because the purlins and other parts of the construction such as posts and knee braces are now partially concealed (Fig. C 1.11a).

If these problems are to be avoided, it is possible to consider leaving the existing construction exposed – frequently an appealing option for the interior architecture. After nailing planed boards or planks to the rafters over the entire roof area and laying a vapour barrier, a new roof is constructed outside the old one – with new rafters, new insulation between the rafters, secondary waterproofing layer and roof covering. Besides the high cost of such an undertaking, it is vital to consider the transitions to the walls, especially at the eaves, with respect to technical (load transfer), constructional (waterproofing), building legislation (new eaves height = greater clearance to adjacent buildings required) and architectural (eaves appearance/overhang) aspects (Fig. C 1.11b).

Where the existing soffit, e.g. plastered woodwool lightweight boards, is or has to be retained, the vapour barrier must be laid on top of this. This is fitted around the rafters and all joints must be on the rafters. The depth of the rafter is now increased by nailing the first counter battens to the rafters (not structurally effective). As this type of construction is hardly likely to be vapourtight, some manufacturers offer so-called smart vapour barriers that guarantee dry thermal insulation when considered as an average over the year. The position of the eaves changes only marginally, which means that the aforementioned problems are not usually relevant (Fig. C 1.11c).

A new structural analysis of the roof structure is necessary because of the additional loads due to insulation, deeper rafters, possibly concrete instead of clay roof tiles and the lining. Whereas attaching additional sections to deepen the rafters is often satisfactory, this approach does not work with the purlins. If the knee braces – which reduce the span of the purlin – are to be removed to allow better use of the roof space, the purlins will almost certainly need to be upgraded structurally. Where possible this should

be carried out symmetrically about the existing loadbearing axis in order to avoid inducing bending in the posts due to eccentric loading. Steel channel sections are ideal because they can be attached on one or both sides with toothed-plate connectors and bolts to create a structural connection between the new steel and the existing timber (Fig. C 1.11d).

The structural upgrading of the purlins, the deepening of the rafters to accommodate the thermal insulation, the trimming of rafters to accommodate new windows (dormer- or Velux-type) and additional work to level the roof structure are the cost factors in roof space conversions. Depending on the condition of the building and the intended measures, a rough comparison with a new, replacement structure is worthwhile because besides the warranty issued with new works, the cost and timing estimates are much more dependable.

Timber joist ends

A form of damage often encountered with timber joist floors is rotten joist ends – and the rotting often extends up to 500 mm from the wall. The possible causes are a change in the moisture balance (different degree of sealing, new thermal insulation, new uses, different user behaviour) or water directly (defective rainwater, waste-water or drinking-water pipes, splashing water, inadequate protection against driving rain).

After determining and rectifying the cause, the replacement of the defective timber members can begin. The joists must be propped during refurbishment, but care must be taken to avoid placing any excessive loads on the floor below. The joist ends are cut back generously to sound timber and replaced by new timber with the same dimensions. Timber splice plates on the sides, connected with toothed-plate connectors and dowels, represent the simplest way of joining new and old (Fig. C 1.12). If a structural analysis reveals that the existing timber members are inadequate for modern loads, steel channel sections can be used instead.

How joist ends supported in masonry pockets should be handled is currently the subject of a

heated debate. Both opinions will be expressed here:

- The joist ends should be finished airtight by building up the wall around them or by some other means. This prevents damp interior air reaching the middle of the masonry and then condensing on the timber.
- A gap should be left between timber and masonry so that air can circulate around the joist ends. This method allows any moisture to dry out again and was the method prescribed in all publications until well into the post-war years.

In either method, bituminous felt can be wrapped around the joist ends in order to provide additional protection against the infiltration of moisture.

Flat roofs

Minor leaks in a flat roof are often not obvious. Even the typical noise of saturated insulation familiar these days – a clear sign of a leak – does not occur with the types of insulation used up until a few decades ago because they are too thin. However, experience shows that older flat roofs are seldom free from defects and so measuring the moisture content of the insulation is highly advisable. In addition, the insulation laid prior to 1970 cannot achieve the thermal performance required today, which means that plans for replacement should be drawn up. The removal of all roof finishes down to the structure is recommended in order to avoid sources of future problems such as saturated insulation and defective vapour barriers. The new roof finishes are laid in the same way as a new-build project and therefore offer the same reliability (covered by warranty). When refurbishing rooftop terraces, the much deeper roof finishes may cause problems at doors, and balustrades or parapets may then be too low.

Many flat roofs built using older methods include eaves details with external gutters just like pitched roofs. When new roof finishes are combined with an external thermal insulation composite system on the walls, the gutter suddenly

C 1.11 Various methods for installing new thermal insulation in an existing pitched roof
   a Increasing the depth of the rafters on the inside where the inner lining does not need to be preserved
   b Existing construction left exposed internally by constructing a new roof on the outside
   c Adding insulation on the outside while retaining the inner lining
   d Structural upgrading of a purlin by means of a steel channel fixed to one side
C 1.12 Splicing a new end on to a rotten timber joist/beam

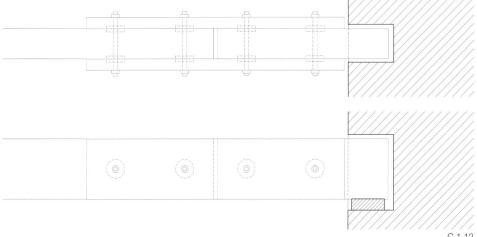

C 1.12

C 1.13

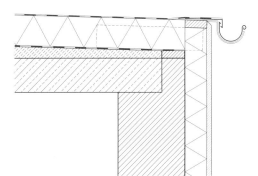

C 1.14

C 1.15

finds itself hanging in mid-air. Timber framing is necessary to rectify this situation (Fig. C 1.14).

Chases, openings, pockets

Chases, openings and pockets in the existing building fabric accompany every conversion project, but are even necessary during normal building services maintenance. In contrast to a new-build project, though, the work sometimes has to be carried out in plastered surfaces and the effects are much greater: a new door requires an opening larger than the door itself, for example. Other parameters therefore have to be taken into account: structural aspects during and after the work, also damage to components that must be preserved. Scouring, chiselling, sawing and drilling are the four ways of cutting away parts of the existing building fabric.

Wall chasers are mainly used for cutting chases for electric cables. Chases up to 30 mm wide with a maximum depth of 40 mm are possible. Larger wall chasers, also electrically operated, are able to cut through masonry up to 500 mm thick, which is why they are popular for installing damp-proof courses (see p. 125). Scouring machines are used in plaster refurbishment because they can remove large areas of plaster or other wall finishes. The advantage of scouring over chiselling is that there is much less vibration and therefore much less damage to the underlying masonry and the adjacent plaster that should remain intact. The disadvantages are the noise and the dust, which places high demands on occupational safety and may also require working areas to be screened off.

The most common method is chiselling with electric tools (for small areas) or pneumatic tools (reinforced concrete, thick masonry). Such tools can also be used to remove finishes such as ceramic tiles or firmly adhering plaster. The main disadvantage of chiselling – besides the vibration – is its coarse nature; chiselling leaves behind very irregular surfaces and edges, which means the follow-up costs are correspondingly high. This disadvantage can be compensated for to certain extent when chiselling is combined with the following methods. The use of an electric circular-saw is always worthwhile when the edge of an area to be cut away has to be exact in terms of position and depth. Such saws are self-propelling, i.e. they travel along a toothed rack mounted on the masonry beforehand. The rack must, however, be firmly attached, which is not possible with every type of masonry (e.g. lightweight concrete bricks). If no suitable anchors are available, one possible solution is to attach the rack with threaded bars that pass through the wall and are secured on the other side with plates. In addition, the saw-blade is water-cooled, and despite extraction it is never possible to rule out saturation of neighbouring components – a problem that virtually precludes sawing above wood-block flooring. Furthermore, the problem of the overcut has to be solved: as the saw-blade is round, the cut at the front of the material extends beyond the planned corner by a

distance that depends on radius of blade and depth of cut. Such a cut cannot be made good in, for example, a fair-face concrete surface. Besides rack-guided saws, hand-held cutting discs are another option. The quality of the cut is, unsurprisingly, only modest, the depth limited to approx. 150 mm and the noise and dust similar to that of scouring. Despite this, the use of such a tool can be very worthwhile as preparation for chiselling work on thinner walls because it minimises the vibration caused by chiselling and ensures reasonably straight edges. Wire saws are used where the component dimensions are large (Fig. C 1.16).

Core drills are used as well as normal drills (Fig. C 1.13). With diameters up to 1.2 m and capable of drilling up to 2 m deep, a whole variety of applications is conceivable: pipe penetrations, preparatory drilling prior to scouring, ventilation and window openings. The method is similar to that of the rack-guided saw and the disadvantages are also the same. However, as the vibration during drilling and sawing is limited, these methods are the most gentle and accurate ways of cutting away existing building materials.

Structural stability during the work

In order to remove building material from load-bearing components, the loads must first be safely diverted. Where a new opening in a wall is more than 1 m wide, two loads must be considered: the loads from suspended floors and the weight of the masonry above the planned opening. With narrower openings, the natural arching effect of the masonry – assuming a solid piece of wall above – is usually sufficient to carry the loads, meaning that temporary props etc. are unnecessary. The loads from a suspended floor should be supported by temporary props and beams approx. 1 m in front of the supporting wall in order to guarantee enough room to carry out the work. It is important to make sure that no unnecessary loads, e.g. building materials, are stored on that floor during the work and that the loads on the temporary props are safely transferred to a load-bearing foundation.

The wall loads can be carried in one of two ways depending on requirements:

Small openings are cut through the wall above the planned new lintel every approx. 600 mm. So-called needles are inserted through these openings, supported on adjustable steel props and wedged up to the underside of the existing masonry so that the loads are securely carried. The removal of the wall below can now be carried out safely. However, this very simple method cannot be employed when cutting an opening in the facade on an upper storey or where for some other reason support on both sides is not feasible. Another disadvantage is that it is not possible to place the new lintel directly below the suspended floor above. In such a situation one solution is to install the new lintel in two stages without the need for any temporary supports. To do this, a horizontal slot is cut in the

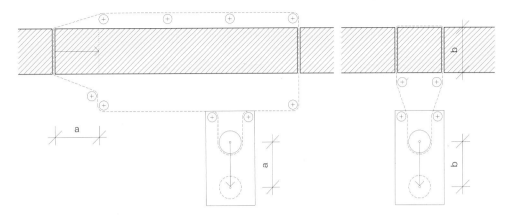

C 1.16

masonry, the depth of which should, however, be no more than half the thickness of the wall. The first lintel, usually a steel I-section, is fitted into this slot and the gap between top flange and underside of masonry filled with grout so that the loads can be safely transferred. Once the grout has cured, the second lintel is installed on the other side of the wall in a similar way. After the grout here has cured, the wall below the new lintels can be broken out (Fig. C 1.17). All measures must be checked by means of a structural analysis and should be well supervised on site. The reactions at the ends of such lintels must be checked because, for example, lightweight masonry often does not have the necessary compressive strength to carry such high point loads. The masonry of the majority of 150–200 mm bearings for such lintels must therefore be replaced by masonry units with a higher compressive strength. In the case of very heavy loads, masonry piers or steel stanchions down to the foundations may even be necessary. In order to prevent settlement, all work, especially above the lintel and the supports, must be carried out with non-shrink grout or mortar. Wherever steel sections are used, adequate space for a fire-resistant casing or a plaster/render background must be allowed for in the design, depending on the circumstances (Fig. C 1.15).

New floor openings
When forming new openings in suspended floors, the loads must be supported in a similar way to that described above. The actual work itself differs depending on the type of floor construction.
Larger openings are hardly possible over vaulting (see "Buildings of the founding years", pp. 135–137). By contrast, in jack arch and timber joist floors, also other types of framed floor constructions, it is possible to remove a whole bay between two supports without having to carry out a structural analysis. However, if more than one bay is involved, the loads carried by the beam to be severed must be diverted to the two intact edge beams by installing trimming beams. The connection options for the trimmers and the loads on the edge beams, which may well need to be upgraded, must all be investi-

gated. These are both problems specific to the material. Timber beams and joists are easy to connect, e.g. by way of timber splice plates on the side, and also easy to strengthen. The same is true of steel beams. But in the case of precast concrete beams, virtually impossible.
In situ concrete floor slabs are comparable with timber joist floors from the structural viewpoint. As reinforcing bars are always severed, the neighbouring, undisturbed zones must carry the loads from the areas either side of a new opening. Many floor slabs are already on the limits of their load-carrying capacity and so only small openings are feasible. Circular openings are particularly favourable because these exhibit the most harmonic flow of forces around the opening. It is also helpful to chisel out openings carefully rather than cutting them. This approach allows the main reinforcing bars

to be exposed and incorporated into the reinforcement of a new edge beam (trimmer within depth of slab).

Support pockets
Unsuitable suspended floors are often replaced by new reinforced concrete slabs. This means that supports have to be formed in the masonry walls. As continuous horizontal slots are not permitted and would also be too costly, individual supports in pockets cut in the masonry have to suffice. These pockets are chiselled out approx. 150 mm deep, their number and width depending on the compressive strength of the masonry. Reinforcement cages are placed in these pockets and connected to reinforcement running along the side of the wall. The slab is now cast up against the wall without any joint (sound insulation) (Fig. C 1.18).

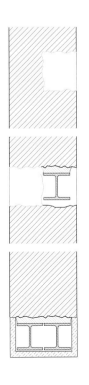

C 1.17

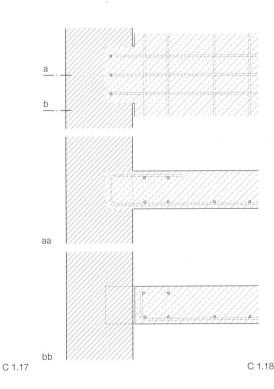

C 1.18

Buildings of the founding years 1870–1920

Georg Giebeler

C 2.1

In the German-speaking countries *Gründerzeit* (= founding years) is an acknowledged expression that designates the first phase of sweeping industrialisation. In the light of the different economic and social situations in the countries of Central Europe, this period can be assumed to begin between 1850 and 1870. In Germany the industrial upswing began in the 1860s and in the following years – following victory in the Franco-Prussian war of 1870/71 and the subsequent French reparations – turned into an economic boom. The founding of the Second German Reich in 1871 also contributed to rapid economic growth.

Industrialisation means mass production, division of labour and working in shifts around the clock. Manufacturing processes began to concentrate at one place, the factory, which required a mass influx of workers from the countryside. The founding years triggered a building boom not linked to any war, the likes of which had never been seen before and have never been seen again since. This also meant that building itself was industrialised. New, reproducible or prefabricated building systems conquered the market, which up until then had been characterised by manual skills. Likewise, the division of labour, i.e. the division into trades, was transferred from manufacturing to the building industry. In terms of the history of building, the founding years was an eclectic period embracing styles such as neo-Gothic, neo-Baroque and neo-Renaissance, which can be combined under the heading of Historicism. Building tasks reflected all conceivable uses, but most of the work in Germany – apart from factories – was devoted to the construction of multi-storey, multi-occupancy housing in the towns and cities (Figs. C 2.1 and 2.2). Similar building methods were used for the large detached houses built during this period for the factory owners and other wealthier citizens. The technical details given in this chapter relate to these two types of housing, unless stated otherwise.

The first phase of industrialisation was accompanied by wholesale social changes that naturally also manifested themselves in the design of buildings. Whereas the houses and villas of the more prosperous citizens offered ample space for living and socialising, the workers were mostly accommodated in deplorable social conditions with an appalling level of hygiene. For example, it was quite normal for shift workers to share a bed – one working, one sleeping. "Living in the dry" – i.e. the housing of tenants in buildings that were just finished for low rents so that they could benefit from the coke stoves necessary for the curing and drying of the building materials – could even lead to health repercussions. The large rooms so popular today were not rooms for socialising, but at best accommodation for large families. Toilets and wash-basins were usually located alongside hallways or stairs and used by all the tenants on one floor. Such conditions provided breeding grounds not only for far-reaching socio-political movements, but also – with the longing for "light and air" – for the ideas of the garden city and, in the end, the Modern Movement.

As the buildings of the founding years represent maximum-profit products, there is often a very great difference between the front and rear elevations of a building. The sides that were seen are richly ornamented facades overlooking wide, often tree-lined, boulevards, and the staircases here are very spacious: wide flights, shallow pitches, large expanses of coloured glass. The opposite of this can very often be found in the same complex: narrow and hence dark backyards overlooked by facades of bare clay brickwork, and narrow, steep staircases leading to small, dark apartments (Fig. C 2.4). Many of these districts with buildings from the founding years still exist today. Their locations in the centres of towns and cities and their good infrastructure make them popular residential areas, also because the density of occupancy has been much reduced compared to earlier times.

Typical strengths and weaknesses
The strengths of buildings from the founding years can be found in their former usage. Large, tall rooms with a floor space often exceeding 20 m² and approx. 3 m high (the Berlin Building Regulations of 1897 prescribed a minimum height of 2.80 m) were advisable in order to accommodate as many persons as possible in one room. Such a structure presumes generously dimensioned, loadbearing internal and

C 2.1 Housing, Hohenzollernring, Cologne (D), 1885,
C. A. Philipp
C 2.2 Housing floor plans, Cologne (D), 1885,
C. A. Philipp
a Ground floor
b 1. 1st floor
C 2.3 Slaking lime and mixing lime mortar on a building
site around 1900
C 2.4 A formerly fully enclosed rear courtyard in Cologne,
now opened on one side

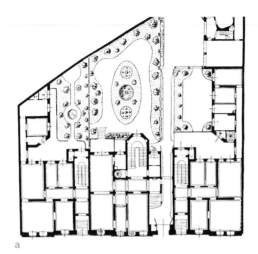
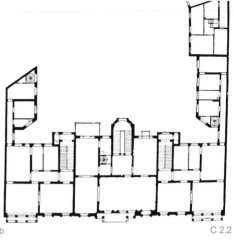

a   b   C 2.2

external walls that, positioned mostly parallel with the facade, result in a simple, orthogonal interior layout. Both attributes are helpful when considering a conversion today. The rooms are suitable for both offices and for more open housing forms; subdivision for uses requiring less floor space is also possible.

The heavyweight form of construction with thick masonry walls (except for the topmost storey in many cases) ensures good sound insulation and adequate thermal mass. On the street side, tall windows ensure a good supply of daylight. The weaknesses are to be found in the "building for maximum profit" philosophy and the lack of technology. Buildings squeezed into back-yards and narrow, dark interior layouts with long access hallways with little or no natural lighting – often lit from one side only without the chance of cross-ventilation – are difficult to let or sell these days. Conversions hardly improve this situation because the daylighting problem cannot be improved. One of the aims of the urban refurbishment schemes of recent decades has therefore been to attempt to "gut" such districts, i.e. to demolish backyard buildings.

Added to these problems are the technical deficits. The lack of or defective waterproofing (horizontal or vertical) to the external walls below ground results in damp basements, sometimes even damp ground floors. In addition, the impact and airborne sound insulation plus the fire resistance of timber joist floors are often inadequate. The joists are also frequently undersized, which leads to visible deflections.

Conversion potential
Buildings of the founding years offer a great potential for conversion. The basic structure is suitable for a multitude of uses, sometimes with very different qualities. After the installation of modern building services, there are usually two problem areas that remain in the conversion reduced to the basic structure: timber joist floors and basement. Improving the floors is possible at reasonable cost up to a certain point. But the situation is different with a damp basement; subsequent damp-proofing is virtually impossible here.

Owing to the many usage options and the great appeal of buildings dating from the founding

years, these problems can be neglected to a certain extent. Complete demolition of individual buildings can be ruled out from the start for economic reasons – unless undertaking an urban renewal scheme.

Basements

In towns and cities that experienced a huge influx of workers and a corresponding shortage of housing in those years, e.g. Berlin, basements were also designed to be habitable rooms. However, their usual purpose was to:

- store food (owing to their consistently cool temperature) or fuel,
- protect against rising damp or splashing water by raising the ground floor more than 400 mm,
- protect against unhealthy "vapours" from the groundwater, which were supposedly the cause of, for example, typhoid.

Basements were therefore usable but not economically lettable floor areas, and their design and construction matches this premise – despite advances in building technology. For example, industrially produced and hence affordable cements and tar-based waterproofing materials had been available since the mid-19th century, but these were either not used at all or not used properly. Basements of the founding years are

C 2.3

therefore mostly stable, but permanently damp. Serious damage is rare, but permanent usage – not to mention habitable rooms – cannot be achieved at reasonable cost (Fig. C 2.7).

Foundations and basement floor slabs
As the buildings of the founding years are all solid masonry constructions, strip footings were the usual type of foundation for normal subsoil conditions. The textbooks of the time specified a depth of 1.0–1.2 m below the level of the site as adequate to prevent frost heave [1]. In order that the permissible bearing pressure of the soil was not exceeded (and rough guidelines were already available), foundations were widened and the masonry was stepped by ¼ brick (imperial format: 65 mm) every second course. The lowest course of the foundation had to provide a flat bearing for the masonry wall above and bridge over minor inconsistencies in the subsoil conditions. Tamped concrete was used in addition to large stone slabs and other large-format rubble stones. The contemporary trade literature contains suggestions for reinforcing the tamped concrete with iron bars or old iron rails [2]. However, old inspection lists seem to indicate that this technique was not widely used [3]. It is probably more realistic to assume that rubble stone was used for the foundations, at least the lowest level. The mortar used either made use of loam from the excavation itself or a very small amount of lime; both of these mortars have only a low strength.

C 2.4

C 2.5

Residential building	Basement	Grd. flr.	1st flr.	2nd flr.	3rd flr.	4th flr.	Attic
				Masonry thickness [cm]			
Front wall	99	77	64	51	51	38	25
Internal wall supporting joists	64	51	51	38	38	38	–
Gable wall not supporting joists, no openings	51	51	38	38	25	25	25
Gable wall supporting joists, no openings	77	64	51	51	38	38	25
Gable wall not supporting joists, with openings	38	38	25	25	25	25	25
Staircase wall for hallway width > 2.50 m	64	51	51	38	38	38	38
Staircase wall for hallway width < 2.50 m	51	38	38	25	25	25	25
Factory building							
Front wall	77	64	51	51	38	38	25
Central wall supporting joists	51	51	38	38	38	38	–
Gable wall not supporting joists	51	38	38	25	25	25	25
Gable wall supporting joists	64	51	51	38	38	38	25
Staircase wall for hallway width > 2.50 m	64	64	51	51	38	38	38
Staircase wall for hallway width < 2.50 m	51	51	38	38	25	25	25

C 2.6

Soil surveys and special foundations using techniques similar to those of today were also not unknown during this time. And as urban planning disregarded the natural features of the landscape such as existing river courses, deep foundations were unavoidable sometimes. Driven timber piles plus a 1–2 m thick "pile cap" of tamped concrete (with a little reinforcement in the bottom) was a frequent solution for multi-storey structures (Fig. C 2.8).

Basements permanently below the water table are very rare because at that time pumps were not in widespread use and that would have meant building "underwater". With a firm sub-soil and a lightweight structure, the lowest layer of the foundation might have been in the form of a timber grillage, which to prevent rotting had to be permanently below the water table. Later, such foundations were built in tamped concrete because the costs dropped over the years (Fig. C 2.11).

Concrete was based on cement and was mixed by hand on the building site. Whenever possible, sand and gravel from the excavation itself were used as the aggregate. Site mixing plus the inclusion of soil in the mix meant that the concrete produced was nowhere near the quality of modern concrete, which also explains the enormous thicknesses of concrete components. The quality of the ground slabs matched the intended usage. Basement floor slabs were preferably positioned at least 200 mm above the highest water table level and as the base-ment was not intended to contain habitable rooms, waterproofing was considered unnec-essary. We therefore encounter two main types of basement floor slab these days: tamped loam or loosely laid clay paving bricks. Neither type of floor can prevent the infiltration of groundwater or rising damp.

Damage and measures
In buildings more than 100 years old, founda-tion problems such as settlement should have been completed or rectified. If no building measures are carried out in the vicinity of the foundations, other refurbishment work will not be worthwhile. One measure to combat rising damp in the basement floor slab is, for example, to install a slab of impermeable concrete at least 250 mm thick on the compacted basement floor. If the surface is floated and rubbed, it can be used as the finished floor. Integrating the slab into the masonry walls and waterproofing the joint is inadvisable even where there is a risk of a rising water table. The existing masonry is not designed for the vertical loads (buoyancy) that would occur at the junction between the concrete and the masonry and considerable damage can occur. It is better to form sufficiently wide joints, e.g. strips of permeable boards, around the perimeter so that the groundwater can infiltrate into the basement (Fig. C 2.5). The floor slab should then fall to a central sump containing a pump from where the water can be pumped out into a suitable sewer.

External walls to basements
The basement walls to buildings dating from the founding years are always in masonry. The surfaces were usually left untreated but occa-sionally limewashed. The prescribed minimum thicknesses are considerable: in Berlin, for example, the building authorities demanded that masonry for external walls below ground be up to 990 mm, i.e. 3½ bricks, thick, depend-ing on the number of storeys (Fig. C 2.6).

Two problems directly associated with this are still relevant today:

The first is that sometimes, in order to save bricks and hence money, only the outer and inner faces are masonry and the intervening cavity is filled with rubble or excavated material held together

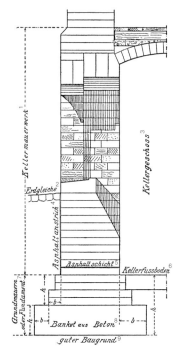

C 2.7

C 2.8

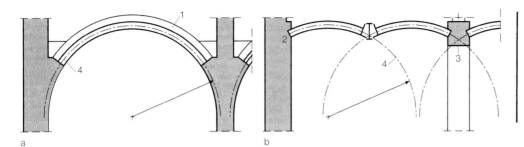
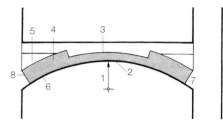

a b

1 Strengthening rib
2 Wall abutment
3 Masonry transverse arch
4 Centre-line of arch

C 2.9

1 Rise   5 Gusset
2 Crown   6 Intrados
3 Extrados   7 Abutment
4 Strengthening   8 Springing

C 2.10

with only a very small amount of binder. Stability is not usually a problem because of the massiveness of these walls (any problems would have manifested themselves before the building was completed). But what can be extremely difficult is the creation of any openings, chases, pockets, etc. because the removal of the material – even when sawing – is very difficult to control. Subsequent, expensive stabilising measures (bricking up) are therefore necessary. In addition, such masonry cannot be waterproofed by injection methods because the voids – sometimes considerable – cannot be reliably filled (see "General refurbishment tasks", p. 126).

The other problem concerns the mortar used. The less expensive non-hydraulic limes often used for masonry mortar require a supply of air for curing. But in order to speed up construction, the excavations were backfilled too early, thus terminating the curing process and leading to unstable joints. But even very lean hydraulic lime mortars still tend to crumble away over the years. Where subsequent filling of the joints is necessary, a lime mortar of similar quality – with the addition of only a small amount of cement – should be used, never pure cement mortar. The latter is unsuitable because of its impermeability and hardness, and it never forms a permanent bond with the existing mortar.

It was realised only a few years ago that basements dating from the founding years should not be damp-proofed even when this is technically possible. The masonry then dries out, especially the lime mortar joints, which suffer a decrease in volume and crumble away even more. The result is settlement and stability problems, especially in thin-walled vaults. Furthermore, the thickness of the masonry walls alone makes the damp-proofing very expensive and the follow-up costs caused by the aforementioned problems are impossible to estimate. Changes of use in basements below buildings from the founding years should therefore be avoided.

Floors over basements

Whereas timber joist floors were mainly used for the upper floors, an airtight and moisture-resistant floor was preferred over the basement, which was almost always in the form of vaulting or a jack arch floor (Figs. C 2.9 and 10). The type of vaulting most frequently used for a suspended floor over a basement is the barrel vault. Only in public, prestigious buildings were domical and groined vaults built for the upper floors as well, especially in staircases and corridors.

Ancient barrel vaults are semicircular in section. No horizontal thrust occurs at the springings of such vaults, which enabled large spans to be built without problems at the abutments. However, the vaults common in the buildings of the founding years describe only a circular arc in order to achieve better use of the space below. Shell-type loadbearing structures of relatively thin masonry are the result. In contrast to flat floor slabs subjected to bending actions, exclusively compressive forces prevail in vaults.

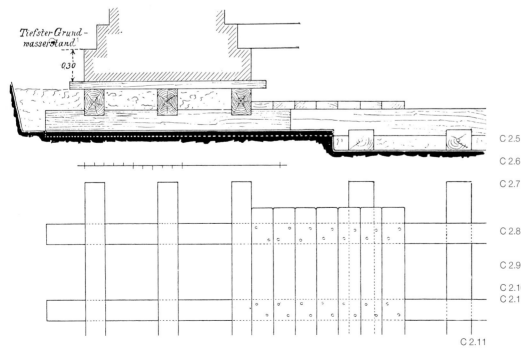

C 2.11

C 2.5   Joint between existing masonry wall and new concrete floor slab in basement
C 2.6   Minimum masonry wall thicknesses according to the Berlin Building Regulations around 1900
C 2.7   Basement perimeter wall and foundation, here in concrete but mostly masonry or rubble stone
([1]Basement masonry, [2]Ground level, [3]Basement storey, [4]Asphalt waterproofing, [5]Asphalt dpc, [6]Basement floor, [7]Foundation, [8]Concrete strip footing, [9]Good subsoil)
C 2.8   Timber piles, tamped concrete foundation cast in layers, strips of iron as reinforcement above second layer
C 2.9   a Barrel vault
        b Jack arch floor
C 2.10 Arch/vault designations
C 2.11 Foundation in groundwater on timber grillage; the uppermost timbers must lie at least 300 mm below the lowest water table.
([1]Lowest water table)

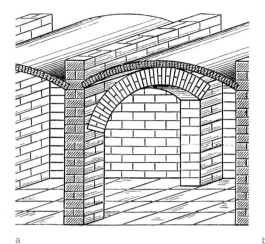

a

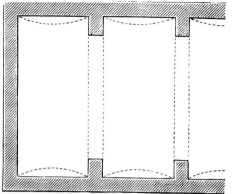

b   C 2.12

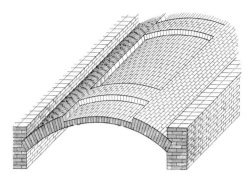

C 2.13

These compressive forces follow the line of thrust within the curve of the vault itself and are resolved into vertical and horizontal forces at the supports. The smaller the rise between springing and crown, the greater is the horizontal thrust that must be resisted by the external wall masonry of the building. To do this, the masonry – already thick – was often strengthened by piers in the region of the transverse arches. In a barrel vault these forces occur only at the springings, and the walls below the vault are not loaded (Fig. C 2.12).

The vaults were built with normal-format clay bricks supported on timber centering. Lime or lime-cement mortar with a small cement content was used as the mortar. The reason for this is the permanent elasticity of the lime mortar, which thus allows the vault to deform, making it less vulnerable to damage. We distinguish between three variations depending on how the bricks were laid:

• "Kuff" bond: the bricks are laid in stretcher bond parallel to the supports, starting at the springings and finishing at the crown (Fig. C 2.13).

• Moller bond: starting at the end walls, rings are constructed one by one so that the bricks are positioned at a right-angle to the springings.
• Herringbone bond: turning the bricks through 45° results in a vault that is self-supporting during construction, meaning that this type of vault could be built without timber centering (Fig. C 2.16).

So-called lunette vaults had to be constructed in the masonry at basement windows or similar openings in the supporting walls; these form a barrel vault intersecting at 90° to the actual vault. Building in transverse arches would have strengthened the groin, but instead a simple mitred arrangement was frequently used.
In order to minimise the rise of the vault, the system spans were often further subdivided. Transverse arches or steel beams (in bending) were then used as the supports. This form of suspended floor construction is referred to as a jack arch floor (Fig. C 2.17).
The steel beams were positioned fairly close together (every 1.5 – 2.5 m), thus limiting the rise of the vault to approx. 300 mm. The beams

used were either I-sections (Fig. C 2.40) or iron rails. One reason for the use of jack arch floors at that time was that even an unqualified bricklayer could construct such a vault. Later, the jack arches were also built using plain concrete or patented special bricks designed for the purpose.
The gussets on top between the walls and the vaults were filled completely with loose material. Clay brick fragments and other debris is often found here in addition to the sand or lighter forms of slag that were actually intended. Timber grounds embedded in this loose fill form the bearers for a nailed subfloor (wooden floorboards with open joints, often laid diagonally) on which the floor finishes for the ground floor were then laid (Fig. C 2.14).

Damage and measures
Vaulted floors are mostly permanently stable, but damage that impairs the loadbearing action is possible. One problem is the loss of material from the joints with the ensuing settlement of the crown of the vault. This subject is also relevant for external walls (see p. 135), but the

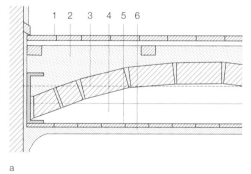

a

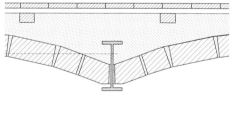

b   C 2.14

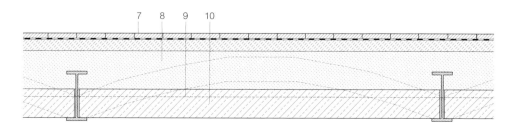

C 2.15

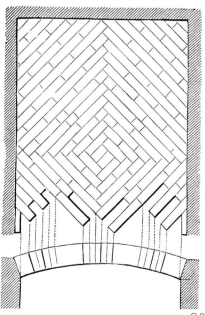

C 2.16

Jack arch span [m]	Rise (1/8 span) [m]	Thickness at crown [cm]	Thickness at support [cm]
2.50	0.31	12	12
3	0.38	12	12, strengthening ribs every 1.50–2.50 m
4	0.50	12	25
5	0.63	25	25

Transverse arch span [m]	Rise (1/4 span) [m]	Thickness [cm]	Width [cm]
2	0.5	38	min. 38
3.5	0.875	51	not specified
6	1.5	63	not specified
8.5	2.125	75	not specified

C 2.17

C 2.18

C 2.19

refurbishment costs for vaults are very much higher. If noticeable settlement has already occurred, the floor bays may need to be replaced, e.g. by a flat reinforced concrete slab (Fig. C 2.15). As the horizontal thrust of the shallow jack arches represents the main load and the steel beams used, or even masonry transverse arches, are not designed for lateral bending, the supports to the remaining, neighbouring floor bays must be restrained laterally prior to demolition, e.g. by way of a compression-resistant connection to steel beams fitted underneath.

Another problem is the rusting of the steel beams in the jack arch floor because the beams were mostly installed without any form of coating and are therefore not protected against corrosion. The bottom flange in particular, which is open to the damp basement, often suffers from considerable flaking. Any beams affected should certainly be investigated by a structural engineer. Where individual beams have to be replaced, the two adjoining jack arches also have to be demolished, and measures must be taken to resist the horizontal thrust of the remaining jack arches. Subsequent strengthening of the beams is not feasible because the different compositions of old and new steel prevent welding. If there is sufficient height in the basement, new steel beams can be placed beneath the existing ones; the construction of new supports is, however, relatively expensive. When several beams have to be replaced, complete replacement of the floor by a flat reinforced concrete floor should be considered.

Demolishing a vaulted floor to an entire room does not usually present any problems but measures to resist the horizontal thrust of any neighbouring vaults are essential. In a row of buildings any vaulting in the neighbouring buildings should also be considered: common fire walls, equal in thickness to internal walls, are probably not sufficiently stable when the horizontal thrust is applied to one side only. Demolition is carried out from above after removing the floor finishes and loose fill. Vaults in Moller and herringbone bond are easier to demolish than those in "Kuff" bond, which fail suddenly as soon as the bricks at the crown are removed.

The easiest way of creating new openings in existing jack arch floors is by removing complete bays and replacing these with reinforced concrete containing the necessary openings. Small openings, e.g. for building services, should be drilled through the vault so that, on the one hand, the flow of forces is disrupted as little as possible and, on the other, the vault is not subjected to any vibration. Holes drilled with core drills up to 150 mm diameter do not usually present any problems.

Ground and upper floors

The storeys above ground level usually begin above the splashing water zone with the raised ground floor and end at the attic storey, which was often unused even though the roofs were sometimes ornamented with gables. Frame constructions for the interior and extensive iron-and-glass roofs, e.g. for department stores, were not unknown to the builders of those times, but the external walls were still heavyweight masonry constructions with a greater or lesser degree of

C 2.12 Jack arch floor over basement between masonry transverse arches
   a Isometric view
   b Plan
C 2.13 Jack arch floor with strengthening ribs
C 2.14 Jack arch floor between steel beams
   a with plaster ceiling on timber boarding
   b without ceiling
   1 Floorboards on wooden subfloor
   2 Filling (slag, sand)
   3 Tie rod
   4 Ceiling joist
   5 Boarding
   6 Plaster/stucco
C 2.15 Jack arch floor replaced by reinforced concrete slab
   7 Floor covering, PE sheeting, floating screed
   8 Filling removed to reduce weight and replaced by loose fill insulation
   9 New tie rod at mid-depth of beams
   10 New concrete slab to replace jack arches
C 2.16 Vault in herringbone bond
C 2.17 Thicknesses of masonry jack arch floors and associated transverse arches
C 2.18 Floor support with step in masonry on both sides of wall
C 2.19 Cantilevering balcony supported on steel beams
C 2.20 Common national and international brick formats around 1900

Formats of backing wall bricks	Length [mm]	Width [mm]	Depth [mm]
German Reich (normal format)	250	120	65
North-west Germany (small format)	220	105	56
Bavaria (large format)	290	140	60
Austria	290	140	65
Italy	220–230	110–170	50–70
France	220	110	60
England	250	110	60
	254	124	76
Belgium and the Netherlands (paving bricks)	240	120	60
Holland	200	100	25
Switzerland (normal format)	250	120	60
Russia	250	120	60
	290	140	80
USA	205	100	60
USA (Roman format)	300	100	40

C 2.20

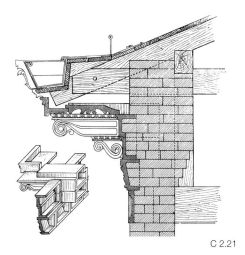

C 2.21

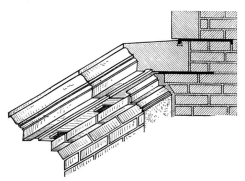

C 2.22

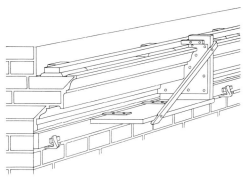

C 2.23

C 2.21 Cornice construction with cantilevering, specially moulded terracotta bricks
C 2.22 Dressed stone moulding anchored to masonry with iron cramps
C 2.23 Rendered moulding formed around masonry corbel with the help of a template
C 2.24 Balcony floor formed by cantilevering floor joists
C 2.25 Window sill and jamb in dressed stone
C 2.26 Rough estimate of the U-value of external masonry in comparison to the Energy Conservation Act

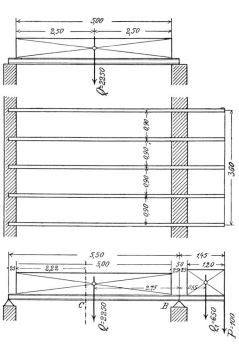

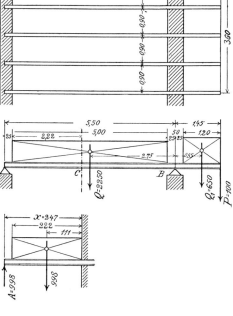

C 2.24

ornamentation and individual windows. The transition from Historicism dominated by manual skills to the technophiliac Modern Movement is already evident in the comparison between the Gothicising facades and stucco ceilings of large detached houses and the simple facades and glazed iron rooflights of factories.

External walls
The external walls of the storeys above ground level consist of clay brickwork in about 95 % of all European buildings dating from the period equivalent to Germany's founding years. The reason for this is the mixture of technical progress (good energy infrastructure for brickworks, good transport infrastructure for supplying building sites) and the traditional building regulations of the time, which permitted the construction of clay brick walls without the need for structural calculations. But in addition to solid external walls, cavity walls were also built (see "Buildings of the inter-war years", pp. 158–159).

Masonry
Masonry constructions include many regional variations owing to, for example, the deposits of stone available locally. The following masonry constructions were used:

- Coursed random rubble masonry: This consists of limestone, sandstone, granite or similar stone types and was frequently used at the bases of walls. The inside face is often in the form of clay brickwork in a masonry bond, which protects against saturation by driving rain and achieves a better level of thermal insulation.
- Rhenish alluvial stone: Pumice or tuffaceous stones that sometimes serve as a basis for man-made masonry units.
- Composite masonry: Walls consisting of outer leaves of clay bricks with a filling of rubble stone were common prior to 1870, also for upper storeys, but in buildings of the founding years were mostly limited to basement walls.
- Clay bricks: In their unsintered form these represent the commonest building material of that period.

In addition, the first manufacturers of calcium silicate and concrete bricks – which can be regarded as the predecessors of the masonry units usual these days – appeared during this period. However, the trade literature of the time treats them as "exotic species", sometimes of low quality, from which we can conclude that they were not used widely until later [4].

Masonry thickness and steps
Owing to different traditions and systems of measurement, clay bricks were manufactured in regional sizes, which led to different wall thicknesses. Attempts at standardisation, like that of German industry and the Chamber of Architects in 1870, led to the so-called Imperial format, which initially asserted itself in Prussia only, however (Fig. C 2.20).
As a rule, masonry thicknesses were in accordance with the building authority stipulations because that meant no structural calculations were necessary. For instance, the masonry walls of a multi-storey residential building in Berlin, built using imperial format bricks, began in the basement at 990 mm thick and decreased by half a brick (= 130 mm) for every storey, with the minimum thickness of the walls to an unoccupied attic storey being 250 mm (Fig. C 2.6). On the other hand, the Bavarian Building Regulations of 1890 specified a minimum thickness of 380 mm for the topmost storey and an increase of half a brick every second storey. Reducing the thickness of the masonry as we proceed up the building, no longer customary, represented an economic realisation of structural principles. The architects of the time were certainly aware of the consequences, e.g. poorer thermal and sound insulation. The changing wall thickness resulted in steps at the floor levels, which were dealt with in one of the following ways:

- Internal step: Each 130 mm step serves as a bearing for the timber joist floor and is located at the position of the underside of the joists.
- Internal and external step: In this detail the axis of the wall remains in the centre of the thickness throughout the height (a better solution structurally), which leads to a 65 mm step on each side. The internal step once

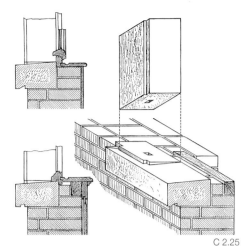

C 2.25

Thickness of masonry[1] [cm]	U-value [W/m²K]	Mandatory upgrade for new render (≥ 0.9 W/m²K)	Internal insulation (U-value min. 0.45 W/m²K), thickness [cm]	External insulation (U-value min. 0.35 W/m²K), thickness [cm]
38	1.16	yes	6	7
51	0.92	possibly	5	7
64	0.76	no	4	6
77	0.65	no	3	5
2 × 25 cm + 6 cm air cavity	0.75	no	4	6

[1] Solid masonry built using clay bricks with a density of approx. 1400 kg/m³, plastered internally, rendered externally

C 2.26

again serves as a bearing for the timber joist floor, the external step is concealed behind a continuous horizontal string course (Fig. C 2.18).

Again and again, such steps lead to misunderstandings during building surveys because they are unusual these days. Therefore, measuring the complete clear depth of the building and the thickness of the external walls in every storey is recommended.

Mortar
The mortar used for masonry was mainly lime mortar, less often cement mortar. The non-hydraulic lime slaked on the building site seems to be the most common. Non-hydraulic lime only cures when there is a supply of air and shrinks considerably while doing so. This led to the following problems during construction:

- The working space for the external walls to basements was backfilled prematurely, thus preventing the mortar from curing.
- In thick masonry walls the mortar in the middle took many years to cure completely, which led to very late settlement or permanently damp walls. Attempts were made to speed up the curing process by building cavity walls or heating the rooms with coke stoves.
- Pointing with cement mortar on the facade took place too early; lime mortar shrinks to a much greater extent than cement mortar and leads to spalling of the brick arrises.
- Plaster/render is applied too soon and cracks due to the ongoing settlement.

In addition, so-called economy lime was frequently used – a lime mortar with loam or earth impurities that cures poorly and has little compressive strength. Lime mortar was also a favourite for render and plaster. Pure cement mortar was used externally on basement walls and the bases of walls, and internally in kitchens and bathrooms. Gypsum and loam plaster were sometimes used internally.

Cantilevers
Historically decorated oriels, balconies and mouldings constitute further features used to break up the facades facing the streets. Canti-levers for balconies and oriels were built as follows:

- Masonry corbels (step-wise thickening of the external wall)
- Continuous steel beams at floor level between or instead of timber joists (Fig. C 2.24)
- Iron brackets (anchoring the upper bracket – in tension – close behind the inner face of the masonry)
- Steel beams built into the masonry (only possible with very thick masonry because the inner lever arm is shorter than the cantilever); to increase the compressive strength at the bearing points, stone bearings were often used (Fig. C 2.19).

Vaulted masonry or flat reinforced concrete slabs were useful balcony floors. Tuffaceous or lightweight sandstones were used for oriel and balcony walls in order to reduce the load on the cantilever.

Mouldings
These are horizontal, structuring features on the facade which depending on their position are called base mouldings, string courses (floors) or cornices (eaves). They are functional as well as decorative. For example, string courses conceal steps in the external wall and allow rain to drip off at every storey. Hood mouldings lend coupled windows flush with the facade some relief and also prevent rain infiltrating the upper joints. Most mouldings have been covered in sheet metal flashings over the years in order to protect them permanently.
The forms of construction are as diverse as the shapes themselves, although they are not always what they might appear at first glance. Wooden mouldings, e.g. at the eaves, are treated in such a way that they appear like dressed stone when viewed from the street; the same is true of rendered mouldings. The method used most frequently to build mouldings on upper floors was to apply render (shaped with the help of a template) to brick corbelling.
Mouldings on prestigious buildings plus hood and base mouldings on simpler buildings are made from dressed stones seated deep within the masonry and sometimes additionally secured with metal cramps. The joints between the dressed stones were often filled with cement mortar, lead or sulphur. Besides the handcrafted shapes, mouldings were also available in industrially prefabricated forms (Figs. C 2.21 – 2.23).

Damage and measures
Damage to external masonry is rather rare. Typical problems are:

- Efflorescence of salts like lime saltpetre, especially at the bases of walls (see "General refurbishment tasks", pp. 126–127).
- Loose or falling render (see "General refurbishment tasks", pp. 124–125).
- External joints crumbling away to a considerable depth: these must be carefully raked out, well wetted to ensure good adhesion and then pointed with a lime or lime-cement mortar having a similar elasticity; pure cement mortar is unsuitable because it drops out of the joint after just a few years.

The upgrading of external walls dating from the founding years involves mainly only thermal performance because the solid form of construction generally complies with fire protection and sound insulation requirements (the topmost storey is a special case). The walls of the lower storeys provide excellent thermal performance during the summer, but in winter only a moderate performance. According to the Energy Conservation Act (EnEV), the thermal insulation of all walls < 510 mm thick must be improved during refurbishment measures (Fig. C 2.26).
When choosing the refurbishment measure, we must distinguish between the front and rear facades of a building. The latter are always in the form of facing masonry or trowelled render purely for economic – not architectural – reasons. Here, external insulation can be attached without disturbing the architecture. The position of the windows must be considered, however, especially coupled windows flush with the outside face.
External insulation is, however, out of the question for prestigious street facades with mouldings and other ornamentation still in their original condition. Internal insulation is the only so-

C 2.27   Masonry lintel with dressed stone window surrounds
         a External elevation
         b Internal elevation
C 2.28   Masonry window lintels
         a Cambered arch
         b with relieving arch
C 2.29   Plan/external elevation of stone window surround
         A Individual stones fitted into masonry bond
         B Larger stone tied back at one point
C 2.30   Window lintel in the form of a cambered arch
         made from ornamental dressed stones
C 2.31   Window lintels in the form of composite steel-
         concrete beams, with integral roller shutter
         a Fixed glazing, roller shutter accessible from below
         b Vienna-type coupled window, roller shutter
         accessible from behind
C 2.32   Window frame fixed with holdfasts
C 2.33   Window frame fixed with ragbolts
C 2.34   Window mullion in the form of overlapping case-
         ments with jaw-type rebates

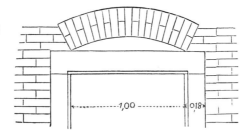

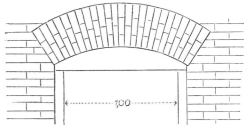

a   b   C 2.27

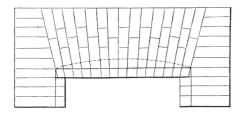

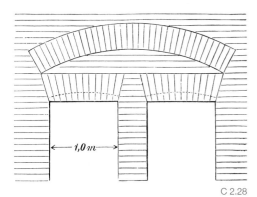

C 2.28

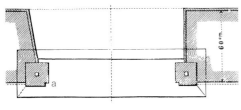

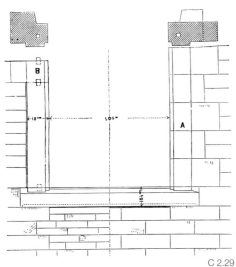

C 2.29

lution in such instances. Fortunately, in build-ings from this period the loadbearing walls are normally parallel to the facade and hence do not touch it at any point and so the problem of thermal bridges can be ignored (see "General refurbishment tasks", pp. 123–124).

Window openings

The windows facing the street are frequently framed by dressed stone mouldings. These function as a nib for the outer frame and at the same time form the window sill and hood moulding protecting the window from water running down the facade. The window sill is usually in one piece and includes a fall, although at the ends it has level stooling for the jambs. The latter are either dressed stones in one piece or several pieces fitted into the masonry bond, extending approx. 300–600 mm into the masonry. The jambs include a nib 80 mm wide for single windows and 120–180 mm wide for coupled windows, and 120–150 mm deep (Figs. C 2.25 and 2.29). The lintel is again in one piece and may be supplemented by a frieze or decorative gable. It carries no load from the masonry above, which is instead car-ried by masonry arches above the lintel (also cambered arches). Two different arches were often used, one equivalent to the depth of the nib, the other for the inner masonry (Figs. C 2.27 and 2.28). Alternatively, loadbearing cam-bered arches made from dressed stones span over the outer window openings and remain visible (Fig. C 2.30).

If there are horizontal window lintels on the in-side of the wall, one of the two following forms of construction is usually involved:

• A non-loadbearing timber beam built into the masonry below a loadbearing masonry arch.
• A steel beam replacing the loadbearing arch and also carrying the loads of the floor above and over wide openings carrying the lintel of dressed stone; this form of construction is frequently encountered in conjunction with roller shutters (Figs. C 2.31a and b).

Windows

The windows of residential buildings dating from the founding years are generally hand-made wooden windows, normally made from Scots pine, occasionally spruce or oak. They were primed and painted with oil-based paints in situ – apart from oak windows, which were steeped in linseed oil and then varnished. The outer frame is fixed to the approx. 70 mm wide masonry nib by means of ragbolts or so-called holdfasts which were driven into the bed joints and sometimes fixed to the outer frame with screws as well. The fixings are frequently con-cealed behind a batten that also hides the junction with the masonry, which is closed off with haired mortar, a mix of animal hair and limewash (Figs. C 2.32 and 2.33).

Large windows were divided into several lights, very frequently in the form of two side-hung casements overlapping in the middle (i.e. no permanent central mullion) and a top light above a fixed transom. The glazing to the lights, sometimes further divided by glazing bars, is held in place with putty. There are very many different types of windows and three will be treated here by way of example.

Roller shutters

The main purpose of roller shutters is to protect against intruders. They are therefore always fit-ted in front of display windows, but in residen-tial buildings frequently only on the ground floor. The housing for the rolled-up shutter is on the inside face and does not provide any insu-lating effect. Although it would seem obvious to replace this by a new housing on the outside, the fascia panel cast together with the other ele-ments often prevents this because it cannot be removed without carrying out some form of structural analysis. If the roller shutters are to be retained, the existing housing must be lined and the roller shutter exchanged for one with a smaller rolled-up diameter.

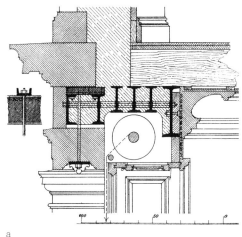

C 2.30   a

Single windows
The weatherproofing of the usually 40 mm wide frames to the opening lights (up to 60 mm for taller lights) is by means of jaw- or S-shaped rebates on the hinge side, a double rebate on all the other sides. Opening lights have battens fitted inside and outside on the hardware side, and a bottom rail with rainwater drip. The vertical joint between opening lights is very often in the form of a jaw-shaped rebate (Fig. C 2.34). As the windows are not completely watertight for the case of driving rain, the window board includes a channel which either drains to the outside or simply allows the water to collect and then evaporate.
The rebate in the dressed stone (Fig. C 2.29, "a") functions as a nib for an auxiliary window, a simple window fitted during the winter months only to improve the thermal insulation.

Graz-type coupled windows
The Graz-type coupled window is basically two single windows in which the opening lights of the outer window open outwards. The form of construction means they must be fitted flush with the facade and are therefore protected against infiltration of driving rain by hood mouldings or window sill-type constructions. In summer the glazing of the outer lights is replaced by louvres (or vice versa: wooden louvres replaced by an auxiliary window in the winter). The disadvantage of this simple and hence inexpensive form of construction is that cleaning the outside of the outer panes, especially the top light, is not for the faint-hearted! The advantage of such windows is the ample ventilation – without draughts – possible by opening the outer window and the top light of the inner window, a feature that no modern window achieves.

Vienna-type coupled windows
This type of window does not suffer from the disadvantage of the outward-opening outer lights. But this has its price: a more elaborate construction, but mainly the smaller clear opening size because the outer lights open inwards. The horizontal transom in particular is much higher. The linings to the reveals are "night shutters", i.e. folding shutters for ensuring privacy at night (Fig. C 2.36).

The Vienna-type coupled window also enabled louvre blinds or roller shutters to be fitted – quite normal on prestigious facades.

Damage and measures
Windows that have been regularly maintained are often still in good condition after 100 years. Rotten wooden parts are sometimes encountered, especially the bottom rails of outer frames. It is possible to replace these, but this is time-consuming and expensive because the whole window has to be removed to do this. When carrying out renovation work, it is important to remember that only oil-based paints may be used for repainting over the existing oil-based paints. However, such an elastic build-up of layers tends to "stick", which can be a nuisance in jaw-type rebates. The alternative is to repaint the window completely after removing all the old paint and primer – a very expensive business.
When renewing windows from the founding years there are, however, two problems: in terms of airtightness and thermal performance, coupled windows do not conform to modern requirements. If toleration of the building stock does not apply, the windows must be upgraded because the 100–150 mm wide layer of stationary air between the two parts of the coupled window does not quite achieve the U-value of 2.0 W/m²K required by German standards. Replacing the single glazing of the inner window with insulating glass would solve the problem, but the slender frames cannot support the extra weight permanently. Depending on the dimensions of the outer frame, it may be possible to replace the inner casement as a whole, but only in the form of a custom, handcrafted construction not covered by the building regulations for new buildings. The installation of completely new windows is probably better from the economic and warranty viewpoints. Such windows can be designed, for example, like old coupled windows. The frames must be increased in size in order to accommodate modern double glazing. Following refurbishment of the ecclesiastical building in Mariazell, the new frame members appear to be as slender as those of the historical windows and the ventilation options have also been retained

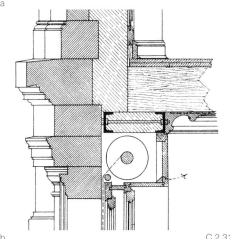

b   C 2.31

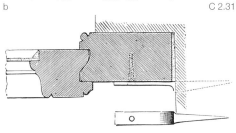

C 2.32

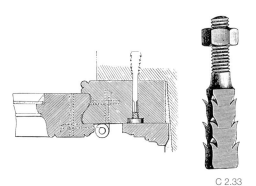

C 2.33

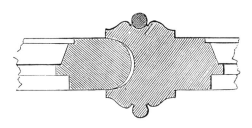

C 2.34

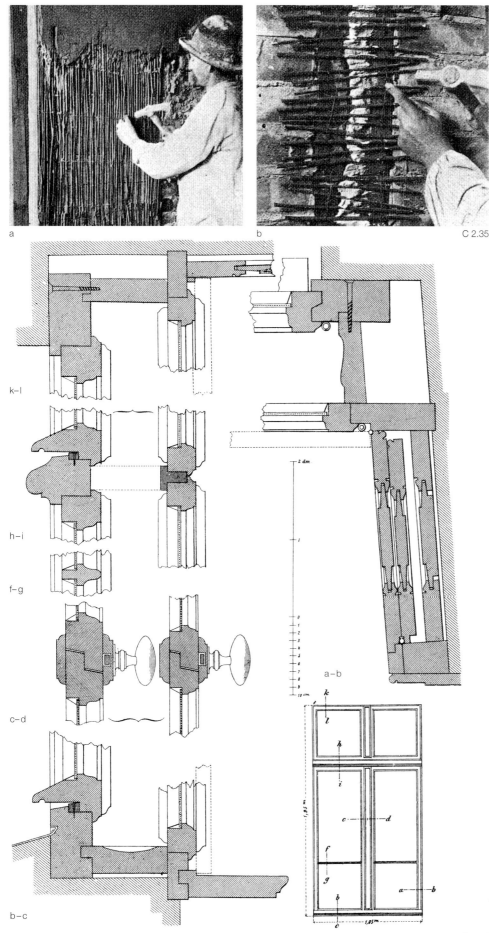

a   b   C 2.35

k–l

h–i

f–g

c–d

b–c

a–b

C 2.36

C 2.35   Reed mats as plaster background
       a   Complete surface
       b   Local reinforcement to prevent cracking
C 2.36   Historic coupled window with an auxiliary window
       inside (Vienna-type coupled window)
C 2.37   Frame construction consisting of cast iron
       columns, steel beams and concrete jack arches,
       warehouse, Berlin (D), c. 1900, R. Guthmann
       ([1] Floor, 4th storey, [2] Conc. jack arch, [3] Section a-b)
C 2.38   Internal view of a new coupled window, ecclesi-
       astical building, Mariazell (A), 1997, Feyferlik/
       Fritzer, with Friedrich Golds
       a   Horizontal section
       b   Left-hand outer opening light
       c   Right-hand outer opening light, push-out
       d   Vertical section

(Fig. C 2.38). In addition, the outer opening lights can now be cleaned from inside thanks to new window hardware.

It is probably better when modern airtightness requirements are not complied with in full (but the building owner must be involved in this decision!). Airtight windows that are opened only infrequently can disrupt the moisture balance of the building (absorption of driving rain by the facade, interstitial condensation in the masonry) to such an extent that irreversible damage is done, e.g. rotting of timber joist floors.

Internal walls and frame constructions
Loadbearing masonry internal walls differ from external walls only in terms of the minimum thicknesses required by the building authorities. The Bavarian Building Regulations of 1890 specified 250 mm for internal walls instead of 380 mm and an increase of 130 mm every second storey. The ensuing steps in the masonry can be arranged on one or both sides of the wall. Like with external walls, most mortar and plaster was based on a lime mix, a cement-based plaster being used only in wet rooms where there are no ceramic tiles.

For non-loadbearing walls, half-brick masonry (imperial format: 130 mm) was used as well as gypsum or pumice planks or timber frames with masonry infill panels. The timber members were also plastered over after nailing on an iron wire mesh embedded in gypsum (patented by the Royal Master Mason of Berlin, Karl Rabitz) or reed mats to form a plaster background (Fig. C 2.35).

For fixing joinery items such as door frames, linings, panelling, etc., timber grounds were often built into the masonry bond to which wooden items could be nailed or screwed later.

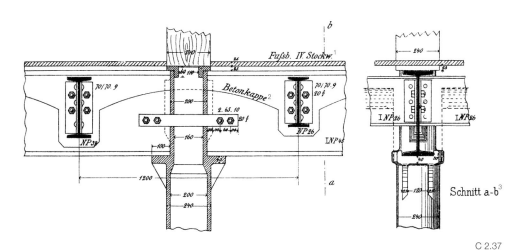

C 2.37

Iron frame constructions

The provision of large openings, e.g. display windows, or spacious, uninterrupted floor areas, as are necessary in industrial buildings or department stores, require part of the building structure to be in the form of a frame. This is where we see very well the transition from manual traditions to industrial production so characteristic of this period. Columns and pillars were indeed manufactured in factories, but to designs by architects, who tried to transfer old handcrafted ornamentation to the industrial process. Cast iron columns were predestined for such treatment but towards the end of the 19th century they became discredited because

they were regarded as unsafe in fire. So in many places fire-resistant cladding was specified or the cast iron columns were replaced by reinforced concrete or wrought iron. A forerunner of steel, wrought iron had a higher (and above all more inconsistent) carbon content than modern steels and so – in contrast to the very brittle cast iron – could accommodate bending stresses. Many frames are therefore hybrid constructions with cast iron columns and steel beams supplemented by timber beams or reinforced concrete for the suspended floors (Fig. C 2.37).

The industrially produced rolled sections were also riveted together to form compound columns

or beams. The sections in use were very similar to those of today, e.g. the very common I-beam in the NP format corresponds roughly to today's IPE section. The designations of the sections used are usually marked on the webs. To prevent corrosion, exposed steel components were usually given an undercoat of red lead and a final coat of oil-based paint. Beams built into masonry were not usually given any protective coating (Fig. C 2.40).

Damage and measures

No further problems have been added to those known at the time (fire protection and corrosion). Thanks to their thick walls (14–30 mm for a

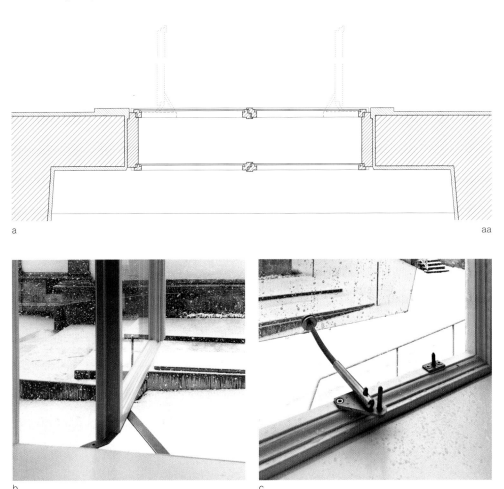

a

aa

b

c

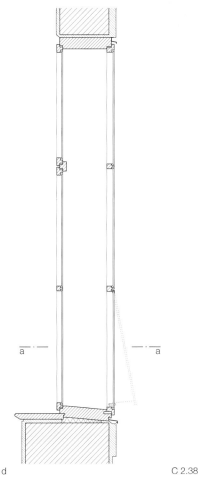

d

C 2.38

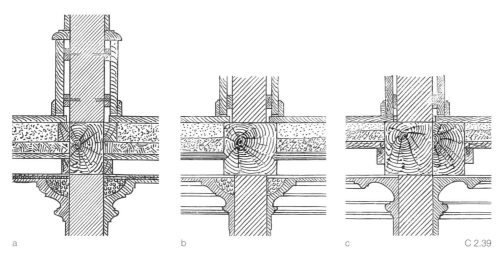

a   b   c   C 2.39

11–19. Deutsche Normalprofile*)

(vereinbart vom Verbande deutscher Architekten- und Ingenieur-Vereine, dem Vereine deutscher Ingenieure und dem technischen Vereine für Eisenhüttenwesen).

Tabelle 11. Normalprofile für I-Eisen.

Bis h = 250 mm ist:
$b = 0{,}4\,h + 10$ mm;
$d = 0{,}03\,h + 1{,}5$ mm

Für h > 250 mm ist:
$b = 0{,}3\,h + 35$ mm;
$d = 0{,}036\,h.$

$t = 1{,}5\,d.$ | $R = d.$ | $r = 0{,}6\,d.$

Bezeichnungen:
h Höhe in mm.
b Breite in mm.
d Stegdicke in mm.
t Flanschstärke in mm.
R und r Abrundungshalbmesser in mm.
F Querschnitt in qcm.
G Gewicht für den m in kg.
Neigung im Flansch 14 Proz.

1	2	3	4	5	6	7	8	9	10	11	12
Profil Nr.	Abmessungen in mm				Querschnitt F qcm	Gewicht f. d. m G kg	Momente bezogen auf die Achse X—X		Momente bezogen auf die Achse Y—Y		Profil Nr.
	h	b	d	t			W	J	w	i	
8	80	42	3,9	5,9	7,57	5,9	19,4	77,7	2,99	6,3	8
9	90	46	4,2	6,3	8,99	7,0	25,9	117	3,81	8,8	9
10	100	50	4,5	6,8	10,6	8,3	34,1	170	4,86	12,2	10
11	110	54	4,8	7,2	12,3	9,6	43,3	238	5,99	16,2	11
12	120	58	5,1	7,7	14,2	11,1	54,5	327	7,38	21,4	12
13	130	62	5,4	8,1	16,1	12,6	67,0	435	8,85	27,4	13
14	140	66	5,7	8,6	18,2	14,2	81,7	572	10,7	35,2	14
15	150	70	6,0	9,0	20,4	15,9	97,9	734	12,5	43,7	15
16	160	74	6,3	9,5	22,8	17,8	117	933	14,7	54,5	16
17	170	78	6,6	9,9	25,2	19,7	137	1 165	17,1	66,5	17
18	180	82	6,9	10,4	27,9	21,7	161	1 444	19,8	81,3	18
19	190	86	7,2	10,8	30,5	23,8	185	1 759	22,6	97,2	19
20	200	90	7,5	11,3	33,4	26,1	214	2 139	25,9	117	20
21	210	94	7,8	11,7	36,3	28,3	244	2 558	29,3	137	21
22	220	98	8,1	12,2	39,5	30,8	278	3 055	33,3	163	22
23	230	102	8,4	12,6	42,6	33,3	314	3 605	36,9	188	23
24	240	106	8,7	13,1	46,1	35,9	353	4 239	41,6	220	24
25	250	110	9,0	13,6	49,7	38,7	396	4 954	46,4	255	25
26	260	113	9,4	14,1	53,3	41,6	441	5 735	50,6	287	26
27	270	116	9,7	14,7	57,1	44,5	491	6 623	56,0	325	27
28	280	119	10,1	15,2	61,0	47,6	541	7 575	60,8	363	28
29	290	122	10,4	15,7	64,8	50,6	594	8 619	66,1	403	29
30	300	125	10,8	16,2	69,0	53,8	652	9 785	71,9	449	30
32	320	131	11,5	17,3	77,7	60,6	781	12 493	84,6	554	32
34	340	137	12,2	18,3	86,7	67,6	922	15 670	98,1	672	34
36	360	143	13,0	19,5	97,0	75,7	1088	19 576	114	817	36
38	380	149	13,7	20,5	107	83,4	1262	23 978	131	972	38
40	400	155	14,4	21,6	118	91,8	1459	29 173	150	1160	40
42½	425	163	15,3	23,0	132	103	1739	36 956	176	1433	42½
45	450	170	16,2	24,3	147	115	2040	45 888	203	1722	45
47½	475	178	17,1	25,6	163	127	2375	56 410	234	2084	47½
50	500	185	18,0	27,0	179	140	2750	68 736	266	2470	50
55	550	200	19,0	30,0	212	166	3602	99 054	349	3486	55

Tabelle 12. Normalprofile für ⌐-Eisen.

$b = 0{,}25\,h + 25$ mm.
Neigung der inneren Flanschflächen 8 Proz.
$R = t;\quad r = \dfrac{t}{2}.$

1	2	3	4	5	6	7	8	9	10	11	12	13	14
Profil Nr.	Abmessungen in mm				F qcm	G kg f. d. m	Momente bezogen auf die Achse X—X		Momente bezogen auf die Achse Y—Y		Zwei zusammengesetzte ⌐=⌐ Eisen. Kleinstes Trägheitsmoment bezogen auf die Schwerachse parallel zum Steg	Schwerpunktsabstand a cm	Profil Nr.
	h	b	d	t			W	J	w	i			
3	30	33	5	7	5,44	4,24	4,3	6,4	2,7	5,3	29,4	1,99	3
4	40	35	5	7	6,21	4,85	7,1	14,1	3,1	6,7	35,4	2,17	4
5	50	38	5	7	7,12	5,55	10,6	26,4	7,3	9,1	45,0	2,43	5
6½	65	42	5,5	7,5	9,03	7,05	17,7	57,5	5,1	14	64,6	2,78	6½
8	80	45	6	8	11,0	8,60	26,5	106	6,2	19	86,4	3,05	8
10	100	50	6	8,5	13,5	10,5	41,1	206	8,4	29	123	3,45	10
12	120	55	7	9	17,0	13,3	60,7	364	11,0	43	173	3,90	12
14	140	60	7	10	20,4	15,9	86,4	605	14,8	63	250	4,25	14
16	160	65	7,5	10,5	24,0	18,7	116	925	18,2	85	332	4,66	16
18	180	70	8	11	28,0	21,8	150	1354	22,4	114	434	5,08	18
20	200	75	8,5	11,5	32,2	25,1	191	1911	27,6	148	556	5,49	20
22	220	80	9	12,5	37,4	29,2	245	2690	33,7	197	736	5,86	22
24	240	85	9,5	13	42,3	33,0	300	3598	39,6	248	916	6,27	24
26	260	90	10	14	48,3	37,7	371	4823	47,7	317	1172	6,64	26
28	280	95	10	15	53,3	41,6	450	6276	57,3	399	1480	6,97	28
30	300	100	10	16	58,8	45,8	535	8026	67,8	495	1848	7,30	30

C 2.40

column 200 mm in diameter), cast iron columns are unlikely to rust right through, unless they are at the same time used as rainwater down-pipes. Replacing or supplementing sections to improve the load-carrying capacity is certainly unsatisfying architecturally because the quality of the materials and fabrication (no parallel flanges) of the old sections do not comply with modern standards. Welded connections were unusual at that time and even today are not feasible because of the different material compositions. The partial replacement of beams where the loadbearing structure is exposed makes it difficult to achieve a satisfactory architectural solution because new beams and connections stand out quite clearly from the historic structure.

Chimneys

Although the first water-filled central heating systems appeared on the market around 1870, most houses of the founding years were still heated with stoves. That meant that all habitable rooms required connections to the chimney, which in turn meant a multitude of flues. The preferred location for the chimney was the centre of the building so that the outlet was as close to the ridge as possible. Chimneys were therefore integrated into masonry internal and fire walls. The smallest cross-sections measure just ½ x ½ brick (imperial format: 140 x 140 mm) and the side walls and walls between the individual flues are also only half a brick thick. When they form part of a 380 mm thick masonry wall, such flues are easily overlooked these days because there is no evidence of them on the outside faces of the wall.

Damage and measures

Chimneys in fire walls between two buildings are a problem. Such constructions do not fulfil modern sound insulation requirements, especially when the connections to the rooms have only been wallpapered over. The flues must be filled with loose material in order to improve the sound insulation.

On the other hand, the now obsolete flues can be used as vertical shafts for all kinds of modern building services. However, even in this case, once the services have been installed, sound insulation measures will be required in the flues to prevent the vertical propagation of airborne sound.

Suspended floors

Up until 1870 masonry vaults or flat timber floors were the norm – techniques that had been used for thousands of years. It was not until technological progress was made in the late 19th century that fundamentally new forms of construction began to develop, e.g. steel beams in conjunction with vaults or reinforced concrete and the solid prefabricated and reinforced concrete floors. As the building boom of the founding years continued, so the new forms of construction became more and more widespread. One reason for this was the rising price of sawn timber, another was the attempt to minimise the known weaknesses of timber joist floors:

C 2.39 Various wall plate details beneath internal walls
    a with battens nailed to the sides for fixing the
      floorboards
    b wider than the wall
    c two-piece construction plus nailed battens
C 2.40 Historic I-sections and channels
C 2.41 Various details for metal anchors (ties)
    ([1] Retaining bar with wedge, [2] Retaining bar, [3] Fixed on top,
    [4] Anchor fixed to side of joist, [5] Continuous tie rod, [6] Decorative
    retaining bar)
C 2.42 Typical timber joist floor
    ([1] Section a-b, [2] Section c-d, [3] Wall, [4] Gable wall)

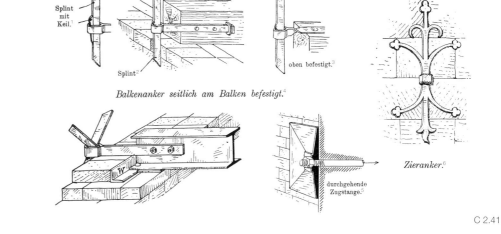

C 2.41

- Poor fire protection
- Poor sound insulation
- Low load-carrying capacity or the severe
deflections of long spans

Timber joist floors
Despite new forms of heavyweight construction, the timber joist floor remained the most
popular solution for upper floors. Almost without exception, the joists were positioned at a
right-angle to the external walls. As the joists
are also used for fixing floorboards and ceilings,
those near the walls were laid first and the other
joists spaced out equally between these. Fig.
C 2.42 shows the various joist types:

- Gable trimmers (g) are wall trimmers alongside the gable, often in the form of a tie beam
for the roof structure.
- Wall trimmers (h) are used for fixing the floorboards and are laid parallel on both sides of
a wall penetrating the floor.
- Header joists are the beams in a timber-frame
wall that may also be used for the internal
walls of the upper floors, but especially as a
sole plate for the tie beam of the roof structure.
- Wall plates (i) often have battens nailed to
both sides or are wider than the wall positioned centrally below in order to fix the floorboards (Fig. C 2.39).
- Continuous joists (k) sometimes form part of
the roof structure in the upper storey but are
regularly spaced in order to brace the external walls. The tension-resistant connection
between joists and wall is achieved by means
of a metal anchor (Fig. C 2.41).

Laid between these "special joists" were the
common joists whose spacing was determined
by economic considerations. For instance, in
the heavily forested regions of southern Germany,
the joists were laid at about 700 mm centres,
but on the coasts of northern Germany this
dimension might be as large as 1.20 m. Two
particular forms of construction show this relationship more distinctly:
British timber joist floor is constructed from joists
100 mm wide and up to 400 mm deep, positioned
at a spacing of approx. 400 mm. Herringbone

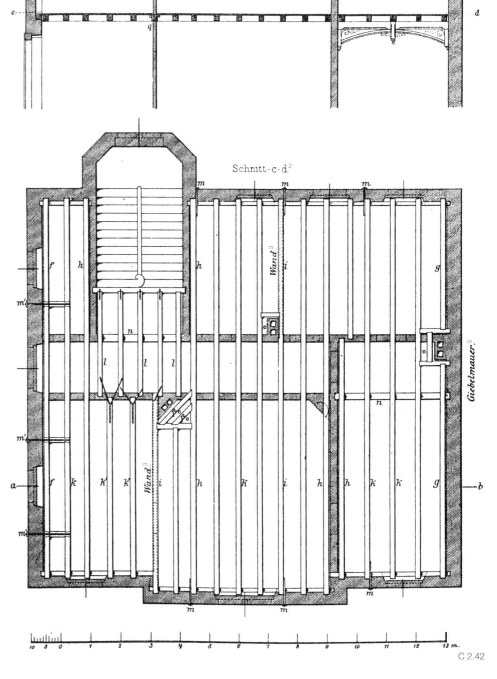

C 2.42

145

a

Joist spacing [cm]	Floorboard thickness [mm]
60	25
60–80	30
80–100	35
100–150	50
100–200	60

C 2.44

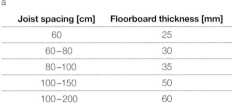

a

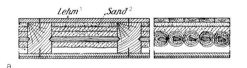

b

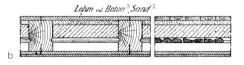

c

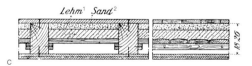

d

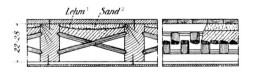

e

C 2.45

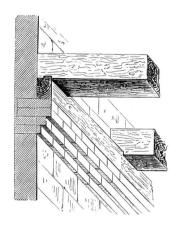

b

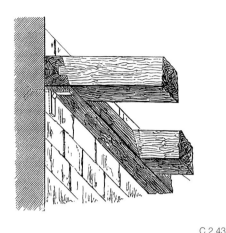

c

C 2.43

strutting and ties every 3 m prevent lateral deflection of the joists. Besides saving timber, such suspended floors also enable longer spans (Fig. C 2.47a).

The situation is totally different with the Austrian timber floor in which the joists form a solid timber component. Circular logs, squared on two sides only, were used mostly. Timber pegs hold the logs together at the joints. A layer of loam and sand was spread over the top of the floor and timber grounds (80 x 50 mm) for fixing the floorboards embedded in this flush with the top of the layer. The considerable self-weight of such suspended floors means that their sound insulation is better than that of standard timber joist floors.

Supports

In Germany timber joist floors are mostly supported on wall plates measuring between 90 x 120 and 120 x 120 mm. Cogged joints were used to form a structural connection between joists and wall plate. We distinguish between two different forms: where the floor rests on a step in the masonry, the wall plate is continuous over the full length, but without a step in the masonry, the wall plate may only be built into the masonry directly below each joist to prevent weakening the wall.

In France the problem of weakening the cross-section of the loadbearing wall in the region of the floor support was overcome by fitting the wall plate in front of the loadbearing wall. The wall plate was fixed by building the ends of the wall plate into the flanking walls at a right-angle to the external wall and driving iron anchors into the wall every 1.20 – 1.80 m (Fig. C 2.43).

Pugging, ceilings, floorboards

Planed floorboards were laid on the joists. As a rule, these are only butt-jointed and the gaps between the boards can vary considerably. The disadvantage of such floors is that dust from the pugging below escapes every time they are walked upon; wood chippings subsequently glued into the gaps prevent this problem. Tongue and groove or loose tongue floorboards, which ensure a dust-tight floor covering and also improve the load distribution across the entire floor area, were used less

often. Softwoods were used mainly, but for high-quality floors and on the ground floor (moisture from below) also oak. The thickness of the boards depends on the span of the floor (Fig. C 2.44).

Pugging between the joists was provided for a variety of purposes such as improving fire resistance, thermal insulation and sound insulation. The first priority when choosing pugging was, however, minimal self-weight. The most common form of construction is the installation of pugging boards 70–120 mm below the top edge of the joists: boards laid loose and with gaps on battens nailed to both sides of the joists. Grooves were frequently cut in the joists – as an alternative to battens – and the boards slotted into these. Sometimes the boards were overlapped instead of leaving gaps, but both types of boarding were covered with straw loam and then filled with sand up to the top of the joists. In practice building debris and other materials such as pumice and slag were often used for pugging (Fig. C 2.45).

Various pugging systems were developed in the search for prefabrication options. Flooring made from hollow clay bricks or gypsum and cement planks replaced both pugging boards and pugging material. The underside was mostly already profiled ready for the plaster of the ceiling. However, such systems were not used often because they required a modular type of construction with all floor bays equal. The trade literature of the time also shows composite forms of construction with timber joists and concrete infills, also infills of reinforced concrete (Fig. C 2.49c).

Ceilings were generally applied to a plaster background (reed mats, Rabitz' patented solution) (see also p. 142). High-quality interiors were finished with panelled wood ceilings. The simplest form was to use planed joists and to leave the pugging boards visible, which were then divided into panels by dummy joists. More elaborate treatments have pugging on pugging boards and a soffit of profiled boards, panels, battens or dummy joists handcrafted by a joiner.

C 2.43　Various joist support details at the external wall
　　　　a　on dressed stone bearing pads
　　　　b　on wall plate supported on brick corbel
　　　　c　French solution: ledger (lambourde) fixed to masonry with iron anchors
C 2.44　Minimum floorboard thicknesses depending on spacing of joists
C 2.45　Various solutions for the pugging to timber joist floors (left: transverse section; right: longitudinal section)
　　　　a　Struts wrapped in straw loam
　　　　　　([1] Loam, [2] Sand)
　　　　b　Pugging on struts inserted into slots
　　　　　　([2] Sand, [3] Loam or concrete)
　　　　c　Pugging boards laid on nailed battens
　　　　　　([1] Loam, [2] Sand)

d　Herringbone strutting as lateral restraint for joists, only necessary for spans > 5 m
　　([1] Loam, [2] Sand)
e　Overlapping boards with decorated boarding fitted underneath
　　([4] Sand or loam)
C 2.46　Dry rot infestation
C 2.47　Various European solutions for timber joist floors
　　　　a　British timber joist floor, transverse and longitudinal sections
　　　　b　Edwin May system (Great Britain): Pugging on sheet metal
　　　　c　Laporte system (France): battens nailed to sides of joists, hollow clay blocks
　　　　d　Ceiling on self-supporting ceiling joists to improve sound insulation or as background for high-quality stucco ceilings

Damage and measures

Timber joist floors can suffer from very many different types of damage. Their loadbearing aspects should be checked, also sound insulation and fire protection aspects, which often do not comply with modern standards. Furthermore, they should also be checked for infestation by insects or fungi. The very common problem of rotten joist ends is dealt with in detail in the chapter "General refurbishment tasks" (see p. 129).

Infestation by insects and fungi

New chemical methods for protecting timber against insects and fungi were already available around 1830. Prior to that, timber components could only be treated with tar; but during the founding years pore-sealing, bactericidal paints appeared, which contained substances like sodium fluoride, dinitrophenols, zinc silicofluoride or magnesium silicofluoride. Steeping and pressure-impregnation treatments were initially used on external components only, e.g. railway sleepers, timber masts or pit props. Impregnation was carried out mainly with tar and aqueous fluoride solutions. Most methods were toxic or least unhealthy, but we can assume that chemical wood preservatives were hardly ever used in interiors for reasons of cost. This also explains the many cases of wood-destroying beetle larvae, e.g. house longhorn beetle, that live exclusively in dead wood (see also "Building materials in refurbishment projects", pp. 86–88). Infestation by larvae can be recognised by the dust that spills out of the boreholes, or in the case of the house longhorn beetle in particular, by the typical scraping noises. The damage can be so serious that the only solution is to replace the components. Cool, damp components (residual moisture content > 10 %) are especially at risk. If the damage is detected early, cutting away the infested layers and treating with chemical wood preservatives (injection) can help; this method is, however, not covered by a standard. DIN 68800-4 prescribes gassing entire rooms with sulphuryl fluoride or, alternatively, heating up the timber components to 60–120 °C with hot air. Both methods certainly kill the larvae reliably, but re-infestation cannot be ruled out.

Much more serious is infestation by dry rot (*Serpula lacrymans*, Fig. C 2.46). This grows on dead wood and requires a damp (min. 20 %), cool (< 26 °C) climate for growth and its wood-destroying metabolism. It belongs to the group of fungi that cause brown rot decay and leaves behind white cotton wool-like mycelia and brownish fruit bodies. Dry rot infestation is therefore easy to see on the surface of the wood; however, the damage often occurs in voids and pugging and so is not always visible. Pugging was often contaminated with earth and it is precisely such conditions that can cause infestation when saturation leads to a favourable climate (21 °C and 30–40 % wood moisture content).

The fungus breaks down the cellulose in the wood and hence its loadbearing structure; infested timber components may appear intact on the surface but still break under gentle pressure. Dry rot is able to destroy softwood joists totally within a year. What is conspicuous about the infestation is the mouldy smell emanating from the fungus, which can also be detected by the reddish-brown spores that form a dust-like layer in unused rooms. Over time, the mycelia also penetrate masonry and concrete, which leads to the need for extensive refurbishment work because dry rot can survive long dry periods (up to 10 years) and so re-infestation cannot be ruled out.

The severe destructive force of this fungus means that radical refurbishment methods are necessary: demolition instead of treatment. To do that, all infested timber components are either cut back generously to sound timber or removed completely and disposed of properly. The same applies to masonry, loose fill and plaster/render: where the material can be removed easily, this is the first choice. After complete elimination of the fungus, the remaining timber components or masonry are treated with a suitable preservative. The new components required for rebuilding in the risk zone may no longer be of timber, and it is especially important that the actual cause of the damage – saturation – is located and permanently rectified.

C 2.46

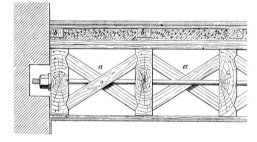

a

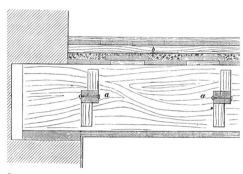

b

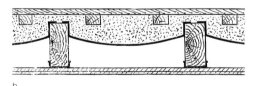

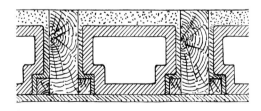

c

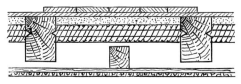

d　　　　　　　　　　　　C 2.47

Floor construction		Weighted impact sound level $L_{n, W (B)}$ [dB]	Airborne sound insulation[1] [dB]
Type A (heavyweight pugging)	• Subfloor: 18 mm gypsum fibreboard, 10 mm insulating board • 24 mm particleboard • 120 x 180 mm timber joists @ 500 mm centres • 24 mm particleboard as pugging boards, with 100 kg/m² sand ballast • 60 x 27 mm resilient channels, 2 No. 12.5 mm plasterboard	Floor finishes without with 57 49	> 60
Type B (lightweight pugging)	• Subfloor: 18 mm gypsum fibreboard, 10 mm insulating board • 24 mm particleboard • 120 x 180 mm timber joists @ 500 mm centres • 160 mm glass wool, approx. 3 kg/m², fitted tightly between joists • 60 x 27 mm resilient channels, 2 No. 12.5 mm plasterboard	Floor finishes without with 55 49	> 60
Type A (heavyweight pugging)	• Subfloor: 18 mm gypsum fibreboard, 10 mm insulating board • 24 mm particleboard • 120 x 180 mm timber joists @ 500 mm centres • 24 mm particleboard as pugging boards, with 100 kg/m² sand ballast • 75 mm self-supporting section, 2 No. 12.5 mm plasterboard	Floor finishes without with 45 38	> 65
Type B (lightweight pugging)	• Subfloor: 18 mm gypsum fibreboard, 10 mm insulating board • 24 mm particleboard • 120 x 180 mm timber joists @ 500 mm centres • 160 mm glass wool, approx. 3 kg/m² fitted tightly between joists • 75 mm self-supporting section, 2 No. 12.5 mm plasterboard	Floor finishes without with 51 41	> 65

[1] The airborne sound reduction indexes are only approximate because the test setup for constructions with airborne sound indexes > 60 dB is not approved.
• The airborne sound insulation of existing floors is very poor: Rw = 46 dB (type A) and 43 dB (type B)
• An improvement of approx. 5 dB can be achieved by using a very simple subfloor (e.g. 18 mm gypsum fibreboard + 10 mm insulating board).

C 2.48

	Load per unit volume [kN/m³]	Layer thickness [cm]	Load per unit area [kN/m²]
Self-weight, floorboards	5	2.4	0.12
Self-weight, pugging	16	12	1.92
Self-weight, ceiling	16.66	3	0.50
(Lime plaster on Rabitz background)			2.54
Imposed load			2.00
			4.54 kN/m²

Assuming normal dimensions (180 x 240 mm solid timber joists @ 900 mm centres), the load per unit area of 4.54 kN/m² produces a line load on each joist of 4.35 kN/m. If we assume a span of 4.75 m for a joist spanning in one direction, the following situation ensues: the bending stress is equal to 99 % of the permissible bending stress of 0.7 kN/cm², the deflection at mid-span is 13.7 mm and therefore below the maximum permissible value of L/300 = 15.8 mm. But the situation is different if we assume a span of 5.50 m: although the deflection is exactly L/300 = 18.3 mm and thus permissible, the bending stress is 0.95 kN/cm² and therefore exceeds the permissible stress by 36 %.

C 2.49

C 2.48   Sound insulation values of a timber joist floor with two different ceilings
C 2.49   Sample calculation for a timber joist floor
C 2.50   Imposed loads in the founding years compared to imposed loads today according to DIN 1055-3:2006-03
C 2.51   Various unreinforced suspended floors, after 1900
   a   Rhenish moulded bricks floor, max. steel beam spacing 1.25 – 2.00 m, total load 5.0 –12.5 kN/m²
     ([1]Slag, [2]Concrete, [3]Floorboards on timber grounds, [4]up to 2000)
   b   "Secura" floor, max. steel beam spacing 1.34 – 3.19 m, block depth 170 – 220 mm, total load 5.2 – 13.3 kN/m²
     ([5]Slag-aggregate concrete, [6]Keystones, [7]Cement screed, [8]up to 3190)
   c   "Förster" floor, max. steel beam spacing 1.00 –1.80 m, block depth 100 – 130 mm, total load 5.0 – 12.5 kN/m²
     ([9]Span up to 1500, [10]Slag, coke ashes)
   d   "Kleinesche" floor
     ([2]Concrete, [11]Starter brick, [3]Fixed on top, [12]Wood-block flooring on wooden subfloor)

Structural aspects
A re-analysis based on modern codes of practice reveals that the cross-sections selected are in most cases undersized. This was not due to lack of knowledge, but rather primarily because of the lower imposed loads assumed at that time for a similar permissible bending stress (0.6 kN/m², similar to today's grade III for solid timber, Fig. C 2.50).
In addition, joists were merely analysed for their loadbearing capacity; checking their serviceability, especially limiting their deflection, was not carried out. The use of sawn timber with wane, common in those days, can be ignored because that is still permissible for grade III solid timber even today. Fig. C 2.49 shows a sample calculation for a suspended floor in housing with loam-sand pugging and span of 4.75 or 5.50 m.

Sound insulation
The main problem with the timber joist floor and hence a key issue in refurbishment is the poor sound insulation, especially in the low-frequency range. Nailed floorboards offer no impact sound insulation whatsoever and the minimal weight desirable for structural reasons reduces the airborne sound insulation as well. Typical self-weights for pugging materials (e.g. loam-sand mix) lie between 150 and 200 kg/m² (1600 kg/m³). This is only a little more than one-third of that of a modern reinforced concrete slab (180 mm = 450 kg/m²) – to which the loads of the subfloor and floor finishes can be added. According to DIN 4109, such a weight per unit area can achieve a sound reduction index of only max. 45 dB – well below the minimum requirement of 52 dB.
Increasing the weight per unit area in order to improve the sound insulation is impossible because the loadbearing capacity of the floor would be exceeded. Added to this is the fact that laying a floating screed on existing floorboards in order to improve the impact sound

insulation would add new, additional loads. The problem is usually solved by reducing the weight per unit area and at the same time decoupling the layers of the floor construction, i.e. upgrading the sound insulation by using a multilayer construction. To do this, the loam-sand pugging and the pugging boards must be removed. This is usually carried out from below because the sound insulation and fire protection requirements mean that the existing soffit cannot be retained anyway, and leaving the floorboards in place simplifies the work.

The new floor should be built according to the DIN 4109 specimen timber floor construction: U-shaped, soft insulating blankets are laid in the floor to avoid flanking transmissions; the soffit is formed by a suspended ceiling (resilient hangers) in dry construction, which also satisfies the fire resistance requirements (Fig. C 2.48). The theoretical sound reduction index of the upgraded construction is 60 dB, with an impact sound insulation reduction index of approx. 20 dB ($L_{n,W}$ approx. 40 dB). As the higher requirements leave very little leeway, the workmanship, especially all junctions, must be supervised very carefully in order to minimise flanking transmissions. In the case of court proceedings, it is not the theoretical value of the suspended floor that counts, but rather the value measured in situ.

Fire protection

A new ceiling can also satisfy current fire protection requirements. Fire-resistant boards just 30 mm thick fixed directly to the joists or metal framing can meet F 90-B requirements on the underside. Two layers of 12.5 mm thick plasterboard, on the other hand, achieves only F 60. Generally speaking, boarding supported by metal framing – assuming adequate height is available for such a solution – is to be preferred in order to achieve a consistent, flat ceiling at reasonable cost. Such suspended ceilings are only approx. 100 mm deep, even allowing for the normal tolerances of existing suspended floors.

Improved fire protection on the top side is also achieved with gypsum-based materials. Prefabricated subfloors or in situ screeds are suitable, but a min. 30 mm thick, lightweight loose fill levelling course is advisable in both instances. A subfloor thickness of 40 mm is adequate for class F 90, although with impact sound insulation and floor covering a total depth of $\geq$ 100 mm should be allowed for. It should be noted that despite this upgrading, an exemption should be applied for in the approval procedure because a timber joist floor can never achieve the F 90-AB requirement (fire resistant with non-combustible loadbearing structure).

Usage	Imposed load, founding years [kN/m²]	Imposed load today [kN/m²]
Housing	1.5	2.0
Schools	2.0	3.0
Places of assembly	3.5–4.0	5.0
Storage	4.0–10.0	> 6.0

C 2.50

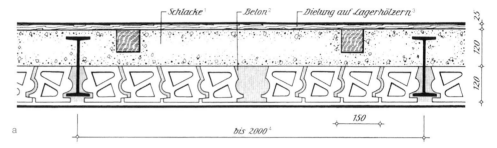

a

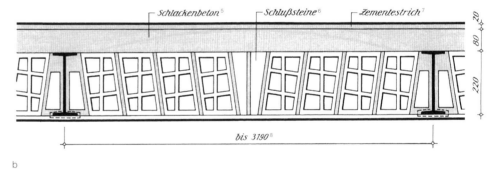

b

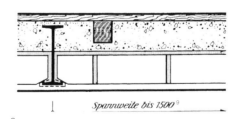

c

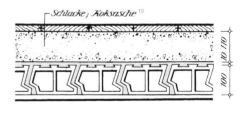

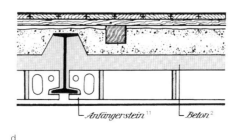

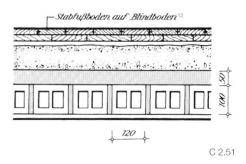

d

C 2.51

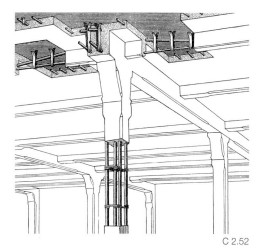

C 2.52

C 2.53

C 2.52 Reinforced concrete construction after François Hennebique, patented in 1886, which became widely known through the World Exposition of 1900 in Paris
C 2.53 Building a staircase of cantilevering dressed stone steps
C 2.54 Various landing details for cantilevering dressed stone stairs
  a Masonry jack arch with sand filling and terrazzo finish
  b Timber joist landing with floorboards
C 2.55 Typical roof structure showing timber components
  ([1] Ridge purlin, [2] Eaves purlin, [3] Post, [4] Intermediate purlin, [5] Collar tie, [6] Eaves, [7] Hip, [8] Hip rafter, [9] Roof truss, [10] Apex, [11] Valley rafter, [12] Common rafter, [13] Gable, [14] Ridge)

Sound insulation and fire protection of stucco ceilings
Stucco ceilings that are to be preserved must be removed prior to carrying out the aforementioned upgrading work. Opening up the floor locally from above reveals whether the ceiling is suspended from the timber joists or – usual with elaborate ceilings – carried on separate ceiling joists, which makes it easy to dismantle the ceiling. To do this, the ceiling is cut into transportable segments and stored safely. The new ceiling should be constructed in a similar way so that the original stucco can be re-attached to it directly (Fig. C 2.47d).

Solid suspended floor slabs
As solid suspended floor slabs were still at the development stage during the founding years, it is hardly surprising that the trade literature of the time describes more than 100 different types. Most of these are further developments of historical forms of construction. Specially shaped, patented bricks designed specifically for suspended floors form, for example, cambered arches between the primary loadbearing steel sections. In addition, there are infill panels in which interlocking bricks carry the bending forces, and unreinforced, flat, concrete infill panels. What all the systems try to do is shorten the construction time. This is achieved by using prefabricated infill panels and flat soffits that can then be plastered without the need for a separate plaster background (Fig. C 2.51). However, these systems were not widely used in housing. Used only rarely in Germany during this period, but important for the history of building are the two systems for reinforced concrete slabs patented by Joseph Monier and François Hennebique in 1878 and 1888, which are based on placing the steel reinforcement for the concrete slabs in the tension zone (Fig. C 2.52). According to the *Allgemeine Baukonstruktionslehre* (general textbook on building construction), the principle was especially popular in France, Belgium and England around 1900 [5]. We can assume that true reinforced concrete construction was first used in highway structures, factories and warehouses.
Suspended floors in the form of true vaults – in contrast to "decorative" vaults (e.g. using a

Rabitz background) – were frequently constructed in prestigious structures such as court buildings, schools, universities, etc., but only over the main stairs, corridors and auditoriums, not everywhere.

Screeds and floor coverings
The screeds of the time – in contrast to those of today – comprised a sand-binder mix, the surface of which was used as the wearing course without any further treatment. They were used wherever timber floors appeared to be unsuitable because of the presence of water or heavy loads. In addition, screeds were often used for fire protection on the topmost floor. The screeds and floor coverings common at that time were:

• Loam screed: used in rural buildings, 150–300 mm thick, sometimes with just an ox blood coating.
• Gypsum screed: only for use in dry rooms, 40 mm thick on a 20 mm thick layer of sand; originally white-reddish, the gypsum was sometimes also pigmented, and with the surface steeped in linseed oil it could be used as a wearing course.
• Lime screed: made from non-hydraulic lime plus fine gravel and cow's blood; during curing a lime-sand mix was worked into the surface, then ground and polished if required.
• Cement screed: a 20 – 30 mm thick sand-cement mix laid on clay paving bricks or concrete (laid while the concrete wall was still wet); floated surfaces were treated with water glass to prevent dusting.
• Asphalt: a layer of natural asphalt laid hot on concrete 120 mm thick.
• Terrazzo: a 10 mm layer of cement plus marble chippings laid over a 20–30 mm thick cement-sand levelling layer while still wet. Concrete 120–150 mm thick or clay paving bricks served as a substrate. The terrazzo was rolled in moist and then ground, polished and rubbed with linseed oil once hard. In many cases the Portland cement used was pigmented in order to create a contrast with the marble chippings. Terrazzo was one of the commonest floor coverings for stairs, halls, corridors and landings, representing an inexpensive imitation of the ancient stone mosaics.

This floor covering was used widely well into the 20th century and only disappeared as the labour costs for terrazzo work became disproportionately expensive. Cracks and holes in such floor coverings can be repaired using a technique similar to the original method of laying, provided skilled workers can be found who can still carry out this work.

• Tiles: laid in a 20–30 mm thick bed of lime mortar on a concrete substrate 100–120 mm thick. Besides terrazzo tiles there are also acid-resistant tiles made from cement and glass. However, high-quality tiles are made from clay (stoneware).
• Floorboards: these also form the floor itself and have already been described on p. 146. The surface was treated with linseed oil and given an additional coat of oil-based paint if required.
• High-quality wood-block flooring: these were laid on a subfloor – rough-sawn softwood floorboards 24 mm thick nailed with approx. 5 mm joints to the joists underneath. Wood-block flooring consisted of prefabricated glued panels measuring about 750 x 750 mm joined together with loose tongue or rebated joints. Perimeter and infill panels often employed different species of wood. The wood-block panels were then either screwed or nailed, occasionally glued, to the subfloor.

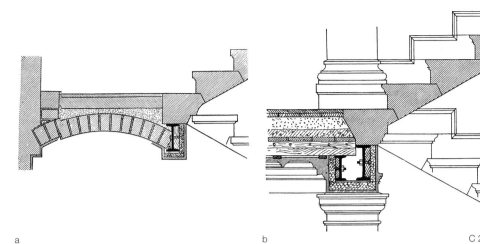

a   b   C 2.54

Stairs

Whereas prior to the founding years wooden stairs were usual, as early as 1853 the Berlin Building Regulations were prescribing "incombustible" stairs, i.e. iron and stone stairs, later reinforced concrete as well. Besides the facades facing the street, the main staircases provided another chance to create an imposing display: wide flights with a shallow pitch, large stairwells, ornamented soffits and landings, richly decorated balustrades and windows with coloured glass were among the usual devices.

One arrangement used very frequently was the cantilevering dressed stone staircase: the individual steps were built into the masonry wall to such a depth that they could cantilever for the full width of the stair flight. The individual steps were not joined together but simply laid on top of each other. Rebates with smooth mating faces enable the loads to be transferred to the adjacent steps. The *Allgemeine Baukonstruktionslehre* describes tests to failure on a 1.41 m wide cantilevering sandstone step with a bearing only 120 mm deep which failed at 1200 kg – corresponding to a uniformly distributed load of 5 kN/m^2 [6] (Fig. C 2.53).

Granite or Jurassic marble was used as well as sandstone. The steps have a trapezoidal cross-section and are given a smooth, sloping soffit, sometimes also tapering towards the stairwell in order to save weight but also to achieve an elegant stringer form. The bearing on the masonry, usually 250 mm deep, was, however, rectangular in cross-section to make it easier to build in. The front edges of landings are carried on steel beams plastered for fire protection reasons (Fig. C 2.54).

Apart from being used for the prefabricated, interlocking steps of spiral stairs, cast iron was favoured for many balustrades. The fixings for the balustrades, however, were mainly steel sections or solid bars cast into the dressed stone. Little damage is found in such solid staircases with their protected steel components. The load-carrying capacities of the rather fragile-looking stair flights of dressed stone cannot be verified even with modern methods of calculation but are adequate in practice.

Roof spaces

We can see from the changing construction laws that it was during the founding years that the roof space first started to change from a utility to a living area. For example, the Berlin Building Regulations of 1853 only mention fire in connection with the roof covering, but the regulations of 1897 also speak of the reliability and properties of habitable rooms under the roof. The reason for this was once again the enormous pressure on the housing market and the economic utilisation of enclosed space. Their reputation as cheap homes for students or "destitute" artists was derived from their quality, Gustav Schönermark remarking around 1900 that "living in rooms beneath clay tile roofs cannot be healthy" [7].

For centuries, roofs had been timber-frame structures erected by carpenters. The constructions of the time were not so very different to those used today. The main differences are the connections – interlocking, handcrafted wood joints at that time – and the dimensions of the loadbearing members. The trade literature of the time contains articles by proponents of structural calculations for such roofs – a clear sign that roof structures were generally still built according to empirical rules, i.e. as economically as possible.

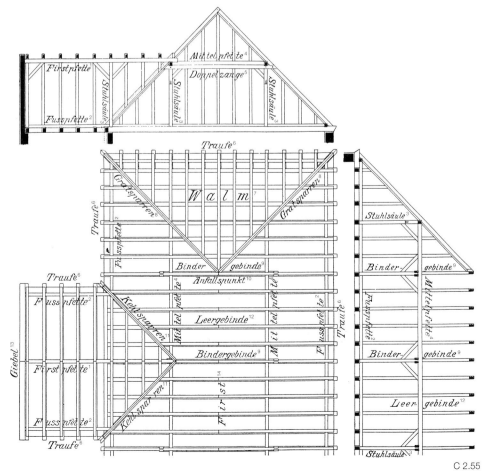

C 2.55

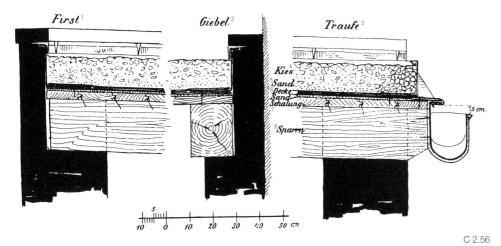

C 2.56

C 2.56 Flat roof construction for a "wood-cement" roof
        with gravel/sand ballast and sheet zinc flashings
        bonded into the waterproofing
        ([1]Ridge, [2]Gable, [3]Eaves, [4]Gravel, [5]Sand, [6]Waterproofing,
        [7]Boarding, [8]Rafter)
C 2.57 Interior view of the roof structure to a residential
        building dating from 1842
C 2.58 Roof space conversion, Vienna (A), 2003,
        Arkan Zeytinoglu

The roof coverings were also similar to those of today. Besides bullnose tiles, interlocking clay tiles had been available since the mid-19th century, also waterproofing materials for flat roofs. Valleys and junctions with masonry were waterproofed with sheet zinc or lead. Only silicone had not yet appeared on the market; instead, haired mortar was used.

Roof structure and floor to roof space
In contrast to all the other floors, the last set of joists was built together with the roof structure by carpenters. This was done for practical reasons, but also because the joists form a rigid system together with the roof trusses, i.e. are interconnected structurally. The trusses were positioned every approx. 4 m; the rafters in between are called common rafters and are irrelevant for the roof structure. The rafters are much further apart than the trusses of modern roof structures: 800–1200 mm. As in the suspended floors, timber members with wane were used; usual cross-sections are 100 x 120 to 120 x 160 mm. Owing to the wider spacing of the rafters, the tiling battens are slightly larger than those common today: 40 x 60 or 50 x 80 mm (Fig. C 2.55).
The ends of the rafters were fitted with cocking pieces because of the thick external walls and also to bridge over the cornice. The ends of the rafters could not be supported on the cornice construction because this would have induced stresses as the masonry settled. Where the eaves is at a higher level than the joists to the topmost floor, the dwarf wall is often in the form of a timber frame. Although the timber frame forms the true loadbearing construction, it is often not visible from outside, also because some building regulations prescribed a masonry facing as well as brick infill panels. The building authorities also required the floor to the roof space to be made from a "fire-resistant" material such as clay paving bricks or a screed material.

Flat roofs

The "tarred felt roof" is a flat roof with a minimal pitch of 1:15, i.e. approx. 7 %. The sheets of tarred felt used were nailed to a layer of boards but not bonded together and are therefore not completely watertight.

The so-called wood-cement roof is waterproof, but the designation "wood-cement" is completely misleading because this is a flat roof waterproofing material based on tar and not a mixture of wood and cement! This form of construction permitted a pitch of 4 %; this is therefore a true flat roof, e.g. laid on boards supported by timber joists. The binder is made up of sulphur, pitch (= viscous tar) and tar with which four layers of felt were bonded together over their full area. The waterproofing "floats" on a layer of sand and is protected from the elements by a layer of gravel. Zinc flashings were fully bonded between the third and fourth layers where required (Fig. C 2.56).

Typical additions and conversions

Besides the aforementioned refurbishment work, there are a few typical building measures that are carried out on the buildings of the founding years, the specific problems of which are investigated below.

Addition of balconies

As many of today's apartments in buildings dating from the founding years were originally planned as accommodation for the masses, balconies – these days regarded as normal for a decent standard of living and an almost indispensable marketing argument – were seen as unnecessary. Two problems must be tackled when considering balconies: planning rules and stability. A balcony cantilevering in the direction of span of a timber joist floor is easy to arrange. After opening up the floor construction locally, steel beams can be installed adjacent to the existing timber joists or certain joists simply replaced by steel beams. These must be secured against uplift at an internal wall (or the other external wall), which is usually guaranteed by the existing vertical load. New bearings in the form of concrete padstones or transverse steel sections are often required to spread the point loads from the beams. It should be remembered that the beams create thermal bridges that must be specially insulated internally.
There are hardly any other alternative solutions for a cantilevering balcony. Brackets anchored

in the masonry, for example, are not possible because there are no fixing systems approved for tension in masonry. Only in very thick masonry with a high vertical load might be possible to anchor a balcony on the rear side of the wall. The simplest way of adding balconies is to erect new columns outside the building, but this does change the existing architecture considerably. It is vital to found these new columns on undisturbed ground and not simply on the former working space for the basement, which will almost certainly lead to damage caused by differential settlement. In order to avoid having to erect new columns for the inner side of the balcony as well, new supports must be fixed to the existing masonry (in chiselled pockets or drilled) because there are no anchor systems approved for such uses.
However, before the structural and constructional problems are tackled, the planning rules for the building plot must be examined. As the density of urban building plots with buildings from the founding years is usually very high, adding balconies often infringes the rules regarding the necessary clearances to neighbouring buildings, a situation that is protected by the notion of toleration of the building stock provided no changes to the building are carried out, e.g. the addition of balconies. In the worst case toleration of the building stock then no longer applies; but in any case the new balconies are not subject to any exemptions and must comply with today's clearances specified for modern buildings. For an exemption to be granted, the neighbours affected must give their permission, and entries in the land register may be necessary, a situation that must be explained to the building owner as early as possible.

C 2.57

Roof space conversions

Anyone who has ever entered an empty roof space to a residential building dating from the founding years cannot fail to have been impressed by the skilled construction and the huge volume – and depending on the location, possibly the view, too. In the initial discussions with the building owner, however, it should be pointed out that the cost of converting the roof space is higher than that of a new construction with the same floor area and, in addition, much of the impressive construction will "disappear" (Fig. C 2.57).

The following problems must be considered during the preliminary planning and cost estimates:

- The existing rafters will not be deep enough for the thermal insulation required these days. Moreover, the permissible deflection will be exceeded by the new loads (insulation plus soffit).

- Deepening the rafters on the outside is critical from the architectural viewpoint because of the cornice; significant deepening of the construction on the outside leads to unsatisfactory constraints at the eaves.
- The above two points make it clear that the rafters must be deepened inwards, e.g. by nailing new rafters to the sides of the existing ones. However, this shifts the intersection of the soffit with the purlin and the knee braces such that the junction is technically (vapour barrier) and architecturally unsatisfactory.
- Intermediate and ridge purlins are undersized for the new loads. They can be strengthened by fixing steel channels to the sides.
- The joists to the topmost floor are not usually designed for normal residential loads. Strengthening them by attaching further timber joists on the sides is very expensive because large areas of the floor construction (from above or below) have to be removed.
- Changing the use from an attic to housing or offices means that the floor loses the protection offered by toleration of the building stock. Fire protection as well as sound and thermal insulation must therefore comply with today's requirements, i.e. in the worst case class F 90-AB, which will mean a complete new floor (reinforced concrete, composite steel-concrete). Even the F 60-B exemption rule cannot be achieved by existing plaster. The entire ceiling of the storey below, usually occupied, must be covered with fire-resistant boards.
- From the legal viewpoint, rooftop terraces are considered to be identical to balconies, and as such the possibilities are limited by the aforementioned planning rules.
- In some towns and cities the existing roofscape is protected by a local byelaws that prohibit large areas of roof covering to be removed or rooftop structures to be built, which means that, for example, only Velux-type windows will be allowed for lighting and views.
- The open area of the roof space is interrupted by large chimneys. If chimneys no longer required are demolished, the flues must be filled and sealed in order to prevent odours.
- The existing pipework will not be designed

for further users and may need to be renewed from basement to roof. Even if unused chimneys are available for new pipes, they must still be opened up on every floor to enable installation.
- The construction work itself is difficult. The storage and transport of debris and building materials usually has to take place on the street in front of the building, which means that part of the street has to be cordoned off for the duration of the work. Depending on the extent of the conversion work, the roof surface has to remain open for longer periods, which can lead to water damage in the storey in use below.

Therefore, demolition of the roof and the subsequent building of a new storey is easier to plan and the costs and timetables are more reliable. Unfortunately, however, the spatial and constructional quality of the existing space is of course lost. On the other hand, this provides the chance for a complete new design (Fig. C 2.58).

Notes:

[1] Schönermark, Gustav; Stüber, Wilhelm: Hochbau Lexikon. Berlin, c. 1900, p. 488
[2] ibid. [1]
[3] Stolz: Hauseinsturz in Buckau, Centralblatt der Bauverwaltung 1887, p. 42. In: Ahnert, Rudolf; Krause, Karl Heinz: Typische Baukonstruktionen von 1860 bis 1960. vol. 1, Berlin, 2006, p. 14
[4] ibid. [2], p. 554
[5] Breymann, Gustav Adolf et al: Allgemeine Baukonstruktionslehre. Teil 1: Die Konstruktionen in Stein. Leipzig, 1903, p. 317
[6] ibid. [5], p. 352
[7] ibid. [1], p. 281

C 2.58

Buildings of the inter-war years 1920–1940

Georg Giebeler

A general spirit of optimism prevailed after the turn of the 20th century which, however, was not consistent with the conservatism of the Germans. The real change did not take place until the end of World War 1, which in addition to death and destruction generated momentum in technical innovation. The "Roaring Twenties" began with the collapse of the monarchies in Russia, Germany and Austria-Hungary, and this political renewal was followed by social and artistic reformations accompanied by technical progress. The founding years were succeeded by the Modern Movement – a radical emancipation. What could be changed, was changed: floating houses, machine-like and aerodynamic buildings, "naked" houses whose internal framework was visible on the outside – those were the avant-garde of architecture. The influence on architecture for the masses did not fail to materialise. The new buzzwords of the day were: honest, functional, utilitarian, light, airy, natural, healthy. The buildings of the founding years were ridiculed as "dilettantish style exercises designed without a natural feeling for art" [1]. Although in political terms the year 1933 marks a turning-point, in terms of architecture there were no radical changes, neither technically nor stylistically – except for the ideologically motivated plans of the National Socialists of course.

The early years of the 20th century witnessed a growth in the formation of groups that were not drawn together because of their hereditary or social status, but rather because they shared the same interests: employers formed trade associations (Association of German Metal-working Industries, 1890), artists formed groups (*Die Brücke*, 1905), the proponents of material correctness formed the Deutscher Werkbund (German Work Federation, 1907). The fact that similar interests could be better asserted via a group while still allowing each individual to prosper also explains the standardisation tendencies in industrial production. Standards organisations, which later would have a considerable influence on construction, were set up in England in 1901 (BSI), Germany in 1917 (DIN, but originally the Standards Committee of German industry, NADI), the USA (ANSI) in 1918, Austria (ÖNorm) in 1920 and

France (AFNOR) in 1926. Such standardisation moves are only feasible and sensible when building materials and/or components can be prefabricated by industry and marketed nationally, even internationally, which in turn presumes communications technologies and a corresponding transport infrastructure plus appropriate on-site machinery. For example, cranes on building sites were virtually unknown at the start of the 1920s; most building materials were moved around by hand.

"Black Tuesday", 24 October 1929, marked the end of the "Roaring Twenties". The collapse of the stock market in the USA initiated the first world economic crisis, the Great Depression, the effects of which would be felt until the outbreak of World War 2. The climax of the crisis around 1930–33 led to drastic economic and social reforms in America, and to the end of democracy in Germany. The depression, preparations for war and the outbreak of war also had an effect on construction methods. As raw materials such as steel were needed for the armaments industry, the state severely restricted methods of construction that were already well established, e.g. reinforced concrete. The methods of the 19th century started to appear again: "The most important thing is to save iron and steel. Wherever possible, they should be replaced by masonry, plain concrete and, if necessary, reinforced concrete, reinforced concrete by plain concrete or masonry, timber by plain concrete, masonry, pumice-aggregate concrete planks, gypsum planks or similar," was the decree of Minister of Labour Franz Seldte in 1937 [2].

The repercussions of the world depression for the building sector were, on the one hand, shortages of and hence expensive building materials and, on the other, a desperate and hence cheap labour force. Together with the new scientific and technical findings, the scarcity of raw materials led to, for example, the use of structural calculations to minimise the dimensions of components [3], which replaced the "empirically based sizing" that had prevailed hitherto. The European building industry suffered a sharp downturn in building work in 1930 and did not recover before the outbreak of war. This chapter therefore deals primarily with the methods of building customary between 1920 and 1930. Buildings built between 1930 and 1945 are very similar to those of the 1920s or make use of techniques from the founding years again (see pp. 132–153).

The radical social change also demanded a radical aesthetic change. Adolf Loos' attack on the decoration of Art Nouveau in his essay *Ornament and Crime* (1908) revealed its drastic effect 10 years later when Art Nouveau and historicising architectural styles were now regarded as the "errors of taste of the 19th century" [4]. However, equating the forms of construction of the 1920s with those of the Bauhaus etc. is an oversimplification because the mass of buildings in Europe cannot be assigned to such movements. Far more decisive were those concepts developed in order to realise the improvement in living conditions of the masses demanded by society as a whole. Dark, stuffy backyards became the symbol of a bygone age that had to be conquered. The picture of the ideal was the low-rise house, possibly in a terrace and with some degree of agricultural self-sufficiency. The concept was based on Ebenezer Howard's ideas for the garden city, which had appeared in his book *To-Morrow: A Peaceful Path to Real Reform* in 1898 and were realised in Letchworth (GB) in 1903 and in Hellerau (D) in 1906.

Where a lower density of development and gardens were not feasible because of high land prices, the very least that could be done was to avoid erecting further buildings within enclosed courtyards. Large residential estates like the Karl Marx Hof project in Vienna included numerous social amenities such as a laundry, pre-school facilities and indoor swimming pool in addition to parks and gardens (Fig. C 3.2).

There are surprising similarities between the socialist-oriented residential developments of the working classes and the garden cities of the conservative middle classes, otherwise thinly veiled by idealistic motives: here the heroic rise of the working classes, there the "back to nature" of the garden cities.

The architects' favourites were, however, office and industrial buildings, where the "New Objectivity" asserted itself most obviously: "The architect has realised that a perfect aesthetic answer to his task ... calls for a design 'from inside to outside'. That is how today's architecture manages without decorative accoutrements and satisfies solely through functional segmentation and utilitarian emphasizing of the building forms and materials created by technology." [5]

Besides the aesthetic preferences, it was primarily the attempt to improve working conditions that played a role here. Unadorned, bulky structures with clean lines appeared (Fig. C 3.1). No factory could manage without its towers – regardless of whether it was in the city or the country. Large expanses of glass revealed the inner workings of the factory and allowed daylight to reach the workplaces, whereas the facades to the offices were usually planned as fenestrated facades with relatively small openings. In constructional terms the buildings were nearly all

steel or reinforced concrete frames with external walls of solid masonry. One consequence of the standardisation euphoria was the modularisation of office buildings, resulting in a grid of 1.25–1.35 m, a standard that is still in use today throughout Europe.

Typical strengths and weaknesses
The residential developments of the 1920s, frequently carried out by cooperative societies, are convincing these days mainly because of their unity. The estates are in the meantime close to town and city centres but nevertheless – as a reaction to the backyards of the 19th century – exhibit a lower density of development and ample greenery. Emphasizing the community in urban planning through the provision of open areas, amenities, parks and gardens, and by keeping the scale of the buildings small promotes a sense of identity and a "human" element. The apartments themselves are characterised by good daylighting and ventilation – most bathrooms, too, have windows. The large urban apartments and detached houses of the 1920s exhibit similar qualities to those of their counterparts dating from the founding years despite being much smaller (Fig. C 3.3). In terms of their construction, the methods of building that were already established by that time – timber joist floors, masonry, pitched roofs – do not generally show any signs of damage.

The desire to build individual apartments for low-income workers required strictly functional, minimal interior layouts (the first edition of Bauentwurfslehre – Architects' Data – by Gropius student Ernst Neufert appeared in 1936, and was sold out in three weeks!). Coupled with the new knowledge of how to save materials through the use of calculations and technology, apartments and houses were built that were regarded at the time as luxurious, although today their size can make them seem oppressive. Further weaknesses are:

- Many small rooms, but mostly enclosed by non-loadbearing walls
- Low room depths between the loadbearing walls
- Narrow stairs with steep flights
- Thin walls and floors with correspondingly poor sound and thermal insulation
- Poor sound insulation in terrace houses because of continuous suspended floors
- Forms of construction vulnerable to damage because of economy measures and lack of knowledge about new technologies such as concrete construction or waterproofing

Conversion potential
The potential for conversion and the need for conversion are very different. It is often possible to continue using houses and apartments without the need for major interventions in the building fabric, a fact that underscores their similarity with the buildings of the founding years. Changes of use, e.g. turning an apartment into an office, are much more difficult

C 3.2

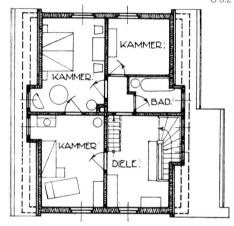
a

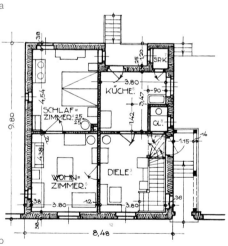
b

c   C 3.3

a

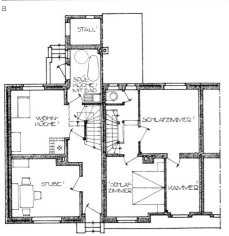

b   C 3.4

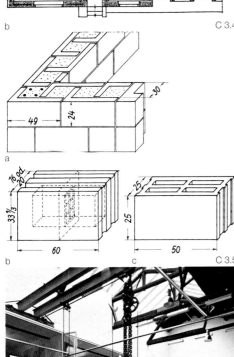

C 3.6

because interior layouts were more closely tailored to certain uses and instead of only one loadbearing internal wall there may be several. The conversion of the small houses of the housing estates is, however, problematic. The unity of a reasonably well-kept residential estate is – if not already protected by a conservation order – usually so impressive that radical interventions are almost out of the question. And it is precisely this characteristic appearance that is so appealing to the owners or buyers of such properties. Difficulties arise in the planning of conversions when attempting to "gain more space". Added to this are problems with sound insulation (terrace houses, Figs. C 3.4a and b), thermal insulation (external walls) and dampness (basement).

Contrasting with the problems of housing are the difficulties experienced with commercial and factory buildings, where the problem of conversion is how to maintain the spaciousness of the framed sheds, mainly when the volume is to be subdivided for new uses.

The similarity with modern commercial structures – modules and frames – enables, however, conversion to virtually any new usage (Fig. C 3.6). However, the building physics problems of sound insulation, thermal insulation and fire protection still remain the same.

Basements

Basements continued to be regarded as ancillary areas for storage purposes only even during the inter-war years. Owing to the poor experiences of the founding years, some building regulations of this time expressly prohibited the creation of rooms for working or accommodation in the basement [6]. Waterproofing technologies had advanced considerably, but were seldom used in basements.

Nevertheless, the basements of this period were built differently to those of the founding years because concrete was used more and more as a building material. At that time it was regarded as inexpensive and waterproof, which was not true in practice and has led again and again to problems of water infiltration and rising damp. The ground floor above the basement was no longer a vaulted construction but instead a flat concrete slab supported on steel beams. However, the global economic crisis forced builders to resort to old building methods more and more because cement was expensive and labour cheap. Apart from the dampness, the basements of these years exhibit very few problems because they were well designed and well built.

Commercial structures rarely have basements. Designed as purely functional buildings, anything that was not regarded as essential for a factory was omitted, e.g. damp-proof courses, damp-proof membranes. As access to such buildings – contrasting with housing – is often at ground level, the problem of water and dampness is also found on the ground floor.

Foundations and ground floor slabs

Foundations of rubble stone or stepped masonry were now only found beneath utility or agricultural buildings. Raft and deep foundations in concrete had been possible since about 1910 because their widespread use had made them cheaper than masonry foundations, and they were also waterproof. The type of cement and its resistance to salts and acids dissolved in the water was pointed out many times, which leads us to conclude that workmanship was poor in this respect. Wide foundations, e.g. on soils with a lower bearing capacity, were reinforced and subjected to bending, which means that similar foundation sizes to those of today can be expected. The permissible bearing capacity of layered sand fill was specified as 100 kN/m² in the first edition of DIN 1054 (1934), and up to 400 kN/m² for firm deposits of gravel or clay. This and the standardised loading assumptions of the day mean that settlement problems are rare.

The improvement in the quality of concrete, the increased use of machinery and ongoing technical developments enabled foundations and basements below the water table, also on a large scale. The methods used were hardly different from those of today and if no problems have arisen so far, can also be regarded as reliable. The situation is different with waterproofing in the case of hydrostatic pressure. The many contradictory construction recommendations led in 1932 to the publication of DIN 4031 ("Water pressure-resistant sealing made from uncoated tarred felts or uncoated asphalt-bitumen felts"). This new standard specified a minimum of three layers of tarred felt continuing at least 300 mm above the highest groundwater level. No waterproofing was required above that level (Fig. C 3.8).

Floor slabs in groundwater were waterproofed on the outside ("tanking"), which unfortunately cannot be repaired if any leaks have appeared in the meantime. Basement floors not subjected to hydrostatic pressure and ground floor slabs without a basement underneath were not waterproofed. The concrete slabs used are normally 120–150 mm thick and generally finished with a bonded screed or clay paving bricks. In the ideal case additives such as "Ceresit" were added to the concrete mix in order to make it waterproof; nevertheless, these floor slabs are not totally watertight. Breaking up the floor and replacing it by a new concrete slab in impermeable quality can minimise this problem at reasonable cost. A completely dry basement is often impossible to achieve because it is not possible to make the junction with the walls completely watertight when hydrostatic pressure is involved, and – depending on the quality of the workmanship – the concrete walls can transport moisture from the soil by way of capillary action.

Ground floor slabs to commercial buildings
Depending on the use of the building, the thicknesses of ground floor slabs in commercial buildings without basements vary considerably: 150 mm is the minimum for lightweight single-storey sheds, the standard is approx. 250 mm, but slabs > 500 mm have even been used (Fig. C 3.7). Reinforcement cannot be presumed because ground floor slabs and foundations were constructed separately, with the top of the foundations frequently flush with the top of the slab. Damp-proof membranes (dpm) and thermal insulation are also rarities.

Both of these aspects create serious problems for a change of use. The simplest answer is to lay a floating screed on a damp-proof membrane which, however, produces a step so that level access is no longer possible. In addition, a floating screed cannot carry heavy loads, thus ruling out certain uses.

In the case of a thin ground slab it is therefore worthwhile considering removing the slab and underlying soil down to approx. 500 mm below finished floor level. A new floor construction with hardcore (to prevent capillary action), blinding layer, thermal insulation, impermeable concrete slab and bonded screed would solve most problems. Only the foundations flush with the top of the slab would represent a potential thermal and moisture bridge which, however, cannot be overcome at reasonable cost. Instead of impermeable concrete, a bituminous damp-proof membrane could be used and joined to new waterproofing at the bases of the walls, waterproofing the foundations at the same time. However, this means the use of an unbonded screed, which increases the overall thickness of the construction even further. Economic considerations frequently preclude the replacement of the ground floor slab; but the lack of thermal insulation infringes the requirements of the Energy Conservation Act and also industrial regulations, even when a damp-proof membrane is laid below a new floor covering. Some architects solve this problem by building platforms, i.e. temporary, raised, dry constructions, on the ground floor, e.g. at workstations (Fig. C 3.6).

External walls to basements
The external walls around basements were frequently of masonry, like in the years before. The recommended wall thicknesses had been reduced since the founding years, but nevertheless were still 510 mm in the basement for a two-and-a-half-storey building. Such huge wall thicknesses mean that damp-proofing such masonry against rising damp is very expensive. Concrete basement walls were not much thinner than masonry ones and – like the floor slabs – not provided with any additional waterproofing. In the presence of slope seepage water or cohesive soils a further cement render or the addition of chemical additives was recommended. Although rising damp in concrete walls is rare, if it does occur it is hardly feasible to remedy the problem. Applying subsequent waterproof-

ing to the outside can usually be carried out without any problems, depending on the soil properties and the local circumstances. Furthermore, concrete walls were often cast up against the soil on the outside, without any separating membrane, until just below ground level. The resulting unevenness of the outer face can amount to several centimetres, which consumes a considerable amount of material to make it level (Fig. 3.9).

The building regulations of 1931 comment on rising damp as follows: "Protection against rising damp should be provided in all external walls and at least in those internal walls in contact with the soil, extending several courses above the adjacent ground level … Buildings without habitable rooms do not need to be protected against moisture in this way." [7] We can conclude from this that damp-proof courses (dpc) were not built into basements at this time.

Floors over basements
Vaults rapidly lost their significance in the 1920s for functional (limited usability, deep floor constructions), economical and also architectural reasons (vaults were regarded as old-fashioned). By the 1930s floors over basements were almost exclusively designed as flat constructions: steel beams with specially moulded bricks, steel beams with concrete, or reinforced concrete. All these floor types were also employed for the upper floors and are described on pp. 165–166.

Ground and upper floors

The increasing use of steel and concrete instead of timber and stone is one of the greatest differences between the upper floors of the inter-war years and those of the founding years. This is very evident in the concrete frames of commercial and large structures, where the new method of construction also led to a new stance, a new aesthetic. Nevertheless, many techniques from the founding years continued to be used virtually unchanged, e.g. solid masonry external walls, also masonry infill panels and facing leaves for frame constructions.

External walls
The recently introduced standardisation of methods of calculation and loading assumptions led to an endeavour to reduce the thicknesses of solid masonry external walls – one of the attempts to save materials and time so typical of the inter-war period. The Berlin Building Regulations of 1929 therefore specified calculations for stability and no minimum thicknesses for particular storeys. External wall thicknesses of just half a brick (120 mm) were permissible for the attic storey. The minimum thickness for a fire wall in the attic storey was also only 120 mm for masonry or 100 mm for concrete.

C 3.4 Houses on a residential estate in Frankfurt-Griesheim (D), c. 1922, H. Hamburger
a External view
b Plan of ground floor
([1] Outhouse, [2] Scullery + bath, [3] Living/kitchen, [4] Drawing room, [5] Bedroom, [6] Bedroom)

C 3.5 Hollow and concrete-filled lightweight concrete blocks
a L-shaped blocks
b "Verokret" aerated concrete block
c Hollow pumice concrete block

C 3.6 Conversion of a former factory building into offices for an advertising agency, Cologne (D), 2005, Georg Giebeler

C 3.7 Thicknesses of ground floor slabs for industrial and commercial buildings (table from 1933), cement: sand mixing ratio

C 3.8 Waterproofing for hydrostatic pressure according to DIN 4031 (for explanation, see p. 275)

C 3.9 Concrete wall to basement cast up against the soil, subsequently waterproofed with a thick coat of bitumen

Imposed load/m²	On undisturbed ground	On filled ground
≤ 1500 kg	150 mm in mix 1:8	200 mm in mix 1:6 to 1:8
≤ 3000 kg	200 mm in mix 1:8	250 mm in mix 1:6 to 1:8
≤ 5000 kg	250 mm in mix 1:8	350 mm in mix 1:6 to 1:8
> 5000 kg	300 mm in mix 1:8	In accord with more detailed investigations

On filled ground the floor construction may need to be reinforced with a grid of steel bars.

C 3.7

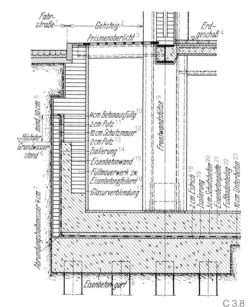

C 3.8

C 3.9

Masonry units

Clay bricks continued to be the first choice for external walls, but they no longer had the market almost exclusively to themselves. The attempts at standardisation during the 19th century began to take effect, and the clay brick now formed the basis for the customary dimensional coordination: from now on in Germany public buildings were built exclusively with imperial-format bricks (normal format at that time: 250 x 120 x 65 mm). Coursed random rubble masonry was now only important as a facing material, e.g. at the bases of walls. In addition, new, factory-made masonry units started to be used because the production processes could now produce materials with a consistently high (standardised) quality.

The calcium silicate bricks of the time correspond to those usual today with a compressive strength of 14–20 MN/m^2, and were also produced in the imperial format.

Hollow bricks were mostly in the form of clay bricks with vertical perforations. They began to be used more and more because of the following advantages: savings in material and weight, faster laying and drying thanks to large formats, and good sound and thermal insulation properties. It was this last aspect in particular that was often seen as an argument in their favour because in the immediate post-war years, and as a result of the economic crisis, there was an acute shortage of fuel. These bricks were mostly somewhat deeper than the normal format (250 x 120 x 104 or 250 x 120 x 142 mm). Their low compressive strength restricted their use to terrace and detached houses.

Lightweight concrete bricks were used for the same reasons as hollow clay bricks (Fig.C 3.5). They were similar to the alluvial- or pumice-stone bricks used previously in certain regions (Rhineland), but now with coal slag as the aggregate. However, they were much bigger units (500 x 250 x 250 mm), indeed, sometimes so large that they could not be laid by hand ("Frankfurter Platte"). Lightweight concrete bricks with dimensions of 250 x 120 x 95 mm for internal walls were also still available.

Mortar

The non-hydraulic limes so common in the past were gradually replaced by hydraulic cement and lime-cement mortars whose quality and strength is similar to that of modern materials. However, the readily workable lime mortar continued to be used for render and plaster mixes. Cement and lime-cement mortars mixed with (additional) lime and sand were used in renders and plasters applied to concrete surfaces, especially soffits.

Masonry thickness and steps

Tables of minimum masonry thicknesses were still used in practice although these had actually been replaced in the building regulations by stability analyses. The thicknesses correspond to the modular system of the imperial format (130±10 mm). The resulting steps were mostly positioned on the inside because the facade architecture of the time rejected the use of string courses as old-fashioned embellishment. The steps served as supports for suspended floors (Fig. C 3.10).

Cavity walls

External walls had been built in the form of cavity walls even during the founding years, especially in northern Germany. A cavity wall is two leaves of masonry either side of an approx. 40–80 mm wide air cavity; the outer leaf is at least 120 mm thick (Fig. C 3.11). This form of construction fulfils three purposes:

- The interior of the masonry gains a supply of air to accelerate the curing of the non-hydraulic lime.
- Provided it is fully enclosed, the layer of air improves the thermal insulation of the external wall.
- Saturation of the facade (clay brickwork, no hard-burned bricks) right through to the interior, e.g. by driving rain, is prevented.

In some cases cavity walls were also integrated into what were actually solid masonry walls, e.g. masonry to spandrel panels. Depending on the purpose, we distinguish between three types of cavity: cavities with a supply of air from inside, cavities with a supply of air from outside, and "closed" cavities whose air is not replenished. In his *Hochbau Lexikon* (building lexicon) of 1900, Gustav Schönermark describes, for example, a form of construction in which the air inlets and outlets are first closed off six months after completion and so can fulfil all three purposes [8].

Cavity walls were built in many different ways because they represented a new method used primarily in the inter-war years. What all the different types have in common is a structural connection between the two leaves achieved by:

Residential building	Basement	Grd. flr.	1st flr.	2nd flr.	3rd flr.	4th flr.	Attic
				Masonry thickness [cm]			
Front wall with openings and floor loads	77	64	51	51	38	38	25
Tall wall without openings but with floor loads	51	51	38	38	38	25	25
Gable wall with openings but without floor loads	51	38	38	38	25	25	25
Gable wall without openings, without floor loads	51	38	38	25	25	25	25
Internal wall with openings and floor loads	51	38	38	38	25	25	–
Staircase wall	38	25	25	25	25	25	25
Factory building							
Front wall with openings and floor loads	90	77	64	51	51	38	25
Tall wall without openings but with floor loads	77	64	51	51	38	38	25
Gable wall without openings, without floor loads	51	51	38	38	25	25	25
Internal wall with openings and floor loads	51	51	51	38	38	38	38
Staircase wall	51	38	38	25	25	25	25

C 3.10

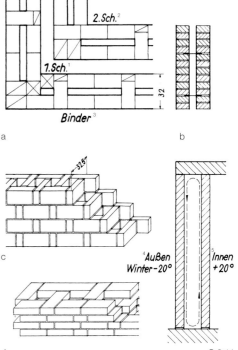

a

b

c

d

e

C 3.11

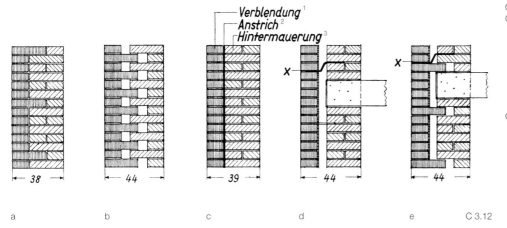

Verblendung [1]
Anstrich [2]
Hintermauerung [3]

a   b   c   d   e   C 3.12

C 3.10   Prescribed minimum wall thicknesses
C 3.11   Various types of cavity wall
    a   "conventional" cavity wall with headers as bonders
      ([1]1st course, [2]2nd course, [3]Header)
    b   with wall ties
    c   "Katona" wall
    d   "Kästel" wall
    e   presumed air circulation in a cavity wall
      ([4]Outside winter -20°, [5]Inside+20°)
C 3.12   Various types of hard-burned brick facing leaves
    a   ½ brick thick with headers as bonders
    b   with offset cavities
    c   ½ brick thick with bituminous coating on rear face of outside leaf
      ([1]Hard-burned brick facing leaf, [2]Coating, [3]Backing wall)
    d   Cavity wall with wall tie (x), open perpend, asphaltic felt above incoming floor joist
    e   Cavity wall with bonders (=headers), otherwise as for d

• Bonders incorporated in the masonry bond with their ends dipped in tar to prevent water penetration
• Wall ties of galvanised steel or cast metal laid in the bed joints (northern Germany, England)
• An offset cavity, i.e. the masonry thicknesses of the inner and outer leaves alternate regularly so that there is no continuous air cavity (north-east Germany)
• Piers of headers in the air cavity at regular intervals but not built into the masonry bond of the other leaf (Fig. C 3.11)

The disadvantage of the reduced stability of double-leaf masonry was reflected in the building regulations, which restricted their use to a maximum of three storeys. The advantages of these walls were seen to be mainly the savings in materials and the shorter drying time [9]. The weather protection and the thermal insulating effect of the air cavity were, however, doubted by many.

Facing brickwork
In line with the notion of doing justice to the material, clay brickwork was now left exposed instead of being rendered, but to improve the resistance to driving rain (and the aesthetics) the outside face was in many cases faced with a 125 mm thick layer of hard-burned or sintered bricks.
The reason for not building walls entirely from these bricks was their higher cost, which also had an effect on the masonry bonds used, with many courses of stretchers. They were mainly bonded into the backing masonry by including headers in the bond, although this meant that moisture (driving rain) could infiltrate into the main part of the wall through hairline cracks and then would only be able to dry out towards the inside because of the impermeability of the facing bricks and the cement mortar used. A higher-quality, but rare form of construction is the double-leaf wall with ventilated and drained air cavity. Wire wall ties or individual headers form the connection to the loadbearing leaf (Fig. C 3.12).
Hard-burned bricks in particular (but also clay bricks) can deviate from the imperial format because masonry units in Hamburg, Oldenburg

or Bavarian format were still produced in some regions.
The facing could also be in the form of natural or reconstituted stone units, tied back to the loadbearing leaf with zinc, bronze or brass wire. The 10–20 mm air cavity between the stone and the masonry meant that the inner and outer leaves could settle independently, preventing restraint stresses in the facing (Fig. C 3.13).

Insulating materials
Various new materials for thermal and sound insulation appeared during the inter-war years. Materials such as compressed, impregnated peat boards ("Torfoleum") were used as impact sound or thermal insulation in walls and suspended floors. These boards measured approx. 500 x 1000 mm, were up to 200 mm thick and had a mass of approx. 0.02 kN/m^2 per 10 mm thickness. There were also cement- or magnesite-bonded lightweight wood-wool boards measuring 500 x 2000 mm in thicknesses between 25 and 150 mm, which were regarded as fire-retardant thermal insulation boards and formed an excellent plaster background. Cork, too, was used very frequently and was available in natural, pressed, bonded (binder: lime or tar) and expanded (twice the volume) forms. "Korkment" consisted of a 4 mm thick cork mat on a jute backing which was laid beneath linoleum to improve the impact sound insulation.

Damage and measures
Damage to external masonry is rather rare. In buildings with basements and a ground floor above the splashing water zone the same applies as for buildings from the founding years, although the damage caused by poor-quality mortar and bricks described in that section now occurs less often thanks to standardisation and quality control.
The situation is different in the case of buildings without basements, where the ground floor is level with the surrounding site – particularly the case with commercial buildings. Here, rising damp due to the lack of or a defective damp-proof course and saturation caused by splashing water – with the well-known consequences such as mould growth on the inside, efflores-

cence inside and outside, and frost-induced spalling on the outside at the bases of walls – can be expected. As composite or rubble-filled walls were now seldom built, the damp-proofing methods described in the chapter "General refurbishment tasks" can be relatively cost-effectively and reliably used (see pp. 125–126). In commercial buildings and multi-storey housing the necessary upgrading measures for external walls are limited to thermal insulation. Rendered facades can be easily and inexpensively upgraded by attaching external insulation without causing any architectural problems and – provided there are no balconies – with few thermal bridges. The situation is more difficult with brickwork facades, as are very common in certain regions, e.g. northern Germany, England and the Benelux countries. If the external appearance is to be retained, internal insulation is the only option. Changing to a multi-layer construction with insulating layer is expensive, and owing to the changed surface, form and colour of the facing bricks, deeper window reveals and freezing moist air on the facade is often unsatisfactory from the architectural viewpoint (see "General refurbishment tasks", pp 122–124). The lightweight concrete or hollow clay brick walls of the small estate houses may also require better sound insulation which, however, is automatically the case when the thermal insulation is improved.

Window openings
Like with vaulted floors over basements, the use of arches over window openings, also cambered arches, gradually gave way to straight beams (in bending), normally standard steel sections, but also timber for openings < 1 m wide and openings in non-loadbearing walls. The lintels over window openings in thick external walls were in the form of several adjacent beams connected together by means of spacer tubes and bolts. They were mostly clad in lime-cement render/plaster on a backing material (e.g. Rabitz background). Window surrounds made from dressed stones – albeit with less decoration than during the founding years – continued to be used, installed in a similar way and bridged over by a relieving arch within the masonry bond.

Reinforced concrete lintels started to become popular later in this period, something that was certainly also partly due to the preparations for war taking place throughout Europe and the associated shortage of steel. In the majority of cases the quality of the concrete and the steel and hence the stability should be adequate for modern requirements, even if this can no longer be verified according to current codes of practice. Only a small amount of steel reinforcement should be presumed, and then only in the bottom of the lintel. The normal concrete cover is 20 mm.

Windows

The windows customary in this period were made from Scots pine and were always painted. The well-known coupled window continued to be used almost unchanged, albeit now with wider rather than tall panes of glass, which characterised the standardisation process. DIN 1240 specified three standard glass formats: 320 x 300, 440 x 300 and 560 x 300 mm. As the same window frame sizes were specified for all glass formats, the largest format represented the most economic and most common one from which standardised window formats were derived by adding several panes together (Fig. C 3.15). Standardisation had been brought about by the desire to produce the windows on an industrial scale.

The widely used single window was subjected to more and more criticism during the years of the depression because the desire for bright interiors, i.e. large expanses of glass, led to large heat losses. Besides the coupled window, double windows and secondary glazing also started to appear. The former consists of an outer single window and a simplified single window in an outer frame and bottom rail. Both types of window were fitted to a ¼ brick nib at mid-depth of wall, which must be taken into account in a survey of the building (Fig. C 3.16). Secondary glazing makes use of similar frame sections which are connected together directly but can still be opened to clean the cavity between the panes. The window illustrated in Fig. C 3.17 also shows for the first time a rainwater channel screwed to the sill of the outer frame. The thermal performance is 50 % better than single windows (coupled and double windows: 100 % improvement). The advantage is the reduced installation work because there is only one junction with the surrounding masonry. Consequently, secondary glazing was particularly popular for the small houses of the new housing estates.

The customary side-hung windows were joined by many patented vertical sliding windows (sash windows), which were widespread in Great Britain. The lower sashes are attached to counterweights and are tilted inwards prior to

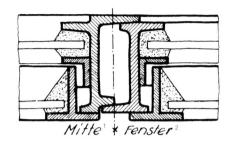

sliding them upwards. As such windows were patented as complete units, they differ in terms of their frame members and hardware. Single-glazed steel windows were installed in the majority of workshops and factories. Such simple windows consist of welded T-, L- and Z-sections and glass panes (standard sizes 180 x 250, 250 x 360 and 360 x 500 mm) held in place by putty on the outside. Where better thermal performance and airtightness were required, special frames were available for forming double rebates for secondary glazing (Fig. C 3.14).

Weaknesses and measures
Old coupled and double windows in good condition are by no means rare. Very little damage is seen at the secure junction between outer frame and window sill on the spandrel panel masonry, and the thermal and sound insulation was adequate over many decades. But owing to more stringent requirements, this is no longer the case, which is why it is advisable to replace these windows. As the mullions and transoms are quite broad, standardised windows with similar frame sizes can be produced. In the case of a double window, the outer window can remain in place and a new inner window fitted behind it. The airtightness of the existing outer window should not be improved because otherwise the condensation that collects in the cavity can no longer evaporate.

Internal walls and frame constructions

Loadbearing internal walls were mostly of masonry during the inter-war years. Compared to the founding years, however, the walls in residential buildings were now much thinner; indeed, wall thicknesses > 380 mm are highly unlikely (Fig. C 3.10). Apart from that there were no other changes to internal walls, meaning that in terms of damage and measures the information given in the chapter "Buildings of the founding years" applies here as well (see p. 142). But two new methods of construction, which were widely used for industrial buildings, started to become widespread: steel and reinforced concrete frames. Both these forms of construction are frequently not apparent from the outside because not only are the walls between the peri-

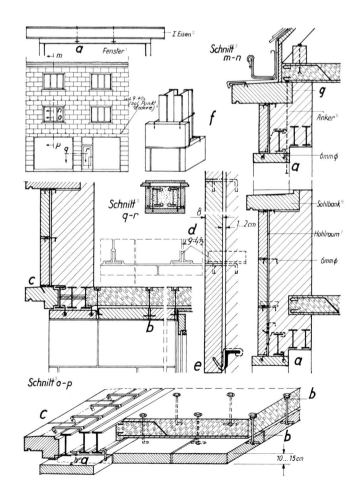

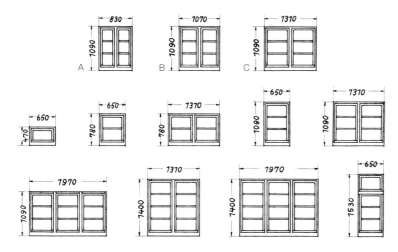

C 3.15

meter columns built in brickwork, but the columns, too, are frequently clad in brickwork. For example, sometimes apparently solid masonry pillars conceal cast iron or steel columns.

The new materials brought about a distinct rationalisation in non-loadbearing internal walls. The otherwise traditional, half-brick thick walls were now built using larger pumice blocks, for example, which besides their lower weight (reduced load on suspended floors) also provided an excellent plaster background. In addition, plank walls were built using gypsum-based boards (50, 60, 70 or 100 mm thick) and lightweight concrete. So-called panel walls are more like plasterboard walls; they consist of finished boarding attached to both sides of a timber framework. The board materials used included cement-bonded boards, lightweight wood-wool boards or other timber boards, also asbestos-cement, which must be checked in advance of any conversion measures. In the trade literature of the time, asbestos was described as "versatile" and, above all, as a "thermal insulating material" [10].

Steel frames

Steel increased in importance during the inter-war years. As long as large quantities of steel were not required for the armaments industry, the "steel framework" was regarded as a cost-effective, efficient substitute for conventional forms of construction. Various types of sus-pended floor supported by steel beams (Fig. C 3.25) superseded vaulting completely and also replaced timber joists floors to a certain extent. Whereas during the founding years steel frames still represented a new method of construction enabling large shed structures, e.g. over railway stations, to be erected, steel was now used increasingly for floor structures, especially for industrial and commercial buildings. Cast iron was quickly replaced by rolled steel sections, produced in grade St 37.12 (tensile strength 37–45 kg/mm^2), with grade St 34.13 rivets and St 38.13 bolts. Grade St 52 was also covered by standards but was not used in the building industry. The sections were joined together by means of gusset plates

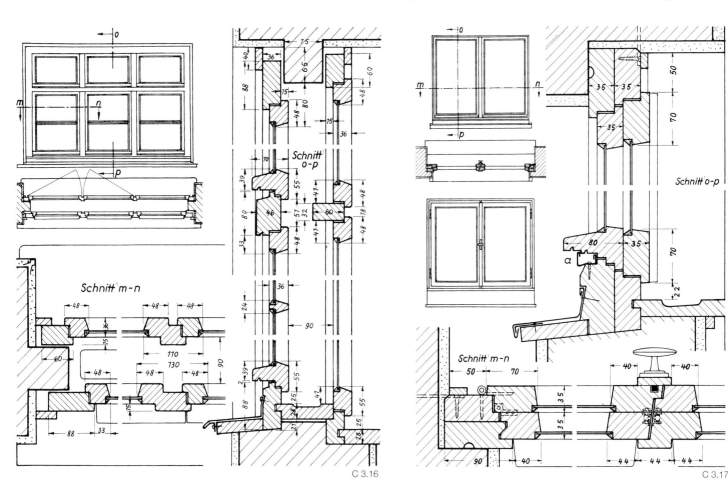

C 3.16

C 3.17

and rivets; bolted connections were explicitly not recommended. Welded connections were already known in the European building industry, but in contrast to the USA were used only rarely because there was a shortage of skilled workers to carry out such work (Fig. C 3.19). Protecting steel components against corrosion was achieved, for example, with chromium and nickel alloys (stainless steel) or copper alloys, but also through the formation of oxide layers that form upon bluing (rubbing with one part bluing salt and three parts olive oil) or black-annealing (rubbing with linseed oil and heating). Galvanising by way of immersion or electro-plating of the components, e.g. with chromium, was also possible, but in most cases two or three coats of paint were applied, with the iron oxide in micaceous iron oxide paint or the lead oxide in red lead protecting against corrosion. The binder used was usually boiled linseed oil, very occasionally synthetic resin (after 1910). It is not advisable to remove any coatings containing lead (also white lead) from complex or compound cross-sections because sand-blasting is the only method and that could release toxic lead that otherwise, i.e. in its bonded state, is not critical. When applying new coats of paint, it is important to check their compatibility with oil paints containing lead.

Fire protection

Fire-resistant coatings based on asbestos are rare, but certainly possible. The same applies here as for paints containing lead. In most cases steel columns are protected by a layer of cement – they were plastered or rendered, encased or filled (hollow sections) with concrete or surrounded completely by masonry. Similar to today, fire protection applied to the loadbearing structure of walls, columns and suspended floors, and in those days a distinction was made between "fire-retardant", which corresponds roughly to class F 15, and "fire-resistant", without specifying the duration of fire resistance exactly. In 1929, for example, the lower requirement "fire-retardant" applied to small houses and stair flights in Berlin.

Apart from the roof covering, roof structures themselves did not have to comply with any requirements, which explains why the loadbearing structures to single-storey sheds remained unprotected. That may well contradict current building regulations or industrial building directives when considering a change of use. Recoating is normally uneconomic because the old coatings have to be completely removed. When cladding is ruled out for architectural reasons, the only solution is to apply for an exemption, which may be granted provided compensatory measures, e.g. installation of smoke and heat vents, fire detectors, perhaps even automatic fire-extinguishing systems (sprinklers) are included in the new design.

Damage and measures

Apart from fire protection, the question of load-bearing capacity is one that must be addressed when confronted with structural steelwork. The loadbearing capacity of steelwork in good condition that has hitherto not been involved in any conversion work does not usually present any problems where external walls, columns and suspended floors are concerned because many changes of use lead to a reduction in the imposed loads (Fig. C 3.23). In 1933 the minimum imposed load according to statutory instruments in Prussia was 5 kN/m², i.e. more than adequate for conversion into offices or housing, for which these days 2 kN/m² is adequate. The situation is different with roof structures; a re-analysis according to current codes of practice usually reveals them to be inadequate. This is due to the real increase in loads because of the addition of soffits and thermal insulation, higher snow loads these days (1933: 0.75 kN/m²) and the verification of serviceability that is now essential (limiting the deflection). If the structural members, e.g. of a trussed girder, have already been reduced to the minimum, which is frequently the case, the only solution is replacement or to distribute the load over additional girders inserted between the existing ones. Strengthening the delicate, riveted constructions is virtually impossible because there is usually insufficient space for additional fasteners at the connections between the members.

a

b
C 3.18

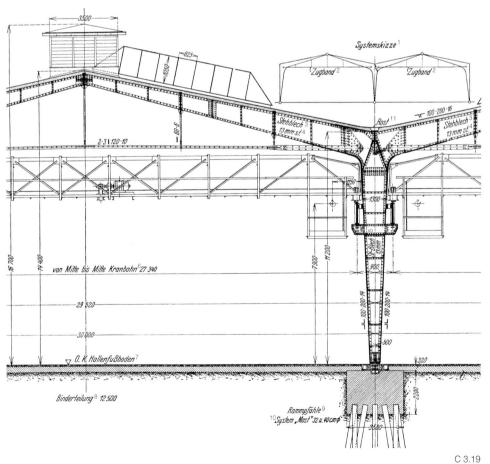

C 3.19

C 3.20

Rust can be neglected because the structural members are internal and also well protected by the red lead. Furthermore, design of the members was based on their weakest cross-section, i.e. reduced by the holes for the rivets. They are therefore otherwise "oversized" and thus have a sufficient loadbearing capacity even in the case of some rust. However, special attention must be paid to the connections with rivets and gusset plates.

Reinforced concrete frames
Multi-storey industrial and office buildings were preferably erected in reinforced concrete instead of steel because of the fire protection requirements. Contemporary arguments against reinforced concrete were the limited spans (max. approx. 10 m) and the poor variability – the latter disadvantage is still valid today (Figs. C 3.18a and b).
The rapid development of reinforced concrete frames is revealed by the fact that many pages were devoted to this subject in the textbooks of the 1920s, whereas 20 years previously only a few pages were necessary [11]. The first German standard covering reinforced concrete construction, DIN 1045, was first published in 1925. Whereas in the USA profiled reinforcing bars were already in use, in Europe L- and T-sections were joined mainly by plain reinforcing bars, also expanded metal in small suspended floor slabs. An understanding of the way reinforced concrete was erected at that time can be gained by considering the loading assumptions, which were hardly any different to those of today, and the relationship between cost of materials (high) and cost of labour (low) in those years. The numbers and sizes of reinforcing bars were just adequate and they were placed in the tension zone only. The same applied to the sizes of concrete components: slender cross-sections and minimised thicknesses prevailed, a fact that led to the inclusion of haunches at beam–column junctions, flared column heads between flat slabs and their supporting columns. With ribbed slabs and beam-and-slab constructions as well, the construction simply followed the structural calculations and labour-intensive formwork was accepted – totally different to the situation these days (Fig. C 3.20).

Damage and measures
Stability does not present any problems with reinforced concrete frames. Damage to the concrete is also rare because the loadbearing structure is not usually exposed to the weather. Exposed reinforcing bars are not critical, either, because the problem is usually due to mechanical damage and not spalling caused by corrosion. Two problems occur during conversion work, however:
Firstly, the addition of building services is difficult. Both the minimised reinforcement and the minimised dimensions of the compression zones of suspended floor slabs cannot be cut away, which makes chases and slots in such structures virtually impossible. The position of the reinforcement should be checked by chiselling away the concrete first before planning any core-drilling. Safer and more economic is certainly a surface-mounted installation, as was preferred in the old days.
The second problem is the inaccurate workmanship often encountered, especially in industrial buildings. Only rarely are the columns of different storeys in vertical alignment; they are more likely several centimetres out of alignment, and out of plumb by a similar amount over their height. This becomes a problem when fitting new components, e.g. partitions, built-in furniture, etc. Adequate tolerances should therefore be allowed for during the planning. In addition, every loadbearing member adjacent to new components must be measured exactly. Choosing a new fitting-out grid offset from the old one does not usually solve the problem because possibly complicated junctions with existing floor beams, haunches, etc. are often overlooked during the planning.

Chimneys
The normal method of constructing chimneys was no different to that of the founding years (see p. 144). New was the use of specially moulded bricks, in some cases containing several flues, e.g. for ventilating rooms distant from the facades. In addition, during the inter-war years stoneware pipes were often inserted into masonry chimneys in order to avoid an accumulation of soot (Fig. C 3.22).

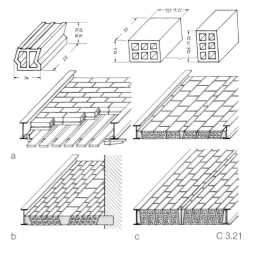

a

b   c   C 3.21

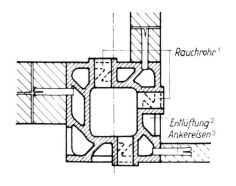

Rauchrohr [1]

Entlüftung [2]
Ankereisen [3]

C 3.22

Usage	Requirement of Prussian building legislation Imposed load [kN/m²]	Proposal for imposed load assumption[1] Imposed load [kN/m²]
Office areas	2.0	3.5
Offices in factory buildings		5.0
Stairs	5.0	
Floors carrying vehicular traffic (e.g. over basement)	8.0	> 8.0
Department stores	5.0	7.5
Light industry	5.0	7.5
Medium-heavy industry		10.0–15.0
Heavy industry		20.0–30.0
Very heavy industry		> 30.0
Ground floor, light industry		10.0
Ground floor, medium-heavy industry		20.0
Ground floor, heavy industry		50.0
Ground floor, fabrication of large machines etc.		100–200

[1] von Heideck, Erich; Leppin, Otto: Der Industriebau. Berlin, 1933

C 3.23

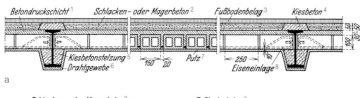

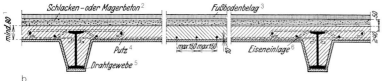

C 3.24

C 3.25

A build-up of soot occurs whenever the exhaust-gas temperatures are too low and the water vapour in the gas condenses in the flue. The sulphur and tar in the gases are dissolved in the water and can penetrate the wall of the chimney, causing brown patches on the outside. Unpleasant odours are also possible. It is, however, not correct to assume that soot accumulations are always linked to the burning of solid fuels; even the very latest gas-fired low-temperature boilers can cause this problem. Inserting a stainless steel or plastic pipe into the masonry flue prevents the condensate from penetrating the masonry.

One simple way of refurbishing the surface is to clad the chimney, e.g. with plasterboard (attached with adhesive). Prior to that, the damaged areas should be covered with plastic sheeting to prevent unpleasant odours. Alternatively, after removing the old plaster, the outside of the masonry can be covered with plastic sheeting and then a plaster background (expanded metal) applied over the whole area ready for new plaster. All other types of barrier on the surface are, by contrast, ineffective over the long-term.

Heating

The main change since the founding years was the introduction of central heating, which slowly became popular depending on the type of use. Individual stoves and their multitude of flues were still common in simple apartment blocks and terrace houses. But in offices (many rooms with an identical heating requirement) the installation of central heating had already become more economic in the 1920s. The systems were mostly fired with solid fuels – wood, peat or coal depending on the local availability. Heat requirement calculations according to DIN 4701 were used to design the systems. There were three types of distribution in those days:

· Pump
· Gravity
· Steam

C 3.23   Imposed loads for industrial buildings, 1933
C 3.24   Part-section through multi-storey building factory building with steel frame
([1]Splice, [2]2nd floor, [3]1st floor, [4]Ground floor, [5]Imposed load, [6]Section, [7]Pipe support, [8]Centre of bldg., [9]Driven piles, [10]"Mast" system, Ø 320 mm)
C 3.25   Solid suspended floors, both types favoured for industrial buildings
a "Kleinesche" floor
([1]Concrete topping, [2]Slag-agg. or lean concrete, [3]Fixed on top, [4]Gravel-agg. concrete, [5]Gravel-agg. conc. block, [6]Wire mesh, [7]Plaster, [8]Steel reinft.)
b Reinforced concrete floor
([1]min. 80, [2]Slag-agg. or lean concrete, [3]Floor covering, [4]Plaster, [5]Wire mesh, [6]Steel reinft.
C 3.26   Heat output of cast iron radiators, output per segment; to convert from calories to watts or from the flow/return temperatures usual at that time (90/70 °C) to those usual today (75/65 °C), multiply the values in the table by 0.25.
C 3.27   Multi-storey industrial building in reinforced concrete, section
([1]End bay, [2]End bay, [3]Imposed load, [4]4th floor, [5]3rd floor, [6]2nd floor [7]1st floor, [8]Ground floor, [9]Basement)
C 3.28   Multi-storey industrial building in reinforced concrete, part-plan of ground floor
([1]Floor over basement, [2]Expansion joint)

A pumped system is a low-pressure hot-water system. It was similar to standard modern heating systems but had an expansion tank and should therefore be regarded as an open system not immune to freezing.

A gravity system does not require a pump. Such a system is only suitable for detached houses because long horizontal runs are not possible. A steam system is normally only found in factories because steam was often available as part of the production process and could be distributed over long distances without the need for any pumps. Such systems are not affected by frost and can react very rapidly, which is very important for shift working. Steam heating systems are still frequently used today. The distribution pipes are generally of iron, and their sizes depend on the type of system: pumped systems require the smallest diameters, steam systems the largest. The pipework can usually continue to be used because leaks are rare and the closed circuits prevent corrosion. It is important to check, though, whether the pipes are badly clogged. The cast iron radiators frequently used at that time can still be used; Fig. C 3.26 lists their heat output.

Suspended floors

The advances in concrete construction also determined the types of floor construction employed. Vaulted floors were hardly built any more, and instead concrete floors supported by steel beams appeared more and more. That was certainly the case for floors over basements, but also those areas of the upper floors such as stair landings and floors to wet areas. Timber joist floors continued to be designed and built, especially for housing. But for industrial structures, concrete floors on steel beams and reinforced concrete floors were used exclusively.

Timber joist floors

Timber joist floors continued to be used for the upper floors of the houses of the new estates and also for multi-storey apartment blocks, even though the disadvantages were well known. But timber joist floors were cheap, dry and quick to erect. Their construction and weaknesses are described in the chapter on buildings of the founding years (see pp. 144–150).

Concrete floors on steel beams

Although this method had been known for some time, it was not used widely until the inter-war years. The form of construction used most often was an in situ, unreinforced, tamped concrete slab supported on the bottom flanges of steel beams. The maximum spans possible were as follows:

- Housing: 1.30 m for a 100 mm deep slab, 1.40 m for 120 mm
- Factories: 1.00 m for a 100 mm deep slab, 1.10 m for 120 mm

The poor room acoustics represents one problem, which led to the introduction of many hol-

	Heavyweight 2-column			Heavyweight 3-column				Lightweight 3-column			Lightweight 4-column			
a	345	495	975	385	480	635	965	555	700	900	450	555	700	900
b	440	590	1080	495	590	745	1080	619	764	964	514	619	764	964
c	180	180	180	235	235	235	235	168	168	168	220	220	220	220

Internal temperature	Heat output [kcal/m²h] with hot-water heating													
15°	470	455	420	420	415	410	385	435	430	415	435	430	425	410
20°	430	420	390	390	385	380	360	400	395	385	400	395	390	380

Internal temperature	Heat output [kcal/m²h] with low-pressure steam heating													
15°	750	720	660	635	620	600	575	660	655	640	660	655	645	630
20°	700	680	620	600	585	570	540	625	615	600	625	615	610	590

C 3.26

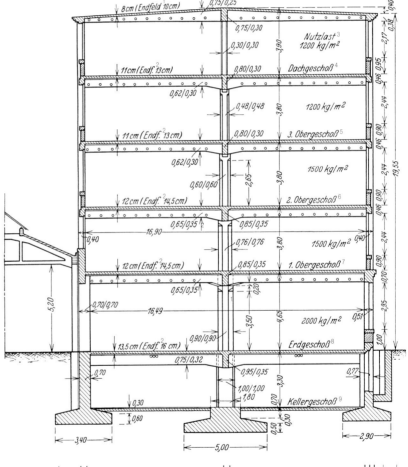

C 3.27

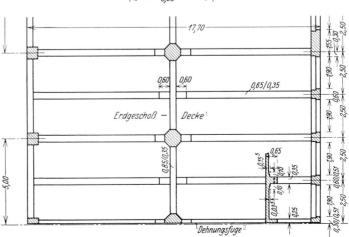

C 3.28

165

low block floors with a concrete topping, but without reinforcement. In addition, there were flat solid slabs made from moulded blocks (Fig. C 3.21).

However, the favourite for factory buildings was the reinforced ribbed slab with infill elements, e.g. the "Kleinesche" floor, the lightweight concrete infill blocks of which normally measured 100 x 150 x 250 mm. The blocks were sometimes given a concrete topping 30–50 mm thick. Such floors were approved for imposed loads up to 7.5 kN/m² and spans up to 6.5 m. The reinforcing bars in the ribs between the blocks were 6 mm diameter plain bars (Fig. C 3.25a). Reinforced concrete slabs without infill elements were supported on steel beams where higher imposed loads were necessary. The minimum depth of the floor according to DIN 1045 –1048 (1932) was merely 70 mm. Fig. C 3.24 shows a steel frame with this type of concrete floor. The depth of the slabs of the approx. 1.8 m span floors is about 150 mm in this example. A structural appraisal reveals that the floor more or less satisfies today's load-carrying and serviceability requirements for the given imposed load (Fig. C 3.25b).

Reinforced concrete floors
Reinforced concrete floors were reinforced mostly in the tension zone only. At the start of the 20th century, the reinforcement in a simply supported slab was in catenary form, i.e. an arch in reverse ("Koenen" haunched slab). Flat slabs, as are customary today, were unusual. On the other hand, ribbed slabs and beam-and-slab constructions or concrete slabs supported on steel beams were common. The reason for this can be found in the formwork customary at that time, which comprised exclusively rough-sawn planks. The work involved in a beam-and-slab floor with haunches was still cheaper than the extra materials required for a flat slab. From the purely structural point of view, the shape of the floor slab made it light and hence economical with respect to the expensive reinforcement. Beam-and-slab floors were often built with primary and secondary beams, with a maximum span of 3 m for the intervening floor bays (spacing of the secondary beams). The primary beams were about 6 – 8 m apart, which led to a relatively small grid for shed-type structures. In addition, flat slabs with flared column heads were often used, especially in the presence of gases and fumes, which could dissipate better

with a "smooth" soffit. According to the edition of DIN 1045 –1048 valid at the time, the minimum depths were 150 mm for flat slabs with flared column heads, 70 mm for flat slabs and 120 mm for slabs over basements carrying vehicular traffic (Figs. C 3.27 and 3.28).
The above in situ concrete slabs were supplemented by many ribbed slab systems with infill elements. The lightweight infill elements made from hollow clay or lightweight concrete units simplified the formwork and also improved the room acoustics. The soffit was usually plastered or a Rabitz plaster background was suspended underneath. The desire for industrial prefabrication led to the first precast concrete floor slabs, albeit with conventional reinforcement, e.g. the "Rapid Floor" comprising 120 x 220 mm I-shaped reinforced concrete beams placed directly adjacent each other. The webs included openings at regular intervals to save weight.

Damage and measures
Lack of experience with reinforced concrete construction manifests itself in, for example, the absence of transverse reinforcing bars to distribute the load. Likewise, contemporary textbooks recommend only butt joints – no hooks

a   C 3.29

C 3.29   a   Drawings for a small apartment block (not built), c. 1930, Hugo Ebinghaus
([1]Date, [2]Drn., [3]Chk., [4]Sheet, [5]Sketch)
     b   Plan of basement, masonry with solid floor slab supported on steel beams
([1]Gas pipe ¾", [2]w. hook for wash, [3]Beam, [4]Heat. pipe, [5]Drying, [6]Opening for ventilation, [7]Water, [8]Basement, [9](1st floor), [10](Ground floor), [11]Washing, [12]Basement, [13](2nd floor), [14]w. lobby, [15]Lobby, [16]Coke, [17]Boiler & coke, [18]Boiler [19]Low-load boiler, [20]Drain, [21]Cable, [22]Petrol trap, [23]Date, [24]Chk., [25]Sheet, [27]Basement)
     c   Layout of joists, upper floor and garage roof
([1]Detail A on stairs to attic, [2]Section a-b, [3]Detail B, [4]Gutter, 6-part, [5]Ruberoid, 2 layers, [6]22 mm boards, [7]220-120 x 60 mm firrings, [8]15 mm boards, [9]Plaster, [10]Plate Ø 200 x 3, [11]Gas pipe 2½", [12]welded, [13]Beam, [14]Opening for stairs, [15]Date, [16]Drn., [17]Chk., [18]Sheet, [19]Upper floor, garage roof)
     d   Roof space, plan on rafters and collars
([1]Gable section a-b, [2]Ruberoid, 2 layers, [3]Boarding, [4]Air cavity, [5]Calcined sand, [6]Straw loam pugging, [7]Pugging boards, [8]Plaster on boarding, [9]Section A-B, [10]Vent, [11]Opening for stairs, [12]Gable side, [13]Date, [14]Drn., [15]Chk., [16]Sheet, [17]Plan on rafters and collars)

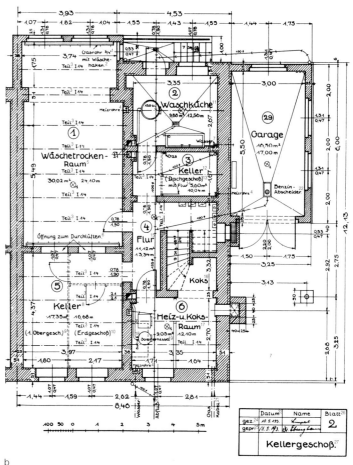

b   C 3.29

or bends – between reinforcing bars in continuous slabs because a tension connection was considered unnecessary [12]. Floors constructed in this way may need to be comprehensively refurbished because of the excessive deflection – like the Hansa Building in Cologne dating from 1925.

The thin concrete slabs to which the floor finishes were applied directly mean that all reinforced concrete floors of the inter-war years suffer from similar problems in terms of sound insulation and fire protection. According to DIN 4109 the sound reduction index R'_w of a 120 mm floor slab is 50 dB, which does not conform to the current minimum requirements. The fire resistance of such a floor slab is also only class F 30 and not the F 90 prescribed these days. The reason for this is the minimum concrete cover to the reinforcement prescribed in those early days: only 10 mm for floor slabs and 15 mm for interior columns; today's standards specify 30–40 mm for class F 90.

Both problems can be solved by adding ceilings to improve sound insulation and fire resistance. A suspended ceiling with fire-resistant boarding (2 No. 20 mm) plus a mineral wool backing (2 No. 40 mm) achieves F 90 without even considering the existing floor slab, but does reduce the clear height in the room by at least 150 mm below the steel beams. Added to this will be any space that might be required for pipes or cables.

Steel columns must also be clad; F 90 is achieved here with boards 25–35 mm thick attached directly. Reinforced concrete columns with their reinforcement not far below the surface do not conform to current F 90 requirements, either. There are two refurbishment options in this situation: increasing the concrete cover or plastering. The concrete cross-section can be increased by applying a layer of sprayed concrete. This method was developed by the Berlin-based Torkret company as early as 1920 and is used these days primarily in civil engineering, e.g. tunnelling, embankments. All loose constituents are removed from the concrete surface beforehand by sand-blasting, water-jetting or shot-peening. Any exposed reinforcing bars with superficial corrosion do not, however, have to be cleaned back to bright metal because the sprayed concrete protects the bars against further rusting.

In the Torkret method a dry to damp concrete mix is pumped under high pressure and not mixed with water until it reaches the nozzle. The mix strikes the surface with a high force, which ensures good adhesion and also obviates the need for any further compacting. As the addition of water at the nozzle in particular requires some experience, this method can only be carried out by specialist contractors. Besides its use for improving fire protection, sprayed concrete can also be applied to strengthen reinforced concrete components because in the verification of loadbearing capacity and serviceability it is permitted to take the sprayed concrete into account to a certain extent. Directly

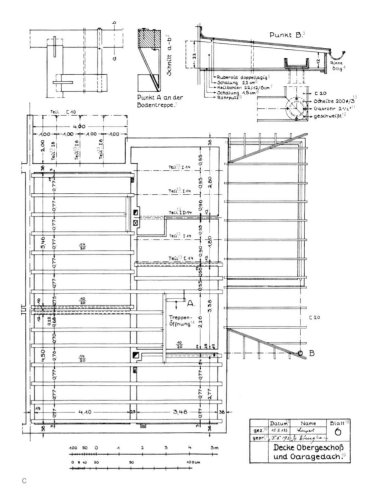

c

C 3.29

d

C 3.29

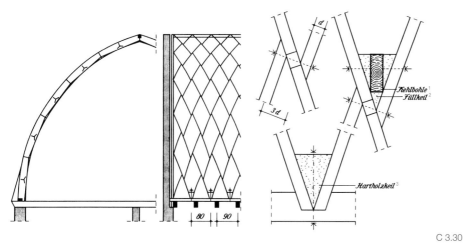

C 3.30

C 3.31

after being applied, the very rough surface of the wet sprayed concrete can be trowelled smooth to achieve a surface not unlike that of fair-face concrete.

If besides upgrading for fire protection reasons no concrete refurbishment works or increases in cross-section are required, components can also be plastered according to DIN 4102. A 10 mm coat of gypsum plaster (or 15 mm lime-cement plaster) is equivalent to 10 mm concrete cover (normal-weight concrete), i.e. the maximum permissible thickness of 25 mm (or 20 mm for lime-cement plaster) should be adequate for class F 90 in most cases. Of course, all loose material must first be removed from the substrate and a coat of bond enhancer applied.

Another problem area is the sound insulation of the party walls between the low-cost terrace or semi-detached houses on the new housing estates. One reason for this is the common party walls of 250 mm thick masonry (sound reduction index R'_w < 50 dB instead of the 55 dB

stipulated), the other is the flanking transmissions through the floor slabs. Reinforced concrete floors, quite properly from the structural engineering viewpoint, were designed as continuous, frame-type timber or steel floors often supported on the party walls. Together with the lack of impact sound insulation, this leads to enormous acoustic problems, and an associated decrease in the value of the properties.

The airborne sound insulation can be markedly improved by installing a non-rigid lining in front of the party wall. The improvement in quality this brings more than makes up for the loss of the approx. 100–120 mm from the width of the room (25 mm air cavity, 50 mm framing, 2 No. 12.5 mm plasterboard).

Improving the impact sound insulation is more difficult. One conceivable solution would be to remove the existing bonded screed and install a new floating screed. Despite the higher loads, this is generally possible – also because the clear room heights were still fairly generous at

this time and so a deeper floor is possible. However, the associated reduction in the clear opening height of the doors is physically and architecturally unsatisfactory. In contrast to the buildings of the founding years, from the 1920s onwards a clear structural opening height of 2.10 m was decided upon in order to accommodate the new, standardised doors. But the main problem with this renovation measure is the fact that in the first place it is the neighbours who benefit, not the occupants of the refurbished accommodation!

Screeds and floor coverings

Screeds and floor coverings are dealt with here only where they differ from those of the founding years because the majority of techniques had hardly changed. However, screeds were used less and less as finished surfaces and instead more and more as a subfloor, especially for linoleum, which had now appeared on the market. Above all, lime and loam screeds were no longer used in the inter-war years. The following screeds and floor coverings were available at that time:

- Flooring cement: a mix of fillers (wood or asbestos chippings) with magnesite and a magnesium chloride solution; used as a subfloor for linoleum or – smoothed with a layer of talcum and oiled with linseed oil – as a finished floor surface; min. 12 mm thick (DIN 272), usually applied in two 10 mm layers. The disadvantages are its sensitivity to moisture and its corrosive effect on metals. The "Dermas Floor" is a flooring cement to which asphalt emulsions have been added to improve the moisture and oil resistance.
- Gypsum screed: in the past used as a wearing course, now primarily as a subfloor for linoleum.
- Cement screed: used as a subfloor for stone, stoneware and terrazzo tiles; mostly laid on a layer of lean concrete.
- Linoleum: a mix of linoxyn (oxidised linseed oil), cork powder or sawdust, pigments and resins (colophonium) on a jute backing (invented in 1863 by Frederick Walton); the composition has remained unchanged to this day. The disadvantages are the odour and its

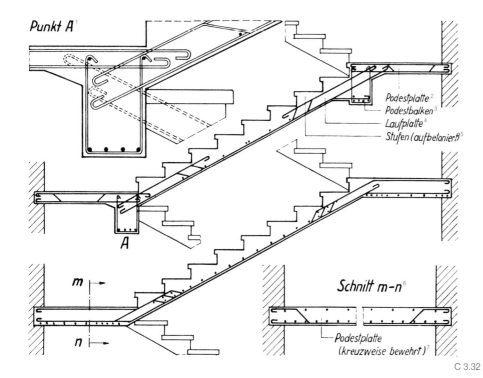

C 3.32

a

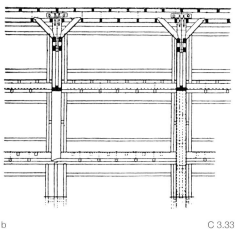

b   C 3.33

C 3.30 "Zollinger" roof
        ([1]Collar, [2]Filler wedge, [3]Hardwood wedge)
C 3.31 "Zollinger" roof for the "German Wine" exhibition,
        Koblenz (D), 1925
C 3.32 Sections through reinforced concrete stairs
        ([1]Detail A, [2]Landing slab, [3]Landing beam, [4]Stair flight, [5]Step (cast on
        top), [6]Section m–n, [7]Landing slab (reinforcement in both directions))
C 3.33 House of the Radio Industry, Berlin (D), 1924,
        Heinrich Straumer, destroyed by fire in 1935
        a Clad timber roof trusses
        b Longitudinal section

lack of moisture and alkali resistance. The
advantages are its resistance to fats and
greases, and its antistatic and fungicidal
properties. It is glued to the substrate over its
whole area by means of terpentine paste
(timber) or resinous linoleum putty (screeds).
· Stragula, balatum: bitumenised paper based
on a wool felt material with a printed oil-paint
finish (sometimes patterned), sold in rolls and
frequently laid loose on floorboards.

Furthermore, there were special industrial floors
which of course could withstand much higher
loads than standard screeds and made no
claims regarding their appearance. The following were in common use:

· Granolithic cement screeds: three layers –
approx. 50 mm lean concrete, 30 mm cement
screed and 5 – 20 mm topping of cement
containing mineral or metallic additives;
divided into bays measuring max. 10 x 10 m,
joints filled with asphalt.
· Xylolite boards: similar to flooring cement but
factory-pressed to form tiles which are then
laid in a 10 mm mortar bed; tile sizes: 160 x
160 or 195 x 195 mm, 12–26 mm thick.
· Mastic and hard asphalt: floor covering comprising asphalt, asphaltic limestone and sand;
surface becomes soft at a temperature of
≥ 35 °C; hard asphalt includes granite, grey-
wacke or basalt; surface becomes soft at a
temperature of ≥ 70 °C; a thickness ≥ 40 mm
is regarded as watertight, therefore waterproofing and floor covering can be provided
with one material.
· End-grain wood-block flooring: a type of floor
frequently used at that time, blocks of Scots
pine or larch 40–100 mm high, square or rectangular in section (60 x 165 mm), factory-
impregnated with tar oil, also available in the
form of prefabricated panels measuring 320 x
500 or 320 x 1000 mm; bonded to concrete
substrate with liquid bitumen, joints filled with
sand.
· Iron plates: 20 mm thick solid cast iron;
"Mammoth Plate" made from 8 mm cast iron,
500 x 500 mm; "Metal Armour Plate" made
from 3 mm sheet steel, 300 x 300 mm; chequer-
plate surface; laid in a bed of cement mortar.

Plasters, renders, paints

Between 1920 and 1940 pure gypsum and
gypsum-lime (1:1) plasters started to be used
more and more for plasterwork in addition to
lime plasters. Pure gypsum plasters were applied in one coat, hard gypsum plasters in two
coats. In the case of the latter, the 5 mm thick
finish coat of finely ground gypsum is very hard
and therefore particularly suitable for spandrel
panels and the bases of walls. Lime, lime-cement
and cement mortar mixed with lime and sand
were used for render. In addition, factory-
mixed, pigmented, dry mortars had been used
increasingly since 1900 for decorative purposes. Applied in a total thickness of 40 mm thick,
they can be worked after they have hardened,
e.g. chiselled, bush-hammered, pointed, to
create the impression of stone. All renders are
applied in at least two coats with an undercoat
thickness of approx. 20 mm.
Besides limewashes, water glass paints – an
invention of Adolf Wilhelm Keim from Munich
(1880) – were now being used outdoors. Water
glass is a solution of sodium or potassium
silicate in water. It creates an insoluble bond
between pigment and substrate. Such paints
are known today as silicate or mineral paints
and their advantage over limewashes is their
improved light fastness with equally good
adhesion. Contrasting with this, paints based
on linseed oil form a film on the surface and are
used on wood (windows) and steel, rarely on
render/plaster. Absorbent substrates such as
render/plaster and timber are primed with a
severely thinned primer, i.e. steeped in linseed
oil. In the 19th century lead was normally added
to accelerate the drying, but in the period
1920–40 this was replaced by cobalt or manganese (desiccant). Oil-based paints tend to crack
when applied too thickly or to form a skin when
they absorb too much oxygen. They are water-
repellent, which is why they were used on
facades, but vapour-permeable.
Distempers based on vegetable or bone glues
were common interior paints. They remain water-
soluble even after drying and are therefore able
to absorb and release water vapour permanently.

Damage and measures
Which type of plaster, render or paint has been
used can be determined by way of laboratory
tests, possibly also by an experienced, skilled
worker. In principle, the refurbishment of plaster,
render or paint does not cause any problems
when the same system is used again. Problems
can occur, however, when weaknesses in the
original finishes have to be rectified through the
use of other materials:

· The elasticity of each coat of plaster/render
must increase from the undercoat to the finish
coat, or at least be identical; this rules out, for
example, applying a new finish coat containing cement to an undercoat based on lime
because this will lead to cracking. All old
plaster/render should therefore be removed
first. Covering the entire area with a reinforcing mesh represents an alternative, popular
solution. However, it is important to ensure
that new render is vapour-permeable because
otherwise the new finishes – mesh, new
render, paint – can become detached from
the old render.
· Oil-based paints on timber cannot always be
refurbished with new paints. The linseed oil
seeps into the timber to such a depth that it
cannot be entirely removed even by sanding
and treating with solvents. Vapours of fats or
esters then can no longer escape and form
blisters beneath the new synthetic resin or
acrylic paints. Oil-based varnishes – which
are now being produced again – are recommended when renovating such surfaces. Oil-
based paints on steel, on the other hand, can
be painted over with synthetic resin or acrylic
paints after rubbing down the old coating.
· Limewashes do not flake off, but tend to
wear. Overpainting with a resin dispersion is
not recommended because the new coat of
paint does not adhere to the old. Potassium
water glass paints represent a good solution
because they bond with the lime substrate.
· Distempers are not waterproof and therefore
cannot be overpainted. They must be
washed off completely.
· Facade surfaces steeped in oil may have
become so hard in the meantime that they
cannot be removed without damaging the sur-

C 3.34

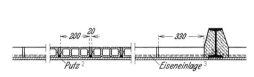

C 3.35

face. The current state of knowledge suggests that an additional mineral paint system following application of a bond enhancer based on water glass can achieve a good result.

Stairs

It was in the new houses of the housing estates of the inter-war years that the staircases were treated as a purely functional area, the size of which was minimised to the benefit of other "more useful" spaces. Stairs with winders, extreme pitches and little headroom were the outcome. The recommended pitch formula of 2 x rise + going = 630 mm was ignored in favour of steeper stairs; rises of 200 mm were common and even with a rise of 220 mm the staircase was still regarded as "usable". The normal headroom of 2.10 m was in some cases reduced to 1.85 m. Spacious entrance areas also became a thing of the past. All these matters present problems today because the only solution is demolition and the redesign of all the areas affected. Reinforced concrete began to replace the dressed stone steps of the preceding years. And when dressed stones cantilevering from the side wall were still required, at least the landings were reinforced concrete with steel members supporting the edges not supported by the walls. Imitations of dressed stone steps in reinforced concrete were also available, but the stair form most frequently encountered is the form we still use today – an inclined reinforced concrete slab with integral steps. The risers were mostly worked subsequently by a mason and the treads were often finished with linoleum or wood (Fig. C 3.32).

Stairs in factories had to comply with a different set of rules. In terms of width, pitch and headroom they comply with current standards. Cantilevering stone steps were not permitted here. Reinforced concrete stringers or spine beams supporting concrete or stone steps were generally favoured. Safety regulations such as hydrants, smoke vents operated from ground floor level and staircase doors that do not constrict the escape route had become standard for industrial buildings. The fitting-out, construction and conception rarely need refurbishment in the case of conversion apart from where mechanical damage has occurred and where

the concrete cover to reinforcement is inadequate (similarly to concrete floor slabs, see p. 167).

Roof spaces

During the 1920s the roof space took on a new significance in small and medium-sized housing. The roof space started to be used more and more purely for economical reasons. The roof surfaces were sometimes continued down into the upper floor and provided with gables. Two aspects now became important: reliable waterproofing for the flat roofs to dormer windows, and functioning thermal insulation in lightweight timber construction. Further technical innovations appeared in timber engineering, which now also permitted the use of connections in tension.

Roof structure

Roof structures were not so very different to those of the founding years. The standardisation of cross-sections and structural calculations, however, led to more slender components that are more advantageous for a roof space conversion. Rafter cross-sections range from 60 x 100 mm to 120 x 140 mm. These are usually inadequate for the additional loads of the interior fitting-out and the new roof covering and much too small for accommodating thermal insulation between the rafters (see also "General refurbishment tasks", pp. 127–129).

The new dowelled connections and glued trusses represented important advances in timber engineering. The shear-plate, split-ring and toothed-plate connectors still used today permitted the fabrication of inexpensive, tension-resistant connections for long-span trussed girders in timber. Because these – like all the innovations of these years – were put to many practical uses, a number of long-span shed roofs were erected in the inter-war years, but sometimes clad in such a way that they looked like solid constructions. This leads us to suspect that some constructions of this type still exist in areas that were spared the ravages of the war. One distinctive design was the "Zollinger" roof patented by Friedrich Zollinger in 1910. The diagonal, intersecting members

(so-called lamellas) support and stabilise each other and hence form a timber lattice shell. The members measure 25 x 150 x 1950 mm or (for long spans) 50 x 300 x 2500 mm and are offset at the joints so that the three intersecting members can be connected with just one bolt. Some of these roofs are still in existence, e.g. the elephant house at Leipzig Zoo. In the event of a fire, these slender sections fail very quickly, and the bolted connections gradually loosen if not regularly maintained. A similar construction was fabricated in 1928, also with aluminium members (Juncker's Zollinger roof), i.e. the timber construction was transferred to steel construction – it's normally the other way around (Figs. C 3.30 and 3.31).

The "Kroher" roof was yet another innovation. Erected for the first time in Munich in 1938, it was a three-dimensional trussed framework of timber lattice girders nailed together such that t needed no further longitudinal bracing. It was intended for spans > 15 m where intervening supports were inconvenient.

In 1906 Otto Hetzer applied for a patent in Weimar for the gluing of individual timber laminations together to form new, curved cross-sections for spanning long distances. His contemporaries discouraged the use of glue, however, although it promised to improve the load-bearing action by 25 %, and advocated nailing the cross-sections instead [13]. But the recommendations that only specialised companies be allowed to fabricate the glued, laminated cross-sections and that the assemblies be especially protected against wetting show that this method was not yet ready for mass production.

American forms of timber construction such as "balloon framing" had already been around for more than 50 years, but it was only now that they began to enter the German market and be adapted to German building methods. The platform-frame and panel forms of construction already standardised in the USA and Australia promised industrial prefabrication, the use of unskilled labour on site and reduced consumption of materials but at the same time better stiffness than conventional methods of timber-frame construction. New building materials such as lightweight wood-wool boards allowed

C 3.34   House for Albert Einstein, Caputh (D), 1929,
          Konrad Wachsmann
C 3.35   Flat roof in the form of a cold deck for an
          industrial building
          ([1] 2 layers of roofing felt, [2] Plaster, [3] Reinforcement)
C 3.36   Conversion of a former factory building dating
          from 1925 into offices, Cologne (D), 2001,
          4000architekten

a   b   C 3.36

the construction of thermally insulated timber structures which, because they were rendered, appeared like solid constructions. Konrad Wachsmann's house for Albert Einstein in Caputh (1929) is not a log construction, even though it appears to be at first glance, but instead makes use of the new, prefabricated, panel and platform-frame methods. The cross-sections used (wall: 60 x 120 mm every 800 mm) do not comply with modern requirements. Moreover, only a few of the buildings from the "new age" of timber construction still remain standing today (Fig. C 3.34).

Roof coverings

The roof coverings of the 19th century did not undergo any significant changes. Bullnose tiles remained the commonest roof covering, but the use of interlocking clay tiles grew during the 1920s. Since the 1930s at the latest, the flat roof has polarised opinions: either regarded as modern or as a "faux pas of taste that disrupts the landscape in the coarsest possible way" [14]. Only for industrial buildings did it become accepted as a low-cost, appropriate roofing form, not entrapped by any ideology. Two or three layers of tarred felt with pitches around 10 % and drainage external to the building via gutters and downpipes was the standard form. Many roofs were built as cold decks, with a relatively large void (crawl space) between the topmost floor and the roof waterproofing. The solid roofs often made use of pumice concrete planks to save weight; 70 mm deep planks could span up to 2.3 m [15] and were sometimes supported on concrete-encased steel beams. A timber framework laid to a fall was built off the solid roof and then waterproofed with felt impregnated with tar or asphalt. To achieve the desired appearance of a true flat roof, the gable walls were frequently raised above the eaves walls to conceal the slope of the roof (Fig. C 3.35).
Double layers of waterproofing on rooftop dormers was a popular solution. The standardised products in use were tarred felt made from distilled coal tar and bitumenised tar felt made from coal tar and natural asphalt. The use of bitumen (crude oil distillation) was, however, still not customary although this could already

be produced on an industrial scale (Ruberoid felt). The polycyclic aromatic hydrocarbons (PAH) contained in tar are regarded as carcinogenic and are released upon heating in particular. The flat roof waterproofing materials of the inter-war years should have long since been replaced because the surface normally becomes brittle after a short time or the backing material (felt) rots. Nevertheless, any "genuine" tarred felts that are found should be completely removed and disposed of in accordance with the appropriate safety regulations. This is because the adhesion between tarred felts and the bituminous felts used today cannot be guaranteed (even though they are supposed to be compatible), and also removal and disposal in the future will be even more expensive.

Conversion of industrial and commercial buildings

The conversion of empty industrial facilities into new housing or offices is one type of project frequently carried out these days. Helped by the fact that these former utility spaces are in the meantime located near town and city centres, they have become popular properties. The problems in the conversion lie in the fundamentally different requirements of the past and future users: whereas at that time stability and dryness were the only important factors, the buildings must now also satisfy higher standards and more stringent regulations.
It is not usually necessary to upgrade the structure because the suspended floors were designed for much higher loads (Fig. C.3.23). But upgrading the fire protection to comply with today's regulations can be very difficult. This applies to structural steelwork in particular, but reinforced concrete structures are also affected because the concrete cover to reinforcement is less than that required today. Furthermore, the relaxations of the "open-plan rule" of the building regulations often no longer apply. If the entire floor area is to be preserved as a whole, exemptions from the fire protection regulations will have to be negotiated, and compensated for by installing, for example, fire detectors, additional escape stairs or smoke vents.
In addition, impact sound insulation must be

improved because the floor finish is likely to be in the form of a bonded screed, which was adequate for the previous uses. Adding a new floating screed is not usually a problem from the structural viewpoint, but does lead to steps at the stairs that are architecturally and functionally unacceptable. The installation of a raised access floor is one alternative, raising the floor level by an amount equal to one step of the existing stairs. This also eases the problem of the installation of the additional pipes and cables needed for the converted premises. The problems of upgrading the thermal insulation for this type of structure are dealt with in the chapter "General refurbishment tasks" (see p. 122–124). For the architect, however, the most important challenge is retaining the expanse and spaciousness of the floor areas in the interior fitting-out – many users require partitions to form individual offices or rooms. Preserving the special character of these interiors therefore calls for good cooperation between architect, building owner and users, all of whom must be prepared to compromise.

Notes:

[1]   Schmidt, Paul: Handbuch des Hochbaus. Nord-
       hausen, 1926 (new ed. by Hugo Ebinghaus), p. 542
[2]   Ahnert, Rudolf; Krause, Karl Heinz: Typische Bau-
       konstruktionen von 1860 bis 1960. vol. 1, Berlin,
       2006
[3]   DIN 1055 Belastungsannahmen im Hochbau, 1934;
       DIN 1050, 1051, 1053 Berechnungsgrundlagen für
       Stahl, Gusseisen und Mauerwerk, 1937
[4]   ibid. [1]
[5]   Heideck, Erich; Leppin, Otto: Der Industriebau.
       Berlin, 1933, p. 1
[6]   Berlin Building Regulations, 1929, cl. 27
[7]   Kommentar zur Bauordnung von Berlin. Berlin,
       1931
[8]   Schönermark, Gustav; Stüber, Wilhelm: Hochbau
       Lexikon. Berlin, c. 1900, p. 644
[9]   Ebinghaus, Hugo: Der Hochbau. Gießen, 1936,
       p. 135
[10]   ibid. [1], p. 27
[11]   Breymann, Gustav Adolf et al.: Allgemeine
       Baukonstruktionslehre. Leipzig, 1903, pp. 65–72
       Esselborn: Lehrbuch des Hochbaus. 2 vols.
       Leipzig, 1922, pp. 721–810
[12]   ibid. [1] Esselborn, p. 781
[13]   ibid. [1], p. 303ff.
[14]   ibid. [1], p. 303ff.
[15]   A depth of 80 mm enables a span of 2.60 m,
       90 mm a span of 3.10 m.

Buildings of the post-war years 1950–1965

Georg Giebeler

C 4.1

Looking back from today, the post-war period spans some 15 years, from 1945 to 1960. But from the point of view of developments in the economy and construction, we can distinguish between two phases: pre- and post-1952. This chapter concentrates on the construction in the second of these two phases.

The period 1945–1952, i.e. the years between the end of the war and the onset of the *Wirtschaftswunder*, the "economic miracle", are dominated by the direct consequences of World War 2: hunger, unemployment, rubble clearance – simply the will to survive. On the level of world politics, it was the beginning of the end of the colonial era (Indian independence in 1948, France's defeat in the Indo-Chinese War in 1954), the splitting of the world into two power blocs (Korean War, 1950–53), and it was the time of radical reforms (currency reforms in West and East Germany in 1948; land reforms: East Germany in 1945, West Germany in 1947). In Europe a gigantic rebuilding programme was set in motion, the Marshall Plan, which between 1947 and 1952 provided approx. 14 billion dollars for Western Europe (3.6 billion for the UK, 3.1 billion for France, 1.6 billion for Italy, 1.4 billion for West Germany and 0.7 billion for western Austria). For the economy of the USA, the only country that had been spared the terrible destruction of World War 2, that meant the chance to export its overproduction, and for Europe a chance to activate economic growth. The years after 1952, on the other hand, are known in Germany as the *Wirtschaftswunderjahre*, the "years of the economic miracle". The national economy and also private prosperity grew at a pace that has never been seen since: in 1955 alone economic growth amounted to 10 %, real earnings grew by a similar amount and the number of new cars on the road increased by 19 %. Whereas at the end of 1940 some two million people were still out of work, by the mid-1950s the first migrant workers were arriving in West Germany to make up the shortfall in labour. The gross national product doubled between 1950 and 1960, and exports quadrupled, which put West Germany in second place in the list of economic powers. Similar phenomena were witnessed in all the countries that benefited from the Marshall Plan, but not in the Eastern Bloc coun-

tries dependent on the Soviet Union. The enormous economic growth continued into the 1960s, but then began to weaken gradually, leading in 1966 to the first post-war recession in West Germany.

The building industry, too, played its part in the economic boom, although there were no fundamental reforms. In his book *Deutsche Architekten. Biographische Verflechtungen 1900–1970* (German architects. Biographical entanglements 1900–1970), the architecture theoretician Werner Durth describes the period from 1920 to 1960 more as a continuum rather than three independent epochs [1]. It is therefore hardly surprising when attitudes, ideologies and forms of construction resemble each other. In the urban planning of the 1950s it was the motif of the "structured and unfettered town" that was pursued, i.e. practically the same idea as that behind the garden city. The "functional town", an expression from the Charter of Athens published in 1941, was actually implemented after the war. Even during the war, plans were being drawn up for towns and cities that would be more suitable for motor traffic, also the functional division into residential, industrial and recreational areas – to a certain extent still contrasting with the towns and cities of the founding years, now almost 100 years old.

The destruction of the war provided the opportunity to realise those plans. In the first years after the war it was practically only the mountains of rubble that grew! Throughout Europe, there was an extreme shortage of housing, whereas 75 % of industrial facilities were intact and production could have begun again if the infrastructure and labour forces had been directly available. The population of Germany in 1950 was approx. 68 million, five million more than in 1925, and they urgently needed new housing. And it was precisely the form of the "structured and unfettered town" that was intended to help here, with rows of housing instead of perimeter blocks, and with generous open spaces between them. In Germany this phase of providing new housing began with the 1st Housebuilding Act of 1950, which facilitated the building of public-sector housing. Besides specifying the sizes of apartments (32–65 m²) this legislation also laid down a maximum rent of 1 DM/m², and it must be borne in mind that the monthly take-home pay of workers at that time was generally less than DM 200. The actual wording of the Act was as follows:

a) Confined living conditions curtail performance at work, both physically and mentally. The ongoing improvement of these conditions is an indispensable prerequisite for the recovery of the German economy.
b) As a result of the shortage of housing, many jobs for skilled workers, mainly in commerce and industry, remain vacant despite the fact that 1.5 million are out of work.
c) As a key industry, the building sector forms the suitable starting point for combating unemployment in general. [2]

By 1954 the number of apartments in West Germany had reached the pre-war level. The statistics for Baden-Württemberg reveal that during the 1950s approx. 70 000 apartments with a total floor space of 5 million m² were built every year. By way of comparison, it is only about half that number today, but with a total floor space amounting to 4 million m². This difference is also reflected in the average size of apartments: in 1950 every occupant had 14 m² of floor space, a figure that rose to 19 m² in 1960, 37 m² in 1990 and today stands at approx. 42 m² per occupant, i.e. three times the 1950 figure.

One special case from the functional viewpoint was the many hostels built. As it was necessary to be near to your place of work, many people had to move because in those early post-war years there were very few private cars and little local public transport. Separate hostels were built for displaced persons and ethnic German emigrants from other countries (in the 1950s almost three million workers left the GDR), also for orphans, mothers raising their families alone, apprentices and students.

One special case from the constructional viewpoint was the reconstruction with "direct recycling". One strategy widely used in the war was setting fire to densely built inner-city districts, which resulted in the total destruction of the apartments with their timber joist floors, but left basements virtually undamaged and indeed even led to "gutted" buildings with essentially intact loadbearing masonry (Fig. C 4.2). These only partially destroyed buildings were initially rebuilt, supplemented with any still usable clay bricks that could be found among the mountains of rubble. When planning a conversion it is therefore important to realise that older methods of construction may still exist in such buildings, mainly in inner-city areas.

Typical strengths and weaknesses
Many buildings on the new residential estates built during the 1950s still attract good prices even though they are seldom located near town centres. The reason for their popularity is the idea of the "unfettered" town and the generous implementation of the demands of the Modern

Movement: functional, sunny, airy, green. Rarely are the buildings more than four storeys high and the clear layout and easy access create neighbourhood-like communities. Almost all apartments have either a balcony or loggia and the distances to adjacent buildings are generous. Amenities such as churches, pre-school facilities, schools and shops are often located in the residential districts, enabling each estate to function as an autonomous unit. The housing estates of the 1950s favoured small-format developments, especially when compared to the large estates built 20 years later (Fig. C 4.8). The small apartments, with their extremely functional layouts, reflect a chief virtue of the post-war years: thriftiness. The dimensions given in Ernst Neufert's *Architects' Data* – these days understood to be minimum sizes – were certainly more like average values in those days [3]. Children's rooms measuring 6 m² are no longer planned, but back in the 1950s a room or even a whole apartment for one person alone was regarded by many people as a luxury. A similar small scale prevailed in kitchens and bathrooms, too; above all, the clear ceiling height was reduced by a further 200 mm compared to the pre-war period – to 2.50 m. This confinement, coupled with loadbearing internal walls (short spans to save money), make conversions difficult, and indeed removing internal walls reinforces the effect of the low ceilings. Frugality was likewise the first rule of construction: shortages of energy and materials (e.g. shortage of wood) led to very economical forms of construction; in addition, the introduction of new components and forms of construction designed to save materials, especially in lightweight masonry, had an impact. The first German legislation on energy-saving construction (DIN 4108) was published in July 1952. Architects were well aware of the weaknesses associated with the methods used for suspended floors, roof structures, roof coverings and windows, and the frugal sizes used, but economical use of materials or heating energy was the priority. Modern conversions therefore have to face problems of poor sound insulation (also the external components) and the lack of reserves in the load-carrying capacity, which mean that additional loads due to refurbishment measures are not permitted.
The materials-saving credo became less significant as the economy grew. Rising wages and better supplies led to the labour-intensive, but materials-saving forms of construction disappearing again towards the end of the 1950s. More and more, forms of construction were assessed from the quality viewpoint. For example, 1959 saw the publication of DIN 4109 Part 1, which specified minimum requirements for impact sound insulation. However, even by the mid-1960s, building technology had not seen any real changes. Multi-layer, insulated external wall components and the triumph of the in situ concrete floor slab did not set new standards until the end of that decade.

C 4.2

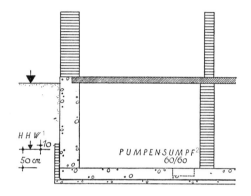

a

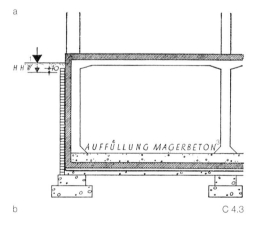

b

C 4.3

C 4.4

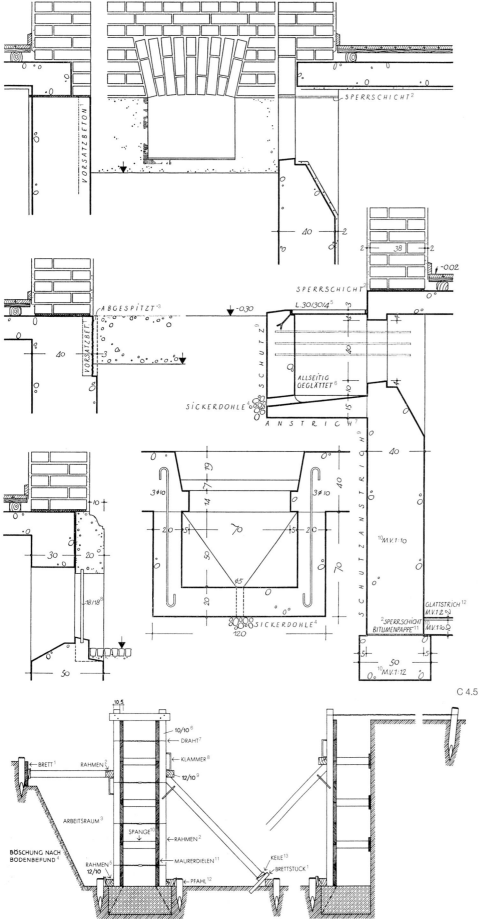

C 4.5

C 4.6

Conversion potential

In terms of conception and urban planning, many buildings dating from the post-war years benefit from good lighting and ample surrounding greenery. The forms of construction, however, exhibit many weaknesses that make conversions awkward. Nevertheless, conversion is still worthwhile in many instances. At the moment there is a backlog of post-war buildings awaiting refurbishment, and those buildings are the main focus of this chapter.

Basements

The weaknesses of the basements of the pre-war years, which can still be found under post-war buildings, have already been discussed in the previous chapters. Many basements built after the war no longer suffer from these weaknesses. Not only had waterproofing using bitumen or asphalt materials become customary in the meantime, but the quality of the workmanship had also improved noticeably. Nevertheless, damp external walls and, in particular, damp basement floors can be found again and again. The reason for this was the poor availability and hence high prices of high-quality waterproofing materials, which is why a "barrier" of cement render had to suffice in many cases. However, as basements were still typically used mainly for storage, this low-cost solution was legitimate.

Foundations and ground floor slabs

It is interesting that the literature of the time now covered special foundations and waterproofing against groundwater in detail [4]. All types of pile foundations replaced the caisson foundations that had been common hitherto. Supporting the sides of excavations and the use of pumps to remove the groundwater had now become customary methods. Shallow foundations were mostly in the form of strip footings. The material typically used was plain tamped concrete in grade B 50 (later B 5, today no longer covered by any standard), which with a stepped foundation was cast in layers 300 mm deep (= tamping depth). Masonry foundations built using hard-burned or even clay bricks picked out from the rubble are certainly possible, and, interestingly, these are stepped at a shallower angle (45 ° instead of 60 °) [5]. The raft foundations common these days were not usual back then; even reinforced foundations were a real exception. Damage to foundations is rather rare because the buildings were not so tall and therefore did not place heavy loads on the subsoil. If, however, poorly fired clay bricks or bricks rescued from the rubble are found in the foundations, it is advisable to investigate them for their durability. The following quote from a 1951 textbook on building illustrates the will to save of those years: "On good subsoil it is sufficient to widen the foundation by 50 mm either side of the wall. This widening also makes it easier to set up the formwork for the concrete and is also provided

Country	Clay brick format		
	Length [cm]	Width [cm]	Height [cm]
Belgium	28.8	13.8	8.8
Germany	24.0	11.5	7.1
England	21.0	10.0	6.5
France	22.0	10.5	6.5
Italy	21.0	10.0	6.5
Netherlands	24.0	11.5	7.1
Austria	25.0	12.0	6.5
Switzerland	25.0	12.0	6.0

C 4.7

C 4.8

C 4.5 External wall to basement in tamped concrete, sections and elevation
([1]Conc. lining, [2]DPC, [3]Chiselled off, [4]Soakaway, [5]L 30 x 30 x 4, [6]All sides trowelled smooth, [7]Coating, [8]18 x 18, [9]Protective coating, [10]Mix, [11]Bitumen felt, [12]Trowelled topping)

C 4.6 External wall to basement in tamped concrete cast between formwork both sides (left) or directly against the soil on one side (right)
([1]Thrust pad, [2]Framing, [3]Working space, [4]Slope depends on soil conditions, [5]Framing 12 x 10, [6]10 x 10, [7]Wire tie, [8]Cramp, [9]12 x 10, [10]Spacer, [11]Planks, [12]Stake, [13]Wedges)

C 4.7 European clay brick formats in the post-war period

C 4.8 Apartment blocks on the Stegerwald Estate, Cologne (D), 1951–56

even when it is not necessary for structural purposes, … this is another possibility for making savings in small houses" (Fig. C 4.5) [6]. Almost all basement floors of the post-war years were of concrete. As these were floors for ancillary purposes, not required to support any heavy loads, they were correspondingly low-cost elements: 100 mm thick, unreinforced, low-grade concrete slabs were very common. The trowelled topping, similar to a monolithic screed, offered no more resistance to rising damp than the concrete slab below.

"Tanking", i.e. waterproofing basement floors and walls with flexible bituminous or synthetic sheeting, had already advanced considerably by this time. Such waterproofing membranes were, however, used only where groundwater was expected, and waterproofing to walls and floors was omitted even on sloping sites. The problems often encountered and their remedies are described in the chapter on buildings of the founding years (see p. 134). Where it was used, the tanking can be regarded as reliable (Fig. C 4.3). Transitions, junctions, steps, fillets and radii and the methods used in general would still apply today if tanking was still employed. The fact that many of these tanked basements have developed leaks is due to the quality of the waterproofing materials used. The standardised waterproofing materials frequently used felt or jute backings, so-called uncoated bitumen or tarred felts. However, these backing materials can become saturated with water and then rot; they then lose their strength and the waterproofing develops cracks. Rotproof glass fleece and synthetic sheeting was still at the development stage in the post-war years and correspondingly expensive; in addition, skilled workers capable of laying such sheeting so that it would remain permanently waterproof were in short supply. As waterproofing against hydrostatic pressure was laid on the outside of the building, refurbishment is not possible. Refurbishment by way of new internal waterproofing is just as unreliable because to guarantee watertightness all internal walls have to be separated from the perimeter walls, which leads to severe stability problems. The economics of such measures should therefore be examined for their reasonableness.

External walls to basements
Masonry or tamped concrete was used for the external walls, the latter 300–400 mm thick. The high material consumption of the past – solid clay brick masonry based on statutory provisions – now had to be minimised. Making the external walls of the basement thinner meant that the depth of the basement below ground level – and not just the number of storeys above – now became critical for the design because of the lateral earth pressure (Fig. C 4.6). A wall thickness of 240 mm was permitted (new dimensional coordination, see "External walls", p. 176), but only up to a height difference of max. 1.25 m between ground level and top of basement floor. Deeper basements required a wall thickness of at least 365 mm.

It would seem that the technique of casting concrete directly against the soil already mentioned in the chapter on buildings of the interwar years (see p. 157) continued to be widely used after the war as well. The wooden spacers were removed as tamping proceeded, so at least this weakness was eliminated. As the external wall could not be further waterproofed with render or coatings, ingress of water was very likely, e.g. through construction joints. The proposals for waterproofing against rising and infiltrating moisture that were made up until 1960 but not standardised (except DIN 4031: "Water pressure-resistant sealing...") nevertheless correspond roughly to today's provisions:

• horizontal waterproofing with bituminous felts or similar above basement floor level
• horizontal waterproofing 300 mm above ground level (= splashing water zone)
• vertical waterproofing of external walls up to the top of the foundations

A damp-proof membrane (dpm) below the basement floor and a damp-proof course (dpc) in the masonry to protect against rising damp were, however, not customary at this time. Furthermore, the aforementioned waterproofing was only intended for "basements in which goods sensitive to water are stored or those containing rooms for persons" [7]. Accordingly, we must assume that these measures were often not carried out. And where waterproofing

was provided, less suitable materials were used, e.g. two coats of cement render as vertical waterproofing, or uncoated bituminous felt, butt-jointed without overlaps, as a horizontal membrane. Even on sloping sites, cement render plus drains was regarded as adequate to protect against the infiltration of moisture from the soil, with the porous clay pipes available, 40–200 mm in diameter, simply laid loosely to a fall adjacent to one another. The lack of flushing points, filter mats and protective measures during backfilling lead us to believe that it is hardly likely that such drainage is still functioning today.

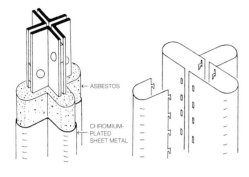

C 4.13

C 4.13 Fire protection to a compound steel column in the form of sprayed asbestos clad in chromium-plated sheet metal
C 4.14 Class F 120 fire protection to a steel column in the form of plastered lightweight concrete blocks plus concrete filling
C 4.15 Reinforcement in a frame-type industrial structure

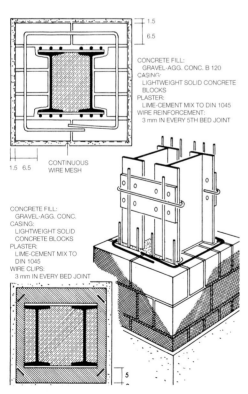

C 4.14

background for plaster and render. This explains their domination of the market well into the 1960s. The magnesite-bonded wood-wool board had been invented in 1908 and manufactured on an industrial scale since the 1930s. The cement-bonded board was invented around the same time but was not produced on a large scale until after the war.

The industrial production of mineral wool insulating materials began in the USA in the 1930s but in Europe they were not fully developed into useful products until after 1955. At first the batts were very heavy (approx. 0.08 kN/m² per 10 mm thickness instead of the 0.01 kN/m² usual today) and therefore in terms of their insulating effect they were comparable with lightweight wood-wool products. Although improved methods of production halved their weight, mineral wool insulating materials did not become established in the marketplace because they were unsuitable as a plaster or render background. In roof spaces as well, lightweight wood-wool boards nailed to the underside of the rafters and then plastered over were preferred to insulation between the rafters. Mineral wool insulating materials were therefore mainly used for improving the room acoustics, i.e. in conjunction with acoustic ceilings and boards. It was not until impact sound insulation became mandatory in 1959 that mineral wool started to be used widely as impact sound insulation in conjunction with floating screeds. In this type of application the lack of biosolubility (cancer risk) of the fibrous materials used is unimportant and can be ignored during refurbishment work, provided the floor screed remains in place.

Cellular glass, too, developed around 1935 in Saint-Gobain, did not become relevant for construction until the early 1960s. It was used as thermal insulation for the flat roofs that were now starting to dominate and replaced the cork insulation that had been used up until then, which in contrast to cellular glass could rot.

Damage and measures

In the past, weaknesses in the external walls had been virtually unknown, but the frugal use of lightweight materials in the buildings of the post-war years now resulted in mediocre thermal insulation and thermal mass, saturated materials, unsatisfactory fixing options and poor sound insulation.

The minimum thermal insulation specified for the first time in 1952 in DIN 4108 divided Germany into thermal insulation areas I – III, each of which had its own limiting values (Figs. C 4.11 and 4.12). The k-values (today U-values) specified did not, however, set a high energy standard, but instead were based on the poor insulating values of solid clay brickwork. For example, in the DIN standard 250 mm thick hollow block masonry was considered to be equivalent to a 460 mm thick solid clay brick wall. According to the corresponding tables, 240 mm thick external walls made from solid lightweight concrete masonry units (density 1.0 MN/m³) were also suitable for area III (mountainous regions).

As even the walls of the founding years do not correspond to the requirements of the latest Energy Conservation Act, this is certainly also the case for the lightweight wool constructions of the post-war years. Added to this is the fact that, for example, capping beams and lintels were cast in normal-weight concrete, which despite the lightweight wood-wool boards laid in the formwork still constituted thermal bridges. Walls in lightweight construction exhibit a lower thermal mass, but in everyday use this does not represent a disadvantage. The low values of DIN 4108 were first improved in 1974 after the oil crisis. Up until that year we must assume that the standard of external components is no better than the DIN 4108 provisions. The application of new external insulation, a typical refurbishment measure these days, is dealt with in the chapter entitled "General refurbishment measures" (see pp. 122–124).

The porous materials are vulnerable to saturation due to driving rain and rising damp, although the occurrence of both phenomena together is rare. As the masonry units form a good substrate for render, and rendering was carried out very carefully at this time, problems with render are unusual. The cement renders continuing out of the ground have mostly been worked (e.g. chiselled) along the bases of walls and so provide protection against moisture. The problem of saturation was known to the architects of the time, which is why they raised habitable storeys above the splashing water zone, i.e. at least 500 mm above ground level. And as the external walls to basements were not built in lightweight masonry (solid clay brickwork or normal-weight concrete), the risk of saturation in the ground and upper storeys was correspondingly reduced, even when damp-proof courses were not completely watertight.

No tensile loads and only low compressive loads can be introduced into hollow block or lightweight concrete masonry. Even the mounting of cupboards on the wall can lead to problems, not to mention a secure anchorage for an intruder-resistant entrance door or the fixings for cantilevering components such as canopies or awnings. Concentrated compressive loads can be transferred relatively easily and safely into the wall by means of bearing pads, e.g. steel plates. But tensile loads are more difficult to handle: the permissible tensile loads on wall anchors are limited to such an extent (0.3–0.8 kN for hollow masonry units, up to 1.7 kN for solid masonry units, and 2.0 kN for lightweight concrete) that, in conjunction with the stipulated minimum hole spacing of 200 mm, even trying to attach a canopy projecting more than 1 m is doomed to failure. In this case the anchor systems can only secure the plate below the canopy against uplift forces. Above the canopy, it may be possible to provide a fixing that passes through the wall, with plates to spread the loads on both the inside and outside of the wall. In the case of a sufficiently deep in situ concrete slab, one alternative worth investigating is a tension anchorage in the edge of the floor slab, but the minimum edge distances of such anchors must be taken into account. The airborne sound insulation – also that of the 240 mm thick internal walls such as those around staircases and between apartments – was unsatisfactory with the new forms of light-weight construction. The "bad soundproofing" of these apartments was general knowledge at the time and that is why the first draft of DIN 4109 appeared in 1959, followed later by further standards on impact sound insulation and the acoustic properties of building materials. A 240 mm thick lightweight concrete wall achieves, for example, approx. 50 dB and is therefore (just) below the minimum requirement for party walls these days. Non-rigid, independent wall linings built in front of such walls can improve the airborne sound insulation easily and at reasonable cost. The lining in front of the wall requires approx. 100 mm space – 25 mm air cavity, 50 mm fully insulated framing, 2 No. 12.5 mm plasterboard (see "Building physics", pp. 42–47). Similar forms of construction for the subsequent improvement of sound insulation were already being discussed in the trade literature of the post-war years [10].

Window openings
The masonry arch, like the vault, rapidly lost its significance. At best, cambered arches were still built, supplemented by the various types of clad steel or reinforced concrete lintels that now dominated the market.

The usual technique with lightweight masonry was to employ specially shaped bricks filled with concrete. The bricks were of lightweight concrete and usually included a nib for mounting the window. Precast concrete lintels were still very rare because suitable hoisting equipment was then necessary, which in those days was not typical on small building sites.

The widespread use of solid in situ concrete slabs, possibly with in situ concrete perimeter beams, led to window lintels being cast monolithically with these other in situ concrete elements. Sometimes the fascia panels to roller shutter housings were also included in this concreting work. They therefore might be only 50 mm thick – when not just a Rabitz background plus render! The reinforcing bars were laid in the lintel and connected to the floor reinforcement. During refurbishment these fascia panels are more of a nuisance than a help because the lintel cannot be simply cut back, which means that the clear window height has to be reduced (see "General refurbishment measures", p. 123). On the other hand, the low concrete cover of 20 mm on external components has seldom led to damage because of the additional render.

Windows
In constructional terms the windows of the 1950s were no different to those of the 1920s (see "Buildings of the inter-war years", p. 160).

The shortfall in imports of timber from the USA (primarily pitch pine) and the poor quality of indigenous timbers in the troubled economy of the post-war period meant that most windows had to be replaced as early as the 1970s. Double glazing, a technique already known and imported from the USA, first really asserted itself after about 1975.

Internal walls and frame constructions
It was during the post-war period that the influences of the Modern Movement – its founders were primarily those who had emigrated to North America – accomplished the transfer from factory buildings to offices, schools and all other buildings where the owners wished to demonstrate their modernity. The fully glazed frame construction of reinforced concrete or steel was adapted to meet the new demands, but the challenge still was to create, for example, offices with an agreeable interior climate and services concealed in the wall, and not simply draughty warehouses with a bare structure. The techniques and experiences of the pre-war years were incorporated into the new designs and also brought about a change in methods of construction. We can therefore say that the frame structures of this period were already quite well developed, even though the frugality typical of this period means that the characteristic weaknesses of housing, e.g. poor sound insulation, excessive deflection, can still be encountered in office buildings.

Steel frames
Experiences with welded constructions and specialist skilled welders were products of wartime production. As a result, the reluctance shown towards welding disappeared and welded connections started to be specified for buildings as well – except for components subjected to dynamic loads, where welded connections were still not recommended. Despite this, riveted forms of construction were still first choice, but were gradually supplanted by bolted connections in the course of the 1950s.

Besides the stability, according to DIN 1050 (1952) it was also necessary to check the maximum deflection (1/300 for spans ≥ 5 m). Steel grades and characteristic values were the same as those before the war, i.e. grade St 37.12 for normal building applications and grade St 52 where a higher strength was required. As the imposed loads had also remained unchanged, we can assume that steel frames from the post-war years also meet modern structural engineering requirements. Where intervention is, however, necessary, and even if this intervention does only concern "subsidiary" components such as additional thermal insulation, severe difficulties can be expected because all cross-sections have been minimised. For example, in a lattice girder it was not uncommon to use different sections for every different member, each designed for its respective load.

The fire protection of the time also roughly corresponds to our modern requirements for

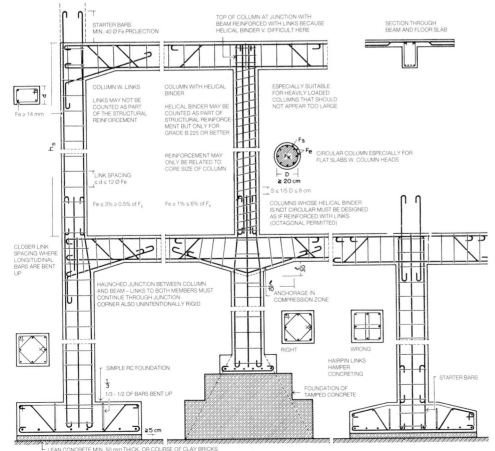

C 4.15

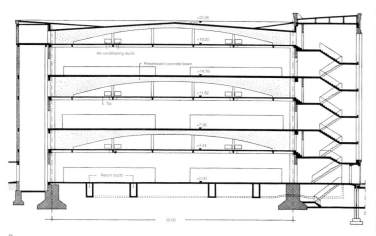

a

b

C 4.16

clad steel sections. Steel beams and columns encased in plastered masonry and with all voids filled with concrete had a minimum cover of 30 mm in the case of concrete and 60 mm for masonry. In Great Britain special bricks were available which were fitted around the flanges. Without such special bricks, though, a masonry casing was labour-intensive work with much cutting of bricks, reinforcing bars in the bed joints and a filling of gravel-aggregate concrete introduced course by course. In addition to concrete and masonry, steel sections were also protected by plaster on a Rabitz background, in some cases two layers with an intermediate air cavity (Fig. C 4.14).

Asbestos cladding products gradually became established. The carcinogenic effect of asbestos was already known and acknowledged as an occupational illness, but it was still used on a large scale well into the 1980s. Even just a thin layer of asbestos offers excellent protection in fire (class F 120 with a suspended asbestos-cement tile 10 mm thick, with 40 mm mineral wool backing), and sprayed asbestos in particular was easy to apply to steel columns. The coatings were always concealed behind ceilings, linings, etc. The removal of such coatings is unavoidable and very expensive. It is recommended to investigate the steel frames of post-war buildings, especially offices and shops. However, fire protection to the steel frames of factory buildings was not common because measures such as sprinklers (rare) and hydrants on every floor level (mandatory) meant that certificates of exemption were issued on a regular basis (Fig. C 4.13).

Reinforced concrete frames

The extensive experience of the previous decades ensured that reinforced concrete technology was properly used in the post-war period, despite economy measures:

- The minimum concrete cover was increased to 15 mm internally and 20 mm externally.
- Fewer plain reinforcing bars we used, and more profiled bars.
- Components were provided with minimum reinforcement at least, and distribution bars.
- Grading curves were now stipulated.

Reinforced concrete frames were primarily used for structures such as office buildings and warehouses because the disadvantage of the reduced flexibility – criticised from all sides – compared to steel frames was unimportant for such uses and reinforced concrete frames behaved better in fire. Whereas for steel structures it was usual to strengthen sections only upon a change of loading (e.g. adding a crane rail), higher imposed loads were assumed as a precaution in reinforced concrete structures, especially in the case of multi-storey warehouses. The labour-intensive formwork construction, the long construction times, the high timber consumption, difficulties when routing services and the lack of recycling options for the building materials after demolition were cited as further disadvantages. But reinforced concrete continued to be chosen instead of structural steelwork because of the high price of steel and the low wages of those days. Furthermore, the reason for the disappearance of haunches at beam-column junctions – even though a haunch improves the flow of forces at this point – was not because of the high cost of constructing the formwork (labour component), but because of the high timber consumption (material component) (Fig. C 3.15).

Reinforced concrete frames dating from this period are copies of steel frames, especially conspicuous because of the columns flush with the outside edges of the floor slabs. Continuous ribbon windows were not common; instead, the frame-type form of construction was highlighted by individual facade bays, with the concrete frame frequently left exposed. Spandrel panels were often of masonry or concrete. The lightweight curtain wall facade first became popular in the USA, and composite steel-concrete construction was used much more frequently in the USA than in Europe.

The prestressed concrete method, perfected by Eugène Freyssinet in the mid-1930s, was introduced into Germany by Franz Dischinger. After the war, though, it was used only for special structures with very long spans, e.g. the Perlon factory in Wuppertal, with its 35 m span, storey-deep arched beams, erected by the contractor Dywidag (Fig. C 4.16).

Damage and measures

Steel and reinforced concrete frames dating from the post-war period are in no way oversized, and in most cases are still adequate structurally; but their fire protection is limited (see p. 163). The main problem of the forms of construction built mainly for offices or similar uses is the fact that frame members are exposed on the facade, which is typical of the architecture of that period but quite naturally creates substantial thermal bridges. If the external appearance is to remain more or less intact, external insulation is ruled out because the columns usually project from the facade and the addition of insulation would make them appear even wider and totally out of scale with the rest of the building. The much-loved spandrel panels of facing masonry also prevent the addition of external insulation. The typical internal appearance, with its exposed columns and beams, is also very difficult architecturally and technically because of the many penetrations (thermal bridges). Internal insulation would also reduce the thermal mass of the walls considerably, which in turn would have a negative effect on the thermal comfort. Furthermore, internal fittings and building services are then difficult to install because the vapour barrier is penetrated. In the case of buildings protected by conservation orders this dilemma often leads – after years of controversy – to total demolition of the building because the facade cannot be refurbished economically while at the same time complying with the conservation stipulations. Facades not protected by conservation orders can be renewed with materials fitted in front of the old facade, i.e. external insulation, but the original appearance is changed completely. Similar problems occur in residential buildings with a box-frame construction where the cross-walls continue through to the outside of the facade to form a feature. Even when, as shown in contemporary details, insulation in the form of lightweight wood-wool or aerated concrete boards has been provided, the insulating values achieved are inadequate. However, refurbishment in this case is much simpler because the new external insulation to the ends of the walls can be cut back at the sides to preserve the original appearance (Figs. C 4.18 and 4.19).

C 4.16 Storey-high prestressed concrete arched beams
with ties for a span of 35 m, factory building,
Wuppertal (D), 1951, B. Halbig
a Section
b Interior view

C 4.17 Floor over basement
a Unreinforced 100 mm deep slab between
steel beams
([1]Long, [2]Cement, [3]Steel)
b Reinforced concrete slabs of different depths
([2]Cement, [3]Steel)

C 4.18 External insulation to the end face of a cross-wall
in a box-frame structure, in situ concrete spandrel
panel with internal insulation

C 4.19 Strips of internal insulation at junction with window, masonry spandrel panel built from hollow
lightweight concrete blocks, box-frame structure

C 4.20 Horizontal and vertical sections through a demountable partition

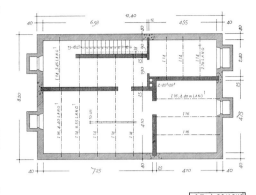

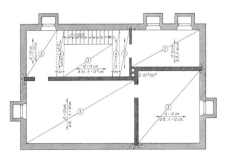

a
b
C 4.17

Internal walls

Internal walls were subjected to even more savings in materials and weight than the external
walls in order to reduce the loads on floors. The
use of new building materials for internal walls
was innovative, but at the same time resulted in
components with poor sound insulation properties:

- Rabitz wall: 50 mm thick, reinforced with
square mesh (5 mm bars @ 400 mm c/c),
self-supporting between two loadbearing
walls, weight 75 kg/m[2].
- Kessler or Pruess wall: 65 mm thick, exposed
clay paving bricks with strips of steel reinforcement, also used as an external wall for
industrial buildings.
- One-sided formwork wall: 50–70 mm thick,
gypsum mortar with a slag aggregate thrown
onto formwork, reinforcement over door
openings only, weight 50–70 kg/m[2]
- Plank wall: 50 mm thick, planks of gypsum,
gypsum slag, pumice concrete or cement
slag, up to 2 m long, weight 40 – 60 kg/m[2].

- Aerated concrete planks: 75, 100 or 150 mm
thick, grooved, 2500 x 500 mm, placed vertically, approved as a fire wall at that time,
weight 60, 80 or 120 kg/m[2].
- Stud wall: 130 or 150 mm thick, lightweight
wood-wool boards fixed to vertical and horizontal 50 x 80 or 80 x 100 mm timber battens,
no filling, weight 60 kg/m[2].

It was at the end of the 1950s that people started
to realise that only frame structures could offer
the necessary variability needed for office
buildings. However, as individual offices were
still the norm, this resulted in new constructional requirements being placed on the partitions
between the individual offices and a number of
demountable partition systems appeared on
the market, which were fitted between floor and
ceiling (Fig. C 4.20). The partitions comprised
timber or metal frames clad with plastic-faced
hardboard or sheet steel panels. The melamine-
faced board was patented by H. Römmler AG
in 1930 and later became well known through
the brand-name "Resopal". In the furniture market it replaced wood veneers in the post-war

period, especially for work surfaces and tables.
The very hard surface was also ideal for demountable, portable, prefabricated partitions. Although
many wall systems had a filling of mineral wool,
the sound insulation value was usually only 30–
35 dB, which was further reduced by flanking
transmissions at the top (acoustic ceilings) and
bottom (continuous screed). The plasterboard
so ubiquitous today – patented in the USA as
long ago as 1894 by Augustine Sackett – was
hardly ever used for walls because such walls
could not be repositioned without having to
repair them afterwards.

Doors

Doors in schools and office buildings were now
being increasingly installed with steel frames,
but wooden frames continued to dominate the
housing market, albeit without the mouldings of
the past. The standard for door leaves included
just five different types, of which "Form 0" was
new: a flush door of plywood, usually without a
filling to the door leaf, and with a correspondingly poor acoustic performance.

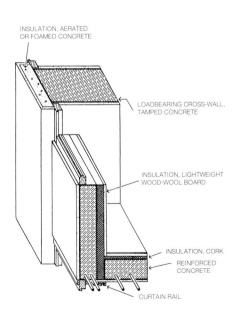

C 4.18

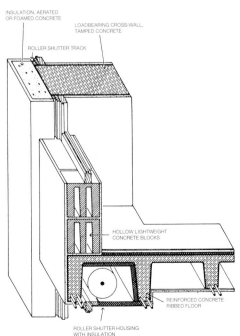

C 4.19

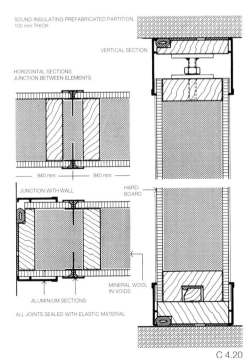

C 4.20

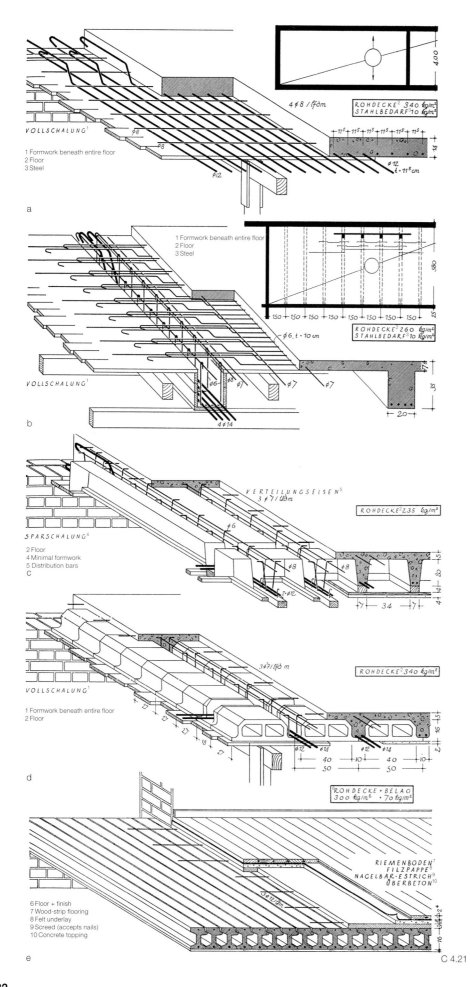

a

VOLLSCHALUNG[1]

1 Formwork beneath entire floor
2 Floor
3 Steel

$4 \phi 8 / lfdm$

ROHDECKE[2] 340 kg/m^2
STAHLBEDARF[3] 10 kg/m^2

b

VOLLSCHALUNG[1]

1 Formwork beneath entire floor
2 Floor
3 Steel

ROHDECKE[2] 260 kg/m^2
STAHLBEDARF[3] 10 kg/m^2

c

SPARSCHALUNG[4]

2 Floor
4 Minimal formwork
5 Distribution bars

VERTEILUNGSEISEN[5]
$3 \phi 7 / lfdm$

ROHDECKE[2] 235 kg/m^2

d

VOLLSCHALUNG[1]

1 Formwork beneath entire floor
2 Floor

$3 \phi 7 / lfdm$

ROHDECKE[2] 340 kg/m^2

e

6 Floor + finish
7 Wood-strip flooring
8 Felt underlay
9 Screed (accepts nails)
10 Concrete topping

RIEMENBODEN[7]
FILZPAPPE[8]
NAGELBAR·ESTRICH[9]
ÜBERBETON[10]

ROHDECKE + BELAG
300 kg/m^2 · 70 kg/m^2

C 4.21

Chimneys and heating

The modified dimensional coordination for masonry units resulted in different clear cross-sections (135 mm, 197.5 mm and 260 mm) that could be built with masonry. Nevertheless, more and more special blocks were built into the masonry bond. The idea of the three-layer special block (smoke-tight earthenware flue, insulation, outer casing) originated in the inter-war period (1927: Plein-Wagner) and solved the problem of excessive soot in masonry chimneys and the risk of leaks. The reason for the increased use of these after the war was the new masonry units, which were not approved for masonry chimneys. Removing such special blocks from post-war buildings can be hazardous because for a long time asbestos was used for the insulation between flue and casing.

Asbestos pipes, besides earthenware and sheet metal pipes, were also used for the gas-fired boilers that were now being installed more and more. Supplies of natural gas were promoted in the post-war years, in some regions even by way of free connections to buildings, which led to the use of many gas cookers and ovens, but fewer gas refrigerators and gas-fired hot-water systems. The majority of new apartments, however, experienced no progress in terms of heating comfort: individual coal- or wood-fired stoves in living room and bathroom – for providing hot water as well – were still the norm. Central heating had not yet become standard, although by this time the systems had reached a good technical standard.

The small apartment sizes prescribed in the 1st Housebuilding Act of 1950, with many rooms plus bathroom, led to many of the latter being positioned within the interior of the building. The ventilation ducts necessary were usually routed alongside the flues and in some cases were again constructed from special blocks. Individual shafts were standard here: "Berlin ventilation" working with fresh air drawn from the neighbouring rooms (door grilles), or "Cologne ventilation" with a separate fresh-air duct for each room. Despite the individual shafts, vertical sound propagation is a problem with both systems, the main reason being the thin partitions between the shafts. The sound insulation can be improved by installing silencers in the exhaust-air openings, which means, however, that fans must also be installed. Only "Berlin ventilation" can be upgraded sensibly – by adding a central fan and heat recovery. From the modern viewpoint, both systems are questionable in terms of energy efficiency, but especially "Cologne ventilation", which in winter constantly introduces cold outside air (see "Building services", p. 67).

Suspended floors

Timber was in short supply in post-war Germany. The primary use of timber for pit props (coal mine expansion), the lack of foreign currency and hence the lack of imports, overuse of forests and state controls ensured that timber construction became less significant. This is particularly evident in the construction of suspended floors. Timber joist floors were mostly replaced by reinforced concrete floors, which in many cases were built as ribbed floors to save concrete and steel, with or without infill elements. Such floors, primarily designed to save materials, did nothing to improve the sound insulation. The floors supported by steel beams known from the inter-war years continued to be used, but only in the sense of reusing materials from the mountain of debris because steel was actually a product in short supply. The Kleinesche and similar patented floor types were also built.

Flat reinforced concrete floors
After more than 25 years experience in reinforced concrete construction, more than half of suspended floors were probably now built using in situ concrete. As the cost of labour did not influence the overall cost to the same extent as the cost of materials, the architects of the time selected forms of construction that although they still comply with the regulations in many aspects, are not built in this way any more (Fig. C 4.17):

• Many loadbearing walls (contrasting with, for example, the loadbearing central wall of the founding years) with changing directions of span (one-way spans in the short direction)
• Changing floor depths within the plan layout and changing reinforcing bar diameters

• Reinforcement in the form of individual bars instead of meshes, but transverse reinforcement to distribute the loads
• Monolithic downstand beams over windows cast together with the floor slabs
• Monolithic downstand beams (occasionally also upstand beams) over non-loadbearing walls, i.e. 115 mm wide, often downstand beams > 250 mm deep to replace loadbearing walls
• Monolithic beams for T-beam floors, haunches at columns
• Continuous slabs for balconies, but mainly butt joints at loadbearing central walls (simply supported slab)

In the post-war period the reinforcement was still very frequently in the form of plain round bars; cold-worked, rolled reinforcement was unusual. The prescribed minimum concrete cover was 15 mm for internal members, 20 mm externally. Flat reinforced concrete floors had a standardised minimum depth of 70 mm; despite this, floors 100–150 mm deep spanning 4 m were normal.
In contrast to structural steelwork, the contemporary literature does not contain any deflection limits for reinforced concrete components. Instead, beam and slab depths were specified according to the spans: simply supported at both ends, the effective depth (centre of reinforcement to top of slab) had to be 1/35 of the span (Figs. C 4.21a and b, also C 4.24).

T-beam, ribbed and waffle floors
The shortage of materials in the post-war years favoured the construction of T-beam and ribbed floors although constructing the formwork and fixing the reinforcement for these in situ concrete floors was very labour-intensive. The slabs (compression zone) spanning from beam to beam were built with the minimum depth of 70 mm. This is why the T-beam floor consumes less concrete despite the longer spans. Ribbed floors (DIN 4158) of in situ concrete achieved further savings in materials (and hence an increase in the formwork requirements): quantity of reinforcement = 7.5 kg/m² for a 5 m span (by way of comparison, we assume approx. 12 kg/m² today). As the slab between the closely spaced ribs (max. spacing 700 mm) could only accommodate compression forces due to longitudinal bending, the transverse bars serve only to distribute the loads; the slab depth between the ribs was sometimes reduced to 50 mm. Ribbed slabs are only economical for spans > 5 m and are therefore found very frequently in schools and offices, but not in housing (Fig. C 4.25).
The labour-intensive formwork consumed huge quantities of timber and resulted in longer construction times. Alternative formwork methods for the structurally efficient T-beam and ribbed floors were therefore required for the mass production of housing. Prefabricated formwork for ribbed floors included:

C 4.22

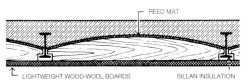

REED MAT

LIGHTWEIGHT WOOD-WOOL BOARDS   SILLAN INSULATION

C 4.23

C 4.21 Various solid floors, in each case showing position of reinforcement and formwork requirements:
  a In situ flat concrete slab
  b In situ T-beam slab
  c Koenen Floor
  d Dahm or Remy Floor
  e Rapid Floor
C 4.22 Robertson Q-Floor (composite steel-concrete floor)
C 4.23 Formwork system for a vaulted lightweight concrete floor
C 4.24 Minimum requirements for flat reinforced concrete slabs
C 4.25 Minimum requirements for ribbed floor slabs

Column spacing [m]	Minimum slab depth [cm]	Weight of steel [kg/m²]	Diameter of reinforcing bars [mm]	Spacing of reinforcement [cm]
2.17	8	4.31	8	14.5
3.13	10	7.37	10	11.0
3.67	12	9.06	12	12.5
4.21	14	10.44	12	10.5
4.70	16	11.70	14	12.5
5.16	18	13.06	14	11.0
5.59	20	14.38	16	13.0

Concrete grade B 160, reinforcement type I (plain), plaster and floor covering 1.26 kN/m², imposed load 2 kN/m²

C 4.24

Column spacing [m]	Hollow element depth [cm]	Compression zone depth [cm]	Total depth [cm]	Steel weight [kg/m²]	Reinforcement [cm²/rib]
2.04	12	5	17	2.4	0.77
2.53	12	5	17	4.0	1.57
2.96	14	5	19	4.7	1.92
3.45	14	5	19	6.2	2.67
3.90	16	5	21	7.0	3.08
4.56	20	5	25	7.9	3.55
5.03	22	5	27	8.9	4.02
5.54	24	5	29	9.9	4.55
6.04	26	6	32	11.0	5.09
6.54	28	6	34	12.2	5.68
7.29	29	7	36	14.7	6.94
7.71	30	7	37	16.1	7.60
8.21	34	8	42	17.5	8.32

Concrete grade B 160, reinforcement type I (plain), rib spacing 500 mm, plaster and floor covering 0.75 kN/m², imposed load 3.5 kN/m²

C 4.25

- Koenen Floor: sheet steel formwork with 500 or 625 mm rib spacing (Fig. C 4.21c)
- Sta-Ka Floor: sheet steel formwork for one-way-span waffle floors with regular transverse ribs; loadbearing ribs 80 x 150 mm, transverse ribs 40 x 150 mm, rib spacing 500 mm
- Montafix Floor: permanent timber formwork, rib spacing 500 or 625 mm, rib depth 115 or 130 mm
- Klimalit Floor: permanent formwork made from lightweight wood-wool boards, rib spacing 500 or 625 mm, rib depth 110, 130, 155, 195 and 230 mm

There were very many systems available for in situ concrete floor slabs with infill elements, which could be built with or without a concrete topping. They helped to reduce the amount of formwork and at the same time provided a flat soffit ready for plastering. Such systems required formwork beneath the entire area of the floor:

- Remy Floor: slag-aggregate or pumice concrete elements 120–340 mm deep, rib spacing 500 mm (Fig. C 4.21d)
- Durisol Floor: hollow lightweight wood-wool elements 100 or 150 mm deep, rib spacing 500 mm
- Pohlmann Floor: hollow elements wrapped in reeds, various depths and spacings, also in the form of T-beams

- Wirus-P Floor: solid lightweight wood-wool elements 140 mm deep, waffle floor with rib spacing of 625 mm

Partially prefabricated floors consist of prefabricated beams and infill elements or floor panels that were reinforced and filled with concrete in situ. They did not require formwork beneath the entire floor area and were therefore more economical in terms of timber consumption:

- F-Floor (DIN 4233): lightweight concrete infill elements between prefabricated ribs, with and without concrete topping, beam spacing 500 or 625 mm, slab depth 200 or 240 mm
- Zech Floor: 150 mm deep prefabricated hollow ribs in normal-weight concrete, 50 mm deep prefabricated floor panels in normal-weight or lightweight concrete, rib spacing 625 mm
- Kaiser-Katzenberger Floor: lightweight sheet steel beams including timber grounds for nails, trapezoidal infill elements made from hollow clay blocks or pumice concrete, rib spacing 500 or 625 mm, floor depth 165, 185, 205 or 225 mm

Prefabricated floors consisted mainly of beams laid directly adjacent to one another (butt joints). To reduce their weight (lifting plant) they were made of lightweight concrete or given a special shape (I-beam, hollow element).

- Rapid Floor: I-shaped beams of normal-weight concrete, 120 x 160 or 120 x 200 mm, up to 6 m long, approx. 30 mm concrete topping with transverse reinforcement (Fig. C 4.21e)
- Schäfer Floor: hollow elements of lightweight concrete (element) and normal-weight concrete (soffit), 330 or 500 mm wide, 120–200 mm deep, up to 5.50 m long, no concrete topping but joints grouted
- Aerated concrete planks: supplied with reinforcement top and bottom, 500 x 140 mm, up to 5 m long, joints grouted

Prestressed concrete beams like those of the Hoyer prestressed wire system were used only occasionally, probably because the economical plan layouts meant that most spans were less than 5 m. These floor types were joined in the 1960s by composite steel-concrete construction, e.g. Robertson Q-Floor, developed in 1931 and still used in the USA today (Fig. C 4.22). In this floor construction two trapezoidal profile steel sheets, one inverted, are joined together and to the 50 mm concrete topping with shear-resistant fixings. The ensuing void between the two steel sheets can be used for routing cables. Fire protection from below is in the form of a suspended ceiling, often still with a plaster finish.

Sound insulation

All forms of floor construction from the post-war period exhibit poor sound insulation properties because of their low weight per unit area. It was for this reason that even back in those days attempts were made to improve the sound insulation by adding resilient layers above and below the floor. For example, a sound reduction index of 41 dB was specified for the Koenen Floor without ceiling; this could be improved to 50 dB by adding a suspended ceiling, but that is still below today's minimum requirements (Fig. C 4.28).

As all the floor types were solely designed to minimise the consumption of materials, all the soffits were concealed – even the appealing aesthetics of ribbed slab soffits. To do this, timber framing was attached to the ribs at the largest possible spacing to provide a supporting construction for lightweight wood-wool boards, which were then plastered. This form of construction gradually replaced the ceilings below timber joist floors as well, which up until then had been in the form of plaster on reed mats or a Rabitz background. Timber plugs or metal rails were integrated into many suspended floor systems in order to ease the fixing of the timber framing. Heinrich Schmitt describes one particularly ingenious form of construction: "Between the steel beams, green timber boards serve as formwork supports, which shrink as the concrete cures and hence become detached from the actual loadbearing vault of clay brick aggregate concrete" (Fig. C 4.23). [11]

Type of floor	Section (example)	Weight [kg/m²]	Airborne sound insulation margin [dB]	Impact sound insulation margin [dB]	DIN 4109 structural floor group
Hollow-block floors between steel or concrete (also in situ) beams Beam floors with voids		180 220 300[1]	-6 -2	-25	I
Solid concrete slabs 100 – 130 mm		200 to 320[1]	-3	-19	I
Solid concrete slabs > 140 mm		> 350[1]	+2	-10	II
Ribbed concrete slabs or T-beam slabs without soffit formwork		160 to 220[1]	-6	-20	I
Ribbed concrete slabs or T-beam slabs with non-rigid ceiling		140 to 220[2]	+1	-9	II
Timber joist floors with slag or loam pugging		180	±0	-9	–

[1] Plaster to the soffit and possibly a screed firmly bonded to the floor must be taken into account when determining the weight.

[2] Excluding the weight of the ceiling.

C 4.26

Only gradually did floor finishes and floor constructions come to be treated as separate items. Up until then all tile and stone finishes, also screeds designed to act as wearing courses, were laid directly on the structural floor. Only the widely used linoleum and cork carpet were laid on 10 mm thick composite boards (2.5 mm hardboard and 7.5 mm softboards). These boards were bonded to the trowelled structural floor over their full area with asphalt – a technique that was also used for wood-block flooring. The improvement in the sound insulation was, however, minimal.

It was only the introduction of DIN 4109 in 1959 that changed the situation; the impact sound improvement values laid down in that draft (adopted in 1962) are, however, still far below today's requirements. When assessing the sound insulation we distinguish between class I structural floors (floors that do not comply with the airborne sound insulation requirements) and class II structural floors (floors that do comply). Almost all the floor constructions of the post-war period belong to class I, with the exception of in situ concrete floor slabs > 140 mm deep. The standard specifies mineral- or plant-based fibrous insulating materials with a minimum thickness of 8 mm in the compressed state for class I floors (Fig. C 4.26).

The screeds laid on these correspond roughly to modern standards in terms of quality of materials, methods of laying and minimum thicknesses. However, the very thin layers of insulation usual in those days meant that the screeds were also correspondingly thin – cement screeds just 35 mm thick were common in practice.

Floor coverings did not undergo any significant further developments. Besides very cheap hardboard and impregnated felts, which are hardly encountered any more, changes were at best due to changing fashions:

• Solnhofener stone slabs from Bavaria, laid in a bed of hydraulic lime mortar, were preferred in entrance halls and corridors, and competed with the terrazzo finishes popular up until this time. These slabs were 20–30 mm thick and were available in formats with side lengths ≥ 250 mm (frequently 300 x 300, 500 x 500 mm, long slabs 350, 250 or 300 mm wide).
• Linoleum (2.2 mm) and cork carpet (4–5 mm) were regarded as bactericidal, easy-care floor finishes warm to the touch and so were laid in schools, hospitals and offices, but also in housing of course. The rolls of material were bonded to the screed or insulating material over the full area of the floor. Cement and gypsum screeds were usually up to 40 mm thick, the latter frequently laid on a thin bed of sand to compensate for any unevenness in the structural floor below and also to improve the curing process. Rubber floor coverings (4 mm) were better, but also more expensive and therefore less common. Synthetic floor coverings were initially laid only occasionally for reasons of cost; the same applies to carpeting.

• Small-format wood-block flooring, much cheaper than true, high-quality wood-strip floors, were used more and more despite the shortage of wood. However, floorboards and wood-strip floors, also subfloors with parquet squares started to disappear because they had to be nailed down and that was not possible on the "new" screeds. Small-format wood-block flooring, on the other hand, could be laid in a 10 mm asphalt bed – later 2 mm asbestos adhesive – applied over the entire floor area, and was therefore better suited to the solid floor constructions.

Damage and measures
The typical weaknesses of floors of the post-war years are the same as those of the timber joist floor: poor sound reduction indexes and limited load-carrying capacity (see "Buildings of the founding years", pp. 145–147). Added to these problems are the use of troublesome building materials and complex forms of construction. Refurbishing such floors is difficult because every new layer designed to overcome existing weaknesses reduces the meagre clear ceiling height even further. As the residential estates of the 1950s are less profitable than, for example, buildings of the founding years and refurbishment of the floors means that the complete building must remain unoccupied for some time, floors are often left unrefurbished.

Sound insulation
Even the minimum requirement for airborne sound insulation at that time (48 dB) was not achieved by some floors, e.g. the Koenen Floor, and none of these lightweight (mostly < 300 kg/m²) floor types can achieve the values required today. Theoretically, the problem could be solved with new resilient ceilings plus new floor finishes. The problems are the loss of clear height in the rooms, which in apartments with only 2.50 m between the structural floors is certainly on the limit anyway, and the additional loads. According to Fig. C 4.24 only 1.26 kN/m² is available for finishes. These loading assumptions are not adequate for a new floating cement screed of normal thickness plus floor covering and plastered or suspended ceiling. The latter would certainly improve the sound insulation considerably, but the space requirement of at least 100 mm means that such ceilings are only possible in office and school buildings. Any measures designed to improve the airborne and structure-borne sound insulation must be of minimal weight. If we assume existing ceiling plaster 15 mm thick and, for example, new wood-block flooring 22 mm thick, only 0.88 kN/m² remains of our 1.26 kN/m². This corresponds to a 40 mm screed on impact sound insulation, or a 30 mm screed plus a ceiling of plaster on lightweight wood-wool boards, which can be achieved in practice with a thin calcium sulphate screed (≥ 35 mm) or mastic asphalt (≥ 20 mm).

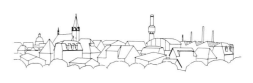

a

b

c   C 4.27

C 4.26 Airborne and impact sound insulation values for floors to DIN 4109 (1959 edition)
C 4.27 Roofscapes, illustrations dating from 1959, Heinrich Schmitt
    a Middle Ages
    b 19th century
    c Future
C 4.28 Minimum sound insulation values to DIN 4109
C 4.29 Shed with arched roof after refurbishment, Cologne (D), 2000, 4000architekten

Component	Requirement, 1959 [dB]	Requirement, today [dB]
Party walls, housing	48	55
Partitions between offices	40	45
Party floors, housing	48	55

C 4.28

C 4.29

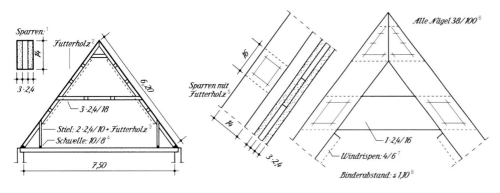

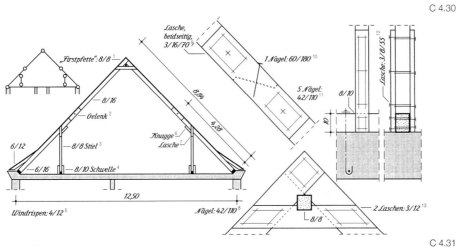

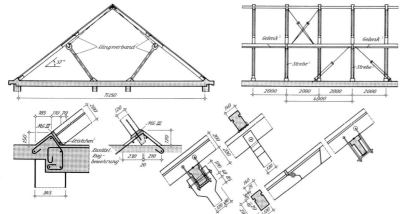

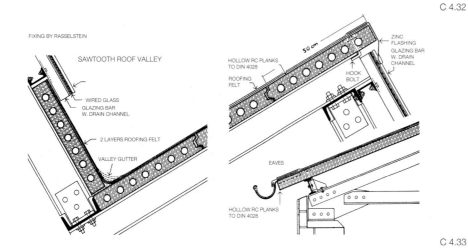

C 4.30

C 4.31

C 4.32

C 4.33

C 4.30   Roof truss made from nailed boards with spacers
([1]Rafters, [2]Spacer, [3]Post: 2 No. 2.4 x 10 + spacer, [4]Sole plate: 10 x 8, [5]Rafters with spacers, [6]All nails 38 x 100, [7]Wind brace: 4 x 6, [8]Truss spacing: max. 1.10)

C 4.31   Pitched roof with spliced rafters (hinged rafters)
([1]"Ridge purlin": 8 x 8, [2]Hinge, [3]8 x 8 post, [4]8 x 10 sole plate, [5]Wind brace: 4 x 12, [6]Cleat, [7]Fishplate, [8]Nails, 42 x 110, [9]Splice plate both sides: 3 x 16 x 70, [10]1 nail: 60 x 180, [11]5 nails: 42 x 110, [12]Fishplate: 3 x 8 x 55, [13]2 collars: 3 x 12)

C 4.32   Purlin roof made from precast concrete elements, used in the GDR since 1946
([1]Longitudinal bracing, [2]Hinge, [3]Strut, [4]Batten, [5]Extra tension reinforcement)

C 4.33   Sawtooth roof construction in the form of hollow concrete planks on structural steelwork

C 4.34   Reinforcement to simply supported slab with cantilever (balcony)

Structural aspects

The current loading assumptions for buildings have not changed much since 1950; the same is true for the principal material parameters. However, in those days there was no need to check for deflection. Normally, it is not necessary to verify the floor construction if this remains unchanged. As shown in Fig. C 4.17b, every suspended floor was optimised with respect to its span and loading, which creates problems when the new floor construction leads to higher loads because the floors usually have no load-bearing reserves. If changes to the floor construction are planned, the existing finishes must be removed, their weights determined and the new finishes adjusted to suit.

Monolithic loadbearing elements

One problem already mentioned in conjunction with upgrading the thermal insulation to the external wall was the monolithic form of construction, e.g. upstand/downstand beams and balcony slabs all cast monolithically with the floors. The positions of the reinforcing bars optimised for this type of construction do not permit any fundamental changes to the floor construction. One simple way of eliminating the thermal bridge at the balcony slab is to cut this off and replace it with a new one built separately in front of the facade (Fig. C 4.34). However, the reinforcement is optimised for the loading case of a continuous slab. Removing the balcony turns the remaining slab into a simply supported member, possibly with inadequate reinforcement in the tension zone near the support. Further problems result from the downstand beams cast together with the floor slab, which extend down to the level of the door intels. This rules out raising the level of the door lintel, meaning that in the case of new floor finishes the existing clear headroom of 2010 mm might well be reduced by 50 mm to 1960 mm. With buildings of the 1950s in particular, it is therefore necessary to work with the existing structure because changes involve too many problems.

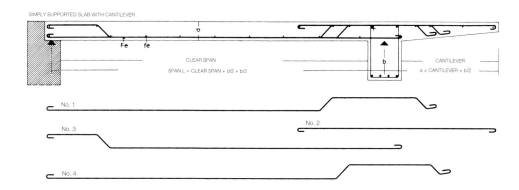

SIMPLY SUPPORTED SLAB WITH CANTILEVER

CLEAR SPAN

SPAN L = CLEAR SPAN + d/2 + b/2

CANTILEVER

a = CANTILEVER + b/2

No. 1

No. 2

No. 3

No. 4

C 4.34

Asphalt adhesive

When it is necessary to remove all floor finishes in order to improve the sound insulation (weight reduction), this can often reveal adhesive compounds containing asphalt that were used to bond floor coverings in the past. These certainly contain tar (carcinogenic) but were not banned until the 1970s. Some of the adhesives used later also includes asbestos fibres. It is hardly possible to remove the layers from the structural floor, and heating them exacerbates the health risk. Removing these adhesives containing PAH or asbestos by planing or grinding is the safest but also the most expensive solution to the problem because such work can only be carried out by specialist contractors. The alternative is to treat the entire area with a two-part epoxy resin primer plus a cement-based filler compound, which seals the material, and then lay a new resilient floor covering (carpet, linoleum). Laying new wood-block flooring on the filler compound is not recommended because the inevitable movement of the wood can shear off the underlying adhesive.

Stairs

It is conspicuous that much space is devoted to stairs and stair shafts in the textbooks of the 1950s [12]. And indeed, they formed an important constructional element in post-war buildings. This is where the architect could satisfy the general desire for brightness and airiness most easily, especially in government offices, schools and other buildings to which the public had access. The attraction of these stairs is, on the one hand, that the architects have not shied away from attempting monumental effects, but, on the other, that they have still followed the credo of thriftiness. The material of choice was reinforced concrete, which could be moulded to suit the architect's desires because the high cost of the formwork was less relevant economically. As the loads correspond to those of today, the lack of sound insulation is acceptable and the constructions are mostly free from defects, conversion is unlikely to be necessary. Indeed, is more important to retain and maintain unusual staircases.

Roof spaces

The majority of the different building styles of the founding years had a considerable impact on the hitherto uniform urban roofscape of simple pitched roofs. The architects of the post-war years attempted to re-create this uniformity, but the question of the roof form split them into two camps: on the one side the proponents of the placid pitched roof without dormer windows, on the other side the advocates of the flat roof, often topped with rooftop terraces in the architectural language of the 1920s avant-garde [13]. For both roof forms, the same applies as for the stairs: they represent a characteristic feature of post-war architecture and should therefore be treated very carefully during conversion work. Added to this is the fact that the forms of construction used for pitched roofs in particular hardly permit any subsequent conversions (Fig. C 4.27).

Roof structure and floor below roof space

The decision regarding the construction of the topmost floor of a building depended mostly on the intended usage and the size of the structure. Only in small residential buildings in which the roof space was unused do we still find the traditional trusses/rafters system (see "Buildings of the founding years", p. 151). Otherwise, the top floors were built similarly to all other upper floors, also because they had to carry the same imposed load of 2 kN/m².

The shortage of wood led to even smaller timber sections on the one hand, but deliberations regarding alternatives such as solid roofs and duo-chord trusses on the other. Solid roofs, e.g. in reinforced concrete, did not become established, however, because they were uneconomical despite the high price of timber. One special case was the long-span shed structure for industrial buildings; the high prices of timber and steel led to more reinforced concrete structures being erected (Fig. C 4.29).

Two further savings options are encountered as well as the smaller sizes of the timber members:

- Shorter spans between supports, e.g. by way of kneebraces below ridge purlins, or collars at a structurally favourable height, neither of

which took any account of headroom requirements.
- Lightweight roof coverings, especially corrugated asbestos-cement sheets: 17 kg/m² instead of the 55 kg/m² for clay tiles.

The usual roof structures have already been described in the chapters on buildings of the founding and inter-war years. The following economic forms of construction were added to these in the 1950s:

- Duo-chord trusses: steep (approx. 50 °) collar roof of compound rafters; two continuous 24 x 140 mm boards nailed together at regular intervals with short 24 x 140 mm spacer blocks (Fig. C 4.30).
- Barffknecht or Birkmann form of construction (1943): I-shaped rafter cross-sections made from boards glued together, e.g. 2 No. 50 x 150 mm with a web measuring 50 x 170 mm in the case of Birkmann, for clear rafter spans of up to 7.5 m.
- Maerz form of construction (1940): similar I-beam construction, but with a web made from hardboard and four squared sections (two top, two bottom) nailed on to form the flanges.
- Hinged rafters: rafters joined together in the middle with a pin-type joint (3-pin beam), which resulted in lower bending moments in the rafters and an empirically designed ridge purlin (Fig. C 4.31).
- Solid-web beams: plate-like I-beams with diagonal, butt-jointed boards forming the web plus connecting and stiffening squared sections to achieve long spans (Fig. C 4.35).

In the mid-1960s the relationship between cost of labour and cost of materials gradually shifted and the shortage of wood became a thing of the past. The frugal forms of roof construction became outdated: "Roof structures requiring a high labour input but a small timber requirement are mostly uneconomical these days … Labour-intensive forms of construction are therefore hardly seen any more." [14]

Roof coverings

The bullnose tiles still common during the inter-war years were gradually replaced by the inter-

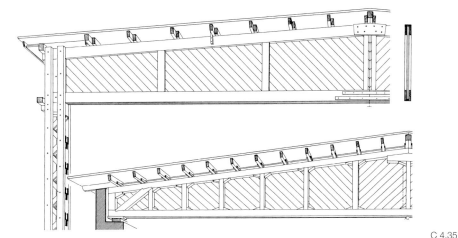

C 4.35

C 4.35 Solid-web beams of nailed boards, span 15 m
C 4.36 Various flat roof edge details with external drainage
         a Gutter lined with two layers of roofing felt
         b Gutter lined with filler compound
         c Rooftop terrace: gutter lined with filler com-
            pound, "Gartenmann" finish on insulation

locking clay roof tiles that had been known since the founding years. There were two reasons for this: the lower weight (55 kg/m² instead of 85) and the shallower roof pitches possible (as low as 15 °), which meant that even low-rise buildings could be provided with a shallower pitched roof to save timber. Concrete roof tiles were also available, but owing to their higher weight and "poor aesthetics should only be used in areas with little clay". [15] The same author expresses the following opinion: "Reflective glazes and the same bright red colours are awful and apart from that not permitted by the standards." [16]

Corrugated asbestos-cement sheets were now used widely. They were light, weather-resistant, incombustible, cheap, easy to saw and drill – but unfortunately contained asbestos. The hazards of this material had been known for a long time; lung cancer as an occupational illness among asbestos workers was acknowledged. But the exceptional durability of this material and the lack of substitutes meant that it was not until the 1990s that the first asbestos bans came into force. Even today, there are still many asbestos-cement sheets on European roofs. Replacing these by non-asbestos fibre-cement sheets with the same profile is the simplest refurbishment measure. Applying a coating to the existing sheets, which bonds the fibres to the surface and therefore eliminates the hazards, still involves a hazardous preliminary treatment in the form of brushing, possibly even water-jetting, in order to ensure that the coating adheres properly.

Asbestos-cement sheets were produced in two depths: 57 and 36 mm for maximum spans of 1450 and 785 mm respectively. The standard sheet size was 915 x 2500 mm; such a sheet weighed only 32 kg and was laid over three supports; accordingly, the spacing of the purlins was 1150 mm. As the purlins replaced the tiling battens, so to speak, the roof structures for corrugated sheets were built the "other way around": there are no rafters between the trusses and the timber or steel purlins span from truss to truss.

Lightweight hollow concrete planks represent a form of pitched roof construction without rafters used for industrial buildings. The 500 mm wide,

50–120 mm deep and max. 3 m long hollow planks were clipped to steel I-sections, for example, and the joints filled with grout. The flexible waterproof sheeting used on flat roofs could be used here, or corrugated Eternit panels (Fig. C 4.33).

Similar prefabricated solid forms of construction were also developed in the GDR, which led to the so-called large-panel construction methods used from the late 1960s onwards. The so-called Menzel Framed Roof was a typical early representative with which prefabricated pitched roofs could be erected [17]. Precast concrete elements 50 mm thick were clipped to the rafters positioned at a spacing of 2 m (140 x 200 mm for all spans) (Fig. C 4.32).

Flat roofs, balconies and loggias

The designation "felt roof" already familiar in the 1950s refers to the very common wool felt backing materials impregnated with bitumen or tar. These waterproofing materials were regarded as especially lightweight, cheap roof coverings for pitched and flat roofs, in particular for "shed roofs and utility buildings with a limited lifespan" [18]. Over the course of time the uncoated felts were increasingly replaced by bituminous felts with granule surfacing both sides that resulted in a more durable roof covering. Rolls of waterproofing materials with glass fleece or metal inlays plus synthetic materials had only just appeared on the market and were hardly used between 1950 and 1960. Like in the inter-war period, tar was often used for impregnating and bonding the materials, the disposal of which is to be recommended for the reasons already mentioned in the chapter on buildings of the inter-war years (see p. 171); the bitumen compounds used in those days may also contain asbestos fibres. The bituminous compounds in use today do not bond reliably to the old waterproofing materials, meaning that it is advisable to remove and dispose of the old layers.

Many felt roofs were laid on timber sheathing. The first layer of felt was always nailed down and only the following layers (when more than one layer was specified) bonded over the full area. Removing these materials does not therefore present any problems. The underlying tim-

ber construction should certainly be inspected for rot at an early stage, e.g. by opening up the ceiling, because leaks and condensation may have caused irreparable damage to such roofs. Nailed materials can also be found on solid roofs – timber battens were cast into the concrete flush with the surface. Otherwise, a maximum of two layers of waterproofing material were bonded to a bituminous preliminary coat applied over the whole area. In contrast to the flat roofs of today, in the post-war years the roof drainage was frequently external. To do this, either the details of pitched roofs were copied (gutter attached to bracket bonded into roof finishes) or a gutter was formed in the solid roof which was then lined with a filler compound or the felt roofing material. Figs. C 4.36a–c show typical perimeter details that cause problems during refurbishment:

- The bonding of the materials along the edge of the gutter has very likely not remained intact. The pumice concrete used as a screed laid to falls (min. fall to DIN = 1.5 ° = 2.6 %) may be saturated.
- The concrete slab forms a thermal bridge and this can only be solved – without disrupting the architecture – by adding internal insulation. In doing so, however, this leads to considerable thermal movements of the roof plate on the masonry.
- The gutter and its connection to the downpipe can only be waterproofed in a similar way – not in accordance with today's flat roof guidelines. In addition, the potential stresses between a normal-weight concrete slab and a lightweight concrete screed prevent permanent liquid-based waterproofing of the gutter.

When carrying out refurbishment work, all edge details should be handled very carefully in order to avoid disrupting the character of the entire building; such cantilevering, tapering and particularly "delicate" edge details are very characteristic of the style. It would be possible to cut off the overhang flush with the masonry (check structural analysis for position of reinforcement) and add a new fair-face precast concrete element separated by a thermal

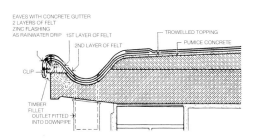

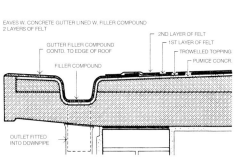

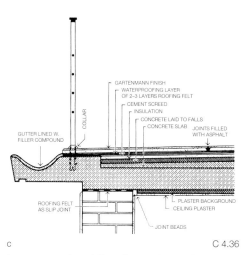

a

b

c   C 4.36

break. A traditional flat roof edge detail with parapet and drainage on the inside will probably be impossible because the depth would be visible (Fig. C 4.36).

Loggias, but also balconies and rooftop terraces, were either not waterproofed at all during the post-war period, or at best with two coats of mastic asphalt (2 No. 20 mm). Quartz sand was worked into the upper coat, which at the time same time served as a wearing course. A cement screed was sometimes used as a finish; this consisted of two layers each 20–30 mm thick, the lower of which was reinforced with wire mesh. This so-called Gartenmann finish was divided into approx. 1 m² bays and the joints filled with asphalt (Fig. C 4.36c). The insulation was mainly in the form of cork tiles. Dubious junctions with other components, poor workmanship and balustrade uprights that penetrate the waterproofing mean that in almost every case these trafficable flat roofs are no longer intact. The insulation and screeds are saturated and mouldy and must be removed completely. The bases of the uprights are usually totally corroded because they have remained permanently wet.

Loggias and rooftop terraces must therefore be completely reconstructed above the structural roof – and not only for energy-efficiency reasons; in doing so, insulation with integral falls and a very low thermal conductivity can help to keep the overall depth of the construction down to a minimum.

Waterproofing techniques developed rapidly during the 1950s. The use of fewer pitched roofs and damage to early flat roofs meant that new solutions were essential. One frequent problem was the formation of blisters in the summer, caused by condensation beneath vapour-tight waterproofing materials. In order to avoid this, the textbooks of the day recommended including a vapour pressure equalisation layer: either the first layer was bonded at discrete points only, or so-called ventilation felts were laid to distribute the water vapour to the edges of the roof where it could escape. Vapour barriers, on the other hand, were rarely used, or only locally, e.g. over wet rooms. Rhepanol, a 1.5 mm thick PIB material applied using the felt-torching method, was intended

not as a waterproofing material, but rather as a vapour barrier. Inorganic materials such as rock wool, cellular glass or rigid polystyrene foam were increasingly used as insulating materials in the 1960s alongside expanded cork or bitumenised wood-wool (Odenwald board). The latter was invented by BASF in 1951 and marketed as a waterproofing material for a flat roofs under the name of "Awatekt". Bitumen felts with factory-applied facings to ease laying were now available. Cellular glass is better in theory because it absorbs less water (vapour) than rigid polystyrene foam, but was hardly used because it was much more expensive. What all the layers of insulation have in common is the fact that they are very thin compared to what we would expect today – mostly < 50 mm. For a time, the screed laid to falls was on top of the layer of the insulation, i.e. directly below the waterproofing, but could not dry out here, between waterproofing and vapour barrier, and so this method was soon abandoned in favour of placing the screed on top of the structural roof. Two layers of grade 500 or three layers of grade 333 felt were usual. Rolls of material with glass fleece or metal foil inlays and synthetic materials had not yet become established. Despite further developments, the lack of experience with (damage at) junctions with vertical components and penetrations plus the forms of construction with several layers of vapour barriers and ventilation felts must be looked at very critically. Accordingly, the finishes to the flat roofs of the 1950s and 1960s should always be completely removed when carrying out refurbishment work.

Refurbishment of cantilevering balcony slabs
One frequent problem encountered with the majority of thermal performance upgrades to external walls is that of the concrete balcony slab cantilevering out from the loadbearing wall. Insulating the slab on all sides is theoretically possible, but results in a thick edge to the slab and a step at the entrance to the balcony. As neither of these details is satisfactory, the slabs are mostly cut off, but the structural calculations must be checked (Fig. C 4.34). New balconies in steel built in front of the facade can utilise the loadbearing external wall as an

inner support and therefore only need new columns to support the outer edges of the balconies. A sufficiently deep, stable foundation is important here; wherever possible, the columns should be founded outside the area of the former excavation (working space) in order to reduce the risk of settlement. To minimise the unavoidable thermal bridges at the supports on the existing wall, the beam under the inside edge of the balcony should be fixed to the loadbearing wall at preferably no more than two points. The problem with forming such supports on the existing wall is usually the limited compressive strength of the lightweight masonry units and the lack of building authority approval for a tension anchor for the new balcony in such masonry units. The support should therefore be fixed to the edge of the concrete floor slab cut off flush with the face of the external wall.

Notes:

[1]   Durth, Werner: Deutsche Architekten, Biographische Verflechtungen 1900–1970. Braunschweig/Wiesbaden, 1986
[2]   1st Housebuilding Act, 1950
[3]   Neufert, Ernst: Architects' Data, Wiesbaden, 2005
[4]   Schmitt, Heinrich: Hochbaukonstruktionen. Ravensburg, 1956, pp. 19–35
[5]   ibid. [4], p. 26
[6]   Hart, Franz: Baukonstruktion für Architekten. Stuttgart, 1951, p. 55
[7]   ibid. [4], p. 44
[8]   ibid. [6], p. 122
[9]   ibid. [6], p. 41
[10] Schmitt, Heinrich: Hochbaukonstruktionen. Ravensburg, 1962, p. 120
[11] ibid. [4], p. 215
[12] Heinrich Schmitt devoted 41 pages to stairs in 1956, twice as many as those on foundations and seven times as many as those on timber joist floors; ibid. [4]
[13] ibid. [4], p. 358
[14] Ahnert, Rudolf; Krause, Karl Heinz: Typische Baukonstruktionen von 1860 bis 1960, vol. 3, Berlin, 2006, source 298: Möhler, K.; Wendler, B.: Hölzerne Hausdächer. Baustoffbedarf, Arbeitsaufwand und Standsicherheitsnachweis. Düsseldorf, 1968
[15] ibid. [4], p. 479
[16] ibid. [4], p. 455
[17] ibid. [14], p. 183
[18] ibid. [4], p. 500

Buildings of the prosperous years 1965–1980

Georg Giebeler

C 5.1

The economy in West Germany in the 1950s was characterised by shortages as a consequence of World War 2. Only gradually did incomes begin to rise, and the post-war upswing remained constant until the first recession in West Germany in the mid-1960s. Essentially, it was a time of full employment, stable governments and few social conflicts. This was reflected in the birth rate, which climbed steadily after 1950 and reached a peak in 1964, when 1.4 million babies were born in Germany – twice as many as in 2006. This, together with an influx of ethnic German and GDR emigrants plus migrant workers led to an increase in the population of West Germany, from 68 million in 1949 to 78 million in 1970. The upturn also became evident in the sizes of apartments: whereas in 1950 every occupant had an average of just 14 m^2 at his or her disposal, this figure had risen to approx. 28 m^2 by 1975. All these factors together meant that there was still a shortage of housing, despite plenty of building activity. The goal of the 2nd Housebuilding Act of 1956 was therefore "to overcome the shortage of housing and create a broad property base for many sectors of the population" [1].

By the mid-1960s the town and city centres had been fully redeveloped – as a result of the great demand, but also because road widths, clearances between buildings and building heights had been specified, which on the whole led to a lower density of development. In order to overcome the housing shortages, new settlements started to appear along the lines of the English "new towns": autonomous estates planned on the drawing board which united the ideas of the garden city – green, airy, bright – and the urban settlement designed around the motor car. Municipal authorities, the property market, the building industry, urban planners and architects were all pursuing the same aims here. The building of these large residential estates started at the beginning of the 1960s and reached its climax in the 1970s (Figs. C 5.1, 5.3 and 5.4). At the start these were very ambitious projects - some were even designed by renowned architects: the Neue Vahr Estate in Bremen was planned by Ernst May, and the true landmark of this new development – a high-rise block – was designed by Alvar Aalto.

The developers of these estates were often cooperative or non-profit-making housebuilding companies with names like "Neue Heimat" (new home). This was a company set up by trade unions which built 100 000 apartments between 1952 and 1959 and thus doubled its property portfolio; another 100 000 had been added by 1963.

The enormous volume of building work, rising wages, falling prices for materials and the outstanding infrastructure called for the introduction of new building methods. The notion of rationalised building, which had first appeared in the 1930s, was now realised in the form of precast concrete construction. A total of 163 apartments were built in Saint-Germain-en-Laye in 1951 using the large-panel form of construction according to the Camus method – a form of construction that was also used in West Germany and Austria from about 1960 onwards, but never really became established. But in the GDR it evolved into the standard method of construction, and was used for building 2.1 million new apartments there between 1960 and 1989.

The architectural avant-garde was exploring new aesthetic and conceptual paths in the early 1960s: Archigram's satellite town (the London-based group of architects named after the architecture journal of the same name that first appeared in 1963), Hans Hollein's "Aircraft Carrier City in the Landscape", or the clip-together plastic modules of the metabolists led by Kisho Kurokawa.

The middle of the 1960s marks the end of the post-war period. Revolts such as the Prague Spring and the student movements plus innovations like colour television, miniskirts and the contraceptive pill led to upheavals in society that also had an effect on architecture and urban planning.

Criticism of the high-rise housing developments grew: as early as 1972, for example, the Pruitt Igoe estate in St. Louis, designed just 20 years previously by Minoru Yamasaki, was partially demolished. The oil crisis of 1973 showed everyone "the limits to growth", which was also the title of a revolutionary study by Dennis L. Meadows, published in 1972 by the Club of Rome [2]. The unconditional belief in the future was destroyed

C 5.1 Residential estate, Cologne (D)
C 5.2 Office landscape, Nordhorn (D), 1963, Quickborner Team
C 5.3 Larger residential estates in East and West Germany (selection)
C 5.4 Residential development dating from the 1970s

by the oil crisis and also reflected in the abandonment of the urban planning policies that had prevailed hitherto. The theoretical basis had already been supplied in the 1960s in books by Jane Jacobs, *The Death and Life of Great American Cities* (1961), and Alexander Mitscherlich, *Die Unwirtlichkeit unserer Städte* (the unreality of our cities) (1965) [3]. In these books they criticise vehemently the so-called slum clearances – the total demolition of old districts in favour of building new estates, in some instances after their owners had been dispossessed. Both authors suggest that the loss of people's homes and hometowns plus the monotony of the content and aesthetics are the reasons for cultural neglect. As a reaction to this, the first small-scale urban redevelopments started to appear in Europe in the 1970s in order to increase the appeal of towns and cities. The first total building refurbishments were carried out in this period. Such measures were urgently required because the majority of the buildings that had survived the wars of the past 100 years were in a deplorable state. For example, in Vienna, which had not been razed to the ground during the war, at the end of the 1970s one-third of the city's inhabitants were still without their own bathroom or toilet!

Conservation, which was defined by the Venice Charter in 1964, no longer protected just individual structures, but more and more also complete urban districts. For example, in 1967 the entire old quarter of Salzburg was covered by a conservation order, and in 1968 it was only the dedication of a group of young Viennese architects that the demolition of the underground station at Karlsplatz (Otto Wagner) was prevented. Today, both of these are tourist attractions whose preservation seems matter-of-course. In office buildings individual offices were being increasingly replaced by open-plan layouts –

an import from the UK and USA. Another development was the so-called office landscape, which had been designed by management consultants in 1963 for a textiles company in Nordhorn. The concept was based on the corporate structure and internal communications; the spacious rooms can be divided into separate areas by means of movable elements (Fig. C 5.2). The spacious storeys needed for open-plan offices were made possible by amending building legislation ("open-plan rule") and by the comparatively cheap energy available in those days for conditioning and lighting the working spaces. The many voluminous office buildings, which often exceeded the limits for tall buildings, are even today still functional and economical in terms of floor area, but are unpopular with employees and costly to run.

Typical strengths and weaknesses
Even though the architectural quality of many buildings dating from the 1970s is debatable, the quality of the construction is certainly very high. The prices of materials had dropped owing to the availability of cheap energy and transport, and the direct and indirect labour costs had not yet reached the level of today. This led to the renunciation of the materials-saving forms of construction that had been practised up until then, the disadvantages of which, e.g. poor sound insulation, had simply been accepted. In addition, the confines of the first post-war buildings gave way to spacious, taller rooms – especially where it was important to display the new prosperity, e.g. in living rooms, or in the foyers to government or office buildings.

The architectural spectrum of this age is enormous: the first architects trained in the post-war years designed, on the one hand, impressive, often sculpted, buildings on a small scale, but

C 5.2

on the other, architecture for the masses with in many instances little artistic sophistication. It is the latter, more than anything else, that is firmly anchored in the public awareness. This leads us to the conclusion that even buildings built to a high constructional standard are doomed to fail in the end when they are based on cheap planning or outdated concepts.

Functionalism, a highly prized concept in the housing sector, too, became the most important and sometimes the sole assessment criterion – at first glance an advantage because, after all, functioning buildings are essential. The only problem was the intensification of a functionalism tailored to the social status quo. Tiny, purely functional kitchens reflected the notion of woman as housewife; likewise, the office landscape was only a reflection of an organisational structure. There are hardly any constructional weaknesses, with the exception of the widespread damage to exposed fair-face concrete surfaces.

Conversion potential
The fact that some buildings dating from the 1970s have already been demolished was not

Estate	Place	Federal state	Start	Completion	Housing units
WK I–IV	Eisenhüttenstadt	Brandenburg	1950	late 1960s	7000
Neue Vahr	Bremen	Bremen	1957	1963	11800
Neustadt	Hoyerswerda	Saxony	1957	mid-1970s	18700
Weststadt	Braunschweig	Lower Saxony	1960	1980s	12000
Nord	Wolfen	Saxony-Anhalt	1960	1980s	13600
Gropiusstadt	West Berlin	Berlin	1962	1975	18500
Märkisches Viertel	West Berlin	Berlin	1963	1974	17000
Neustadt	Halle/Saale	Saxony-Anhalt	1964	1990s	40600
Mettenhof	Kiel	Schleswig-Holstein	1965	1970s	8000
Lütten Klein	Rostock	Mecklenburg-W. Pomerania	1965	1969	10600
Nord	Erfurt	Thuringia	1965	1990	16400
Lobeda	Jena	Thuringia	1966	1986	10000
Oggersheim-West	Ludwigshafen	Rhineland Palatinate	1967	1970s	9500
Osdorfer Born	Hamburg	Hamburg	1967	1972	10600
Schönwalde I + II	Greifswald	Mecklenburg-W. Pomerania	1969	1980	10000
Mümmelmannsberg	Hamburg	Hamburg	1970	1979	18800
Lusan	Gera	Thuringia	1972	1980s	15000
Chorweiler	Cologne	North Rhine-Westphalia	1972	1980s	20000
Großer Dreesch I–III	Schwerin	Mecklenburg-W. Pomerania	1972	mid-1980s	20100
Neuperlach	Munich	Bavaria	1974	1979	24000
Fritz Heckert Estate	Chemnitz	Saxony	1974	1990s	31300
Lichtenhagen	Rostock	Mecklenburg-W. Pomerania	1974	1976	6900
Grünau	Leipzig	Saxony	1976	late 1980s	38500
Hellersdorf	East Berlin	Berlin	1977	late 1980s	42200
Lichtenberg	East Berlin	Berlin	1977	late 1980s	48000
Marzahn	East Berlin	Berlin	1977	late 1980s	58200
Neuberesinchen	Frankfurt/Oder	Brandenburg	1978	1990s	8300
Neu-Olvenstedt	Magdeburg	Saxony-Anhalt	1981	late 1980s	18900

C 5.3

C 5.4

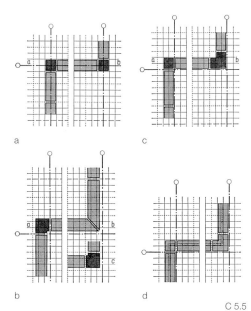

a

c

b

d

C 5.5

due to the quality of the workmanship. It was instead the monofunctionalism and the urban planning structures, which made conversion difficult. Office landscapes with 400 m² of floor area and a clear ceiling height of 2.75 m cannot be let these days. Large residential estates suffer from structural problems that have social as well as architectural roots, e.g. the functional and economical, but inhospitable access concepts via central corridors. Added to this are the difficulties encountered when attempting energy-efficiency upgrades, caused by the peculiarities of the design (e.g. balconies, garden windows) or the facade surfaces (e.g. fair-face concrete, facing brickwork). Accordingly, the conversion potential varies considerably from building to building. Presumably, buildings from these years will therefore only survive the coming decades with the help of special initiatives.

When comparing those constructions with the buildings of today, it is conspicuous that our modern concepts are hardly different to those of the late 1970s. At the latest, it was the Energy Conservation Act (EnEG) of 1976 that ensured major changes to all external components and hence completely new constructional conditions. Many forms of construction that are standard today originated in this period: after 1970 office and industrial buildings made use of frame structures almost exclusively, and reinforced concrete became the material of choice for members in bending and heavily loaded components. Furthermore, the inverted roof, curtain wall facades, double glazing, synthetic resin floors, oriented strand boards, external thermal insulation composite systems and many other inventions and developments appeared at this time. When planning a conversion we can therefore assume similar forms of construction and materials to those still in use today. The main differences are to be found in the dimensions and the ecological evaluation: the thickness of thermal insulation back then was minimal (< 60 mm), which is why thermal bridges played a subsidiary role, and materials such as asbestos, or substances such as lindane or PCP were used without question.

Modularisation and industrialised building
Easily procured, easily transported masonry units remained the favourite materials for walls during the post-war years. Dimensional coordination was therefore based on the clay brick. The boom in new building work in the mid-1960s, however, took place under new conditions:
• New buildings were built on green-field sites.
• Only with large-format concrete components, either in situ or precast, was it possible to erect large building volumes in a short time.
• The erection of tall buildings called for the stacking of identical plan layouts.

Identical plan layouts using large-format components represent a very rational and therefore inexpensive form of construction, which, how-

ever, calls for precise planning. Consequently, new modular and grid systems became established: structural, fitting-out, modular or facade grids formed the prerequisites for industrialised building. The book *Baukonstruktionslehre 1* (theory of building design) by Otto Frick and Karl Knöll, published in 1963, did not include the term "dimensional coordination", but in the revised edition of 1979 they had the following to say: "The values given here for system and element provide the planner with fundamental incentives for the design of the building … Plan layout and overall construction depend to a certain extent on the dimensions and construction details of the prefabricated elements." [4] So the architect turned to the planning of systems in order to be able to plan at all.

In 1966 the Committee on Housing, Building Construction & Planning of the UN Economic Commission for Europe reached agreement on the new European module, which was based on the basic module M = 10 cm. The resulting so-called multimodules such as 183 M (1830 cm) or submodules such as M/10 (1 cm), from which controlling dimensions (grid dimensions), coordinating sizes (sizes of elements including allowance for fitting and jointing) and work sizes (theoretical element dimensions without taking into account manufacturing tolerances) evolved. This mathematical approach to architecture was only partially successful because the theoretical discussion alone with merely two-dimensional modular systems exposed the geometrical weaknesses (Fig. C 5.5).

Basements

Rooms (partially) below ground level were increasingly used as proper, habitable spaces; basements and semi-basements for pursuing hobbies or holding parties became a must for every modern family, and tax rebates encouraged the letting of semi-basement rooms. The question of well-being was subsidiary to economic and functional criteria. In addition, buildings were planned in new areas without taking proper account of the subsoil properties, which resulted in the need for high-quality waterproofing as well as elaborate, expensive foundation and excavation works. Both phenomena – usable space below ground level and planning without considering topographical aspects – were developments that showed similarities with the founding years, which were also characterised by a phase of private-sector house-building on a massive scale. The waterproofing methods and machinery now available, however, turned usable basements into a mass phenomenon.

Foundations and basement floor slabs
Masonry or unreinforced, tamped concrete foundations – the customary methods of the post-war period – were now replaced by reinforced concrete foundations because the higher building loads of multi-storey forms of con-

C 5.6

struction and the use of heavier building materials (sound insulation) led to the need for better-quality foundations. Deep foundations making use of piles that transfer their loads via end bearing or skin friction were also used, especially for high-rise buildings. Raft foundations were popular, too, distributing the high building loads adequately over a wider area. The diaphragm wall, an excavation method involving a bentonite-filled trench, was also developed in this period. It was used to build multi-level basements on confined urban sites.

For the first time, basement floors were now waterproofed. Simple cement screed floors or tamped concrete slabs were hardly used any more. The norm became reinforced concrete slabs 80–120 mm deep with a damp-proof membrane laid on top to protect against moisture from the soil – but only when it was necessary for the basement to remain permanently dry. Where demands were lower, the waterproofing was omitted and instead a so-called waterproof concrete – with a high cement content, specific grading curve and additives – used to protect against moisture: either in the form of a 30 mm topping on a lean concrete slab or as a 100 mm thick ground slab.

Damage and measures
Settlement – either already completed or still ongoing – may be a problem with buildings dating from the early 1960s. The standards of foundation construction in those years were no better than the post-war days, but the larger buildings resulted in heavier loads and in some cases the subsoil was poor.

Serious moisture damage is rare even where basement floors are not 100 % watertight. Any small amounts of moisture that infiltrate into basements can usually be absorbed by the interior

air, meaning that although the amount of moisture is measurable, a mouldy smell does not ensue.

External walls to basements
Many external walls to the basements of detached houses continued to be built in masonry or tamped concrete of low quality. But for apartment blocks and high-rise buildings the basement walls were now of reinforced concrete. Waterproofing to prevent the ingress of moisture became an important topic. Vertical waterproofing in the form of bituminous coatings and paints were added to the traditional cement render. Damp-proof courses (usually of simple bituminous felt) to prevent rising damp were now included in masonry walls. The standard work of the 1960s, *Hochbaukonstruktionen* (building construction) by Heinrich Schmitt, introduced a number of moisture barriers that even today are erroneously included in new buildings: the lowest moisture barrier is frequently 100 mm above the top of the basement floor instead of at the same level as the damp-proof membrane to the basement floor. In historical terms this form of construction originates from the time of the basements used solely for storage, where watertight floors were unknown. In those days such a damp-proof course was only intended to protect the masonry, not ensure a dry basement. Even today, connecting the damp-proof membrane with the damp-proof course is still shown in some textbooks in the form of hollow fillets and waterproof renders. Another barrier often still included these days is a course of bricks beneath the floor over the basement, but this is only sensible when the ground floor is located above the splashing water zone, and serves as a barrier to moisture rising in the base of the wall. The fact that such brickwork is still built even when the basement is totally below ground level is based on a misunderstanding.

The further development of waterproof concrete enabled the construction of basements without tanking from the 1970s onwards. The materials and dimensions used correspond almost exactly with those prescribed today. Even as this method of constructing basement was being introduced, it was pointed out that bending stresses were not allowed because otherwise hairline cracks would develop. And this is exactly the main cause of problems in such basements.

Ground and upper floors

New methods, but primarily new forms of construction, changed the external appearance of buildings fundamentally: concrete frames and the box-frame (or cross-wall) method of construction permitted a totally unrestricted facade design, e.g. with curtain walls or lightweight walls of fibre-cement panels, but also precast concrete elements in fair-face quality. Furthermore, the regulations regarding permissible building heights were relaxed: whereas in the 1930s only low-rise buildings were permitted on the edges of the towns, many new buildings, especially on large housing estates, now reached the limit for tall buildings, even exceeded them in some cases.

External walls
The method of building apartments that prevailed in the 1950s, i.e. loadbearing longitudinal (= external) walls was increasingly superseded by the box-frame method, i.e. loadbearing internal walls, during the 1960s. This form of construction permitted considerably greater building depths and was therefore regarded as more economic. The amount of incoming daylight was reduced, but this was partly compen-

C 5.5 Problems at the internal and external corners of a wall in a modular system
    a Wall grid and planning grid coincide. Corner elements at external corner (a) and internal corner (b) have identical overall dimensions. wall elements have different widths.
    b Wall elements offset from planning grid. Corner elements (a and c) with identical dimensions are possible, likewise wall elements with the same width. However, left- and right-hand wall elements are necessary (corner vulnerable to transport damage).
    c Wall element faces positioned on planning grid. Two different corner elements are required for internal and external corners. Wall elements are the same width.
    d The problem of the internal and external corners is obvious here just from the schematic drawing of the wall elements showing different layer thicknesses and different layer materials. With the joints indicated here, only one internal and one external corner element are required. All wall elements are the same width.
C 5.6 Sand-blasted fair-face concrete, Bensberg Town Hall (D), 1971, Gottfried Böhm
C 5.7 Box-frame construction, spandrel panels ensure longitudinal stability
C 5.8 Box-frame construction with cantilevering supports, Cologne-Chorweiler (D), 1972

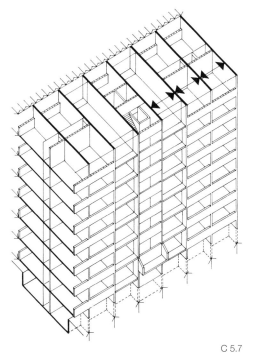

C 5.7

C 5.8

C 5.9 Calcium silicate facing masonry
C 5.10 External cladding of fibre-cement sheeting, Cologne (D)
C 5.11 Building site with large-format system formwork for in situ concrete construction, around 1970
C 5.12 Spandrel panel cladding made from precast concrete elements (exposed aggregate finish), Colonia Tower, Cologne (D), 1973, Henrik Busch
C 5.13 Terraced houses in in situ concrete, Graz (A), 1978, Werkgruppe Graz

C 5.9

C 5.10

sated for by the larger amounts of glass in the facade without the need for any intruding lintels (Figs. C 5.7 and 5.8).

Turning the span of the floors through 90 ° for apartments had far-reaching functional and aesthetic consequences:

- Loggias replaced balconies, which 10 years earlier had represented a logical form of construction because the floor slab could then continue beyond the loadbearing external wall.
- Great building depths resulted in dark zones in the middle of the building: bathrooms and kitchens were shifted from the external walls to the interiors – with no natural ventilation or daylighting.
- The box-frame method of construction for apartments permitted the use of short floor spans which, however, led to standardised, narrow rooms – the dimensions of double bed, circulation space and wardrobe measured approx. 3.60 m in total.

Besides the box-frame method of construction, there were also structures with loadbearing transverse and longitudinal walls with floor slabs spanning in both directions, particularly for high-rise buildings.

Solid walls

Reinforced concrete was now often used as a wall material. But now normal-weight concrete was used instead of the lightweight or clay brick aggregate concretes of the post-war period. The reason for this was the high dead loads of the concrete floors and walls, which increased with the number of floors. This also explains why solid bricks started to appear in masonry construction again and lightweight forms of construction were favoured for detached houses only. High compressive strengths meant good sound insulation and fire protection, but this fact was often exploited in order to reduce the thickness of the components (counter-productive in terms of sound insulation and fire protection). Loadbearing walls just 115 mm thick were common in terrace houses, and the walls of multi-storey buildings were often only 175 mm thick. In Germany calcium silicate masonry

units enjoyed their heyday. This was due to their appearance and also their better accuracy compared to clay bricks, but especially because of the large-format varieties, which could be laid very economically (Fig. C 5.9). The neutral colouring of the calcium silicate brick made it the preferred choice for facing masonry in this period because colour was gradually disappearing from surfaces. This phenomenon was particularly evident in kitchens: whereas in the post-war years most buyers preferred pastel shades, after 1965 white and grey surfaces took an almost exclusive hold on the market. Formwork systems replaced traditional timber formwork for in situ concrete construction. The Doka large-format formwork system – three-ply core plywood, timber and steel framing – was developed in 1965. This system allowed in situ concrete walls to be constructed at affordable prices (Fig. C 5.11). Climbing formwork originally developed for large civil engineering structures such as bridge piers began to be used for high-rise buildings as well. Table forms, i.e. movable large-format formwork, was used for box-frame construction, and identical room

widths rationalised this technique even further. The Hünnebeck company from Düsseldorf developed "room formwork" at this time, which allowed the formwork to walls and floors to be set up the same time; in section this formwork was the shape of an upturned "U". To strike the formwork, the entire "U" was lowered and the two side walls pulled inwards. The steel formwork was then lifted out with the help of an L-shaped grab and moved up to the next storey. Heinrich Schmitt summarised the progress in figures: whereas traditional timber formwork required approx. 75 min/m² from setup to striking, large-format systems needed only 15 min/m² [5]. This also shows that it was the no longer the cost of materials that was critical for the overall cost of construction, but increasingly the cost of labour. The rational and hence relatively adaptable combination of in situ concrete and ready-made formwork systems was preferred in Western Europe, whereas in Eastern Europe the building boom was mastered with the help of fully prefabricated methods – large-panel construction.

C 5.11

Thermal performance and insulating materials
That most important virtue of the post-war period – thriftiness – was regarded as out of date in the years of prosperity. Structures built after 1965 are characterised neither by frugality of material consumption nor by energy efficiency, a situation that did not change until the first oil crisis in 1973. The German government reacted to this drastic event by publishing a supplement to DIN 4108 (thermal performance) within two years and finally a completely revised set of rules in 1977: the Thermal Insulation Act. This also meant, however, that buildings built or refurbished before the oil crisis were considered to be based on the thermal performance criteria of the founding years. Although the materials required had long since been available, it was only now that they started to be used, as required by the new statutory provisions. The 1977 Thermal Insulation Act represented a radical change: the requirements for thermal performance were raised – for roof surfaces by a factor of 3.5, for instance. In addition, double glazing was now stipulated, although the U-value of 3.3 W/m²K specified at that time was still very high compared to today.
The values specified could no longer be achieved economically with solid masonry walls. Calcium silicate brick walls 365 mm, which according to DIN 4108 were adequate in Cologne or Hamburg (thermal insulation area I) prior to 1974, were now nowhere near sufficient. Besides the renewed triumph of porous masonry units, especially aerated concrete for detached family homes, it was the use of insulating materials in apartment blocks that changed building construction permanently.
Some double-leaf masonry walls, an invention of the founding years to improve resistance to driving rain, were now built with insulating materials (cavity insulation) instead of an air cavity. Mineral wool just 60 mm thick was regarded as adequate insulation for a building!
Cladding to external walls (with an air space between structure and cladding) was generally built without insulation prior to 1977. Its only purpose was to protect against driving rain, but otherwise was similar to modern forms of cladding. After the oil crisis, rigid polystyrene foam – invented in 1951 and first used as a backing material for the first external thermal insulation composite systems (ETICS) towards the end of the 1950s – quickly became the favourite material for adding thermal insulation to external walls. Here again, an insulation thickness of just 40 mm was considered adequate!
Besides stone slabs, asbestos fibre cement sheets were used almost exclusively for the cladding (with ventilation cavity). Both small-format, tile-like panels (300 x 600 mm) and large-format sheets (up to 1250 x 3580 mm) were available on the market. In contrast to the rendered facades still popular in the 1950s, these inexpensive sheets and panels represented a dry trade, could be erected quickly and required little maintenance, which is why they were used on a massive scale for multi-

storey housing in particular (Fig. C 5.10). Asbestos fibres were successively replaced by synthetic fibres between 1980 and 1990.

Damage and measures
The durability and quality of construction of the majority of external wall forms is undisputed – with the exception of the early lightweight external walls of the 1960s. The latter are, however, no longer often encountered in their original condition. But thermal performance upgrades are very difficult: besides the unavoidable thermal bridges at loggias (see p. 200), the fair-face concrete spandrel panels favoured in those days represent a problem. Where these are precast concrete elements, they can be removed, although their high weight means that this is no easy task. Spandrel panels of in situ concrete present a greater problem because they frequently form the lateral restraints to the cross-walls (bracing against horizontal loads). Simply removing these without providing a new form of lateral restraint is therefore impossible, but leaving them in place without any insulation equally impossible because the in situ concrete spandrel panels constitute an inadmissible thermal bridge due to their connection with the external wall. It is precisely these fair-face concrete elements that are typical of the architecture of this period; a thermal performance upgrade destroys the architecture for ever (Fig. C 5.12).
It is a similar situation with external walls because the fair-face concrete or facing masonry cannot be insulated sensibly on the inside. The thermal bridges caused by the cross-walls and floor slabs – differently to the longitudinal walls of the founding years – are unacceptable. The only solution is to attach insulation on the outside – in terms of building physics the better solution for housing anyway. However, the character of the building is changed completely because the "brutality" of the construction so typical of this period disappears behind a modern skin.
The terraced housing that became fashionable after 1970 (Fig. C 5.13) exploited the new freedoms of the box-frame former construction most consequently. Owing to the thermal bridges caused by the cross-walls and terraces, an energy-efficiency upgrade is economically and aesthetically hardly feasible, which might move some owners to consider demolition. Similar problems can be found in the ambitious projects of the 1970s that used in situ concrete techniques – which in the meantime had become affordable – to express a new architectural language. But in the case of buildings with cladding to the facade and an air cavity that is not yet insulated, adding further thermal insulation is relatively straightforward. The only problem here is the disposal of the fibre-cement panels containing asbestos. However, the cost of this is generally overestimated because it is instinctively likened to the cost of removing sprayed asbestos from heating systems – a totally different case. Mineral wool insulation from this period must also

C 5.12

be removed and disposed of; the fibres' lack of biosolubility can be accepted only in the case of fully encapsulated components such as impact sound insulation.

Concrete deterioration
In addition to the lack of thermal insulation, many fair-face concrete components suffer from damage to their surfaces due to rusting reinforcement. The concrete cover as specified in DIN 1045 and used throughout the 1970s was not substantially increased until a new edition of the standard appeared in 1988. In 1975 a concrete cover of just 20 mm was considered adequate for external components, and this could even be reduced to 15 mm in the case of precast concrete elements. Large building volumes, short building times and inadequate curing represent further sources of problems that have led to corrosion of the steel reinforcement. This corrosion starts with the carbonation process, which due to the influence of carbon dioxide converts the calcium hydroxide protecting against rust into calcium carbonate. This causes the original pH value of the con-

C 5.13

Class	Surface protection	Thickness [μm]	Binder
OS-A	Hydrophobic treatment	0	Silane, siloxane
OS-B	Coating for non-trafficable surfaces	80	Polyurethane, epoxy resin
OS-C	Coating for non-trafficable surfaces with increased impermeability	80	Polyurethane, epoxy resin
OS-D I	Coating for non-trafficable surfaces with minimal crack bridging at least based on polymer cement	2000	Polymer, cement
OS-D II	As for OS-D I but based purely on polymer	300	Polymer dispersion
OS-E	Coating with enhanced crack bridging for non-trafficable surfaces	1000	Polyurethane, acrylate, epoxy resin
OS-F	Coating with enhanced crack bridging for trafficable surfaces	1500–3000	Polyurethane

C 5.14

Type of deterioration	Exposure class		Examples	Concrete cover[3,4] [mm]			Min. strength class of concrete[5]
				c_{min}	c	c_{nom}	
Deterioration induced by carbonation[1]	XC 1	Dry or permanently wet	Interiors with normal humidity, components permanently underwater	10	10	20	C 16/20 LC 16/18
	XC 2	Wet, seldom dry	Parts of water tanks, foundation components	20		35	
	XC 3	Moderate humidity	Open sheds, garages, interiors with high humidity		15		C 20/25 LC 20/22
	XC 4	Alternately wet and dry	Extern. components exposed to direct rainfall, components in alternate wet/dry zones	25		40	C 25/30 LC 25/28
Deterioration induced by chlorides[1]	XD 1	Moderate moisture	Components within range of spray water from traffic pavements, detached garages				C 30/37 LC 30/33
	XD 2	Wet, seldom dry	Swimming pools, brine baths, components exposed to indust. waste water with chlorides	40	15	55	
	XD 3	Alternately wet and dry	Components in splashing water zone of traffic pave. wi. de-icing salts, park deck w. direct traffic[2]				C 35/45 LC 35/38
Deterioration induced by chlorides in seawater[1]	XS 1	Salt-laden air but no direct contact with seawater	External components in coastal regions				C 30/37 LC 30/33
	XS 2	Underwater	Components in port facilities constantly underwater	40	15	55	
	XS 3	Within tidal range, splashing and spray water	Quay walls in port facilities				C 35/45 LC 35/38
With concrete simultaneously affected by wear (without concrete technology measures)[1]	XM 1	Moderate abrasion	Directly trafficked components with moderate traffic	Increase c_{min} by 5 mm			
	XM 2	Severe abrasion	Components directly exposed to heavy forklift truck traffic, directly trafficked components in industrial facilities, silos	Increase c_{min} by 10 mm			C 30/37 LC 30/33
	XM 3	Very severe abrasion	Components directly exposed to tracked vehicle traffic	Increase c_{min} by 15 mm			C 35/45 LC 35/38

[2] Additional surface protection necessary for directly trafficked parking decks, e.g. coating.

[3] The following applies in the case of lightweight concrete (except exposure class XC 1): $c_{min} \geq d_{gl} + 5$ mm (d_{gl} = max. particle size of lightweight aggregate).

[4] When concreting against uneven surfaces, $\triangle c$ must be increased by the difference of the unevenness, but by 20 mm at least; when concreting directly against the soil, $\triangle c$ must be increased by 50 mm.

[5] Provided no higher figures apply due to the exposure classes for concrete deterioration.

C 5.15

C 5.14 Surface protection systems for refurbished fair-face concrete components
C 5.15 Minimum concrete cover and concrete grades to DIN 1045-1
C 5.16 Refurbishment operations for damaged fair-face concrete components:
 a Exposing the corroded reinforcing bars
 b Applying a coat of anti-corrosion agent
 c Making good with PCC mortar

crete to drop from 13; and if the value falls below 9, the outer layer of the steel reinforcement begins to corrode and the increase in volume causes the concrete cover to break away. This natural process is accelerated by mechanical damage or chemical attack, large pores in the concrete or defects such as cracks and honeycombing. Incidentally, the process stops sooner indoors than outdoors – there is usually insufficient moisture for corrosion and so spalling is unusual on internal components.

The first steps that should be taken when refurbishing concrete are normally as follows:

- Establish the strength of the damaged areas (rebound hammer, tests on cores), check the pH value (phenolphthalein solution), the moisture levels in the components (see "Planning refurbishment works", p. 23) plus the positions and sizes of the reinforcement (electromagnetic location systems).
- Cut away all loose concrete.
- Clean the exposed reinforcement by means of sand-blasting, shot-peening or high-pressure water jets (flame-cleaning is not recommended) back to firm concrete and quality level Sa 2.5 (bright metal) when refurbishing with PCC mortar; only removal of flaking rust (Sa 1) is necessary when applying sprayed concrete.

There are two ways of carrying out the actual refurbishment:

- Refurbishment with PCC mortar (polymer-modified mix): In this method an initial protective coating is applied in two operations (low- or zero-solvent epoxy resin or cement emulsion coatings, sometimes containing red lead or zinc oxide). Afterwards, a bond enhancer based on a reaction resin or cementitious synthetic resin (somewhat easier to use) is applied, into which the PCC mortar is worked while the bond enhancer is still wet. PCC mortar consists of cement mortar with the addition of synthetic binders and is used for reconstructing the original profile. Systems are available without carbonation resistance (M1), with carbonation resistance

a

b

c

C 5.16

(M2) and for loadbearing components (M3). However, the latter can only be used in certain situations because of the high elastic modulus and the combustibility in some instances (not class A to DIN 4102).
• Refurbishment with sprayed concrete: In this method the initial protective coating and the bond enhancer are unnecessary. Instead, sprayed concrete to DIN 18551 (e.g. Torkret method) is applied to the damaged areas – but this should not be confused with PCC sprayed concrete, which, like the first method, must be built up. Cement-based sprayed concrete adheres excellently to the substrate and provides natural corrosion protection. Depending on its thickness, it can also represent an upgrade in terms of loadbearing capacity and fire protection. The stipulation that sprayed concrete should only be applied to a firm substrate, i.e. all carbonated concrete must be removed first, is currently disputed.

With either of the above methods, small areas of damage can be made good with a repair mortar based on a PCC or epoxy resin mix. A carbonation retarder can be applied, too. This is a special sealing treatment based on siloxane or acrylic resin, usually with the addition of a pigment. Some products are water-repellent but at the same time vapour-permeable (Fig. C 5.14).
The values given in Fig. C 5.15 should be regarded as the minimum dimensions for the concrete cover after refurbishment. Although a smaller concrete cover is permitted by the German Reinforced Concrete Committee (DAfStb) directive covering the protection and repair of concrete components, a new analysis of the component's stability must then be carried out. Damaged concrete caused by corroded reinforcement is a very common problem with concrete spandrel panel elements. If these are precast components suspended in front of the structure, their fixings (reinforcing bars or anchors, depending on year of construction) must be checked. It was many years before these were produced in stainless steel and any mild steel fixings may have already corroded, which in the worst case can lead to the entire element falling from the building!

High-rise buildings
It was the new reinforced concrete methods that rendered possible tall buildings at reasonable cost for the first time, and such buildings became more and more popular with architects. Whereas up until the early 1960s high-rise buildings were used only for offices in city centres, apartment blocks in the suburbs plus hotels and hospitals now accounted for the majority of high-rise structures.
In Germany the Study Group for Urban Planning, Building & Housing published guidelines for the building of high-rise structures in the 1970s; many of the points are similar to today's regulations for tall buildings. Unacceptable today, however, are the escape stairs permissible at that time (800 mm flight width, 200/200 rise/going ratio) as a second means of escape from tall buildings with up to 12 storeys plus the mandatory inclusion of rubbish chutes in high-rise housing.
At the start of the 1960s, some high-rise buildings were still built in masonry (a trend that first began in Switzerland), e.g. 240 mm thick internal walls and 500 mm external walls of calcium silicate bricks. As the cutting of chases and slots was prohibited, even during erection, and the walls and their openings cannot be changed, such buildings cannot be converted. Such interventions prove to be problematic in concrete high-rise buildings as well because the loadbearing walls are often < 200 mm thick, i.e. their loadbearing capacity is fully exploited, especially in the lower storeys.

Loadbearing internal walls and frame constructions
The change from the loadbearing external to the loadbearing internal wall (box-frame construction) has already been described (see p. 193). The frame structures already known from the 1950s developed into the sole means of construction for department stores, offices, industrial buildings, etc. during the 1960s. However, steel frames rapidly lost their significance in the course of this development – for the following reasons:
• The poor performance in fire had to be improved by encasing or cladding the steel members.
• The external columns normally within the

facade required protection against corrosion.
• Formwork techniques had developed to such an extent that concrete frames could now be erected just as economically.

The basic form of reinforced concrete frames plus their external appearance were very similar to those of the post-war period. The only difference was the new formwork systems, which were no longer compatible with the haunches at the column-beam junctions that had been common up until then. Ribbed floors with their complicated formwork also gradually disappeared and were replaced by flat floors with simple rectangular downstand beams. As the density of building services started to increase considerably (telephones, air-conditioning), albeit still far less than today, the distribution networks were frequently routed through openings in the frame construction, which was readily possible with in situ concrete (Fig. C 5.18). The use of fair-face concrete internally was uncommon; all columns, beams and soffits were clad – the latter only rarely with prefabricated systems, which became popular in the 1980s, but instead with plaster on a suitable background (e.g. lightweight wood-wool boards).

Damage and measures
Minimal reinforcement and the resulting restrictions on serviceability are characteristics that hardly apply to the buildings erected between 1965 and 1980, which means that the problems of refurbishment are mostly limited to remedying concrete deterioration.

Facade systems
The erection of high-rise buildings called for the development of new facade systems: precast concrete (large-panel construction) and the curtain walls of extruded aluminium sections that had been widely used in America for a long time. The latter generally match the forms of construction used today, although the U-values of the panels and glazing employed then no longer conform to modern requirements. The development of facade systems caused the loadbearing frame to be shifted to the interior, where it could no longer divide up the facade as it had done in the past. The posts of

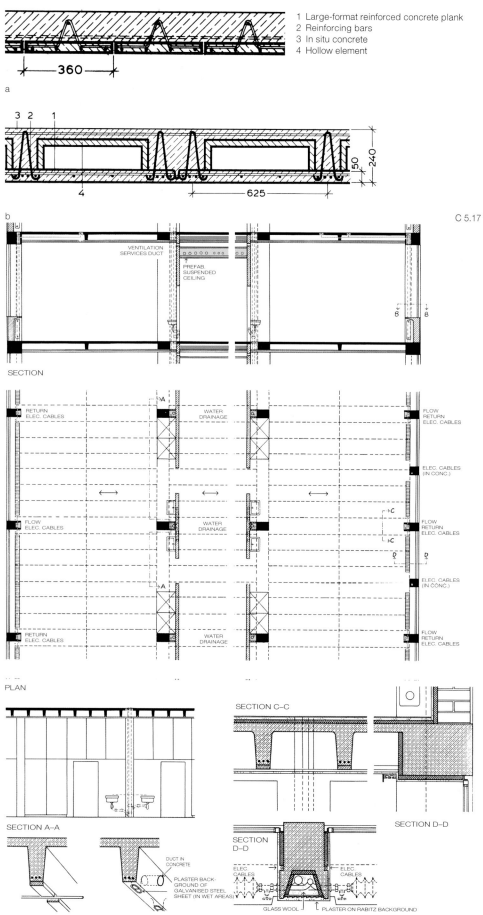

1 Large-format reinforced concrete plank
2 Reinforcing bars
3 In situ concrete
4 Hollow element

a

b

C 5.17

VENTILATION SERVICES DUCT

PREFAB. SUSPENDED CEILING

B   B

SECTION

RETURN ELEC. CABLES

WATER DRAINAGE

FLOW RETURN ELEC. CABLES

ELEC. CABLES (IN CONC.)

A

FLOW ELEC. CABLES

WATER DRAINAGE

FLOW RETURN ELEC. CABLES

C

C

D

D

ELEC. CABLES (IN CONC.)

A

RETURN ELEC. CABLES

WATER DRAINAGE

FLOW RETURN ELEC. CABLES

PLAN

SECTION C-C

SECTION A-A

SECTION D-D

SECTION D-D

DUCT IN CONCRETE

PLASTER BACK-GROUND OF GALVANISED STEEL SHEET (IN WET AREAS)

ELEC. CABLES

ELEC. CABLES

GLASS WOOL   PLASTER ON RABITZ BACKGROUND

C 5.18

the curtain wall – designed for horizontal loads only – together with the closed spandrel panels – to prevent the propagation of fire – were now responsible for the segmentation of the facade, which led to a certain uniformity in the architecture of high-rise office buildings. The closed spandrel panels of in situ concrete were often used to brace the building horizontally, which rules out their removal during conversion. Besides these post-and-rail elevations, experiments were also carried out with suspended sandwich panels consisting of a weather-resistant outer face (e.g. aluminium), a core of rigid foam insulation and an internal vapour barrier (e.g. plastic panel) (Figs. C 5.19 and 5.20). In contrast to earlier post-and-rail solutions with no thermal break, these panels had the advantage that there were no thermal bridges. The thickness of the insulation, however, no longer meets the latest requirements.

Damage and measures
The sound insulation of facades is often unsatisfactory because the details at the junctions with suspended floors and internal walls had not yet been adequately developed to suppress flanking transmissions (internal) or because of lightweight forms of construction and a lack of regulations (external). The situation regarding thermal performance is similar, with thermal insulation that is too thin for today's standards and many thermal bridges. The only solution for refurbishment is to rebuild the facade completely. Re-creating the delicateness of the original sections even only approximately requires a certain degree of skill and a client who is not put off by the cost.
Buildings with a loadbearing structure visible on the outside usually have only minimal insulation – if at all – on the inside to prevent condensation. Here again, the building must be deconstructed back to the loadbearing structure. The new facade is then erected in front of the columns instead of between them. This means that the refurbished building is hardly distinguishable from office buildings planned and built today.
One irksome task, even when planning such buildings these days, is compensating for the differences between the tolerances of the structure and those of the cladding, mainly because the facade now encloses the entire building and any discrepancies are no longer disguised by the columns and beams dividing up the facade. Although the tolerances of concrete structures built between 1965 and 1980 were certainly much better than those of buildings erected directly after the war, primarily because of new formwork techniques, considerable inaccuracies still remain in certain instances. These were not improved until the appearance of DIN 18202 (flatness tolerances) in 1977. Therefore, when planning refurbishment measures, relatively adaptable details – nevertheless satisfying acoustic and fire requirements – must be devised for the junctions with suspended floors and columns or internal walls.

Windows

Double glazing become became compulsory with the publication of the Thermal Insulation Act in 1977. Up until 1975 it had been usual in the warmer regions of Germany to install single windows with single glazing – a solution that even during the founding years had been used for ancillary rooms only. The U-values of the first insulating glass units were about twice as good as those of single glazing but were still around 3.0 W/m²K. It is only since 1995 that the inner faces of the panes in insulating glass units have been coated with metal oxides, a development that cut the U-value from 3.0 to 1.3 W/m²K overnight. Some manufacturers print the date of manufacture on the spacer between the panes, which allows an estimate of the window's performance. Without further investigations, however, an original window dating from the period 1965–80 cannot be classed as upgradable because the frames are usually not stiff enough to accommodate new glazing and the airtightness and operation no longer conform to modern ideas of comfort and convenience. In addition, there is a high risk that wooden windows have been treated with preservatives that are now prohibited (e.g. lindane, PCP), also on the inside, a fact that, incidentally, can apply to all wooden linings.

Render, paints, coatings

The well-known mineral renders continued to be used for multi-storey buildings and these were joined by synthetic resin mixes, the latter designated in DIN 18558 as "coatings with a render-type appearance". They quickly became significant as a finish coat because they could be relatively easily applied even by unskilled labour. For a long time nothing else was used as the finish coat to external thermal insulation composite systems. Suitable synthetic resin or similar film-forming coatings were used as a

final coat, also for later renovation work. Although the vapour permeability is guaranteed by the manufacturers, it is only possible when applied properly, i.e. in a thin coat. Multiple renovation coats and excessive render thicknesses lead again and again, however, to impermeable layers, large areas of which become detached from the substrate. Such finishes must be removed back to the substrate by scouring or shot-blasting and a new system applied. In the coming years this refurbishment measure will certainly also become necessary with the early external thermal insulation composite systems as well, the insulation thicknesses of which are only just adequate according to the latest standards.

Lightweight and prefabricated partitions

Partitions in dry construction without a loadbearing function have been around for a long time, but it was not until modularisation progressed that their widespread use became worthwhile. Lightweight partitions made from plastered boards on framing were replaced by prefabricated demountable walls, e.g. plasterboard on galvanised steel sections. Walls in dry construction had been produced since the 1940s, but not until now had they been used on such a huge scale. This resulted in the new DIN 18183 (1985) covering prefabricated walls made from plasterboard. Demountable partitions were also used in housing. Although their advantages could not be fully exploited here, the timber framing was often replaced by metal framing, e.g. extruded aluminium or pressed steel sections (Fig. C 5.21).

Suspended floors

From the mid-1960s onwards, the flat reinforced concrete floor replaced virtually all other known suspended floor systems. With their homogeneous loadbearing behaviour and flat soffits,

C 5.19

C 5.17 Partially prefabricated reinforced concrete suspended floor systems
a Plank floor with smooth soffit
b Plank floor with smooth soffit and hollow elements to reduce the weight
C 5.18 Reinforced concrete frame construction showing routing of services, downstand beams spanning in the longitudinal direction, ribbed floor spanning across the building; example from 1978
C 5.19 Postal Cheque Office, Essen (D), 1968, Building Dept. of Düsseldorf Regional Postal Service
C 5.20 Postal Cheque Office, Essen
a Part-elevation on facade
b Horizontal section AA through spandrel panel element and movable sunshading panel
c Vertical section BB through glazing and spandrel panel

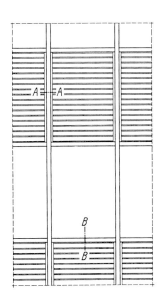

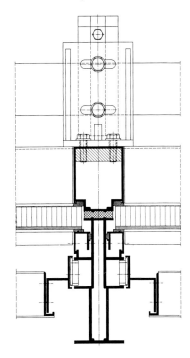

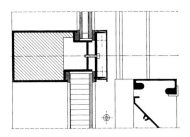

a

b

c

C 5.20

internal walls were possible anywhere, something that was just not feasible with timber joist floors (dead load of wall) or T-beam floors (detail at top of wall). Over time, the in situ concrete floor was joined by more and more partially and fully prefabricated floor systems. Both these latter forms of suspended floor enabled rapid progress on site because formwork was eliminated, and the partially prefabricated version had the further advantage of low weight, which eased transport and erection. Thoroughly rationalised plan layouts were, however, essential for both systems. But the new European modular dimensions could not assert themselves even here, a fact that becomes obvious when we study the grid sizes, which continued to be based on masonry dimensions. The differences between in situ and precast concrete floors can be ignored in the event of refurbishment work – except when new openings are planned. In such cases it is important to remember that the principal reinforcement in precast elements – contrasting with the mesh reinforcement of in situ concrete – is usually of a larger diameter but at a wider spacing (Fig. C 5.17).

Composite steel-concrete floors, e.g. with trapezoidal profile steel sheeting, were used more and more in high-rise and industrial buildings.

Balconies and loggias

In contrast to prefabricated construction, suspended floors and/or loadbearing walls of in situ concrete usually continued from inside to outside without any thermal break. The ensuing thermal bridge was acknowledged, but ignored: "Columns and continuous cross-walls form thermal bridges at balconies and loggias. They are not critical where the lintel or masonry is thicker (> 300 mm). The work required to prevent these is complicated and totally disproportionate to the disadvantage of the minimal heat losses or the gradual blackening of the edge of the floor." [6] Only rarely was an approx. 500 mm wide strip of thin thermal insulation laid in the bottom of the formwork or incorporated in the masonry (Figs. C 5.22 and 5.23).

An improvement in terms of building physics is problematic owing to the lack of separation between the components. Subsequent separation – similar to a separated balcony – is impossible because the wall plates that support the floors are designed as continuous. Attaching insulation on all sides – on a loggia that means floor, side walls and soffit – is just as complicated if the flat roof guidelines are to be observed (turning up the waterproofing at the door). Firstly, there would be a step at least 200 mm high at the door to the loggia, and secondly, the insulation to the soffit would reduce the clear headroom by at least 100 mm; the clear height in the loggia might be as little as 2.20 m. One possible solution is to renew the facade completely, turning the loggias into unheated conservatories, which, however, presumes that the facade faces approximately south. The alternative is to convert the loggias into heated living spaces and build constructionally independent balconies in front of the facade. Increasing the usable floor area represents an economic advantage for the building owner, providing the apartment is unoccupied at the time and a new rental agreement is possible. If the apartment continues to be occupied by the same tenant, only a modernisation surcharge can be charged.

Floor finishes

DIN 4109 "Sound insulation in buildings" was introduced in 1962 and remained valid until the end of the 1970s. Compared to the bonded screeds of the post-war years, it represented a considerable improvement, but still lagged far behind today's limiting values. In box-frame construction unfavourable structure-borne sound propagation through the entire structure, especially from the stair flights and lifts without any acoustic separation, results from the fact that the concrete floors are continuous over the party walls. As impact sound insulation is only very thin, the floating cement screed on top can be reduced to 35 mm. The total depth of the floor finishes is therefore only 50–60 mm, which in a total refurbishment project means it is necessary to deal with the change in levels at junctions with staircases that are to be retained. Besides traditional wet screeds, dry subfloors were often used – frequently one layer of 19 or 22 mm thick tongue and groove particleboards, possibly asbestos-cement boards in wet areas.

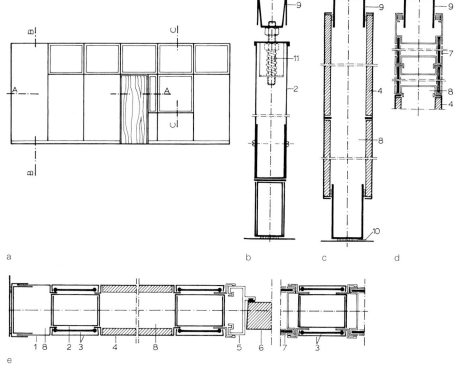

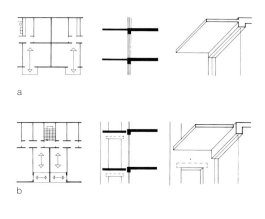

a
b
c
d

e

1 Wall channel
2 Stud
3 Cover section with spring clip
4 Wall element:
  coated sheet steel with plasterboard
5 Aluminium door frame

6 Door leaf
7 Glazing in aluminium glazing bars
8 Rock wool filling
9 Ceiling channel
10 Elastic floor steel
11 Screw adjuster

C 5.21

C 5.22

C 5.21 Demountable partition
  a Elevation on partition
  b Section BB, post with screw adjuster
  c Section BB, plain wall element
  d Section CC, detail of junction with ceiling above fanlight
  e Horizontal section AA
C 5.22 Sketches of balcony/loggia construction principles
  a Balcony slabs cantilevering beyond longitudinal loadbearing walls
  b Separate loggia slabs spanning between masonry side walls
C 5.23 Various balcony/loggia details
  a In situ concrete in the form of a cantilevering slab with bituminous waterproofing
  b Precast concrete elements, waterproof according to the opinions at the time, spanning between the side walls
C 5.24 Floor finishes for underfloor heating with stainless steel pipes

Both should be removed during refurbishment work; particleboards are generally contaminated with formaldehyde.

Underfloor heating had first appeared at the start of the 1970s. Besides grids of cables laid directly in the screed, hot-water systems were also on offer, which, however, did not become really established until the 1980s. Initially, the pipes were not embedded in the screed, but rather separated from the screed by way of plastic or profiled sheeting in order to allow for the expansion and contraction of the metal pipes used at that time (Fig. C 5.24).

Like with concrete floors and internal walls, in the 1970s developers were looking for practical – i.e. quickly installed, dry – floor coverings. For example, in situ terrazzo was replaced by prefabricated terrazzo (reconstituted stone flags). Most wooden floors were fixed in place with adhesive, but now the tar adhesives of the past had been replaced by synthetic resin adhesives and small-format wood-block flooring had replaced floorboards. But the majority of floor coverings were now PVC and carpeting fixed with adhesive. Needle-punch carpets in particular were very popular. Up until that time carpets had been a luxury article, but new production methods (tufting) and the use of synthetic fibres meant that there were now floor coverings on the market that were even cheaper than linoleum or mosaic parquet.

Roof spaces

The pitched roof was almost completely ousted by the "modern" flat roof. Only the case of single family homes did pitched roofs still prevail.

Flat roofs

It was precisely at the beginning of this period that flat roof constructions were sometimes of an experimental nature. The introduction of DIN 18338 "Roof covering and roof sealing works" in 1974 was intended to limit the resulting abundance of failures. Textbooks published as late as 1978 were still describing what we today would call risky forms of construction. But Heinrich Schmitt, for one, was still hoping that "research ... would solve the problems to such an extent that there would be no further serious problems with flat roofs today" [7].

The fact that even now the flat roof still has a poor reputation among the general public can be attributed to the damage-prone designs of the 1970s. The defects were in the first place due to the planners' lack of experience (research work was carried out on the building itself, so to speak), the thermal stresses due to the thin thermal insulation, and the contractors' lack of experience with the materials and details. In the 1970s the flat roof was regarded not only as more modern than the pitched roof, but also less expensive, which leads us to suspect a not so very high standard of workmanship. Many flat roofs were literally just that – flat, i.e.

designed and built without falls to roof outlets. Otherwise, a fall of min. 2 % was created mostly by a layer of normal-weight concrete on top of the structure. One early form of insulation with integral falls was in the form of a layer of in situ lightweight concrete (10–12 kN/m³) – with no further insulation, no vapour barrier.

The multitude of roof designs used can be divided into three groups still in use today: cold deck, warm deck and inverted roof.

The cold deck is a common form of construction with insulation plus ventilation cavity. It is regarded as generally reliable because there are no problems with saturation and the roof covering, as an independent component, can be built with adequate falls. The space between the insulation and the roof covering is frequently formed by way of timber framing. Sheathing attached to rafters or battens on this framing is then nailed over the entire area of the roof to create an air space above the insulation. The timber framing is either fixed directly to the concrete roof slab or is itself the loadbearing roof structure which is clad on the underside with plasterboard.

In a warm deck, i.e. roof without ventilation cavity and thermal insulation below the waterproofing, condensation both in the insulation and the structural slab must be presumed for roof constructions dating from the 1970s. This water evaporates when the sun shines on the roof and causes blisters below the vapour barrier. So-called vapour pressure equalisation layers

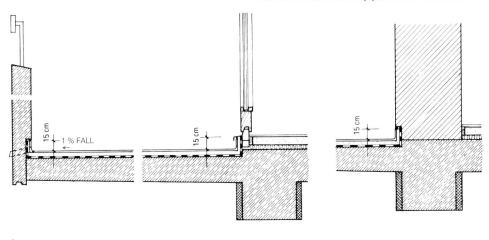

a

b   C 5.23

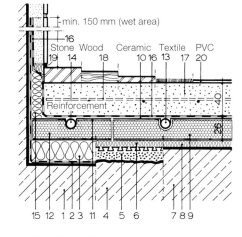

1   Concrete floor slab (no basement below, top)
2   Damp-proof membrane
3   Thermal insulation (e.g. Tecto-Tel boards)
4   Solid slab (uneven)
5   Loose fill for levelling (e.g. Bituperl) covered with corrugated card
6   Impact sound insulation if required
7   Solid slab (floated finish)
8   Impact sound and thermal insulation
9   JOCO large-format element (factory-prefabricated) with backing plate of PUR foam
10 Heat diffusion surface of sheet aluminium with grooves for pipes
11 Aluminium foil facing
12 JOCO perimeter element
13 Stainless steel pipe in the form of a grid within JOCO element, factory-fitted
14 Connecting pipe between distributor and element
15 Perimeter insulation, 10 mm
16 JOCO 5-ply foil, weldable
17 Cement screed, min. 40 mm thick
18 Reinforcement (heavy loads only)
19 Permanently elastic joint between stone floor finish and wall or skirting board
20 Floor coverings

C 5.24

Thermal resistance [m²K/W]	Thermal conductivity index [W/m²K]		
	0.035 Polyurethane [mm]	0.041 Polystyrene [mm]	0.052 Cellular glass [mm]
0.86	30.0	35.0	45.0
1.08	37.5	43.8	56.3
1.29	45.0	52.5	67.5
1.51	52.5	61.3	78.8
1.72	60.0	70.0	90.0

C 5.25

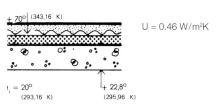

C 5.26

C 5.25 Insulation thicknesses required for a flat roof to DIN 4108 (1969 edition)
C 5.26 Flat roof vent for vapour pressure equalisation layer in warm deck
  a Gravel
  b Waterproofing (several layers)
  c Upper vapour pressure equalisation layer
  d Flat roof vent
  e Thermal insulation
  f Vapour barrier
  g Lower vapour pressure equalisation layer
C 5.27 Various flat roof constructions (warm deck, cold deck and reservoir roof) with their associated U-values
C 5.28 Large-panel construction wall systems and their thermal performance upgrades
C 5.29 Large-panel construction type P 2

Warm deck with insufficient thermal insulation

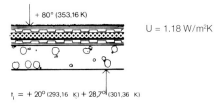

U = 1.18 W/m²K

$t_i = +20°$ (293,16 K) $+ 28,7°$ (301,36 K)

Gravel, waterproofing
2nd vapour pressure equalisation layer (ventilation felt)
Insufficient thermal insulation
Vapour barrier
1st vapour pressure equalisation layer (ventilation felt)
Undercoat
150 mm reinforced concrete

Warm deck

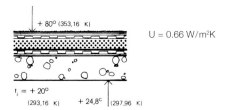

U = 0.66 W/m²K

$t_i = +20°$ (293,16 K) $+ 24,8°$ (297,96 K)

Gravel, waterproofing
2nd vapour pressure equalisation layer (ventilation felt)
Sufficient thermal insulation
Vapour barrier
1st vapour pressure equalisation layer
Undercoat
150 mm reinforced concrete

Warm deck

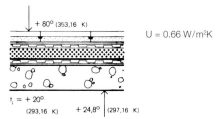

U = 0.66 W/m²K

$t_i = +20°$ (293,16 K) $+ 24,8°$ (297,16 K)

30 mm fine-grained conc., 30 mm coarse-grained conc.
Textured copper or aluminium foil as protective layer
2nd vapour pressure equalisation layer (ventilation felt)
Sufficient thermal insulation
Vapour barrier
1st vapour pressure equalisation layer (ventilation felt)
Undercoat
150 mm reinforced concrete

Cold deck

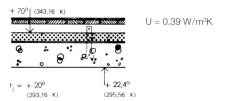

U = 0.46 W/m²K

$t_i = 20°$ (293,16 K) $+ 22,8°$ (295,96 K)

2 layers of bituminous felt
Screed with waterproofing additive
Corrugated asbestos-cement sheeting
50 mm expanded cork or polystyrene insulation
150 mm reinforced concrete

Cold deck

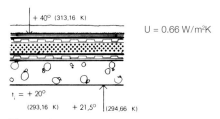

U = 0.39 W/m²K

$t_i = +20°$ (293,16 K) $+ 22,4°$ (295,56 K)

2 layers of bituminous felt
20 mm timber sheathing
50 mm air space
50 mm expanded cork or polystyrene insulation
150 mm reinforced concrete

Reservoir roof

U = 0.66 W/m²K

$t_i = +20°$ (293,16 K) $+ 21,5°$ (294,66 K)

50 mm water
Gravel, waterproofing
Plastic sheeting with welded joints
2nd vapour pressure equalisation layer (ventilation felt)
Thermal insulation
Vapour barrier
1st vapour pressure equalisation layer (ventilation felt)
Undercoat, 150 reinforced concrete

C 5.27

below the vapour barrier and below the waterproofing were an attempt to avoid this problem (Fig. C 5.27). Such a function is achieved by bonding the vapour barrier and waterproofing only at discrete points, or by laying a special material with a facing of perforated glass fleece or corrugated card on the underside.

As the planners of that period assumed that the vapour in these layers spread horizontally, numerous vents were included, the intention of which was to allow the water vapour to escape, but because these vents penetrate the roof covering they represent a potential source of problems (Fig. C 5.26).

One special form of the warm deck was based on the low water absorption of the newly developed insulating material cellular glass, which required neither a vapour barrier nor a levelling layer. No vapour barriers were laid on flat roofs of trapezoidal profile steel sheeting, either, because these were regarded as vapour-tight. The so-called reservoir roof is usually a warm deck construction with a raised roof outlet that ensures an approx. 50 mm deep pond of water on the roof, the intention of which is to reduce the thermal load on the roof, especially during the summer.

The inverted or upside-down roof – a new development of the 1970s – represented an application for extruded thermal insulation with its low water absorption, which in the meantime had now reached such a stage of development that it was ready for the market. In this type of roof the insulation is laid on top of the waterproofing, rendering a vapour barrier unnecessary.

Damage and measures
On cold decks the lack of a stack effect in horizontal layers of air and the resulting saturation of the mineral wool normally used has proved to be a problem. The fact that this had not yet been recognised in the 1970s is revealed by a design in which corrugated fibre-cement sheets laid loose on the insulation and covered with a screed laid to falls were intended to act as the ventilation cavity. In many cases cold decks were, however, built with deep air spaces (100–200 mm), and most of these do not suffer from problems. In a refurbishment project this deep air space can be used to install additional ther-

mal insulation. After removing the soffit materials and existing insulation (mostly non-biosoluble mineral wool), a vapour barrier should be attached to prevent permanently any saturation of the thermal insulation (membrane function). On warm decks the insulation is often completely saturated. The contractors' lack of practical experience, numerous penetrations (e.g. vents), the lack of falls, deformations due to inadequately sized or missing insulation at parapets and poorly laid or missing vapour barriers represent the main sources of damage. In the case of refurbishment we should therefore always assume removal of all roof finishes and a new construction, which, however, also means changes to the parapet because this is usually not high enough for the insulation thicknesses necessary these days.

Inverted roofs should have remained intact where the waterproofing was laid properly. It is possible to add further insulation to comply with the latest requirements of the Energy Conservation Act. In the case of very early inverted roofs, the renewal of all details and junctions should be considered at least.

Pitched roofs

Traditional carpentry joints were superseded after the mid-1960s by punched metal plate fasteners of galvanised steel, which had been available in Germany since 1952. As synthetic resin adhesives became more reliable, so nailed trusses were replaced by glued ones. The glued laminated trusses known from the inter-war years now became very popular. Although manufacturers had required a permit for gluing loadbearing timber components (DIN 1052) since the 1940s, all glued trusses should nevertheless be examined for their serviceability. The mandatory stamp on the truss helps when trying to identify the construction.

Special forms of construction

The shortage of affordable housing in Europe was met by prefabrication on a massive scale. The fabrication of transportable elements (in terms of size and weight) in the factory and the subsequent erection on the building site turned building into an industrial operation. For example, detached family homes were more and more in the form of system houses chosen from catalogues and then adapted to suit the buyer's requirements, and in multi-storey housing, fully prefabricated building methods (large-panel construction) were introduced.

External wall variant/material	Section	Concrete			Existing		Refurbishment with extra insulation	
		Conc. grade	Density	Standard cube strength R^n	Thermal resistance[1] $1/\Lambda$	Thermal transmittance (U-value)[1]	Thermal conductivity group 040, min. thk.	Thermal transmittance (U-value)[1]
			[kg/dm³]	[N/mm²]	[m²K/W]	[W/m²K]	[mm]	[W/m²K]
1 layer Long. ext. wall Gable ext. wall Lightweight conc. (aerated conc.)		B 50	1.25	4.1	0.57	1.35	80	0.36
2 layers (»Cottbus«) Loggia ext. wall Lightweight conc. Wood-wool bd.		B 225	1.7	18.4	0.82	1.01	80	0.33
Gable wall w. window opening Normal-wt. conc. Wood-wool bd.		B 160	2.25	13.1	0.67	1.19	80	0.35
2 layers (»Berlin«) Long. ext. wall Loggia ext. wall Normal-wt. conc. Wood-wool bd.		B 225	2.3	18.4	0.63	1.25	80	0.36
Gable wall (double) Normal-wt. conc. Polystyrene board		B 225	2.3	18.4	1.37	0.65	80	0.28
3 layers Long. ext. wall Loggia ext. wall Normal-wt. conc. Polystyrene board		B 225	2.3	18.4	1.34	0.66	80	0.28
Gable wall Normal-wt. conc. Polystyrene board		B 225	2.3	18.4	1.35	0.66	80	0.28

[1] without thermal bridges

C 5.28

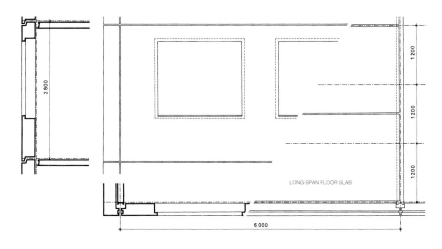

LONG-SPAN FLOOR SLAB

C 5.29

Large-panel construction

Attempts to reduce the cost of housing and speed up the work by using prefabricated forms of construction had been carried out in Eastern Europe again and again since the mid-1950s. This industrialised method of building continued to be developed and, based on a maximum element weight, was divided into the following load categories in the ex-GDR:

- 0.8 t: block construction, since 1952, storey height divided into three strips, 650 000 housing units
- 1.1 t: further development of 0.8 t block construction, since 1977, 47 100 housing units
- 2.0 t: strip method, since 1966, similar to 0.8 t block construction, 43 100 housing units
- 5.0 t: large-panel construction, since 1966, storey-high, types P 1 and P 2, 363 600 housing units (Fig. C 5.29)
- 6.3 t: large-panel construction, since 1976, storey-high, type WBS 70, 644 900 housing units

Large-panel construction in particular was "exported" from the GDR to other socialist countries, and used in a similar way in those states. The plan layouts of these (usually) 5- or 11-storey buildings employ controlling dimensions that with a storey height of 2.80 m are based on a multiple of 1.20 m. All the following information is based on type P 2.

Basements
Whereas the external walls to basements, 2.40 m high, were originally still built of in situ concrete, later they were in the form of single-leaf prefabricated normal-weight concrete elements 150 – 260 mm thick depending on the number of storeys. The vertical joints were mostly sealed with the permanently elastic "Morinol" putty, which contains asbestos. The damp-proof membrane for the floor was in the form of a single coat of bitumen. Leaking joints and defects in the damp-proof membrane are frequent problems.

External walls
The external walls of type P 2, 220–320 mm thick, were based on room sizes (e.g. 3.60 x 2.80 m) and consist of between one and three layers. Single-layer 300 mm thick elements were produced in lightweight concrete and rendered outside, plastered inside. Two-layer elements with external insulation ("Cottbus") made from lightweight or normal-weight concrete were again mostly rendered outside, plastered inside. The outside elevation of the two-layer, internally insulated element in normal-weight concrete ("Berlin") was rendered or finished with ceramic tiles. The insulation was in the form of 50 mm thick lightweight wood-wool boards. The core insulation to the three-layer panels was also 50 mm thick, but made from rigid polystyrene foam (Fig. C 5.28). The anchors between the 120 or 150 mm thick inner leaf and the 60 mm

thick weatherproof leaf were made of stainless steel, like the anchors to loggia panels. Standard lengths for all external elements were 2.40, 3.60 and 6.00 m.
All external walls have little thermal insulation. In addition, the insulation of the two-layer systems has frequently been saturated by driving rain (external insulation) or condensation (internal insulation) and is thus essentially ineffective. For reasons of cost, the thermal insulation is usually upgraded by adding min. 80 mm thick external insulation in the form of a composite system with render. The refurbishment of the three-layer elements presents problems. They do not need to be upgraded from the thermal insulation viewpoint, but most panels exhibit damage to the surface caused by poor on-site workmanship. These, too, are therefore frequently provided with an external thermal insulation composite system, which reduces the problematic thermal stresses in the outer leaf. As the 60 mm thick weatherproof leaf is sometimes only 30 mm thick and there are frequently corroded, exposed reinforcing bars owing to the poor compaction, the load-carrying capacity of such panels must be checked and upgraded if necessary. The mechanical fasteners for the external thermal insulation composite system are mostly attached to the inner leaf, i.e. through the weatherproof leaf and the layer of insulation.

Suspended floors and floor finishes
The floor elements of type P 2 were manufactured in two variants: either with conventional reinforcement in concrete grade B 225 or prestressed in concrete grades ≥ B 300. The conventionally reinforced solid concrete slabs were produced in system lengths (spans) of 2.40 and 3.60 m, were 110 or 140 mm deep and up to 4.80 m wide. The 600 – 1800 mm wide prestressed solid concrete slabs were also 140 mm

deep and available in system lengths of 4.80 and 6.00 m as well. Prestressed hollow planks – 600 mm wide and 240 mm deep – could span up to 7.20 m (Fig. C 5.31).
The anchorages (not supports) in the bracing external walls were mostly in the form of pockets filled with in situ concrete, which then formed a capping beam flush with the floor. In some cases the floors were finished only with bonded screeds, but floating screeds on lightweight wood-wool boards were also used (both calcium sulphate screeds). Floating dry subfloors consist of 30 mm thick rigid insulating boards on a 30 mm deep loose sand or slag fill. The normal overall depth of all systems was 75 mm.
There is no cause to doubt the load-carrying capacity of the suspended floors, which were always designed for an imposed load of min. 1.5 kN/m² (hollow planks up to 10 kN/m²), even if the planned depth of bearings on loadbearing internal walls has not been achieved in practice due to erection inaccuracies. The airborne sound insulation is also adequate because the weight of the floors always exceeded 300 kg/m². Impact sound insulation, on the other hand, is often only guaranteed by the resilient floor coverings used. Replacing the floor finishes by a floating screed that is not much deeper but much better from the acoustics viewpoint is often not carried out for reasons of cost. In addition, any new floor finishes may not exceed a self-weight of 100 kg/m².

Internal walls
Large-panel construction was always erected in the form of a box frame, so there are no loadbearing external walls, which serve only for the horizontal stability. The loadbearing internal walls were produced in normal-weight concrete and are 150 mm thick. All other internal walls, e.g. concrete or gypsum walls 40–70 mm thick,

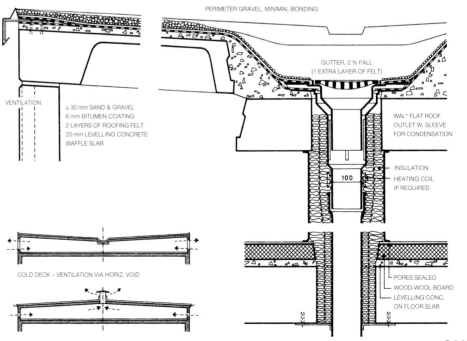

PERIMETER GRAVEL, MINIMAL BONDING

VENTILATION

≥ 30 mm SAND & GRAVEL
6 mm BITUMEN COATING
2 LAYERS OF ROOFING FELT
20 mm LEVELLING CONCRETE
WAFFLE SLAB

COLD DECK – VENTILATION VIA HORIZ. VOID

GUTTER, 2 % FALL
(1 EXTRA LAYER OF FELT)

WAL* FLAT ROOF
OUTLET W. SLEEVE
FOR CONDENSATION

INSULATION
HEATING COIL
IF REQUIRED

100

PORES SEALED
WOOD-WOOL BOARD
LEVELLING CONC.
ON FLOOR SLAB

C 5.30

have no structural function whatsoever and can be removed during a conversion.

Roofs

The internal height of the roof spaces is generally much less than 2.0 m. The roof erected above a normal upper floor consists of panels – mostly 240 mm deep concrete waffle slabs, occasionally also 100 mm deep solid slabs. The roofs mostly drained inwards (fall: 5–10 %) to a longitudinal gutter of in situ concrete (valley roof). The thermal insulation was in the form of a layer of max. 60 mm thick mineral wool boards which were ventilated via the roof space (cold deck). The waterproofing was in the form of two layers of bituminous felt sheeting protected by a topping of gravel.

It is relatively easy to add additional thermal insulation in the roof void, likewise just as easy to provide new waterproofing (Fig. C 5.30).

Loggias and balconies

The 1.20 m deep and 3.60 m (conventional reinforcement) or 6.00 m (prestressed concrete) wide loggias were independent loadbearing constructions built in front of the facade. They were fixed to the building with stainless steel anchors in the loadbearing side walls. The spandrel panels comprising steel frames with asbestos-cement or fair-face concrete infill panels do not provide any loadbearing or bracing functions.

Besides the usual surface refurbishment measures, e.g. concrete repairs, replacing the spandrel panels and renewing the waterproofing, it is important to check that the bearing depth on the side walls is adequate. The condition of the stainless steel anchors should also be investigated. As these loggias are already separated from the building, they do not present any problems when upgrading the thermal performance (Fig. C 5.32).

Notes:
[1] 2nd Housebuilding Act, 1956
[2] Meadows, Dennis, L. et al.: The Limits to Growth, A Report for the Club of Rome's Project on the Predicament of Mankind, Stuttgart, 1972
[3] Jacobs, Jane: The Death and Life of Great American Cities, New York, 1961
     Mitscherlich, Alexander: Die Unwirtlichkeit unserer Städte, Frankfurt, 1965
[4] Frick, Otto; Knöll, Karl; Neumann, Friedrich (ed.): Baukonstruktionslehre, 2 vols., Stuttgart, 1979, p. 382
[5] Schmitt, Heinrich: Hochbaukonstruktionen, Ravensburg, 1978, p. 322
[6] ibid. [5], p. 298
[7] ibid. [5], p. 593

C 5.30 Vertical section through cold deck (waffle slab)
C 5.31 Connection details at external longitudinal wall (non-loadbearing)
C 5.32 Vertical sections through loggia and junction with floor slab

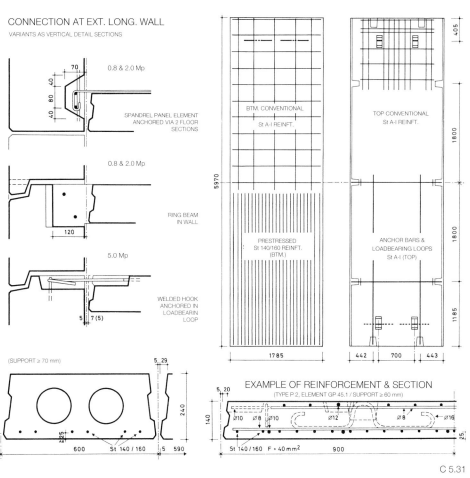

CONNECTION AT EXT. LONG. WALL
VARIANTS AS VERTICAL DETAIL SECTIONS

SPANDREL PANEL ELEMENT ANCHORED VIA 2 FLOOR SECTIONS

RING BEAM IN WALL

WELDED HOOK ANCHORED IN LOADBEARIN LOOP

EXAMPLE OF REINFORCEMENT & SECTION
(TYPE P 2, ELEMENT GP 45.1 / SUPPORT ≥ 60 mm)

C 5.31

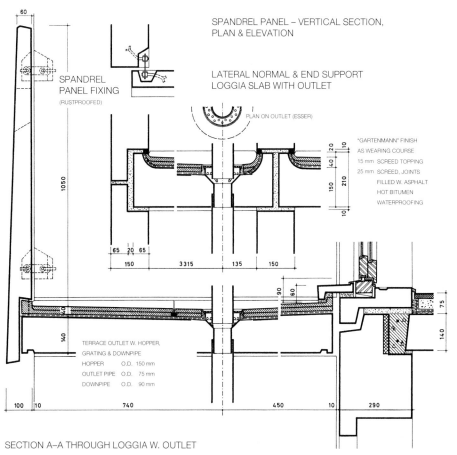

SPANDREL PANEL FIXING
(RUSTPROOFED)

SPANDREL PANEL – VERTICAL SECTION, PLAN & ELEVATION

LATERAL NORMAL & END SUPPORT LOGGIA SLAB WITH OUTLET

PLAN ON OUTLET (ESSER)

"GARTENMANN" FINISH AS WEARING COURSE
15 mm SCREED TOPPING
25 mm SCREED, JOINTS FILLED W. ASPHALT
HOT BITUMEN
WATERPROOFING

TERRACE OUTLET W. HOPPER, GRATING & DOWNPIPE
HOPPER   O.D. 150 mm
OUTLET PIPE   O.D. 75 mm
DOWNPIPE   O.D. 90 mm

SECTION A–A THROUGH LOGGIA W. OUTLET

C 5.32

205

Part D   Case Studies

Fig. D   Arched roof shed, refurbishment, Cologne (D),
2000, 4000architekten

Example 01

Holiday home

Scaiano, CH 1850/2004

Architects:
Markus Wespi Jérôme de Meuron
Architekten, Caviano
Structural engineer:
Paolo de Giorgi, Tegna

On the edge of the village of Scaiano in Ticino on the eastern banks of Lake Maggiore, a ruined stable and barn building has been converted into a holiday home for a family. The steeply sloping plot is entered via the garden, and the entrance to the three-storey house itself is on the upper floor. A few steps lead down to the living room with its fireplace, which heats all the rooms in winter via a hot-air system. The storey below contains study, children's room and bathroom, the basement below that a bedroom and storage room. The subdivision of the interior space has hardly been modified and includes changes of level connected via steep, narrow stairs, lending the building a sort of labyrinth character. The architects decided to retain the coursed random rubble masonry and thus preserve the seemingly ancient nature of the building. But the wooden veranda and pitched roof were completely removed and the rotten timber joist floors replaced by concrete slabs. With its new flat roof, the building has been reduced to a simple cube form. A bathroom was essential for the new usage and so this was excavated out of the hillside on the lower level in order to prevent disturbing the clear, historic lines of the building. The existing window openings were retained and only enlarged slightly in a few instances. The new concrete lintels have been left exposed and thus reveal the refurbishment measures. Inside the building the existing masonry was insulated with cellular glass, plastered and subsequently given a glaze finish to match the beige-brown colouring of the painted cement screed floor.

- Demolition of pitched roof and suspended floors, integration of concrete floor slabs
- Internal thermal insulation
- Extension for bathroom
- Pointing to produce half rendered effect on existing coursed random rubble masonry walls

📖 Baumeister 08/2006

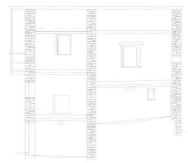

aa, existing

Sections · Plans
Scale 1:200

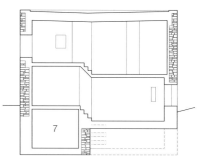

bb

1	Entrance	4	Children's room
2	Kitchen/	5	Study
	dining room	6	Bathroom
3	Living room	7	Bedroom

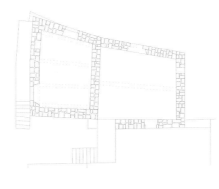

Upper floor, existing

Upper floor

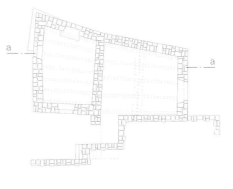

Lower floor, existing

Lower floor

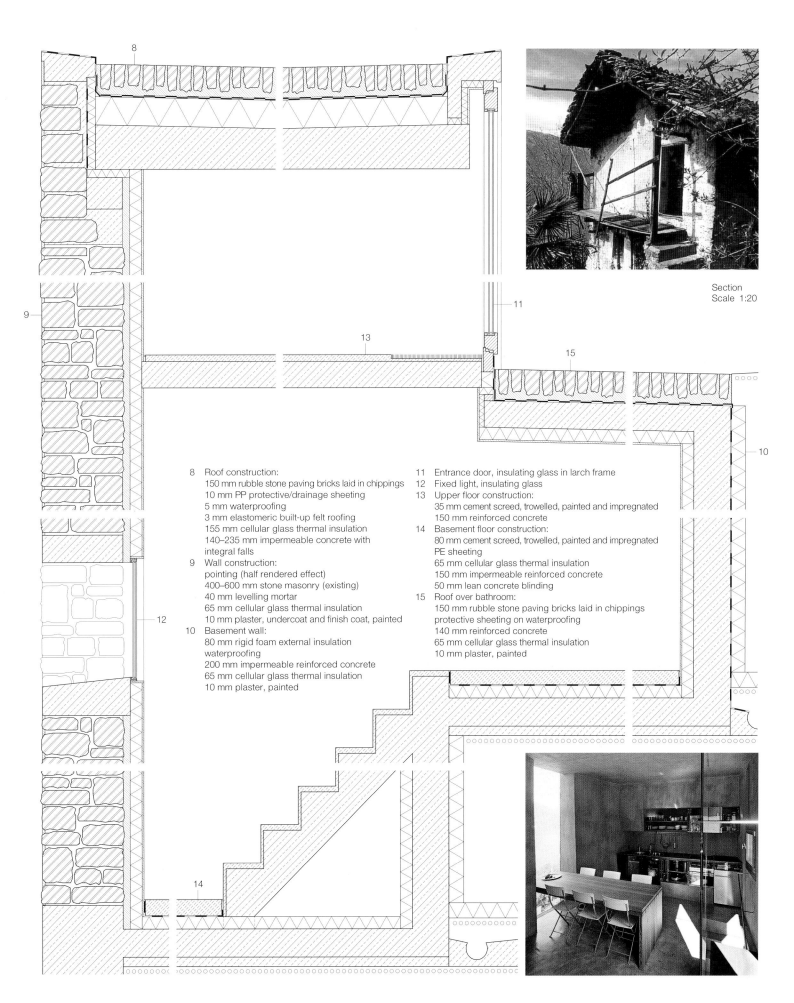

Section
Scale 1:20

8 Roof construction:
150 mm rubble stone paving bricks laid in chippings
10 mm PP protective/drainage sheeting
5 mm waterproofing
3 mm elastomeric built-up felt roofing
155 mm cellular glass thermal insulation
140–235 mm impermeable concrete with
integral falls
9 Wall construction:
pointing (half rendered effect)
400–600 mm stone masonry (existing)
40 mm levelling mortar
65 mm cellular glass thermal insulation
10 mm plaster, undercoat and finish coat, painted
10 Basement wall:
80 mm rigid foam external insulation
waterproofing
200 mm impermeable reinforced concrete
65 mm cellular glass thermal insulation
10 mm plaster, painted

11 Entrance door, insulating glass in larch frame
12 Fixed light, insulating glass
13 Upper floor construction:
35 mm cement screed, trowelled, painted and impregnated
150 mm reinforced concrete
14 Basement floor construction:
80 mm cement screed, trowelled, painted and impregnated
PE sheeting
65 mm cellular glass thermal insulation
150 mm impermeable reinforced concrete
50 mm lean concrete blinding
15 Roof over bathroom:
150 mm rubble stone paving bricks laid in chippings
protective sheeting on waterproofing
140 mm reinforced concrete
65 mm cellular glass thermal insulation
10 mm plaster, painted

Example 02

Monastery library

Fitero, E, 1247/1614/2001

Architects:
Miguel Alonso del Val and
Rufino Hernández Minguillón, Pamplona
Project team:
Eduardo Arilla Alvarez, Maria José Prieto
Rodríguez, Victor Hernández Barricarte,
Patricia Sánchez Delgado, Joaquín Aliaga
Montes
Structural engineers:
Susana Iturralde Mendive, Pamplona

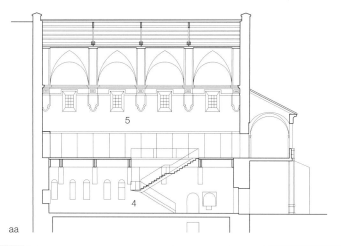

aa

Cistercian monks founded the monastery in
Fitero in 1140 – one of their first monasteries in
Spain. The architectural highlight of the complex
is the two-storey cloister with its pointed-arch
arcades and external buttressing. The upper
floor was completed in 1614 and its purist aesthetic is reminiscent of the style of the "El Escorial".
The conversion measures focused on the
former kitchen, the adjoining refectory and the
library above. A timber pavilion roof was built
on top of the restored, extended walls to the
kitchen as a reference to the former dome. The
pyramid-shaped construction is topped by a
glazed lantern, which admits daylight to highlight the geometrical structure of the roof framing. This room serves as an access zone for
the new exhibition rooms and the cloister. In the
adjoining former refectory, the semi-darkness of
the room is ideal for audio-visual presentations.
The exhibits on display are all relics of monastery
life dating from the Middle Ages. The historic
stone corbels now serve as supports for the new
timber floor. Visitors gain access to the Baroque
monastery library via a staircase in the centre
of the room. Apart from the extensive restoration
work, the architects limited their intervention here
to the glass display cabinets for the collection
of Baroque books, engravings and clothing. To
avoid spoiling the effect of the interior space,
which is dominated by the painted barrel vault
ceiling, the glass display cabinets are arranged
in a very restrained fashion along the outer walls.

• Masonry refurbishment and extensions
• Addition of a timber pavilion roof
• New timber suspended floor

Detail 10/2003

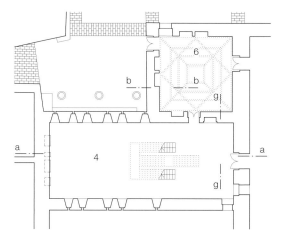

1 Abbey
2 Chapter house
3 Dormitory
4 Refectory dating from
   Middle Ages/
   exhibition
5 Library/
   exhibition
6 Kitchen/entrance
7 Cloister
8 Baroque
   refectory
9 Abbot's palace
10 Hostel
11 Vestry
12 Chapel
13 Home for the elderly

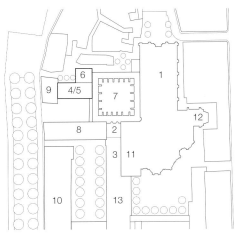

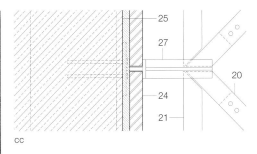

cc

Section · Plan
Scale 1:400
Location drawing
Scale 1:2500
Horizontal section · Vertical section
Scale 1:20

14 Roof to lantern:
 1 mm sheet zinc
 geotextile separating
 layer
 20 mm MDF
 framing laid to falls
 60 mm polystyrene
 thermal insulation
 20 mm MDF
15 Insulating glass, 4 mm
 + 6 mm cavity + 4 mm
16 Steel framing,
 30 x 50 mm
 hollow sections
17 Steel channel, 180 mm
18 Roof construction:
 clay roof tiles
 25 x 50 mm battens
 60 mm polystyrene
 thermal insulation

20 mm Scots pine
 sheathing
19 Secondary beam,
 80 x 200 mm glulam
20 Diagonal member,
 100 x 260 mm glulam
21 Perimeter beam,
 100 x 400 mm glulam
22 Gutter,
 3 mm sheet zinc
23 Masonry backing
24 Sandstone, 70 mm
25 Reinforced concrete
 ring beam
26 Sandstone wall,
 restored and extended,
 approx. 1400 mm thick
27 Bracket of welded
 steel flats,
 12 mm and 15 mm

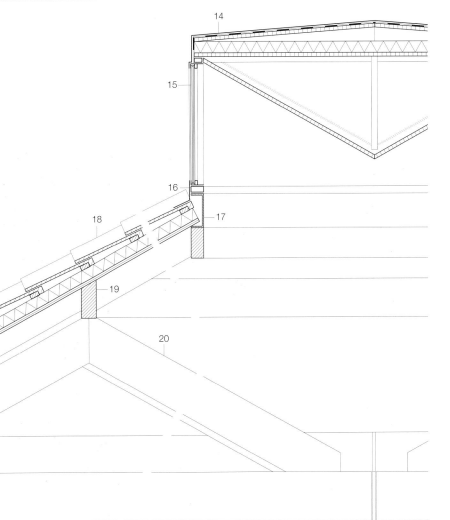

bb

Example 02

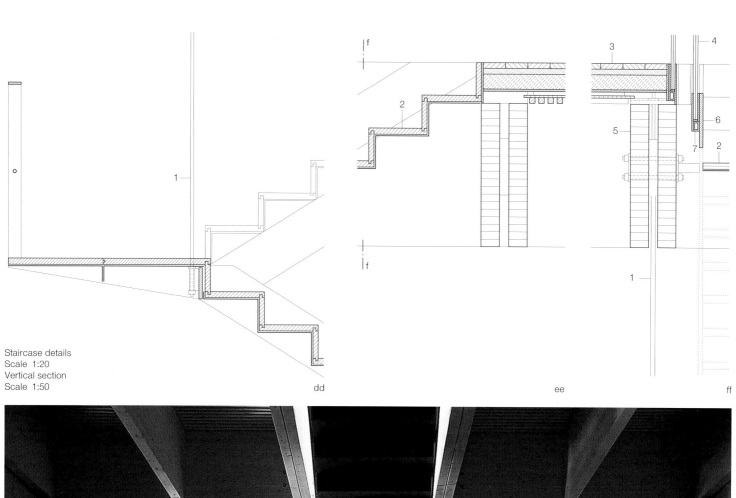

Staircase details
Scale 1:20
Vertical section
Scale 1:50

dd

ee

ff

1 Hanger for landing, Ø16 mm steel rod
2 Stair flight:
   30 mm oak tread
   25 mm oak riser
   2 mm sheet steel, painted
3 Floor construction:
   30 mm ceramic tiles on
   30 mm mortar bed
   80 mm screed on
   1.2 mm sheet steel
   20 x 20 mm battens
   12 mm particleboard
   30 x 30 mm battens, waxed Scots pine
4 Balustrade, 2 No. 4 mm laminated
   safety glass, EPDM bearing pads
5 Glulam beam, 760 x 100 mm
6 Steel plate stringer, 320 x 20 mm
7 Steel hollow section, 50 x 20 mm

8 Double-leaf loadbearing masonry:
   175 mm clay bricks
   300 mm air cavity and wall ties
   125 mm clay bricks, plastered
9 MDF, 2 No. 16 mm,
   with 30 x 30 mm steel hollow sections between
10 Uplight
11 Display cabinet,
   2 No. 4 mm laminated safety glass
12 Sandstone, 70 mm
13 Reinforced concrete ring beam
14 Sandstone corbel (existing)
   with new bearing pad of 20 mm steel plate
   + 20 mm EPDM
15 Double-leaf loadbearing masonry:
   450 mm sandstone
   300 mm air cavity and wall ties
   450 mm sandstone

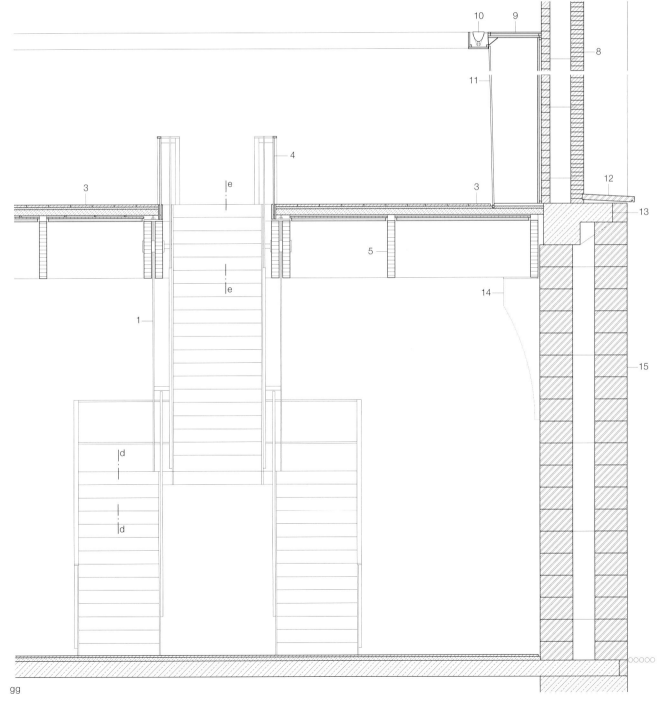

gg

Example 03

University building

Vaduz, FL, 1890/2002

Architects:
Karl + Probst, Munich
Ludwig Karl, Markus Probst
Project team:
Birgit Dierolf, Norbert Engelhardt,
Sebastian Hrycyk, Rafael Malenka,
Carolin Ruckdeschel, Carola Seifert
Structural engineers:
Vogt Ingenieurbüro, Vaduz

One of the first factories to be built in Liechtenstein was this former cotton mill on the northern edge of Vaduz. It dates from 1882 and up until the 1970s it was repeatedly converted and extended. The factory finally closed in 1992 and by the end of the 1990s it had been decided to convert this piece of industrial heritage into facilities for the University of Liechtenstein. One of the aims of the conversion and refurbishment work was to preserve the external appearance and the internal structure as far as possible.
No thermal insulation was added to the existing external walls of coursed random rubble masonry up to 800 mm thick, which were supplemented where necessary and given new coats of render outside, plaster inside. All the windows were provided with new low E glass and glazing bars to match the original windows.
The character of the two former spinning halls with their north-facing sawtooth roofs was able to be retained for the new usage (study rooms and lecture theatres). Clear internal heights of more than 5 m enabled galleries to be built.
The glazing and roof coverings to both sheds are new; in fact the entire roof structure of the southern shed was demolished and renewed because the damage here was too extensive.
As part of the work, the cast iron columns were removed, cleaned to remove all corrosion, and – after applying new corrosion protection – re-erected in their original positions. It has also been possible to preserve the original, spacious character of the former cotton warehouse, a 12 m high central area which is now used for exhibitions and events. In order that the roof structure could remain exposed, the existing roof was provided with insulation between the new rafters. The library and cafeteria are housed in an all-new narrow elevated structure in front of the west facade – clearly demarcating old and new.

• External walls and internal columns retained and restored
• Windows, roof glazing, roof coverings, eaves and verge details are all new, corresponding to their original condition

📖 Baumeister 10/2002
Deutsche Bauzeitung 10/2002
Hochparterre 10/2002

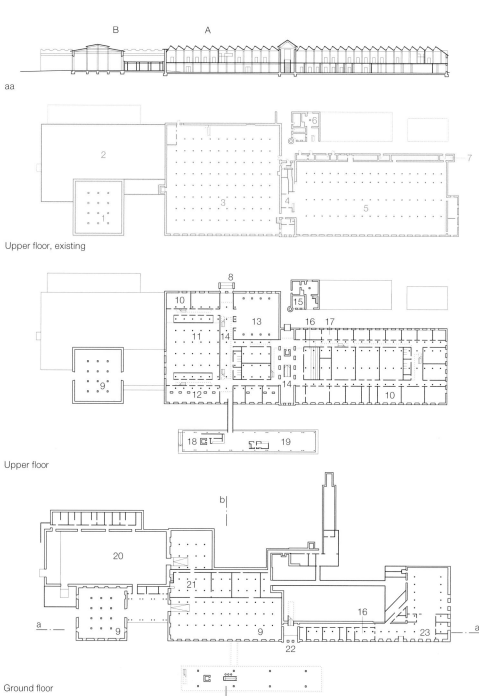

aa

Upper floor, existing

Upper floor

Ground floor

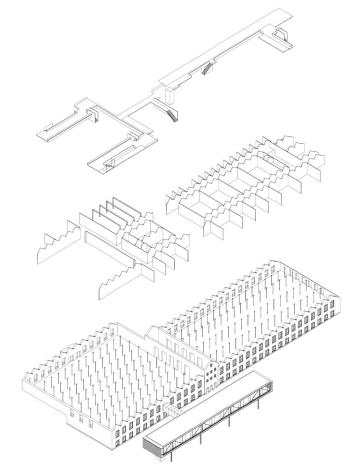

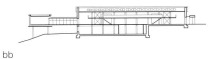

bb

Sections · Plans
Scale 1:1500
Isometric views of sheds, new walls
and galleries
Not to scale

1   Bales store (1889):
    former cotton warehouse
2   Arched roof shed (1973):
    former machine hall
3   North shed (1890):
    former spinning hall
4   Connecting block (1882):
    former offices and stores building
5   South shed (1890):
    former spinning hall
6   Boiler house
7   Former equipment rooms, demolished
8   East entrance
9   Exhibitions/events
10 Seminar rooms
11 Workroom,
    Institute of Architecture & Planning
12 Workroom for lecturers
13 Conference hall/auditorium
14 Foyer
15 Caretaker's office
16 Lecture theatre
17 Group rooms
18 Cafeteria
19 Library
20 Multipurpose hall
21 Store/workshop
22 West (main) entrance
23 Youth centre

Example 03

Vertical section through
sawtooth roof
North hall
Vertical section through
bales store
Scale 1:20

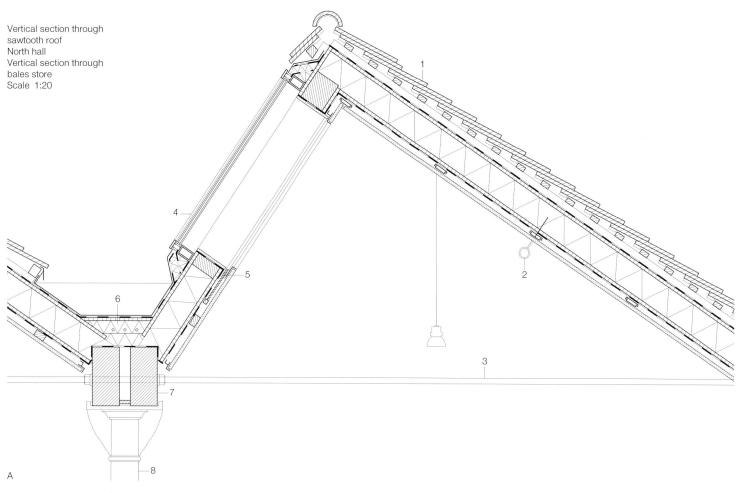

A

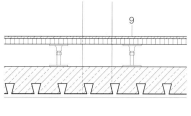

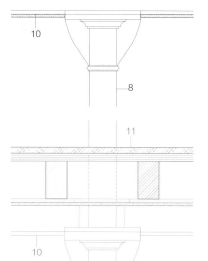

1   Roof construction: bullnose tiles, 50 x 30 mm battens,
    50 x 30 mm counter battens, waterproofing, 18 mm
    OSB, 140 mm rafters (existing) with thermal insulation
    between, 18 mm OSB, PE vapour barrier, 30 x 50 mm
    battens, 40 mm void, 18 mm magnesite-bonded
    wood-wool acoustic board
2   Sprinklers
3   Tie bar (existing), Ø30 mm
4   Windows, low E glass in powder-coated aluminium
    frames
5   Pleated blackout blind: polyester fabric
6   Valley gutter heating
7   Timber beams (existing), 2 No. 150 x 315 mm,
    repainted
8   Cast iron columns (existing), Ø150 mm, with new
    corrosion protection
9   New floor construction: 12 mm flooring cement, 148 mm
    void, sheet steel decking, 140 mm concrete topping,
    suspended ceiling
10 Primary beam (existing), 130 x 200 mm cast iron
11 Old floor construction: 30 mm flooring cmt., 42 mm
    boards, 170 x 210 mm timber joists, gypsum boards
12 Roof construction: 0.6 mm stainless steel w. double
    welted joints, bitumen felt, 24 mm sheathing, 50 mm
    counter battens, waterproofing, 100 x 180 mm rafters,
    160 mm thermal insulation, 0.4 mm separating layer
13 Roof construction (existing): sheathing, rafters, roof
    structure, beams scrubbed
14 Timber cornice (existing), removed/reaffixed higher
15 Wall construction: render (existing), coursed rubble
    stone masonry (existing) up to 800 mm thick, 2 coats
    of lime plaster
16 Wooden windows according to original design and
    colouring, low E glass, 30 mm thermal insulation to
    reveals, 25 mm plaster
17 Stone window surround (existing), cleaned/modified
18 Ground floor construction: 12 mm flooring cement,
    73 mm cement screed with underfloor heating, 0.4 mm
    separating layer, 20 mm impact sound insulation, 60 mm
    polystyrene insulation, 5 mm bitumen felt waterproof-
    ing, 20 mm levelling layer, lean concrete (existing)

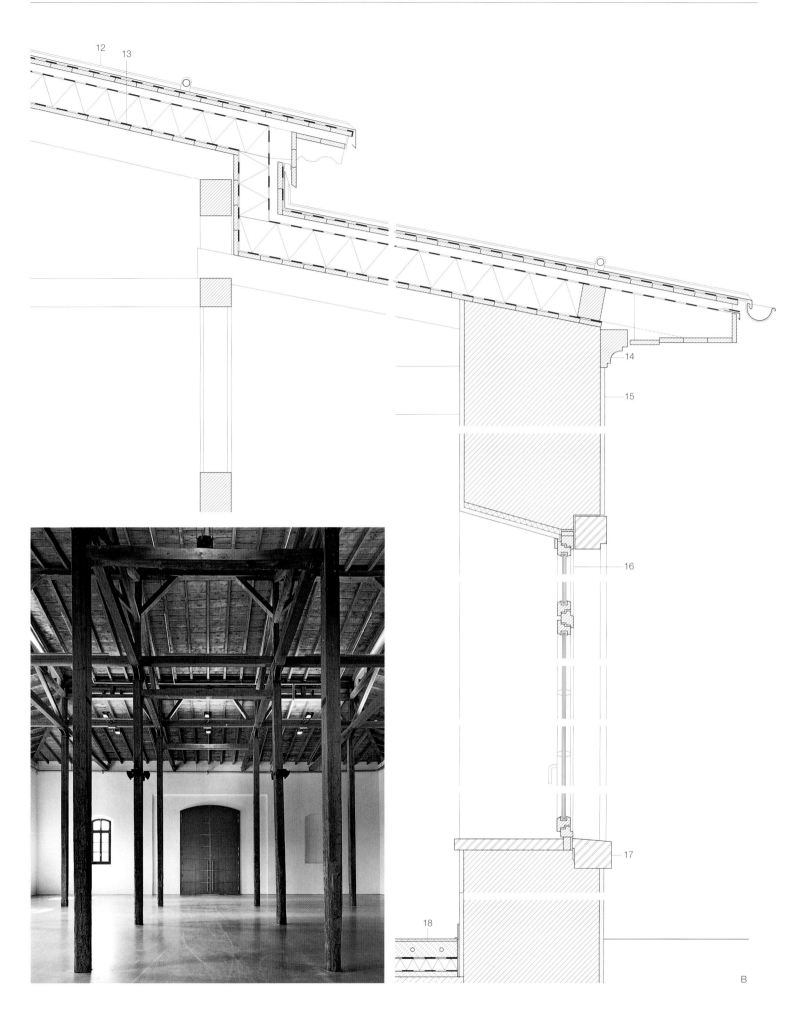

B

Example 04

Hotel

Barth, D, 1896/1997
Architect:
Volker Giencke, Graz
Project team:
Wolfgang Feyferlik,
Susi Fritzer, Claudius Pratsch
Structural engineer:
Alois Winkler, Graz

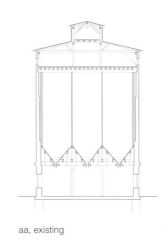

aa, existing

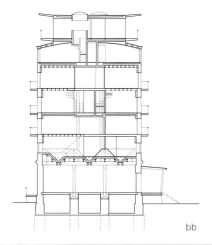

bb

The little town of Barth on the Baltic Sea coast has a number of warehouses dating from the late 19th century which have been empty since the early 1990s. The largest of these, a cereals store in clay brick masonry directly in the port itself and opposite the Zingst peninsula, has been converted into a hotel with 47 rooms and apartments. The construction of the store is simple and functional. The external walls decrease from 770 mm at the base to 250 mm at the top, the steps in the masonry forming the supports for the timber joists or steel beams. The store was originally divided into two parts: the northern section with cast iron columns for storing sacks, the southern section in the form of a silo for cereals, with 21 narrow, shaft-like chambers the full height of the building consisting of 30–50 mm thick timber planks stacked and nailed together to resemble glued laminated timber.

New internal walls now divide the four levels of the sack store into double bedrooms and suites. In the former silo new suspended floors have been built to create two-storey maisonettes the full depth of the building and just 2.50 or 2.65 m wide. These are dominated by the timber walls of the silo because these have been left exposed. Openings have been cut in these timber walls for corridors and glazed doors, and small balconies and windows with white sliding shutters have been added to the formerly windowless silo section. A two-storey rooftop extension was added to the existing building – a concrete structure with a perimeter rooftop terrace. The former ramp on the west facade has been replaced by a covered, partly glazed terrace. At the southern end a spiral staircase serves as an alternative means of escape, and at the northern end each suite has a conservatory-type extension.

- Retention of external walls, columns, silo walls and hoppers
- Enlarged window openings, new balconies
- Rooftop extension, new extensions
- Addition of new internal walls, suspended floors, bathrooms

Architektur Aktuell 210, 1997
Bauwelt 31 – 32/1997
The Architectural Review 09/1998

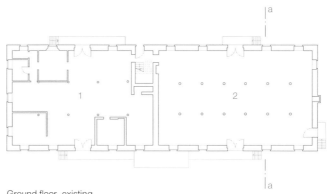

Ground floor, existing

Sections · Plans
Scale 1:500

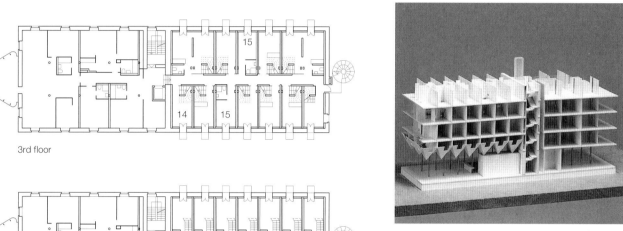

15

14   15

3rd floor

13

14

2nd floor

14   15

10

11   12

1st floor

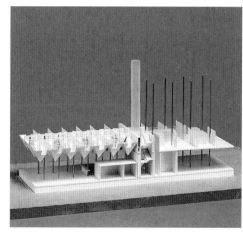

|b

5

3   4   6

9

7   8

⊗ Ground floor

|b

1   Former sack store
2   Former silo (cereals store)
3   Conservatory
4   Ballroom
5   Kitchen
6   Restaurant
7   Glazed extension
8   Terrace
9   External stairs: access to hotel and
     alternative means of escape
10 Seminar room
11 Reception
12 Staff room
13 Suite
14 Maisonette
15 Hotel bedroom

Example 04

1 External wall (existing), 390 mm, silo wall (existing),
   80 mm nailed laminated timber, surface scrubbed
2 Balustrade, Ø15 mm stainless steel tubes
3 Wooden floor, 30 mm bongossi with routed grooves
4 Edge beam, 120 x 65 x 2 mm steel channel
5 Soffit, sheet steel painted white
6 Fixing, stainless steel, anchored with sleeves cast into
   concrete pocket in masonry
7 Sliding shutter, 20 mm plywood painted white, steel
   flat track, plastic rollers
8 Steel angle, 120 x 80 mm
9 Lining to reveal, 20 mm plywood painted white
10 Clay brick lintel with reinforcement, 340 x 70 mm
11 Wooden grating, 30 mm bongossi with routed grooves,
   20 mm insulation, sheet steel covering, bitumen felt,
   mortar
12 Insulating glass in spruce frame, painted white

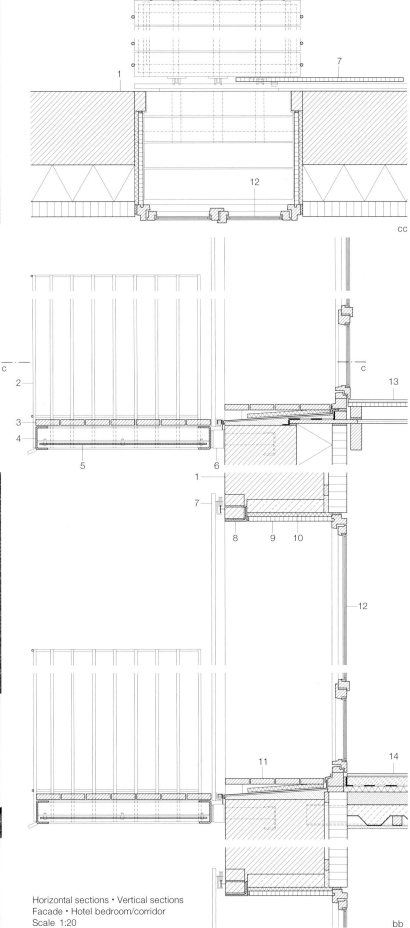

Horizontal sections · Vertical sections
Facade · Hotel bedroom/corridor
Scale 1:20

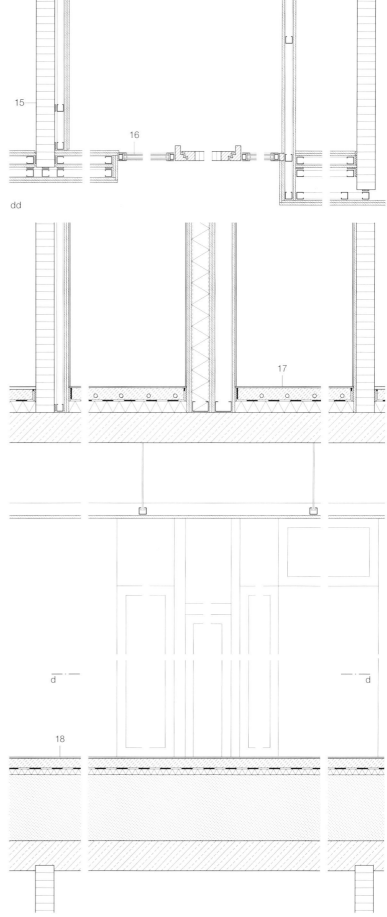

13 Floor construction: 16 mm maple wood-block flooring, 20 mm wood-based board product, 60 x 60 mm timber bearers, felt strips, 20 mm sheathing (soffit), 60 x 140 mm joists

14 Floor construction: 16 mm maple wood-block flooring, 50 mm screed, bitumen felt, 30 mm impact sound insulation, 70 mm loose fill, trapezoidal profile steel decking with 60 mm concrete topping

15 Silo wall (existing): 100 mm nailed laminated timber, surface scrubbed, lining of 2 No. 20 mm plasterboard

16 Fire-resistant glazing, wired glass in 50 x 20 mm steel frame

17 Floor construction, bathroom: 5 mm mosaic tiles in tile adhesive, 65 mm heated screed, separating layer, 60 mm impact sound insulation, 160 mm reinforced concrete slab, 400 mm services void, 15 mm plasterboard suspended ceiling

18 Floor construction, corridor: 6 mm carpet, 50 mm screed, PE sheeting, 30 mm impact sound insulation, services routed in 350 mm expanded clay granulates loose fill, 160 mm reinforced concrete slab

Example 05

Residential building

Cologne, D, 1904/2005

Architect:
Boris Enning, Cologne
Project team:
Susanne Hageböke, Rosemarie Barnickel
Structural engineer:
Klaus Hoppert, Cologne

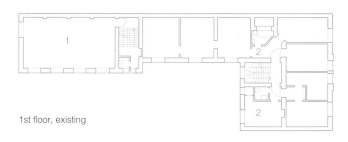

1st floor, existing

1 Workshop
2 Apartment
3 Rooftop terrace
4 Loft apartment

Around 1900 a joiner in Cologne had a building for several tenants built together with a clay brick workshop building in the rear court. This combination of housing and workshop so typical of this period has now been refurbished in accordance with the conservation order covering the building and the rooms of the workshop converted into loft apartments. The decorated render facade and the roof of the apartment building were renewed after extensive discussions with the local Heritage Protection Department. The interior layouts originally comprised very small rooms identical on every floor, but now these have been redesigned and rooms ranging in size from 48 to 100 m^2 permit ample flexibility in terms of usage. Stucco ceilings and wooden floorboards have been renewed and the walls given a coat of lime plaster mixed with marble dust to produce a very smooth appearance. In contrast to this, the interior of the former workshop has a somewhat coarser character to reflect the former usage. The clay brick walls have been left exposed here, the existing concrete jack arch floors spanning between steel beams only roughly sand-blasted. In order that the building achieves a low-energy house standard, insulation was added to roof, external walls and the floor over the basement to comply with the different requirements. Where the facade was worthy of preservation, the external appearance was retained by adding an insulating plaster internally, but elsewhere an external thermal insulation composite system was used. The external masonry walls to the semi-basement were damp-proofed so that this can now be used as additional living accommodation. Steel balconies were built in front of the facades facing the rear court, and the court itself was turned into garden ideal for families and children.

- Renewal of roof and facade
- Addition of steel balconies
- Internal insulation behind facade protected by conservation order
- External thermal insulation composite system
- Damp-proofing to semi-basement
- Renewal of building services

 Baumeister 10/2006

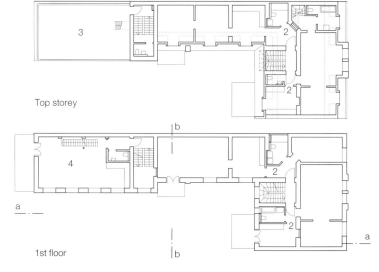

Top storey

1st floor

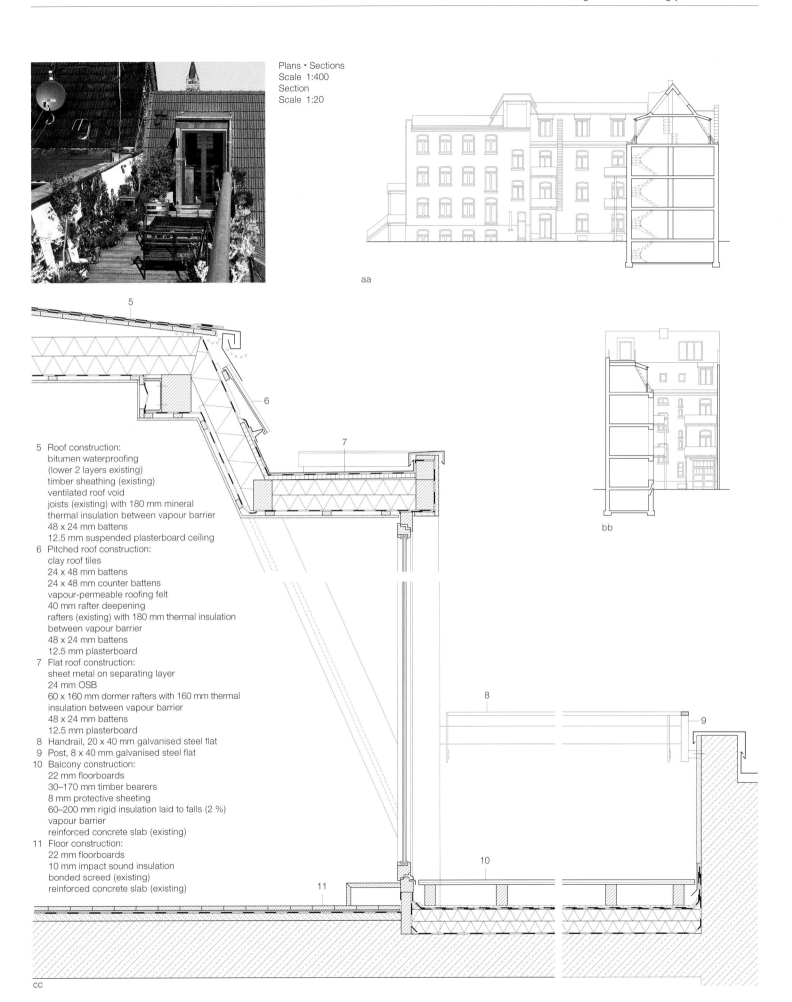

Plans · Sections
Scale 1:400
Section
Scale 1:20

aa

bb

5 Roof construction:
  bitumen waterproofing
  (lower 2 layers existing)
  timber sheathing (existing)
  ventilated roof void
  joists (existing) with 180 mm mineral
  thermal insulation between vapour barrier
  48 x 24 mm battens
  12.5 mm suspended plasterboard ceiling
6 Pitched roof construction:
  clay roof tiles
  24 x 48 mm battens
  24 x 48 mm counter battens
  vapour-permeable roofing felt
  40 mm rafter deepening
  rafters (existing) with 180 mm thermal insulation
  between vapour barrier
  48 x 24 mm battens
  12.5 mm plasterboard
7 Flat roof construction:
  sheet metal on separating layer
  24 mm OSB
  60 x 160 mm dormer rafters with 160 mm thermal
  insulation between vapour barrier
  48 x 24 mm battens
  12.5 mm plasterboard
8 Handrail, 20 x 40 mm galvanised steel flat
9 Post, 8 x 40 mm galvanised steel flat
10 Balcony construction:
  22 mm floorboards
  30–170 mm timber bearers
  8 mm protective sheeting
  60–200 mm rigid insulation laid to falls (2 %)
  vapour barrier
  reinforced concrete slab (existing)
11 Floor construction:
  22 mm floorboards
  10 mm impact sound insulation
  bonded screed (existing)
  reinforced concrete slab (existing)

cc

Example 06

House and studio

London, GB, 1900/2002

Architects:
Adjaye Associates, London
Project team:
Josh Carver, Amy Lau
Structural engineers:
Techniker, London

This building, formerly a warehouse for a factory, is located in Shoreditch, to the north-east of the centre of London. Following complete gutting and the addition of a new storey, it now serves as a house and studio for two young artists. The entrance hall and the two studios extend over two storeys, a room for guests and a bathroom are on the first floor. The living accommodation is on the topmost floor and is reached via a staircase without having to pass through the studios. The bedrooms, bathroom and rooftop terrace surround the central living area, the latter being separated from the terrace by full-height glazing. The loadbearing external walls of clay brick masonry have been retained and extended by building a parapet for the top floor. Slender steel columns on the inside stabilise the existing external walls and serve as additional supports for the floors. The voids are filled with insulation. Most of the original window openings have been retained and fitted with fixed lights. At ground level reflective panes flush with the outer face of the wall prevent inquisitive passers-by from peering into the studios. "Dirty House" owes its name to the black anti-graffiti paint on the facade, which is used on all street lighting and electricity distribution cabinets in this part of the city. The set-back top storey is fully glazed on two sides. It represents a stark contrast to the dark box below and thus demonstrates the different uses. In order to suggest the idea of a "floating" roof, the perimeter rainwater gutter was integrated into the roof. Lighting at the base of the parapet illuminates the underside of the roof and reinforces the "floating" idea.

Gutting
· Additional storey
· Reinforcing the external walls with steel columns, plus thermal insulation in the voids
· Anti-graffiti paint finish

A+U 10/2003
Bauwelt 05/2003
DBZ 03/2003

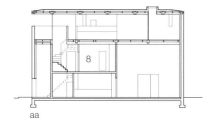

aa

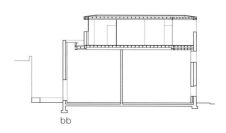

bb

Ground floor

2nd floor

Ground floor, existing

Sections
Plans
Scale 1:400

1 Entrance
2 WC
3 Kitchen
4 Studio
5 Living room
6 Bathroom
7 Bedroom
8 Room for guests

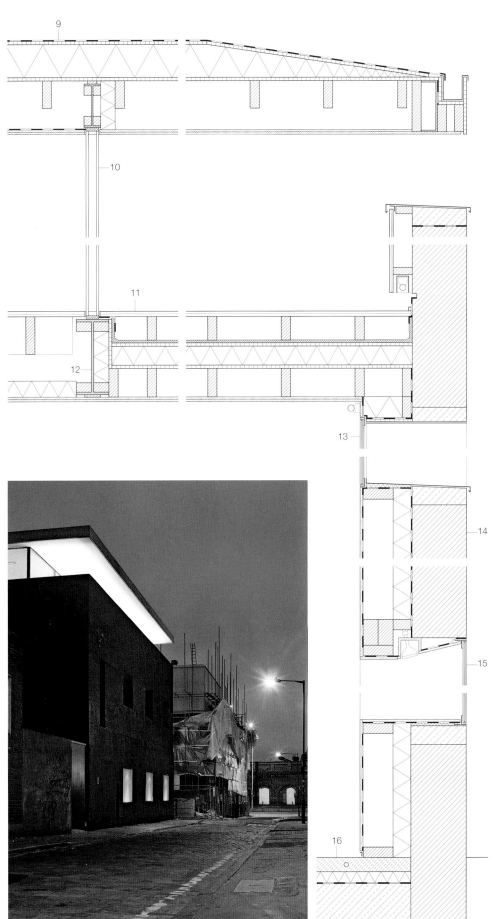

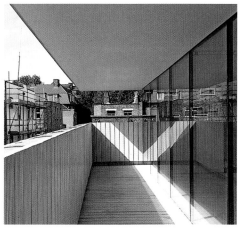

Section through facade
Scale 1:20

9 Roof construction:
1 layer of synthetic felt waterproofing
18 mm plywood
175 mm thermal insulation
18 mm plywood
150 x 50 mm rafters
vapour barrier
2 No. 12.5 mm impregnated plasterboard, painted
10 Glass facade:
insulating glass, 12 mm toughened safety glass
+ 40 mm cavity + 12 mm toughened safety glass,
with 12 x 65 mm galvanised posts
11 Floor construction:
28 mm impregnated softwood floorboards
120 x 50 mm timber joists
between existing steel beams
synthetic felt waterproofing
18 mm plywood
100 mm thermal insulation
18 mm plywood
150 x 50 mm timber joists
2 No. 12.5 mm plasterboard,
soffit perforated
12 Steel beam, IPE 400
13 Fixed light, insulating glass,
8 mm toughened safety glass + 16 mm cavity
+ 8 mm toughened safety glass, frameless
14 Wall construction:
anti-graffiti paint
300 mm clay brickwork (existing)
airtight membrane
thermal insulation
between IPB 100 mm steel columns
vapour barrier
12.5 mm plasterboard
15 Fixed light, insulating glass,
8 mm toughened safety glass + 16 mm cavity
+ 8 mm toughened safety glass, frameless,
inner pane sand-blasted, outer pane reflective
16 Floor construction:
epoxy resin coating
75 mm heated screed
60 mm thermal insulation
PE sheeting
200 mm reinforced concrete ground slab (existing)

Example 07

Office building

Berlin, D, 1928/2001

Architects:
Kahlfeldt Architekten, Berlin
Petra and Paul Kahlfeldt
Project team:
Pascal Dworak, Alexander Khorrami,
Karin Willke, Angela Schoen
Structural engineers:
Jockwer & Partner, Berlin

The retention of the structure and the careful conversion of this piece of industrial heritage were the key tasks involved in the refurbishment of the transformer substation in Berlin-Charlottenburg dating from 1928. This building originally housed the equipment for the electricity supplies to this part of the city, although the strictly organised clay brick facade does not reveal anything of the technical functions and complexity of the plant within located in the most diverse rooms on nine floors. The building became defunct in 1984 and all the machinery and technical installations were removed, which left an empty shell for which various uses were explored. Following consultations with the tenant, a communications company, the structure and character of this historical building was able to be preserved because the interior layout could be adapted to the new usage with only minimal intervention.

On the floors for the former switchgear there are now spacious rooms for project teams, meeting rooms and individual offices. The former oil circuit-breaker bays provide quiet areas for creative thinking, the "Think Tanks". The phase-shift hall on the ground floor and the adjoining transformer bays are now used for project presentations and exhibitions. The three-storey crane hall now forms the central entrance foyer. The loadbearing steel frame was also preserved along with the clay brickwork of the facade plus its windows with their many glazing bars. Large insulating glass windows and internal insulation represent new additions. The lightwell, once open to the sky, was given a glass roof so in this atrium-like interior space the existing brick walls do not require any insulation.

· Retention of steel loadbearing structure and clay brick masonry
· Retention of original steel windows, frames repainted, glass renewed
· New inner windows with insulating glass
· Internal insulation
· Glass roof to lightwell

📖 Deutsche Bauzeitung 09/2001
Kahlfeldt, Petra und Paul:
Moderne Architektur. Berlin 2006
l'architecture d'aujourd'hui 349, 2003

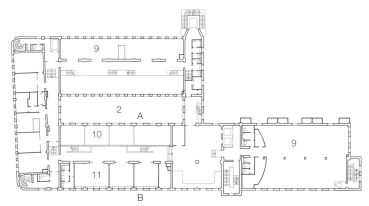

5th floor

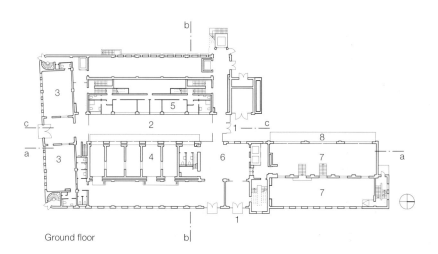

Ground floor

Plans · Sections
Scale 1:750

1 Entrance
2 Lightwell with new glass roof
3 Office
4 Exhibitions (former transformer bays)
5 Think Tank (former oil circuit-breaker bay)
6 Reception
7 Office (former transformer bay)
8 Terrace
9 Team room/office
10 Office/management
11 Meeting room

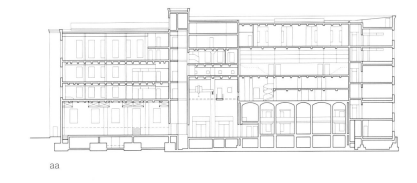

aa

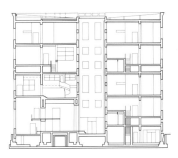

bb

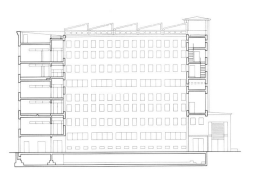

cc

Example 07

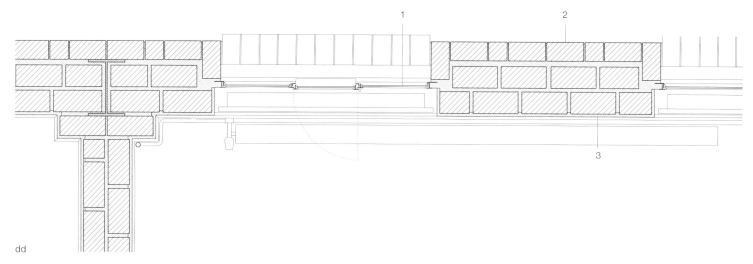

dd

Horizontal sections · Vertical sections
Lightwell, outer facade
Scale 1:20

1 Steel window (existing), repainted, glass renewed
2 Clay brickwork (existing), 430 mm,
 brick format 200 x 100 x 50 mm
3 Plaster, 15 mm
4 Steel window (existing), repaired, glass renewed,
 converted from side-hung to hopper opening,
 new hardware
5 Opening light: insulating glass in silver anodised
 aluminium frame
6 Insulation to window reveal
7 Internal insulation:
 10 mm plaster finish coat
 bond enhancer
 vapour barrier
 10 mm plaster intermediate coat with fabric
 reinforcement
 50 mm insulating plaster with polystyrene beads
 expanded metal
8 Anti-glare protection: aluminium louvre blind,
 reflective on one side, perforated
9 Fresh-air inlet in spandrel panel, manually regulated
10 Sound-insulated fresh-air element
11 Floor construction:
 7 mm carpet
 50 mm screed
 existing clay hollow element floor with 150 mm
 concrete topping
 soffit sprayed white

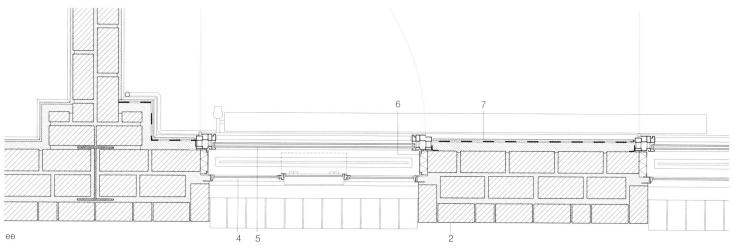

ee

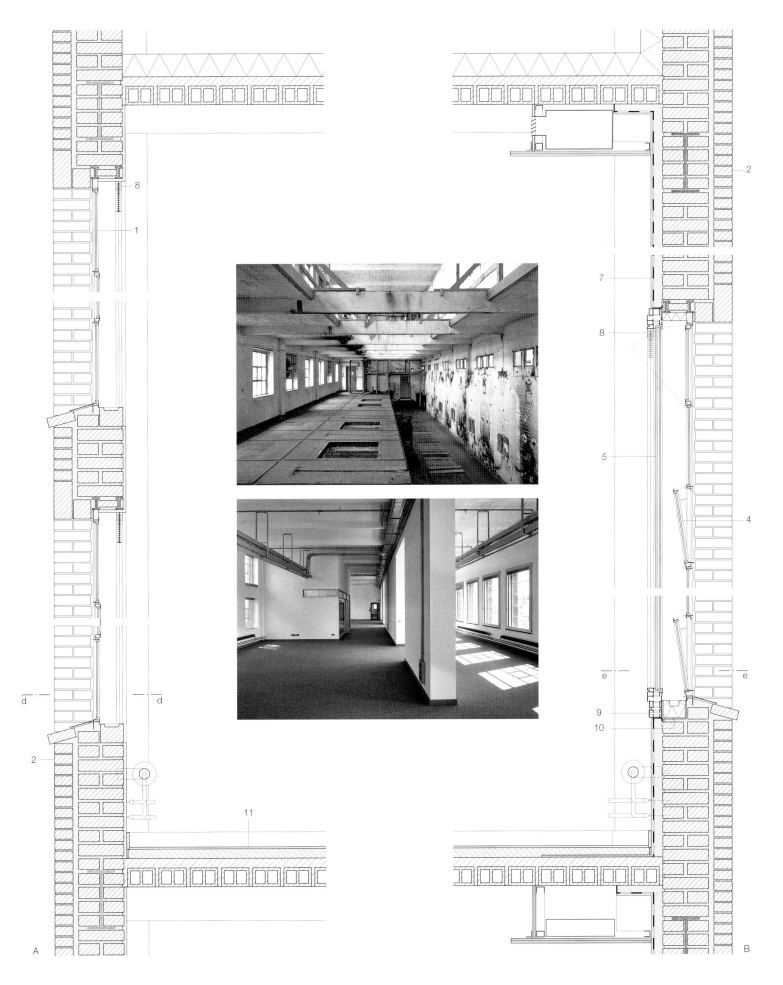

Example 08

Museum

Chemnitz, D, 1930/2007

Architects:
Staab Architekten, Berlin
Project team:
Madina von Arnim, Alexander Böhme,
Oliver Kampmann, Corinna Moesges
Jens Achtermann, Stefan Ernst, Daniel Angly,
Per Pedersen, Birgit Knicker, Daniela Krause,
Manuela Jochheim, Uwe-Christian Metz,
Franz Schommers, Gerd Eder, Oskar Söllner,
Frank Kotzerke, Johann Göhler
Structural engineers:
C & E Consulting & Engineering, Chemnitz

The treatment of the construction and architecture
of the existing building was a crucial design
parameter for the conversion of this former bank
– protected by a conservation order – in the
centre of Chemnitz. The building was first stripped
back to its loadbearing structure – external
walls, loadbearing columns, ribbed floors and
stabilising stair shafts. Simple interventions,
also visible in the architecture, were employed
to emphasize the specific spatial qualities of
the existing building and at the same time to
adapt it to the needs of the museum. The former
banking hall has been rebuilt with its illuminated
ceiling to serve as a central exhibition area that
can also be used occasionally for special events.
Light-permeable screens fitted to the windows
of the upper floors facing the internal lightwell
filter the incoming daylight and thus ensure
even, non-glare illumination in the rooms of the
museum. The new fitting-out elements are limited
to the exhibition walls in a lightweight construction, the stairs providing a direct link between
the four levels of the new museum, and the
cloakroom, cafeteria and ticket desks in the
form of sand-coloured aluminium boxes.
As part of the refurbishment work all damaged
travertine stone facade panels were replaced
and insulation was added to the inside of the
external walls. The rendered facade that replaced
the travertine stone on the side wing in the
1950s was rebuilt as an insulated construction
with ventilation cavity. The cornice was reconstructed and the curving glass front to the
entrance foyer was returned to its original condition.

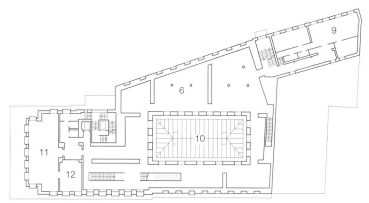

1st floor

- Deconstruction back to loadbearing structure
- Creation of spacious exhibition areas
- Repairs to travertine stone facades, internal
  insulation
- Reconstruction of travertine stone facade,
  with insulation and ventilation cavity
- Reconstruction of illuminated ceiling

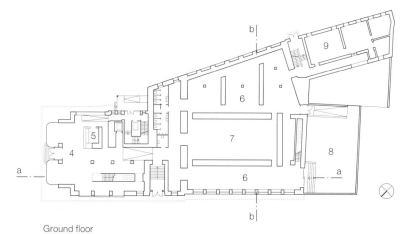

Ground floor

Metamorphose 01/2008
Bauwelt 7/2008
Borgelt, Christiane; Jost, Regina:
Kunstsammlungen Chemnitz – Museum
Gunzenhauser. Die Neuen Architekturführer,
vol. 117. Berlin, 2007

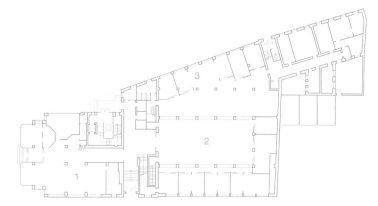

Ground floor, existing

Plans · Sections
Scale 1:750

1 Self-service
   restaurant
2 Banking hall
3 Office
4 Entrance foyer
5 Tickets, café,
   cloakroom
6 Exhibition

7 Temporary exhibitions/
   events
8 Open-air display area
   for sculptures
9 Workshop/store
10 Lightwell
11 Meeting room
12 Library

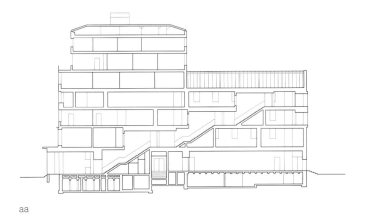

aa

bb

Example 08

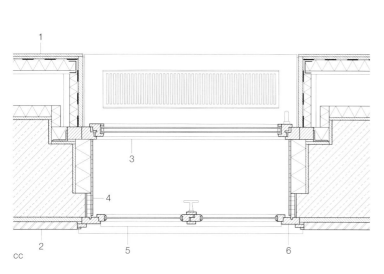

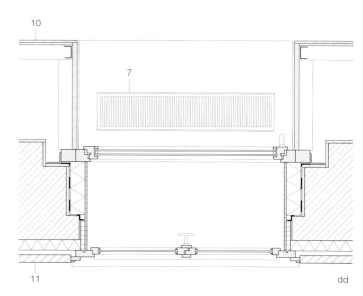

cc

dd

1   Independent wall lining: 2 No. 12.5 mm plasterboard,
    vapour barrier, 40 mm mineral wool
2   Wall construction:
    40 mm travertine stone cladding (existing), mortar
    backing, 290–520 mm reinforced concrete external
    wall (existing), 15 mm plaster (renewed)
    60 mm cellular glass internal insulation
3   Inner window: wooden frame, painted white,
    $U_f \leq 2.2$ W/m²K, $U_g \leq 1.1$ W/m²K
4   Plywood lining to reveal (outside), 5 mm, painted,
    on existing wooden lining
5   Existing wooden frame repaired, 4 mm float glass
    (existing)
6   Outer frame painted white

7   Wooden slotted ventilation grille in window board,
    30 mm, painted white
8   Slotted skirting board
9   Floor construction:
    35 mm ground mastic asphalt, separating layer, 20 mm
    expanded perlite insulation, 20 mm mineral wool
    insulation, 5–25 mm loose fill levelling layer, reinforced
    concrete slab (existing)
10 Independent wall lining: 2 No. 12.5 mm plasterboard
11 Reconstructed travertine stone facade:
    40 mm travertine stone slabs, joints filled with elastic
    compound and finished with quartz sand, 20 mm
    ventilation cavity, 60 mm mineral wool insulation,
    290–520 mm reinforced concrete external wall

    (existing), 15 mm plaster (existing)
12 Vapour-tight sheeting
13 Additional masonry to spandrel panel
14 Beam supporting glass roof over lightwell (existing)
15 Fabric sunshade/glare protection, horizontal guides
16 Fluorescent lighting
17 Steel section, IPE 80
18 Steel section, IPE 270
19 Steel T-section, 270 x 135 x 20 mm, with endplate,
    fitted into existing masonry
20 Steel rod hanger, Ø12 mm
21 Satin-finish plastic panel, 1760 x 830 x 10 mm, with
    slots on rear face for attaching to hangers
22 Ventilation grille

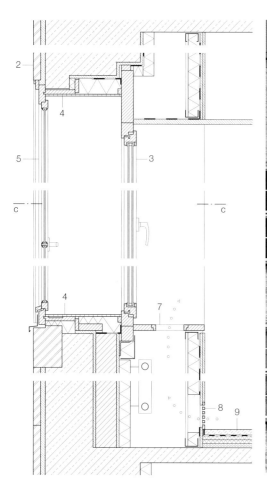

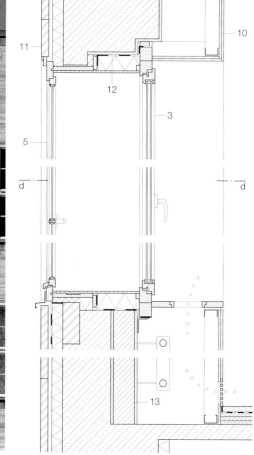

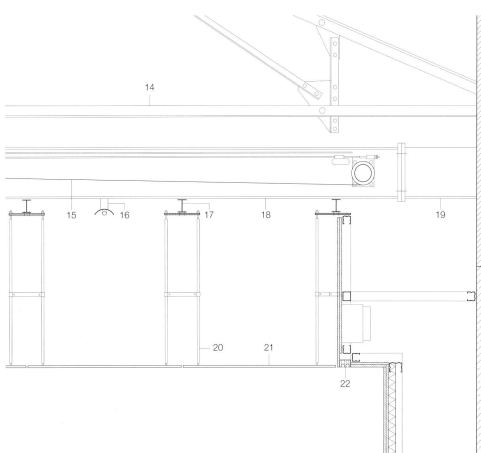

Travertine stone facade (existing) with internal insulation
Reconstructed travertine stone facade
Horizontal sections · Vertical sections
Illuminated ceiling
Scale 1:20

Example 09

Housing development

Chur, CH, 1944/2000

Architects:
Dieter Jüngling and
Andreas Hagmann, Chur
Structural engineer:
Georg Liesch, Chur

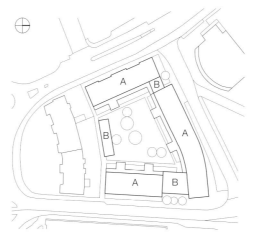

Location drawing
Scale 1:2000
Plans
Scale 1:500

A Existing
B New

1 Living room
2 Room
3 Kitchen
4 Loggia

The "Tivoli" estate of apartment blocks opposite the station in Chur was designed by Karl Beer in 1942. It is a nondescript complex, but here in these poorly defined surroundings it represents a worthwhile preservation project. The apartments, however, with their small-format interior layouts no longer conformed to modern standards and expectations, and were therefore difficult to let. The aim therefore was to adapt the interior layouts to today's requirements and at the same time update the old staircases to comply with the latest legislation and standards. Owing to the central location of the estate it also seemed sensible to integrate shops and offices and thus increase the density of the existing site. This resulted in the three individual existing buildings being carefully refurbished and supplemented by new structures to create a perimeter development surrounding a landscaped inner court. Transferring the staircases to the outside enabled additional living space to be created. The new architecture of the buildings is also visible from the inner court, where an outer leaf in the form of a loggia extension was built in front of the original facade. Apart from the extra floor space and the higher standard of the apartments, this also resulted in the chance to provide the old facade with external insulation and use the loggias as a buffer zone, thus improving the energy balance of the compact structure quite crucially.

· Demolition of existing staircases
· External thermal insulation
· Loggia extensions
· Repositioning of staircases
· Infill development to create perimeter block

Detail 06/2001

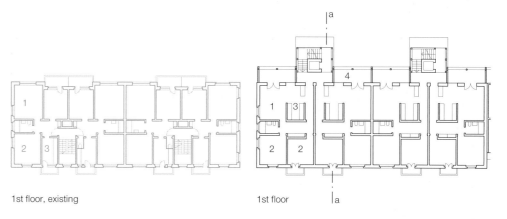

1st floor, existing

1st floor

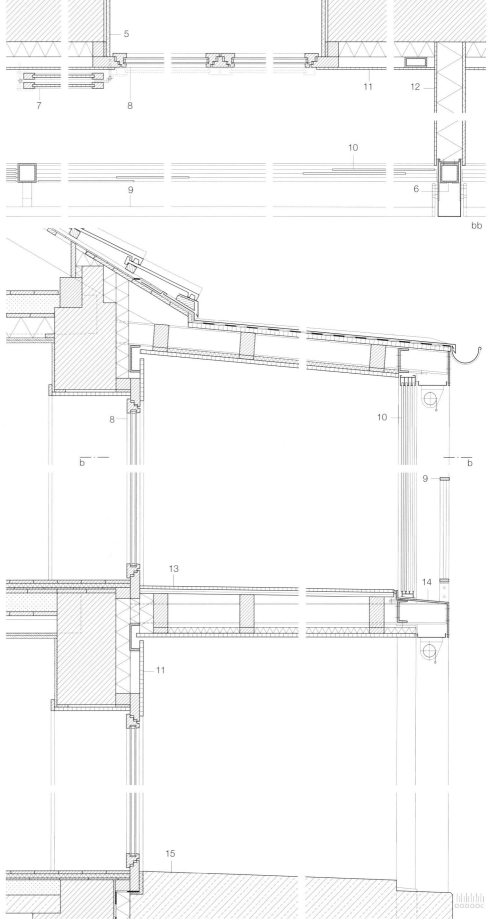

Horizontal section
Vertical section
Loggia extension facing inner court
Scale 1:20

5   Cement-bonded particleboard, 16 mm
6   Steel hollow section, 100 x 100 mm,
     sheet aluminium cladding, 2 mm
7   Folding shutters with 32 x 48 mm fir frame and
     12 mm phenolic resin-faced plywood infill panels
8   Wooden window, fir, 65 mm, with insulating glass
9   Balustrade of 50 x 15 mm steel flats and Ø15 mm
     steel rods
10   Sliding element, 10 mm toughened safety glass in
     aluminium track
11   Facade construction:
     12 mm veneer plywood
     120 x 60 mm steel hollow section
     80 mm thermal insulation
     350–410 mm masonry (existing)
     15 mm plaster
12   Wall construction:
     12 mm veneer plywood
     140 mm thermal insulation
     16 mm cement-bonded particleboard
13   Floor construction:
     15 mm veneer plywood on 24 mm timber sheathing
     80 x 171 mm timber joists with 120 mm steel I-section
     80 x 30 mm battens, 30 mm thermal insulation
     12 mm perforated veneer plywood
14   Sheet steel, 6 mm, factory-bent
15   Reinforced concrete ground slab, finely rubbed

Example 09

Section
Scale 1:500
Horizontal section
Vertical section
Staircase tower facing
inner court
Scale 1:20

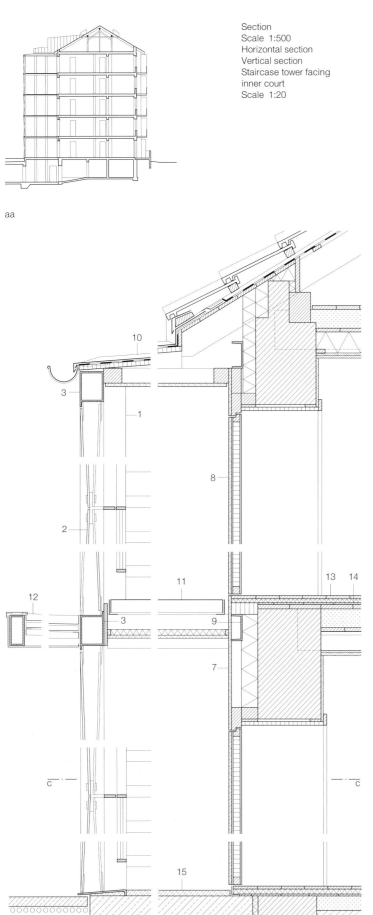

aa

cc

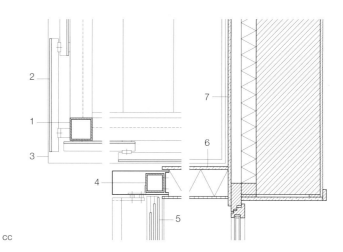

1   Steel hollow section, 120 x 120 mm
2   Glass louvre, 10 mm toughened safety glass with point fixings, 115 x 50 x 5 mm steel flats
3   Steel hollow section, 160 x 120 mm
4   Steel hollow section, 100 x 100 mm, sheet aluminium cladding, 2 mm
5   Sliding element, 10 mm toughened safety glass in aluminium track
6   Wall construction:
    16 mm cement-bonded particleboard
    140 mm thermal insulation
    12 mm veneer plywood
7   Wall construction:
    16 mm cement-bonded particleboard
    steel hollow section, 120 x 60 mm
    80 mm thermal insulation
    350–410 mm masonry (existing)
    15 mm plaster
8   Cement-bonded particleboard, 16 mm, added to existing door leaf
9   Steel channel, 140 x 60 mm
10 Roof construction:
    sheet copper with standing seams
    built-up felt roofing
    27 mm 3-ply core plywood
    100 x 80 mm timber joists

16 mm cement-bonded particleboard
11 Floor construction: 5–7 mm profiled sheet metal, factory-bent perimeter frame, 100 x 50 mm steel angle
    180 x 100 mm steel hollow section
    30 mm insulation to void
    16 mm cement-bonded particleboard
12 Canopy: 2 mm sheet steel, coated with liquid plastic
    30 mm trapezoidal profile steel sheeting perimeter frame, 30 x 30 mm steel angle
    160 x 80 mm steel hollow section
13 Floor construction:
    13 mm oak wood-block flooring
    2 mm fleece
    16 mm impact sound insulation
14 Floor construction (existing):
    9 mm beech wood-block flooring
    21 mm fir floorboards
    120 x 220 mm timber joists with 100 mm pugging
    21 mm fir pugging boards
    24 mm gypsum boards
    28 mm gypsum plaster
15 Granolithic screed, 30 mm, on 250 mm reinforced concrete

Museum

Ingolstadt, D, 1954/2000

Architects:
Fischer Architekten, Munich
Florian Fischer, Erhard Fischer
Project team:
Ralf Emmerling, Sieglinde Neyer
Structural engineers:
Muck Ingenieure, Ingolstadt

This shed with sawtooth roof dating from the 1950s is located directly on the former city wall of Ingolstädt and was originally used for car production. It was in a desolate condition when it was purchased by a museum foundation. However, the architects have turned it into an elegant, memorable exhibition facility using very simple means. On three sides the structure was given a new "skin" of aluminium sandwich panels bent back to form very sharp arrises at the corners of the building. The 250 mm wide ventilation space behind the panels now also accommodates the existing rainwater down-pipes from the sawtooth roof. Whereas the doors in the aluminium skin are just visible in outline, the ventilation openings and the windows to the offices are hidden behind perforated sheet aluminium – nothing disturbs the effect of the material and the clarity of the volume. On the north side the plain facade was replaced by an approx. 2 m deep steel-and-glass extension – the "display window" that permits a good view of the exhibition areas inside the building. This is also the location of the main entrance. Inside the building all existing fitting-out items and building services were removed and the original basic structural condition of the building restored. An unconventional solution was chosen for heating the interior: heating pipes laid in the bases of the external walls to heat up the components. Thermal insulation was added to the roof and the roof covering and glazing renewed. The local building authority agreed to the omission of insulation in the external walls.

· Facade cladding with aluminium sandwich panels
· Construction of steel-and-glass extension
· Removal of all fitting-out items
· Insulation to roof

▱ Detail 06/2001

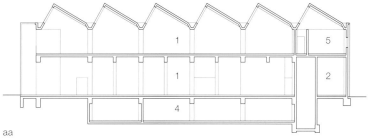

aa

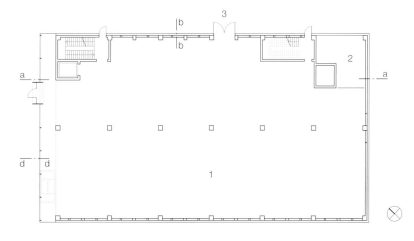

Section · Plan
Scale 1:500

1 Exhibitions
2 Store
3 Deliveries
4 Workshop
5 Management

Example 10

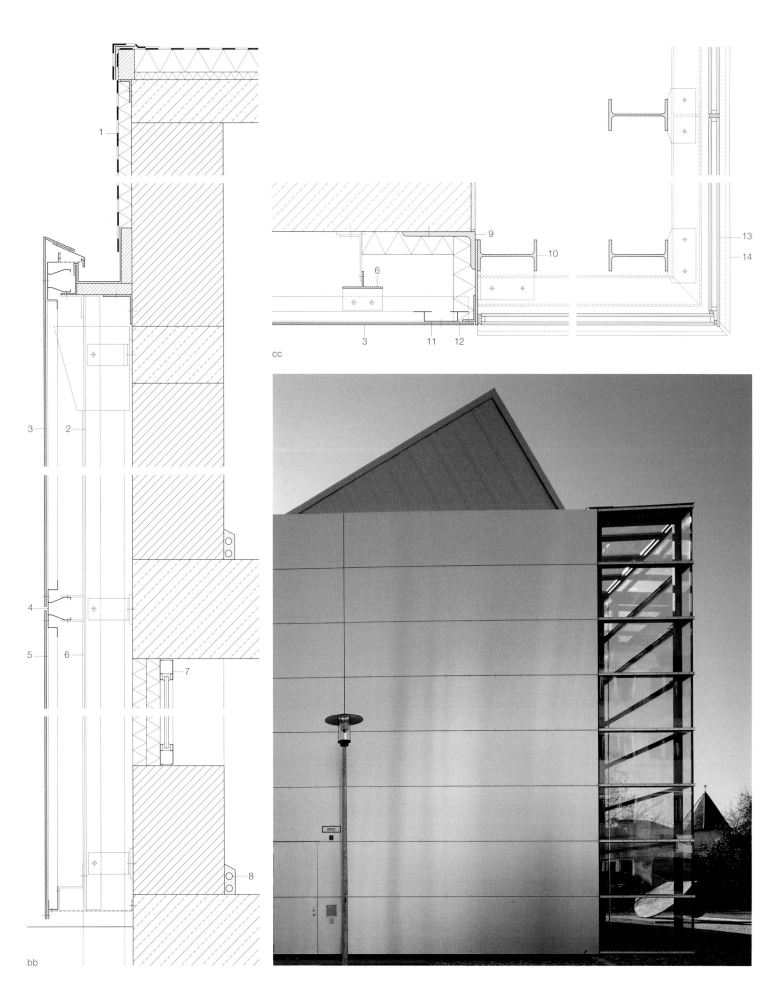

Vertical sections
Horizontal section
Scale 1:10

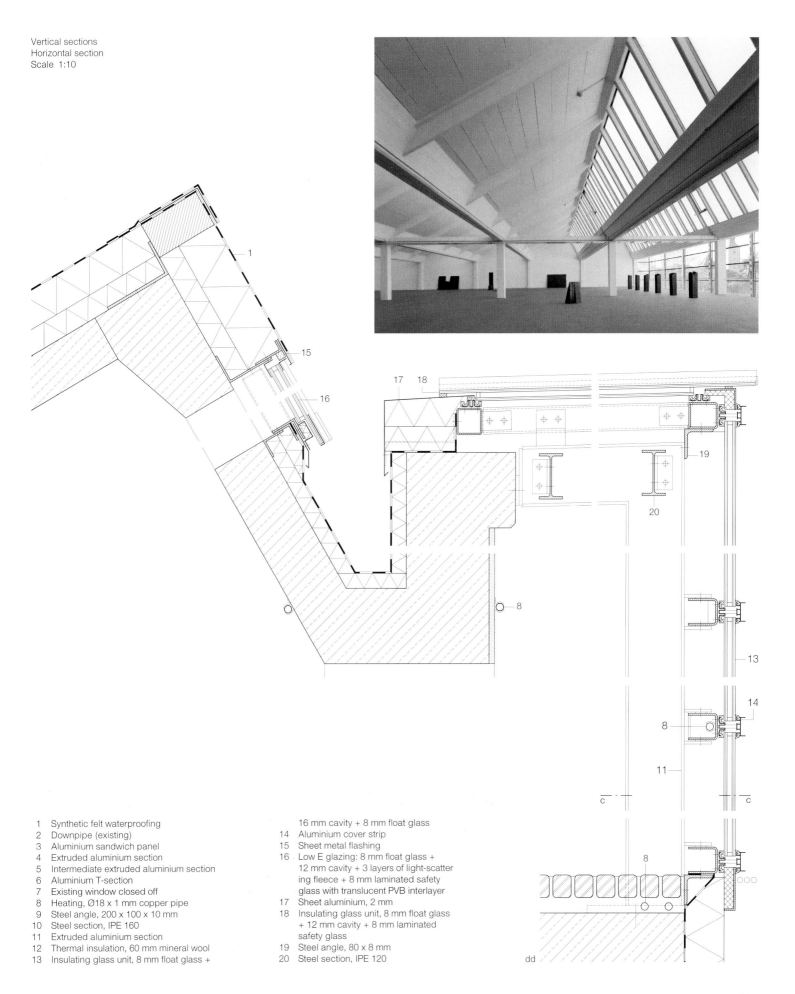

1   Synthetic felt waterproofing
2   Downpipe (existing)
3   Aluminium sandwich panel
4   Extruded aluminium section
5   Intermediate extruded aluminium section
6   Aluminium T-section
7   Existing window closed off
8   Heating, Ø18 x 1 mm copper pipe
9   Steel angle, 200 x 100 x 10 mm
10 Steel section, IPE 160
11 Extruded aluminium section
12 Thermal insulation, 60 mm mineral wool
13 Insulating glass unit, 8 mm float glass +

16 mm cavity + 8 mm float glass
14 Aluminium cover strip
15 Sheet metal flashing
16 Low E glazing: 8 mm float glass +
    12 mm cavity + 3 layers of light-scatter
    ing fleece + 8 mm laminated safety
    glass with translucent PVB interlayer
17 Sheet aluminium, 2 mm
18 Insulating glass unit, 8 mm float glass
    + 12 mm cavity + 8 mm laminated
    safety glass
19 Steel angle, 80 x 8 mm
20 Steel section, IPE 120

Example 11

Arched roof shed

Cologne, D, 1950/2000

Architects:
4000architekten, Cologne
Georg Giebeler
Project assistant:
Anke Josat

Achieving maximum effect with minimum intervention – this was the goal pursued by the architects when given the task of converting a production building dating from the 1950s into the sales depot for a book wholesaler. After removing all fitting-out items and non-loadbearing components from this building, which had stood empty for years, all that remained was the delicate reinforced concrete frame construction spanning 38 m. The concrete surfaces were revealed by sand-blasting and – totally in keeping with the notion of conservation – instead of being made good, for example, were preserved together with all their superficial defects by applying a coat of clear varnish! A new walkway provides quick access between the facilities on the ground floor and the offices on the first floor. The black steel plates of the walkway, also treated with clear varnish, stand out from the prevailing grey of the concrete structure. On the side facing the open hall, the offices on both floors have full-height, frameless glazing. The width of the butt-jointed panes matches that of the standard doors, which are fitted into simple steel frames. Apart from a few panes at the ends, every one has the same format, which means that the doors can be repositioned at any time if required. Thanks to the use of standardised components, the project was completed in just four weeks – from award of contract to completion of refurbishment measures. This also helped to keep the costs down to a minimum.

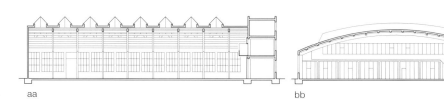

aa   bb

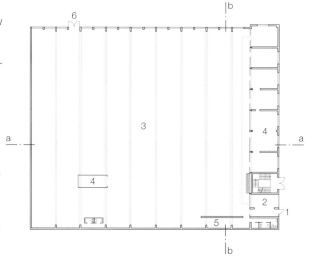

Sections
Plan
Scale 1:750

1   Entrance
2   Reception
3   Book
    storage
4   Offices
5   Plant room
6   Deliveries

- Demolition of all non-loadbearing internal components
- Uncovering all concrete surfaces
- Application of clear varnish to protect exposed reinforcement
- Integration of storey-high frameless glazing
- Construction of a cantilevering walkway to provide access to the upper floor

Bauwelt 42–43/2001
db 09/2002

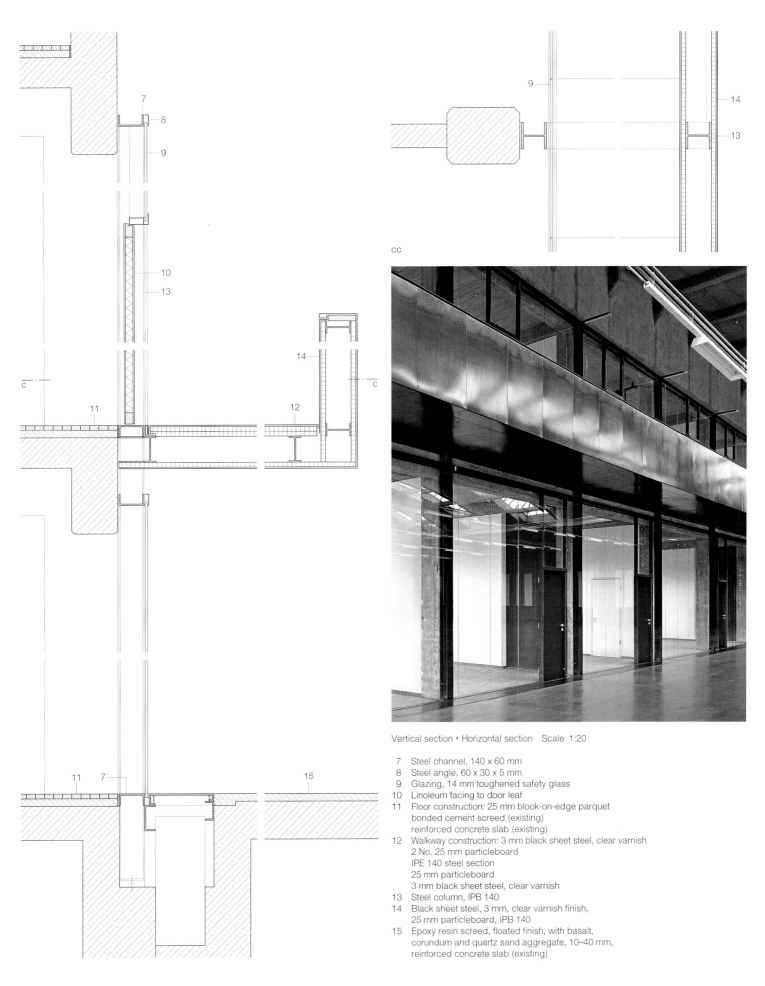

cc

Vertical section · Horizontal section   Scale 1:20

7   Steel channel, 140 x 60 mm
8   Steel angle, 60 x 30 x 5 mm
9   Glazing, 14 mm toughened safety glass
10 Linoleum facing to door leaf
11 Floor construction: 25 mm block-on-edge parquet
    bonded cement screed (existing)
    reinforced concrete slab (existing)
12 Walkway construction: 3 mm black sheet steel, clear varnish
    2 No. 25 mm particleboard
    IPE 140 steel section
    25 mm particleboard
    3 mm black sheet steel, clear varnish
13 Steel column, IPB 140
14 Black sheet steel, 3 mm, clear varnish finish,
    25 mm particleboard, IPB 140
15 Epoxy resin screed, floated finish, with basalt,
    corundum and quartz sand aggregate, 10–40 mm,
    reinforced concrete slab (existing)

241

Example 12

Office building

Düsseldorf, D, 1950/1998

Architects:
Petzinka Pink Architekten, Düsseldorf
Project team:
Christian Dortschy, Mathias Stamminger,
Michael Marx, Miquel Nieto, Bruno Dercks
Structural engineers:
Gehlen, Düsseldorf

This corner block is part of an inner-city complex dating from the 1950s. Flaws in the facade and an outdated interior layout led to this building being left unoccupied for many years. The building was gutted while retaining most of the form, reorganised and clad with specially developed facade elements. As the existing loadbearing structure could not accommodate any additional imposed loads, some of the existing components were replaced by others made from lightweight materials. The reinforced concrete frame with cantilevering floor slabs was retained, whereas spandrel panels, downstand beams and facade cladding panels were removed. The reinforcing meshes in the floor slabs were exposed on the top side and additional reinforcement inserted, which increased the load-carrying capacity from 1.8 to 3.5 kN/m². All internal partitions are non-loadbearing in accordance with the variable usage concept. The low-tech solar facade consists of prefabricated tray elements made from toughened safety glass and lightweight wood-wool boards, which alternate with the pairs of opening lights with low E glass and aluminium frames. The plan layouts are completely flexible, with no predetermined divisions, and the plain wall areas of the facade provide connection options for lightweight partitions. In addition, the cable trunking in the plane of the facade – in front of the floor edges and accessible from outside – guarantee flexibility in the use of the interior spaces and also future technical upgrades.

- Gutting
- Upgrading the loadbearing structure for new usage concepts by means of additional reinforcement
- Lightweight, modular, prefabricated facade
- Flexible plan layout
- Cables in horizontal trunking in the facade, accessible from outside

Petzinka, Karl-Heinz; Pink, Thomas: Technologische Architektur – Petzinka Pink Architekten. Basel 2004

5th floor

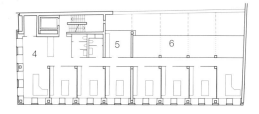

2nd floor

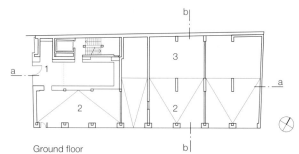

Ground floor

Plans • Sections
Scale 1:500

1 Entrance foyer
2 Parking
3 Double-decker parking
4 Office
5 Tea kitchen
6 Void
7 Apartment

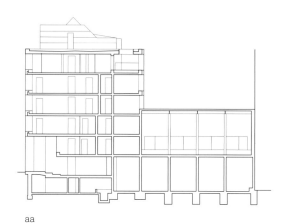

aa

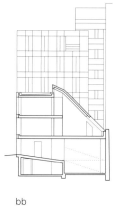

bb

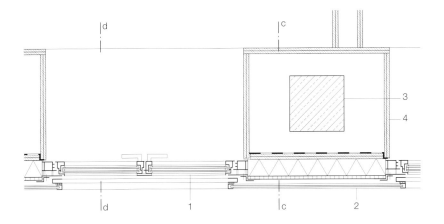

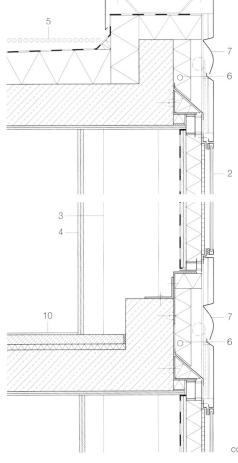

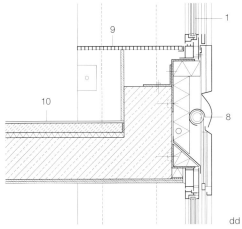

Horizontal section · Vertical section
Scale 1:20

1 Low E glass in aluminium frame
2 Prefabricated lightweight element:
8 mm toughened safety glass
35 mm air space
15 mm lightweight wood-wool board,
red finish
85 mm fibrous insulating material
2 No. 12 mm waterproof plasterboard
vapour barrier
3 Reinforced concrete column (existing),
300 x 300 mm
4 Column cladding, 2 No. 12 mm
plasterboard
5 Roof construction:
50 mm gravel, waterproofing,

100–180 mm thermal insulation with
integral falls, 220 mm reinforced concrete slab (existing), 20 mm plaster
6 Cable trunking
7 Anodised sheet aluminium fascia
panel, 3 mm, opened from outside
8 Fabric roller blind, aluminium vacuum
metallised finish
9 Window board, 3 mm anodised sheet
aluminium, on grating
10 Floor construction:
carpet, 50 mm screed, 30 mm impact
sound insulation, 220 mm reinforced
concrete slab (existing), 20 mm plaster

Example 13

Private house

Bochum, D, 1950/2001

Architect:
Anja Köster, Bochum

Plans
Scale 1:200

1 Entrance
2 Bathroom/WC
3 Kitchen
4 Living room
5 Bedroom
6 Dining room
7 Study

For the owner of this house, demolition to make way for a new building was not even considered. Instead, the owner, the grandson of the original builder, decided to carry out a total refurbishment of the building so typical for the suburbs of the post-war period. Once the first floor became vacant, this was the chance to combine the two lower floors to form one house. Turning the plan layout through 180° meant that the living room could now face south-west, overlooking the garden, placing the kitchen and dining room on the road side. The creation of large openings in the walls to all rooms resulted in new relationships and increased the interior space visually. The upper floor is reached via an open staircase, which is actually a stepped kitchen cupboard tailor-made by a joiner! A spacious study, the bedroom and the modernised, enlarged bathroom are located here. With the exception of the bathrooms, the widened window openings now extend down to floor level in both storeys and admit more daylight into the interior. Low E glass and an external thermal insulation composite system guarantee a better energy balance for the building. The rooms under the roof constitute a separate apartment that is reached via the existing staircase and can be let separately.

· New plan layout, wall openings
· External thermal insulation composite system
· New windows with low E glass
· Enlarged window openings

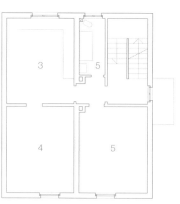

1st floor, existing

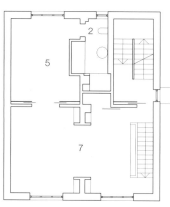

1st floor

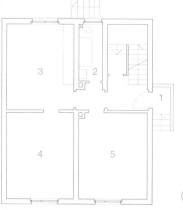

Ground floor, existing

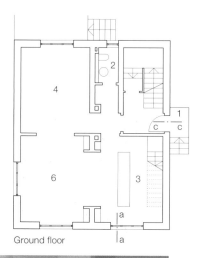

Ground floor

244

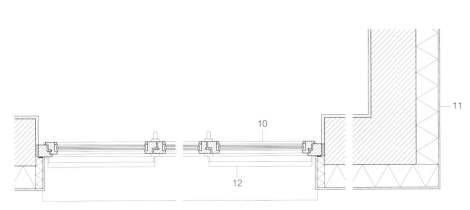

bb

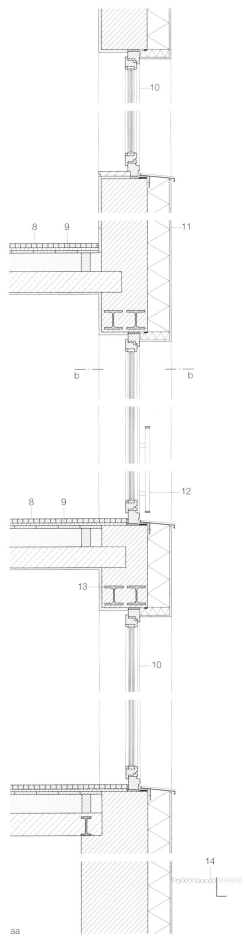

Horizontal section
Vertical section
Scale 1:20

8 Oak block-on-edge parquet, 22 mm,
   bonded over full area
9 Existing floor construction:
   13 mm particleboard as levelling layer
   15 mm floorboards
   50 x 100 mm timber bearers
   between slag/ash loose fill
   110 mm reinforced concrete slab
   10 mm lime-gypsum plaster
10 Wooden window with low E glass
   (U = 1.1 W/m²K), 5 mm + 16 mm cavity + 5 mm

11 Wall construction:
   10 mm mineral render
   lightweight reinforcing mortar with glass
   fibre fabric
   120 mm rigid polystyrene foam insulation
   250 mm clay/pumice masonry (existing)
   15 mm lime-gypsum plaster
12 Balustrade, 5 x 25 mm galvanised steel flats
13 Steel section, HEB 100
14 Gravel, basalt, black

aa

Example 13

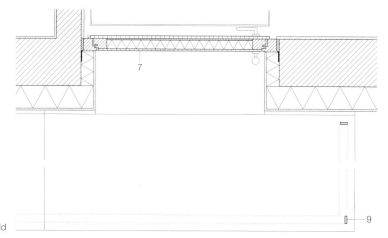

dd

9

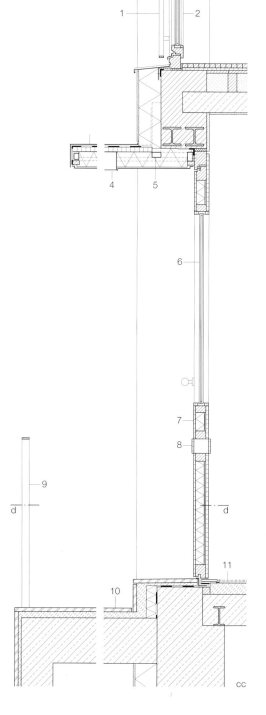

1

2

4

5

6

7

8

9

d

d

10

11

cc

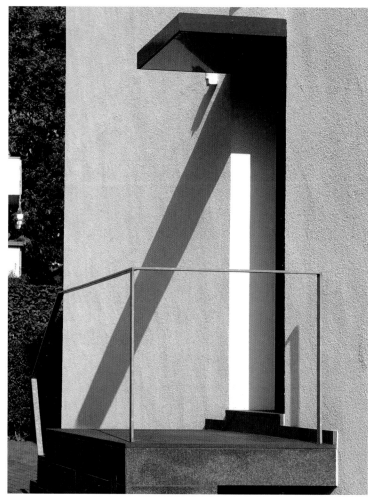

Horizontal section · Vertical section
Scale 1:20

1 Balustrade, 5 x 25 mm galvanised steel flats
2 Wooden window
with insulating glass (U = 1.1 W/m²K),
5 mm + 16 mm cavity + 5 mm
3 Canopy construction:
2 mm stove-enamelled aluminium
PE sheeting
25 mm waterproof particleboard
50 x 30 x 3 mm steel hollow section
100 mm mineral wool thermal insulation
2 mm stove-enamelled aluminium
4 Lamp

5 50 x 30 x 3 mm steel hollow section
6 Insulating glass unit,
4 mm + 16 mm cavity + 4 mm
7 Framed and braced door with steel
reinforcement, faced both sides
8 Letter plate
9 Balustrade, 10 x 40 mm steel flats
10 Landing construction:
20 mm granite tiles in trass-cement
mortar
masonry/concrete steps (existing)
11 Floor construction, entrance hall:
sisal mat
60 mm bonded screed
180 mm reinforced concrete (existing)

Private house

Kaufbeuren, D, 1960/2004

Architects:
kehrbaumarchitekten, Augsburg
Klaus Kehrbaum
Project team:
Simon Habel, Markus Groß
Structural engineers:
GBD, Dornbirn

This box-frame construction dating from the 1960s is situated on a south-facing slope on the edge of a small nature conservation area. From the windows there is an uninterrupted view of the mountains. The building originally contained 10 separate apartments but these have now been combined and converted into one spacious house. The form of the building was changed only very little by the architects, but now the contours are much more apparent. The anthracite colouring of the new slate roof and slate cladding to the walls lends the building an almost ancient, sculpted appearance. The internal layout adheres to the original concept of the building. In the large living rooms the original loadbearing structure has been opened up, but in the guest and children's rooms the original structure is still obvious. Besides the galleries to the apartments, the converted roof space now contains an archive. The loggias direct the view southwards and provide screening against the wind and sunshading for the large areas of glass. In order to avoid thermal bridges, the loggias were insulated with cellular glass, which is also used on the walls facing the prevailing wind. Cellular insulation was blown into the voids of the timber joists floors. A rooflight runs the full length of the building and illuminates the corridor below. The energy concept includes 40 m² of solar collectors that feed a tank for the hot-water and heating systems. Downstream of the system there are five water tanks that act as a thermal mass to keep the temperature within the house comfortable. Heating pipes have been laid in the floors and ceilings. The generously sized (120 m²) photovoltaic installation produces more electricity than this low-energy house needs; the excess energy is fed into the public electricity grid.

- Internal insulation
- Cellulose installation in the timber joists floors
- New wall and floor openings
- Slate roof covering and wall cladding

Detail 11/2006

Plans
Scale 1:400

1	Gravel garden	9	Dressing room
2	Atrium garden	10	Boiler room
3	Pergola	11	Utility room
4	Swimming pool	12	Sauna
5	Guest room	13	Cellar
6	Living room	14	Thermal mass
7	Study	15	Apartment
8	Bedroom	16	Storage
		17	Gallery
		18	Archive
		19	Rooflight

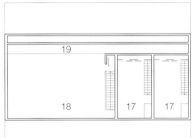

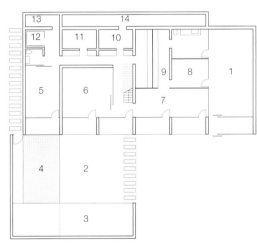

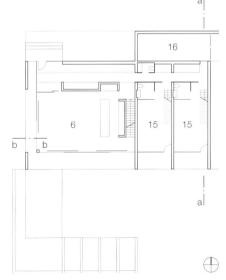

Example 14

aa

Section
Scale 1:400
Vertical sections
Scale 1:20

A   Solar roof, south side
B   Rooflight, north side

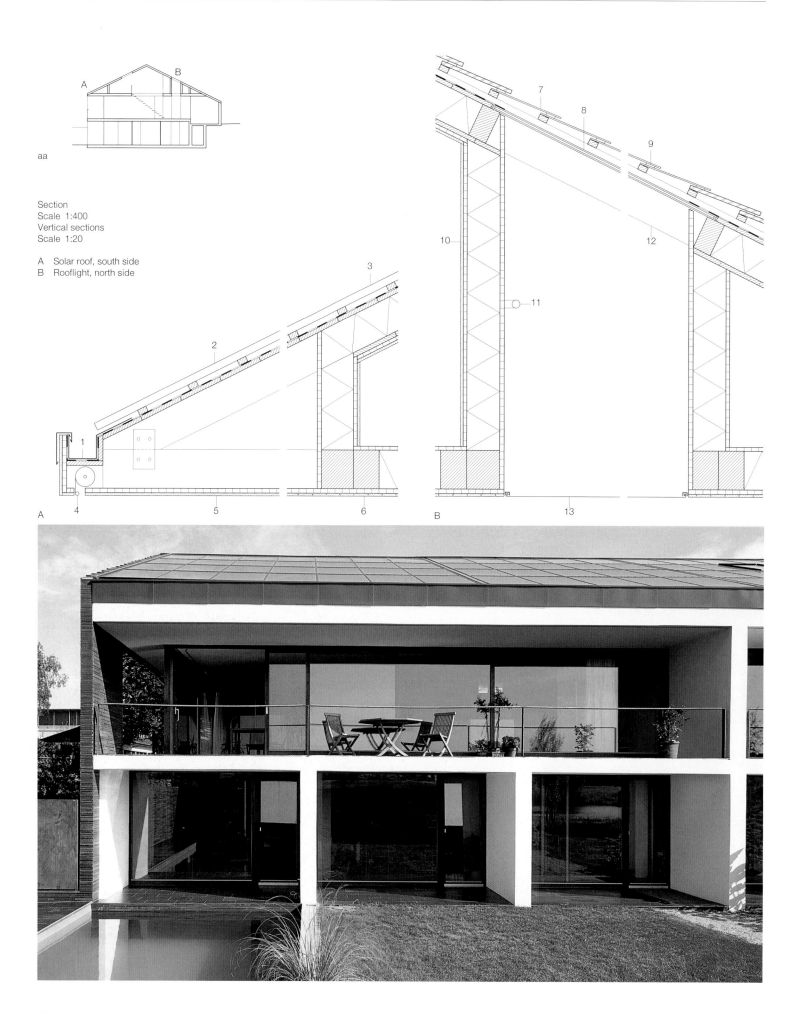

A

B

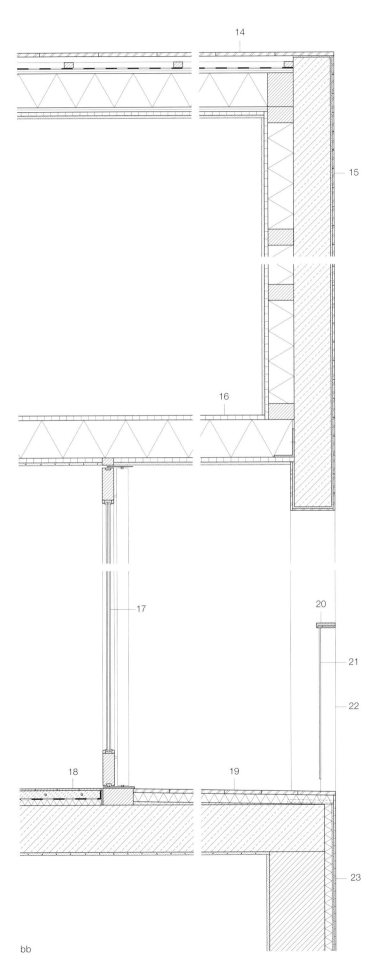

1 Rainwater gutter, sheet aluminium,
   concealed
2 Solar roof construction, south side:
   photovoltaic element/thermal collector
   30 x 50 mm timber battens
   vapour-permeable roofing felt
   24 mm timber sheathing
   rafters (existing)
3 Roof over converted roof space:
   photovoltaic element
   30 x 50 mm timber battens
   vapour-permeable roofing felt
   24 mm timber sheathing
   180 mm thermal insulation
   20 mm OSB, 15 mm plaster
4 Roller blind (sunshade)
5 Soffit: 15 mm plaster, 20 mm OSB
6 Floor construction:
   plaster with ceiling heating
   20 mm OSB
   200 mm timber joists (existing)/thermal
   insulation
   20 mm OSB
   paint finish
7 Toughened safety glass, 6 mm, printed,
   anti-reflection coating
8 Insulating glass,
   6 mm + 12 mm cavity + 6 mm,
   as water run-off layer
9 Sealing tape
10 Wall construction:
   15 mm plaster, 20 mm OSB
   170 mm thermal insulation
   20 mm OSB, painted white
11 Fluorescent lighting
12 Rafters (existing), painted white
13 Translucent ceiling, matt white plastic
   sheeting

14 Roof construction: 20 mm slates
   30 x 50 mm battens
   30 x 50 mm counter battens
   vapour-permeable roofing felt
   24 mm timber sheathing
   180 mm thermal insulation
   24 mm timber sheathing
   20 mm OSB, 15 mm plaster
15 Wall construction:
   10 mm slate cladding in mortar bed
   200 mm reinforced concrete
   140 mm thermal insulation
   20 mm OSB, 15 mm plaster
16 Floor construction: 20 mm OSB
   200 mm timber joists (existing)/thermal
   insulation
   20 mm OSB, 15 mm plaster
17 Sliding insulating glass element,
   6 mm + 12 mm cavity + 6 mm
18 Floor construction:
   10 mm wood-block flooring
   40 mm screed, separating layer
   30 mm impact sound insulation
   250 mm RC slab (existing)
   plaster with ceiling heating
19 Loggia floor: 20 mm slates
   50 mm thermal insulation on screed
   laid to fall
   250 mm RC slab (existing)
   15 mm plaster
20 Handrail, black anodised aluminium
   section, 90 x 15 mm
21 Perspex, 8 mm
22 Uprights, 80 x 10 mm steel flats
23 Wall construction:
   10 mm slate cladding in mortar bed
   40 mm thermal insulation
   masonry (existing), 15 mm plaster

bb

Example 15

School

Schulzendorf, D, 1965/2006

Architects:
zanderroth architekten, Berlin
Sascha Zander, Christian Roth,
with Guido Neubeck, Berlin
Project assistant:
Hanael Fesz
Structural engineer:
Ingenieurbüro für Bauwesen
Volker Krienitz, Schulzendorf

Like a giant basket, a facade of woven willow
canes surrounds this extended school building
in Schulzendorf. The expanding community
here on the southern edge of Berlin required
new classrooms for the growing number of children of primary school age. The plot containing
a school dating from the 1930s also contained
a multipurpose hall dating from the 1990s and
a newer pre-school facility as well as a school
building in large-panel construction – type
Magdeburg – which was built in 1965. In order
to reinforce the ensemble as a whole, the architects suggested extending this latter construction instead of erecting another separate building. This would create a larger building with a
greater urban presence. On two sides the old
building has now been supplemented by new
classroom wings; the dreary, plain gable ends
have been covered up and the previously open
courtyards have been incorporated into the
new overall structure in the form of two glass-
roofed atria. Access to all the classrooms is via
galleries open to these atria. Wider circulation
zones between the two atria provide internal
meeting points. Outside, an envelope of willow
canes woven in situ has been suspended in
front of the facades of the new and old buildings, joining them together to make one single
block. Returns at ground floor level create
space for covered recreational and entrance
areas and open-air seating for the school canteen.
The entrance merges with the auditorium for
school events, which is open over the full height
of the building via the two atria. A bold colour
scheme has been used for the circulation and
public zones. Different plain colours cover entire
walls, spandrel panels, floors and ceilings in
the storeys around the two atria. The local library
is also housed on the ground floor plus the
school canteen, which also serves as a meeting room for the local council.

· Building extensions
· New facade cladding
· New roofs over courtyards

Bauwelt 47/2007
Detail 11/2007

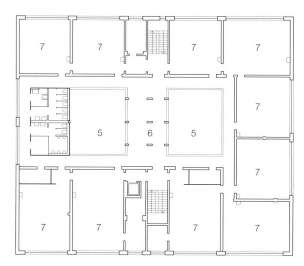

2nd floor

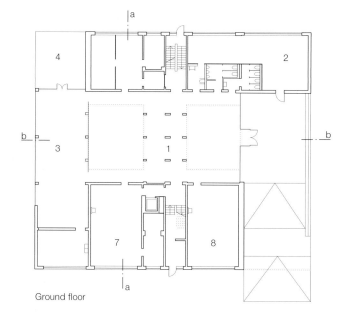

Ground floor

Plans	1	Auditorium/ foyer	7	Classroom
Sections	2	Library	8	Staff room
Scale 1:500	3	Canteen	9	School (1930s)
Location drawing	4	Terrace	10	Pre-school facility
Scale 1:5000	5	Atrium	11	Gymnasium
	6	Gallery	12	Extended school

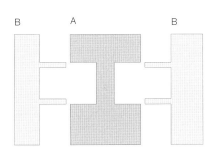

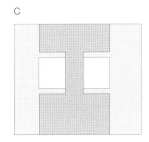

A   Existing large-panel construction (1965)
B   Extensions to both sides

C   Plan on new primary school

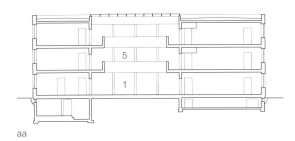

aa

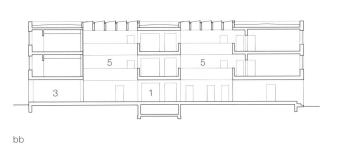

bb

Example 15

1 Roof construction:
  bitumen felt waterproofing, slate granule surfacing
  180 mm thermal insulation, rigid polystyrene foam
  vapour barrier, synthetic felt
  concrete laid to falls
  240 mm reinforced concrete
  120 mm acoustic ceiling on metal framing, with
  mineral-fibre insulation, fibrous fleece, 12.5 mm
  perforated plasterboard
2 Sunshading insulating glass unit,
  6 mm toughened safety glass + 16 mm cavity
  + 8 mm laminated safety glass on steel sections
3 Floor construction:
  PUR finish, 65 mm cement screed
  35 mm mineral wool impact sound insulation
  250 mm reinforced concrete
  110 mm acoustic ceiling
4 High-gloss acrylic paint, 12.5 mm plasterboard, all
  joints filled and ground smooth, levelling battens,
  150 mm reinforced concrete

5 Glued laminated timber parapet, 220 x 610 mm
6 Glued laminated timber beam, 280 x 970 mm
7 Insulating glass (U = 1.1 W/m²K)
  in wood-aluminium frame, opening outwards
8 Lining to reveal, 1 mm sheet titanium-zinc
9 Wall construction:
  woven debarked willow canes, boiled,
  pressure-impregnated, 200–240 mm long,
  15–20 mm diameter
  vapour-permeable UV-resistant sheeting
  120 mm rock wool with foil facing
  250 mm reinforced concrete
  15 mm gypsum plaster
10 Steel tube, Ø 21.3 mm
11 Steel flat, 40 x 10 mm, with locating pin
12 Mineral wool, 140 mm
13 Floor construction, foyer:
  2.5 mm linoleum
  80 mm cement screed with underfloor heating
  120 mm PUR rigid foam thermal insulation

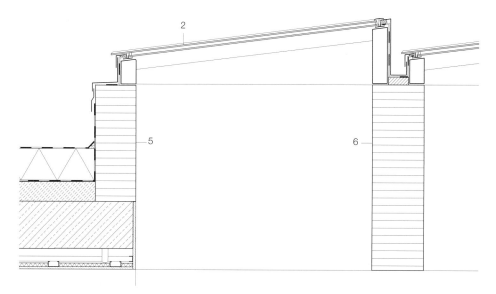

cc

Horizontal section
Vertical sections
Scale 1:20

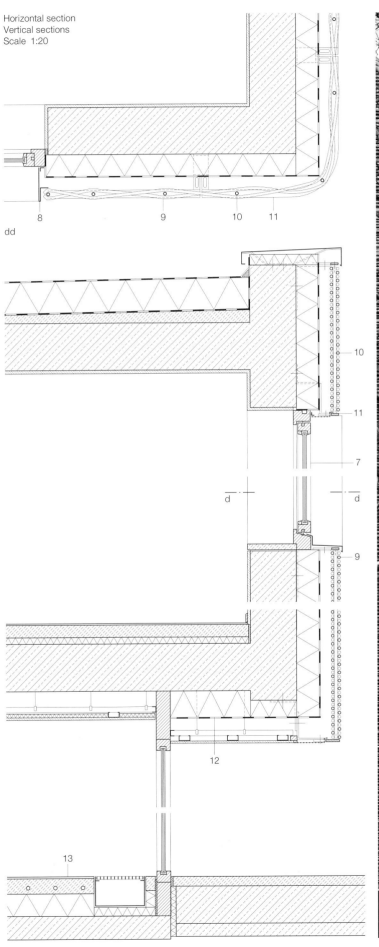

dd

8
9
10
11

10

11

7

d

d

9

12

13

Example 16

Community centre

Munich, D, 1970/2001

Architects:
Allmann Sattler Wappner, Munich
Project team:
Markus Kuntscher, Jan Schabert, Dirk Bauer
Structural engineers:
Hagl Ingenieurgesellschaft, Munich

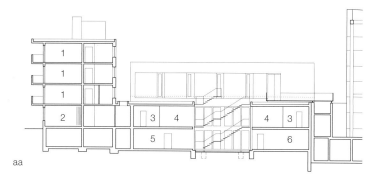

aa

The Herz Jesu Community Centre originally
built in 1970 consists of an apartment block with
club for senior citizens, a pre-school facility,
youth centre and the local parish hall. In terms
of its construction, it is closely related to the
nearby Herz Jesu Church and the vicarage
dating from the founding years. The agglomer-
ation of buildings is typical of the 1970s, with
different, complex spatial volumes, although
the different uses are clearly evident from the
outside. As the parish centre no longer conformed to modern needs, the refurbishment
included rectifying defects in the construction
and the fire safety requirements plus functional
deficits in the communal areas. The brief was
to preserve the spirit of the 1970s architecture,
but at the same time the interventions should
be clearly visible and create a reference to the
late 1990s. The sturdiness of the individual
buildings has been emphasized by adding full
thermal insulation to the buildings finished with
a pigmented mineral render in a uniform colour.
Reflecting the different forms of construction,
the windows to the framed facade have been
linked together to form dark bands, whereas
individual windows have been used for the solid
construction. By lowering the floor of the atrium
to the same level as the basement and linking
all levels of building via a steel staircase, right
up to the rooftop terrace, the complex has been
given a focal point. The adjoining rooms gain
more daylight and natural ventilation via the open
atrium. The parish hall with its uninterrupted
glazing between the structural members opens
out onto a spacious terrace, which can also be
reached via a ramp from the church square.
The steel construction of the terrace with its
larch flooring is raised above the level of the
existing roof.

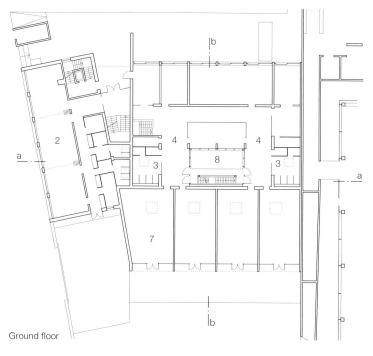

Ground floor

• External thermal insulation composite system
• Lowering of atrium floor
• Linking of building levels

◫ Detail 10/2002

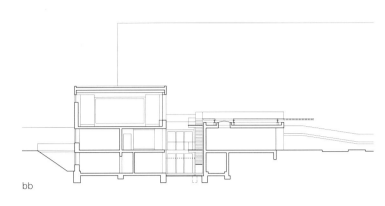

bb

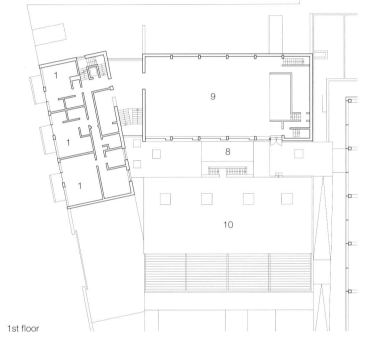

9

8

10

1st floor

Sections	1	Apartment	6	Youth centre
Plans	2	Club for senior citizens	7	Common room, pre-school
Scale 1:500	3	Washroom, pre-school	8	Atrium
Location drawing	4	Cloakroom, pre-school	9	Parish hall
Scale 1:1500	5	Sports room, pre-school	10	Rooftop terrace

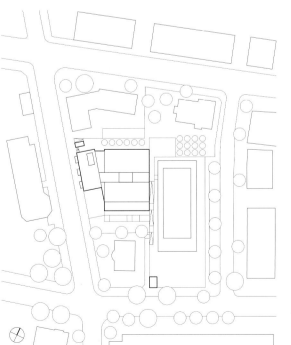

Example 16

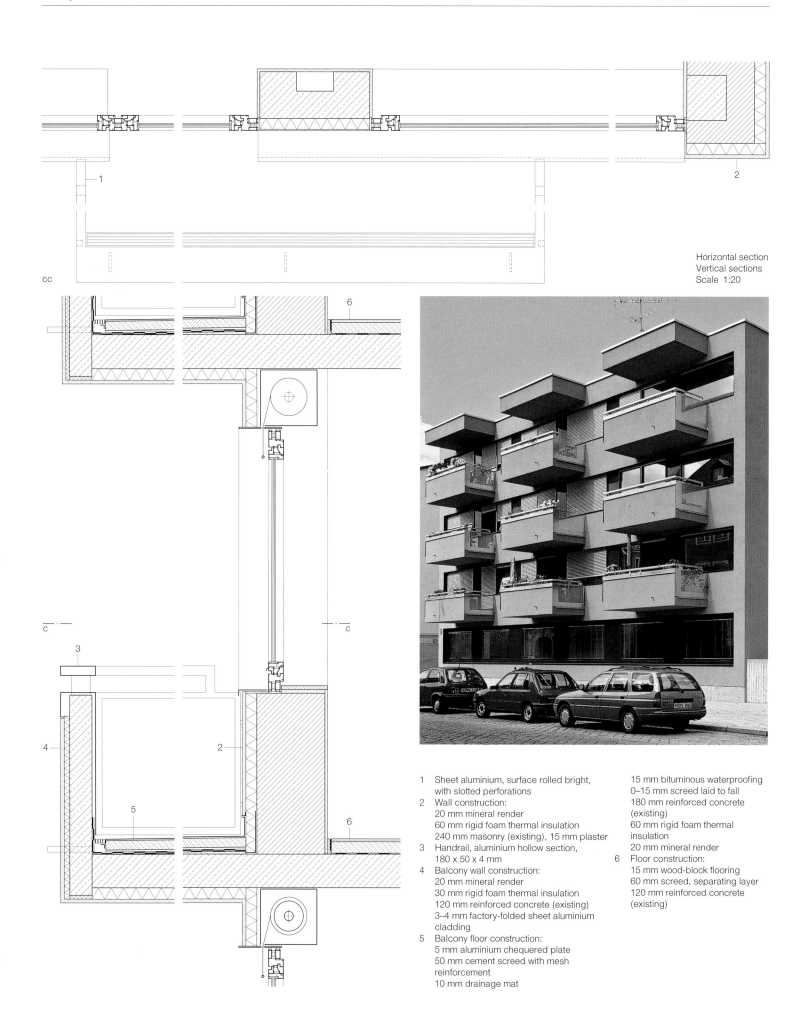

cc

Horizontal section
Vertical sections
Scale 1:20

c — c

cc

1   Sheet aluminium, surface rolled bright, with slotted perforations
2   Wall construction:
    20 mm mineral render
    60 mm rigid foam thermal insulation
    240 mm masonry (existing), 15 mm plaster
3   Handrail, aluminium hollow section, 180 x 50 x 4 mm
4   Balcony wall construction:
    20 mm mineral render
    30 mm rigid foam thermal insulation
    120 mm reinforced concrete (existing)
    3–4 mm factory-folded sheet aluminium cladding
5   Balcony floor construction:
    5 mm aluminium chequered plate
    50 mm cement screed with mesh reinforcement
    10 mm drainage mat

15 mm bituminous waterproofing
0–15 mm screed laid to fall
180 mm reinforced concrete (existing)
60 mm rigid foam thermal insulation
20 mm mineral render
6   Floor construction:
    15 mm wood-block flooring
    60 mm screed, separating layer
    120 mm reinforced concrete (existing)

7 Steel flat, 30 x 10 mm
8 Steel flat, 30 x 6 mm
9 Larch planks, 50 mm, on neoprene pads
10 Secondary beam, HEA 140 steel section
11 Bracket, 40 x 40 mm steel hollow section
12 Roof construction:
  50 mm gravel
  synthetic roofing felt
  rigid foam ≤ 180 mm
  glass fleece-bitumen roofing felt
  perforated glass fleece, bitumen primer
  240 mm reinforced concrete slab
  12.5 mm suspended perforated plasterboard ceiling
13 Primary beam, HEA 200 steel section
14 Post-and-rail facade, aluminium with insulating glass
15 Reinforced concrete post, Ø100 mm
16 Rigid foam, 60 mm, mineral render, 20 mm
17 Sunshade, aluminium Z-sections
18 Steel channel, 200 mm

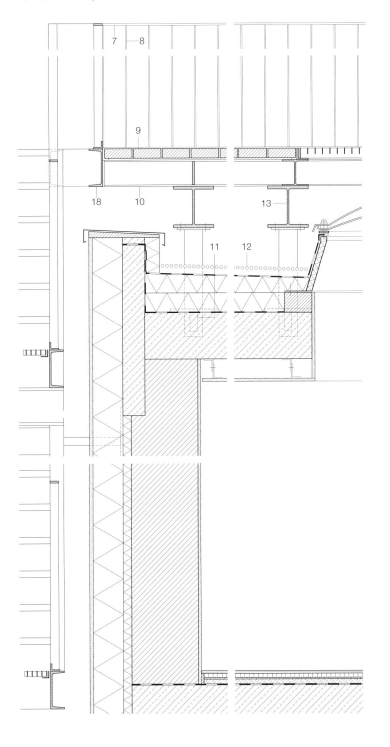

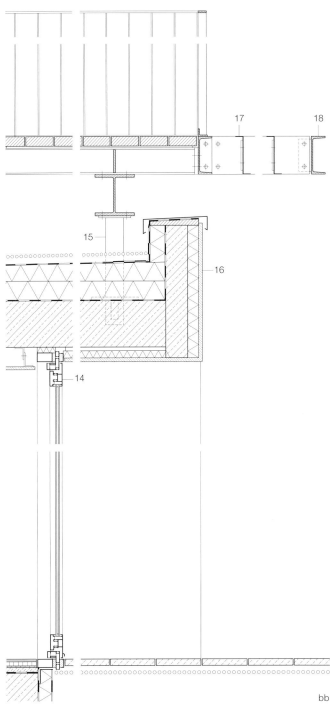

bb

Example 17

Residential development

Zurich, CH, 1970/2005

Architects:
Urs Primas, Zurich
Proplaning, Basel
Project team:
Franziska Schneider, Peter Sutter,
Hans Meyer
Structural engineers:
Proplaning, Basel
Grob & Partner, Winterthur

The refurbishment of a residential development consisting of one 19-storey and two six-storey blocks dating from 1970 provided the opportunity to change the layout of the apartments in the high-rise block in addition to carrying out an energy-efficiency upgrade and other constructional improvements. At the bottom of the high-rise block the architect combined some small apartments to form maisonettes, although each floor of which, having its own entrance and bathroom, is also essentially an autonomous area. At the top of the high-rise block, some smaller apartments on the same floor have been combined to create more spacious, L-shaped living/dining areas plus space for an additional entrance and separate bathroom with shower. This estate therefore offers a range of accommodation somewhat different from that usually available. All three buildings have been provided with external insulation clad with corrugated aluminium in a bronze colour. Loggias painted a bright colour form accents seemingly cut out of the metal skin. To protect against the more severe weather that can be expected above the sixth floor of the high-rise block, the loggias to the apartments here have been provided with folding/sliding windows, thus enabling the spaces to be used as conservatories or extensions to the internal living space. In the high-rise building controlled mechanical ventilation for the apartments was installed in order to achieve the Swiss Minergie standard, which prescribes a maximum energy consumption of 80 kWh/m²a for refurbishment projects. The incoming fresh air is fed from a riser in the facade construction on the north side to the rooms and extracted via disc valves, a system that enables optimum cross-ventilation. The exhaust air is extracted from the wet areas so that in most apartments only one exhaust-air duct in the corridor is necessary. The incoming and outgoing air installations are connected via a run-around circuit for heat recovery.

- External insulation with new cladding
- New plan layouts
- Installation of controlled ventilation for apartments
- Conversion of some loggias into conservatories

 Detail 11/2006

Standard floor, building C

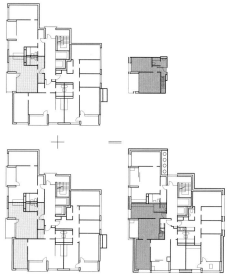

Existing   Maisonette type 1

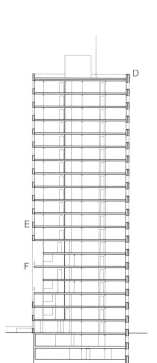

aa   Section, building B

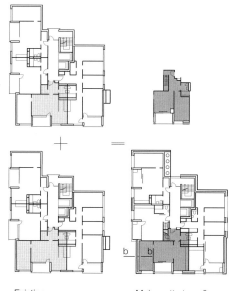

Existing   Maisonette type 2

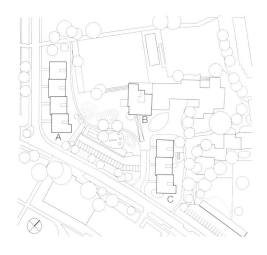

Plans
Section
Scale 1:750
Location drawing
Scale 1:3000

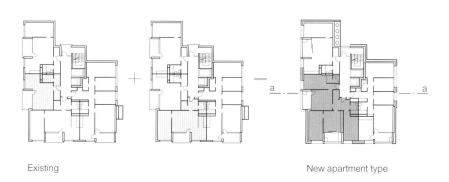

Existing

New apartment type

Example 17

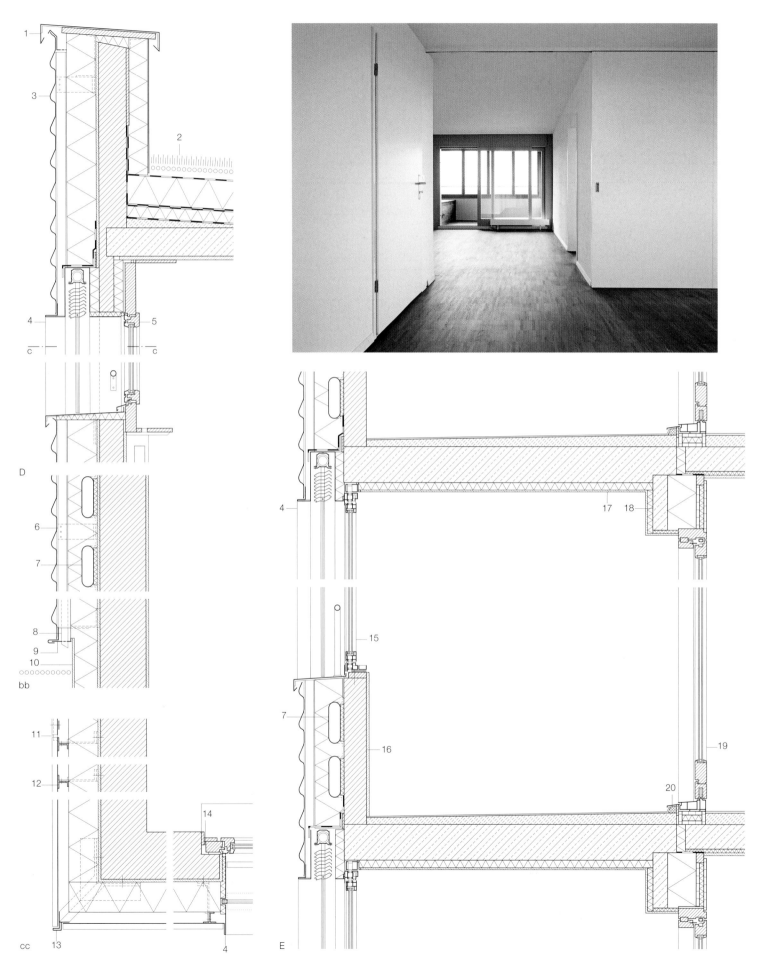

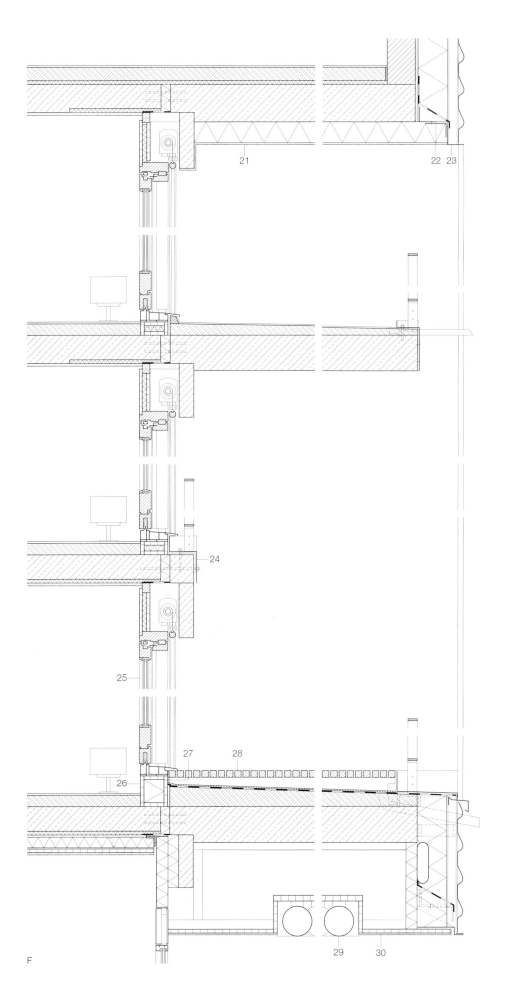

Vertical section · Horizontal section, facade
Vertical section, conservatory
Vertical section, loggia
Scale 1:20

1 Parapet capping, 2 mm sheet stainless steel
2 Roof construction: 80 mm extensive planting
  10 mm waterproofing, 2 layers of bitumen felt
  120 mm rock wool thermal insulation
  60 mm roof finishes (existing)
  150 mm reinforced concrete slab (existing)
  15 mm plaster
3 Wall construction: corrugated aluminium sheeting,
  170 x 30 x 1 mm, coated
  50 mm ventilation cavity
  160 mm mineral wool thermal insulation
  250–300 mm masonry of concrete-filled wood-chip
  hollow blocks (existing)
4 Window frame, 2 mm sheet aluminium, coated
5 Wood-aluminium window with insulating glass
6 Fixing bracket, aluminium
7 Fresh-air duct, alum., on acoustic pads, 213 x 57 mm
8 Rainwater outlet from loggia, ground floor
9 Aluminium section, perforated
10 Thermal insulation, 140 mm, base of wall rendered
11 Backing piece behind cladding joint
12 Aluminium section, continuous, 50 x 50 x 4–7 mm
13 Corner profile, coated aluminium
14 Permanently resilient seal
15 Sliding/folding window, alum. frame/insulating glass
16 Spandrel panel, 125 mm clay brickwork, reinforced
17 Plaster, 10 mm, with fabric reinforcement, 40 mm
   mineral wool thermal insulation attached with adhesive
18 Lintel (existing), 160 mm rock wool thermal insulation
19 Lifting/sliding wooden door with insulating glass
20 Epoxy resin fillet fixed to floor (existing)
21 Plaster, 100 mm mineral wool thermal insulation
22 Fixing angle, aluminium
23 Continuous aluminium section
24 Frame, 4 mm coated sheet steel, factory-bent
25 Lifting/sliding wooden door with insulating glass
26 Frame widening, wood-based product, thermally
   insulated
27 Waterproofing to junction with window, liquid plastic
28 Loggia floor construction:
   grating of oak battens, 35 x 35 mm, arrises chamfered
   40 mm tapered oak bearers
   8 mm rubber granulate mat
   12 mm polymer-modified bitumen roofing felt, 2 layers
   70–110 mm screed laid to fall
   190 mm reinforced concrete
29 Lamp
30 Plaster background, cement-bonded wood-based
   product

F

Example 18

Mixed residential and commercial development

Hamburg, D, 1979/2007

Architects:
Kleffel Papay Warncke, Hamburg
Project team:
Michael Krüger, Marion Kleine,
David Lagemann, Stephen Perry
Structural engineers:
Wetzel & von Seht, Hamburg

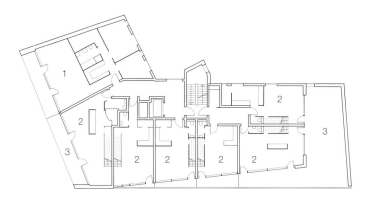

6th floor

This eight-storey office block built in the old part of Hamburg in the late 1970s was due for extensive modernisation. Firstly, decontamination was necessary, i.e. the removal of all fitting-out items containing dangerous substances. Only after that was it possible to remove all the remaining fitting-out components, the facade construction and the reinforced concrete spandrel panels. The sixth and seventh floors were completely demolished apart from the service cores, which together with the two gable walls on the south and east elevations stabilise the building. Extensions to the reinforced concrete floors eliminated the former set-backs in the facade prior to the building of the storey-high post-and-rail facade. The window elements are framed by a "meandering" band of anodised and etched sheet aluminium. In front of the opening vents, which are filled with an insulating element, there is a safety barrier – a frame with an infill of steel flat louvres that can be opened outwards. The direction of the zig-zag windows alternates between storeys. A sunshade in front of the fixed lights – together with the new building services – contributes to a pleasant climate in the offices. The two set-back top storeys in lightweight construction accommodate maisonettes. The rooftop terraces on the top floors help the new building volume to fit into its surroundings because they match the height of the existing neighbouring buildings.

- Removal of dangerous substances
- Demolition of loadbearing structure, facade construction and reinforced concrete spandrel panels
- Additions to loadbearing structure
- Complete demolition of the sixth and seventh floors with subsequent rebuilding
- New post-and-rail facade
- New building services

📖 Hamburg Chamber of architects: Architektur in Hamburg, Jahrbuch 2007. Hamburg 2007

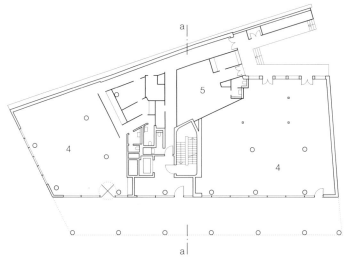

Ground floor

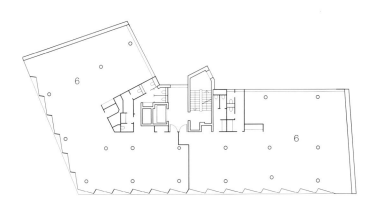

5th floor

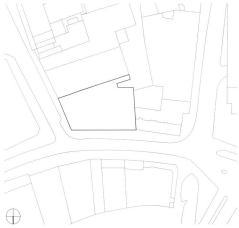

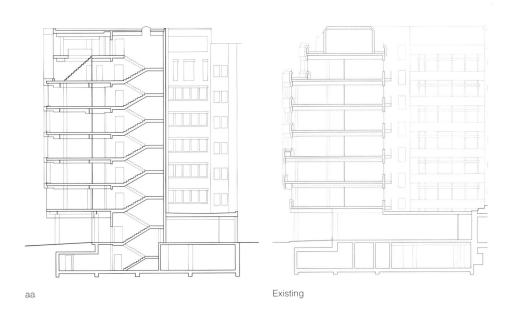

aa   Existing

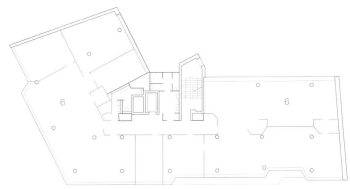

5th floor, existing

Plans
Sections
Scale 1:500
Location drawing
Scale 1:2000

1   Apartment
2   Maisonette
3   Rooftop terrace
4   Shop
5   Store
6   Office

Example 18

Vertical sections
Horizontal section
Scale 1:20

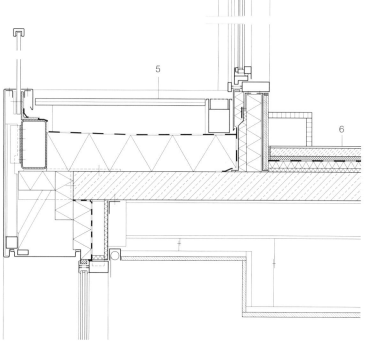

1 Roof construction:
 built-up felt waterproofing, 2 layers,
 upper layer with slate granule surfacing
 140–208 mm insulation with integral falls
 vapour barrier, bitumen primer
 120 mm reinforced concrete
 12.5 mm suspended plasterboard ceiling
2 Sheet aluminium, etched and anodised
3 Post-and-rail construction
4 Floor construction:
 10 mm wood-block flooring,
 bonded over entire area
 50 mm cement screed
 separating layer
 30 mm EPS impact sound insulation
 levelling layer
 60 mm polystyrene
 160 mm reinforced concrete slab (new)
 12.5 mm suspended plasterboard ceiling
5 Grooved timber planks, 35 mm, timber
 bearers, protective mat

6 Floor construction:
 10 mm wood-block flooring,
 bonded over entire area
 43 mm cement screed
 22 mm profiled sheeting
 separating layer
 30 mm EPS impact sound insulation
 20 mm levelling layer
 150 mm reinforced concrete slab (existing)
7 Steel flat louvres, 4 mm
8 Opening vent, 55 mm sandwich panel
9 Insulating glass: 10 mm toughened
 safety glass + 16 mm cavity + 8 mm
 toughened safety glass
10 Floor construction:
 10 mm carpet
 35 mm bonded screed
 18 mm wood-based board product
 57 mm void
 150 mm reinforced concrete slab
 (existing/extended)

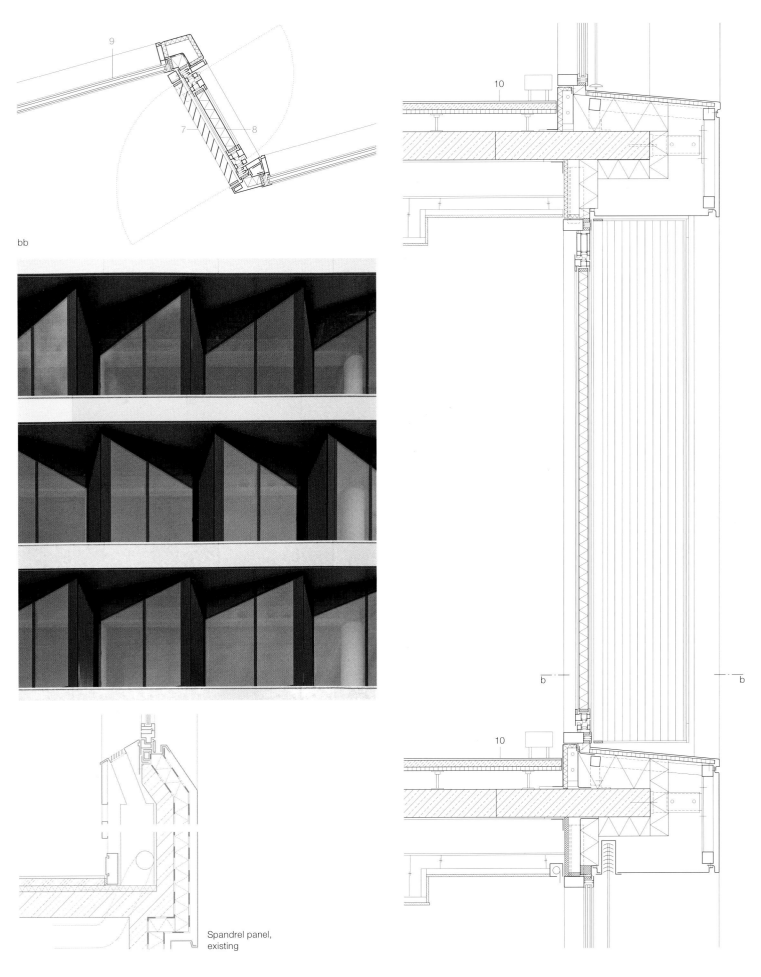

bb

Spandrel panel,
existing

Building physics

Thermal performance and moisture control

Dew point temperature
If the temperature drops below the dew point either within a building component or on its surface, the water vapour in the air condenses because the saturation moisture level has been reached.

Relative humidity
The relative humidity specifies the moisture content in the interior air in relation to the maximum possible moisture content. The maximum moisture content (saturation) is heavily dependent on the temperature. In summer the relative humidity is normally 50–70 %, in winter 30–60 %, depending on the air change rate in the building and the moisture loads.

Specific heat capacity
The specific heat capacity of buildings or components is especially important when considering the summertime thermal performance. How much thermal energy a building material can store over a certain period of time depends on its specific heat capacity and thermal conductivity. This is described by the effective heat capacity.

Temperature amplitude ratio and phase lag
The temperature amplitude ratio (TAR) of a building component layer describes the relationship between the two surface temperatures of that layer. For a wall this is the ratio of the inner to the outer surface (or external) temperature. In conjunction with the summertime thermal performance, the TAR can be used to deduce how the rise in temperature of the outer surfaces has an effect on the inner surfaces. The phase lag (or phase shift) specifies the length of time it takes for a change in the outer surface temperature to become noticeable on the inside.

Thermal bridge
According to a general definition, a thermal bridge is the coincidence of components with one-dimensional U-values. How such a point junction influences the heat losses and the surface temperatures can only be determined with two-dimensional finite element or finite difference methods. If the junctions are linear, the influence is characterised by a thermal bridge loss coefficient (Ψ-value). In most cases point thermal bridges have only a minor influence on the energy requirement, but can lead to moisture problems.

Thermal conductivity
The thermal conductivity of a material is its ability to transport thermal energy and this value is used as an input when calculating U-values. The thermal conductivity group (WLG) values used in the past have now been superseded by the thermal conductivity design values, and only the latter should be used in analyses.

Thermal transmittance (U-value)
The thermal quality of a building component is described by its U-value, which specifies how much heat energy passes through 1 m^2 of the component for a temperature difference of 1 K between the two sides of the component.

DIN EN 6946 is used for calculating the U-values of external components (except doors and windows). The U-values of doors and windows are determined according to DIN EN 10077. To do that requires the U-values of the glass (to DIN EN 673) and the frame to be known plus the properties of the insulating glass spacer and the dimensions of the window. All this data can be supplied by the manufacturer. A simplified method of calculation is given in DIN 4108. Glazing bars are included in the calculation.

Total energy transmittance (g-value)
The total energy transmittance specifies the proportion of solar energy incident on glazing that passes through to the interior and hence is available as an energy gain in the winter. It is calculated according to DIN EN 410.

Sound insulation

Airborne sound
Soundwaves generated by sound sources (e.g. people, machines) that propagate in the air surrounding those sources.

Frequency
The frequency is a measure of the pitch of a soundwave. Low frequencies lie between about 50 and 250 Hz, medium frequencies between about 250 and 1000 Hz, and high frequencies up to several thousand hertz. The frequency range for assessing the sound insulation is 100–3150 Hz, and this covers all noises typical in residential buildings; the extended frequency range is 50–5000 Hz.

Impact sound
Impact sound is the structure-borne sound in a floor that is generated by persons walking across that floor and radiated in the form of airborne sound by the components affected.

Normalised impact sound level L_n
The normalised impact sound (pressure) level L_n is the variable for assessing the sound level in a neighbouring room (usually below) generated by a standard tapping machine. It is important to remember that the normalised impact sound level Ln depends on the frequency, but in contrast to the sound reduction index R is hardly reliant on the frequency on solid floors. An additional floating screed reduces the transmission of impact sound to a greater extent as the frequency increases. This is why footsteps on a floating screed are perceived as muffled – more of the low-frequency components in the noise of footsteps are transmitted than the high-frequency components.

Sound pressure level
The sound pressure level is a logarithmic measure of the physical pressure of the soundwaves in decibels (dB).

Sound reduction index R
The sound reduction index R is the variable for assessing the difference in the sound pressure levels between a loud room (sound source) and a room requiring acoustic protection. It is important to remember that the sound reduction index R of a component depends on the frequency – it is generally much lower for low frequencies than for high ones. This is why the noises we hear from neighbouring apartments are always muffled (high bass component). The low high-frequency components of noises are insulated to a lesser extent than the high-frequency components – the acoustic make-up of the noise is altered.

Soundwave
A soundwave is the elastic and locally propagating deformation of a substance (air, liquid, solid) for the transport of energy, triggered by a moving body within that substance (vocal cords, loudspeaker, footsteps, etc.).

Structure-borne sound
Soundwaves generated through direct contact with a building component in which the sound propagates (e.g. hammering on a wall, pressure peaks upon shutting off taps, a jet of water striking a shower tray).

Construction terms

Bonder

Bonders are used to secure stone facings or – usually in the form of headers – facing brickwork to a backing masonry wall. Whether of stone or brick, they are built into the bond of the facing masonry. In the case of a stone facing, the connection to the other stones not bonded into the backing masonry wall is normally by way of spigots and pockets in the stones themselves plus grout.

Cocking piece

A cocking piece (or sprocket) is a timber component at the eaves of a pitched roof. It is required for wall thicknesses exceeding about 250 mm. As for structural reasons the eaves purlin is usually supported on the inside of the wall and that means the rainwater gutter cannot be connected directly to this, the cocking piece bridges the distance between eaves purlin and outer edge of wall. This means that the pitch of the roof in the region of the cocking piece is shallower than that of the main part of the roof. The inner end of the cocking piece is usually cut at an angle and nailed to the top of every rafter.

Cogged joint

This is a form of joint that can be used to prevent the horizontal displacement of two pieces of wood. For example, cutting the end of a timber joist to resemble a hook, which then fits into a matching notch cut in a timber wall plate, thus enabling tensile forces to be transferred as well.

Haunch

A haunch is an inclined transition between a column and a downstand beam. These were common in reinforced concrete construction in the past but are now used only for bridges and in structural steelwork. The gradual deepening of the downstand beam adjacent to the support has the effect of increasing the moment of resistance of a continuous beam where it is heavily loaded at the support and also improving the force transfer into the column.

Masonry nib

A masonry nib helps to ensure reliable waterproofing of the joint between door or window and external wall. An external nib was usually formed, i.e. the window opening was on the outer face of the wall and smaller than the clear internal dimensions. The nib created a mounting surface for the frame, which was pressed up against this and sealed. Contrasting with this, windows that open outwards only – common in windy regions – were built with an internal nib. A central nib was sometimes built for coupled windows constructed in two parts.

Propped beam

A propped beam is a (usually) long-span timber construction in which the vertical forces, e.g. imposed loads, are not transferred to the supports indirectly by way of bending, but instead directly via inclined struts. In contrast to the trussed frame, a related form of construction, a propped beam normally has only two diagonal struts instead of several. Besides their use as a loadbearing timber construction, propped beams were also used as concealed framing to internal walls above timber joist

floors. In such cases they extended over the full height of the storey and spanned from the external to the central wall.

Pugging boards

Pugging boards (or soundboarding) are the boards used to carry the pugging (= loose fill) in traditional timber joist floors. These are usually loose-laid, low-quality boards with wane and other defects, normally supported on battens nailed to the sides of the joists, occasionally inserted into grooves cut in the sides of the joists.

Rabitz background

The Rabitz plaster background is a form of construction that was patented in 1878 by the Royal Master Mason of Berlin, Karl Rabitz, and is still used in a similar form to this day. In this solution the plaster mix is applied to a wire mesh. It was often used as a substitute for the reed mats that were commonly used up until that time to form the ceilings below timber joist floors. The wire mesh can also be shaped as required, e.g. to form dummy vaults.

Timber ground

Nailed floorboards require timber grounds when they cannot be nailed directly to the loadbearing floor, e.g. over vaults. Timber grounds are mostly in the form of planed softwood battens measuring approx. 80 x 50 mm, i.e. wider than they are deep. They are frequently "worked into" the loose fill so that their top side is flush with the top of the loose fill.

Tongue and groove joint

A tongue and groove (t & g) joint is the connection of two pieces of wood by way of a protruding continuous strip on one piece that fits into a continuous housing in the other (both tongue and groove being cut directly out of the wood itself). A special form of this joint is the loose tongue joint in which two pieces of wood each with a continuous housing are joined by a separate strip of wood. Joints where the tongues and grooves are a dovetail shape in cross-section are also possible.

Transverse arch

Transverse arches were constructed to strengthen barrel vault or jack arch floors and were built into the masonry bond of the vault or floor. They are mostly supported on masonry piers.

Wane

Wane (or waney edge) is the presence of the original rounded surface of a log, with or without bark, on any face or edge of a piece of sawn timber. This happens, for example, when a log is merely trimmed on four sides instead of being sawn to form 90° arrises. This is an economy measure and beams or joists can be allocated to various quality classes according to DIN 4074 depending on the ratio between the member depth and the width of wane.

Wooden subfloor

Wooden subfloors are used for fixing high-quality, elaborate wood-block or parquet flooring or wooden floorboards. Rough-sawn softwood boards are mostly used which are nailed directly to the loadbearing timber joists or timber grounds. Generous gaps are left between the boards to allow for expansion and contraction. The wooden subfloor forms the structural layer to which the wooden floor covering is nailed.

Wood-strip flooring

The pieces of wood used for wood-strip flooring are much longer and wider than those used for wood-block or parquet flooring. And another difference between this type of floor finish and wood-block or parquet flooring is that these narrow planks usually have a loadbearing function as well. They are nailed directly to the timber joists – secret nailing in the joints often being employed when the strips are connected via tongue and groove joints.

Statutory instruments, directives, standards

The EU has issued directives for a number of products, the particular aim of which is to ensure the safety and health of users. These directives must be implemented in the EU member states in the form of compulsory legislation and regulations.

The directives themselves do not contain any technical details, but instead only lay down the mandatory underlying requirements. The corresponding technical values are specified in associated sets of technical rules (e.g. codes of practice) and in the form of EN standards harmonised throughout Europe.

Generally, the technical rules provide advice and information for everyday activities. They are not statutory instruments, but rather give users decision-making aids, guidelines for implementing technical procedures correctly and/or practical information for turning legislation into practice. The use of the technical rules is not compulsory; only when they have been included in government legislation or other statutory instruments do they become mandatory, or when the parties to a contract include them in their conditions.

In Germany the technical rules include DIN standards, VDI directives and other publications such as the Technical Rules for Hazardous Substances.

The standards are divided into product, application and testing standards. They often relate to just one specific group of materials or products, and are based on: the corresponding testing and calculation methods for the respective materials and components. The latest edition of a standard – which should correspond with the state of the art – always applies. A new or revised standard is first published as a draft for public discussion before (probably with revisions) it is finally adopted as a valid standard. The origin and area of influence of a standard can be gleaned from its designation:

- DIN plus number (e.g. DIN 4108) is essentially a national document (drafts are designated with "E" and preliminary standards with "V").
- DIN EN plus number (e.g. DIN EN 335) is a German edition of a European standard–drawn up by the European Standardisation Organisation CEN – that has been adopted without amendments.
- DIN EN ISO (e.g. DIN EN ISO 13786) is a standard with national, European and worldwide influence. Based on: a standard from the International Standardisation Organisation ISO, a European standard was drawn up, which was then adopted as a DIN standard.
- DIN ISO (e.g. DIN ISO 2424) is a German edition of an ISO standard that has been adopted without amendments.

The following compilation represents a selection of statutory instruments, directives and standards that reflects the state of the art regarding building materials and building material applications as of August 2008.

General

Energieeinsparverordnung (EnEV –
Energy Conservation Act). 2007-07

Part B   Principles

Building physics
DIN 4102-1 Fire behaviour of building materials and building components – Part 1: Building materials; concepts, requirements and tests. 1998-05

DIN 4102-4 Fire behaviour of building materials and building components; synopsis and application of classified building materials, components and special components. 1994-03

DIN 4108 supp. 2 Thermal insulation and energy economy in buildings – Thermal bridges – Examples for planning and performance. 2006-03

DIN 4108-2 Thermal protection and energy economy in buildings – Part 2: Minimum requirements for thermal insulation. 2007-07

DIN 4109 Sound insulation in buildings; requirements and testing. 1989-11

DIN 18005-1 Noise abatement in town planning – Part 1: Fundamentals and directions for planning. 2002-07

DIN 18183-1 Partitions and wall linings with gypsum boards on metal framing – Part 1: Cladding with gypsum plasterboards. 2009-05

DIN 18230-1 Structural fire protection in industrial buildings – Part 1: Analytically required fire resistance time. 1998-05

DIN EN 410 Glass in building – Determination of luminous and solar characteristics of glazing. 1998-12

DIN EN 673 Glass in building – Determination of thermal transmittance (U-value) – Calculation method. 2003-06

DIN EN 6946 Building components and building elements – Thermal resistance and thermal transmittance – Calculation method. 2008-04

DIN EN 10077-1 Thermal performance of windows, doors and shutters – Calculation of thermal transmittance – Part 1: General. 2006-12

DIN EN 13501-1 Fire classification of construction products and building elements – Part 1: Classification using data from reaction to fire tests. 2007-05

DIN EN ISO 7730 Ergonomics of the thermal environment – Analytical determination and interpretation of thermal comfort using calculation of the PMV and PPD indices and local thermal comfort criteria. 2007-06

DIN V 4108-4 (pre-standard) Thermal insulation and energy economy in buildings – Part 4: Hygrothermal design values. 2007-06

DIN 1946-6 (draft standard) Ventilation and air conditioning – Part 6: Ventilation for residential buildings; general requirements, requirements for measuring, performance and labelling, delivery/acceptance (certification) and maintenance. 2006-12

VDI 2566 sht. 1/2: Technical rules – Acoustical design for lifts with/without machine room. 2001/2004

VDI 2719 Technical rule – Sound isolation of windows and their auxiliary equipment. 1987-08

VDI 4100 Technical rule – Noise control in dwellings – Criteria for planning and assessment. 2007-08

Building services
ATV-DVWK-M 143/DWA-M 143-3 (refurbishment of drainage systems external to buildings). Parts 1–20. 2003-12

ATV-M 101 (planning of drainage systems; new-build, refurbishment and renewal measures). 1996-05

ATV-M 149 (surveys, classification and assessment of drainage systems external to buildings). 1999-04

BHKS Rule 5005 (leak tests of waste-water and rainwater pipes in buildings and below ground; testing with water). 2005-10

BHKS Rule 5006 (leak tests of waste-water and rainwater pipes in buildings and below ground; testing with air). 2007-05

BHKS Rule 5007 (leak tests of waste-water and rainwater pipes in buildings and below ground; testing with vacuum). 2007-04

DIN 1946-6 (draft standard) Ventilation and air conditioning – Part 6: Ventilation for residential buildings; general requirements, requirements for measuring, performance and labelling, delivery/acceptance (certification) and maintenance. 2006-12

DIN 1986-100 Drainage systems on private ground – Part 100: Specifications in relation to DIN EN 752 and DIN EN 12056. 2008-05

DIN 1986-3 Drainage systems on private ground – Part 3: Specifications for service and maintenance. 2004-11

DIN 1986-30 Drainage systems on private ground – Part 30: Maintenance. 2003-02

DIN 1988-1 Drinking water supply systems; general (DVGW code of practice). 1988-12

DIN 1988-2 Drinking water supply systems; materials, components, appliances, design and installation (DVGW code of practice). 1988-12

DIN 1988-3 Drinking water supply systems; pipe sizing (DVGW code of practice). 1988-12

DIN 1988-7 Turnbuckles made from steel tubes or round steel bars. 2004-12

DIN 1989-1 Rainwater harvesting systems – Part 1: Planning, installation, operation and maintenance. 2002-04

DIN 4102-4 Fire behaviour of building materials and building components; synopsis and application of classified building materials, components and special components. 1994-03

DIN 4102-6 Fire behaviour of building materials and building components; ventilation ducts; definitions, requirements and tests. 1977-09

DIN 4102-9 Fire behaviour of building materials and elements; seals for cable penetrations; concepts, requirements and testing. 1990-05

DIN 4102-11 Fire behaviour of building materials and building components; pipe encasements, pipe bushings, service shafts and ducts, and barriers across inspection openings; terminology, requirements and testing. 1985-12

DIN 4109 Sound insulation in buildings; requirements and testing. 1989-11

DIN 4261-1 Small sewage treatment plants – Part 1: Plants for waste-water in front of treatment. 2009-02

DIN 4702-1 Boilers for central heating; terms, requirements, testing, marking. 1990-03

DIN 4702-4 Boilers for central heating; boilers for wood, straw and similar fuels; terms requirements, testing. 1990-03

DIN 4702-6 Central heating boilers; condensing boilers for gaseous fuels. 1990-03

DIN 4703-1 Heating appliances – Part 1: Dimensions of sectional radiators. 1999-12

DIN 4703-3 Heating appliances – Part 3: Conversion of the standard thermal output. 2000-10

DIN 4708-1 Central hot-water installations; terms and calculation-basis. 1994-04

DIN 4708-2 Central hot-water installations; rules for the determination of the water-heat-demand in dwelling houses. 1994-04

DIN 4719 Ventilation and air conditioning – Requirements, performance testing and labelling. 2006-12

DIN 4725-200 Floor heating, systems and components - Part 200: Determination of the thermal output, pipe coverings larger than 0.065 m. 2001-03

DIN 4726 Warm water surface heating systems and radiator connecting systems – Plastics piping systems and multilayer piping systems. 2008-10

DIN 4747-1 Heating plants for district heating – Part 1: Safety requirements for domestic substations, stations and domestic systems to be connected to hot-water district heating networks. 2003-11

DIN 4753-1 Water heaters and water heating installations for drinking water and service water; requirements, marking, equipment and testing. 1988-03

DIN 5035-6 Artificial lighting – Part 6: Measurement and evaluation. 2006-11

DIN 5035-7 Artificial lighting – Part 7: Lighting of interiors with visual display workstations. 2004-08

DIN 6280-14 Generating sets – Reciprocating internal combustion engines driven generating sets – Part 14: Combined heat and power system (CHPS) with reciprocating internal combustion engines; basics, requirements, components and application. 1997-08

DIN 8901 Refrigerating systems and heat pumps – Protection of soil, ground and surface water – Safety and environmental requirements and testing. 2002-12

DIN 18012 House service connections facilities – Principles for planning. 2008-05

DIN 18014 Foundation earth electrode – General planning criteria. 2007-09

DIN 18015-1 Electrical installations in residential buildings – Part 1: Planning principles. 2007-09

DIN 18015-2 Electrical installations in residential buildings – Part 2: Nature and extent of minimum equipment. 2004-08

DIN 18015-3 Electrical installations in residential buildings – Part 3: Wiring and disposition of electrical equipment. 2007-09

DIN 18017-1 Ventilation of bathrooms and WCs without outside windows; single shaft systems without ventilators. 1987-02

DIN 18017-3 Ventilation of bathrooms and WCs without outside windows by fans. 1990-08

DIN 44576-4 Electric room heating; thermal storage floor heating; characteristics of performance; calculation for room heating. 1987-03

DIN 50930-6 Corrosion of metals – Corrosion of metallic materials under corrosion load by water inside of tubes, tanks and apparatus – Part 6: Influence of the composition of drinking water. 2001-08

DIN EN 307 Heat exchangers – Guidelines to prepare installation, operating and maintenance instructions required to maintain the performance of each type of heat exchanger. 1998-12

DIN EN 378-1 Refrigerating systems and heat pumps – Safety and environmental requirements – Part 1: Basic requirements, definitions, classification and selection criteria. 2008-06

DIN EN 752 Drain and sewer systems outside buildings. 2008-04

DIN EN 806-1 Specifications for installations inside buildings conveying water for human consumption – Part 1: General. 2001-12

DIN EN 806-2 Specification for installations inside buildings conveying water for human consumption – Part 2: Design. 2005-02

DIN EN 806-3 Specifications for installations inside buildings conveying water for human consumption – Part 3: Pipe sizing – Simplified method. 2006-07

DIN EN 1264-3 Floor heating – Systems and components – Part 3: Dimensioning. 1997-11

DIN EN 1264-4 Floor heating – Systems and components – Part 4: Installation. 2001-12

DIN EN 1717 Protection against pollution of potable water installations and general requirements of devices to prevent pollution by backflow – Technical rule of the DVGW. 2001-05

DIN EN 12056-1 Gravity drainage systems inside buildings – Part 1: General and performance requirements. 2001-01

DIN EN 12056-2 Gravity drainage systems inside buildings – Part 2: Sanitary pipework, layout and calculation. 2001-01

DIN EN 12097 Ventilation for buildings – Ductwork – Requirements for ductwork components to facilitate maintenance of ductwork systems. 2006-11

DIN EN 12098-1 Controls for heating systems – Part 1: Outside temperature compensated control equipment for hot water heating systems. 1996-09

DIN EN 12098-2 Controls for heating systems – Part 2: Optimum start-stop control equipment for hot water heating systems. 2001-10

DIN EN 12566-3 Small waste-water treatment systems for up to 50 PT – Part 3: Packaged and/or site assembled domestic wastewater treatment plants. 2005-10

DIN EN 12665 Light and lighting – Basic terms and criteria for specifying lighting requirements. 2002-09

DIN EN 12828 Heating systems in buildings – Design of water-based heating systems. 2003-06

DIN EN 12831 Heating systems in buildings – Method for calculation of the design heat load. 2003-08

DIN EN 12977-3 Thermal solar systems and components – Custom built systems – Part 3: Performance test methods for solar water heater stores. 2008-11

DIN EN 13465 Ventilation for buildings – Calculation methods for the determination of air flow rates in dwellings. 2004-05

DIN EN 13779 Ventilation for non-residential buildings – Performance requirements for ventilation and room-conditioning systems. 2007-09

DIN EN 14336 Heating systems in buildings – Installation and commissioning of water based heating systems. 2005-01

DIN EN 14337 Heating systems in buildings – Design and installation of direct electrical room heating systems. 2006-02

DIN EN 14511-1 Air conditioners, liquid chilling packages and heat pumps with electrically driven compressors for space heating and cooling – Part 1: Terms and definitions. 2008-02

DIN EN 14706 Thermal insulation products for building equipment and industrial installations – Determination of maximum service temperature. 2006-03

DIN EN 15243 Ventilation for buildings – Calculation of room temperatures and of load and energy for buildings with room conditioning systems. 2007-10

DIN EN 15251 Indoor environmental input parameters for design and assessment of energy performance of buildings addressing indoor air quality, thermal environment, lighting and acoustics. 2007-08

DIN EN 50164-2/DIN VDE 0185-202 Lightning Protection Components (LPC) – Part 2: Requirements for conductors and earth electrodes. 2009-03

DIN EN 62305-1 (VDE 0185-305-1) Protection against lightning – Part 1: General principles. 2006-10

DIN EN 62305-3 (VDE 0185-305-3) Protection against lightning – Part 3: Physical damage to structures and life hazard. 2007-01

DIN EN ISO 10077-1 Thermal performance of windows, doors and shutters – Calculation of thermal transmittance – Part 1: General. 2006-12

DIN EN ISO 13786 Thermal performance of building components – Dynamic thermal characteristics – Calculation methods. 2008-04

DIN V 4701-10 (pre-standard) Energy efficiency of heating and ventilation systems in buildings – Part 10: Heating, domestic hot water supply, ventilation. 2003-08

DIN V 4701-12 (pre-standard) Energetic evaluation of heating and ventilation systems in existing buildings – Part 12: Heat generation and domestic hot water generation. 2004-02

DIN V 4759-2 (pre-standard) Heating installations for different sources of energy; use of heat pumps including electrically operated compressors in bivalent heating installations. 1986-05

DIN V 18599 (pre-standard) Energy efficiency of buildings – Calculation of the net, final and primary energy demand for heating, cooling, ventilation, domestic hot water and lighting. 2007-02

DIN V ENV 61024 (VDE V 0185 part 100) Lightning protection structural facilities. 2002-11

DIN VDE 0100-410 Low-voltage electrical installations – Part 4-41: Protection for safety – Protection against electric shock. 2007-06

DIN VDE 0100-701 Low-voltage electrical installations – Part 7-701: Requirements for special installations or locations – Locations containing a bath or shower. 2008-10

DIN VDE 0100-737 Erection of low-voltage installations – Humid and wet areas and locations, outdoor installations. 2002-01

DIN VDE 0298-3 Application of cables and cords in power installations – Part 3: Guide to use of non-harmonised cables. 2006-06

DIN VDE 0298-4 Application of cables and cords in power installations – Part 4: Recommended current-carrying capacity for sheathed and non-sheathed cables for fixed wirings in and around buildings and for flexible cables and cords. 2003-08

DVGW W 551 Drinking water heating and drinking water piping systems; technical measures to reduce legionella growth; design, construction, operation and rehabilitation of drinking water installations. 2004-04

DVGW W 553 (design of secondary circuits in central drinking water heating systems). 1998-12

DWA-A 138 (planning, construction and operation of installations for the seepage of rainwater). 2004-05

Energieeinsparverordnung (EnEV – Energy Conservation Act). 2007-07

Heizungsanlagen-Verordnung (HeizanlV – Heating Plant Act). 1998-05

Muster-Richtlinie über brandschutztechnische Anforderungen an Leitungsanlagen (MLAR – Model Pipe & Cable Routing Directive). 2005-11

RAL-RG 678 Technical rule (requirements for electrical installations in dwellings). 2004-09

Directive 2002/91/EC of the European Parliament and of the Council of 16 December 2002 on the Energy Performance of Buildings.

TRB 610 Technical rule – Pressure vessels – Installation of pressure vessels for the storage of gases. 1995-11

TRB 801 No. 25 (special pressure vessels according to annex II to cl. 12 of the German pressure vessels act – pressure vessels for non-corrosive gases or gas mixtures). 1996-01

TRF Technical rules for LPG. vol. 1, 1996/vol. 2, 1997

Trinkwasserverordnung (TrinkwV – Drinking Water Act). 2001-05

VDI 2035 sht. 1 Technical rule – Prevention of damage in water heating installations – Scale formation in domestic hot water supply installations and water heating installations. 2005-12

VDI 2050 sht. 1 Technical rule – Requirements at technique centres – Technical basis for planning and execution. 2006-12

VDI 2055 Technical rule – Thermal insulation for heated and refrigerated industrial and domestic installations – Calculations, guarantees, measuring and testing methods, quality assurance, supply conditions. 1994-07

VDI 2067 sht. 1 Technical rule – Economic efficiency of building installations – Fundamentals and economic calculation. 2000-09

VDI 2087 Technical rule – Air ducts – Operating and construction fundamentals. 2006-12

VDI 3803 Technical rule – Air-conditioning systems – Structural and technical principles. 2002-10

VDI 3817 Technical rule – Listed buildings – Building services. 2000-10

VDI 4640 sht. 1 Technical rule – Thermal use of the underground – Fundamentals, approvals, environmental aspects. 2000-12

VDI 4640 sht. 2 Technical rule – Thermal use of the underground – Ground source heat pump systems. 2001-09

VDI 4640 sht. 4 Technical rule – Thermal use of the underground – Direct uses. 2004-09

VDI 6000 sht. 1 Technical rule – Provision and installation of sanitary facilities – Private housing. 2008-02

VDI 6001 sht. 1 Technical rule – Reconstruction of tap-water installations – Water intended for human consumption. 2004-07

VDI 6022 sht. 1 Technical rule – Hygienic requirements for ventilating and air-conditioning systems and air-handling units. 2006-04

VDI 6023 sht. 1 Technical rule – Hygiene for drinking water supply systems – Requirements for planning, design, operation, and maintenance. 2006-07

VDMA 24186-1 (range of services for the maintenance of mechanical ventilation and other technical equipment in buildings – mechanical ventilation plant and installations). 2002-09

VDMA 24186-2 (range of services for the maintenance of technical installations and equipment in buildings – heating plant and installations). 2002-09

VDMA 24186-3 (range of services for the maintenance of technical installations and equipment in buildings – refrigeration plant and installations for cooling and heating purposes). 2002-09

Wasserhaushaltsgesetz (WHG – Water Management Act). 1957-07

Conservation

Baugesetzbuch (BauGB – Federal Building Code). 2004

The Venice Charter for the Conservation and Restoration of Monuments and Sites. 1964

Heritage Protection Act of the City of Hamburg. 1973

Heritage Protection Act of the Federal State of Saxony-Anhalt. 1991

Heritage Protection Act of the Federal State of Mecklenburg-Western Pomerania. 1998

European Cultural Convention. 1955

Convention for the Protection of the Architectural Heritage of Europe. 1985

Act for the Protection and Care of Heritage in the Federal State of Brandenburg. 2004

Act for the Protection of Cultural Heritage. Baden-Württemberg. 1983

Act for the Protection of Cultural Heritage. Schleswig-Holstein. 1996

Act for the Protection of Cultural Heritage. Hesse. 1986

Act for the Protection and Care of Heritage in the Federal State of North Rhine-Westphalia. 1980

Act for the Protection and Care of Heritage. Bavaria. 1973

Act for the Protection and Care of Cultural Heritage in the Federal State of. 1993

Act for the Protection of Heritage in Berlin. 1995

Act for the Protection and Care of Cultural Heritage. Bremen. 1975

Hague Convention for the Protection of Cultural Property in the Event of Armed Conflict. 1954. Second protocol of 1999

Federal Act for the Protection and Care of Cultural Monuments. Rhineland-Palatinate. 1978

Lower Saxony Heritage Protection Act. 1978

Saarland Heritage Protection Act. 2004

Thuringia Act for the Protection and Care of Cultural Heritage. 2004

UNESCO Convention Concerning the Protection of World Cultural and Natural Heritage. 1972

Building materials in refurbishment projects

German Reinforced Concrete Committee (DAfStb) Directive: "Schutz und Instandsetzung von Betonbauteilen" (repairs directive)

DIN 1052 Design of timber structures – General rules and rules for buildings. 2008-12

DIN 1053-1 Masonry – Part 1: Design and construction. 1996-11

DIN V 18550 (pre-standard) Plastering/rendering and plastering/rendering systems – Execution. 2005-04

DIN 52161-1 Testing of wood preservatives – Detection of wood preservatives in wood – Sampling from structural timber in service. 2006-06

DIN 52175 Wood preservation; concept, principles. 1975-01

DIN EN ISO 12944-1 Paints and varnishes – Corrosion protection of steel structures by protective paint systems – Part 1: General introduction. 1998-07 (supersedes DIN 55928-1:1991-05)

DIN 68800-1 Protection of timber used in buildings; general specifications. 1974-05

DIN 68800-2 Protection of timber – Part 2: Preventive constructional measures in buildings. 1996-05

DIN 68800-3 Protection of timber; preventive chemical protection. 1990-04

DIN 68800-4 Wood preservation; measures for the eradication of fungi and insects. 1992-11

DIN 68800-5 Protection of timber used in buildings; preventive chemical protection for wood based materials. 1978-05

DIN EN 335-1 Durability of wood and wood-based products – Definition of use classes – Part 1: General. 2006-10

DIN EN 350-1 Durability of wood and wood based products – Natural durability of solid wood – Part 1: Guide to the principles of testing and classification of the natural durability of wood. 1994-10

DIN EN 460 Durability of wood and wood-based products – Natural durability of solid wood – Guide to the durability requirements for wood to be used in hazard classes. 1994-10

DIN EN 1504-1 Products and systems for the protection and repair of concrete structures – Definitions, requirements, quality control and evaluation of conformity – Part 1: Definitions. 2005-10

DIN EN 13318 Screed material and floor screeds – Definitions. 2000-12

DIN EN ISO 12944-1 Paints and varnishes – Corrosion protection of steel structures by protective paint systems – Part 1: General introduction. 1998-07

Dangerous substances in the building stock

BGR 128 (rules for contaminated areas) cl. 1, scope: previous regulation: EU Safety Data Sheets Directive 91/155/ EWG, superseded since 1 June 2007 by REACH regulation (Registration, Evaluation, Authorisation and Restriction of Chemicals) No. 1907/2006

Chemikalien Gesetz (ChemG – Chemicals Act). 2002-06 (last amended 2006-10)

Act for the Implementation of Directive 98/8/EC of 16 February 1998 concerning the placing of biocidal products on the market.

Council Directive 98/24/EC of 7 April 1998 on the protection of the health and safety of workers from the risks related to chemical agents at work

Directive 98/8/EC of the European Parliament and of the Council of 16 February 1998 concerning the placing of biocidal products on the market

Wertermittlungsrichtlinien – WertR – Valuation Directive). 2006-03

StGB § 325 Luftverunreinigung

Verordnung über Verbote und Beschränkungen des Inverkehrbringens gefährlicher Stoffe, Zubereitungen und Erzeugnisse nach dem Chemikaliengesetz (Chem-VerbotsVO – Chemicals Prohibition Act). 2003-03

Verordnung zum Schutz vor Gefahrstoffen (GefStoffV – Dangerous Substances Act). 2004-12

Part C Historical periods

DIN 105-1 Clay bricks; solid bricks and vertically perforated bricks. 2002-06

DIN 105-2 Clay bricks; lightweight vertically perforated bricks. 2002-06

DIN 105-3 Clay bricks; high-strength bricks and high-strength engineering bricks. 1984-05

DIN 105-4 Clay bricks; ceramic engineering bricks. 1984-05

DIN 106-1 Sand-lime bricks and blocks; solid bricks, perforated bricks, solid blocks, hollow blocks. 2003-02

DIN 107 Building construction; identification of right and left side. 1974-04

DIN 1045-1 Concrete, reinforced and prestressed concrete structures – Part 1: Design and construction. 2008-08

DIN 1052-1 Timber structures; design and construction. 1988-04

DIN 1053-1 Masonry – Part 1: Design and construction. 1996-11

DIN 1055-1 Action on structures – Part 1: Densities and weights of building materials, structural elements and stored materials. 2002-06

DIN 1055-3 Action on structures – Part 3: Self-weight and imposed load in building. 2006-03

DIN 1101 Wood wool slabs and multilayered slabs as insulating materials in building – Requirements, testing. 2000-06

DIN 1249-11 Glass in building; glass edges; concept, characteristics of edge types and finishes. 1986-09

DIN 1259-1 Glass – Part 1: Terminology for glass types and groups. 2001-09

DIN 1946-6 Ventilation and air conditioning – Part 6: Ventilation for residential buildings; requirements, performance, acceptance (VDI ventilation code of practice). 1998-10

DIN 4070-1 Softwood; cross-sectional dimensions and static values for sawn timber, square timber stock and roof battens. 1958-01

DIN 4099-1 Welding of reinforcing steel – Part 1: Execution. 2003-08

DIN 4103-1 Internal non-loadbearing partitions; requirements, testing. 1984-07

DIN 4103-2 Internal non-loadbearing partitions; gypsum wallboard partitions. 1985-12

DIN 4103-4 Internal non-loadbearing partitions; partitions with timber framing. 1988-11

DIN 4108-3 Thermal protection and energy economy in buildings – Part 3: Protection against moisture subject to climate conditions; Requirements and directions for design and construction. 2001-07

DIN 4109 Sound insulation in buildings; requirements and testing. 1989-11

DIN 4121 Hanging wire-plaster ceilings; plaster ceilings with plaster-bearing steel-inserts, Rabitz ceilings, directions for the execution. 1978-07

DIN 4165-100 (pre-standard) Autoclaved aerated concrete masonry units – Part 100: High-precision units and elements with specific properties. 2005-10

DIN 4172 Modular coordination in building construction. 1955-07

DIN 4420-1 Service and working scaffolds – Part 1: Service scaffolds – Performance requirements, general design, structural design. 2004-03

DIN 7864-1 Sheets of elastomers for waterproofing; terms of delivery. 1984-04

DIN 13494 Thermal insulation products for building applications – Determination of the tensile bond strength of the adhesive and of the base coat to the thermal insulation material. 2003-02

DIN 13495 Thermal insulation products for building applications – Determination of the pull-off resistance of external thermal insulation composite systems (ETICS) (foam block test). 2003-02

DIN 13964 Suspended ceilings – Requirements and test methods. 2007-02

DIN 14489 Sprinkler extinguishing systems; general fundamentals. 1985-05

DIN 14675 Fire detection and fire alarm systems – Design and operation. 2003-11

DIN 18017-1 Ventilation of bathrooms and WCs without outside windows; single shaft systems without ventilators. 1987-02

DIN 18025-1 Accessible dwellings; dwellings for wheelchair users, design principles. 1992-12

DIN 18055 Windows; air permeability of joints, water tightness and mechanical strain; requirements and testing. 1981-10

DIN 18065 Stairs in buildings – Terminology, measuring rules, main dimensions. 2000-01

DIN V 18073 (pre-standard) Roller shutters, awnings, rolling doors and other blinds and shutters in buildings – Terms and requirements. 2008-03

DIN 18100 Doors; wall openings for doors with dimensions in accordance with DIN 4172. 1983-10

DIN 18111-1 Door frames – Steel door frames – Part 1: Standard door frames for rebated doors in masonry. 2004-08

DIN 18148 Lightweight concrete hollow boards. 2000-10

DIN V 18151-100 (pre-standard) Lightweight concrete hollow blocks – Part 100: Hollow blocks with specific properties. 2005-10

DIN V 18152-100 (pre-standard) Lightweight concrete solid bricks and blocks – Part 100: Solid bricks and blocks with specific properties. 2005-10

DIN V 18153-100 (pre-standard) Concrete masonry units (normal-weight concrete) – Part 100: Masonry units with specific properties. 2005-10

DIN 18156-2 Materials for ceramic linings by thin mortar bed technique; hydraulic mortar. 1978-03

DIN 18157-1 Execution of ceramic linings by thin mortar bed technique; hydraulic mortar. 1979-07

DIN 18162 Lightweight concrete wallboards – unreinforced. 2000-10

DIN 18164-1 Thermal insulating products for building applications; insulating materials for thermal insulation. 1992-08

DIN 18164-2 Thermal insulating products for building applications; insulating materials for impact sound insulation; polystyrene particle foam materials. 2001-09

DIN 18165-1 Fibre insulation materials; thermal insulation materials. 1991-07

DIN 18165-2 Fibre insulating building materials; impact sound insulating materials. 2009-09

DIN 18168-1 Ceiling linings and suspended ceilings with gypsum plasterboards – Part 1: Requirements for construction. 2007-04

DIN 18180 Gypsum plasterboards – Types and requirements. 2007-01

DIN 18181 Gypsum plasterboards for building construction – Application. 2008-10

DIN 18183-1 Partitions and wall linings with gypsum boards on metal framing – Part 1: Cladding with gypsum plasterboards. 2008-01

DIN 18184 Gypsum plaster boards with polystyrene or polyurethane rigid foam as insulating material. 2008-10

DIN 18195 Waterproofing of buildings. 2000-08

DIN 18201 Tolerances in building: terminology, principles, application, testing. 1997-04

DIN 18255 Building hardware – Door lever handles, backplates and escutcheons – Definitions, dimensions, requirements and marking. 2002-05

DIN 18299 to 18459 German construction contract procedures – Part C: General technical specifications for building works

DIN V 18500 (pre-standard) Cast stones – Terminology, requirements, testing, inspection. 2006-12

DIN 18516-1 Cladding for externals walls, ventilated at rear – Part 1: Requirements, principles of testing. 1999-12

DIN 18531-1 Waterproofing of roofs – Sealings for non-utilised roofs – Part 1: Terms and definitions, requirements, design principles. 2005-11

DIN 18540 Sealing of exterior wall joints in building using joint sealants. 2006-12

DIN 18542 Sealing of outside wall joints with impregnated

sealing tapes made of cellular plastics – Impregnated sealing tapes – Requirements and testing. 1999-01

DIN V 18550 (pre-standard) Plastering/rendering and plastering/rendering systems – Execution. 2005-04

DIN 18558 Synthetic resin plasters; terminology, requirements, application. 1985-01

DIN 18560-1/A1 (draft standard) Floor screeds in building construction – Part 1: General requirements, testing and construction. 2008-07

DIN 18560-2/A1 (draft standard) Floor screeds in building construction – Part 2: Floor screeds and heating floor screeds on insulation layers. 2008-07

DIN 18560-4 Floor screeds – Part 4: Screeds laid on separated layer. 2004-04

DIN 18800-5 Steel structures – Part 5: Composite structures of steel and concrete – Design and construction. 2007-03

DIN 18807 Trapezoidal sheeting in building; trapezoidal steel sheeting. 1987-06

DIN 18808 Steel structures; structures made from hollow sections subjected to predominantly static loading. 1984-10

DIN 52128 Bituminous roof sheeting with felt core; definition, designation, requirements. 1977-03

DIN 52130 Bitumen sheeting for waterproofing of roofs – Concepts, designation, requirements. 1995-11

DIN 52131 Bitumen waterproof sheeting for fusion welding – Concepts, designation, requirements. 1995-11

DIN 52132 Polymer bitumen sheeting for waterproofing of roofs – Concepts, designation, requirements. 1996-05

DIN 52133 Polymer bitumen waterproof sheeting for fusion welding – Terms and definitions, designation, requirements. 1995-11

DIN 52143 Bitumen roofing felt with glass fleece base; terms and definitions, designation, requirements. 1985-08

DIN 55699 Application of thermal insulation composite systems. 2005-02

DIN 68119 Wood shingles. 1996-09

DIN 68121-1 Timber profiles for windows and window doors; dimensions, quality requirements. 1993-09

DIN 68365 Sawn timber for carpentry – Appearance grading – Softwood. 2008-12

DIN 68702 Wood paving. 2001-04

DIN 68706-1 Interior doors made from wood and wood-based panels – Part 1: Door leaves; concepts, sizes, requirements. 2002-02

DIN 68800-1 Protection of timber used in buildings; general specifications. 1974-05

DIN 68800-4 Wood preservation; measures for the eradication of fungi and insects. 1992-11

DIN CEN/TS 81-82 (pre-standard) Safety rules for the construction and installation of lifts – Existing lifts – Part 82: Improvement of the accessibility of existing lifts for persons including persons with disability. 2008-09

DIN CEN/TS 12872 (pre-standard) Wood-based panels – Guidance on the use of loadbearing boards in floors, walls and roofs. 2007-10

DIN CEN/TS 15717 (pre-standard) Parquet flooring – General guideline for installation. 2008-07

DIN EN 81-1 Safety rules for the construction and installation of lifts – Part 1: Electric lifts. 2000-05

DIN EN 197-1 Cement – Part 1: Composition, specifications and conformity criteria for common cements. 2004-08

DIN EN 206-1 Concrete – Part 1: Specification, performance, production and conformity. 2001-07

DIN EN 300 Oriented Strand Boards (OSB) – Definitions, classification and specifications. 2006-09

DIN EN 309 Particleboards – Definition and classification. 2005-04

DIN EN 312-5 Particleboards. Specifications. Requirements for loadbearing boards for use in humid conditions. 1997-06

DIN EN 316 (draft standard) Wood fibreboards – Definition, classification and symbols. 2008-07

DIN EN 335 Durability of wood and wood-based products – Definition of use classes. 2006-10

DIN EN 356 Glass in building – Security glazing – Testing and classification of resistance against manual attack. 2000-02

DIN EN 357 Glass in building – Fire-resistant glazed ele-

ments with transparent or translucent glass products – Classification of fire resistance. 2005-02

DIN EN 386 Glued laminated timber – Performance requirements and minimum production requirements. 2002-04

DIN EN 413-1 Masonry cement – Part 1: Composition, specifications and conformity criteria. 2004-05

DIN EN 459-1 Building lime – Part 1: Definitions, specifications and conformity criteria. 2002-02

DIN EN 490 Concrete roofing tiles and fittings for roof covering and wall cladding – Product specifications. 2006-09

DIN EN 492 Fibre cement slates and fittings – Product specification and test methods. 2006-12

DIN EN 501 Roofing products from metal sheet – Specification for fully supported roofing products from zinc sheet. 1994-11

DIN EN 548 Resilient floor coverings – Specification for plain and decorative linoleum. 2004-11

DIN EN 572-1 Glass in building – Basic soda lime silicate glass products – Part 1: Definitions and general physical and mechanical properties. 2004-09

DIN EN 622-1 Fibreboards – Specifications – Part 1: General requirements. 2003-09

DIN EN 634-1 Cement-bonded particleboards – Specifications – Part 1: General requirements. 1995-04

DIN EN 1062-1 Paints and varnishes – Coating materials and coating systems for exterior masonry and concrete – Part 1: Classification. 2004-08

DIN EN 1279-1 Glass in building – Insulating glass units – Part 1: Generalities, dimensional tolerances and rules for the system description. 2004-08

DIN EN 1304 Clay roofing tiles and fittings – Product definitions and specifications. 2008-07

DIN EN 1307 Textile floor coverings – Classification of pile carpets. 2008-08

DIN EN 1313-1 (draft standard) Round and sawn timber – Permitted deviations and preferred sizes – Part 1: Softwood sawn timber. 2008-08

DIN EN 1470 Textile floor coverings – Classification of needled floor coverings except for needled pile floor coverings. 2009-02

DIN EN 1849-1 Flexible sheets for waterproofing – Determination of thickness and mass per unit area – Part 1: Bitumen sheets for roof waterproofing. 2000-01

DIN EN 1849-2 Flexible sheets for waterproofing – Determination of thickness and mass per unit area – Part 2: Plastic and rubber sheets for roof waterproofing. 2001-09

DIN EN 1991-1-1 Eurocode 1: Actions on structures – Part 1-1: General actions; densities, self-weight, imposed loads for buildings. 2002-10

DIN EN 1991-1-2 Eurocode 1 – Actions on structures – Part 1-2: General actions; actions on structures exposed to fire. 2003-9

DIN EN 1991-1-3 Eurocode 1 – Actions on structures – Part 1-3: General actions – Snow loads. 2004-09

DIN EN 1992-1-1 Eurocode 2: Design of concrete structures – Part 1-1: General rules and rules for buildings. 2005-10

DIN EN 1992-1-2 Eurocode 2: Design of concrete structures – Part 1-2: General rules – Structural fire design. 2006-10

DIN EN 1993-1-1 Eurocode 3: Design of steel structures – Part 1-1: General rules and rules for buildings. 2005-07

DIN EN 1993-1-2 Eurocode 3: Design of steel structures – Part 1-2: General rules – Structural fire design. 2006-10

DIN EN 1994-1-1 Eurocode 4: Design of composite steel and concrete structures – Part 1-1: General rules and rules for buildings. 2006-07

DIN EN 1994-1-2 Eurocode 4: Design of composite steel and concrete structures – Part 1-2: General rules – Structural fire design. 2006-11

DIN EN 1995-1-1 Eurocode 5: Design of timber structures – Part 1-1: General – General rules and rules for buildings. 2008-09

DIN EN 1995-1-2 Eurocode 5: Design of timber structures – Part 1-2: General – Structural fire design. 2006-10

DIN EN 10080 Steel for the reinforcement of concrete – Weldable reinforcing steel – General. 2005-08

DIN EN 12004 Adhesives for tiles – Requirements, evaluation of conformity, classification and designation. 2007-11

DIN EN 12150-1 Glass in building – Thermally toughened soda lime silicate safety glass – Part 1: Definition and description. 2000-11

DIN EN 12152 Curtain walling – Air permeability – Performance requirements and classificationDIN EN 12153 Curtain walling – Air permeability – Test methods. 2000-09

DIN EN 12154 Curtain walling – Watertightness – Performance requirements and classification. 2000-06

DIN EN 12217 Doors – Operating forces – Requirements and classification. 2004-05

DIN EN 12464-1 Light and lighting – Lighting of work places – Part 1: Indoor workplaces. 2003-03

DIN EN 12467 Fibre cement flat sheets – Product specification and test methods. 2006-12

DIN EN 12620 Aggregates for concrete. 2008-07

DIN EN 12825 Raised access floors. 2002-04

DIN EN 12859 Gypsum blocks – Definitions, requirements and test methods. 2008-06

DIN EN 13055-1 Lightweight aggregates – Part 1: Lightweight aggregates for concrete, mortar and grout. 2002-08

DIN EN 13162 Thermal insulation products for buildings – Factory-made mineral wool (MW) products – Specification. 2009-02

DIN EN 13163 Thermal insulation products for buildings – Factory-made products of expanded polystyrene (EPS) – Specification. 2009-02

DIN EN 13164 Thermal insulation products for buildings – Factory made products of extruded polystyrene foam (XPS) – Specification DIN EN 13166 Thermal insulation products for buildings – Factory-made products of phenolic foam (PF) – Specification. 2009-02

DIN EN 13165 Thermal insulation products for buildings – Factory made rigid polyurethane foam (PUR) products – Specification DIN EN 13171 Thermal insulating products for buildings – Factory-made wood fibre (WF) products – Specification. 2009-02

DIN EN 13226 (draft standard) Wood flooring – Solid wood parquet elements with grooves and/or tongues. 2008-11

DIN EN 13318 Screed material and floor screeds – Definitions. 2000-12

DIN EN 13363-1 Solar protection devices combined with glazing – Calculation of solar and light transmittance – Part 1: Simplified method. 2007-09

DIN EN 13488 Wood flooring – Mosaic parquet elements. 2003-05

DIN EN 13658-1 Metal lath and beads – Definitions, requirements and test methods – Part 1: Internal plastering. 2005-09

DIN EN 13658-2 Metal lath and beads – Definitions, requirements and test methods – Part 2: External renderingDIN EN 13859-2 Flexible sheets for waterproofing – Definitions and characteristics of underlays – Part 2: Underlays for walls. 2009-01

DIN EN 13950 Gypsum plasterboard thermal/acoustic insulation composite panels – Definitions, requirements and test methods. 2006-02

DIN EN 18202 (tolerances in building). 2008

DIN EN ISO 150 Raw, refined and boiled linseed oil for paints and varnishes – Specifications and methods of test. 2007-05

DIN EN ISO 2424 Textile floor coverings – Vocabulary. 1999-01

DIN EN ISO 4618 Paints and varnishes – Terms and definitions. 2007-03

DIN EN ISO 10211 Thermal bridges in building construction – Heat flows and surface temperatures – Detailed calculations. 2008-04

DIN EN ISO 12543-1 (draft standard) Glass in building – Laminated glass and laminated safety glass – Part 1: Definitions and description of component parts. 2008-07

DIN EN ISO 13791 Thermal performance of buildings – Calculation of internal temperatures of a room in summer without mechanical cooling – General criteria and validation procedures. 2005-02

DIN EN ISO 14683 Thermal bridges in building construction – Linear thermal transmittance – Simplified methods and default values. 2008-04

Bibliography

Part B   Principles

Planning refurbishment works
Clancy, Brian P.: New buildings from old – some views on refurbishment projects. In: The Structural Engineer. vol. 73, No. 20, 1995

Ebinghaus; Hugo: Der Hochbau. Nordhausen, 1936

Kleemann, Manfred; Hansen, Patrik: Evaluierung der CO2-Minderungsmaßnahmen im Gebäudebereich. Jülich, 2005

Lippok, Jürgen; Korth, Dietrich: Abbrucharbeiten – Grundlagen, Vorbereitung, Durchführung. Cologne, 2004

Paterson, James, Perry, Paul: A systematic approach to refurbishment. In: The Structural Engineer. vol. 80, No. 9, 2002

Building physics
Becker, Klausjürgen; Pfau, Jochen; Tichelmann, Karsten: Trockenbau-Atlas, Teil 1. Cologne, 2004

Becker, Klausjürgen; Pfau, Jochen; Tichelmann, Karsten: Trockenbau-Atlas, Teil 2. Cologne, 2006

German Energy Agency (dena) (ed.): Besser als ein Neubau – EnEV-minus-30 %. Planungshilfe. Berlin, 2007

German Energy Agency (dena) (ed.): Thermische Behaglichkeit im Niedrigenergiehaus – Teil 1: Winterliche Verhältnisse. Berlin, 2007

Fanger, Ole: Thermal Comfort – Analysis and Applications in Environmental Engineering. Copenhagen, 1970

Feist, Wolfgang et al.: PHPP 2007 – Passive House Planning Package. Passive House Institute (ed.). Darmstadt, 2007

Fraunhofer Institute for Building Physics (ed.): WUFI und WUFI 2D. Holzkirchen, 2007

Gösele, Karl: Schallschutz-Entwicklungen in den letzten 30 Jahren. In: Deutsche Bauzeitung 122/1988

Informationsdienst Holz (ed.): Holzbau Handbuch. Reihe 1. Teil 14. Folge 1 – Modernisierung von Altbauten. Munich, 2001

Informationsdienst Holz (ed.): Holzbau Handbuch. Reihe 3. Teil 3. Folge 3 – Schalldämmende Holzbalken- und Brettstapeldecken. Munich, 1999

Informationsdienst Holz (ed.): Holzbau Handbuch. Reihe 3. Teil 3. Folge 4 – Schallschutz Wände und Dächer. Bonn/Munich, 2004

Informationsdienst Holz (ed.): Holzbau Handbuch. Reihe 3. Teil 4. Folge 2 – Feuerhemmende Holzbauteile (F 30). Munich, 2001

Informationsdienst Holz (ed.): Holzbau Handbuch. Reihe 7. Teil 3. Folge 1 – Erneuerung von Fachwerkbauten. Bonn/Munich 2004

Institut für Bauforschung e.V. (ed.): U-Werte alter Bauteile. Hannover, 2005

Institute for Building Climatology, Dresden TU (ed.): Delphin.

Kah, Oliver; Feist, Wolfgang: Wirtschaftlichkeit von Wärmedämmmaßnahmen im Gebäudebestand. Darmstadt, 2005

Kötz, Wolf-Dietrich: Erhebung zum Stand der Technik beim baulichen Schallschutz. Fortschritte der Akustik. 1988

Kordina, Karl; Meyer-Ottens, Claus: Holz-Brandschutz-Handbuch. Munich, 1994

Krämer, Georg; Pfau, Jochen; Tichelmann, Karsten: Handbuch Sanierung. Knauf Gips KG (ed.). Iphofen, 2002

Lutz, Jenisch; et al.: Lehrbuch der Bauphysik. Stuttgart, 2002

Passive House Institute (ed.): Study group for low-cost passive houses. Proceedings vol. 24. Einsatz von Passivhaustechnologien bei der Altbau-Modernisierung. Darmstadt, 2003

Passive House Institute (ed.): Study group for low-cost passive houses. Proceedings vol. 32. Faktor 4 auch bei sensiblen Altbauten–Passivhauskomponenten + Innendämmung. Darmstadt, 2005

Rabold, Andreas; et al.: Forschungsvorhaben – Holzbalkendecken in der Altbausanierung. Final report, available from the German Society for Wood Research

Scholze, Jürgen: Bauphysik 17. Berlin, 1995

Stiegel, Horst; Hauser, Gerd: Wärmebrückenkatalog für Modernisierungs- und Sanierungsmaßnahmen zur Vermeidung von Schimmelpilzen. Stuttgart, 2006

Veres, Eva; Brandstetter, Klaus; Ertel, Hanno: Bauphysik 11. Berlin, 1989

Building services
Arendt, Claus: Modernisierung alter Häuser: Planung, Bautechnik, Haustechnik. Munich, 2003/Baden-Baden, 2006

Bundesarbeitskreis Altbauerneuerung: Almanach Kompetenz Bauen im Bestand. Cologne, 2006

BINE Informationsdienst: Solare Luftsysteme. Bonn, 2002

BINE Informationsdienst: Thermische Nutzung der Sonnenenergie. Bonn, 2002

Bohne, Dirk: Ökologische Gebäudetechnik. Stuttgart, 2004

Daniels, Klaus: Gebäudetechnik. Ein Leitfaden für Architekten und Ingenieure. Munich/Zurich, 2000

Eckermann, Wulf; Preißler, Hans Albert: Altbaumodernisierung, Haustechnik. Stuttgart/Munich, 2000

Eschenfelder, Dieter: Altbausanierung mit moderner Haustechnik – gesetzliche Grundlagen, Sanierungskonzepte, ökologische und ökonomische Aspekte. Munich, 2005

Guenzel, Winfried: Sanierung von Hausanschlussleitungen. Verfahren – Einsatzmöglichkeiten – Praxisbeispiele. Renningen, 2002

Informationszentrum Energie: Biogene Brennstoffe. No. 1–4. Baden-Württemberg, 2005

Informationszentrum Energie: Brennwertnutzung, Energiesparende und umweltschonende Wärmeerzeugung. Baden-Württemberg, 2002

Initiativkreis Erdgas & Umwelt: Gas-Brennwertheizung. Essen, 2008

Laasch, Thomas; Laasch, Erhard: Haustechnik. Grundlagen – Planung – Ausführung. Wiesbaden, 2005

Lenz, Joachim; John, Hans-Joachim: Ertüchtigung, Sanierung, Erneuerung von Druckrohrleitungen. Essen, 1996

Pistohl, Wolfram: Handbuch der Gebäudetechnik – Planungsgrundlagen und Beispiele. vols. 1 & 2. Düsseldorf, 2007

Ranft, Fred; Haas-Arndt, Doris: Energieeffiziente Altbauten. Durch Sanierung zum Niedrigenergiehaus. Cologne, 2004

Rau, Otfried; Braune, Ute: Der Altbau – Renovieren, Restaurieren, Modernisieren. Leinfelden-Echterdingen, 2004

Scholze, Georg: Leitungswasserschäden – Vermeidung – Sanierung – Haftung. Renningen, 2003

Sichla, Frank: Blitz- und Überspannungsschutz für Antennen, Geräte und Anlagen. Baden-Baden, 2006

Vogel, Markus: Kanalinstandhaltung – Von der Zustandserfassung zur nachhaltigen Sanierung von Entwässerungskanälen und -leitungen. Renningen, 2002

Wagner, Volker: Inspektion und Sanierung von Abwasserkanälen. Renningen, 2000

Waldner, Paul: Kompendium der elektrotechnischen und elektronischen Gebäudetechnik. Düsseldorf, 2003

Wellpott, Edwin; Bohne, Dirk: Technischer Ausbau von Gebäuden. Stuttgart, 2006

Baden-Württemberg Trade & Industry Ministry: Energie sparen durch Wärmepumpen. Stuttgart, 2006

Baden-Württemberg Trade & Industry Ministry: Holzenergienutzung, Technik, Planung und Genehmigung. Stuttgart, 2005

Baden-Württemberg Trade & Industry Ministry: Kleine Blockheizkraftwerke, Technik, Planung und Genehmigung. Stuttgart, 2005

Baden-Württemberg Trade & Industry Ministry: Mittelgroße Wärmepumpenanlagen. Stuttgart, 2005

Baden-Württemberg Trade & Industry Ministry: Thermische Solaranlagen zur Warmwasserbereitung und Heizungsunterstützung. Stuttgart, 2005

Conservation
Cramer, Johannes; Breitling, Stefan: Architecture in Existing Fabric: Planning, Design, Building. Basel/Boston/Berlin, 2007

Deutsches Nationalkomitee für Denkmalschutz (ed.): Denkmalschutz. Texte zum Denkmalschutz und zur Denkmalpflege. Pub. by Deutsches Nationalkomitee für Denkmalschutz. Bonn, 1996

Deutsches Nationalkomitee für Denkmalschutz (ed.): Denkmalschutzgesetze. Pub. by Deutsches Nationalkomitee für Denkmalschutz. Bonn, 2005

Hubel, Achim: Denkmalpflege – Geschichte, Themen, Aufgaben. Stuttgart, 2006

Hume, Ian J.: The structural engineer in conservation. In: The Structural Engineer, vol. 75, No. 3, 1997

Huse, Norbert: Denkmalpflege – Deutsche Texte aus drei Jahrhunderten. Munich, 1996

Kiesow, Gottfried: Denkmalpflege in Deutschland. Darmstadt, 2000

Martin, Dieter J.; Krautzberger, Michael: Handbuch Denkmalschutz und Denkmalpflege. Munich, 2006

Petzet, Michael; Mader, Gert: Praktische Denkmalpflege. Stuttgart/Berlin/Cologne, 1993

Vereinigung der Landesdenkmalpfleger in der Bundesrepublik Deutschland (ed.): Entstaatlichung der Denkmalpflege? Von der Provokation zur Diskussion. Berlin, 2000.

Building materials in refurbishment projects
Arendt, Claus: Altbausanierung – Leitfaden zur Erhaltung und Modernisierung alter Häuser. Stuttgart, 1993

Balkow, Dörte: Bauen im Bestand. Schäden, Maßnahmen und Bauteile. Katalog für die Altbauerneuerung. Cologne, 2006

Balkowski, Michael: Handbuch der Bauerneuerung. Angewandte Bauphysik für die Modernisierung von Wohngebäuden. Cologne, 2006

Bates, W.: Historical Structural Steelwork Handbook. British Constructional Steelwork Association. London, 1984

Barnickel, Ulrich: Metall an historischen Gebäuden – Geschichte, Gestaltung, Restaurierung. Stuttgart/Munich, 2003

Blaich, Jürgen: Bauschäden – Analyse und Vermeidung. Stuttgart, 1999

Erler, Klaus: Alte Holzbauwerke. Beurteilen und Sanieren. Berlin, 2004

Frössel, Frank: Handbuch Putz und Stuck – Herstellung, Beschichtung und Sanierung für Neu- und Altbau. Munich, 2003

Grassegger, Gabriele: Neue Natursteinrestaurierungsergebnisse und messtechnische Erfassung. Stuttgart, 2005

Großmann, G. Ulrich: Einführung in die historische Bauforschung. Darmstadt, 1993

Hankammer, Gunter: Schäden an Gebäuden erkennen und beurteilen. Cologne, 2005

Hegger, Manfred; Auch-Schwelk, Volker; Fuchs, Matthias; Rosenkranz, Thorsten: Construction Materials Manual. Basel/Boston/Berlin, 2006

Hegger, Manfred; Fuchs, Matthias; Stark, Thomas; Zeumer, Martin: Energy Manual – Sustainable Architecture. Basel/Boston/Berlin, 2008

Karsten, Rudolf: Bauchemie. Mit Ursachen, Verhütung und Sanierung von Bauschäden. Heidelberg, 2003

Lenze, Wolfgang: Fachwerkhäuser restaurieren, sanieren, modernisieren – Materialien und Verfahren für eine dauerhafte Instandsetzung. Stuttgart, 2007

Lißner, Karin; Rug, Wolfgang: Holzbausanierung. Grundlagen und Praxis der sicheren Ausführung. Berlin/Heidelberg/New York, 2000

Maier, Josef: Handbuch Historisches Mauerwerk – Untersuchungsmethoden und Instandsetzungsverfahren. Basel/Boston/Berlin, 2002

Oswald, Rainer; Abel, R.: Hinzunehmende Unregelmäßigkeiten bei Gebäuden: Typische Erscheinungsbilder, Beurteilungskriterien, Grenzwerte. Wiesbaden, 2005

Pfundstein, Margit; Gellert, Roland; Spitzner, Martin H.; Rudolphi, Alexander: Insulating Materials. Principles, Materials, Applications. Munich, 2008

Piepenburg, Werner: Mörtel, Mauerwerk, Putz – Die Putzfibel für Baustelle und Bauleitung. Munich, 1961

Rentmeister, Andreas: Instandsetzung von Natursteinmauerwerk. Stuttgart/Munich, 2003

Reul, Horst: Handbuch Bautenschutz und Bausanierung – Leitfaden für die Sanierungsbranche. Cologne, 1989

Richarz, Clemens; Schulz, Christina; Zeitler, Friedemann: Energy-Efficiency Upgrades – Principles, Details, Examples. Munich, 2007

Rosenbaum, Erich: Problemkreis Fußboden. Entstehung und Behebung von Schäden an Unterkonstruktionen und deren Nutzschichten. Cologne, 1985

Ruffert, Günther: Schäden an Betonbauwerken – Ursachen, Analysen, Beispiele. Cologne-Braunsfeld, 1982

Schönburg, Kurt: Schäden an Sichtflächen. Bewerten, Beseitigen, Vermeiden. Berlin, 2003

Snethlage, Rolf: Leitfaden Steinkonservierung – Planung von Untersuchungen und Maßnahmen zur Erhaltung von Denkmälern aus Naturstein. Stuttgart, 2005

Stahr, Michael: Bausanierung – Erkennen und Beheben von Bauschäden. Braunschweig, 2004

Stark, Jochen; Wicht, Bernd: Geschichte der Baustoffe. Wiesbaden/Berlin, 1998

Weber, Helmut: Fassadenschutz und Bausanierung. Renningen-Malmsheim, 1994

Weber, Jürgen; Goschka, Ines: Bauwerksabdichtung in der Altbausanierung – Verfahren und juristische Betrachtungsweise. Wiesbaden, 2006

Zimmermann, Günter: Schadenfreies Bauen. vols. 1–20. Stuttgart, 2007

Dangerous substances in the building stock

Bremer Umweltinstitut e.V.: Gift im Holz, Bremen, 1994

Advisory council for environmentally relevant legacy materials (BUA), German Chemical Society (GDCh): Phenol – BUA-Stoffbericht 209. 1998

Deutsche Forschungsgemeinsaft: MAK- und BAT-Werte-Liste 2000. Senate Commission for investigating materials hazardous to health. Weinheim, 2000

Streit, Bruno: Lexikon Ökotoxikologie. Weinheim, 1994

Part C   Historical periods

Ahnert, Rudolph; Krause, Karl Heinz: Typische Baukonstruktionen von 1860 bis 1960. vol. 1. Berlin, 2000

Ahnert, Rudolph; Krause, Karl Heinz: Typische Baukonstruktionen von 1860 bis 1960. vol. 2, Berlin, 2001

Ahnert, Rudolph; Krause, Karl Heinz: Typische Baukonstruktionen von 1860 bis 1960. vol. 3. Berlin, 2002

Collins, A. Richard (ed.): Structural Engineering – two centuries of British achievement. Institution of Structural Engineers. London, 1983

Fasold, Wolfgang; Veres, Eva: Schallschutz und Raumakustik in der Praxis. Berlin, 2003

Gerner, Manfred: Fachwerk – Entwicklung, Instandsetzung, Neubau. Munich, 2007

Klein-Meynen, Dieter et al.: Kölner Wirtschaftsarchitektur – von der Gründerzeit bis zum Wiederaufbau. Cologne, 1996

Ruffert, Günther: Lexikon der Betonsanierung. Stuttgart, 1999

Simon, Katja: Fertighausarchitektur in Deutschland seit 1945. Oberhausen, 2005

General refurbishment tasks

Balak, Michael; Pech, Anton: Mauerwerkstrockenlegung. Vienna, 2003

Chandler, Ian: Repair and refurbishment of modern buildings. London, 1991

Hettmann, Dieter: Mauerwerksinjektionen gegen kapillar aufsteigende Feuchtigkeit. vol. 1. Vienna, 1992

Highfield, David: Refurbishment and upgrading of buildings. London, 2000

Institution of Structural Engineers: Aspects of Cladding. London, 1995

Weber, Helmut: Fassadenschutz und Bausanierung. Renningen-Malmsheim, 1983

Buildings of the founding years 1890–1920

Breymann, Gustav Adolf et al.: Allgemeine Baukonstruktionslehre. Die Konstruktionen in Stein. vol. 1. Leipzig, 1903

Breymann, Gustav Adolf et al.: Allgemeine Baukonstruktionslehre. Die Konstruktionen in Holz. vol. 2. Leipzig, 1900

Breymann, Gustav Adolf et al.: Allgemeine Baukonstruktionslehre. Die Konstruktionen in Eisen. vol. 3. Leipzig, 1902

Breymann, Gustav Adolf et al.: Allgemeine Baukonstruktionslehre. Verschiedene Konstruktionen. vol. 4. Leipzig, 1900

Issel, Hans (ed.); Opderbecke, Adolf: Der Maurer. Leipzig, 1910

Schönermark, Gustav; Stüber, Wilhelm: Hochbau-Lexikon. Berlin, c. 1900

Trier, Eduard; Weyres, Willy: Kunst des 19. Jahrhunderts im Rheinland – Architektur II. vol. 2. Düsseldorf, 1980

Buildings of the inter-war years 1920–1940

Deutscher Beton-Verein, Wirtschaftsgruppe Bauindustrie und Deutscher Zement-Bund (ed.): Neues Bauen in Eisenbeton. Berlin, 1937

Emperger, Fritz von (ed.): Handbuch für Eisenbetonbau in 14 Bänden. Berlin, 1907–1931

Esselborn (ed.); bearbeitet von Brennecke, L. et al.: Lehrbuch des Hochbaues. vol. 1. Leipzig, 1922

Esselborn (ed.); bearbeitet von Durm, Josef; Durm, Rudolf: Lehrbuch des Hochbaues. vol. 2. Leipzig, 1926

Frick, Otto; Knöll, Karl: Baukonstruktionslehre. Teil 1. Leipzig/Berlin, 1936

Frick, Otto; Knöll, Karl: Baukonstruktionslehre. Teil 2. Leipzig/Berlin, 1935

Heideck, Erich; Leppin, Otto: Der Industriebau. vol. 2. Berlin, 1933

Schmidt, Paul; bearbeitet von Hugo Ebinghaus: Handbuch des Hochbaues. Nordhausen, 1926

Buildings of the post-war years 1950–1965

Durth, Werner: Deutsche Architekten – Biografische Verflechtungen 1900–1970. Stuttgart/Zurich, 2001

Frick, Otto: Frick/Knöll – Baukonstruktionslehre. Teil 1: Steinbau. Bielefeld, 1951

Frick, Otto: Frick/Knöll – Baukonstruktionslehre. Teil 1: Holzbau. Leipzig, 1953

Hart, Franz: Baukonstruktion für Architekten. vol. 1. Stuttgart, 1951

Henn, Walter: Bauten der Industrie – Ein internationaler Querschnitt. Munich, 1955

Henn, Walter: Bauten der Industrie – Planung, Entwurf, Konstruktion. Munich, 1955

Hess, Friedrich: Konstruktion und Form im Bauen. Stuttgart, 1949

Merinsky, J. K.: Raumbaukonstruktionslehre. Vienna, 1948

Mittag, Martin: Baukonstruktionslehre. Gütersloh, 1960

Neufert, Ernst and Peter: Architects' Data. 3rd ed. Oxford, 2002

Ortner, Rudolf: Baukonstruktionen und Ausbau – Bauen und Wissen. 2 vols. Gotha, 1951

Schmitt, Heinrich: Hochbaukonstruktionen. Ravensburg, 1956

Schmitt, Heinrich: Hochbaukonstruktionen. Ravensburg, 1962

Wiel, Leopold; Deutschmann, Eberhard: Baukonstruktionen unter Anwendung der Maßordnung im Hochbau. Leipzig, 1955

Zbinden, Fritz: Der Massiv-Hochbau – Grundlagen der Konstruktion und Ausführung. Zurich, 1949

Buildings of the prosperous years 1965–1980

Neumann, Friedrich (ed.): Frick/Knöll – Baukonstruktionslehre. Teil 1. Stuttgart, 1963

Neumann, Friedrich (ed.): Frick/Knöll – Baukonstruktionslehre. Teil 2. Stuttgart, 1964

Neumann, Friedrich (ed.): Frick/Knöll – Baukonstruktionslehre. Teil 1. Stuttgart, 1979

Neumann, Friedrich (ed.): Frick/Knöll – Baukonstruktionslehre. Teil 2. Stuttgart, 1979

Schmitt, Heinrich: Hochbaukonstruktionen, Ravensburg, 1978

Wiel, Leopold; Dittmann, Heinz: Baukonstruktionen des Wohnungsbaues. Leipzig, 1974

Wieschemann, Paul Gerhard; Gatz, Konrad: Betonkonstruktionen im Hochbau. Munich, 1968

Picture credits

The authors and publishers would like to express their sincere gratitude to all those who have assisted in the production of this book, be it through providing photos or artwork or granting permission to reproduce their documents or providing other information. Photographs not specifically credited were taken by the architects or are works photographs or were supplied from the archives of the magazine DETAIL. Despite intensive endeavours we were unable to establish copyright ownership in just a few cases; however, copyright is assured. Please notify us accordingly in such instances. The numbers refer to the figures.

Part A   Introduction

A   Jan Maly, Prag

Definitions
A 1.1   Jochen Helle/artur, Essen
A 1.2   Eneko Ametzaga, Bilbao
A 1.4   VAN HAM Art Auctions, Cologne
A 1.6   Jean-Luc Valentin, Frankfurt am Main
A 1.7   Veit Landwehr, Cologne
A 1.8   Michael Heinrich, Munich
A 1.9   Ulrich Schwarz, Berlin
A 1.10   Stefan Müller-Naumann, Munich
A 1.11   Christa Lachenmaier, Cologne

Further building work...
A 2.1   Fabio Galli
A 2.2   from: Baumeister 10/1981
A 2.3   Papa Balaguer Dezcallar
A 2.4–5   Paul Ott, Graz

Part B   Principles

B   Ruedi Walti, Basel

Planning refurbishment works
B 1.2–3   according to data from: Kleemann, Manfred; Hansen, Patrik: Evaluierung der CO_2-Minderungsmaßnahmen im Gebäudebereich. Jülich, 2005
B 1.5   based on: Ahnert, Rudolph; Krause, Karl Heinz: Typische Baukonstruktionen von 1860 bis 1960. vol. 1. Berlin, 2000, p. 68
B 1.6   Detail 11/2007, p. 1326
B 1.7   Testo AG, Lenzkirch
B 1.9   based on: Ebinghaus, Hugo: Der Hochbau. Nordhausen, 1936, p. 476
B 1.11   see B 1.2
B 1.12   Liebherr Hydraulikbagger GmbH, Kirchdorf/Iller
B 1.13–14 Hilti Deutschland GmbH, Kaufering
B 1.15   according to data from: Lippok, Jürgen; Korth, Dietrich: Abbrucharbeiten. Cologne, 2004, p. 382

Building physics
B 2.1   www.thermografie-seminare.de
B 2.3   based on: Arbeitsgemeinschaft Energiebilanz
B 2.4   according to: DIN EN ISO 7730
B 2.7a–b based on: Passive House Institute, Darmstadt
B 2.8–9   according to data from: German Energy Agency (dena) (ed.): Besser als ein Neubau – EnEV minus 30 %. Planungshilfe. Berlin, 2007
B 2.10   according to: DIN 4108-2
B 2.13–14 based on: Sto AG, Stühlingen
B 2.15   according to data from: German Energy Agency (dena) and DIN V 4108-4
B 2.20   Passive House Institute, Darmstadt
B 2.21   see B 2.8
B 2.23   see B 2.7
B 2.24   see B 2.7
B 2.25   according to data from: Passive House Institute, Darmstadt
B 2.26a–b Burkhard Schulze Darup, Nuremberg

B 2.26c   see B 2.7
B 2.27a–b see B 2.7
B 2.28   from: Energieeinsparverordnung (EnEV): Verordnung über energiesparenden Wärmeschutz und energiesparende Anlagentechnik in Gebäuden. Berlin, 2007
B 2.43–44 according to data from: VHT, Darmstadt
B 2.45–46 based on: VHT, Darmstadt
B 2.47   Saint-Gobain Rigips GmbH, Düsseldorf
B 2.48–50 Knauf Gips KG, Iphofen

Building services
B 3.1   www.ak-pictures.de
B 3.4   according to data from: Pistohl, Wolfram: Handbuch der Gebäudetechnik. vol. 1. Cologne, 2007
B 3.6   based on: Pistohl, Wolfram: Handbuch der Gebäudetechnik. vol. 1. Cologne, 2007
B 3.7   see B 3.4
B 3.8   Volker Pröstler/prodonator
B 3.10   Vienna TU, TVFA
B 3.11   Doyma GmbH & Co., Oyten
B 3.12   GEVI Rohrinnensanierung mbH
B 3.13   Sachverständigenbüro für Gebäudetechnik SGN, Berlin
B 3.14   Kai Breker, Kiel
B 3.16   Dehoust GmbH, Leimen/Heidelberg
B 3.17   IMS Robotics, Ottendorf-Okrilla
B 3.18   Gullyver Gesellschaft für mobile Inspektionssysteme mbH, Bremen
B 3.19   see B 3.4
B 3.20–21 SAERTEX multiCOM GmbH, Saerbeck
B 3.23   according to data from: German Energy Agency (dena) (ed.): Leitfaden Energieausweis – Energiebedarfsausweis für Wohngebäude – Modernisierungsempfehlungen. Teil 2. Berlin, 2007
B 3.24–25 Dorsch Umwelttechnik GmbH, Baiersdorf
B 3.26–28 according to data from: Darmstadt TU, Department of Design & Building Technology
B 3.29–30 see B 3.6
B 3.31–33 see B 3.26
B 3.34   EMCO Bau- und Klimatechnik GmbH & Co. KG, Lingen
B 3.35   Rupert Ganzer, Frankfurt am Main
B 3.36   TROX GmbH, Neukirchen-Vluyn
B 3.38   according to data from: Darmstadt TU, Department of Design & Energy-Efficient Construction
B 3.40   SorTech AG, Halle/Saale
B 3.41–43 see B 3.26
B 3.45   according to data from: Gerner, Manfred (ed.): Altbaumodernisierung – Haustechnik. series 4. Stuttgart, 2000
B 3.46   according to: RAL
B 3.47   according to: VDE 0250
B 3.48   according to: EN V 61 024-1
B 3.50–51 Studiengemeinschaft für Fertigbau e.V., Koblenz

Conservation
B 4.1   Jörg von Bruchhausen, Berlin
B 4.2   from: Roman-Germanic Central Museum, Mainz (ed.): Führer zu vor- und frühgeschichtlichen Denkmälern – Trier. Teil 2. vol. 32. Mainz, 1977, p. 155
B 4.3   Architecture Museum, Berlin TU
B 4.4   Rheinisches Bildarchiv, Cologne
B 4.5a–b Numismatic Collection, State Museums, Berlin – Prussian collection
B 4.6   Deutscher Kunstverlag GmbH, Munich/Berlin
B 4.7   from: Huse, Norbert (ed.): Denkmalpflege – Deutsche Texte aus drei Jahrhunderten. Munich, 1996, p. 112
B 4.8   see B 4.7, p. 113
B 4.9   Baden-Württemberg Industrial Archive, Stuttgart
B 4.10a   Richard Peter sen./SLUB Dresden/Deutsche Fotothek
B 4.10b   Daniel Scholz/SLUB Dresden/Deutsche Fotothek
B 4.11   State of Hesse Conservation Agency/Cover-

fotos: Thomas Wiegand, Kassel
B 4.12   Rolf Zöllner/Berlin State Archive
B 4.13   Franz Moerscher/Völklingen Ironworks World Heritage Site, Völklingen/Saarbrücken
B 4.15   German Foundation for Monument Protection (DSD), Bonn
B 4.16   Kerstin Hähner/PantherMedia, Munich
B 4.17   Alexandra Restaurierungen Gerschler and Splett GbR, Berlin
B 4.18   courtesy of: Johannes Cramer, Berlin
B 4.19   Klaus Block, Berlin
B 4.22   Waldemar Titzenthaler/Berlin State Archive
B 4.23   Berlin State Archive
B 4.25–26 Stefane Jacob/Berlin State Archive

Building materials in refurbishment projects
B 5.1   Holzabsatzfonds, Bonn
B 5.3   according to: DIN EN 350-2
B 5.14   Mike Frajese/PIXELIO
B 5.31   Jean Jannon/PIXELIO
B 5.34   EvilSemmy/PIXELIO

Dangerous substances in the building stock
B 6.1   Gesellschaft für Ökologische Bautechnik Berlin mbH (GFöB), Berlin
B 6.2   www.gefahrstoffe-im-griff.de
B 6.3–10 see B 6.1
B 6.11   Deutsches Institut für Gütesicherung und Kennzeichnung e.V. (RAL); Deutsches Institut Bauen und Umwelt e.V. (DIBU); Gemeinschaft umweltfreundlicher Teppichboden e.V. (GUT); Internationaler Verein für zukunftsfähiges Bauen und Wohnen e.V. (natureplus)
B 6.12–28 see B 6.1

Part C   Historical periods

C   Nigel Young/Foster & Partners

General refurbishment tasks
C 1.1   Ignacio Martinez, Lustenau
C 1.4–7   based on: Balak, Michael; Pech, Anton: Mauerwerkstrockenlegung. Vienna, 2003, pp. 150–153
C 1.8   based on: Weber, Helmut: Fassadenschutz und Bausanierung. Renningen-Malmsheim, 1983
C 1.9   based on: Hettmann, Dietmar: Mauerwerksinjektionen gegen kapillar aufsteigende Feuchtigkeit, seminar vol. 1. Vienna, 1992
C 1.10   see C 1.4, p. 162
C 1.13   Hilti Deutschland GmbH, Kaufering
C 1.15   Daniela Kluth, Cologne
C 1.16   see C 1.4, p. 154

Buildings of the founding years 1870–1920
C 2.1–2   from: Trier, Edurard; Weyres, Willy: Kunst des 19. Jahrhunderts im Rheinland. Architektur II. vol. 2. Düsseldorf, 1980, pp. 440–441
C 2.3   from: Schönermark, Gustav; Stüber, Wilhelm: Hochbau-Lexikon. Berlin, c. 1900, p. 653
C 2.6   according to data from: Schönermerk, Gustav; Stüber, Wilhelm: Hochbau-Lexikon. Berlin, c. 1900, p. 625
C 2.7   see C 2.3, p. 488
C 2.8   see C 2.3, p. 497
C 2.9   from: Ahnert, Rudolph; Krause, Karl Heinz: Typische Baukonstruktionen von 1860 bis 1960. vol. 2. Berlin 2001, p. 47
C 2.10   see C 2.9, p. 46
C 2.11   see C 2.3, p. 490
C 2.12a–b from: Breymann et al.: Allgemeine Baukonstruktionslehre. Die Konstruktionen in Stein. Leipzig, 1903, p. 166
C 2.13   see C 2.12, p. 176
C 2.14–15 based on: Ahnert, Rudolph; Krause, Karl Heinz: Typische Baukonstruktionen von 1860 bis 1960. vol. 2. Berlin, 2001, p. 47
C 2.16   see C 2.12, p. 184
C 2.17   see C 2.6, p. 897
C 2.18   see C 2.3, p. 16

C 2.19   see C 2.3, p. 83
C 2.20   see C 2.6, p. 75
C 2.21   see C 2.12, p. 102
C 2.22   see C 2.12, p. 115
C 2.23   see C 2.3, p. 706
C 2.24   see C 2.3, p. 81
C 2.25   see C 2.12, p. 120
C 2.27a–b see C 2.12, p. 125
C 2.28   see C 2.12, p. 126
C 2.29   see C 2.12, p. 121
C 2.30   see C 2.12, p. 128
C 2.31a–b see C 2.12, plate 27
C 2.32   from: Breymann et al.: Allgemeine Baukon-
          struktionslehre. Die Konstruktionen in Holz.
          Leipzig, 1900, p. 323
C 2.33   see C 2.32, p. 322
C 2.34   see C 2.32, p. 324
C 2.35a–b see C 2.3, p. 165
C 2.36   see C 2.32, p. 104
C 2.37   from: Breymann et al.: Allgemeine Baukon-
          struktionslehre. Die Konstruktionen in Eisen.
          Leipzig, 1902, plate 5
C 2.38b–c Wolfgang Feyferlik, Graz
C 2.39a–c see C 2.32, p. 71
C 2.40   see C 2.37, Tab. 17
C 2.41   see C 2.3, p. 41
C 2.42   see C 2.32, plate 13
C 2.43a–c see C 2.32, p. 76
C 2.44   according to: Breymann et al.: Allgemeine
          Baukonstruktionslehre. Die Konstruktionen in
          Holz. Leipzig, 1900, p. 285
C 2.45a–e from: Esselborn (ed.); revised by Brennecke,
          L. et al.: Lehrbuch des Hochbaues, vol. 1,
          Leipzig, 1922, pp. 290–291
C 2.46   Bürogemeinschaft Sachverständigenbüro für
          Holzschutz, Hannover
C 2.47a   see C 2.32, p. 74
C 2.47b   see C 2.32, p. 91
C 2.47c   see C 2.32, p. 87
C 2.47d   see C 2.32, p. 75
C 2.48   according to data from: Knauf Gips KG,
          Iphofen
C 2.50   see C 2.44, p. 110
C 2.51a–d see C 2.9, pp. 56–57
C 2.52   see C 2.12, p. 318
C 2.53   see C 2.3, p. 839
C 2.54a–b see C 2.12, p. 356
C 2.55   see C 2.3, p. 257
C 2.56   see C 2.3, p. 301
C 2.57   Paul Ott, Graz
C 2.58   Alexander Koller, Vienna

Buildings of the inter-war years 1920–1940
C 3.1   Volkswagen AG, Wolfsburg
C 3.2   Christian Schittich, Munich
C 3.3a–c from: Schmidt, Paul: Handbuch des Hoch-
          baues. Nordhausen, 1926, pp. 550–551
C 3.4a–b see C 3.3, pp. 558–559
C 3.5   from: Ebinghaus, Hugo: Der Hochbau.
          Nordhausen, 1936, p. 148
C 3.6   Paul Ott, Graz
C 3.7   according to data from: Heideck, Erich;
          Leppin, Otto: Der Industriebau. vol. 2. Berlin,
          1933, p. 120
C 3.8   from: Heideck, Erich; Leppin, Otto:
          Der Industriebau. vol. 2. Berlin, 1933, p. 34
          ([1] Road, [2] Footpath, [3] Overhead light, [4] Ground floor,
          [5] min. 300 mm, [6] Max. water table; [7] 40 mm radius,
          [8] RC footing, [9] Front wall column, [10] 40 mm conc. fill,
          [11] 20 mm render, [12] 120 mm bwk., [13] 20 mm render,
          [14] Insulation, [15] RC wall, [16] Infill bwk. between RC cols.,
          [17] Glazed finish, [18] 20 mm screed, [19] Insulation, [20] 50 mm
          concrete, 21 RC slab, 22 floor covering, 23 100 mm blinding)
C 3.10   according to data from: Ebinghaus, Hugo:
          Der Hochbau. Nordhausen, 1936, pp. 118–119
C 3.11   see C 3.5, p. 134
C 3.12   see C 3.5, p. 136
C 3.13   see C 3.5, p. 157
C 3.14   see C 3.5, p. 365
C 3.15   see C 3.5, p. 489
C 3.16   see C 3.5, p. 492
C 3.17   see C 3.5, p. 494
C 3.18a   see C 3.5, p. 67
C 3.18b   Tobias Kneschke/Berlin.de, Berlin

C 3.19   see C 3.8, p. 52
C 3.20   see C 2.45, p. 780
C 3.21   see C 3.5, p. 190
C 3.22   see C 3.5, p. 143
C 3.23   see C 3.7, p. 11
C 3.24   see C 3.8, p. 58
C 3.25a–b see C 3.8, p. 72
C 3.26   see C 3.7, p. 203
C 3.27   see C 3.8, p. 59
C 3.28   see C 3.8, p. 60
C 3.29a–b see C 3.5, pp. 764–765
C 3.29c–d see C 3.5, pp. 769–770
C 3.30   from: Ahnert, Rudolph; Krause, Karl Heinz:
          Typische Baukonstruktionen von 1860 bis
          1960. vol. 3. Berlin, 2002, p. 161
C 3.31   see C 3.5, p. 319
C 3.32   see C 3.30, p. 55
C 3.33a–b see C 3.5, pp. 310–311
C 3.34   Hans Bach, Potsdam (courtesy of: Einstein
          Forum, Potsdam)
C 3.35   see C 3.8, p. 73
C 3.36a–b Paul Ott, Graz

Buildings of the post-war years 1950–1965
C 4.1   from: Henn, Walter: Bauten der Industrie –
          Planung, Entwurf, Konstruktion. Munich, 1955,
          p. 185
C 4.2   from: Durth, Werner: Deutsche Architekten –
          Biografische Verpflechtungen 1900–1970.
          Stuttgart/Zurich, 2001, p. 187
C 4.3   from: Hart, Franz: Baukonstruktion für Archi-
          tekten. Stuttgart, 1951, p. 53
C 4.5   see C 4.3, p. 50
C 4.6   from: Schmitt, Heinrich: Hochbaukonstruktionen.
          Ravensburg, 1956, p. 159
C 4.9   see C 4.3, p. 43
C 4.10   see C 4.3, p. 57
C 4.11   see C 4.6, p. 68
C 4.12   according to data from: Schmitt, Heinrich:
          Hochbaukonstruktionen. Ravensburg, 1956,
          p. 69
C 4.13   see C 4.6, p. 346
C 4.14   see C 4.6, p. 344
C 4.15   see C 4.6, p. 354
C 4.16a   see C 4.1, p. 160
C 4.16b   from: Henn, Walter: Bauten der Industrie.
          Ein internationaler Querschnitt. Munich, 1955,
          p. 50
C 4.17a–b see C 4.3, p. 101
C 4.18–19 see C 4.6, p. 265
C 4.20   from: Schmitt, Heinrich: Hochbaukonstruktionen.
          Ravensburg, 1962, p. 122
C 4.21a–b see C 4.3, p. 103
C 4.21c–d see C 4.3, p. 107
C 4.21e   see C 4.3, p. 109
C 4.22   see C 4.20, p. 256
C 4.23   see C 4.6, p. 215
C 4.24–25 see C 4.12, p. 240
C 4.26   based on: Schmitt, Heinrich: Hochbau-
          konstruktionen. Ravensburg, 1962, p. 99
C 4.27   see C 4.6, p. 193
C 4.29   Paul Ott, Graz
C 4.30   see C 3.30, plate 51
C 4.31   see C 3.30, plate 52
C 4.32   see C 3.30, plate 62
C 4.33   see C 4.6, p. 485
C 4.34   see C 4.6, p. 226
C 4.35   see C 4.6, p. 439
C 4.36a–b see C 4.6, p. 510
C 4.36c   see C 4.6, p. 514

Buildings of the prosperous years 1965–1980
C 5.2   from: Wankum, Alfons: Mobiliarordnung in der
          Bürolandschaft. Teambrief No. 27. Quickborn,
          1967
C 5.4   J. H. Darchinger/darchinger.com
C 5.5   from: Neumann, Friedrich (ed.): Frick/Knöll –
          Baukonstruktionslehre. Teil 1. Stuttgart, 1979,
          p. 379
C 5.6   Peter Mattes, Bergisch Gladbach
C 5.7   from: Schmitt, Heinrich: Hochbaukonstruktionen.
          Ravensburg, 1978, p. 307

C 5.8   N. Nehring, Wuppertal
C 5.11   Doka Schalungstechnik, Amstetten
C 5.13   Paul Ott, Graz
C 5.14   according to data from: Ruffert, Günther:
          Lexikon der Betonsanierung. Stuttgart, 1999,
          p. 238
C 5.15   according to data from: www.beton.org
C 5.16a–c maxit Deutschland GmbH, Marke Deitermann,
          Datteln
C 5.17   from: Neumann, Friedrich (ed.): Frick/Knöll –
          Baukonstruktionslehre. Teil 2. Stuttgart, 1979,
          p. 193
C 5.18   see C 5.7, p. 359
C 5.19   Christoph Schäfer, Hamburg
C 5.20a–c see C 5.17, p. 171
C 5.21   see C 5.17, p. 181
C 5.22   see C 5.7, p. 296
C 5.23   see C 5.7, p. 297
C 5.24   see C 5.17, p. 256
C 5.25   according to data from: Schmitt, Heinrich:
          Hochbaukonstruktionen. Ravensburg, 1978,
          p. 601
C 5.26   see C 5.7, p. 612
C 5.27   based on: Schmitt, Heinrich: Hochbau-
          konstruktionen. Ravensburg, 1978, p. 605
C 5.28   based on: www.iemb.de
C 5.29   from: Wiel, Leopold; Dittmann, Heinz:
          Baukonstruktionen des Wohnungsbaues.
          Leipzig, 1974, p. 31
C 5.30   see C 5.29, p. 80
C 5.31   see C 5.29, p. 53
C 5.32   see C 5.29, p. 98

Part D   Case studies

D   Paul Ott, Graz

pp. 208–209   Hannes Henz, Zurich
pp. 210–213   José Manuel Cutillas, Barañain (E)
p. 218   Paul Ott, Graz
pp. 220 bottom, 221   Ralph Richter/archenova,
                      Düsseldorf
pp. 222–223   Axel Hartmann, Cologne
pp. 224 left, 225   Lyndon Douglas, London
p. 226 left   Stefan Müller, Berlin
p. 226 right   Bewag Archive, Berlin
p. 227   Stefan Müller, Berlin
p. 228   Michael Zalewski, Berlin
p. 229 top   Udo Hesse, Berlin
p. 229 bottom   Stefan Müller, Berlin
pp. 230–232   Werner Huthmacher, Berlin
p. 233 bottom   Werner Huthmacher, Berlin
p. 233 top   Chemnitz Art Collections –
                      Gunzenhauser Museum
p. 234   Ralph Feiner, Malans
pp. 235 top, 236   Schenk+Campell, Lüen
p. 237 top   Michael Heinrich, Munich
pp. 238, 239   Michael Heinrich, Munich
pp. 240–241   Paul Ott, Graz
pp. 242, 243 left   Tomas Riehle/artur, Essen
p. 244 bottom   Jörg Hempel, Aachen
pp. 245, 246 right   Jörg Hempel, Aachen
p. 247 top   Stefan Müller-Naumann, Munich
pp. 248, 249   Stefan Müller-Naumann, Munich
p. 251   Frank Kaltenbach, Munich
pp. 252–253   Andrea Kroth, Berlin
p. 254 right   Florian Holzherr, Munich
p. 255 top   Florian Holzherr, Munich
p. 256   Florian Holzherr, Munich
p. 257   Andreas Gabriel, Munich
pp. 258, 259 bottom   Andrea Helbling, Zurich
pp. 260, 261   Andrea Helbling, Zurich
pp. 262, 264, 265   Oliver Heissner, Hamburg

Index

Authors

Georg Giebeler

Born 1963
Studies in architecture at Graz TU and Städel School, Frankfurt am Main
Assistant to Prof. Giencke, Graz
Scientific assistant to Prof. Döring, Aachen
1995 to date: architectural practice in Cologne (4000architekten)
2004 to date: Professor for Building Design, Wismar University of Applied Sciences, Technology, Business & Design; work and research focus: building with the building stock, the estate of Ulrich Müther, numerous publications about his own structures

Rainer Fisch

Born 1970
Studies in architecture in Trier
1997–1998: freelance assistant at State of Hesse Conservation Agency
1998 to date: member of staff at Federal Office for Building & Regional Planning (BBR); entrusted with building measures for Prussian Cultural Heritage Foundation: Friedrichs-werder Church, Museums Island (Berlin), National Library
2007: successful completion of doctorate studies (Dr.-Ing.) at TU-Berlin; theme: conversion of church buildings

Harald Krause

Born 1962
Studies and doctorate (Dr. rer. nat.) in physics at Munich TU
1993–1998: in charge of R&D at Institute for Window Technology, Rosenheim; projects on highly thermally insulating windows, summertime thermal performance, solar energy
1998 to date: own consulting engineering practice for energy-efficient construction, numerous passive house projects in Germany, Italy, France, Ireland
1995 to date: Professor for Building Physics & Building Services at Rosenheim University of Applied Sciences; research projects in the fields of energy-efficiency upgrades and ventilation of residential accommodation
Member of Conference Committee of International Conference on Passive Houses

Florian Musso

Born 1956
Studies in architecture at University of Stuttgart and University of Virginia
Partner in architectural practice LorenzMusso architectes in Sion (CH) since 1989 and in Munich since 2002
2002 to date: Professor for Building Design, Materials Science & Design at Munich TU; research and publications in the fields covered by this chair, especially subsystems in industrialised building

Karl-Heinz Petzinka

Born 1956
Studies in architecture at RWTH Aachen University
Freelance assistant with O. M. Ungers
Scientific assistant to Prof. Döring, Aachen
Visiting lecturer at University of Wuppertal
Visiting professor at RWTH Aachen University and Düsseldorf Academy of Art
1994 to date: Professor for Design & Building Technology at Darmstadt TU
Designer of numerous international buildings as freelance architect (PetzinkaPink)
Co-founder of brand-name "Technologische Architektur", with emphasis on technology in architecture, lightweight construction, energy-efficiency upgrades

Alexander Rudolphi

Born 1952
Studies in construction engineering at Darmstadt TU and Berlin TU
Own consulting engineering practice plus research and teaching at Berliner Zentrum für Bau- und Erhaltungstechnik e.V.
1995 to date: Managing Director of Gesellschaft für ökologische Bautechnik Berlin mbH
Specialist for timber and building damage
Founder and Managing Director of RAL Gütegemeinschaft Holzschutz und Bautenschutz
Consultancy and research activities concerning sustainable building, quality assurance and quality determination of assemblies and materials plus development of certification methods
Honorary professor at Eberswalde University of Applied Sciences